D1128821

CHRYSLER

CIRRUS/STRATUS/SEBRING/AVENGER/BREEZE 1995-98 REPAIR MANUAL

CHILTON'S

Covers all U.S. and Canadian models of Chrysler Cirrus, Sebring, Dodge Avenger, Stratus and Plymouth Breeze

by Matthew E. Frederick, A.S.E., S.A.E.

CHILTON *Automotive Books*

PUBLISHED BY **HAYNES NORTH AMERICA.** Inc.

AUTOMOTIVE PARTS & ACCESSORIES ASSOCIATION MEMBER

Manufactured in USA
© 1998 Haynes North America, Inc.
ISBN 0-8019-9090-4
Library of Congress Catalog Card No. 98-71355
4567890123 9876543210

Haynes Publishing Group
Sparkford Nr Yeovil
Somerset BA22 7JJ England

Haynes North America, Inc
861 Lawrence Drive
Newbury Park
California 91320 USA

ABCDE
FGHIJ
K

8E1

Contents

Contents

SAFETY NOTICE

Proper service and repair procedures are vital to the safe, reliable operation of all motor vehicles, as well as the personal safety of those performing repairs. This manual outlines procedures for servicing and repairing vehicles using safe, effective methods. The procedures contain many NOTES, CAUTIONS and WARNINGS which should be followed, along with standard procedures to eliminate the possibility of personal injury or improper service which could damage the vehicle or compromise its safety.

It is important to note that repair procedures and techniques, tools and parts for servicing motor vehicles, as well as the skill and experience of the individual performing the work vary widely. It is not possible to anticipate all of the conceivable ways or conditions under which vehicles may be serviced, or to provide cautions as to all possible hazards that may result. Standard and accepted safety precautions and equipment should be used when handling toxic or flammable fluids, and safety goggles or other protection should be used during cutting, grinding, chiseling, prying, or any other process that can cause material removal or projectiles.

Some procedures require the use of tools specially designed for a specific purpose. Before substituting another tool or procedure, you must be completely satisfied that neither your personal safety, nor the performance of the vehicle will be endangered.

Although information in this manual is based on industry sources and is complete as possible at the time of publication, the possibility exists that some car manufacturers made later changes which could not be included here. While striving for total accuracy, the authors or publishers cannot assume responsibility for any errors, changes or omissions that may occur in the compilation of this data.

PART NUMBERS

Part numbers listed in this reference are not recommendations by Haynes North America, Inc. for any product brand name. They are references that can be used with interchange manuals and aftermarket supplier catalogs to locate each brand supplier's discrete part number.

SPECIAL TOOLS

Special tools are recommended by the vehicle manufacturer to perform their specific job. Use has been kept to a minimum, but where absolutely necessary, they are referred to in the text by the part number of the tool manufacturer. These tools can be purchased, under the appropriate part number, from your local dealer or regional distributor, or an equivalent tool can be purchased locally from a tool supplier or parts outlet. Before substituting any tool for the one recommended, read the SAFETY NOTICE at the top of this page.

ACKNOWLEDGMENTS

The publisher expresses appreciation to Chrysler Corporation for their generous assistance.

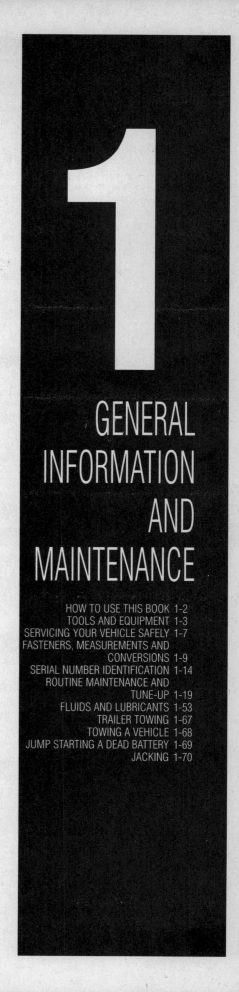

1

GENERAL INFORMATION AND MAINTENANCE

HOW TO USE THIS BOOK

Chilton's Total Car Care manual for the 1995–98 Cirrus, Stratus, Breeze, Sebring convertible, Sebring coupe and Avenger is intended to help you learn more about the inner workings of your vehicle while saving you money on its upkeep and operation.

The beginning of the book will likely be referred to the most, since that is where you will find information for maintenance and tune-up. The other sections deal with the more complex systems of your vehicle. Operating systems from engine through brakes are covered to the extent that the average do-it-yourselfer becomes mechanically involved. This book will not explain such things as rebuilding a transaxle for the simple reason that the expertise required and the investment in special tools make this task uneconomical. It will, however, give you detailed instructions to help you change your own brake pads and shoes, replace spark plugs, and perform many more jobs that can save you money, give you personal satisfaction and help you avoid expensive problems.

A secondary purpose of this book is a reference for owners who want to understand their vehicle and/or their mechanics better. In this case, no tools at all are required.

Where to Begin

Before removing any bolts, read through the entire procedure. This will give you the overall view of what tools and supplies will be required. There is nothing more frustrating than having to walk to the bus stop on Monday morning because you were short one bolt on Sunday afternoon. So read ahead and plan ahead. Each operation should be approached logically and all procedures thoroughly understood before attempting any work.

All sections contain adjustments, maintenance, removal and installation procedures, and in some cases, repair or overhaul procedures. When repair is not considered practical, we tell you how to remove the part and then how to install the new or rebuilt replacement. In this way, you at least save the labor costs. Backyard repair of some components is just not practical.

Avoiding Trouble

Many procedures in this book require you to "label and disconnect . . ." a group of lines, hoses or wires. Don't be lulled into thinking you can remember where everything goes—you won't. If you hook up vacuum or fuel lines incorrectly, the vehicle will run poorly, if at all. If you hook up electrical wiring incorrectly, you may instantly learn a very expensive lesson.

You don't need to know the official or engineering name for each hose or line. A piece of masking tape on the hose and a piece on its fitting will allow you to assign your own label such as the letter A or a short name. As long as you remember your own code, the lines can be reconnected by matching similar letters or names. Do remember that tape will dissolve in gasoline or other fluids; if a component is to be washed or cleaned, use another method of identification. A permanent felt-tipped marker can be very handy for marking metal parts. Remove any tape or paper labels after assembly.

Maintenance or Repair?

It's necessary to mention the difference between maintenance and repair. Maintenance includes routine inspections, adjustments, and replacement of parts which show signs of normal wear. Maintenance compensates for wear or deterioration. Repair implies that something has broken or is not working. A need for repair is often caused by lack of maintenance. Example: draining and refilling the automatic transmission fluid is maintenance recommended by the manufacturer at specific mileage intervals. Failure to do this can ruin the transaxle, requiring very expensive repairs. While no maintenance program can prevent items from breaking or wearing out, a general rule can be stated: MAINTENANCE IS CHEAPER THAN REPAIR.

Two basic mechanic's rules should be mentioned here. First, whenever the left side of the vehicle or engine is referred to, it is meant to specify the driver's side. Conversely, the right side of the vehicle means the passenger's side. Second, most screws and bolts are removed by turning counterclockwise, and tightened by turning clockwise.

Safety is always the most important rule. Constantly be aware of the dangers involved in working on an automobile and take the proper precautions. See the information in this section regarding SERVICING YOUR VEHICLE SAFELY and the SAFETY NOTICE on the acknowledgment page.

Avoiding the Most Common Mistakes

Pay attention to the instructions provided. There are 3 common mistakes in mechanical work:

1. Incorrect order of assembly, disassembly or adjustment. When taking something apart or putting it together, performing steps in the wrong order usually just costs you extra time; however, it CAN break something. Read the entire procedure before beginning disassembly. Perform everything in the order in which the instructions say you should, even if you can't immediately see a reason for it. When you're taking apart something that is very intricate, you might want to draw a picture of how it looks when assembled at one point in order to make sure you get everything back in its proper position. We will supply exploded views whenever possible. When making adjustments, perform them in the proper order; often, one adjustment affects another, and you cannot expect even satisfactory results unless each adjustment is made only when it cannot be changed by any other.

2. Overtorquing (or undertorquing). While it is more common for overtorquing to cause damage, undertorquing may allow a fastener to vibrate loose causing serious damage. Especially when dealing with aluminum parts, pay attention to torque specifications and utilize a torque wrench in assembly. If a torque figure is not available, remember that if you are using the right tool to perform the job, you will probably not have to strain yourself to get a fastener tight enough. The pitch of most threads is so slight that the tension you put on the wrench will be multiplied many times in actual force on what you are tightening. A good example of how critical torque is can be seen in the case of spark plug installation, especially where you are putting the plug into an aluminum cylinder head. Too little torque can fail to crush the gasket, causing leakage of combustion gases and consequent overheating of the plug and engine parts. Too much torque can damage the threads or distort the plug, changing the spark gap.

There are many commercial products available for ensuring that fasteners won't come loose, even if they are not torqued just right (a very common brand is Loctite®). If you're worried about getting something together tight enough to hold, but loose enough to avoid mechanical damage during assembly, one of these products might offer substantial insurance. Before choosing a threadlocking compound, read the label on the package and make sure the product is compatible with the materials, fluids, etc. involved.

3. Crossthreading. This occurs when a part such as a bolt is screwed into a nut or casting at the wrong angle and forced. Crossthreading is more likely to occur if access is difficult. It helps to clean and lubricate fasteners, then to start threading with the part to be installed positioned straight in. Then, start the bolt, spark plug, etc. with your fingers. If you encounter resistance, unscrew the part and start over again at a different angle until it can be inserted and turned several times without much effort. Keep in mind that many parts, especially spark plugs, have tapered threads, so that gentle turning will automatically bring the part you're threading to the proper angle, but only if you don't force it or resist a change in angle. Don't put a wrench on the part until it's been tightened a couple of turns by hand. If you suddenly encounter resistance, and the part has not seated fully, don't force it. Pull it back out to make sure it's clean and threading properly.

Always take your time and be patient; once you have some experience, working on your vehicle may well become an enjoyable hobby.

TOOLS AND EQUIPMENT

♦ **See Figures 1 thru 15**

Naturally, without the proper tools and equipment it is impossible to properly service your vehicle. It would also be virtually impossible to catalog every tool that you would need to perform all of the operations in this book. Of course, It would be unwise for the amateur to rush out and buy an expensive set of tools on the theory that he/she may need one or more of them at some time.

The best approach is to proceed slowly, gathering a good quality set of those tools that are used most frequently. Don't be misled by the low cost of bargain tools. It is far better to spend a little more for better quality. Forged wrenches, 6 or 12-point sockets and fine tooth ratchets are by far preferable to their less expensive counterparts. As any good mechanic can tell you, there are few worse experiences than trying to work on a vehicle with bad tools. Your monetary savings will be far outweighed by frustration and mangled knuckles.

Begin accumulating those tools that are used most frequently: those associated with routine maintenance and tune-up. In addition to the normal assortment of screwdrivers and pliers, you should have the following tools:

- Wrenches/sockets and combination open end/box end wrenches in sizes from ⅛–¾ in. or 3mm–19mm (depending on whether your vehicle uses standard or metric fasteners) and a ¹³⁄₁₆ in. or ⅝ in. spark plug socket (depending on plug type).

➡ **If possible, buy various length socket drive extensions. Universal-joint and wobble extensions can be extremely useful, but be careful when using them, as they can change the amount of torque applied to the socket.**

- Jackstands for support.
- Oil filter wrench.
- Spout or funnel for pouring fluids.
- Grease gun for chassis lubrication (unless your vehicle is not equipped with any grease fittings—for details, please refer to information on Fluids and Lubricants, later in this section).
- Hydrometer for checking the battery (unless equipped with a sealed, maintenance-free battery).
- A container for draining oil and other fluids.
- Rags for wiping up the inevitable mess.

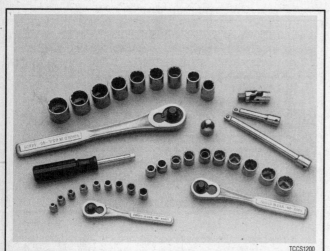

Fig. 1 All but the most basic procedures will require an assortment of ratchets and sockets

TCCS1200

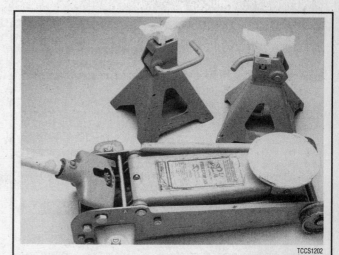

Fig. 3 A hydraulic floor jack and a set of jackstands are essential for lifting and supporting the vehicle

TCCS1202

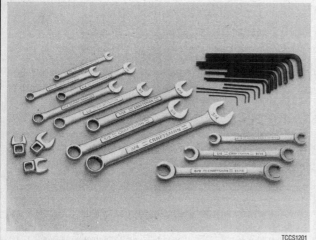

Fig. 2 In addition to ratchets, a good set of wrenches and hex keys will be necessary

TCCS1201

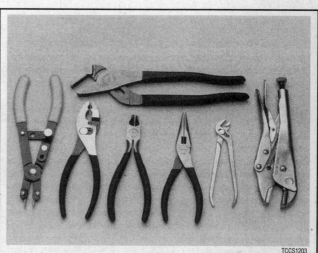

Fig. 4 An assortment of pliers, grippers and cutters will be handy for old rusted parts and stripped bolt heads

TCCS1203

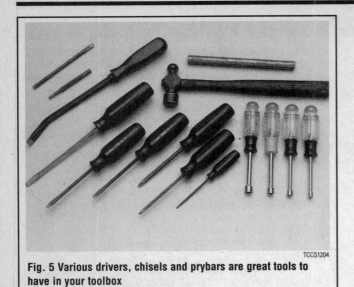

Fig. 5 Various drivers, chisels and prybars are great tools to have in your toolbox

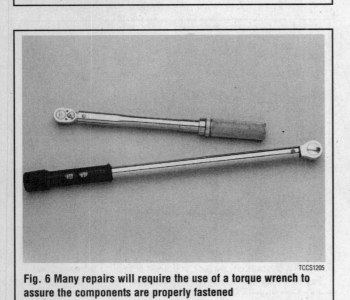

Fig. 6 Many repairs will require the use of a torque wrench to assure the components are properly fastened

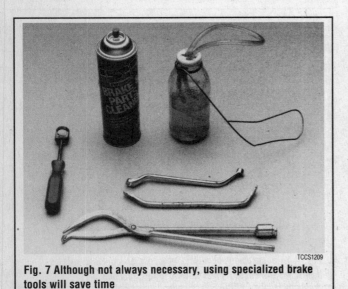

Fig. 7 Although not always necessary, using specialized brake tools will save time

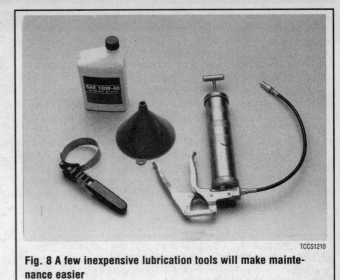

Fig. 8 A few inexpensive lubrication tools will make maintenance easier

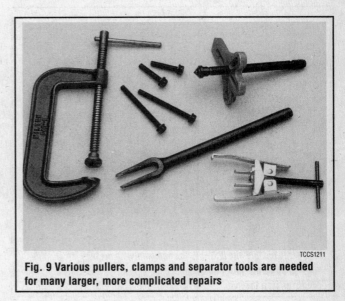

Fig. 9 Various pullers, clamps and separator tools are needed for many larger, more complicated repairs

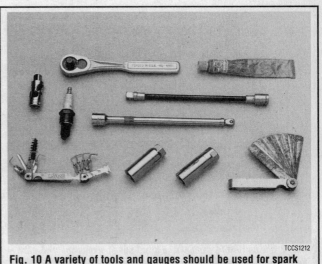

Fig. 10 A variety of tools and gauges should be used for spark plug gapping and installation

In addition to the above items there are several others that are not absolutely necessary, but handy to have around. These include Oil Dry® (or an equivalent oil absorbent gravel—such as cat litter) and the usual supply of lubricants, antifreeze and fluids, although these can be purchased as needed. This is a basic list for routine maintenance, but only your personal needs and desire can accurately determine your list of tools.

After performing a few projects on the vehicle, you'll be amazed at the other tools and non-tools on your workbench. Some useful household items are: a large turkey baster or siphon, empty coffee cans and ice trays (to store parts), ball of twine, electrical tape for wiring, small rolls of colored tape for tagging lines or hoses, markers and pens, a note pad, golf

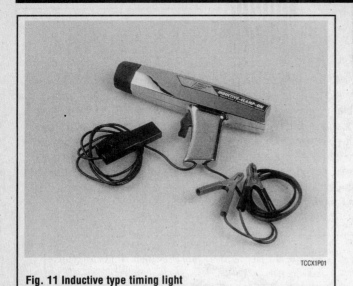

Fig. 11 Inductive type timing light

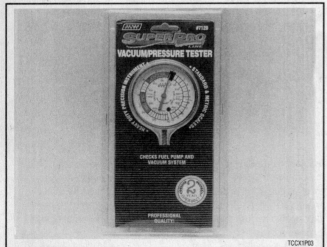

Fig. 12 A screw-in type compression gauge is recommended for compression testing

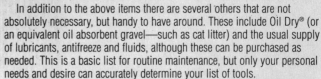
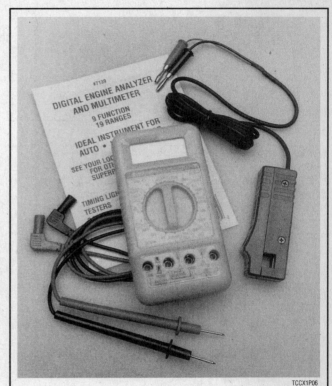

Fig. 14 Most modern automotive multimeters incorporate many helpful features

Fig. 13 A vacuum/pressure tester is necessary for many testing procedures

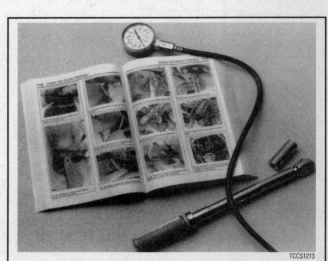

Fig. 15 Proper information is vital, so always have a Chilton Total Car Care manual handy

DIAGNOSTIC TEST EQUIPMENT

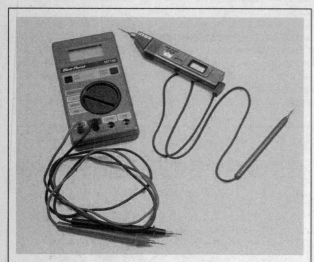

Digital multimeters come in a variety of styles and are a "must-have" for any serious home mechanic. Digital multimeters measure voltage (volts), resistance (ohms) and sometimes current (amperes). These versatile tools are used for checking all types of electrical or electronic components

Modern vehicles equipped with computer-controlled fuel, emission and ignition systems require modern electronic tools to diagnose problems. Many of these tools are designed solely for the professional mechanic and are too costly and difficult to use for the average do-it-yourselfer. However, various automotive aftermarket companies have introduced products that address the needs of the average home mechanic, providing sophisticated information at affordable cost. Consult your local auto parts store to determine what is available for your vehicle.

Trouble code tools allow the home mechanic to extract the "fault code" number from an on-board computer that has sensed a problem (usually indicated by a Check Engine light). Armed with this code, the home mechanic can focus attention on a suspect system or component

Sensor testers perform specific checks on many of the sensors and actuators used on today's computer-controlled vehicles. These testers can check sensors both on or off the vehicle, as well as test the accompanying electrical circuits

Hand-held scanners represent the most sophisticated of all do-it-yourself diagnostic tools. These tools do more than just access computer codes like the code readers above; they provide the user with an actual interface into the vehicle's computer. Comprehensive data on specific makes and models will come with the tool, either built-in or as a separate cartridge

tees (for plugging vacuum lines), metal coat hangers or a roll of mechanics's wire (to hold things out of the way), dental pick or similar long, pointed probe, a strong magnet, and a small mirror (to see into recesses and under manifolds).

A more advanced set of tools, suitable for tune-up work, can be drawn up easily. While the tools are slightly more sophisticated, they need not be outrageously expensive. There are several inexpensive tach/dwell meters on the market that are every bit as good for the average mechanic as a professional model. Just be sure that it goes to a least 1200–1500 rpm on the tach scale and that it works on 4, 6 and 8-cylinder engines. (If you have one or more vehicles with a diesel engine, a special tachometer is required since diesels don't use spark plug ignition systems). The key to these purchases is to make them with an eye towards adaptability and wide range. A basic list of tune-up tools could include:

- Tach/dwell meter.
- Spark plug wrench and gapping tool.
- Feeler gauges for valve or point adjustment. (Even if your vehicle does not use points or require valve adjustments, a feeler gauge is helpful for many repair/overhaul procedures).

A tachometer/dwell meter will ensure accurate tune-up work on vehicles without electronic ignition. The choice of a timing light should be made carefully. A light which works on the DC current supplied by the vehicle's battery is the best choice; it should have a xenon tube for brightness. On any vehicle with an electronic ignition system, a timing light with an inductive pickup that clamps around the No. 1 spark plug cable is preferred.

In addition to these basic tools, there are several other tools and gauges you may find useful. These include:

- Compression gauge. The screw-in type is slower to use, but eliminates the possibility of a faulty reading due to escaping pressure.
- Manifold vacuum gauge.
- 12V test light.
- A combination volt/ohmmeter
- Induction Ammeter. This is used for determining whether or not there is current in a wire. These are handy for use if a wire is broken somewhere in a wiring harness.

As a final note, you will probably find a torque wrench necessary for all but the most basic work. The beam type models are perfectly adequate, although the newer click types (breakaway) are easier to use. The click type torque wrenches tend to be more expensive. Also keep in mind that all types of torque wrenches should be periodically checked and/or recalibrated. You will have to decide for yourself which better fits your purpose.

Special Tools

Normally, the use of special factory tools is avoided for repair procedures, since these are not readily available for the do-it-yourself mechanic. When it is possible to perform the job with more commonly available tools, it will be pointed out, but occasionally, a special tool was designed to perform a specific function and should be used. Before substituting another tool, you should be convinced that neither your safety nor the performance of the vehicle will be compromised.

Special tools can usually be purchased from an automotive parts store or from your dealer. In some cases special tools may be available directly from the tool manufacturer.

SERVICING YOUR VEHICLE SAFELY

▶ **See Figures 16, 17, 18 and 19**

It is virtually impossible to anticipate all of the hazards involved with automotive maintenance and service, but care and common sense will prevent most accidents.

The rules of safety for mechanics range from "don't smoke around gasoline," to "use the proper tool(s) for the job." The trick to avoiding injuries is to develop safe work habits and to take every possible precaution.

Do's

- Do keep a fire extinguisher and first aid kit handy.
- Do wear safety glasses or goggles when cutting, drilling, grinding or prying, even if you have 20–20 vision. If you wear glasses for the sake of vision, wear safety goggles over your regular glasses.

- Do shield your eyes whenever you work around the battery. Batteries contain sulfuric acid. In case of contact with the eyes or skin, flush the area with water or a mixture of water and baking soda, then seek immediate medical attention.
- Do use safety stands (jackstands) for any undervehicle service. Jacks are for raising vehicles; jackstands are for making sure the vehicle stays raised until you want it to come down. Whenever the vehicle is raised, block the wheels remaining on the ground and set the parking brake.
- Do use adequate ventilation when working with any chemicals or hazardous materials. Like carbon monoxide, the asbestos dust resulting from some brake lining wear can be hazardous in sufficient quantities.
- Do disconnect the negative battery cable when working on the electrical system. The secondary ignition system contains EXTREMELY HIGH VOLTAGE. In some cases it can even exceed 50,000 volts.

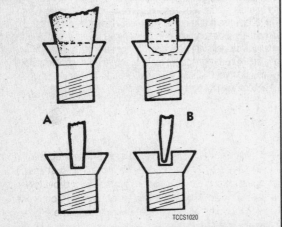

Fig. 16 Screwdrivers should be kept in good condition to prevent injury or damage which could result if the blade slips from the screw

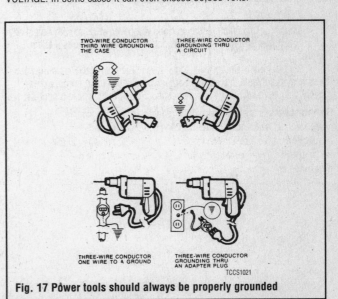

Fig. 17 Power tools should always be properly grounded

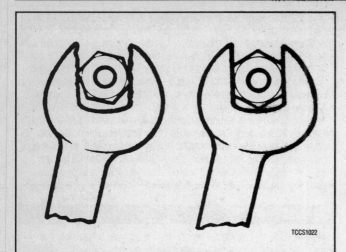

TCCS1022

Fig. 18 Using the correct size wrench will help prevent the possibility of rounding off a nut

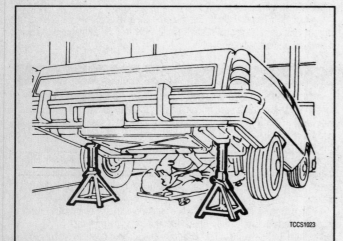

TCCS1023

Fig. 19 NEVER work under a vehicle unless it is supported using safety stands (jackstands)

• Do follow manufacturer's directions whenever working with potentially hazardous materials. Most chemicals and fluids are poisonous if taken internally.

• Do properly maintain your tools. Loose hammerheads, mushroomed punches and chisels, frayed or poorly grounded electrical cords, excessively worn screwdrivers, spread wrenches (open end), cracked sockets, slipping ratchets, or faulty droplight sockets can cause accidents.

• Likewise, keep your tools clean; a greasy wrench can slip off a bolt head, ruining the bolt and often harming your knuckles in the process.

• Do use the proper size and type of tool for the job at hand. Do select a wrench or socket that fits the nut or bolt. The wrench or socket should sit straight, not cocked.

• Do, when possible, pull on a wrench handle rather than push on it, and adjust your stance to prevent a fall.

• Do be sure that adjustable wrenches are tightly closed on the nut or bolt and pulled so that the force is on the side of the fixed jaw.

• Do strike squarely with a hammer; avoid glancing blows.

• Do set the parking brake and block the drive wheels if the work requires a running engine.

Don'ts

• Don't run the engine in a garage or anywhere else without proper ventilation—EVER! Carbon monoxide is poisonous; it takes a long time to leave the human body and you can build up a deadly supply of it in your system by simply breathing in a little every day. You may not realize you are slowly poisoning yourself. Always use power vents, windows, fans and/or open the garage door.

• Don't work around moving parts while wearing loose clothing. Short sleeves are much safer than long, loose sleeves. Hard-toed shoes with neoprene soles protect your toes and give a better grip on slippery surfaces. Jewelry such as watches, fancy belt buckles, beads or body adornment of any kind is not safe working around a vehicle. Long hair should be tied back under a hat or cap.

• Don't use pockets for toolboxes. A fall or bump can drive a screwdriver deep into your body. Even a rag hanging from your back pocket can wrap around a spinning shaft or fan.

• Don't smoke when working around gasoline, cleaning solvent or other flammable material.

• Don't smoke when working around the battery. When the battery is being charged, it gives off explosive hydrogen gas.

• Don't use gasoline to wash your hands; there are excellent soaps available. Gasoline contains dangerous additives which can enter the body through a cut or through your pores. Gasoline also removes all the natural oils from the skin so that bone dry hands will suck up oil and grease.

• Don't service the air conditioning system unless you are equipped with the necessary tools and training. When liquid or compressed gas refrigerant is released to atmospheric pressure it will absorb heat from whatever it contacts. This will chill or freeze anything it touches. Although refrigerant is normally non-toxic, R-12 becomes a deadly poisonous gas in the presence of an open flame. One good whiff of the vapors from burning refrigerant can be fatal.

• Don't use screwdrivers for anything other than driving screws! A screwdriver used as a prying tool can snap when you least expect it, causing injuries. At the very least, you'll ruin a good screwdriver.

• Don't use a bumper or emergency jack (that little ratchet, scissors, or pantograph jack supplied with the vehicle) for anything other than changing a flat! These jacks are only intended for emergency use out on the road; they are NOT designed as a maintenance tool. If you are serious about maintaining your vehicle yourself, invest in a hydraulic floor jack of at least a 1½ ton capacity, and at least two sturdy jackstands.

FASTENERS, MEASUREMENTS AND CONVERSIONS

Bolts, Nuts and Other Threaded Retainers

♦ **See Figures 20, 21, 22 and 23**

Although there are a great variety of fasteners found in the modern car or truck, the most commonly used retainer is the threaded fastener (nuts, bolts, screws, studs, etc). Most threaded retainers may be reused, provided that they are not damaged in use or during the repair. Some retainers (such as stretch bolts or torque prevailing nuts) are designed to deform when tightened or in use and should not be reinstalled.

Whenever possible, we will note any special retainers which should be replaced during a procedure. But you should always inspect the condition of a retainer when it is removed and replace any that show signs of damage. Check all threads for rust or corrosion which can increase the torque necessary to achieve the desired clamp load for which that fastener was originally selected. Additionally, be sure that the driver surface of the fastener has not been compromised by rounding or other damage. In some cases a driver surface may become only partially rounded, allowing the driver to catch in only one direction. In many of these occurrences, a fastener may be installed and tightened, but the

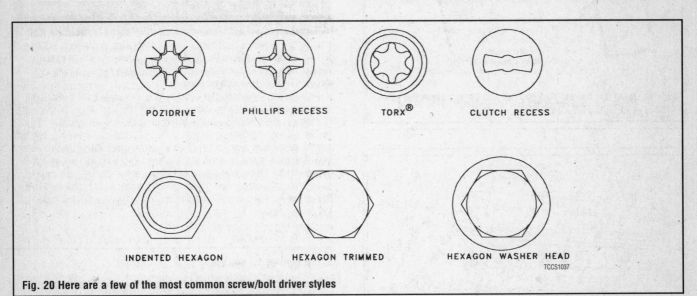

POZIDRIVE　　PHILLIPS RECESS　　TORX®　　CLUTCH RECESS

INDENTED HEXAGON　　HEXAGON TRIMMED　　HEXAGON WASHER HEAD

TCCS1037

Fig. 20 Here are a few of the most common screw/bolt driver styles

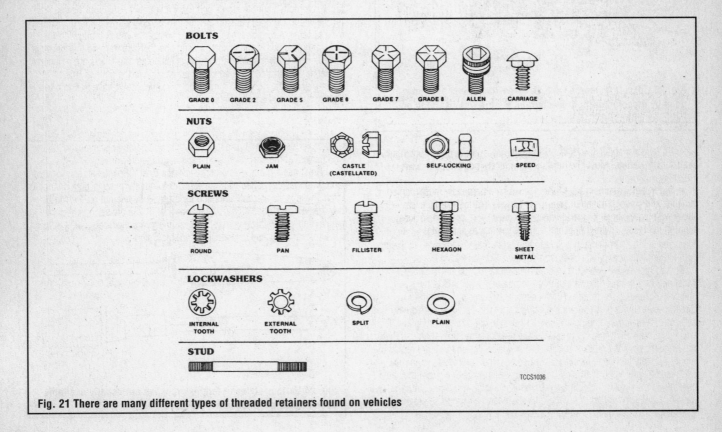

BOLTS

GRADE 0　GRADE 2　GRADE 5　GRADE 6　GRADE 7　GRADE 8　ALLEN　CARRIAGE

NUTS

PLAIN　　JAM　　CASTLE (CASTELLATED)　　SELF-LOCKING　　SPEED

SCREWS

ROUND　　PAN　　FILLISTER　　HEXAGON　　SHEET METAL

LOCKWASHERS

INTERNAL TOOTH　　EXTERNAL TOOTH　　SPLIT　　PLAIN

STUD

TCCS1036

Fig. 21 There are many different types of threaded retainers found on vehicles

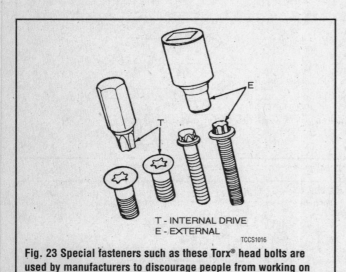

A - Length
B - Diameter (major diameter)
C - Threads per inch or mm
D - Thread length
E - Size of the wrench required
F - Root diameter (minor diameter)

TCCS1038

Fig. 22 Threaded retainer sizes are determined using these measurements

T - INTERNAL DRIVE
E - EXTERNAL

TCCS1016

Fig. 23 Special fasteners such as these Torx® head bolts are used by manufacturers to discourage people from working on vehicles without the proper tools

driver would not be able to grip and loosen the fastener again. (This could lead to frustration down the line should that component ever need to be disassembled again).

If you must replace a fastener, whether due to design or damage, you must ALWAYS be sure to use the proper replacement. In all cases, a retainer of the same design, material and strength should be used. Markings on the heads of most bolts will help determine the proper strength of the fastener. The same material, thread and pitch must be selected to assure proper installation and safe operation of the vehicle afterwards.

Thread gauges are available to help measure a bolt or stud's thread. Most automotive and hardware stores keep gauges available to help you select the proper size. In a pinch, you can use another nut or bolt for a thread gauge. If the bolt you are replacing is not too badly damaged, you can select a match by finding another bolt which will thread in its place. If you find a nut which threads properly onto the damaged bolt, then use that nut to help select the replacement bolt. If however, the bolt you are replacing is so badly damaged (broken or drilled out) that its threads cannot be used as a gauge, you might start by looking for another bolt (from the same assembly or a similar location on your vehicle) which will thread into the damaged bolt's mounting. If so, the other bolt can be used to select a nut; the nut can then be used to select the replacement bolt.

In all cases, be absolutely sure you have selected the proper replacement. Don't be shy, you can always ask the store clerk for help.

✳✳ WARNING

Be aware that when you find a bolt with damaged threads, you may also find the nut or drilled hole it was threaded into has also been damaged. If this is the case, you may have to drill and tap the hole, replace the nut or otherwise repair the threads. NEVER try to force a replacement bolt to fit into the damaged threads.

Torque

Torque is defined as the measurement of resistance to turning or rotating. It tends to twist a body about an axis of rotation. A common example of this would be tightening a threaded retainer such as a nut, bolt or screw. Measuring torque is one of the most common ways to help assure that a threaded retainer has been properly fastened.

When tightening a threaded fastener, torque is applied in three distinct areas, the head, the bearing surface and the clamp load. About 50 percent of the measured torque is used in overcoming bearing friction. This is the friction between the bearing surface of the bolt head, screw head or nut face and the base material or washer (the surface on which the fastener is rotating). Approximately 40 percent of the applied torque is used in overcoming thread friction. This leaves only about 10 percent of the applied torque to develop a useful clamp load (the force which holds a joint together). This means that friction can account for as much as 90 percent of the applied torque on a fastener.

TORQUE WRENCHES

▶ **See Figures 24 and 25**

In most applications, a torque wrench can be used to assure proper installation of a fastener. Torque wrenches come in various designs and most automotive supply stores will carry a variety to suit your needs. A torque wrench should be used any time we supply a specific torque value for a fastener. A torque wrench can also be used if you are following the general guidelines in the accompanying charts. Keep in mind that because there is no worldwide standardization of fasteners, the charts are a general guideline and should be used with caution. Again, the general rule of "if you are using the right tool for the job, you should not have to strain to tighten a fastener" applies here.

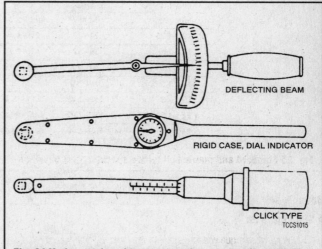

DEFLECTING BEAM

RIGID CASE, DIAL INDICATOR

CLICK TYPE

TCCS1015

Fig. 24 Various styles of torque wrenches are usually available at your local automotive supply store

Standard Torque Specifications and Fastener Markings

In the absence of specific torques, the following chart can be used as a guide to the maximum safe torque of a particular size/grade of fastener.
- There is no torque difference for fine or coarse threads.
- Torque values are based on clean, dry threads. Reduce the value by 10% if threads are oiled prior to assembly.
- The torque required for aluminum components or fasteners is considerably less.

U.S. Bolts

SAE Grade Number	1 or 2			5			6 or 7		
Number of lines always 2 less than the grade number.									
Bolt Size (Inches)—(Thread)	**Maximum Torque**			**Maximum Torque**			**Maximum Torque**		
	Ft./Lbs.	Kgm	Nm	Ft./Lbs.	Kgm	Nm	Ft./Lbs.	Kgm	Nm
¼ — 20	5	0.7	6.8	8	1.1	10.8	10	1.4	13.5
— 28	6	0.8	8.1	10	1.4	13.6			
5/16 — 18	11	1.5	14.9	17	2.3	23.0	19	2.6	25.8
— 24	13	1.8	17.6	19	2.6	25.7			
3/8 — 16	18	2.5	24.4	31	4.3	42.0	34	4.7	46.0
— 24	20	2.75	27.1	35	4.8	47.5			
7/16 — 14	28	3.8	37.0	49	6.8	66.4	55	7.6	74.5
— 20	30	4.2	40.7	55	7.6	74.5			
½ — 13	39	5.4	52.8	75	10.4	101.7	85	11.75	115.2
— 20	41	5.7	55.6	85	11.7	115.2			
9/16 — 12	51	7.0	69.2	110	15.2	149.1	120	16.6	162.7
— 18	55	7.6	74.5	120	16.6	162.7			
5/8 — 11	83	11.5	112.5	150	20.7	203.3	167	23.0	226.5
— 18	95	13.1	128.8	170	23.5	230.5			
¾ — 10	105	14.5	142.3	270	37.3	366.0	280	38.7	379.6
— 16	115	15.9	155.9	295	40.8	400.0			
7/8 — 9	160	22.1	216.9	395	54.6	535.5	440	60.9	596.5
— 14	175	24.2	237.2	435	60.1	589.7			
1 — 8	236	32.5	318.6	590	81.6	799.9	660	91.3	894.8
— 14	250	34.6	338.9	660	91.3	849.8			

Metric Bolts

Relative Strength Marking	4.6, 4.8			8.8		
Bolt Markings						
Bolt Size Thread Size x Pitch (mm)	**Maximum Torque**			**Maximum Torque**		
	Ft./Lbs.	Kgm	Nm	Ft./Lbs.	Kgm	Nm
6 x 1.0	2–3	.2–.4	3–4	3–6	4–.8	5–8
8 x 1.25	6–8	.8–1	8–12	9–14	1.2–1.9	13–19
10 x 1.25	12–17	1.5–2.3	16–23	20–29	2.7–4.0	27–39
12 x 1.25	21–32	2.9–4.4	29–43	35–53	4.8–7.3	47–72
14 x 1.5	35–52	4.8–7.1	48–70	57–85	7.8–11.7	77–110
16 x 1.5	51–77	7.0–10.6	67–100	90–120	12.4–16.5	130–160
18 x 1.5	74–110	10.2–15.1	100–150	130–170	17.9–23.4	180–230
20 x 1.5	110–140	15.1–19.3	150–190	190–240	26.2–46.9	160–320
22 x 1.5	150–190	22.0–26.2	200–260	250–320	34.5–44.1	340–430
24 x 1.5	190–240	26.2–46.9	260–320	310–410	42.7–56.5	420–550

TCCS1098

Fig. 25 Standard and metric bolt torque specifications based on bolt strengths—WARNING: use only as a guide

Beam Type
♦ **See Figure 26**

The beam type torque wrench is one of the most popular types. It consists of a pointer attached to the head that runs the length of the flexible beam (shaft) to a scale located near the handle. As the wrench is pulled, the beam bends and the pointer indicates the torque using the scale.

Click (Breakaway) Type
♦ **See Figure 27**

Another popular design of torque wrench is the click type. To use the click type wrench you pre-adjust it to a torque setting. Once the torque is reached, the wrench has a reflex signaling feature that causes a momentary breakaway of the torque wrench body, sending an impulse to the operator's hand.

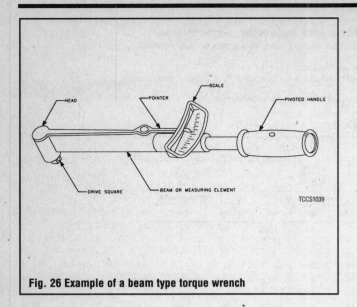

Fig. 26 Example of a beam type torque wrench

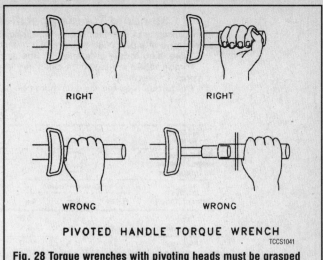

Fig. 28 Torque wrenches with pivoting heads must be grasped and used properly to prevent an incorrect reading

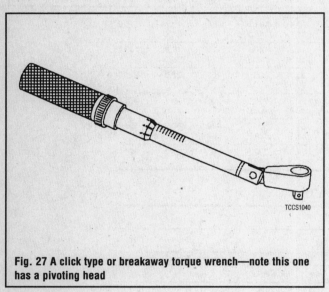

Fig. 27 A click type or breakaway torque wrench—note this one has a pivoting head

Pivot Head Type

▶ **See Figures 27 and 28**

Some torque wrenches (usually of the click type) may be equipped with a pivot head which can allow it to be used in areas of limited access. BUT, it must be used properly. To hold a pivot head wrench, grasp the handle lightly, and as you pull on the handle, it should be floated on the pivot point. If the handle comes in contact with the yoke extension during the process of pulling, there is a very good chance the torque readings will be inaccurate because this could alter the wrench loading point. The design of the handle is usually such as to make it inconvenient to deliberately misuse the wrench.

➡️ It should be mentioned that the use of any U-joint, wobble or extension will have an effect on the torque readings, no matter what type of wrench you are using. For the most accurate readings, install the socket directly on the wrench driver. If necessary, straight extensions (which hold a socket directly under the wrench driver) will have the least effect on the torque reading. Avoid any extension that alters the length of the wrench from the handle to the head/driving point (such as a crow's foot). U-joint or wobble extensions can greatly affect the readings; avoid their use at all times.

Rigid Case (Direct Reading)

▶ **See Figure 29**

A rigid case or direct reading torque wrench is equipped with a dial indicator to show torque values. One advantage of these wrenches is that they can be held at any position on the wrench without affecting accuracy. These wrenches are often preferred because they tend to be compact, easy to read and have a great degree of accuracy.

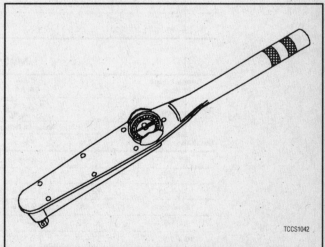

Fig. 29 The rigid case (direct reading) torque wrench uses a dial indicator to show torque

TORQUE ANGLE METERS

▶ **See Figure 30**

Because the frictional characteristics of each fastener or threaded hole will vary, clamp loads which are based strictly on torque will vary as well. In most applications, this variance is not significant enough to cause worry. But, in certain applications, a manufacturer's engineers may determine that more precise clamp loads are necessary (such is the case with many aluminum cylinder heads). In these cases, a torque angle method of installation would be specified. When installing fasteners which are torque angle tightened, a predetermined seating torque and standard torque wrench are usually used first to remove any compliance from the joint. The fastener is then tightened the specified additional portion of a turn measured in degrees. A torque angle gauge (mechanical protractor) is used for these applications.

Standard and Metric Measurements

▸ **See Figure 31**

Throughout this manual, specifications are given to help you determine the condition of various components on your vehicle, or to assist you in their installation. Some of the most common measurements include length (in. or cm/mm), torque (ft. lbs., inch lbs. or Nm) and pressure (psi, in. Hg, kPa or mm Hg). In most cases, we strive to provide the proper measurement as determined by the manufacturer's engineers.

Though, in some cases, that value may not be conveniently measured with what is available in your toolbox. Luckily, many of the measuring devices which are available today will have two scales so the Standard or Metric measurements may easily be taken. If any of the various measuring tools which are available to you do not contain the same scale as listed in the specifications, use the accompanying conversion factors to determine the proper value.

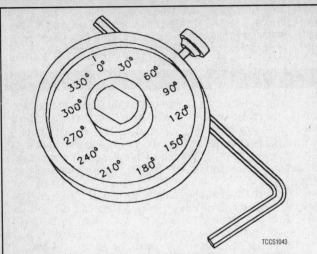

Fig. 30 Some specifications require the use of a torque angle meter (mechanical protractor)

TCCS1043

CONVERSION FACTORS

LENGTH–DISTANCE

Inches (in.)	x 25.4	= Millimeters (mm)	x .0394 = Inches
Feet (ft.)	x .305	= Meters (m)	x 3.281 = Feet
Miles	x 1.609	= Kilometers (km)	x .0621 = Miles

VOLUME

Cubic Inches (in3)	x 16.387	= Cubic Centimeters	x .061 = in3
IMP Pints (IMP pt.)	x .568	= Liters (L)	x 1.76 = IMP pt.
IMP Quarts (IMP qt.)	x 1.137	= Liters (L)	x .88 = IMP qt.
IMP Gallons (IMP gal.)	x 4.546	= Liters (L)	x .22 = IMP gal.
IMP Quarts (IMP qt.)	x 1.201	= US Quarts (US qt.)	x .833 = IMP qt.
IMP Gallons (IMP gal.)	x 1.201	= US Gallons (US gal.)	x .833 = IMP gal.
Fl. Ounces	x 29.573	= Milliliters	x .034 = Ounces
US Pints (US pt.)	x .473	= Liters (L)	x 2.113 = Pints
US Quarts (US qt.)	x .946	= Liters (L)	x 1.057 = Quarts
US Gallons (US gal.)	x 3.785	= Liters (L)	x .264 = Gallons

MASS–WEIGHT

Ounces (oz.)	x 28.35	= Grams (g)	x .035 = Ounces
Pounds (lb.)	x .454	= Kilograms (kg)	x 2.205 = Pounds

PRESSURE

Pounds Per Sq. In. (psi)	x 6.895	= Kilopascals (kPa)	x .145 = psi
Inches of Mercury (Hg)	x .4912	= psi	x 2.036 = Hg
Inches of Mercury (Hg)	x 3.377	= Kilopascals (kPa)	x .2961 = Hg
Inches of Water (H_2O)	x .07355	= Inches of Mercury	x 13.783 = H_2O
Inches of Water (H_2O)	x .03613	= psi	x 27.684 = H_2O
Inches of Water (H_2O)	x .248	= Kilopascals (kPa)	x 4.026 = H_2O

TORQUE

Pounds–Force Inches (in–lb)	x .113	= Newton Meters (N·m)	x 8.85 = in–lb
Pounds–Force Feet (ft–lb)	x 1.356	= Newton Meters (N·m)	x .738 = ft–lb

VELOCITY

Miles Per Hour (MPH)	x 1.609	= Kilometers Per Hour (KPH)	x .621 = MPH

POWER

Horsepower (Hp)	x .745	= Kilowatts	x 1.34 = Horsepower

FUEL CONSUMPTION*

Miles Per Gallon IMP (MPG)	x .354	= Kilometers Per Liter (Km/L)
Kilometers Per Liter (Km/L)	x 2.352	= IMP MPG
Miles Per Gallon US (MPG)	x .425	= Kilometers Per Liter (Km/L)
Kilometers Per Liter (Km/L)	x 2.352	= US MPG

*It is common to covert from miles per gallon (mpg) to liters/100 kilometers (1/100 km), where mpg (IMP) x 1/100 km = 282 and mpg (US) x 1/100 km = 235.

TEMPERATURE

Degree Fahrenheit (°F) = (°C x 1.8) + 32
Degree Celsius (°C) = (°F – 32) x .56

TCCS1044

Fig. 31 Standard and metric conversion factors chart

The conversion factor chart is used by taking the given specification and multiplying it by the necessary conversion factor. For instance, looking at the first line, if you have a measurement in inches such as "free-play should be 2 in." but your ruler reads only in millimeters, multiply 2 in. by the conversion factor of 25.4 to get the metric equivalent of 50.8mm. Likewise, if the specification was given only in a Metric measurement, for example in Newton Meters (Nm), then look at the center column first. If the measurement is 100 Nm, multiply it by the conversion factor of 0.738 to get 73.8 ft. lbs.

SERIAL NUMBER IDENTIFICATION

Vehicle

♦ See Figure 32

The Vehicle Identification Number (VIN) is stamped on a metal plate located on the top left-hand side (driver's side) of the instrument panel, so that it can be seen by looking through the lower corner of the windshield. The VIN is made up of 17 digits in a combination of numbers and letters that contain specific information regarding the vehicle:

- The 1st digit represents the country of manufacture: 1 or 4—USA., 3—Mexico.
- The 2nd digit will be the letter B, C or P, which represents the make of the vehicle: Dodge, Chrysler or Plymouth, respectively.
- The 3rd digit represents vehicle type; this is a 3 and means passenger vehicle.

- The 4th digit represents the safety restraint features with which that particular car was produced: A—passive restraint seat belts with a driver's side air bag (except Avenger and Sebring coupe), or driver's and passenger's side air bags (Avenger and Sebring coupe); H—active restraint seat belts with driver's and passenger's side air bags; X—driver's side air bag with passenger manual seat belts; E—active driver's and passenger's side air bags.
- The 5th digit represents the particular line of vehicle: J—Cirrus/Stratus/Breeze; L—Sebring convertible; U—Avenger/Sebring coupe.
- The 6th digit represents the vehicle series: 4—High Line; 5—Premium; 6—Sport.
- The 7th digit represents the body style of the vehicle: 6—4-door Sedan; 5—Convertible; 2—Coupe.
- The 8th digit indicates with what engine the vehicle is equipped: C—2.0L 4 cyl. 16V SOHC engine with MFI; Y—2.0L 4 cyl. 16V DOHC engine with MFI; H or N—2.5L V6 24V SOHC engine with MFI; X—2.4L 4 cyl. 16V DOHC engine with MFI.
- The 9th digit is a check digit for all vehicles.
- The 10th digit indicates the model year: S for 1995; T for 1996; V for 1997; W for 1998.
- The 11th digit represents the manufacturing plant where the vehicle was assembled: N—Sterling Heights, Michigan; T—Toluca; E—DSM/Mitsubishi of America plant.
- The 12th through 17th digits indicate the production sequence number.

90901P29

Fig. 32 Location of the Vehicle Identification Number (VIN) code plate at the left side of the instrument panel

Engine

♦ See Figures 33, 34, 35 and 36

The engine identification code is contained within the VIN as the 8th digit and identifies the engine type, displacement and fuel system. The VIN can be found on the instrument panel. See the Engine Identification chart for engine VIN codes.

The engine identification code is also located on the rear of the engine block, just below the cylinder head on the 2.5L engine, on the left rear side of the engine block behind the starter on the 2.0L engine for 1995–98, as well as the 2.4L engine for 1995–96, and at the rear of the engine block on the 2.4L engine for 1997–98 models. This code supplies information about the manufacturing plant location and time of manufacture.

VEHICLE IDENTIFICATION CHART

Engine (ID/VIN)	Displacement Liters (cc)	Cubic Inches	No. of Cylinders	Fuel System	Eng. Mfg.	Code	Year
C	2.0 (1996)	122	4	MFI	Chrysler	S	1995
Y	2.0 (1996)	122	4	MFI	Chrysler	T	1996
X	2.4 (2429)	148	4	MFI	Chrysler	V	1997
H	2.5 (2497)	152	6	MFI	Mitsubishi	W	1998
N	2.5 (2497)	152	6	MFI	Mitsubishi		

MFI: Multi-port Fuel Injection

90901C01

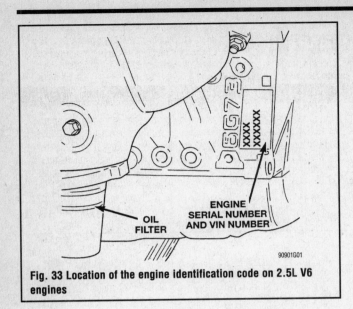

Fig. 33 Location of the engine identification code on 2.5L V6 engines

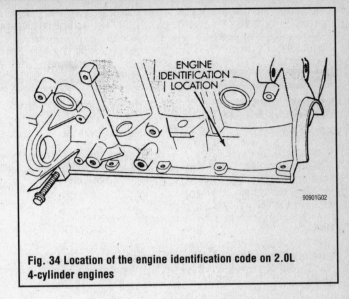

Fig. 34 Location of the engine identification code on 2.0L 4-cylinder engines

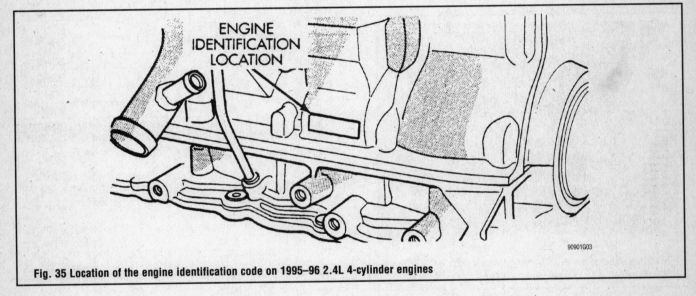

Fig. 35 Location of the engine identification code on 1995–96 2.4L 4-cylinder engines

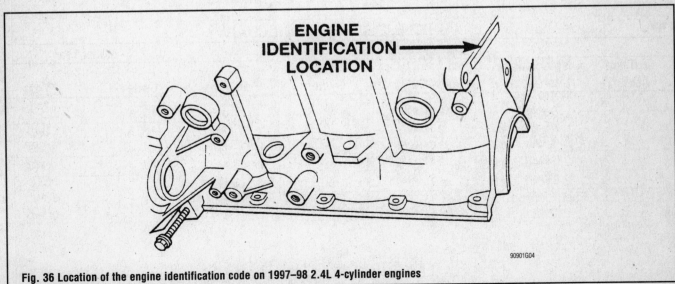

Fig. 36 Location of the engine identification code on 1997–98 2.4L 4-cylinder engines

ENGINE IDENTIFICATION

Year	Model	Engine Displacement Liters (cc)	Engine Series (ID/VIN)	Fuel System	No. of Cylinders	Engine Type
1995	Cirrus	2.5 (2497)	H	MFI	6	SOHC
	Sebring Coupe	2.0 (1996)	Y	MFI	4	DOHC
	Sebring Coupe	2.5 (2497)	N	MFI	6	SOHC
	Avenger	2.0 (1996)	Y	MFI	4	DOHC
	Avenger	2.5 (2497)	N	MFI	6	SOHC
	Stratus	2.0 (1996)	C	MFI	4	SOHC
	Stratus	2.4 (2429)	X	MFI	4	DOHC
	Stratus	2.5 (2497)	H	MFI	6	SOHC
1996	Cirrus	2.4 (2429)	X	MFI	4	DOHC
	Cirrus	2.5 (2497)	H	MFI	6	SOHC
	Sebring Conv.	2.4 (2429)	X	MFI	4	DOHC
	Sebring Conv.	2.5 (2497)	H	MFI	6	SOHC
	Sebring Coupe	2.0 (1996)	Y	MFI	4	DOHC
	Sebring Coupe	2.5 (2497)	N	MFI	6	SOHC
	Avenger	2.0 (1996)	Y	MFI	4	DOHC
	Avenger	2.5 (2497)	N	MFI	6	SOHC
	Stratus	2.0 (1996)	C	MFI	4	SOHC
	Stratus	2.4 (2429)	X	MFI	4	DOHC
	Stratus	2.5 (2497)	H	MFI	6	SOHC
	Breeze	2.0 (1996)	C	MFI	4	SOHC
1997	Cirrus	2.4 (2429)	X	MFI	4	DOHC
	Cirrus	2.5 (2497)	H	MFI	6	SOHC
	Sebring Conv.	2.4 (2429)	X	MFI	4	DOHC
	Sebring Conv.	2.5 (2497)	H	MFI	6	SOHC
	Sebring Coupe	2.0 (1996)	Y	MFI	4	DOHC
	Sebring Coupe	2.5 (2497)	N	MFI	6	SOHC
	Avenger	2.0 (1996)	Y	MFI	4	DOHC
	Avenger	2.5 (2497)	N	MFI	6	SOHC
	Stratus	2.0 (1996)	C	MFI	4	SOHC
	Stratus	2.4 (2429)	X	MFI	4	DOHC
	Stratus	2.5 (2497)	H	MFI	6	SOHC
	Breeze	2.0 (1996)	C	MFI	4	SOHC
1998	Cirrus	2.5 (2497)	H	MFI	6	SOHC
	Sebring Conv.	2.4 (2429)	X	MFI	4	DOHC
	Sebring Conv.	2.5 (2497)	H	MFI	6	SOHC
	Sebring Coupe	2.0 (1996)	Y	MFI	4	DOHC
	Sebring Coupe	2.5 (2497)	N	MFI	6	SOHC
	Avenger	2.0 (1996)	Y	MFI	4	DOHC
	Avenger	2.5 (2497)	N	MFI	6	SOHC
	Stratus	2.0 (1996)	C	MFI	4	SOHC
	Stratus	2.4 (2429)	X	MFI	4	DOHC
	Stratus	2.5 (2497)	H	MFI	6	SOHC
	Breeze	2.0 (1996)	C	MFI	4	SOHC
	Breeze	2.4 (2429)	X	MFI	4	DOHC

DOHC - Dual Overhead Cam
SOHC - Single Overhead Cam
MFI - Multi-port Fuel Injection

90901C02

GENERAL ENGINE SPECIFICATIONS

Year	Engine ID/VIN	Engine Displacement Liters (cc)	Fuel System Type	Net Horsepower @ rpm	Net Torque @ rpm (ft. lbs.)	Bore x Stroke (in.)	Compression Ratio	Oil Pressure (psi) @ idle rpm
1995	C	2.0 (1996)	MFI	132 @ 6000	129 @ 5000	3.44 x 3.27	9.8:1	4 @ 600-1300
	Y	2.0 (1996)	MFI	140 @ 6000	130 @ 4800	3.44 x 3.27	9.6:1	4 @ 700-900
	X	2.4 (2429)	MFI	150 @ 5200	167 @ 4000	3.44 x 3.98	9.4:1	4 @ 600-1300
	H	2.5 (2497)	MFI	164 @ 5900	163 @ 4350	3.29 x 2.99	9.4:1	6 @ 500-1100
	N	2.5 (2497)	MFI	155 @ 5500	161 @ 4400	3.29 x 2.99	9.5:1	11.4 @ 600-800
1996	C	2.0 (1996)	MFI	132 @ 6000	129 @ 5000	3.44 x 3.27	9.8:1	4 @ 600-1300
	Y	2.0 (1996)	MFI	140 @ 6000	130 @ 4800	3.44 x 3.27	9.6:1	4 @ 700-900
	X	2.4 (2429)	MFI	150 @ 5200	167 @ 4000	3.44 x 3.98	9.4:1	4 @ 600-1300
	H	2.5 (2497)	MFI	168 @ 5800	170 @ 4350	3.29 x 2.99	9.4:1	6 @ 500-1100
	N	2.5 (2497)	MFI	163 @ 5800	170 @ 4400	3.29 x 2.99	9.5:1	11.4 @ 650-850
1997	C	2.0 (1996)	MFI	132 @ 6000	129 @ 5000	3.44 x 3.27	9.8:1	4 @ 600-1300
	Y	2.0 (1996)	MFI	140 @ 6000	130 @ 4800	3.44 x 3.27	9.6:1	4 @ 700-900
	X	2.4 (2429)	MFI	150 @ 5200	165 @ 4000	3.44 x 3.98	9.4:1	4 @ 600-1300
	H	2.5 (2497)	MFI	168 @ 5800	170 @ 4350	3.29 x 2.99	9.4:1	6 @ 500-1100
	N	2.5 (2497)	MFI	163 @ 5500	170 @ 4350	3.29 x 2.99	9.5:1	11.4 @ 650-850
1998	C	2.0 (1996)	MFI	132 @ 6000	128 @ 5000	3.44 x 3.27	9.8:1	4 @ 600-1300
	Y	2.0 (1996)	MFI	140 @ 6000	130 @ 4800	3.44 x 3.27	9.6:1	4 @ 700-900
	X	2.4 (2429)	MFI	150 @ 5200	167 @ 4000	3.44 x 3.98	9.4:1	4 @ 600-1300
	H	2.5 (2497)	MFI	168 @ 5800	170 @ 4350	3.29 x 2.99	9.4:1	6 @ 500-1100
	N	2.5 (2497)	MFI	163 @ 5500	170 @ 4350	3.29 x 2.99	9.4:1 ①	11.4 @ 650-850

MFI -Multiport Fuel Injection
① Compression ratio for California - 9.0:1

90901C04

Transaxle

MANUAL

♦ **See Figures 37, 38 and 39**

On all models, except the Avenger and Sebring coupe, the transaxle model, assembly number and build date can be found on a metal identification plate which is attached to the end cover of the transaxle. This information is also shown on a bar code label that is secured to the front of the transaxle.

The last eight digits of the VIN are stamped on the case, below the back-up lamp switch.

On the Avenger and Sebring coupe, the transaxle model, assembly number and build date can be found on a bar code label that is secured to the front of the transaxle, and up on top of the bell housing.

➡ **There are four different versions of this transaxle. There aren't any visible differences between the models, so make sure to refer to the ID tag to determine with which transaxle your vehicle is equipped.**

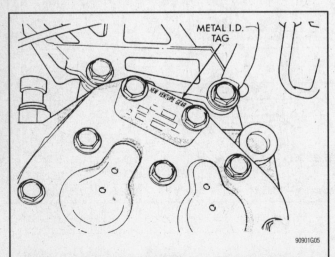

Fig. 37 Location of the metal identification tag on the transaxle rear case cover

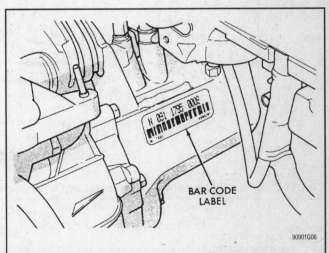

Fig. 38 Location of the bar code label on the front of the transaxle

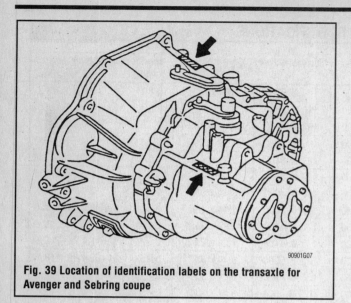

Fig. 39 Location of identification labels on the transaxle for Avenger and Sebring coupe

AUTOMATIC

♦ **See Figures 40 and 41**

On 1995 Cirrus and Stratus vehicles, the model, assembly number and build date can be found on an identification tag, which is located on the transaxle case, next to the solenoid assembly.

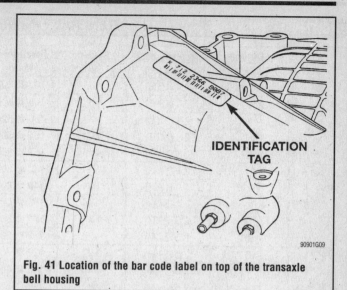

Fig. 41 Location of the bar code label on top of the transaxle bell housing

On all other vehicles, the model, assembly number and build date can be found on a bar code label which is located on the transaxle case, up on the bell housing.

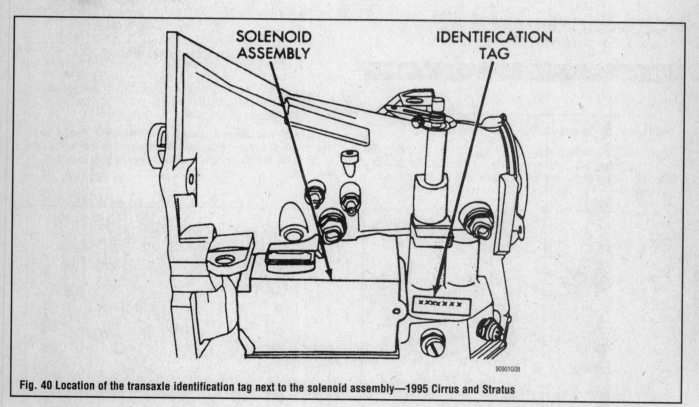

SOLENOID ASSEMBLY

IDENTIFICATION TAG

Fig. 40 Location of the transaxle identification tag next to the solenoid assembly—1995 Cirrus and Stratus

ROUTINE MAINTENANCE AND TUNE-UP

UNDERHOOD MAINTENANCE COMPONENT LOCATIONS—6-CYLINDER ENGINE

1. Coolant overflow tank fill cap
2. Washer fluid reservoir
3. Power steering fluid reservoir
4. Timing belt (beneath cover)
5. Accessory drive belt
6. PCV valve
7. Spark plugs and wires
8. Oil level dipstick
9. Vehicle Emissions Control Information (VECI) label
10. Engine oil fill cap
11. Brake fluid reservoir
12. Transaxle fluid level dipstick (automatic)
13. Positive battery terminal remote connector
14. Upper coolant hose
15. Negative battery terminal remote connector
16. Air cleaner housing

90901P31

UNDERHOOD MAINTENANCE COMPONENT LOCATIONS—4-CYLINDER ENGINE

1. Automatic transaxle fluid level dipstick
2. Windshield washer fluid reservoir
3. Engine oil fill cap
4. Oil level dipstick
5. Upper radiator hose
6. Spark plugs
7. Brake fluid reservoir
8. Battery
9. Air cleaner
10. PCV valve
11. Power steering fluid reservoir
12. Coolant overflow tank
13. Timing belt cover (belt underneath)

90901P97

Proper maintenance and tune-up is the key to long and trouble-free vehicle life, and the work can yield its own rewards. Studies have shown that a properly tuned and maintained vehicle can achieve better gas mileage than an out-of-tune vehicle. As a conscientious owner and driver, set aside a Saturday morning, say once a month, to check or replace items which could cause major problems later. Keep your own personal log to jot down which services you performed, how much the parts cost you, the date, and the exact odometer reading at the time. Keep all receipts for such items as engine oil and filters, so that they may be referred to in case of related problems or to determine operating expenses. As a do-it-yourselfer, these receipts are the only proof you have that the required maintenance was performed. In the event of a warranty problem, these receipts will be invaluable.

The literature provided with your vehicle when it was originally delivered includes the factory recommended maintenance schedule. If you no longer have this literature, replacement copies are usually available from the dealer. A maintenance schedule is provided later in this section, in case you do not have the factory literature.

Air Cleaner (Element)

REMOVAL & INSTALLATION

▶ See Figures 42, 43, 44 and 45

1. Unfasten the retaining clips on the air cleaner housing cover.
2. Lift the cover off of the air cleaner housing.
3. Remove the air cleaner element from the housing.

To install:

4. Wipe the air cleaner housing out using a damp cloth. Check the lid gasket, if so equipped, to ensure that it has a tight seal; replace it if necessary.
5. Position the replacement air cleaner element in the housing.
6. Install the air cleaner cover and secure by snapping the retaining clips.

Fuel Filter

On the Cirrus, Stratus, Breeze and Sebring convertible, a frame-mounted fuel filter is located on the frame rail, above the rear of the fuel tank. On the 1995 Avenger and Sebring coupe, the fuel filter is located on the left side of the engine compartment firewall. On the 1996–98 Avenger and Sebring coupe, the fuel filter is located underneath the vehicle, back near the fuel tank, along with the pressure regulator.

Fig. 43 After disengaging the retaining clips, lift the cover up to access the air filter

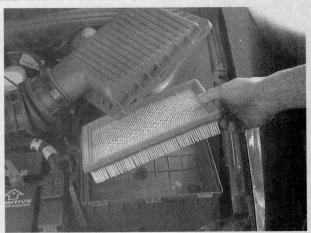

Fig. 44 Remove the air cleaner filter from the housing

Fig. 42 Unsnap the air cleaner housing cover retaining clips

Fig. 45 Using a damp cloth, clean any dirt or debris from the inside of the air cleaner housing

REMOVAL & INSTALLATION

Cirrus, Stratus, Breeze and Sebring Convertible

▶ See Figure 46

> ⁕⁕ **CAUTION**
>
> Observe all applicable safety precautions when working around fuel. Whenever servicing the fuel system, always work in a well ventilated area. Do not allow fuel spray or vapors to come in contact with a spark or open flame. Keep a dry chemical fire extinguisher near the work area. Always keep fuel in a container specifically designed for fuel storage; also, always properly seal fuel containers to avoid the possibility of fire or explosion.

1. Properly relieve the fuel system pressure, as outlined in Section 5 of this manual.
2. If not already done, disconnect the negative battery cable remote connection at the left strut tower.
3. From inside the trunk, disconnect the fuel pump module wiring jumper from the main body harness. The 4-pin electrical connector is located underneath the mat on the left side of the trunk, near the base of the shock tower. Locate the body grommet for the jumper near the bottom of the rear seat. Push out the grommet and route the jumper completely through the hole in the body.
4. Loosen the fuel filler cap slowly, then remove it to release the pressure in the fuel tank.
5. Raise and safely support the vehicle. Place a transmission jack, or equivalent support device underneath the fuel tank.
6. Place an approved fuel container, with at least a 16-gallon capacity, under the fuel tank drain plug. The drain plug is located on the bottom left edge of the fuel tank. Remove the plug and drain the fuel.
7. After the fuel is finished draining, install the plug and tighten to 32 inch lbs. (3.6 Nm).
8. Remove the driver's side fuel tank strap. Loosen, but do not remove, the passenger side fuel tank strap just enough to allow the filler neck to contact the rear suspension crossmember.
9. Place a shop rag below the fuel line connections to catch any fuel spill. Disengage the quick-connect fittings from the fuel pump and the fuel filter. Refer to Section 5 for information regarding quick-connect fittings.
10. Remove the fuel filter from the vehicle.

To install:

➡The fuel lines are permanently attached to the fuel filter. The ends of the fuel supply and return lines have different size quick-connect fittings. The larger quick-connect fittings attach to the large nipple (supply side) on the fuel pump module. The smaller fitting connects to the small nipple (return side) on the fuel pump module.

11. Apply a thin coating of clean engine oil to the fuel filter nipples, then attach the quick-connect fuel lines. Refer to Section 5 for details.
12. Carefully raise the fuel tank into position and install the retaining straps. Install the front bolts first, then the rear bolts and tighten to 250 inch lbs. (23 Nm). As the fuel tank is being raised, install the fuel pump module wiring harness grommet into the body.
13. Carefully lower the vehicle, and connect the fuel pump module wiring harness.
14. Fill up the fuel tank.
15. Connect the negative battery cable.

1995 Avenger and Sebring Coupe

▶ See Figure 47

> ⁕⁕ **CAUTION**
>
> Observe all applicable safety precautions when working around fuel. Whenever servicing the fuel system, always work in a well ventilated area. Do not allow fuel spray or vapors to come in contact with a spark or open flame. Keep a dry chemical fire extinguisher near the work area. Always keep fuel in a container specifically designed for fuel storage; also, always properly seal fuel containers to avoid the possibility of fire or explosion.

1. Properly relieve the fuel system pressure, as outlined in Section 5 of this manual.
2. If not already done, disconnect the negative battery cable.
3. Disconnect the positive battery cable. Unfasten the hold-down device and remove the battery from the vehicle.
4. Remove the air intake hose.

➡Wrap shop towels around the fitting that is being disconnected to absorb residual fuel in the lines.

5. Cover the hose connection with shop towels to prevent any splash of fuel that could be caused by residual pressure in the fuel pipe line. Hold the fuel filter nut securely with a back-up wrench and remove the eye bolt

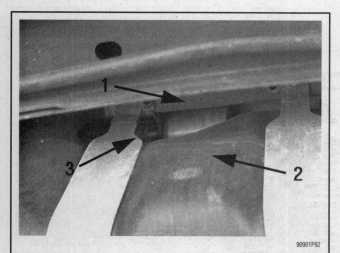

Fig. 46 Location of the fuel filter on the frame rail (1) and above the fuel tank (2). Note the use of quick-connect fittings (3)

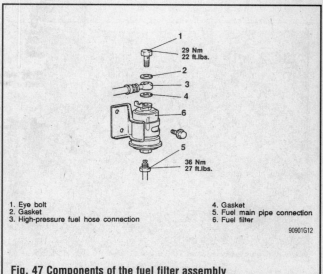

1. Eye bolt
2. Gasket
3. High-pressure fuel hose connection
4. Gasket
5. Fuel main pipe connection
6. Fuel filter

1 — 29 Nm / 22 ft.lbs.
5 — 36 Nm / 27 ft.lbs.

Fig. 47 Components of the fuel filter assembly

from the filter. Disconnect the high-pressure fuel line from the filter. Remove and discard the gaskets.

6. While holding the fuel filter nut securely with a back-up wrench, loosen the main pipe flare nut. Separate the flare nut connection from the filter.

7. Remove the mounting bolts and remove the fuel filter. If necessary, remove the fuel filter bracket.

To install:

8. Install the filter in its mounting bracket. Install the bracket bolt only finger-tight. Movement of the filter will ease attachment of the fuel lines.

➡**Make sure new O-ring gaskets are installed prior to installation.**

9. Insert the main pipe at the connector part of the filter and screw in the main pipe's flare nut finger-tight; do not overtighten.

10. Position the high pressure fuel line in place and install the eye bolt, along with new O-ring gaskets. Tighten the eye bolt to 22 ft. lbs. (29 Nm). Tighten the main pipe flare nut to 27 ft. lbs. (36 Nm), with a back-up wrench on the nut.

11. Tighten the filter mounting bolts to 10 ft. lbs. (14 Nm).

12. Install the air intake hose.

13. Install the battery into the vehicle. Connect the positive battery cable.

14. Connect the negative battery cable. Turn the key to the **ON** position to pressurize the fuel system and check for leaks.

➡**If repairs of a leak are required, remember to relieve the fuel pressure before opening the fuel system.**

1996–98 Avenger and Sebring Coupe

♦ **See Figure 48**

✳✳ CAUTION

Observe all applicable safety precautions when working around fuel. Whenever servicing the fuel system, always work in a well ventilated area. Do not allow fuel spray or vapors to come in contact with a spark or open flame. Keep a dry chemical fire extinguisher near the work area. Always keep fuel in a container specifically designed for fuel storage; also, always properly seal fuel containers to avoid the possibility of fire or explosion.

1. Properly relieve the fuel system pressure, as outlined in Section 5 of this manual.

2. If not already done, disconnect the negative battery cable.

3. Raise and safely support the vehicle.

➡**Wrap shop towels around the fitting that is being disconnected to absorb residual fuel in the lines.**

4. Cover the hose connection with shop towels to prevent any splash of fuel that could be caused by residual pressure in the fuel pipe line. Hold the fuel filter nut securely with a back-up wrench, then remove the eye bolt. Disconnect the high pressure fuel line from the filter. Remove and discard the gaskets.

5. While holding the fuel filter nut securely with a back-up wrench, loosen and remove the main pipe eye bolt. Disconnect the fuel main pipe from the filter. Remove and discard the gaskets.

6. Unfasten the mounting bolt and remove the fuel filter. If necessary, remove the fuel filter bracket.

To install:

7. Install the filter to its bracket only finger-tight. Movement of the filter will ease attachment of the fuel lines.

➡**Make sure new O-rings are installed prior to installation.**

8. Insert the main pipe at the connector part of the filter and manually screw in the main pipe's flare nut.

9. While holding the fuel filter nut, on each end of the filter, with a back-up wrench, tighten the eye bolts to 22 ft. lbs. (29 Nm).

10. Tighten the filter mounting bolts to 10 ft. lbs. (14 Nm).

11. Carefully lower the vehicle, then connect the negative battery cable.

12. Turn the key to the **ON** position to pressurize the fuel system and check for leaks.

➡**If repairs of a leak are required, remember to release the fuel pressure before opening the fuel system.**

PCV Valve

The Positive Crankcase Ventilation (PCV) valve is part of a system which is designed to protect the atmosphere from harmful vapors. Blow-by gas from the crankcase, as well as fumes from crankcase oil, are diverted into the combustion chamber where they are burned during engine operation. Proper operation of this system will improve engine performance, as well as decrease the amount of harmful vapors released into the atmosphere.

REMOVAL & INSTALLATION

♦ **See Figures 49, 50, 51 and 52**

1. If necessary, use a pair of pliers to unfasten the crankcase hose retaining clamps, then disconnect the ventilation hoses from the PCV valve.

2. Remove the PCV valve from the camshaft (rocker) cover or the hose, as applicable.

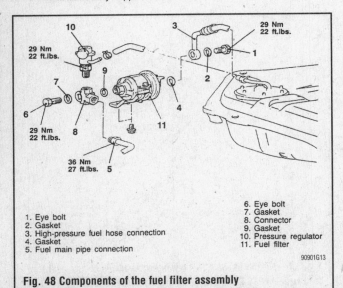

1. Eye bolt
2. Gasket
3. High-pressure fuel hose connection
4. Gasket
5. Fuel main pipe connection
6. Eye bolt
7. Gasket
8. Connector
9. Gasket
10. Pressure regulator
11. Fuel filter

90901G13

Fig. 48 Components of the fuel filter assembly

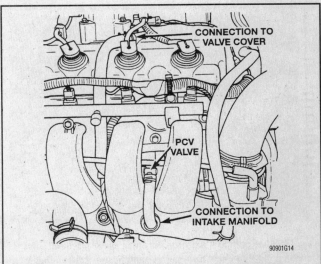

CONNECTION TO VALVE COVER

PCV VALVE

CONNECTION TO INTAKE MANIFOLD

90901G14

Fig. 49 Location of the PCV valve on the 2.0L SOHC engine

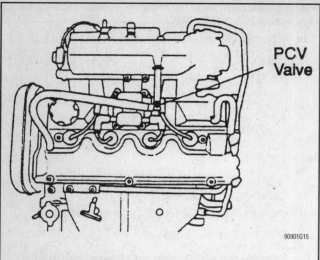

Fig. 50 Location of the PCV valve on the 2.0L DOHC engine

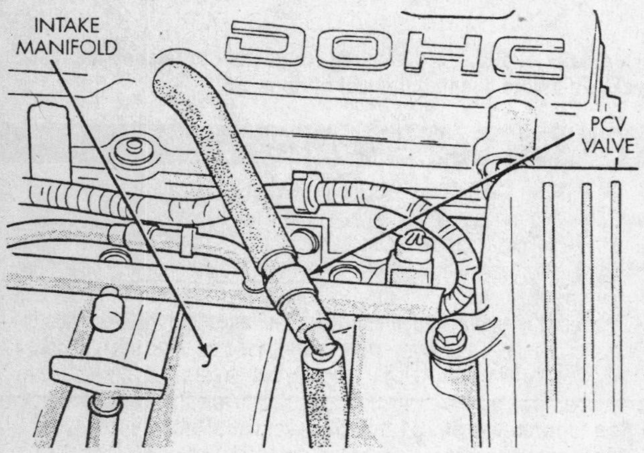

Fig. 51 Location of the PCV valve on the 2.4L engine

Fig. 52 After pulling it out from the valve cover grommet, disconnect the PCV valve from the vacuum hose—2.5L engine shown

To install:

3. Install the PCV valve into the rocker cover or attach it to the hose, as necessary.

4. Reconnect the ventilation hoses to the valve. If necessary, use a pair of pliers to secure the hose clamps.

5. Connect the negative battery cable.

Evaporative Canister

This system is designed to contain gasoline vapor, which normally escapes from the fuel tank and intake manifold, from discharging into the atmosphere. Vapor absorption is accomplished through the use of a charcoal canister, which stores the vapors until they can be removed and burned in the combustion process.

SERVICING

▶ See Figures 53, 54 and 55

For all 1995–97 models including 1998 Sebring convertibles, the evaporative canister is mounted to a bracket located behind the front fascia on the passenger's side of the vehicle.

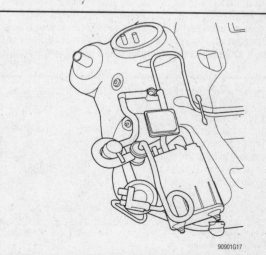

Fig. 53 Pull back the inner fender well shield ahead of the right front wheel to access the canister on 1995–97 vehicles, as well as on the 1998 Sebring convertible

Fig. 54 Location of the EVAP canister assembly on top of the fuel tank—1998 Cirrus, Stratus and Breeze models

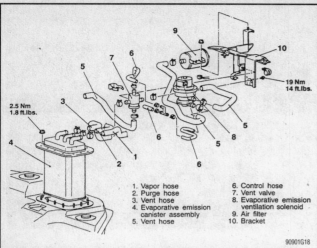

1. Vapor hose
2. Purge hose
3. Vent hose
4. Evaporative emission canister assembly
5. Vent hose
6. Control hose
7. Vent valve
8. Evaporative emission ventilation solenoid
9. Air filter
10. Bracket

90901G18

Fig. 55 Location of the fuel tank mounted EVAP canister assembly—1998 Sebring and Avenger coupes

For 1998 models, except Sebring convertible, the evaporative canister is mounted to a bracket located on top of the fuel tank at the rear of the vehicle.

Check the evaporative emission control system every 15,000 miles (24,000 km). The evaporative canister is a sealed, maintenance-free unit. Inspect the fuel vapor lines and the vacuum hoses for proper connections and correct routing, as well as condition. Replace clogged, damaged or deteriorated parts as necessary. Refer to the Vehicle Emission Control Information (VECI) label, located under the hood, for routing of the canister hoses.

➡**The evaporative system uses special type hoses. If it becomes necessary to replace any of the hoses, use only fuel resistant hoses.**

Battery

PRECAUTIONS

✳✳ CAUTION

Always use caution when working on or near the battery. Never allow a tool to bridge the gap between the negative and positive battery terminals. Also, be careful not to allow a tool to provide a ground between the positive cable/terminal and any metal component on the vehicle. Either of these conditions will cause a short circuit, leading to sparks and possible personal injury.

Do not smoke, have an open flame or create sparks near a battery; the gases contained in the battery are very explosive and, if ignited, could cause severe injury or death.

All batteries, regardless of type, should be carefully secured by a battery hold-down device. If this is not done, the battery terminals or casing may crack from stress applied to the battery during vehicle operation. A battery which is not secured may allow acid to leak out, making it discharge faster; such leaking corrosive acid can also eat away at components under the hood.

Always visually inspect the battery case for cracks, leakage and corrosion. A white corrosive substance on the battery case or on nearby components would indicate a leaking or cracked battery. If the battery is cracked, it should be replaced immediately.

GENERAL MAINTENANCE

▶ **See Figure 56**

A battery that is not sealed must be checked periodically for electrolyte level. You cannot add water to a sealed maintenance-free battery (though not all maintenance-free batteries are sealed); however, a sealed battery must also be checked for proper electrolyte level, as indicated by the color of the built-in hydrometer "eye."

Always keep the battery cables and terminals free of corrosion. Check these components at least once a year. Refer to the removal, installation and cleaning procedures outlined in this section.

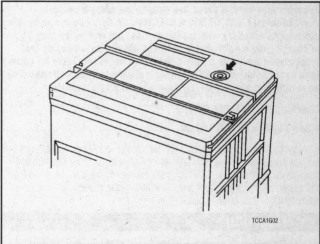

TCCA1G02

Fig. 56 A typical location for the built-in hydrometer on maintenance-free batteries

Keep the top of the battery clean, as a film of dirt can help completely discharge a battery that is not used for long periods. A solution of baking soda and water may be used for cleaning, but be careful to flush this off with clear water. DO NOT let any of the solution into the filler holes. Baking soda neutralizes battery acid and will de-activate a battery cell.

Batteries in vehicles which are not operated on a regular basis can fall victim to parasitic loads (small current drains which are constantly drawing current from the battery). Normal parasitic loads may drain a battery on a vehicle that is in storage and not used for 6–8 weeks. Vehicles that have additional accessories such as a cellular phone, alarm system or other devices that increase parasitic load may discharge a battery sooner. If the vehicle is to be stored for 6–8 weeks in a secure area and the alarm system, if present, is not necessary, the negative battery cable should be disconnected at the onset of storage to protect the battery charge.

Remember that constantly discharging and recharging will shorten battery life. Take care not to allow a battery to be needlessly discharged.

BATTERY FLUID

Check the battery electrolyte level at least once a month, or more often in hot weather or during periods of extended vehicle operation. On non-sealed batteries, the level can be checked either through the case on translucent batteries or by removing the cell caps on opaque-cased types. The electrolyte level in each cell should be kept filled to the split ring inside each cell, or the line marked on the outside of the case.

If the level is low, add only distilled water through the opening until the level is correct. Each cell is separate from the others, so each must be checked and filled individually. Distilled water should be used, because the chemicals and minerals found in most drinking water are harmful to the battery and could significantly shorten its life.

If water is added in freezing weather, the vehicle should be driven several miles to allow the water to mix with the electrolyte. Otherwise, the battery could freeze.

Although some maintenance-free batteries have removable cell caps for access to the electrolyte, the electrolyte condition and level on all sealed maintenance-free batteries must be checked using the built-in hydrometer "eye." The exact type of eye varies between battery manufacturers, but most apply a sticker to the battery itself explaining the possible readings. When in doubt, refer to the battery manufacturer's instructions to interpret battery condition using the built-in hydrometer.

➡**Although the readings from built-in hydrometers found in sealed batteries may vary, a green eye usually indicates a properly charged battery with sufficient fluid level. A dark eye is normally an indicator of a battery with sufficient fluid, but one which may be low in charge. And a light or yellow eye is usually an indication that electrolyte supply has dropped below the necessary level for battery (and hydrometer) operation. In this last case, sealed batteries with an insufficient electrolyte level must usually be discarded.**

Checking the Specific Gravity

▶ **See Figures 57, 58 and 59**

A hydrometer is required to check the specific gravity on all batteries that are not maintenance-free. On batteries that are maintenance-free, the specific gravity is checked by observing the built-in hydrometer "eye" on the top of the battery case. Check with your battery's manufacturer for proper interpretation of its built-in hydrometer readings.

✳✳ CAUTION

Battery electrolyte contains sulfuric acid. If you should splash any on your skin or in your eyes, flush the affected area with plenty of clear water. If it lands in your eyes, get medical help immediately.

The fluid (sulfuric acid solution) contained in the battery cells will tell you many things about the condition of the battery. Because the cell plates must be kept submerged below the fluid level in order to operate, maintaining the fluid level is extremely important. And, because the specific gravity of the acid is an indication of electrical charge, testing the fluid can be an aid in determining if the battery must be replaced. A battery in a vehicle with a properly operating charging system should require little maintenance, but careful, periodic inspection should reveal problems before they leave you stranded.

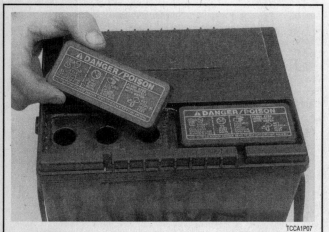

Fig. 57 On non-maintenance-free batteries, the fluid level can be checked through the case on translucent models; the cell caps must be removed on other models

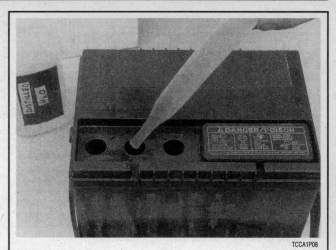

Fig. 58 If the fluid level is low, add only distilled water through the opening until the level is correct

Fig. 59 Check the specific gravity of the battery's electrolyte with a hydrometer

As stated earlier, the specific gravity of a battery's electrolyte level can be used as an indication of battery charge. At least once a year, check the specific gravity of the battery. It should be between 1.20 and 1.26 on the gravity scale. Most auto supply stores carry a variety of inexpensive battery testing hydrometers. These can be used on any non-sealed battery to test the specific gravity in each cell.

The battery testing hydrometer has a squeeze bulb at one end and a nozzle at the other. Battery electrolyte is sucked into the hydrometer until the float is lifted from its seat. The specific gravity is then read by noting the position of the float. If gravity is low in one or more cells, the battery should be slowly charged and checked again to see if the gravity has come up. Generally, if after charging, the specific gravity between any two cells varies more than 50 points (0.50), the battery should be replaced, as it can no longer produce sufficient voltage to guarantee proper operation.

CABLES

▶ **See Figures 60, 61, 62, 63 and 64**

Once a year (or as necessary), the battery terminals and the cable clamps should be cleaned. Loosen the clamps and remove the cables, negative cable first. On batteries with posts on top, the use of a puller specially

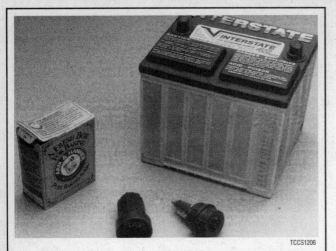

Fig. 60 Maintenance is performed with household items and with special tools like this post cleaner

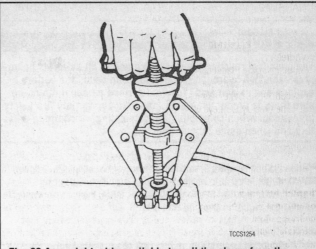

Fig. 63 A special tool is available to pull the clamp from the post

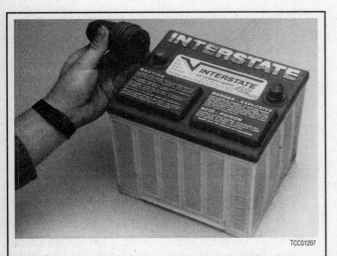

Fig. 61 The underside of this special battery tool has a wire brush to clean post terminals

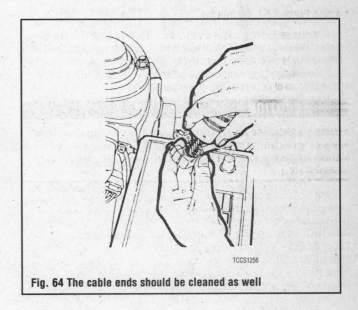

Fig. 64 The cable ends should be cleaned as well

made for this purpose is recommended. These are inexpensive and available in most auto parts stores. Side terminal battery cables are secured with a small bolt.

Clean the cable clamps and the battery terminal with a wire brush, until all corrosion, grease, etc., is removed and the metal is shiny. It is especially important to clean the inside of the clamp thoroughly (an old knife is useful here), since a small deposit of foreign material or oxidation there will prevent a sound electrical connection and inhibit either starting or charging. Special tools are available for cleaning these parts, one type for conventional top post batteries and another type for side terminal batteries. It is also a good idea to apply some dielectric grease to the terminal, as this will aid in the prevention of corrosion.

After the clamps and terminals are clean, reinstall the cables, negative cable last; DO NOT hammer the clamps onto battery posts. Tighten the clamps securely, but do not distort them. Give the clamps and terminals a thin external coating of grease after installation, to retard corrosion.

Check the cables at the same time that the terminals are cleaned. If the cable insulation is cracked or broken, or if the ends are frayed, the cable should be replaced with a new cable of the same length and gauge.

Fig. 62 Place the tool over the battery posts and twist to clean until the metal is shiny

CHARGING

> ※※ **CAUTION**
>
> **The chemical reaction which takes place in all batteries generates explosive hydrogen gas. A spark can cause the battery to explode and splash acid. To avoid serious personal injury, be sure there is proper ventilation and take appropriate fire safety precautions when connecting, disconnecting, or charging a battery and when using jumper cables.**

A battery should be charged at a slow rate to keep the plates inside from getting too hot. However, if some maintenance-free batteries are allowed to discharge until they are almost "dead," they may have to be charged at a high rate to bring them back to "life." Always follow the charger manufacturer's instructions on charging the battery.

REPLACEMENT

◆ **See Figures 65 thru 77**

When it becomes necessary to replace the battery, select one with an amperage rating equal to or greater than the battery originally installed. Deterioration and just plain aging of the battery cables, starter motor, and associated wires makes the battery's job harder in successive years. The slow increase in electrical resistance over time makes it prudent to install a new battery with a greater capacity than the old.

The Sebring coupe and Avenger models are equipped with a battery that is removed and installed in the conventional manner. However, the Cirrus, Stratus, Breeze and Sebring convertible models have the battery mounted within the fender well area, just ahead of the left front wheel, with a remote negative terminal location on the left, front shock tower. To replace the battery on these vehicles only, perform the following procedure.

1. With all accessories turned **OFF**, place the ignition switch in the **OFF** position.
2. Disconnect the negative battery cable at the remote location on the left front shock tower. Secure the cable so that it does not accidentally make contact with the post by placing the small eye of the cable over the stud as illustrated.
3. Turn the steering wheel to the full left position. If more access is needed, remove the left front wheel instead.
4. Remove the battery shield after twisting the four plastic screws ¼ turn.

Fig. 65 The Cirrus' battery is located behind the access panel, just ahead of the left front wheel—Stratus, Breeze and Sebring convertible similar

Fig. 66 Disconnect the negative battery cable by first loosening the retaining nut on the threaded stud at the left strut tower . . .

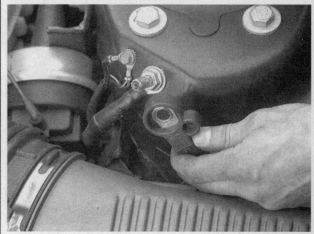

Fig. 67 . . . then separate the cable from the stud

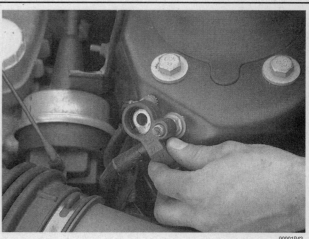

Fig. 68 To prevent the negative battery cable from contacting the stud, secure the cable by placing its small eye onto the stud

Fig. 69 After twisting the four plastic screws (arrows), disengage the retaining tabs from its lower portion and remove the access panel from the vehicle

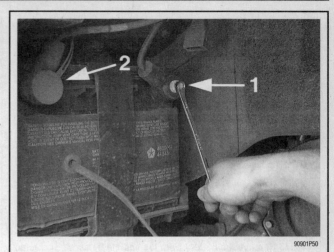

Fig. 72 Disconnect the negative cable at the battery (1), followed by the positive cable (2)

Fig. 70 If the vehicle is equipped with a battery heater blanket and/or engine block heater, the extension cord is located under the hood, near the air cleaner housing

Fig. 73 Loosen the battery's upper and lower retaining strap bolts . . .

Fig. 71 If so equipped, disengage the battery heater blanket cord

Fig. 74 . . . then remove the battery retaining strap

Fig. 75 Remove the battery from the vehicle by carefully sliding it out of the tray. Be careful not to tip it or spill any of the battery acid

Fig. 76 If necessary, remove the battery heater blanket by first disengaging the retaining clasp . . .

5. If equipped, disengage the battery blanket heater cord.

6. Disconnect the negative cable at the battery, then the positive cable.

7. Remove the upper and lower battery retaining strap bolts.

8. Remove the battery from the vehicle. If the edge of the battery tray has a bottom lip, it may be necessary to move the battery to the rear of the tray and lift. Be careful not to tip the battery, so that acid will not spill out.

9. If equipped, remove the battery heater blanket.

To install:

10. Install the battery heater blanket, if so equipped. Install the battery into the vehicle.

11. Install the battery hold-down bracket and strap. Tighten the hold-down bracket and strap bolts to 160 inch lbs. (14 Nm).

12. Connect the positive cable first, then the negative cable to the battery.

13. Connect the battery heater blanket cord, if so equipped.

Fig. 77 . . . then unwrapping it from around the battery

14. Install the battery shield and secure with the four plastic screws.

15. Connect the negative battery cable to the remote location at the shock tower.

Belts

INSPECTION

▶ **See Figures 78 thru 83**

Inspect the belts for signs of glazing or cracking. A glazed belt will be perfectly smooth from slippage, while a good belt will have a slight texture of fabric visible. Cracks will usually start at the inner edge of the belt and run outward. All worn or damaged drive belts should

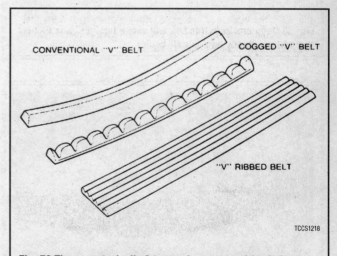

CONVENTIONAL "V" BELT   COGGED "V" BELT

"V" RIBBED BELT

TCCS1218

Fig. 78 There are typically 3 types of accessory drive belts found on vehicles today

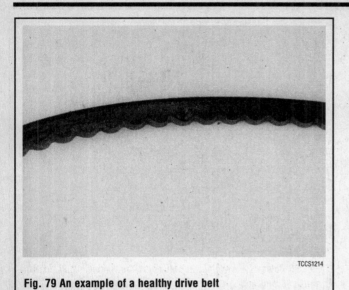

Fig. 79 An example of a healthy drive belt

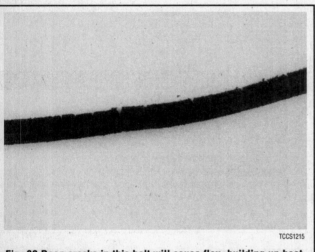

Fig. 80 Deep cracks in this belt will cause flex, building up heat that will eventually lead to belt failure

Fig. 81 The cover of this belt is worn, exposing the critical reinforcing cords to excessive wear

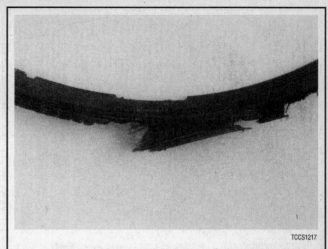

Fig. 82 Installing too wide a belt can result in serious belt wear and/or breakage

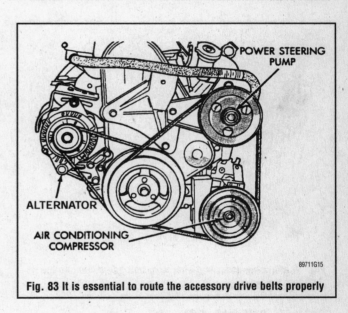

POWER STEERING PUMP

ALTERNATOR

AIR CONDITIONING COMPRESSOR

Fig. 83 It is essential to route the accessory drive belts properly

be replaced immediately. It is best to replace all drive belts at one time, as a preventive maintenance measure, during this service operation.

ADJUSTMENT

Cirrus, Stratus, Breeze and Sebring Convertible

A/C COMPRESSOR AND ALTERNATOR DRIVE BELT

▶ See Figures 84 and 85

1. If equipped with the 2.0L or 2.4L engine, loosen the locknut at the top and pivot bolt at the bottom of the alternator. If equipped with a 2.5L engine, loosen the idler pulley locking bolt.

2. Adjust the belt by rotating the adjusting bolt until the correct tension is reached. A new belt should be adjusted to 130–150 lbs. tension. A used belt should be adjusted to 80–90 lbs. tension.

3. After the belt is properly adjusted, tighten the pivot bolt and locknut on 2.0L and 2.4L engines to 40 ft. lbs. (54 Nm). Tighten the idler pulley locking bolt on 2.5L engines to 40 ft. lbs. (54 Nm).

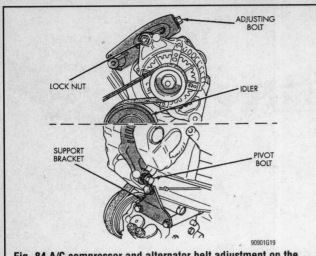

Fig. 84 A/C compressor and alternator belt adjustment on the 2.0L SOHC and 2.4L engines

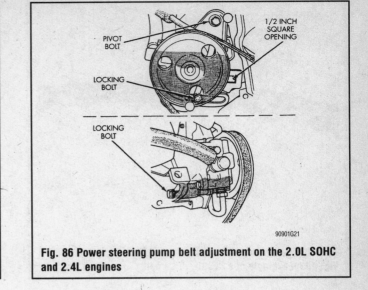

Fig. 86 Power steering pump belt adjustment on the 2.0L SOHC and 2.4L engines

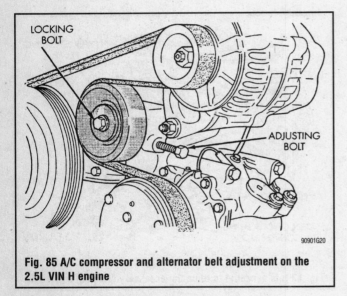

Fig. 85 A/C compressor and alternator belt adjustment on the 2.5L VIN H engine

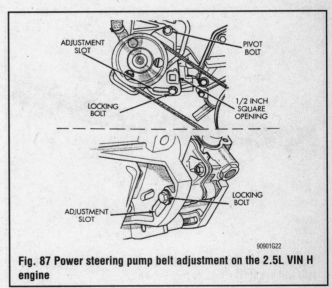

Fig. 87 Power steering pump belt adjustment on the 2.5L VIN H engine

POWER STEERING PUMP DRIVE BELT

▶ See Figures 86 and 87

1. From above the vehicle, loosen the pivot bolt at the top of the power steering pump.

2. Raise and safely support the front of the vehicle securely on jackstands.

3. From underneath the vehicle, loosen the locking bolts at the bottom of the power steering pump.

4. Use a ½ inch breaker bar inserted in the square opening of the mounting bracket to adjust the belt tension. A new belt should be adjusted to 130–150 lbs. tension. A used belt should be adjusted to 80–90 lbs. tension.

5. After the belt is adjusted properly, tighten the locking bolts to 40 ft. lbs. (54 Nm), except for the rear locking bolt on the 2.5L V6 engine, which is tightened to 250 inch lbs. (28 Nm).

6. Lower the vehicle.
7. Tighten the pivot bolt to 40 ft. lbs. (54 Nm).

Sebring Coupe and Avenger (2.0L DOHC Engine)

ALTERNATOR BELT

▶ See Figures 88 and 89

1. Place a straightedge along the bottom edge of the belt and across the 2 pulleys. Allow both ends of the straightedge to rest on the bottom of each pulley for support.

2. Measure the deflection of the belt from the straightedge with a force of about 22 lbs. applied midway between the 2 pulleys. Deflection should be 0.35–0.45 inch (9.0–11.5mm).

3. To adjust the tension on the alternator drive belt, loosen the adjusting bolt and the pivot locknut at the alternator. Then, move the alternator by turning the adjusting bolt. Once the desired value is reached, secure

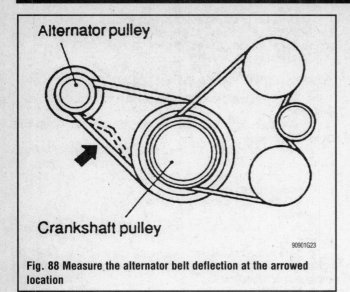

Fig. 88 Measure the alternator belt deflection at the arrowed location

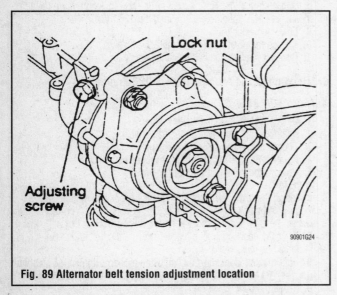

Fig. 89 Alternator belt tension adjustment location

the bolt and locknut. Tighten the pivot bolt to 40 ft. lbs. (54 Nm) and the locknut to 45 ft. lbs. (61 Nm). Recheck the belt tension.

POWER STEERING PUMP BELT—VEHICLES WITHOUT A/C

1. Press on the belt, about midway between the power steering pump pulley and the crankshaft pulley. With reasonable pressure applied (about 22 lbs.), the belt should deflect about 0.43–0.55 inches (11–14mm).
2. Adjustment can be made by loosening the 3 bolts that hold the pump. Place a suitable bar or lever between the body of the pump and gently pry to achieve the desired tension.
3. Retighten the 3 bolts to 29 ft. lbs. (39 Nm).
4. Rotate the crankshaft one or more full rotations, then check the belt tension again.

POWER STEERING PUMP AND A/C BELT

▶ See Figure 90

1. Press the belt in, at about the center between the power steering pump pulley and the crankshaft pulley. With reasonable pressure applied (about 22 lbs.) the belt should deflect about 0.39–0.43 inches (10–11mm).
2. Adjustment can be made by loosening the tensioner pulley nut and turning the adjuster bolt until the desired tension is attained.
3. Tighten the pulley nut and check the belt tension again.

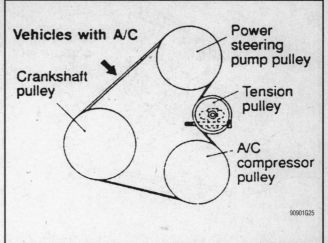

Fig. 90 Depress/measure the power steering pump and A/C belt deflection at the arrowed location

Sebring Coupe and Avenger (2.5L VIN N Engine)

ALTERNATOR AND POWER STEERING PUMP BELT

▶ See Figure 91

1. Press the belt in, midway between the power steering pump pulley and the alternator pulley. With reasonable pressure applied (about 22 lbs.), the belt should deflect about 0.45–0.49 inches (11.5–12.5mm).
2. Adjustment can be made by loosening the tensioner pulley nut and turning the adjuster bolt until the desired tension is attained.
3. Tighten the pulley nut and check the belt tension again. Tighten the locknut to 17 ft. lbs. (23 Nm).

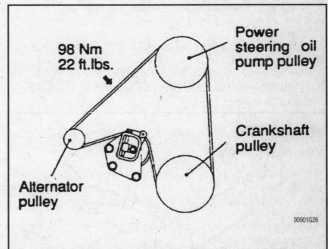

Fig. 91 Measure the alternator and power steering pump belt deflection at the arrowed location

AIR CONDITIONING COMPRESSOR BELT

▶ See Figure 92

1. Press the belt in, midway between the crankshaft pulley and the tensioner pulley. With reasonable pressure applied (about 22 lbs.), the belt should deflect about 0.32–0.35 inches (8–9mm).
2. Adjustment can be made by loosening the tensioner pulley nut and turning the adjuster bolt until the desired tension is attained.
3. Tighten the pulley nut and check the belt tension again.

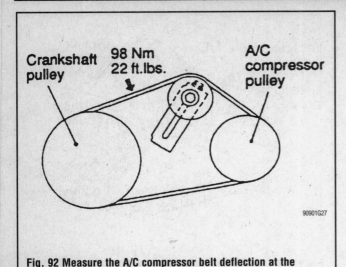

Fig. 92 Measure the A/C compressor belt deflection at the arrowed location

REMOVAL & INSTALLATION

Cirrus, Stratus, Breeze and Sebring Convertible

▶ See Figure 93

A/C COMPRESSOR AND ALTERNATOR DRIVE BELT

1. Disconnect the negative battery cable remote connection at the left strut tower.
2. If equipped with the 2.0L or 2.4L engine, loosen the locknut at the top and pivot bolt at the bottom of the alternator. If equipped with a 2.5L engine, loosen the idler pulley lockbolt.
3. Rotate the adjuster screw to decrease the belt tension.
4. Take note of the exact routing of the belt prior to removal. Lift the drive belt from the pulleys and remove it from the engine compartment.

To install:
5. Position the replacement belt around the pulleys, making sure the belt routing is correct.
6. Adjust the belt by rotating the adjusting bolt until the correct tension is reached. Refer to the procedure earlier in this section for belt adjustment.

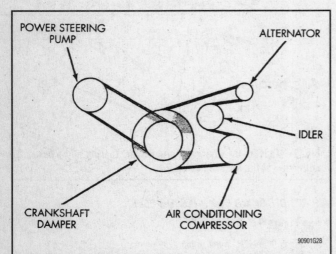

Fig. 93 Accessory drive belt routing for 2.0L SOHC, 2.4L and 2.5L VIN H engines

7. After the belt is installed and/or properly adjusted, tighten the pivot bolt and locknut on 2.0L and 2.4L engines to 40 ft. lbs. (54 Nm); on 2.5L engines, tighten the locking bolt to 40 ft. lbs. (54 Nm).
8. Connect the negative battery cable.

POWER STEERING PUMP DRIVE BELT

1. Disconnect the negative battery cable remote connection at the left strut tower.
2. From above the vehicle, loosen the pivot bolt at the top of the power steering pump.
3. Raise and safely support the front of the vehicle securely on jackstands.
4. From underneath the vehicle, loosen the locking bolts at the bottom of the power steering pump.
5. With the tension released, remove the drive belt.

To install:
6. Install the drive belt around the crankshaft and power steering pump pulleys.
7. Use a ½ inch breaker bar inserted in the square opening of the mounting bracket to adjust the belt tension. Refer to the procedure earlier in this section for belt adjustment.
8. After the belt is installed and/or adjusted properly, tighten the locking bolts to 40 ft. lbs. (54 Nm), except for the rear locking bolt on the 2.5L V6 engine, which is tightened to 250 inch lbs. (28 Nm).
9. Lower the vehicle.
10. Tighten the pivot bolt to 40 ft. lbs. (54 Nm).
11. Connect the negative battery cable.

Sebring Coupe and Avenger (2.0L DOHC Engine)

ALTERNATOR BELT

1. Disconnect the negative battery cable.
2. Remove the undercover right side panel.
3. Loosen the adjusting bolt and the pivot locknut at the alternator.
4. Rotate the adjusting bolt to decrease the belt tension.
5. Remove the drive belt from the engine.

To install:
6. Install the drive belt around the crankshaft and alternator pulleys.
7. Adjust the belt by rotating the adjusting bolt until the correct tension is reached. Refer to the procedure earlier in this section for belt adjustment.
8. Once the desired value is reached, secure the bolt and locknut. Recheck the belt tension.
9. After the belt is installed and adjusted properly, tighten the pivot nut to 40 ft. lbs. (54 Nm). Then, tighten the locknut to 45 ft. lbs. (61 Nm).
10. Install the undercover right side panel.
11. Connect the negative battery cable.

POWER STEERING PUMP BELT—VEHICLES WITHOUT A/C

1. Disconnect the negative battery cable.
2. Loosen the 3 bolts that secure the power steering pump.
3. Move the pump to decrease the belt tension.
4. Remove the drive belt from the engine.

To install:
5. Route the drive belt around the crankshaft and power steering pump pulleys.
6. Place a suitable bar or lever between the body of the pump and gently pry to get the desired tension. Refer to the procedure earlier in this section for belt adjustment.
7. Tighten the 3 bolts to 29 ft. lbs. (39 Nm) and check belt tension again.
8. Connect the negative battery cable.

POWER STEERING PUMP AND A/C BELT

1. Disconnect the negative battery cable.
2. Loosen the tension pulley locknut.
3. Rotate the adjusting bolt to decrease the belt tension.
4. Remove the drive belt from the engine.

To install:

5. Position the replacement belt around the pulleys, making sure the belt routing is correct.

6. Adjust the belt by rotating the adjusting bolt until the correct tension is reached. Refer to the procedure earlier in this section for belt adjustment.

7. Once the desired tension is reached, secure the locknut. Recheck the belt tension.

8. After the belt is installed and adjusted properly, tighten the locknut.

9. Connect the negative battery cable.

Sebring Coupe and Avenger (2.5L VIN N Engine)

1. Disconnect the negative battery cable.
2. Loosen the tension pulley locknut.
3. Rotate the adjusting bolt to decrease the belt tension.
4. Remove the drive belt from the engine.

To install:

5. Position the replacement belt around the pulleys, making sure the belt routing is correct.

6. Adjust the belt by rotating the adjusting bolt until the correct tension is reached. Refer to the procedure earlier in this section for belt adjustment.

7. Once the desired tension is reached, secure the locknut. Recheck the belt tension.

8. After the belt is installed and adjusted properly, tighten the locknut to 17 ft. lbs. (23 Nm).

9. Connect the negative battery cable.

Timing Belt

INSPECTION

▶ **See Figures 94 thru 101**

All engines covered by this manual utilize timing belts to drive the camshaft from the crankshaft's turning motion and to maintain proper valve timing. Some manufacturers schedule periodic timing belt replacement to assure optimum engine performance, to make sure the motorist is not stranded should the belt break (as the engine will stop instantly), and for some (manufacturers with interference motors), to prevent the possibility of severe internal engine damage should the belt break.

Because the engines are classified as interference motors (listed by the manufacturer as an engine whose valves might contact the pistons if the camshaft was rotated separately from the crankshaft), Chrysler corporation recommends changing the timing belt at 105,000 miles (169,000 km) for Cirrus, Stratus, Sebring convertible or Breeze, and 100,000 miles (161,000 km) for Sebring and Avenger coupes.

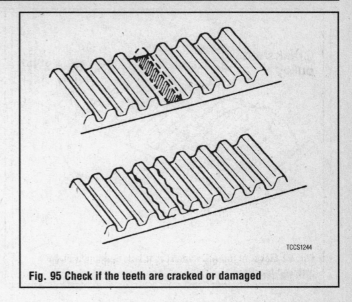

TCCS1244

Fig. 95 Check if the teeth are cracked or damaged

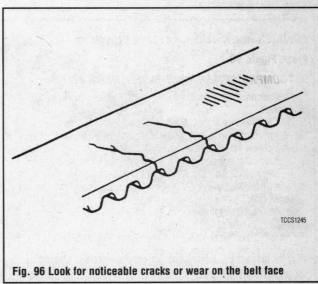

TCCS1245

Fig. 96 Look for noticeable cracks or wear on the belt face

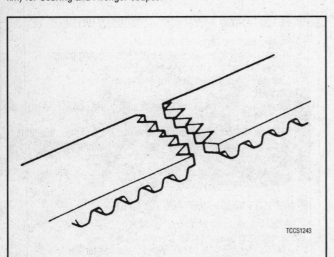

TCCS1243

Fig. 94 Check for premature parting of the belt

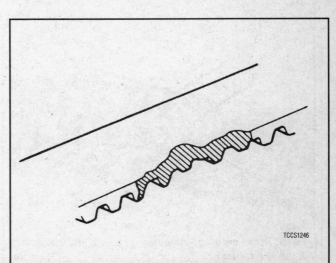

TCCS1246

Fig. 97 You may only have damage on one side of the belt; if so, the guide could be the culprit

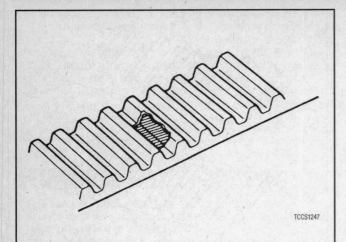

Fig. 98 Foreign materials can get in between the teeth and cause damage

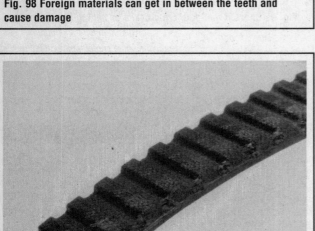

Fig. 99 Inspect the timing belt for cracks, fraying, glazing or damage of any kind

Fig. 100 Damage on only one side of the timing belt may indicate a faulty guide

Fig. 101 ALWAYS replace the timing belt at the interval specified by the manufacturer

Regardless of whether or not you decide to replace the timing belt, you would be wise to check it periodically to make sure it has not become damaged or worn. Generally speaking, a severely worn belt may cause engine performance to drop dramatically, but a damaged belt (which could give out suddenly) may not give as much warning. In general, any time the engine timing cover(s) is (are) removed, you should inspect the belt for premature parting, severe cracks or missing teeth. Also, an access plug is provided in the upper portion of the timing cover so that camshaft timing can be checked without cover removal. If timing is found to be off, cover removal and further belt inspection or replacement is necessary.

Hoses

INSPECTION

▶ **See Figures 102, 103, 104 and 105**

Upper and lower radiator hoses, along with the heater hoses, should be checked for deterioration, leaks and loose hose clamps at every oil change or at least every 15,000 miles (24,000 km). It is also wise to check the hoses periodically in early spring and at the beginning of the fall or winter

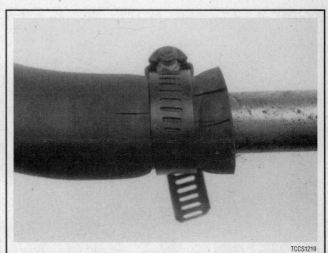

Fig. 102 The cracks developing along this hose are a result of age-related hardening

Fig. 103 A hose clamp that is too tight can cause older hoses to separate and tear on either side of the clamp

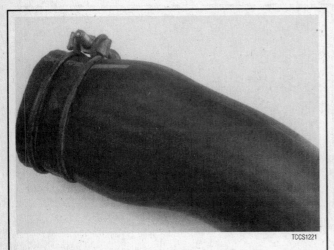

Fig. 104 A soft spongy hose (identifiable by the swollen section) will eventually burst and should be replaced

Fig. 105 Hoses are likely to deteriorate from the inside if the cooling system is not periodically flushed

when you are performing other maintenance. A quick visual inspection could discover a weakened hose which might have left you stranded if it had remained unrepaired.

Whenever you are checking the hoses, make sure the engine and cooling system are cold. Visually inspect for cracking, rotting or collapsed hoses, and replace as necessary. Run your hand along the length of the hose. If a weak or swollen spot is noted when squeezing the hose wall, the hose should be replaced.

REMOVAL & INSTALLATION

1. Remove the radiator pressure cap.

✷✷ CAUTION

Never remove the pressure cap while the engine is running, or personal injury from scalding hot coolant or steam may result. If possible, wait until the engine has cooled to remove the pressure cap. If this is not possible, wrap a thick cloth around the pressure cap and turn it slowly to the stop. Step back while the pressure is released from the cooling system. When you are sure all the pressure has been released, use the cloth to turn and remove the cap.

2. Position a clean container under the radiator and/or engine drain-cock or plug, then open the drain and allow the cooling system to drain to an appropriate level. For some upper hoses, only a little coolant must be drained. To remove hoses positioned lower on the engine, such as a lower radiator hose, the entire cooling system must be emptied.

✷✷ CAUTION

When draining coolant, keep in mind that cats and dogs are attracted by ethylene glycol antifreeze, and are quite likely to drink any that is left in an uncovered container or in puddles on the ground. This will prove fatal in sufficient quantity. Always drain coolant into a sealable container. Coolant may be reused unless it is contaminated or several years old.

3. Loosen the hose clamps at each end of the hose requiring replacement. Clamps are usually either of the spring tension type (which require pliers to squeeze the tabs and loosen) or of the screw tension type (which require screw or hex drivers to loosen). Pull the clamps back on the hose away from the connection.

4. Twist, pull and slide the hose off the fitting, taking care not to damage the neck of the component from which the hose is being removed.

➡If the hose is stuck at the connection, do not try to insert a screwdriver or other sharp tool under the hose end in an effort to free it, as the connection and/or hose may become damaged. Heater connections especially may be easily damaged by such a procedure. If the hose is to be replaced, use a single-edged razor blade to make a slice along the portion of the hose which is stuck on the connection, perpendicular to the end of the hose. Do not cut deep so as to prevent damaging the connection. The hose can then be peeled from the connection and discarded.

5. Clean both hose mounting connections. Inspect the condition of the hose clamps and replace them, if necessary.
   To install:
6. Dip the ends of the new hose into clean engine coolant to ease installation.
7. Slide the clamps over the replacement hose, then slide the hose ends over the connections into position.
8. Position and secure the clamps at least ¼ in. (6.35mm) from the ends of the hose. Make sure they are located beyond the raised bead of the connector.
9. Close the radiator or engine drains and properly refill the cooling system with the clean drained engine coolant or a suitable mixture of ethylene glycol coolant and water.

10. If available, install a pressure tester and check for leaks. If a pressure tester is not available, run the engine until normal operating temperature is reached (allowing the system to naturally pressurize), then check for leaks.

✳✳ CAUTION

If you are checking for leaks with the system at normal operating temperature, BE EXTREMELY CAREFUL not to touch any moving or hot engine parts. Once temperature has been reached, shut the engine OFF, and check for leaks around the hose fittings and connections which were removed earlier.

CV-Boots

INSPECTION

♦ See Figures 106 and 107

The CV (Constant Velocity) boots should be checked for damage each time the oil is changed and any other time the vehicle is raised for service. These boots keep water, grime, dirt and other damaging matter from enter-

TCCS1011

Fig. 106 CV-boots must be inspected periodically for damage

TCCS1010

Fig. 107 A torn boot should be replaced immediately

ing the CV-joints. Any of these could cause early CV-joint failure which can be expensive to repair. Heavy grease thrown around the inside of the front wheel(s) and on the brake caliper/drum can be an indication of a torn boot. Thoroughly check the boots for missing clamps and tears. If the boot is damaged, it should be replaced immediately. Please refer to Section 7 for procedures.

Spark Plugs

♦ See Figure 108

A typical spark plug consists of a metal shell surrounding a ceramic insulator. A metal electrode extends downward through the center of the insulator and protrudes a small distance. Located at the end of the plug and attached to the side of the outer metal shell is the side electrode. The side electrode bends in at a 90⁻ angle so that its tip is just past and parallel to the tip of the center electrode. The distance between these two electrodes (measured in thousandths of an inch or hundredths of a millimeter) is called the spark plug gap.

The spark plug does not produce a spark but instead provides a gap across which the current can arc. The coil produces anywhere from 20,000 to 50,000 volts (depending on the type and application) which travels

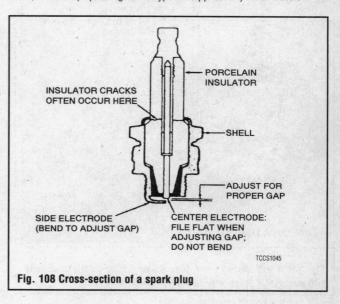

TCCS1045

Fig. 108 Cross-section of a spark plug

through the wires to the spark plugs. The current passes along the center electrode and jumps the gap to the side electrode, and in doing so, ignites the air/fuel mixture in the combustion chamber.

SPARK PLUG HEAT RANGE

♦ See Figure 109

Spark plug heat range is the ability of the plug to dissipate heat. The longer the insulator (or the farther it extends into the engine), the hotter the plug will operate; the shorter the insulator (the closer the electrode is to the block's cooling passages) the cooler it will operate. A plug that absorbs little heat and remains too cool will quickly accumulate deposits of oil and carbon since it is not hot enough to burn them off. This leads to plug fouling and consequently to misfiring. A plug that absorbs too much heat will have no deposits but, due to the excessive heat, the electrodes will burn away quickly and might possibly lead to preignition or other ignition problems. Preignition takes place when plug tips get so hot that they glow sufficiently to ignite the air/fuel mixture before the actual spark occurs. This early ignition will usually cause a pinging during low speeds and heavy loads.

The general rule of thumb for choosing the correct heat range when picking a spark plug is: if most of your driving is long distance, high speed

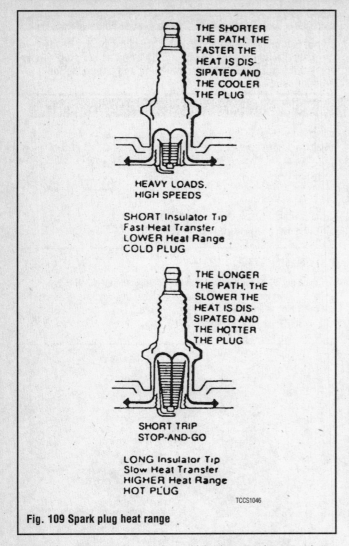

THE SHORTER THE PATH, THE FASTER THE HEAT IS DISSIPATED AND THE COOLER THE PLUG

HEAVY LOADS, HIGH SPEEDS

SHORT Insulator Tip
Fast Heat Transfer
LOWER Heat Range
COLD PLUG

THE LONGER THE PATH, THE SLOWER THE HEAT IS DISSIPATED AND THE HOTTER THE PLUG

SHORT TRIP STOP-AND-GO

LONG Insulator Tip
Slow Heat Transfer
HIGHER Heat Range
HOT PLUG

TCCS1046

Fig. 109 Spark plug heat range

Fig. 110 Label each spark plug wire before disengaging and/or disconnecting them one at a time

Fig. 111 Be certain that the socket is squarely seated over the spark plug; otherwise, damage to the ceramic insulator could occur, making removal extremely difficult

travel, use a colder plug; if most of your driving is stop and go, use a hotter plug. Original equipment plugs are generally a good compromise between the 2 styles and most people never have the need to change their plugs from the factory-recommended heat range.

REMOVAL & INSTALLATION

◆ **See Figures 110, 111, 112 and 113**

A set of spark plugs usually requires replacement after about 30,000 miles (48,000 km), depending on your style of driving. However, some engines today can reach 100,000 miles (161,000 km) before the spark plugs require replacement. In any case, it is recommended that the spark plugs be replaced according to the maintenance interval chart located in the vehicle owner's manual or at the end of this section. In normal operation plug gap increases about 0.001 in. (0.025mm) for every 2500 miles (4000 km). As the gap increases, the plug's voltage requirement also increases. It requires a greater voltage to jump the wider gap and about two to three times as much voltage to fire the plug at high speeds than at idle. The improved air/fuel ratio control of modern fuel injection combined with the higher voltage output of modern ignition systems will often allow an engine to run significantly longer on a set of standard spark plugs, but keep in mind that efficiency will drop as the gap widens (along with fuel economy and power).

When you're removing spark plugs, work on one at a time. Don't start by removing the plug wires all at once, because, unless you number them, they may become mixed up. Take a minute before you begin and number

the wires with tape.

1. Disconnect the negative battery cable and, if the vehicle has been run recently, allow the engine to thoroughly cool. On Cirrus, Stratus, Sebring convertible and Breeze models, disconnect the remote negative battery cable connection at the left strut tower.

➡**Note: On 2.5L engines it is necessary to remove the upper intake plenum to gain access to the rear spark plugs (see Chapter 3).** ◄

2. Carefully twist the spark plug wire boot to loosen it, then pull upward and remove the boot from the plug. Be sure to pull on the boot and not on the wire, otherwise the connector located inside the boot may become separated.

3. Using compressed air, blow any water or debris from the spark plug well to assure that no harmful contaminants are allowed to enter the combustion chamber when the spark plug is removed. If compressed air is not available, use a rag or a brush to clean the area.

➡**Remove the spark plugs when the engine is cold, if possible, to prevent damage to the threads. If removal of the plugs is difficult, apply a few drops of penetrating oil or silicone spray to the area around the base of the plug, and allow it a few minutes to work.**

4. Using a spark plug socket equipped with a rubber insert to properly

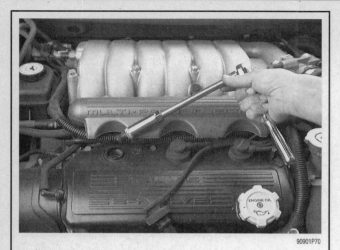

Fig. 112 Depending on the tightness of the socket fit and the engine, carefully pull the spark plug out of the bore

Fig. 113 After removing it from the socket, inspect the spark plug for signs of wear

hold the plug, turn the spark plug counterclockwise to loosen and remove the spark plug from the bore.

✳✳ WARNING

Be sure not to use a flexible extension on the socket. Use of a flexible extension may allow a shear force to be applied to the plug. A shear force could break the plug off in the cylinder head, leading to costly and frustrating repairs.

To install:

5. Inspect the spark plug boot for tears or damage. If a damaged boot is found, the spark plug wire must be replaced.

6. Using a wire feeler gauge, check and adjust the spark plug gap. When using a gauge, the proper size should pass between the electrodes with a slight drag. The next larger size should not be able to pass, while the next smaller size should pass freely.

7. Carefully thread the plug into the bore by hand. If resistance is felt before the plug is almost completely threaded, back the plug out and begin threading again. In small, hard to reach areas, an old spark plug wire and boot could be used as a threading tool. The boot will hold the plug while you twist the end of the wire and the wire is supple enough to twist before it would allow the plug to crossthread.

✳✳ WARNING

Do not use the spark plug socket to thread the plugs. Always carefully thread the plug by hand or by using an old plug wire to prevent the possibility of crossthreading and damaging the cylinder head bore.

8. Carefully tighten the spark plug to 20 ft. lbs. (28 Nm).

9. Apply a small amount of silicone dielectric compound to the end of the spark plug lead or inside the spark plug boot to prevent sticking, then install the boot to the spark plug and push until it clicks into place. The click may be felt or heard, then gently pull back on the boot to assure proper contact.

10. If removed, connect the spark plug wire to its corresponding ignition coil or distributor terminal.

11. Connect the negative battery cable.

INSPECTION & GAPPING

▶ **See Figures 114 thru 123**

Check the plugs for deposits and wear. If they are not going to be replaced, clean the plugs thoroughly. Remember that any kind of deposit will decrease the efficiency of the plug. Plugs can be cleaned on a spark plug cleaning machine, which can sometimes be found in service stations,

Fig. 114 A normally worn spark plug should have light tan or gray deposits on the firing tip

or you can do an acceptable job of cleaning with a stiff brush. If the plugs are cleaned, the electrodes must be filed flat. Use an ignition points file, not an emery board or the like, which will leave deposits. The electrodes must be filed perfectly flat with sharp edges; rounded edges reduce the spark plug voltage by as much as 50%.

Check spark plug gap before installation. The ground electrode (the L-shaped one connected to the body of the plug) must be parallel to the cen-

ter electrode and the specified size wire gauge (please refer to the Tune-Up Specifications chart for details) must pass between the electrodes with a slight drag.

➡**NEVER adjust the gap on a used platinum type spark plug.**

Always check the gap on new plugs as they are not always set correctly at the factory. Do not use a flat feeler gauge when measuring the gap on a

Fig. 115 A carbon fouled plug, identified by soft, sooty, black deposits, may indicate an improperly tuned vehicle. Check the air cleaner, ignition components and engine control system

Fig. 117 A physically damaged spark plug may be evidence of severe detonation in that cylinder. Watch that cylinder carefully between services, as a continued detonation will not only damage the plug, but could also damage the engine

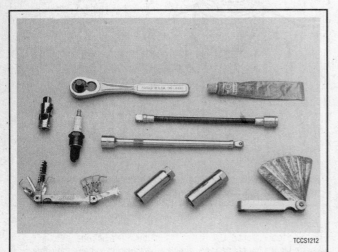

Fig. 116 A variety of tools and gauges are needed for spark plug service

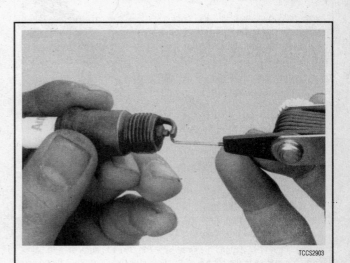

Fig. 118 Checking the spark plug gap with a feeler gauge

Fig. 119 An oil fouled spark plug indicates an engine with worn piston rings and/or bad valve seals allowing excessive oil to enter the chamber

Fig. 121 This spark plug has been left in the engine too long, as evidenced by the extreme gap—plugs with such an extreme gap can cause misfiring and stumbling accompanied by a noticeable lack of power

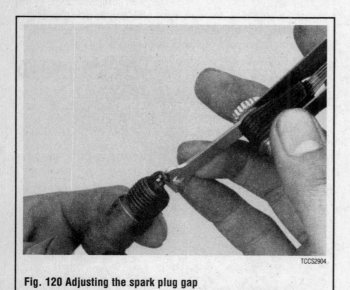

Fig. 120 Adjusting the spark plug gap

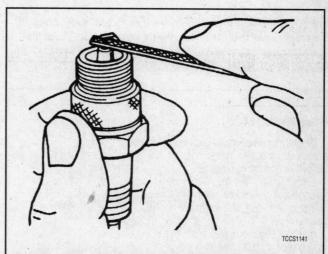

Fig. 122 If the standard plug is in good condition, the electrode may be filed flat—WARNING: do not file platinum plugs

used plug, because the reading may be inaccurate. A round-wire type gapping tool is the best way to check the gap. The correct gauge should pass through the electrode gap with a slight drag. If you're in doubt, try one size smaller and one larger. The smaller gauge should go through easily, while the larger one shouldn't go through at all. Wire gapping tools usually have a bending tool attached. Use that to adjust the side electrode until the proper distance is obtained. Absolutely never attempt to bend the center electrode. Also, be careful not to bend the side electrode too far or too often

Fig. 123 A bridged or almost bridged spark plug, identified by a build-up between the electrodes caused by excessive carbon or oil build-up on the plug

as it may weaken and break off within the engine, requiring removal of the cylinder head to retrieve it.

Spark Plug Wires

TESTING

▶ **See Figure 124**

At every tune-up/inspection, visually check the spark plug cables for burns cuts, or breaks in the insulation. Check the boots and the nipples on the coil or distributor, if equipped. Replace any damaged wiring.

Every 50,000 miles (80,000 km) or 60 months, the resistance of the wires should be checked with an ohmmeter. Wires with excessive resistance will cause misfiring, and may make the engine difficult to start in damp weather.

To check resistance, disconnect the spark plug wire from the plug and ignition coil or distributor, then use an ohmmeter to measure the resistance.

For the 2.0L DOHC engine, the resistance should measure no more than 8000 ohms maximum.

For 2.0L SOHC and 2.4L DOHC engines for 1995, the resistance should be 250–1000 ohms per inch or 3,000–12,000 ohms per foot.

For 2.0L SOHC and 2.4L DOHC engines for 1996–98, the resistance should be follows:
- Cables #1 and #4: 3,500–4,900 ohms.
- Cables #2 and #3: 2,950–4,100 ohms.

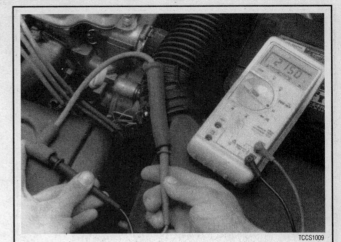

Fig. 124 Checking individual plug wire resistance with a digital ohmmeter

For the 2.5L SOHC engine for 1995, the resistance should be 250–550 ohms per inch or 3,000–6,600 ohms per foot.

For the 2.5L SOHC engine for 1996–98, the resistance should be 250–560 ohms per inch or 3,000–6,700 ohms per foot.

If resistance falls outside of specifications, the cable(s) should be replaced with new ones.

REMOVAL & INSTALLATION

➡ **As the spark plug wires must be routed and connected properly, if all of the wires must be disconnected from the spark plugs or from the ignition coil pack/distributor at the same time, be sure to tag the wires to assure proper reconnection.**

When installing a new set of spark plug wires, replace the wires one at a time so there will be no mix-up. Start by replacing the longest cable first. Twist the boot of the spark plug wire ½ turn in each direction before pulling if off. Install the boot firmly over the spark plug. Route the wire exactly the same as the original. Insert the nipple firmly onto the tower on the ignition coil or distributor, if equipped. Be sure to apply silicone dielectric compound to the spark plug wire boots and tower connectors prior to installation.

Distributor Cap and Rotor

The 2.4L DOHC, 2.0L SOHC and DOHC 4-cylinder engines are equipped with distributorless ignition systems. Only the 2.5L SOHC V6 engine is equipped with a distributor.

REMOVAL & INSTALLATION

▶ **See Figures 125 thru 133**

1. Disconnect the negative battery cable. On Cirrus, Stratus and Sebring convertible models, disconnect the remote negative battery cable connection at the left strut tower.
2. If necessary for access, do the following:
   a. Remove the bolt attaching the air inlet resonator to the intake manifold.
   b. Loosen the clamps holding the air cleaner cover to the air cleaner housing.
   c. Remove the PCV make-up air hose from the air inlet tube.
   d. Loosen the hose clamp at the throttle body.
   e. Remove the air cleaner cover, resonator and inlet tube.
   f. Remove the EGR tube, as described in Section 4.
3. Mark for identification, if necessary, and remove the spark plug wires from the distributor cap.

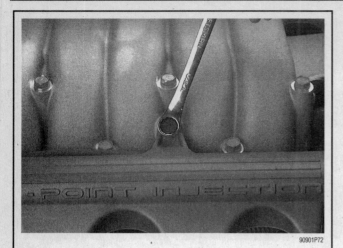

Fig. 125 Remove the bolt holding the air inlet resonator to the top of the intake manifold

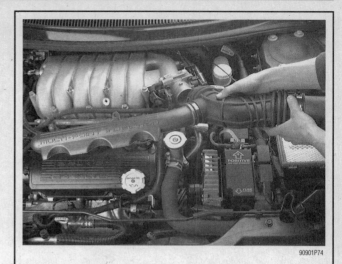

Fig. 128 Removal of the air cleaner/inlet resonator assembly

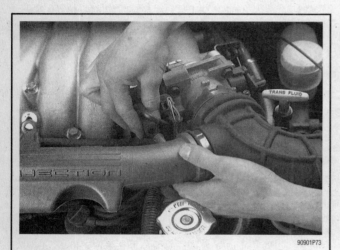

Fig. 126 After disengaging the air cleaner housing cover clamps, disconnect the PCV hose from the air inlet resonator

Fig. 129 Number the spark plug wires to match the distributor cap before removal

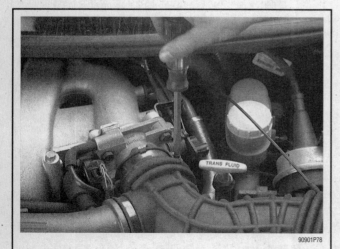

Fig. 127 Loosening the air inlet tube hose clamp at the throttle body

Fig. 130 Loosen the distributor cap hold-down screws

Fig. 131 Removal of the distributor cap

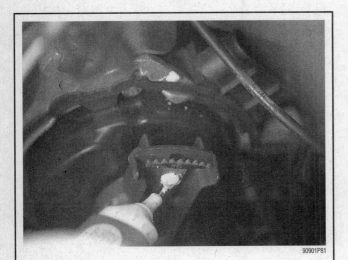

Fig. 132 Marking the rotor position-to-distributor

4. Loosen the hold-down screws and remove the distributor cap.

5. Mark the rotor position. A scribe mark indicates where to position the rotor when reinstalling. Remove the rotor.

To install:

6. Install the rotor onto the distributor.

7. Verify proper rotor alignment using the mark made at disassembly.

8. Install the distributor cap.

9. Connect the spark plug cables, following the identification marks made at disassembly.

10. If removed earlier, install the following:

   a. Install the EGR tube and tighten the mounting bolts to 95 inch lbs. (11 Nm).

Fig. 133 Remove the distributor rotor—rotor's underside shown

   b. Install the air cleaner cover, resonator and inlet tube.

   c. Tighten the hose clamp at the throttle body.

   d. Install the PCV hose.

   e. Tighten the clamps holding the air cleaner cover to the air cleaner housing.

   f. Install the bolt attaching the air inlet resonator to the intake manifold.

11. Reconnect the negative battery cable.

INSPECTION

Inspect the distributor cap for cracks or burned electrodes. Inspect the rotor for cracks or a burned electrode. Replace if defective.

Ignition Timing

GENERAL INFORMATION

All engines in the vehicles covered by this manual are equipped with a "fixed" ignition system. This means that ignition timing is controlled by the Powertrain Control Module (PCM) and is not adjustable.

Valve Lash

All engines in the vehicles covered by this manual are equipped with hydraulic valve lifters that do not require periodic valve lash adjustment. Proper adjustment is maintained automatically by hydraulic pressure in the valves.

Idle Speed and Mixture Adjustment

Idle speed and mixture for all engines covered by this manual are electronically controlled by a computerized fuel injection system. Adjustments are neither necessary nor possible.

GASOLINE ENGINE TUNE-UP SPECIFICATIONS

Year	Engine ID/VIN	Engine Displacement Liters (cc)	Spark Plugs Gap (in.)	Ignition Timing (deg.) MT	Ignition Timing (deg.) AT	Fuel Pump (psi)	Idle Speed (rpm) MT	Idle Speed (rpm) AT	Valve Clearance In.	Valve Clearance Ex.
1995	C	2.0 (1996)	0.033 - 0.038	①	①	47-51	①	①	HYD	HYD
	Y	2.0 (1996)	0.048 - 0.053	①	①	47-50	①	①	HYD	HYD
	X	2.4 (2429)	0.048 - 0.053	①	①	47-51	①	①	HYD	HYD
	H	2.5 (2497)	0.038 - 0.043	①	①	47-51	①	①	HYD	HYD
	N	2.5 (2497)	0.039 - 0.043	①	①	38	①	①	HYD	HYD
1996	C	2.0 (1996)	0.033 - 0.038	①	①	48	①	①	HYD	HYD
	Y	2.0 (1996)	0.048 - 0.053	①	①	47-50	①	①	HYD	HYD
	X	2.4 (2429)	0.048 - 0.053	①	①	48	①	①	HYD	HYD
	H	2.5 (2497)	0.038 - 0.043	①	①	47-51	①	①	HYD	HYD
	N	2.5 (2497)	0.039 - 0.043	①	①	47-50	①	①	HYD	HYD
1997	C	2.0 (1996)	0.033 - 0.038	①	①	49	①	①	HYD	HYD
	Y	2.0 (1996)	0.048 - 0.053	①	①	47-50	①	①	HYD	HYD
	X	2.4 (2429)	0.048 - 0.053	①	①	49	①	①	HYD	HYD
	H	2.5 (2497)	0.038 - 0.043	①	①	47-51	①	①	HYD	HYD
	N	2.5 (2497)	0.039 - 0.043	①	①	47-50	①	①	HYD	HYD
1998	C	2.0 (1996)	0.033 - 0.038	①	①	49	①	①	HYD	HYD
	Y	2.0 (1996)	0.048 - 0.053	①	①	47-50	①	①	HYD	HYD
	X	2.4 (2429)	0.048 - 0.053	①	①	49	①	①	HYD	HYD
	H	2.5 (2497)	0.038 - 0.043	①	①	47-51	①	①	HYD	HYD
	N	2.5 (2497)	0.039 - 0.043	①	①	47-50	①	①	HYD	HYD

HYD Hydraulic valve lifters

① Regulated by the PCM and therefore not adjustable.

90901C03

Air Conditioning System

SYSTEM SERVICE & REPAIR

▶ See Figure 134

➡**It is recommended that the A/C system be serviced by an EPA Section 609 certified automotive technician utilizing a refrigerant recovery/recycling machine.**

The do-it-yourselfer should not service his/her own vehicle's A/C system for many reasons, including legal concerns, personal injury, environmental damage and cost. The following are some of the reasons why you may decide not to service your own vehicle's A/C system.

According to the U.S. Clean Air Act, it is a federal crime to service or repair (involving the refrigerant) a Motor Vehicle Air Conditioning (MVAC) system for money without being EPA certified. It is also illegal to vent R-134a refrigerant into the atmosphere.

State and/or local laws may be more strict than the federal regulations, so be sure to check with your state and/or local authorities for further information. For further federal information on the legality of servicing your A/C system, call the EPA Stratospheric Ozone Hotline.

➡**Federal law dictates that a fine of up to $25,000 may be levied on people convicted of venting refrigerant into the atmosphere. Additionally, the EPA may pay up to $10,000 for information or services leading to a criminal conviction of the violation of these laws.**

When servicing an A/C system, you run the risk of handling or coming in contact with refrigerant, which may result in skin or eye irritation, or frostbite. Although low in toxicity (due to chemical stability), inhalation of concentrated refrigerant fumes is dangerous and can result in death; cases of fatal cardiac arrhythmia have been reported in people accidentally subjected to high levels of refrigerant. Some early symptoms include loss of concentration and drowsiness.

Also, refrigerants can decompose at high temperatures (near gas heaters or open flame), which may result in hydrofluoric acid, hydrochloric acid and phosgene (a fatal nerve gas).

R-134a refrigerant is a greenhouse gas which, if allowed to vent into the atmosphere, will contribute to global warming (the Greenhouse Effect).

It is usually more economically feasible to have a certified MVAC automotive technician perform A/C system service to your vehicle. While it is illegal to service an A/C system without the proper equipment, the home mechanic would have to purchase an expensive refrigerant recovery/recycling machine to service his/her own vehicle.

Fig. 134 Example of an A/C refrigerant information label located in the engine compartment

PREVENTIVE MAINTENANCE

Although the A/C system should not be serviced by the do-it-yourselfer, preventive maintenance can be practiced and A/C system inspections can be performed to help maintain the efficiency of the vehicle's A/C system. For preventive maintenance, perform the following:

• The easiest and most important preventive maintenance for your A/C system is to be sure that it is used on a regular basis. Running the system for five minutes each month (no matter what the season) will help ensure that the seals and all internal components remain lubricated.

➡**Some newer vehicles automatically operate the A/C system compressor whenever the windshield defroster is activated. When running, the compressor lubricates the A/C system components; therefore, the A/C system would not need to be operated each month.**

• In order to prevent heater core freeze-up during A/C operation, it is necessary to maintain a proper antifreeze protection. Use a hand-held coolant tester (hydrometer) to periodically check the condition of the antifreeze in your engine's cooling system.

➡**Antifreeze should not be used longer than the manufacturer specifies.**

• For efficient operation of an air conditioned vehicle's cooling system, the radiator cap should have a holding pressure which meets manufacturer's specifications. A cap which fails to hold these pressures should be replaced.

• Any obstruction of or damage to the condenser configuration will restrict air flow which is essential to its efficient operation. It is, therefore, a good rule to keep this unit clean and in proper physical shape.

➡**Bug screens which are mounted in front of the condenser (unless they are original equipment) are regarded as obstructions.**

• The condensation drain tube expels any water, which accumulates on the bottom of the evaporator housing, into the engine compartment. If this tube is obstructed, the air conditioning performance can be restricted and condensation buildup can spill over onto the vehicle's floor.

SYSTEM INSPECTION

Although the A/C system should not be serviced by the do-it-yourselfer, preventive maintenance can be practiced and A/C system inspections can be performed to help maintain the efficiency of the vehicle's A/C system. For A/C system inspection, perform the following:

The easiest and often most important check for the air conditioning system consists of a visual inspection of the system components. Visually inspect the air conditioning system for refrigerant leaks, damaged compressor clutch, abnormal compressor drive belt tension and/or condition, plugged evaporator drain tube, blocked condenser fins, disconnected or broken wires, blown fuses, corroded connections and poor insulation.

A refrigerant leak will usually appear as an oily residue at the leakage point in the system. The oily residue soon picks up dust or dirt particles from the surrounding air and appears greasy. Through time, this will build up and appear to be a heavy dirt impregnated grease.

For a thorough visual and operational inspection, check the following:

• Check the surface of the radiator and condenser for dirt, leaves or other material which might block air flow.

• Check for kinks in hoses and lines. Check the system for leaks.

• Make sure the drive belt is properly tensioned. When the air conditioning is operating, make sure the drive belt is free of noise or slippage.

• Make sure the blower motor operates at all appropriate positions, then check for distribution of the air from all outlets with the blower on **HIGH** or **MAX**.

➡**Keep in mind that under conditions of high humidity, air discharged from the A/C vents may not feel as cold as expected, even if the system is working properly. This is because vaporized moisture in humid air retains heat more effectively than dry air, thereby making humid air more difficult to cool.**

• Make sure the air passage selection lever is operating correctly. Start the engine and warm it to normal operating temperature, then make sure the temperature selection lever is operating correctly.

Windshield Wiper (Elements)

ELEMENT (REFILL) CARE & REPLACEMENT

▶ **See Figures 135 thru 144**

For maximum effectiveness and longest element life, the windshield and wiper blades should be kept clean. Dirt, tree sap, road tar and so on will cause streaking, smearing and blade deterioration if left on the glass. It is advisable to wash the windshield carefully with a commercial glass cleaner at least once a month. Wipe off the rubber blades with the wet rag afterwards. Do not attempt to move wipers across the windshield by hand; damage to the motor and drive mechanism will result.

To inspect and/or replace the wiper blade elements, place the wiper switch in the **LOW** speed position and the ignition switch in the **ACC** position. When the wiper blades are approximately vertical on the windshield, turn the ignition switch to **OFF**.

Fig. 137 Pylon® wiper blade and adapter

Fig. 135 Bosch® wiper blade and fit kit

Fig. 138 Trico® wiper blade and fit kit

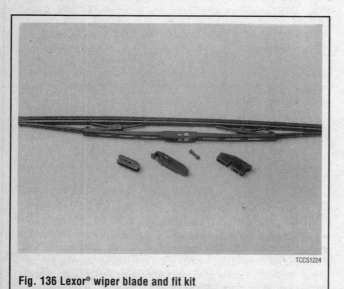

Fig. 136 Lexor® wiper blade and fit kit

Fig. 139 Tripledge® wiper blade and fit kit

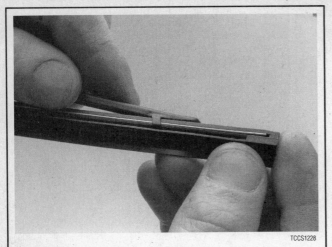

Fig. 140 To remove and install a Lexor® wiper blade refill, slip out the old insert and slide in a new one

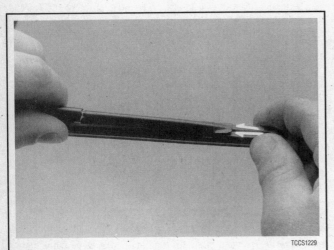

Fig. 141 On Pylon® inserts, the clip at the end has to be removed prior to sliding the insert off

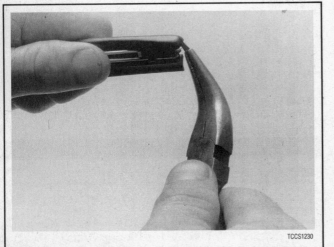

Fig. 142 On Trico® wiper blades, the tab at the end of the blade must be turned up . . .

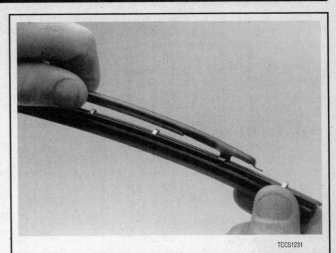

Fig. 143 . . . then the insert can be removed. After installing the replacement insert, bend the tab back

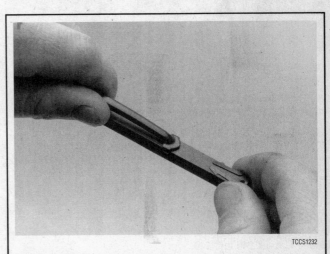

Fig. 144 The Tripledge® wiper blade insert is removed and installed using a securing clip

Examine the wiper blade elements. If they are found to be cracked, broken or torn, they should be replaced immediately. Replacement intervals will vary with usage, although ozone deterioration usually limits element life to about one year. If the wiper pattern is smeared or streaked, or if the blade chatters across the glass, the elements should be replaced. It is easiest and most sensible to replace the elements in pairs.

If your vehicle is equipped with aftermarket blades, there are several different types of refills and your vehicle might have any kind. Aftermarket blades and arms rarely use the exact same type blade or refill as the original equipment. Here are some typical aftermarket blades; not all may be available for your vehicle:

The Anco® type uses a release button that is pushed down to allow the refill to slide out of the yoke jaws. The new refill slides back into the frame and locks in place.

Some Trico® refills are removed by locating where the metal backing strip or the refill is wider. Insert a small screwdriver blade between the frame and metal backing strip. Press down to release the refill from the retaining tab.

Other types of Trico® refills have two metal tabs which are unlocked by squeezing them together. The rubber filler can then be withdrawn from the frame jaws. A new refill is installed by inserting the refill into the front frame jaws and sliding it rearward to engage the remaining frame jaws.

There are usually four jaws; be certain when installing that the refill is engaged in all of them. At the end of its travel, the tabs will lock into place on the front jaws of the wiper blade frame.

Another type of refill is made from polycarbonate. The refill has a simple locking device at one end which flexes downward out of the groove into which the jaws of the holder fit, allowing easy release. By sliding the new refill through all the jaws and pushing through the slight resistance when it reaches the end of its travel, the refill will lock into position.

To replace the Tridon® refill, it is necessary to remove the wiper blade. This refill has a plastic backing strip with a notch about 1 in. (25mm) from the end. Hold the blade (frame) on a hard surface so that the frame is tightly bowed. Grip the tip of the backing strip and pull up while twisting counterclockwise. The backing strip will snap out of the retaining tab. Do this for the remaining tabs until the refill is free of the blade. The length of these refills is molded into the end and they should be replaced with identical types.

Regardless of the type of refill used, be sure to follow the part manufacturer's instructions closely. Make sure that all of the frame jaws are engaged as the refill is pushed into place and locked. If the metal blade holder and frame are allowed to touch the glass during wiper operation, the glass will be scratched.

Tires and Wheels

Common sense and good driving habits will afford maximum tire life. Fast starts, sudden stops and hard cornering are hard on tires and will shorten their useful life span. Make sure that you don't overload the vehicle or run with incorrect pressure in the tires. Both of these practices will increase tread wear.

➡️**For optimum tire life, keep the tires properly inflated, rotate them often and have the wheel alignment checked periodically.**

Inspect your tires frequently. Be especially careful to watch for bubbles in the tread or sidewall, deep cuts or underinflation. Replace any tires with bubbles in the sidewall. If cuts are so deep that they penetrate to the cords, discard the tire. Any cut in the sidewall of a radial tire renders it unsafe. Also look for uneven tread wear patterns that may indicate the front end is out of alignment or that the tires are out of balance.

TIRE ROTATION

▶ **See Figures 145 and 146**

Tires must be rotated periodically to equalize wear patterns that vary with a tire's position on the vehicle. Tires will also wear in an uneven way as the

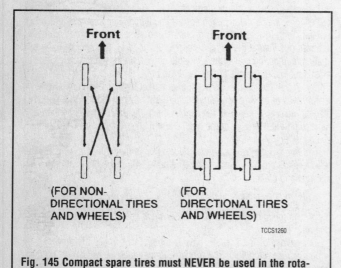

Fig. 145 Compact spare tires must NEVER be used in the rotation pattern

TCCS1234

Fig. 146 Unidirectional tires are identifiable by sidewall arrows and/or the word "rotation"

front steering/suspension system wears to the point where the alignment should be reset.

Rotating the tires will ensure maximum life for the tires as a set, so you will not have to discard a tire early due to wear on only part of the tread. Regular rotation is required to equalize wear.

When rotating "unidirectional tires," make sure that they always roll in the same direction. This means that a tire used on the left side of the vehicle must not be switched to the right side and vice-versa. Such tires should only be rotated front-to-rear or rear-to-front, while always remaining on the same side of the vehicle. These tires are marked on the sidewall as to the direction of rotation; observe the marks when reinstalling the tire(s).

Some styled or "mag" wheels may have different offsets front to rear. In these cases, the rear wheels must not be used up front and vice-versa. Furthermore, if these wheels are equipped with unidirectional tires, they cannot be rotated unless the tire is remounted for the proper direction of rotation.

➡️**The compact or space-saver spare is strictly for emergency use. It must never be included in the tire rotation or placed on the vehicle for everyday use.**

TIRE DESIGN

▶ **See Figure 147**

For maximum satisfaction, tires should be used in sets of four. Mixing of different types (radial, bias-belted, fiberglass belted) must be avoided. In most cases, the vehicle manufacturer has designated a type of tire on which the vehicle will perform best. Your first choice when replacing tires should be to use the same type of tire that the manufacturer recommends.

When radial tires are used, tire sizes and wheel diameters should be selected to maintain ground clearance and tire load capacity equivalent to the original specified tire. Radial tires should always be used in sets of four.

✳️✳️ CAUTION

Radial tires should never be used on only the front axle.

When selecting tires, pay attention to the original size as marked on the tire. Most tires are described using an industry size code sometimes referred to as P-Metric. This allows the exact identification of the tire specifications, regardless of the manufacturer. If selecting a different tire size or brand, remember to check the installed tire for any sign of interference with the body or suspension while the vehicle is stopping, turning sharply or heavily loaded.

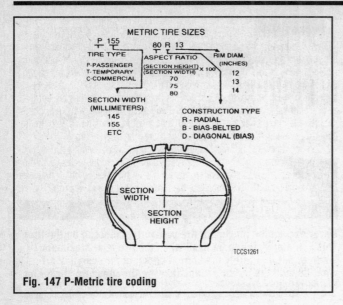

Fig. 147 P-Metric tire coding

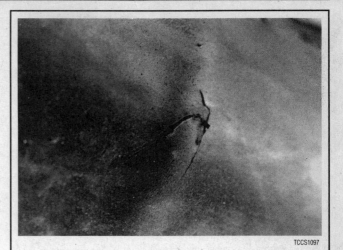

Fig. 148 Tires should be checked frequently for any sign of puncture or damage

Snow Tires

Good radial tires can produce a big advantage in slippery weather, but in snow, a street radial tire does not have sufficient tread to provide traction and control. The small grooves of a street tire quickly pack with snow and the tire behaves like a billiard ball on a marble floor. The more open, chunky tread of a snow tire will self-clean as the tire turns, providing much better grip on snowy surfaces.

To satisfy municipalities requiring snow tires during weather emergencies, most snow tires carry either an M + S designation after the tire size stamped on the sidewall, or the designation "all-season." In general, no change in tire size is necessary when buying snow tires.

Most manufacturers strongly recommend the use of 4 snow tires on their vehicles for reasons of stability. If snow tires are fitted only to the drive wheels, the opposite end of the vehicle may become very unstable when braking or turning on slippery surfaces. This instability can lead to unpleasant endings if the driver can't counteract the slide in time.

Note that snow tires, whether 2 or 4, will affect vehicle handling in all non-snow situations. The stiffer, heavier snow tires will noticeably change the turning and braking characteristics of the vehicle. Once the snow tires are installed, you must re-learn the behavior of the vehicle and drive accordingly.

➡**Consider buying extra wheels on which to mount the snow tires. Once done, the "snow wheels" can be installed and removed as needed. This eliminates the potential damage to tires or wheels from seasonal removal and installation. Even if your vehicle has styled wheels, see if inexpensive steel wheels are available. Although the look of the vehicle will change, the expensive wheels will be protected from salt, curb hits and pothole damage.**

TIRE STORAGE

If they are mounted on wheels, store the tires at proper inflation pressure. All tires should be kept in a cool, dry place. If they are stored in the garage or basement, do not let them stand on a concrete floor; set them on strips of wood, a mat or a large stack of newspaper. Keeping them away from direct moisture is of paramount importance. Tires should not be stored upright, but in a flat position.

INFLATION & INSPECTION

▶ **See Figures 148 thru 156**

The importance of proper tire inflation cannot be overemphasized. A tire employs air as part of its structure. It is designed around the supporting strength of the air at a specified pressure. For this reason, improper inflation drastically reduces the tire's ability to perform as intended. A tire will

Fig. 149 Tires with deep cuts, or cuts which show bulging, should be replaced immediately

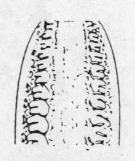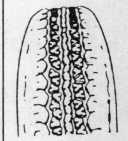

- **DRIVE WHEEL HEAVY ACCELERATION**
- **OVERINFLATION**

- **HARD CORNERING**
- **UNDERINFLATION**
- **LACK OF ROTATION**

Fig. 150 Examples of inflation-related tire wear patterns

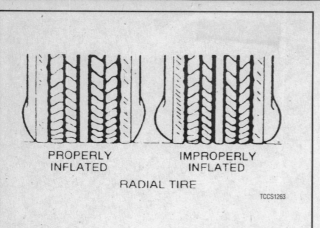

Fig. 151 Radial tires have a characteristic sidewall bulge; don't try to measure pressure by looking at the tire. Use a quality air pressure gauge

lose some air in day-to-day use; having to add a few pounds of air periodically is not necessarily a sign of a leaking tire.

Two items should be a permanent fixture in every glove compartment: an accurate tire pressure gauge and a tread depth gauge. Check the tire pressure (including the spare) regularly with a pocket type gauge. Too often, the gauge on the end of the air hose at your corner garage is not accurate because it suffers too much abuse. Always check tire pressure when the tires are cold, as pressure increases with temperature. If you must move the vehicle to check the tire inflation, do not drive more than a mile before checking. A cold tire is generally one that has not been driven for more than three hours.

A plate or sticker is normally provided somewhere in the vehicle (driver door, post, hood, tailgate or trunk lid) which shows the proper pressure for the tires. Never counteract excessive pressure build-up by bleeding off air pressure (letting some air out). This will cause the tire to run hotter and wear quicker.

❋❋ CAUTION

Never exceed the maximum tire pressure embossed on the tire! This is the pressure to be used when the tire is at maximum loading, but it is rarely the correct pressure for everyday driving. Consult the owner's manual or the tire pressure sticker for the correct tire pressure.

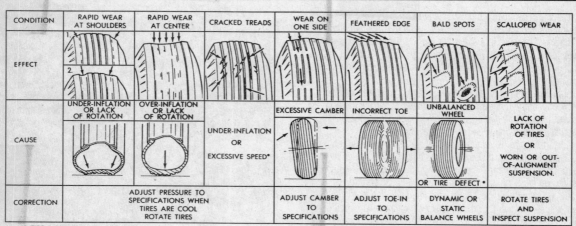

Fig. 152 Common tire wear patterns and causes

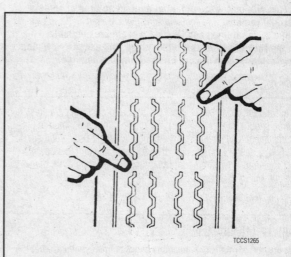

Fig. 153 A sticker showing recommended tire sizes and pressures is located on the inside of the driver's door

Fig. 154 Tread wear indicators will appear when the tire is worn

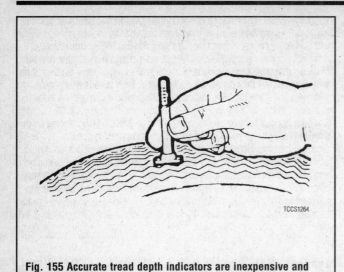

Fig. 155 Accurate tread depth indicators are inexpensive and handy

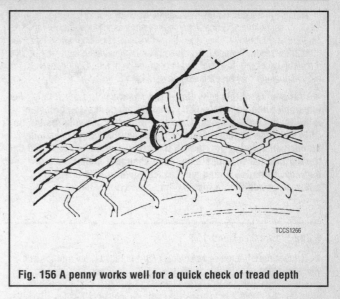

Fig. 156 A penny works well for a quick check of tread depth

Once you've maintained the correct tire pressures for several weeks, you'll be familiar with the vehicle's braking and handling personality. Slight adjustments in tire pressures can fine-tune these characteristics, but never change the cold pressure specification by more than 2 psi. A slightly softer tire pressure will give a softer ride but also yield lower fuel mileage. A slightly harder tire will give crisper dry road handling but can cause skidding on wet surfaces. Unless you're fully attuned to the vehicle, stick to the recommended inflation pressures.

All tires made since 1968 have built-in tread wear indicator bars that show up as ½ in. (13mm) wide smooth bands across the tire when 1/16 in. (1.5mm) of tread remains. The appearance of tread wear indicators means that the tires should be replaced. In fact, many states have laws prohibiting the use of tires with less than this amount of tread.

You can check your own tread depth with an inexpensive gauge or by using a Lincoln head penny. Slip the Lincoln penny (with Lincoln's head upside-down) into several tread grooves. If you can see the top of Lincoln's head in 2 adjacent grooves, the tire has less than 1/16 in. (1.5mm) tread left and should be replaced. You can measure snow tires in the same manner by using the "tails" side of the Lincoln penny. If you can see the top of the Lincoln memorial, it's time to replace the snow tire(s).

CARE OF SPECIAL WHEELS

If you have invested money in magnesium, aluminum alloy or sport wheels, special precautions should be taken to make sure your investment is not wasted and that your special wheels look good for the life of the vehicle.

Special wheels are easily damaged and/or scratched. Occasionally check the rims for cracking, impact damage or air leaks. If any of these are found, replace the wheel. But in order to prevent this type of damage and the costly replacement of a special wheel, observe the following precautions:

• Use extra care not to damage the wheels during removal, installation, balancing, etc. After removal of the wheels from the vehicle, place them on a mat or other protective surface. If they are to be stored for any length of time, support them on strips of wood. Never store tires and wheels upright; the tread may develop flat spots.

• When driving, watch for hazards; it doesn't take much to crack a wheel.

• When washing, use a mild soap or non-abrasive dish detergent (keeping in mind that detergent tends to remove wax). Avoid cleansers with abrasives or the use of hard brushes. There are many cleaners and polishes for special wheels.

• If possible, remove the wheels during the winter. Salt and sand used for snow removal can severely damage the finish of a wheel.

• Make certain the recommended lug nut torque is never exceeded or the wheel may crack. Never use snow chains on special wheels; severe scratching will occur.

FLUIDS AND LUBRICANTS

Fluid Disposal

Used fluids such as engine oil, transmission fluid, antifreeze and brake fluid are hazardous wastes and must be disposed of properly. Before draining any fluids, consult with your local authorities; in many areas, waste oil, coolant, etc. is being accepted as a part of recycling programs. A number of service stations and auto parts stores are also accepting waste fluids for recycling.

Be sure of the recycling center's policies before draining any fluids, as many will not accept different fluids that have been mixed together.

Fuel and Engine Oil Recommendations

➡**Some fuel additives contain chemicals that can damage the catalytic converter and/or oxygen sensor. Read all of the labels carefully before using any additive in the engine or fuel system.**

All Cirrus, Stratus, Breeze, Avenger, Sebring coupe and convertibles are designed to run on unleaded fuel. The use of a leaded fuel in a car requiring unleaded fuel will plug the catalytic converter and render it inoperative. It will also increase exhaust backpressure to the point where engine output will be severely reduced. The minimum octane rating of the unleaded fuel being used must be at least 87, which usually means regular unleaded, but some high performance engines may require higher ratings. Fuel should be selected for the brand and octane which performs best with your engine. Judge a gasoline by its ability to prevent pinging, its engine starting capabilities (cold and hot) and general all weather performance.

As far as the octane rating is concerned, refer to the General Engine Specifications chart earlier in this section to find your engine and its compression ratio. If the compression ratio is 9.0:1 or lower, a regular grade of unleaded gasoline can be used in most cases. If the compression ratio is higher than 9.0:1, use a premium grade of unleaded fuel.

The use of a fuel too low in octane (a measure of anti-knock quality) will result in spark knock. Since many factors such as altitude, terrain, air temperature and humidity affect operating efficiency, knocking may result even though the recommended fuel is being used. If persistent knocking occurs, it may be necessary to switch to a higher grade of fuel. Continuous or heavy knocking may result in engine damage.

➡**Your engine's fuel requirement can change with time, mainly due to carbon build-up, which will, in turn, change the compression ratio. If your engine pings, knocks or diesels (runs with the ignition OFF) switch to a higher grade of fuel. Sometimes, just changing brands will cure the problem. If it becomes necessary to retard the timing from the specifications, don't change it more than a few degrees. Retarded timing will reduce power output and fuel mileage, in addition to making the engine run hotter.**

OIL

▶ **See Figures 157 and 158**

The Society Of Automotive Engineer (SAE) grade number indicates the viscosity of the engine oil and, thus, its ability to lubricate at a given temperature. The lower the SAE grade number, the lighter the oil; the lower the viscosity, the easier it is to crank the engine in cold weather. Oil viscosities should be chosen from those oils recommended for the lowest anticipated temperatures during the oil change interval. With the proper viscosity, you will be assured of easy cold starting and sufficient engine protection.

Multi-viscosity oils (5W-30, 10W-30, etc.) offer the important advantage of being adaptable to temperature extremes. They allow easy starting at low temperatures, yet they give good protection at high speeds and engine temperatures. This is a decided advantage in changeable climates or in long distance driving.

The American Petroleum Institute (API) designation indicates the classification of engine oil used under certain given operating conditions. Only oil designated for Service SH, or the latest superseding oil grade, should be used. Oils of the SH type perform a variety of functions inside the engine in addition to their basic function as a lubricant. Through a balanced system of metallic detergents and polymeric dispersants, engine oil prevents the formation of high and low temperature deposits and also keeps sludge and particles of dirt in suspension. Acids, particularly sulfuric acid, as well as other byproducts of combustion, are neutralized. Both the SAE grade number and the API designation can be found on the side of the oil bottle.

Synthetic Oils

There are excellent synthetic and fuel-efficient oils available that, under the right circumstances, can help provide better fuel mileage and better engine protection. However, these advantages come at a price, which can be significantly more than the price per quart of conventional motor oils.

Before pouring any synthetic oils into your car's engine, you should consider the condition of the engine and the type of driving you do. It is also wise to check the vehicle manufacturer's position on synthetic oils.

Generally, it is best to avoid the use of synthetic oil in both brand new and older, high mileage engines. New engines require a proper break-in, and the synthetics are so slippery that they can impede this; most manufacturers recommend that you wait at least 5,000 miles (8,000 km) before switching to a synthetic oil. Conversely, older engines which have worn parts tend to leak more oil; synthetics will slip past worn parts more readily than regular oil. If your car already leaks oil, (due to worn parts or bad seals/gaskets), it may leak more with a synthetic inside.

Consider your type of driving. If most of your accumulated mileage is on the highway at higher, steadier speeds, a synthetic oil will reduce friction and probably help deliver better fuel mileage. Under such ideal highway conditions, the oil change interval can be extended, as long as the oil filter can continue to operate effectively for the extended life of the oil. If the filter can't do its job for this extended period, dirt and sludge will build up in your engine's crankcase, sump, oil pump and lines, no matter what type of oil is used. If using synthetic oil in this manner, you should continue to change the oil filter at the recommended intervals.

Cars used under harder, stop-and-go, short hop circumstances should always be serviced more frequently; for these cars, synthetic oil may not be a wise investment. Because of the necessary shorter change interval needed for this type of driving, you cannot take advantage of the long recommended change interval of most synthetic oils.

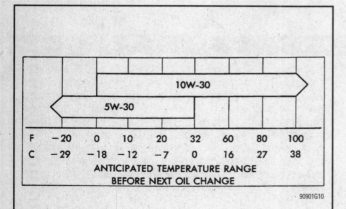

TCCS1235

Fig. 157 Look for the API oil identification label when choosing your engine oil

Fig. 158 Recommended SAE engine oil viscosity grades for gasoline engines

90901G10

Engine

OIL LEVEL CHECK

▶ **See Figures 159, 160, 161, 162 and 163**

Every time you stop for fuel, check the engine oil, after making sure the engine has fully warmed and the vehicle is parked on a level surface. Because it takes some time for the oil to drain back to the oil pan, you should wait a few minutes before checking your oil. If you are doing this at a fuel stop, first fill the fuel tank, then open the hood and check the oil, but don't get so carried away as to forget to pay for the fuel! Most station attendants won't believe that you forgot.

1. Make sure the car is parked on level ground.
2. When checking the oil level, it is best for the engine to be at normal operating temperature, although checking the oil immediately after stopping will lead to a false reading. Wait a few minutes after turning off the engine to allow the oil to drain back into the crankcase.

3. Open the hood and locate the dipstick, which will be in a guide tube located in the front of the engine compartment. Pull the dipstick from its tube, wipe it clean (using a clean, lint-free rag) and then reinsert it.

4. Pull the dipstick out again and, holding it horizontally, read the oil level. The oil should be between the SAFE and ADD, MIN and MAX or the upper and lower notch marks on the dipstick. If the oil is below the ADD, MIN, or lower notch marks, add oil of the proper viscosity through the capped opening in the top of the valve cover. See the oil and fuel recommendations listed earlier in this section for the proper viscosity and rating of oil to use.

5. Insert the dipstick and check the oil level again after adding any oil. Approximately one quart of oil will raise the level from the ADD, MIN, or lower notch marks to the SAFE, MAX, or upper notch marks. Be sure not to overfill the crankcase. Excess oil will generally be consumed at an accelerated rate and may cause problems.

✷✷ WARNING

DO NOT overfill the crankcase. It may result in oil fouled spark plugs, oil leaks caused by oil seal failure, or engine damage due to oil foaming.

6. Close the hood.

Fig. 161 Remove the oil filler cap from the top of the valve cover. Examine the condition of the cap and rubber seal; replace if worn or damaged

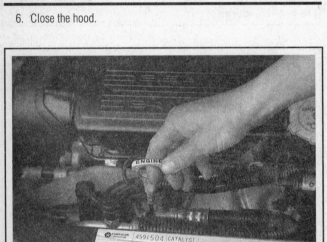

Fig. 159 Locate the engine oil dipstick in the front of the engine compartment toward the right

Fig. 162 Hold the oil container with the spout on top to avoid splashing, and pour in the proper amount of the correct viscosity engine oil

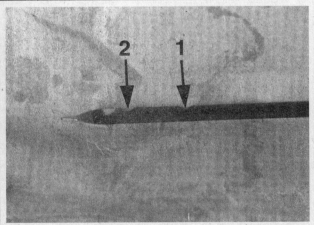

Fig. 160 The engine oil level should measure between the upper (1) and lower (2) notch marks

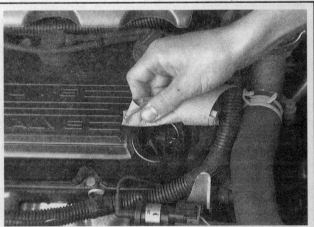

Fig. 163 Always wipe the oil fill hole area clean of any dirt or spilled oil before installing the filler cap

OIL & FILTER CHANGE

▶ **See Figures 164 thru 175**

✳✳ CAUTION

The EPA warns that prolonged contact with used engine oil may cause a number of skin disorders, including cancer! You should make every effort to minimize your exposure to used engine oil. Protective gloves should be worn when changing the oil. Wash your hands and any other exposed skin areas as soon as possible after exposure to used engine oil. Soap and water, or water-less hand cleaner should be used.

The manufacturer's recommended oil change interval is 7500 miles (12,000 km) under normal operating conditions. We recommend an oil change interval of 3000–3500 miles (4800–5600 km) under normal conditions; more frequently under severe conditions such as when the average trip is less than 4 miles (6 km), the engine is operated for extended periods at idle or low speed, when towing a trailer or operating in dusty areas.

In addition, we recommend that the filter be replaced EVERY time the oil is changed.

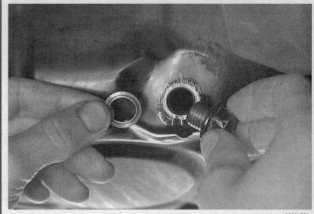

Fig. 166 Examine the the drain plug and gasket for wear or damage, and replace if necessary. The drain plug must always be installed with a gasket

Fig. 164 After the drain pan is in correct position, loosen the oil pan drain plug

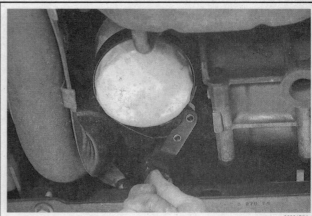

Fig. 167 The oil filter can be loosened with a variety of special tools made specifically for that purpose, such as a strap-type filter wrench . . .

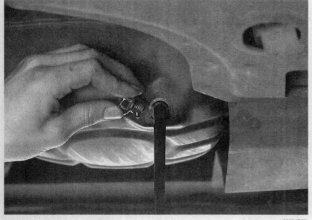

Fig. 165 Remove the plug and allow the oil to drain until it stops dripping. Be careful not to drop the plug into the pan

Fig. 168 . . . or an end cap-type oil filter wrench with a ratchet tool

➥**Please be considerate of the environment. Dispose of waste oil properly by taking it to a service station, municipal facility or recycling center.**

1. Run the engine until it reaches normal operating temperature. Then turn the engine **OFF**.

2. Remove the oil filler cap.

3. Raise and safely support the front of the vehicle using jackstands.

4. Slide a drain pan of at least 5 quarts (4.7 liters) capacity under the oil pan. Wipe the drain plug and surrounding area clean using an old rag.

5. Loosen the drain plug using a ratchet, short extension and socket, or a box wrench. Turn the plug out by hand, using a rag to shield your fingers from the hot oil. By keeping an inward pressure on the plug as you unscrew it, oil won't escape past the threads and you can remove it without being burned by hot oil. Quickly withdraw the plug and move your hands out of the way, but be careful not to drop the plug into the drain pan, as fishing it out can be an unpleasant mess. Allow the oil to drain completely.

6. Examine the condition of the drain plug for thread damage or stretching, then examine the plug gasket for cracks or wear. Replace the drain plug, gasket or both if damaged.

7. Install the drain plug and gasket. Tighten the drain plug to 20–25 ft. lbs. (27–34 Nm) on 4-cylinder engines or 29 ft. lbs. (40 Nm) on 6-cylinder engines. Do not overtighten the plug.

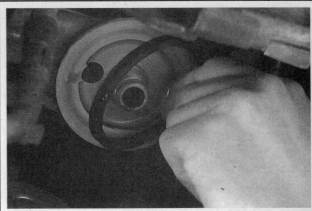

90901P61

Fig. 171 If the old filter mounting gasket is stuck to the adapter surface, remove it immediately before installing the new filter, or oil leakage will occur

90901P59

Fig. 169 During removal, always keep the opening of the filter straight up to prevent any of the old oil, still contained in the filter, from spilling

90901P62

Fig. 172 Be sure to wipe the mounting surface of the filter adapter using a clean shop towel

90901P60

Fig. 170 Always check the filter adapter surface once the old filter is removed. The filter mounting gasket may have remained stuck to the surface

TCCS1901

Fig. 173 Before installing a new oil filter, lightly coat the rubber gasket with clean oil

Fig. 174 Pour some fresh oil into the new filter before installation to lubricate the engine quicker during initial start-up

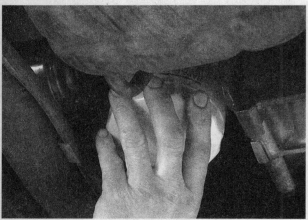

Fig. 175 Install the new oil filter onto the adapter and hand-tighten only. Be careful not to overtighten the filter

8. Move the drain pan under the oil filter. Use a strap-type or end cap-type wrench to loosen the oil filter. Cover your hand with a rag and spin the filter off by hand, but turn it slowly. Keep in mind that it's holding about one quart of dirty, hot oil.

➡**Be careful when removing the oil filter, because the filter contains about 1 quart of hot, dirty oil.**

9. Empty the old oil filter into the drain pan, then properly dispose of the filter.

10. Using a clean shop towel, wipe off the filter adapter on the engine block. Be sure the towel does not leave any lint which could clog an oil passage.

11. Coat the rubber gasket and pour some fresh oil into the new filter before installation; this will lubricate the engine quicker during initial startup. Spin the filter onto the adapter by hand until it contacts the mounting surface, then tighten it an additional ½–¾ turn. Do NOT overtighten the filter.

12. Carefully lower the vehicle.

13. Refill the crankcase with the correct amount of fresh engine oil. Please refer to the Capacities chart later in this section.

14. Install the oil filler cap.

15. Check the oil level on the dipstick. It is normal for the level to be a bit above the full mark until the engine is run and the new filter is filled with oil. Start the engine and allow it to idle for a few minutes.

✳ WARNING

Do not run the engine above idle speed until it has built up oil pressure, as indicated when the oil light goes out.

16. Shut off the engine and allow the oil to flow back to the crankcase for a minute, then recheck the oil level. Check around the filter and drain plug for any leaks, and correct as necessary.

When you have finished this job, you will notice that you now possess four or five quarts of dirty oil. The best thing to do is to pour it into plastic jugs, such as milk or old antifreeze containers. Then, locate a service station or automotive parts store where you can pour it into their used oil tank for recycling.

➡**Improperly disposing of used motor oil not only pollutes the environment, it violates federal law. Dispose of waste oil properly.**

Manual Transaxle

FLUID RECOMMENDATIONS

The proper fluid for all manual transaxles is Mopar® type M.S. 9417 manual transaxle fluid. Do NOT use Hypoid gear lube, engine oil and/or automatic transmission fluid, as these may cause damage. The manufacturer does not give an interval for manual transaxle fluid change; however, the fluid should be drained and refilled if water contamination is suspected. If the oil is foamy or looks milky, it should be replaced.

LEVEL CHECK

You should check the manual transaxle for leaks and proper fluid level each time the vehicle is raised. To check the oil level, perform the following:

1. Raise and safely support the vehicle. Make sure the vehicle is raised level and evenly for an accurate reading.

➡**The transaxle fill plug is accessible through the left fender well.**

2. Remove the fill plug from the transaxle side cover. If the fluid level is within ³⁄₁₆ in. (5mm) of the fill plug opening, the fluid level is fine.

3. If the fluid level is ³⁄₁₆ in. (5mm) below the bottom of the fill plug opening or lower, you should add the proper type of fluid through the filler hole, until the proper level is reached.

DRAIN & REFILL

1. Raise and safely support the vehicle in a level position.

2. Place a suitable drain pan under the transaxle drain plug.

3. Remove the rubber fill plug, located on the left side of the transaxle differential area.

4. Use a wrench to loosen the drain plug, then remove the drain plug from the transaxle and allow the fluid to drain completely into the pan.

5. After the fluid has drained completely, install the drain plug and tighten to 20 ft. lbs. (28 Nm).

6. Add the proper type and amount of fluid to the transaxle through the filler hole, then install the rubber filler plug.

7. Wipe the outside of the transaxle if any fluid spills.

8. Carefully lower the vehicle.

Automatic Transaxle

FLUID RECOMMENDATIONS

When adding fluid or refilling the transaxle, use MOPAR® ATF Plus 3 type 7176 fluid. If this is not available, you can use Mopar Dexron III® automatic transmission fluid, or equivalent.

LEVEL CHECK

▶ **See Figures 176 and 177**

1. Park the vehicle on a level surface.
2. Start the engine and let it run at curb idle for at least one minute.
3. Apply the parking brake and block the drive wheels.
4. With the brakes applied, move the shift lever through all the gear ranges, ending in **P**.

➡**The fluid level must be checked with the engine running at slow idle, with the car level, and the fluid at least at room temperature. The correct fluid level cannot be read if you have just driven the car for a long time at high speed, city traffic in hot weather, or if the car has been pulling a trailer. In these cases, wait at least 30 minutes for the fluid to cool down.**

5. Remove the dipstick, then determine if the fluid is hot or warm. Hot fluid is about 180°F (82°C), which is the normal operating temperature after the vehicle has been driven at least 15 miles (24 km). The fluid is too hot to touch. Warm fluid is about 85–125°F (29–52°C).
6. Wipe the dipstick clean, with a lint-free rag, then reinsert it to the fully seated position.

Fig. 176 Pull up on the transaxle fluid level dipstick and remove it from the engine

7. Remove the dipstick again and note the reading. If the fluid is hot, the reading should be within the crosshatched area marked "HOT" between the upper two holes in the dipstick. If the fluid level is warm, the fluid level should be within the lower two holes in the area marked "WARM".
8. If the fluid level is low, use a funnel to add the proper type and amount of transaxle fluid to bring it to the correct level, through the dipstick tube. It generally takes less than a pint. DO NOT overfill the transaxle! If the fluid level is within specifications, simply push the dipstick back into the filler tube completely.

> ✳✳ **WARNING**
>
> **To avoid getting any dirt or water in the transaxle, always make sure the dipstick is fully seated in the tube.**

DRAIN & REFILL

▶ **See Figures 178 thru 189**

The car should be driven approximately 10 miles (16 km) to warm the transaxle fluid before the pan is removed.

➡**The fluid should be drained while the transaxle is warm.**

1. Raise and safely support the vehicle with jackstands.
2. Place a suitable drain pan under the transaxle fluid pan.
3. If necessary, remove the splash shield below the transaxle pan by pulling down on the fasteners.
4. Loosen the automatic transaxle fluid pan bolts.

> ✳✳ **WARNING**
>
> **Be careful not to damage the mating surfaces of the oil pan and case. Any damage could result in fluid leaks.**

5. Lightly tap the pan at one corner with a rubber mallet or carefully pry the fluid pan loose, and allow the fluid to drain.
6. Remove the remaining bolts, then remove the pan. Thoroughly clean the gasket mating surfaces.
7. If necessary, unfasten any retaining screws or clips, then remove the filter.

To install:

8. If removed, install a new filter and O-ring gasket on the throttle valve body.
9. Clean the oil pan and magnet. Apply a ⅛ inch (3mm) bead of

Fig. 177 If the fluid is warm, the level should be within the lower two holes of the dipstick (1). If the fluid is hot, the reading should be within the two upper holes of the dipstick (2)

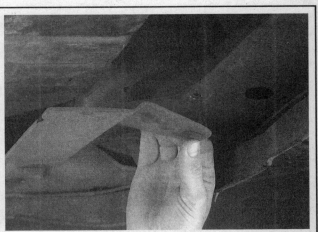

Fig. 178 Remove the splash shield for access to all the transaxle pan bolts

Fig. 179 Loosen all of the transaxle fluid pan bolts

Fig. 180 Tap the pan loose with a rubber faced hammer

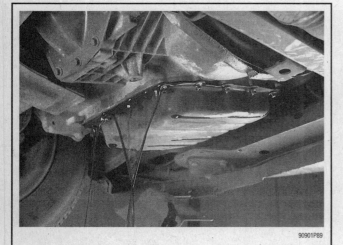

Fig. 181 Allow the pan to hang down slightly, enabling the fluid to drain into a suitable container

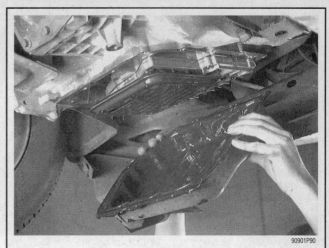

Fig. 182 After the fluid has fully drained, remove the remaining bolts and then the pan

Fig. 183 Remove the transaxle fluid filter

Fig. 184 Do not forget to remove the O-ring gasket and replace it with a new one, if installing a new filter

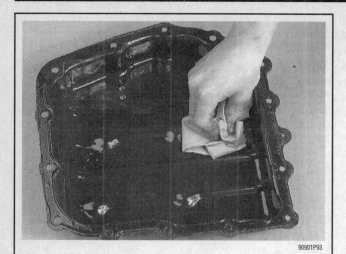

Fig. 185 Be sure to thoroughly clean the oil pan before installation

Fig. 188 Applying a bead of RTV sealant to the oil pan

Fig. 186 Clean the oil pan magnet of any metallic shavings

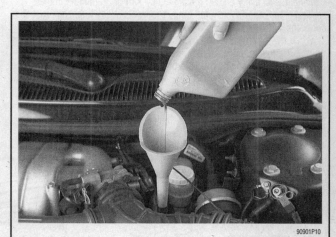

Fig. 189 To avoid a mess in the engine compartment and on the ground, always use a funnel when pouring automatic transmission fluid into the transaxle

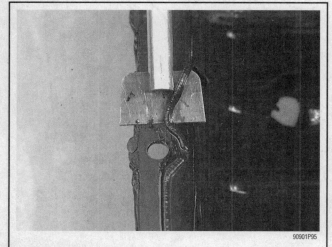

Fig. 187 Clean the oil pan of all old gasket material using an appropriate surface scraping tool

MOPAR® RTV sealant or equivalent on the transaxle pan, then install the pan and secure with the retaining bolts. Tighten the bolts to 14 ft. lbs. (19 Nm).

10. Carefully lower the vehicle.

11. Pour 4 quarts (3.8 liters) of the proper automatic transaxle fluid through the dipstick tube. Be sure to use a funnel to avoid making a mess!

12. Start the engine and allow to idle for at least a minute. With the parking brake set and the brakes depressed, move the gear selector through each position, ending in the Park or Neutral position.

13. Check the fluid level and add just enough fluid to bring the level to ⅛ inch (3mm) below the ADD mark.

14. Allow the engine to fully warm up to normal operating temperature, then check the fluid level. The fluid level should be in the HOT range. If not, add the proper amount of fluid to bring it up to that level. If the fluid level is within specifications, simply push the dipstick back into the filler tube completely.

✳✳ WARNING

To avoid getting any dirt or water in the transaxle, always make sure the dipstick is fully seated in the tube.

Cooling System

▶ See Figure 190

❄ CAUTION

Never remove the radiator cap under any conditions while the engine is hot! Failure to follow these instructions could result in damage to the cooling system, engine and/or personal injury. To avoid having scalding hot coolant or steam blow out of the radiator, use extreme care whenever you are removing the radiator cap. Wait until the engine has cooled, then wrap a thick cloth around the radiator cap and turn it slowly to the first stop. Step back while the pressure is released from the cooling system. When you are sure the pressure has been released, press down on the radiator cap (with the cloth still in position), then turn and remove the cap.

FLUID RECOMMENDATIONS

The cooling system should be inspected, flushed and refilled with fresh coolant at least every 30,000 miles (48,000 km) or 36 months. If the coolant is left in the system too long, it loses its ability to prevent rust and corrosion.

When the coolant is being replaced, use a good quality ethylene glycol or equivalent type antifreeze that is safe to be used with aluminum cooling system components. The ratio of antifreeze to water should always be a 50/50 mixture. This ratio will ensure the proper balance of cooling ability, corrosion protection and antifreeze protection. At this ratio, the antifreeze protection should be good to -34°F (-37°C). If greater antifreeze protection is needed, the ratio should not exceed 70% antifreeze to 30% water.

LEVEL CHECK

▶ See Figure 191

➡ **When checking the coolant level, the radiator cap need not be removed. Simply check the coolant level in the recovery bottle or surge tank.**

Check the coolant level in the recovery tank, usually mounted near the firewall, to the right of the passenger side strut tower. The coolant recovery tank level should be between the ADD and FULL marks on the side of the

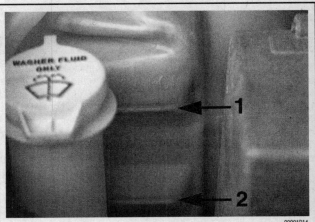

90901P14

Fig. 191 Check the coolant level at the recovery tank. A proper level is between the FULL HOT (1) and ADD (2) marks on the side of the tank. Add coolant if necessary

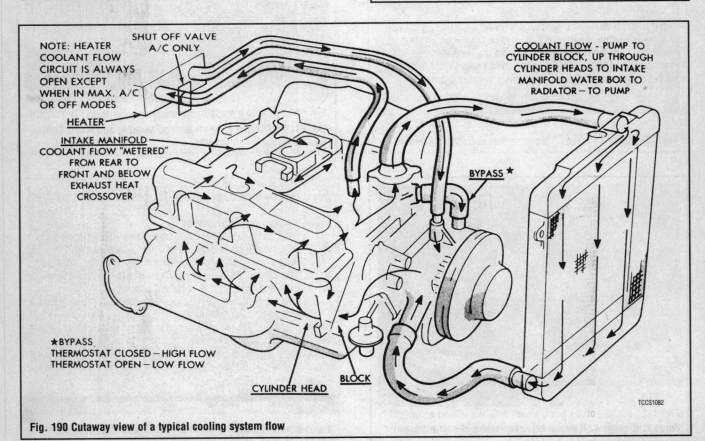

NOTE: HEATER COOLANT FLOW CIRCUIT IS ALWAYS OPEN EXCEPT WHEN IN MAX. A/C OR OFF MODES

SHUT OFF VALVE A/C ONLY

HEATER

INTAKE MANIFOLD COOLANT FLOW "METERED" FROM REAR TO FRONT AND BELOW EXHAUST HEAT CROSSOVER

COOLANT FLOW - PUMP TO CYLINDER BLOCK, UP THROUGH CYLINDER HEADS TO INTAKE MANIFOLD WATER BOX TO RADIATOR — TO PUMP

BYPASS ★

★BYPASS THERMOSTAT CLOSED — HIGH FLOW THERMOSTAT OPEN — LOW FLOW

CYLINDER HEAD

BLOCK

TCCS1082

Fig. 190 Cutaway view of a typical cooling system flow

recovery tank, when the engine is at normal operating temperature. Only add coolant to the recovery tank as necessary to bring the system up to a proper level.

> ### ✳✳ CAUTION
>
> **Should it be necessary to remove the radiator cap, make sure the system has had time to cool, reducing the internal pressure.**

DRAIN & REFILL

▶ **See Figures 192 thru 198**

> ### ✳✳ CAUTION
>
> **When draining the coolant, keep in mind that cats and dogs are attracted by ethylene glycol antifreeze and are quite likely to drink any that is left in an uncovered container or in puddles on the ground. This will prove fatal in sufficient quantity. Always drain the coolant into a sealable container. Coolant should be reused until it is contaminated or several years old. To avoid injuries from scalding fluid and steam, DO NOT remove the radiator cap while the engine and radiator are still hot.**

1. Before draining the cooling system, place the heater's temperature selector to the full WARM position while the engine is running. This will provide vacuum for system operation.

2. Turn the engine off before it gets hot and the system builds pressure.

3. Make sure the engine is still cool and the vehicle is parked on a level surface.

4. Remove the recovery tank cap.

➡**If the radiator draincock on Cirrus, Stratus and Sebring convertible models equipped with the 2.5L engine cannot be located, remove the right lower fog light unit from the front vehicle bumper/fascia. Then, loosen the mounting fastener and swing the horn out of the way. If necessary, unplug the wiring connectors.**

5. Place a fluid catch pan under the radiator. Turn the radiator draincock counterclockwise to open, then allow the coolant to drain. The coolant should drain out of the recovery tank first. On Cirrus, Stratus and Sebring convertible models equipped with the 2.5L engine, use a 3 inch long, ⅜ inch drive extension and a 19mm socket with universal joint.

Fig. 193 With the horn removed, the draincock is accessible

Fig. 194 Coolant draining through an opening and into a suitable container

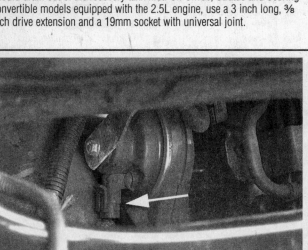

Fig. 192 Location of the horn, which must be moved aside on many 2.5L models. If necessary, also detach the horn's electrical connector (arrow)

Fig. 195 While pressing down on the radiator cap, rotate it counterclockwise to remove

Fig. 196 Clean the radiator cap's rubber gasket of any dirt to achieve a proper seal

Fig. 197 Be sure to fill the cooling system to the bottom of the filler neck with a 50/50 mixture of ethylene glycol (or other suitable) antifreeze and water. Always use a funnel to avoid spills

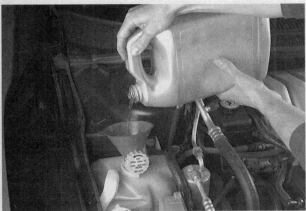

Fig. 198 Fill the coolant recovery tank to the proper level after filling the cooling system at the engine. Always use a funnel to avoid spills

6. Remove the radiator cap by performing the following:
   a. Slowly rotate the cap counterclockwise to the detent.
   b. If any residual pressure is present, WAIT until the hissing stops.
   c. After the hissing noise has ceased, press down on the cap and continue rotating it counterclockwise to remove it.
7. Allow the coolant to drain completely from the vehicle.
8. Close the radiator draincock.

➡ **When filling the cooling system, be careful not to spill any coolant on the drive belts or alternator.**

9. Using a 50/50 mixture of antifreeze and clean water, fill the radiator to the bottom of the filler neck and the coolant tank to the FULL mark.
10. Install the radiator cap, then place the cap back on the recovery bottle or surge tank.
11. Start the engine. Select heat on the climate control panel and turn the temperature valve to full WARM. Run the engine until it reaches normal operating temperature. Check to make sure there is hot air flowing from the floor ducts.
12. Check the fluid level in the recovery tank, and add as necessary.

FLUSHING & CLEANING

1. Drain the cooling system, as described in the preceding drain and refill procedure.
2. Close the drain valve.

➡ **A flushing solution may be used. Ensure that it is safe for use with aluminum cooling system components, and follow the directions on the container.**

3. If using a flushing solution, remove the thermostat, then reinstall the thermostat housing.
4. Add sufficient water to fill the system.
5. Start the engine and run it for a few minutes. Drain the system.
6. If using a flushing solution, disconnect the heater hose that connects the cylinder head to the heater core (that end of the hose which connects to the fitting on the firewall). Connect a water hose to the end of the heater hose that runs to the cylinder head and run water into the system until it begins to flow out of the top of the radiator.
7. Allow the water to flow out of the radiator until it is clear.
8. Reconnect the heater hose.
9. Drain the cooling system.
10. Reinstall the thermostat.
11. Empty the coolant reservoir or surge tank and flush it.
12. Fill the cooling system, using the correct ratio of antifreeze and water, to the bottom of the filler neck. Fill the reservoir or surge tank to the FULL mark.
13. Install the radiator cap, making sure that the arrows align with the overflow tube.

Brake Master Cylinder

FLUID RECOMMENDATIONS

Use only MOPAR®, or equivalent brake fluid meeting DOT 3 specifications from a clean, sealed container. Using any other type of fluid may result in severe brake system damage.

❊❊ WARNING

Brake fluid damages paint. It also absorbs moisture from the air; never leave a container or the master cylinder uncovered longer than necessary. All parts in contact with the brake fluid (master cylinder, hoses, plunger assemblies, etc.) must be kept clean, since any contamination of the brake fluid will adversely affect braking performance.

LEVEL CHECK

▶ **See Figures 199, 200, 201 and 202**

It should be obvious how important the brake system is to safe operation of your vehicle. The brake fluid is key to the proper operation of your vehicle. Low levels of fluid indicate a need for service (there may be a leak in the system or the brake pads may just be worn and in need of replacement). In any case, the brake fluid level should be inspected at least during every oil change, but more often is desirable. Every time you open the hood is a good time to glance at the master cylinder reservoir.

To check the fluid level, look on the side of the reservoir to see how high the fluid level is against the markings on the side of the reservoir. The level should be at the FULL mark. If not, remove the reservoir cap, then add the proper amount of DOT 3 brake fluid to bring the level up to FULL.

When making additions of brake fluid, use only fresh, uncontaminated brake fluid which meets or exceeds DOT 3 standards. Be careful not to spill any brake fluid on painted surfaces, as it will quickly eat the paint. Do not allow the brake fluid container or the master cylinder to remain open any longer than necessary; brake fluid absorbs moisture from the air, reducing the fluid's effectiveness and causing corrosion in the lines.

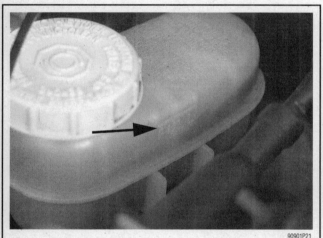

Fig. 199 When checking the fluid level, the level should be at the FULL line. Add the proper amount of fluid if necessary

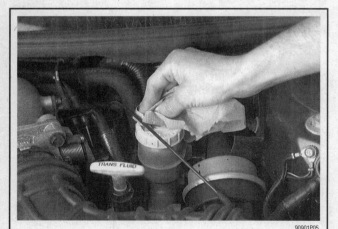

Fig. 200 Avoid hydraulic system contamination by wiping the master cylinder reservoir cap and surrounding area clean of any dirt or debris

Fig. 201 Inspect the inner rubber seal of the reservoir cap for any dirt, and clean as necessary

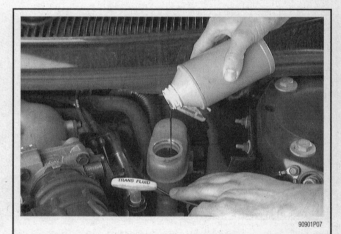

Fig. 202 Pour in enough DOT 3 quality brake fluid until it reaches the FULL level. Be careful not to spill any brake fluid, as it can damage painted surfaces

Clutch Master Cylinder

FLUID RECOMMENDATIONS

When adding or changing the fluid in the hydraulic clutch system, use a quality brake fluid conforming to DOT 3 specifications such as MOPAR® Brake Fluid, or equivalent. Never reuse old brake fluid.

LEVEL CHECK

The fluid in the clutch master cylinder is key to the proper clutch actuation on your vehicle. Low levels of fluid indicate a need for service (there may be a leak in the system or the clutch pad lining may just be worn and in need of replacement). In any case, the fluid level should be inspected at least during every oil change, but more often is desirable. Every time you open the hood is a good time to glance at the master cylinder reservoir.

1. Wipe the clutch master cylinder reservoir cap and the surrounding area clean with a shop towel.

2. Inspect the fluid in the reservoir, making sure the fluid is between the MAX and MIN marks.

3. If required, remove the clutch master cylinder reservoir lid, then add fresh fluid to bring the level up to the MAX mark on the reservoir.

When making additions of fluid, use only fresh, uncontaminated brake fluid which meets DOT 3 standards. Do not allow the brake fluid container or the master cylinder to remain open any longer than necessary; brake fluid absorbs moisture from the air, reducing the fluid's effectiveness and causing corrosion in the lines.

✴✴ WARNING

Be careful to avoid spilling any brake fluid on painted surfaces, because the paint coat will become discolored or damaged.

4. Reinstall the lid onto the clutch master cylinder.

Power Steering Pump

FLUID RECOMMENDATIONS

When adding fluid, or making a complete fluid change, Cirrus, Stratus, Sebring convertible and Breeze models require only Mopar® Power Steering Fluid or equivalent; NEVER add automatic transmission fluid. However, Sebring and Avenger coupes require only MOPAR® ATF Plus type 7176 transmission fluid, Dexron II® automatic transmission fluid, or equivalent. Failure to use the proper fluid may cause hose and seal damage, and fluid leaks.

LEVEL CHECK

▶ **See Figures 203, 204 and 205**

1. Park the vehicle on a level surface with the engine at normal operating temperatures, then turn the engine **OFF** and remove the ignition key.
2. Use a rag to clean all the dirt and oil residue from the power steering pump reservoir cap/dipstick.
3. Remove the reservoir cap/dipstick and wipe off the fluid.
4. Install the cap/dipstick, making sure it is properly seated.
5. Unscrew the cap again, then check the fluid level while holding the cap above the tip of the dipstick. If the level is at or below the ADD mark on the dipstick, add fluid until the level reaches the FULL mark. Be careful not to overfill, as this will cause fluid loss and seal damage. A large loss in fluid volume may indicate a problem, which should be inspected and repaired at once.

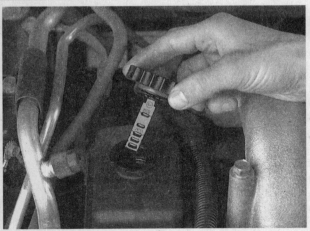

Fig. 203 Unscrew the cap by turning counterclockwise and lifting it out of the reservoir

Fig. 204 If the engine is cold, the fluid level should reach the FULL COLD mark. If the engine is hot, the fluid should be between the HOT and ADD marks

Fig. 205 Pour in power steering fluid to the correct level. Use a funnel to avoid any fluid spills. Do not spill any fluid on the drive belt or deterioration will occur

Chassis Greasing

▶ **See Figures 206 and 207**

On all models except Sebring and Avenger coupes, there are only 2 areas which require regular chassis greasing: the front upper control arm ball joint fittings and the rear upper control arm ball joint fittings. These parts should be greased every 12 months or 7,500 miles (12,000 km) with Mopar, multi-mileage lube or equivalent.

If you choose to do this job yourself, you will need to purchase a hand operated grease gun, if you do not own one already, and a long flexible extension hose to reach the various grease fittings. You will also need a cartridge of the appropriate grease.

First, use a clean cloth to wipe the dirt from around the grease fitting and joint seal. Press the fitting of the grease gun hose onto the grease fitting of the suspension component. Pump a few shots of grease into the fitting, until the rubber boot on the joint begins to expand, indicating that the joint is full. Remove the gun from the fitting. Be careful not to overfill the joints, which will rupture the rubber boots, allowing the entry of dirt. You can keep the grease fittings clean by covering them with a small square of aluminum foil.

90901P32

Fig. 206 Location of the front ball joint grease fitting on top of the front upper control arm

90901P34

Fig. 207 Location of the rear ball joint grease fitting on top of the rear upper control arm

Body Lubrication and Maintenance

The body mechanisms and linkages should be inspected, cleaned and lubricated, as necessary, to preserve correct operation and to avoid wear and corrosion. Before you lubricate a component, make sure to wipe any dirt or grease from the surface with a suitable rag. If necessary, you can also use a suitable cleaning solvent to clean off the surface. And don't forget to wipe any excess lubricant off the component when finished.

To be sure the hood latch works properly, use engine oil to lubricate the latch, safety catch and hood hinges, as necessary. Apply Mopar® or equivalent multi-purpose grease sparingly to all pivot and slide contact areas.

Use engine oil to lubricate the following components:
- Door hinges—hinge pin and pivot points
- Hood hinges—pivot points
- Trunk lid hinges—pivot points

Use Mopar® Lubriplate or equivalent on the following components:
- Door check straps
- Ashtray slides
- Fuel fill door latch mechanism
- Parking brake moving parts
- Front seat tracks

Wheel Bearings

All Cirrus, Stratus, Breeze, Avenger, Sebring coupe and convertible vehicles are equipped with sealed hub and bearing assemblies. The hub and bearing assembly is non-serviceable. If the assembly is damaged, the complete unit must be replaced. Refer to Section 8 for the hub and bearing removal and installation procedure.

TRAILER TOWING

General Recommendations

Trailer towing is absolutely NOT recommended for the Sebring coupe or Avenger models. However, it is okay for any Cirrus, Stratus, Sebring convertible or Breeze models to tow a trailer, provided that certain rules and criteria are met. Your vehicle was primarily designed to carry passengers and cargo. It is important to remember that towing a trailer will place additional loads on your vehicle's engine, drive train, steering, braking and other systems. However, if you decide to tow a trailer, using the prior equipment is a must.

Local laws may require specific equipment such as trailer brakes or fender mounted mirrors. Check your local laws.

✳✳ WARNING

Installing the trailer brakes to the vehicle's brake system lines can place an excessive load and cause a possible failure to the system. If the system fails when the brakes are needed, tragic consequences could result.

Trailer Weight

The weight of the trailer is the most important factor. A good weight-to-horsepower ratio is about 35:1, 35 lbs. of Gross Combined Weight (GCW) for every horsepower your engine develops. Multiply the engine's rated horsepower by 35 and subtract the weight of the vehicle, passengers and luggage. The number remaining is the approximate ideal maximum weight you should tow, although a numerically higher axle ratio can help compensate for heavier weight.

Hitch (Tongue) Weight

◆ See Figure 208

Calculate the hitch weight in order to select a proper hitch. The weight of the hitch is usually 9–11% of the trailer gross weight and should be measured with the trailer loaded. Hitches fall into various categories: those that mount on the frame and rear bumper, the bolt-on type, or the weld-on distribution type used for larger trailers. Axle mounted or clamp-on bumper hitches should never be used.

Check the gross weight rating of your trailer. Tongue weight is usually figured as 10% of gross trailer weight. Therefore, a trailer with a maximum gross weight of 2000 lbs. will have a maximum tongue weight of 200 lbs. Class I trailers fall into this category. Class II trailers are those with a gross weight rating of 2000–3000 lbs., while Class III trailers fall into the 3500–6000 lbs. category. Class IV trailers are those over 6000 lbs. and are for use with fifth wheel trucks, only.

When you've determined the hitch that you'll need, follow the manufacturer's installation instructions, exactly, especially when it comes to fastener torques. The hitch will be subjected to a lot of stress and good hitches come with hardened bolts. Never substitute an inferior bolt for a hardened bolt.

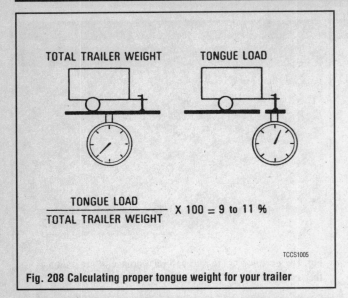

Fig. 208 Calculating proper tongue weight for your trailer

$$\frac{\text{TONGUE LOAD}}{\text{TOTAL TRAILER WEIGHT}} \times 100 = 9 \text{ to } 11\,\%$$

TCCS1005

Cooling

ENGINE

Overflow Tank

One of the most common, if not THE most common, problems associated with trailer towing is engine overheating. If you have a cooling system without an expansion tank, you'll definitely need to get an aftermarket expansion tank kit, preferably one with at least a 2 quart capacity. These kits are easily installed on the radiator's overflow hose, and come with a pressure cap designed for expansion tanks.

Oil Cooler

Aftermarket engine oil coolers are helpful for prolonging engine oil life and reducing overall engine temperatures. Both of these factors increase engine life. While not absolutely necessary in towing Class I and some Class II trailers, they are recommended for heavier Class II and all Class III towing. Engine oil cooler systems usually consist of an adapter, screwed on in place of the oil filter, a remote filter mounting and a multi-tube, finned heat exchanger, which is mounted in front of the radiator or air conditioning condenser.

TRANSAXLE

An automatic transaxle is usually recommended for trailer towing. Modern automatics have proven reliable and, of course, easy to operate, in trailer towing. The increased load of a trailer, however, causes an increase in the temperature of the automatic transaxle fluid. Heat is the worst enemy of an automatic transaxle. As the temperature of the fluid increases, the life of the fluid decreases.

It is essential, therefore, that you install an automatic transaxle cooler. The cooler, which consists of a multi-tube, finned heat exchanger, is usually installed in front of the radiator or air conditioning compressor, and hooked in-line with the transaxle cooler tank inlet line. Follow the cooler manufacturer's installation instructions.

Select a cooler of at least adequate capacity, based upon the combined gross weights of the vehicle and trailer.

Cooler manufacturers recommend that you use an aftermarket cooler in addition to, and not instead of, the present cooling tank in your radiator. If you do want to use it in place of the radiator cooling tank, get a cooler at least two sizes larger than normally necessary.

➡**A transaxle cooler can, sometimes, cause slow or harsh shifting in the transaxle during cold weather, until the fluid has a chance to come up to normal operating temperature. Some coolers can be purchased with or retrofitted with a temperature bypass valve which will allow fluid flow through the cooler only when the fluid has reached above a certain operating temperature.**

Handling a Trailer

Towing a trailer with ease and safety requires a certain amount of experience. It's a good idea to learn the feel of a trailer by practicing turning, stopping and backing in an open area such as an empty parking lot.

TOWING THE VEHICLE

▶ **See Figure 209**

When towing is required, the vehicle should be flat bedded or towed with the front wheels off of the ground on a wheel lift, to prevent damage to the transaxle. DO NOT allow your vehicle to be towed by a sling type tow truck, if it is at all avoidable. If it is necessary to tow the vehicle from the rear, a wheel dolly should be placed under the front tires.

Regardless of whether the vehicle is equipped with a manual transaxle, push starting the vehicle IS NOT RECOMMENDED under any circumstance.

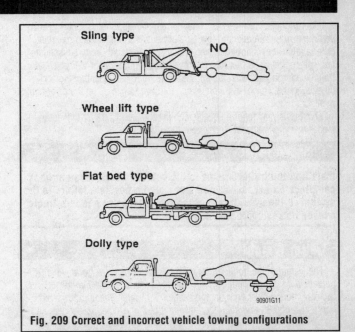

Sling type
NO
Wheel lift type
Flat bed type
Dolly type

90901G11

Fig. 209 Correct and incorrect vehicle towing configurations

JUMP STARTING A DEAD BATTERY

▶ **See Figure 210**

Whenever a vehicle is jump started, precautions must be followed in order to prevent the possibility of personal injury. Remember that batteries contain a small amount of explosive hydrogen gas which is a by-product of battery charging. Sparks should always be avoided when working around batteries, especially when attaching jumper cables. To minimize the possibility of accidental sparks, follow the procedure carefully.

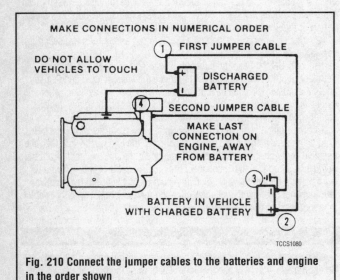

Fig. 210 Connect the jumper cables to the batteries and engine in the order shown

❊❊ CAUTION

NEVER hook up the batteries in a series circuit, or the entire electrical system will go up in smoke, including the starter!

Vehicles equipped with a diesel engine may utilize two 12 volt batteries. If so, the batteries are connected in a parallel circuit (positive terminal to positive terminal, negative terminal to negative terminal). Hooking the batteries up in parallel circuit increases battery cranking power without increasing total battery voltage output. Output remains at 12 volts. On the other hand, hooking two 12 volt batteries up in a series circuit (positive terminal to negative terminal, positive terminal to negative terminal) increases total battery output to 24 volts (12 volts plus 12 volts).

Jump Starting Precautions

• Be sure that both batteries are of the same voltage. Vehicles covered by this manual and most vehicles on the road today utilize a 12 volt charging system.
• Be sure that both batteries are of the same polarity (have the same terminal, in most cases NEGATIVE grounded).
• Be sure that the vehicles are not touching or a short could occur.
• On serviceable batteries, be sure the vent cap holes are not obstructed.
• Do not smoke or allow sparks anywhere near the batteries.
• In cold weather, make sure the battery electrolyte is not frozen. This can occur more readily in a battery that has been in a state of discharge.
• Do not allow electrolyte to contact your skin or clothing.

Jump Starting Procedure

▶ **See Figures 211 and 212**

1. Make sure that the voltages of the 2 batteries are the same. Most batteries and charging systems are of the 12 volt variety.
2. Pull the jumping vehicle (with the good battery) into a position so the jumper cables can reach the dead battery and that vehicle's engine. Make sure that the vehicles do NOT touch.
3. Place the transmissions/transaxles of both vehicles in **Neutral** (MT) or **P** (AT), as applicable, then firmly set their parking brakes.

➡**If necessary for safety reasons, the hazard lights on both vehicles may be operated throughout the entire procedure without significantly increasing the difficulty of jumping the dead battery.**

4. Turn all lights and accessories OFF on both vehicles. Make sure the ignition switches on both vehicles are turned to the **OFF** position.
5. Cover the battery cell caps with a rag, but do not cover the terminals.
6. Make sure the terminals on both batteries are clean and free of corrosion or proper electrical connection will be impeded. If necessary, clean the battery terminals before proceeding.
7. Identify the positive (+) and negative (-) terminals on both batteries.

➡**All Cirrus, Stratus, Sebring convertible and Breeze models have the battery mounted in the fender well area in front of the left front wheel. The positive (+) and negative (-) battery terminals are available for jump starting purposes by way of remote terminal connections in the engine compartment. The positive (+) remote connection is located behind the fuse box, next to the air cleaner housing. The negative (-) remote connection is located on the left strut tower.**

8. Connect the first jumper cable to the positive (+) terminal of the dead battery, then connect the other end of that cable to the positive (+) terminal of the booster (good) battery.
9. Connect one end of the other jumper cable to the negative (-) terminal on the booster battery and the final cable clamp to an engine bolt head,

Fig. 211 Location of the negative battery cable remote connection on the left side strut tower

Fig. 212 Location of the positive battery cable remote connection behind the engine compartment fuse box

alternator bracket or other solid, metallic point on the engine with the dead battery. Try to pick a ground on the engine that is positioned away from the battery in order to minimize the possibility of the 2 clamps touching should one loosen during the procedure. DO NOT connect this clamp to the negative (–) terminal of the bad battery.

JACKING

▶ **See Figures 213 thru 220**

Your vehicle was supplied with a jack for emergency road repairs. This jack is fine for changing a flat tire or other short term procedures not requiring you to go beneath the vehicle. If it is used in an emergency situation, carefully follow the instructions provided either with the jack or in your owner's manual. Do not attempt to use the jack on any portions of the vehicle other than those specified by the vehicle manufacturer. Always block the diagonally opposite wheel when using a jack.

A more convenient way of jacking is the use of a garage or floor jack. On Sebring coupe and Avenger models, you may use the floor jack to raise the front of the vehicle by placing the jack under the jacking pad located on the front centermember of the vehicle. After raising the vehicle, be sure to place jackstands between the two notches at the body pinch weld on each side to

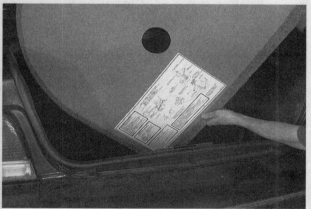

Fig. 213 Jacking instructions for the manufacturer-supplied jack, as well as the contact points, are explained and illustrated in the owner's manual and inside the spare tire cover

✱✱ CAUTION

Be very careful to keep the jumper cables away from moving parts (cooling fan, belts, etc.) on both engines.

10. Check to make sure that the cables are routed away from any moving parts, then start the donor vehicle's engine. Run the engine at moderate speed for several minutes to allow the dead battery a chance to receive some initial charge.

11. With the donor vehicle's engine still running at idle, try to start the vehicle with the dead battery. Crank the engine for no more than 15 seconds at a time and let the starter cool for at least 15 minutes between tries. If the vehicle does not start in 3 tries, it is likely that something else is also wrong or that the battery needs additional time to charge.

12. Once the vehicle is started, allow it to run at idle for a few seconds to make sure that it is operating properly.

13. Turn ON the headlights, heater blower and, if equipped, the rear defroster of both vehicles in order to reduce the severity of voltage spikes and subsequent risk of damage to the vehicles' electrical systems when the cables are disconnected. This step is especially important to any vehicle equipped with computer control modules.

14. Carefully disconnect the cables in the reverse order of connection. Start with the negative cable that is attached to the engine ground, then the negative cable on the donor battery. Disconnect the positive cable from the donor battery and finally, disconnect the positive cable from the formerly dead battery. Be careful when disconnecting the cables from the positive terminals not to allow the alligator clips to touch any metal on either vehicle or a short and sparks will occur.

safely support the vehicle. On Cirrus, Stratus, Sebring convertible and Breeze models, you may use the floor jack to raise the front of the vehicle by placing the jack under the jacking pad located at the front of the unibody frame rail, just behind each front wheel well. After raising the vehicle, be sure to place jackstands under the frame rails to safely support the vehicle. To raise the rear of all vehicles covered by this manual, place the floor jack under the center of the rear crossmember, then place jackstands under each unibody frame rail.

Never place the jack under the radiator, engine or transaxle components. Severe and expensive damage will result when the jack is raised. Additionally, never jack under the floorpan or bodywork; the metal will deform.

Whenever you plan to work under the vehicle, you must support it on jackstands or ramps. Never use cinder blocks or stacks of wood to support the vehicle, even if you're only going to be under it for a few minutes. Never

Fig. 214 To avoid scuffing or distorting the wheel cover, use the small prying end of the lug wrench for removal

Fig. 215 Using the vehicle's combination jack crank/lug nut tool, loosen, but do not remove the lug nuts with the wheel still on the ground

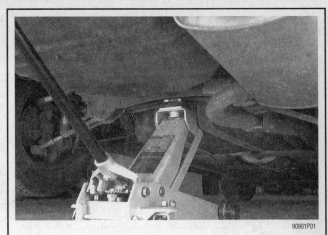

Fig. 218 To raise the rear, place the contact pad of a hydraulic floor jack at the center point of the rear suspension crossmember

Fig. 216 When utilizing the vehicle's emergency jack, always make sure it is properly positioned under the pointed location at each corner pinch weld

Fig. 219 Safely suspend the rear wheels from the ground by placing jackstands under each unibody frame rail

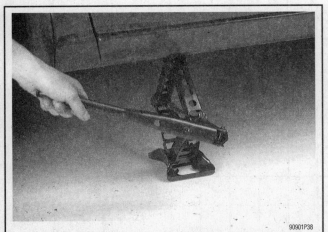

Fig. 217 Always make sure that the vehicle is parked on a level surface with the emergency brake applied when utilizing the emergency jack

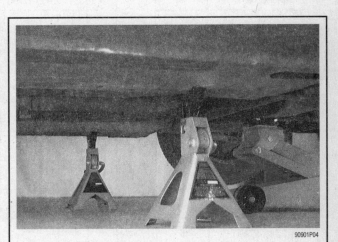

Fig. 220 Safely suspend the front wheels above the ground by placing jackstands under each unibody frame rail—Cirrus, Stratus, Sebring convertible and Breeze

crawl under the vehicle when it is supported only by the tire changing jack or other floor jack.

➡ **Always position a block of wood or small rubber pad on top of the jack or jackstand to protect the lifting point's finish when lifting or supporting the vehicle.**

Small hydraulic, screw, or scissors jacks are satisfactory for raising the vehicle. Drive-on trestles or ramps are also a handy and safe way to both raise and support the vehicle. Be careful though, some ramps may be too steep to drive your vehicle onto without scraping the front bottom panels. Never support the vehicle beneath any suspension member (unless specifically instructed to do so by a repair manual) or by an underbody panel.

Jacking Precautions

The following safety points cannot be overemphasized:
- Always block the opposite wheel or wheels to keep the vehicle from rolling off the jack.
- When raising the front of the vehicle, firmly apply the parking brake.
- When the drive wheels are to remain on the ground, leave the vehicle in gear to help prevent it from rolling.
- Always use jackstands to support the vehicle when you are working underneath. Place the stands beneath the vehicle's jacking brackets. Before climbing underneath, rock the vehicle a bit to make sure it is firmly supported.

SCHEDULED MAINTENANCE INTERVALS (NORMAL SERVICE)
(Cirrus, Stratus, Sebring Convertible and Breeze)

TO BE SERVICED	TYPE OF SERVICE	VEHICLE MILEAGE INTERVAL (x1000)														
		Km 12	24	36	48	60	72	84	96	108	120	132	144	156	160	168
		Miles 7.5	15	22.5	30	37.5	45	52.5	60	67.5	75	82.5	90	97.5	100	105
Engine oil	R	✓	✓	✓	✓	✓	✓	✓	✓	✓	✓	✓	✓	✓		✓
Engine oil filter (2.0L & 2.4L engines)	R	✓	✓	✓	✓	✓	✓	✓	✓	✓	✓	✓	✓	✓		✓
Engine oil filter (2.5L engine)	R		✓		✓		✓		✓		✓		✓			✓
Disc brake pads and brake shoe linings	S/I			✓			✓			✓			✓			
Accessory	A		✓		✓		✓				✓		✓			✓
drive belts	R								✓							
Automatic transaxle fluid and filter	R				✓				✓				✓			
PCV valve	S/I								✓				✓			
Front and rear upper control arm ball joints	L				✓				✓				✓			
Air cleaner filter element	R				✓				✓				✓			
Exhaust system	S/I	✓	✓	✓	✓	✓	✓	✓	✓	✓	✓	✓	✓	✓		✓
Brake lines & hoses	S/I	✓	✓	✓	✓	✓	✓	✓	✓	✓	✓	✓	✓	✓		✓
CV-joints, suspension component boots & seals	S/I	✓	✓	✓	✓	✓	✓	✓	✓	✓	✓	✓	✓	✓		✓
Tire rotation	-	✓	✓	✓	✓	✓	✓	✓	✓	✓	✓	✓	✓	✓		✓
Coolant level, hoses & clamps	S/I	✓	✓	✓	✓	✓	✓	✓	✓	✓	✓	✓	✓	✓		✓
Spark plugs (2.0L & 2.4L engines)	R				✓				✓				✓			
Spark plug wires (2.0L & 2.4L engines)	R								✓							
Spark plugs and wires (2.5L engine)	R														✓	
Manual transaxle fluid level	S/I	✓	✓	✓	✓	✓	✓	✓	✓	✓	✓	✓	✓	✓		✓
Timing belt	R															✓
Engine coolant	R				✓				✓				✓			

R - Replace   S/I - Inspect and service, if needed   L - Lubricate   A - Adjust

90901C06

SCHEDULED MAINTENANCE INTERVALS (SEVERE SERVICE)
(Cirrus, Stratus, Sebring Convertible and Breeze)

TO BE SERVICED	TYPE OF SERVICE	Km	5	10	14	19	24	29	34	38	43	48	53	58	62	67	72	77	82	86	91	96
		Miles	3	6	9	12	15	18	21	24	27	30	33	36	39	42	45	48	51	54	57	60
Engine oil	R		✓	✓	✓	✓	✓	✓	✓	✓	✓	✓	✓	✓	✓	✓	✓	✓	✓	✓	✓	✓
Engine oil filter (2.0L & 2.4L engines)	R		✓	✓	✓	✓	✓	✓	✓	✓	✓	✓	✓	✓	✓	✓	✓	✓	✓	✓	✓	✓
Engine oil filter (2.5L engine)	R			✓		✓		✓		✓		✓		✓		✓		✓		✓		✓
Disc brake pads and brake shoe linings	S/I					✓				✓				✓				✓				✓
Accessory	A						✓					✓					✓					
drive belts	R																					✓
Automatic transaxle fluid and filter	R						✓					✓					✓					✓
PCV valve	S/I											✓										✓
Front and rear upper control arm ball joints	L											✓										✓
Air cleaner	S/I		✓	✓	✓	✓	✓	✓	✓	✓	✓	✓	✓	✓	✓	✓	✓	✓	✓	✓	✓	✓
filter element	R											✓										✓
Exhaust system	S/I		✓	✓	✓	✓	✓	✓	✓	✓	✓	✓	✓	✓	✓	✓	✓	✓	✓	✓	✓	✓
Brake lines & hoses	S/I		✓	✓	✓	✓	✓	✓	✓	✓	✓	✓	✓	✓	✓	✓	✓	✓	✓	✓	✓	✓
CV-joints, suspension component boots & seals	S/I		✓	✓	✓	✓	✓	✓	✓	✓	✓	✓	✓	✓	✓	✓	✓	✓	✓	✓	✓	✓
Tire rotation	-		✓	✓	✓	✓	✓	✓	✓	✓	✓	✓	✓	✓	✓	✓	✓	✓	✓	✓	✓	✓
Coolant level, hoses & clamps	S/I		✓	✓	✓	✓	✓	✓	✓	✓	✓	✓	✓	✓	✓	✓	✓	✓	✓	✓	✓	✓
Spark plugs (2.0L & 2.4L engines)	R											✓										✓
Spark plug wires (2.0L & 2.4L engines)	R																					✓
Spark plugs and wires (2.5L engine)	R		Replace at 75,000 miles																			
Engine coolant flush	R													✓					✓			

R - Replace   S/I - Inspect and service, if needed   L - Lubricate   A - Adjust

FREQUENT OPERATION MAINTENANCE (SEVERE SERVICE)

If a vehicle is operated under any of the following conditions it is considered severe service:

- Towing a trailer or using a camper or car-top carrier.
- Repeated short trips of less than 5 miles in temperatures below freezing, or trips of less than 10 miles in any temperature.
- Extensive idling or low-speed driving for long distances as in heavy commercial use, such as delivery, taxi or police cars.
- Operating on rough, muddy or salt-covered roads.
- Operating on unpaved or dusty roads.
- Driving in extremely hot (over 90°F) conditions.

90901C07

SCHEDULED MAINTENANCE INTERVALS (NORMAL SERVICE)
(Sebring and Avenger Coupes)

TO BE SERVICED	TYPE OF SERVICE	VEHICLE MILEAGE INTERVAL (x1000)														
		Km 12	24	36	48	60	72	84	96	108	120	132	144	156	160	168
		Miles 7.5	15	22.5	30	37.5	45	52.5	60	67.5	75	82.5	90	97.5	100	105
Engine oil	R		✓	✓	✓	✓	✓	✓	✓	✓	✓	✓	✓	✓		✓
Engine oil filter	R		✓		✓		✓		✓		✓		✓			✓
CV-joint boots	S/I		✓		✓		✓		✓		✓		✓			✓
Steering linkage and ball joint seals	S/I				✓				✓				✓			
Accessory drive belts	S/I				✓				✓				✓			
Rear drum brake shoe linings and wheel cylinders	S/I				✓				✓				✓			
Automatic transaxle fluid	S/I		✓		✓		✓		✓		✓		✓			✓
Disc brake pads	S/I		✓		✓		✓		✓		✓		✓			✓
Distributor cap and rotor (2.5L engine)	S/I								✓							
Air cleaner filter element	R				✓				✓				✓			
Exhaust system (muffler connections, pipe and heat shields)	S/I				✓				✓				✓			
Brake lines & hoses	S/I		✓		✓		✓		✓		✓		✓			✓
Timing belt	R														✓	
Evaporative emission control system (except canister)	S/I								✓							
Fuel hoses	S/I				✓				✓				✓			
Spark plugs (2.0L engine)	R				✓				✓				✓			
Spark plug wires	R								✓							
Spark plugs (2.5L engine)	R														✓	
Manual transaxle fluid level	S/I				✓				✓				✓			
Fuel system (tank, lines, connections and filler cap)	S/I								✓							
Engine coolant	R				✓				✓				✓			

R - Replace   S/I - Inspect and service, if needed

90901C08

SCHEDULED MAINTENANCE INTERVALS (SEVERE SERVICE)
(Sebring and Avenger Coupes)

TO BE SERVICED	TYPE OF SERVICE	VEHICLE MILEAGE INTERVAL (x1000)																			
		Km 5	10	14	19	24	29	34	38	43	48	53	58	62	67	72	77	82	86	91	96
		Miles 3	6	9	12	15	18	21	24	27	30	33	36	39	42	45	48	51	54	57	60
Engine oil	R	✓	✓	✓	✓	✓	✓	✓	✓	✓	✓	✓	✓	✓	✓	✓	✓	✓	✓	✓	✓
Engine oil filter	R		✓		✓		✓		✓		✓		✓		✓		✓		✓		✓
Air cleaner filter element	R					✓					✓					✓					✓
Spark plugs	R					✓					✓					✓					✓
Manual transaxle fluid	R										✓										✓
Automatic transaxle fluid	R					✓					✓					✓					✓
Disc brake pads	S/I		✓		✓		✓		✓		✓		✓		✓		✓		✓		✓
Rear drum brake linings and wheel cylinders	S/I					✓					✓					✓					✓

R - Replace   S/I - Inspect and service, if needed

FREQUENT OPERATION MAINTENANCE (SEVERE SERVICE)

If a vehicle is operated under any of the following conditions it is considered severe service:

- Towing a trailer or using a camper or car-top carrier.
- Repeated short trips of less than 5 miles in temperatures below freezing, or trips of less than 10 miles in any temperature.
- Extensive idling or low-speed driving for long distances as in heavy commercial use, such as delivery, taxi or police cars.
- Operating on rough, muddy or salt-covered roads.
- Operating on unpaved or dusty roads.
- Driving in extremely hot (over 90°F) conditions.

90901C09

CAPACITIES

Year	Model	Engine ID/VIN	Engine Displacement Liters (cc)	Engine Oil with Filter (qts.)	Transaxle (qts.)		Fuel Tank (gal.)	Cooling System (qts.)
					5-Spd	Auto.		
1995	Cirrus	H	2.5 (2497)	4.5	-	4.0 ①	16	10.5
	Sebring Coupe	Y	2.0 (1996)	4.5	2.2	4.0 ①	16.9	7.4
	Sebring Coupe	N	2.5 (2497)	4.5	-	4.0 ①	16.9	7.4
	Avenger	Y	2.0 (1996)	4.5	2.2	4.0 ①	16.9	7.4
	Avenger	N	2.5 (2497)	4.5	-	4.0 ①	16.9	7.4
	Stratus	C	2.0 (1996)	4.5	2.2	4.0 ①	16	8.5
	Stratus	X	2.4 (2429)	4.5	-	4.0 ①	16	9.0
	Stratus	H	2.5 (2497)	4.5	-	4.0 ①	16	10.5
1996	Cirrus	X	2.4 (2429)	5.0	-	4.0 ①	16	9.0
	Cirrus	H	2.5 (2497)	4.5	-	4.0 ①	16	10.5
	Sebring Conv.	X	2.4 (2429)	5.0	-	4.0 ①	16	9.0
	Sebring Conv.	H	2.5 (2497)	4.5	-	4.0 ①	16	10.5
	Sebring Coupe	Y	2.0 (1996)	4.5	2.2	4.0 ①	16.9	7.4
	Sebring Coupe	N	2.5 (2497)	4.5	-	4.0 ①	16.9	7.4
	Avenger	Y	2.0 (1996)	4.5	2.2	4.0 ①	16.9	7.4
	Avenger	N	2.5 (2497)	4.5	-	4.0 ①	16.9	7.4
	Stratus	C	2.0 (1996)	4.5	2.2	4.0 ①	16	8.5
	Stratus	X	2.4 (2429)	5.0	-	4.0 ①	16	9.0
	Stratus	H	2.5 (2497)	4.5	-	4.0 ①	16	10.5
	Breeze	C	2.0 (1996)	4.5	2.2	4.0 ①	16	8.5
1997	Cirrus	X	2.4 (2429)	5.0	-	4.0 ①	16	9.0
	Cirrus	H	2.5 (2497)	4.5	-	4.0 ①	16	10.5
	Sebring Conv.	X	2.4 (2429)	5.0	-	4.0 ①	16	9.0
	Sebring Conv.	H	2.5 (2497)	4.5	-	4.0 ①	16	10.5
	Sebring Coupe	Y	2.0 (1996)	4.5	2.2	4.0 ①	16.9	7.4
	Sebring Coupe	N	2.5 (2497)	4.5	-	4.0 ①	16.9	7.4
	Avenger	Y	2.0 (1996)	4.5	2.2	4.0 ①	16.9	7.4
	Avenger	N	2.5 (2497)	4.5	-	4.0 ①	16.9	7.4
	Stratus	C	2.0 (1996)	4.5	2.2	4.0 ①	16	8.5
	Stratus	X	2.4 (2429)	5.0	-	4.0 ①	16	9.0
	Stratus	H	2.5 (2497)	4.5	-	4.0 ①	16	10.5
	Breeze	C	2.0 (1996)	4.5	2.2	4.0 ①	16	8.5
1998	Cirrus	H	2.5 (2497)	4.5	-	4.0 ①	16	10.5
	Sebring Conv.	X	2.4 (2429)	5.0	-	4.0 ①	16	9.0
	Sebring Conv.	H	2.5 (2497)	4.5	-	4.0 ①	16	10.5
	Sebring Coupe	Y	2.0 (1996)	4.5	2.2	4.0 ①	16.9	7.4
	Sebring Coupe	N	2.5 (2497)	4.5	-	4.0 ①	16.9	7.4
	Avenger	Y	2.0 (1996)	4.5	2.2	4.0 ①	16.9	7.4
	Avenger	N	2.5 (2497)	4.5	-	4.0 ①	16.9	7.4
	Stratus	C	2.0 (1996)	4.5	2.2	4.0 ①	16	8.5
	Stratus	X	2.4 (2429)	5.0	-	4.0 ①	16	9.0
	Stratus	H	2.5 (2497)	4.5	-	4.0 ①	16	10.5
	Breeze	C	2.0 (1996)	4.5	2.2	4.0 ①	16	8.5
	Breeze	X	2.4 (2429)	5.0	-	4.0 ①	16	9.0

① Overhaul fill capacity - 9.1 qts.

90901C05

ENGLISH TO METRIC CONVERSION: MASS (WEIGHT)

Current mass measurement is expressed in pounds and ounces (lbs. & ozs.). The metric unit of mass (or weight) is the kilogram (kg). Even although this table does not show conversion of masses (weights) larger than 15 lbs, it is easy to calculate larger units by following the data immediately below.

To convert ounces (oz.) to grams (g): multiply th number of ozs. by 28
To convert grams (g) to ounces (oz.): multiply the number of grams by .035

To convert pounds (lbs.) to kilograms (kg): multiply the number of lbs. by .45
To convert kilograms (kg) to pounds (lbs.): multiply the number of kilograms by 2.2

lbs	kg	lbs	kg	oz	kg	oz	kg
0.1	0.04	0.9	0.41	0.1	0.003	0.9	0.024
0.2	0.09	1	0.4	0.2	0.005	1	0.03
0.3	0.14	2	0.9	0.3	0.008	2	0.06
0.4	0.18	3	1.4	0.4	0.011	3	0.08
0.5	0.23	4	1.8	0.5	0.014	4	0.11
0.6	0.27	5	2.3	0.6	0.017	5	0.14
0.7	0.32	10	4.5	0.7	0.020	10	0.28
0.8	0.36	15	6.8	0.8	0.023	15	0.42

ENGLISH TO METRIC CONVERSION: TEMPERATURE

To convert Fahrenheit (°F) to Celsius (°C): take number of °F and subtract 32; multiply result by 5; divide result by 9

To convert Celsius (°C) to Fahrenheit (°F): take number of °C and multiply by 9; divide result by 5; add 32 to total

Fahrenheit (F)	Celsius (C)			Fahrenheit (F)	Celsius (C)			Fahrenheit (F)	Celsius (C)		
°F	°C	°C	°F	°F	°C	°C	°F	°F	°C	°C	°F
−40	−40	−38	−36.4	80	26.7	18	64.4	215	101.7	80	176
−35	−37.2	−36	−32.8	85	29.4	20	68	220	104.4	85	185
−30	−34.4	−34	−29.2	90	32.2	22	71.6	225	107.2	90	194
−25	−31.7	−32	−25.6	95	35.0	24	75.2	230	110.0	95	202
−20	−28.9	−30	−22	100	37.8	26	78.8	235	112.8	100	212
−15	−26.1	−28	−18.4	105	40.6	28	82.4	240	115.6	105	221
−10	−23.3	−26	−14.8	110	43.3	30	86	245	118.3	110	230
−5	−20.6	−24	−11.2	115	46.1	32	89.6	250	121.1	115	239
0	−17.8	−22	−7.6	120	48.9	34	93.2	255	123.9	120	248
1	−17.2	−20	−4	125	51.7	36	96.8	260	126.6	125	257
2	−16.7	−18	−0.4	130	54.4	38	100.4	265	129.4	130	266
3	−16.1	−16	3.2	135	57.2	40	104	270	132.2	135	275
4	−15.6	−14	6.8	140	60.0	42	107.6	275	135.0	140	284
5	−15.0	−12	10.4	145	62.8	44	112.2	280	137.8	145	293
10	−12.2	−10	14	150	65.6	46	114.8	285	140.6	150	302
15	−9.4	−8	17.6	155	68.3	48	118.4	290	143.3	155	311
20	−6.7	−6	21.2	160	71.1	50	122	295	146.1	160	320
25	−3.9	−4	24.8	165	73.9	52	125.6	300	148.9	165	329
30	−1.1	−2	28.4	170	76.7	54	129.2	305	151.7	170	338
35	1.7	0	32	175	79.4	56	132.8	310	154.4	175	347
40	4.4	2	35.6	180	82.2	58	136.4	315	157.2	180	356
45	7.2	4	39.2	185	85.0	60	140	320	160.0	185	365
50	10.0	6	42.8	190	87.8	62	143.6	325	162.8	190	374
55	12.8	8	46.4	195	90.6	64	147.2	330	165.6	195	383
60	15.6	10	50	200	93.3	66	150.8	335	168.3	200	392
65	18.3	12	53.6	205	96.1	68	154.4	340	171.1	205	401
70	21.1	14	57.2	210	98.9	70	158	345	173.9	210	410
75	23.9	16	60.8	212	100.0	75	167	350	176.7	215	414

ENGLISH TO METRIC CONVERSION: LENGTH

To convert inches (ins.) to millimeters (mm): multiply number of inches by 25.4

To convert millimeters (mm) to inches (ins.): multiply number of millimeters by .04

Inches		Decimals	Milli-meters	Inches to millimeters		Inches		Decimals	Milli-meters	Inches to millimeters	
				inches	mm					inches	mm
	1/64	0.051625	0.3969	0.0001	0.00254		33/64	0.515625	13.0969	0.6	15.24
1/32		0.03125	0.7937	0.0002	0.00508	17/32		0.53125	13.4937	0.7	17.78
	3/64	0.046875	1.1906	0.0003	0.00762		35/64	0.546875	13.8906	0.8	20.32
1/16		0.0625	1.5875	0.0004	0.01016	9/16		0.5625	14.2875	0.9	22.86
	5/64	0.078125	1.9844	0.0005	0.01270		37/64	0.578125	14.6844	1	25.4
3/32		0.09375	2.3812	0.0006	0.01524	19/32		0.59375	15.0812	2	50.8
	7/64	0.109375	2.7781	0.0007	0.01778		39/64	0.609375	15.4781	3	76.2
1/8		0.125	3.1750	0.0008	0.02032	5/8		0.625	15.8750	4	101.6
	9/64	0.140625	3.5719	0.0009	0.02286		41/64	0.640625	16.2719	5	127.0
5/32		0.15625	3.9687	0.001	0.0254	21/32		0.65625	16.6687	6	152.4
	11/64	0.171875	4.3656	0.002	0.0508		43/64	0.671875	17.0656	7	177.8
3/16		0.1875	4.7625	0.003	0.0762	11/16		0.6875	17.4625	8	203.2
	13/64	0.203125	5.1594	0.004	0.1016		45/64	0.703125	17.8594	9	228.6
7/32		0.21875	5.5562	0.005	0.1270	23/32		0.71875	18.2562	10	254.0
	15/64	0.234375	5.9531	0.006	0.1524		47/64	0.734375	18.6531	11	279.4
1/4		0.25	6.3500	0.007	0.1778	3/4		0.75	19.0500	12	304.8
	17/64	0.265625	6.7469	0.008	0.2032		49/64	0.765625	19.4469	13	330.2
9/32		0.28125	7.1437	0.009	0.2286	25/32		0.78125	19.8437	14	355.6
	19/64	0.296875	7.5406	0.01	0.254		51/64	0.796875	20.2406	15	381.0
5/16		0.3125	7.9375	0.02	0.508	13/16		0.8125	20.6375	16	406.4
	21/64	0.328125	8.3344	0.03	0.762		53/64	0.828125	21.0344	17	431.8
11/32		0.34375	8.7312	0.04	1.016	27/32		0.84375	21.4312	18	457.2
	23/64	0.359375	9.1281	0.05	1.270		55/64	0.859375	21.8281	19	482.6
3/8		0.375	9.5250	0.06	1.524	7/8		0.875	22.2250	20	508.0
	25/64	0.390625	9.9219	0.07	1.778		57/64	0.890625	22.6219	21	533.4
13/32		0.40625	10.3187	0.08	2.032	29/32		0.90625	23.0187	22	558.8
	27/64	0.421875	10.7156	0.09	2.286		59/64	0.921875	23.4156	23	584.2
7/16		0.4375	11.1125	0.1	2.54	15/16		0.9375	23.8125	24	609.6
	29/64	0.453125	11.5094	0.2	5.08		61/64	0.953125	24.2094	25	635.0
15/32		0.46875	11.9062	0.3	7.62	31/32		0.96875	24.6062	26	660.4
	31/64	0.484375	12.3031	0.4	10.16		63/64	0.984375	25.0031	27	690.6
1/2		0.5	12.7000	0.5	12.70						

ENGLISH TO METRIC CONVERSION: TORQUE

To convert foot-pounds (ft. lbs.) to Newton-meters: multiply the number of ft. lbs. by 1.3

To convert inch-pounds (in. lbs.) to Newton-meters: multiply the number of in. lbs. by .11

in lbs	N-m	in lbs	N-m	in lbs	N-m	in lbs	N-m	in lbs	N-m
0.1	0.01	1	0.11	10	1.13	19	2.15	28	3.16
0.2	0.02	2	0.23	11	1.24	20	2.26	29	3.28
0.3	0.03	3	0.34	12	1.36	21	2.37	30	3.39
0.4	0.04	4	0.45	13	1.47	22	2.49	31	3.50
0.5	0.06	5	0.56	14	1.58	23	2.60	32	3.62
0.6	0.07	6	0.68	15	1.70	24	2.71	33	3.73
0.7	0.08	7	0.78	16	1.81	25	2.82	34	3.84
0.8	0.09	8	0.90	17	1.92	26	2.94	35	3.95
0.9	0.10	9	1.02	18	2.03	27	3.05	36	4.0

ENGLISH TO METRIC CONVERSION: TORQUE

Torque is now expressed as either foot-pounds (ft./lbs.) or inch-pounds (in./lbs.). The metric measurement unit for torque is the Newton-meter (Nm). This unit—the Nm—will be used for all SI metric torque references, both the present ft./lbs. and in./lbs.

ft lbs	N-m	ft lbs	N-m	ft lbs	N-m	ft lbs	N-m
0.1	0.1	33	44.7	74	100.3	115	155.9
0.2	0.3	34	46.1	75	101.7	116	157.3
0.3	0.4	35	47.4	76	103.0	117	158.6
0.4	0.5	36	48.8	77	104.4	118	160.0
0.5	0.7	37	50.7	78	105.8	119	161.3
0.6	0.8	38	51.5	79	107.1	120	162.7
0.7	1.0	39	52.9	80	108.5	121	164.0
0.8	1.1	40	54.2	81	109.8	122	165.4
0.9	1.2	41	55.6	82	111.2	123	166.8
1	1.3	42	56.9	83	112.5	124	168.1
2	2.7	43	58.3	84	113.9	125	169.5
3	4.1	44	59.7	85	115.2	126	170.8
4	5.4	45	61.0	86	116.6	127	172.2
5	6.8	46	62.4	87	118.0	128	173.5
6	8.1	47	63.7	88	119.3	129	174.9
7	9.5	48	65.1	89	120.7	130	176.2
8	10.8	49	66.4	90	122.0	131	177.6
9	12.2	50	67.8	91	123.4	132	179.0
10	13.6	51	69.2	92	124.7	133	180.3
11	14.9	52	70.5	93	126.1	134	181.7
12	16.3	53	71.9	94	127.4	135	183.0
13	17.6	54	73.2	95	128.8	136	184.4
14	18.9	55	74.6	96	130.2	137	185.7
15	20.3	56	75.9	97	131.5	138	187.1
16	21.7	57	77.3	98	132.9	139	188.5
17	23.0	58	78.6	99	134.2	140	189.8
18	24.4	59	80.0	100	135.6	141	191.2
19	25.8	60	81.4	101	136.9	142	192.5
20	27.1	61	82.7	102	138.3	143	193.9
21	28.5	62	84.1	103	139.6	144	195.2
22	29.8	63	85.4	104	141.0	145	196.6
23	31.2	64	86.8	105	142.4	146	198.0
24	32.5	65	88.1	106	143.7	147	199.3
25	33.9	66	89.5	107	145.1	148	200.7
26	35.2	67	90.8	108	146.4	149	202.0
27	36.6	68	92.2	109	147.8	150	203.4
28	38.0	69	93.6	110	149.1	151	204.7
29	39.3	70	94.9	111	150.5	152	206.1
30	40.7	71	96.3	112	151.8	153	207.4
31	42.0	72	97.6	113	153.2	154	208.8
32	43.4	73	99.0	114	154.6	155	210.2

TCCS1C03

ENGLISH TO METRIC CONVERSION: FORCE

Force is presently measured in pounds (lbs.). This type of measurement is used to measure spring pressure, specifically how many pounds it takes to compress a spring. Our present force unit (the pound) will be replaced in SI metric measurements by the Newton (N). This term will eventually see use in specifications for electric motor brush spring pressures, valve spring pressures, etc.

To convert pounds (lbs.) to Newton (N): multiply the number of lbs. by 4.45

lbs	N	lbs	N	lbs	N	oz	N
0.01	0.04	21	93.4	59	262.4	1	0.3
0.02	0.09	22	97.9	60	266.9	2	0.6
0.03	0.13	23	102.3	61	271.3	3	0.8
0.04	0.18	24	106.8	62	275.8	4	1.1
0.05	0.22	25	111.2	63	280.2	5	1.4
0.06	0.27	26	115.6	64	284.6	6	1.7
0.07	0.31	27	120.1	65	289.1	7	2.0
0.08	0.36	28	124.6	66	293.6	8	2.2
0.09	0.40	29	129.0	67	298.0	9	2.5
0.1	0.4	30	133.4	68	302.5	10	2.8
0.2	0.9	31	137.9	69	306.9	11	3.1
0.3	1.3	32	142.3	70	311.4	12	3.3
0.4	1.8	33	146.8	71	315.8	13	3.6
0.5	2.2	34	151.2	72	320.3	14	3.9
0.6	2.7	35	155.7	73	324.7	15	4.2
0.7	3.1	36	160.1	74	329.2	16	4.4
0.8	3.6	37	164.6	75	333.6	17	4.7
0.9	4.0	38	169.0	76	338.1	18	5.0
1	4.4	39	173.5	77	342.5	19	5.3
2	8.9	40	177.9	78	347.0	20	5.6
3	13.4	41	182.4	79	351.4	21	5.8
4	17.8	42	186.8	80	355.9	22	6.1
5	22.2	43	191.3	81	360.3	23	6.4
6	26.7	44	195.7	82	364.8	24	6.7
7	31.1	45	200.2	83	369.2	25	7.0
8	35.6	46	204.6	84	373.6	26	7.2
9	40.0	47	209.1	85	378.1	27	7.5
10	44.5	48	213.5	86	382.6	28	7.8
11	48.9	49	218.0	87	387.0	29	8.1
12	53.4	50	224.4	88	391.4	30	8.3
13	57.8	51	226.9	89	395.9	31	8.6
14	62.3	52	231.3	90	400.3	32	8.9
15	66.7	53	235.8	91	404.8	33	9.2
16	71.2	54	240.2	92	409.2	34	9.4
17	75.6	55	244.6	93	413.7	35	9.7
18	80.1	56	249.1	94	418.1	36	10.0
19	84.5	57	253.6	95	422.6	37	10.3
20	89.0	58	258.0	96	427.0	38	10.6

TCCS1C04

ENGLISH TO METRIC CONVERSION: LIQUID CAPACITY

Liquid or fluid capacity is presently expressed as pints, quarts or gallons, or a combination of all of these. In the metric system the liter (l) will become the basic unit. Fractions of a liter would be expressed as deciliters, centiliters, or most frequently (and commonly) as milliliters.

To convert pints (pts.) to liters (l): multiply the number of pints by .47
To convert liters (l) to pints (pts.): multiply the number of liters by 2.1
To convert quarts (qts.) to liters (l): multiply the number of quarts by .95

To convert liters (l) to quarts (qts.): multiply the number of liters by 1.06
To convert gallons (gals.) to liters (l): multiply the number of gallons by 3.8
To convert liters (l) to gallons (gals.): multiply the number of liters by .26

gals	liters	qts	liters	pts	liters
0.1	0.38	0.1	0.10	0.1	0.05
0.2	0.76	0.2	0.19	0.2	0.10
0.3	1.1	0.3	0.28	0.3	0.14
0.4	1.5	0.4	0.38	0.4	0.19
0.5	1.9	0.5	0.47	0.5	0.24
0.6	2.3	0.6	0.57	0.6	0.28
0.7	2.6	0.7	0.66	0.7	0.33
0.8	3.0	0.8	0.76	0.8	0.38
0.9	3.4	0.9	0.85	0.9	0.43
1	3.8	1	1.0	1	0.5
2	7.6	2	1.9	2	1.0
3	11.4	3	2.8	3	1.4
4	15.1	4	3.8	4	1.9
5	18.9	5	4.7	5	2.4
6	22.7	6	5.7	6	2.8
7	26.5	7	6.6	7	3.3
8	30.3	8	7.6	8	3.8
9	34.1	9	8.5	9	4.3
10	37.8	10	9.5	10	4.7
11	41.6	11	10.4	11	5.2
12	45.4	12	11.4	12	5.7
13	49.2	13	12.3	13	6.2
14	53.0	14	13.2	14	6.6
15	56.8	15	14.2	15	7.1
16	60.6	16	15.1	16	7.6
17	64.3	17	16.1	17	8.0
18	68.1	18	17.0	18	8.5
19	71.9	19	18.0	19	9.0
20	75.7	20	18.9	20	9.5
21	79.5	21	19.9	21	9.9
22	83.2	22	20.8	22	10.4
23	87.0	23	21.8	23	10.9
24	90.8	24	22.7	24	11.4
25	94.6	25	23.6	25	11.8
26	98.4	26	24.6	26	12.3
27	102.2	27	25.5	27	12.8
28	106.0	28	26.5	28	13.2
29	110.0	29	27.4	29	13.7
30	113.5	30	28.4	30	14.2

TCCS1C05

ENGLISH TO METRIC CONVERSION: PRESSURE

The basic unit of pressure measurement used today is expressed as pounds per square inch (psi). The metric unit for psi will be the kilopascal (kPa). This will apply to either fluid pressure or air pressure, and will be frequently seen in tire pressure readings, oil pressure specifications, fuel pump pressure, etc.

To convert pounds per square inch (psi) to kilopascals (kPa): multiply the number of psi by 6.89

Psi	kPa	Psi	kPa	Psi	kPa	Psi	kPa
0.1	0.7	37	255.1	82	565.4	127	875.6
0.2	1.4	38	262.0	83	572.3	128	882.5
0.3	2.1	39	268.9	84	579.2	129	889.4
0.4	2.8	40	275.8	85	586.0	130	896.3
0.5	3.4	41	282.7	86	592.9	131	903.2
0.6	4.1	42	289.6	87	599.8	132	910.1
0.7	4.8	43	296.5	88	606.7	133	917.0
0.8	5.5	44	303.4	89	613.6	134	923.9
0.9	6.2	45	310.3	90	620.5	135	930.8
1	6.9	46	317.2	91	627.4	136	937.7
2	13.8	47	324.0	92	634.3	137	944.6
3	20.7	48	331.0	93	641.2	138	951.5
4	27.6	49	337.8	94	648.1	139	958.4
5	34.5	50	344.7	95	655.0	140	965.2
6	41.4	51	351.6	96	661.9	141	972.2
7	48.3	52	358.5	97	668.8	142	979.0
8	55.2	53	365.4	98	675.7	143	985.9
9	62.1	54	372.3	99	682.6	144	992.8
10	69.0	55	379.2	100	689.5	145	999.7
11	75.8	56	386.1	101	696.4	146	1006.6
12	82.7	57	393.0	102	703.3	147	1013.5
13	89.6	58	399.9	103	710.2	148	1020.4
14	96.5	59	406.8	104	717.0	149	1027.3
15	103.4	60	413.7	105	723.9	150	1034.2
16	110.3	61	420.6	106	730.8	151	1041.1
17	117.2	62	427.5	107	737.7	152	1048.0
18	124.1	63	434.4	108	744.6	153	1054.9
19	131.0	64	441.3	109	751.5	154	1061.8
20	137.9	65	448.2	110	758.4	155	1068.7
21	144.8	66	455.0	111	765.3	156	1075.6
22	151.7	67	461.9	112	772.2	157	1082.5
23	158.6	68	468.8	113	779.1	158	1089.4
24	165.5	69	475.7	114	786.0	159	1096.3
25	172.4	70	482.6	115	792.9	160	1103.2
26	179.3	71	489.5	116	799.8	161	1110.0
27	186.2	72	496.4	117	806.7	162	1116.9
28	193.0	73	503.3	118	813.6	163	1123.8
29	200.0	74	510.2	119	820.5	164	1130.7
30	206.8	75	517.1	120	827.4	165	1137.6
31	213.7	76	524.0	121	834.3	166	1144.5
32	220.6	77	530.9	122	841.2	167	1151.4
33	227.5	78	537.8	123	848.0	168	1158.3
34	234.4	79	544.7	124	854.9	169	1165.2
35	241.3	80	551.6	125	861.8	170	1172.1
36	248.2	81	558.5	126	868.7	171	1179.0

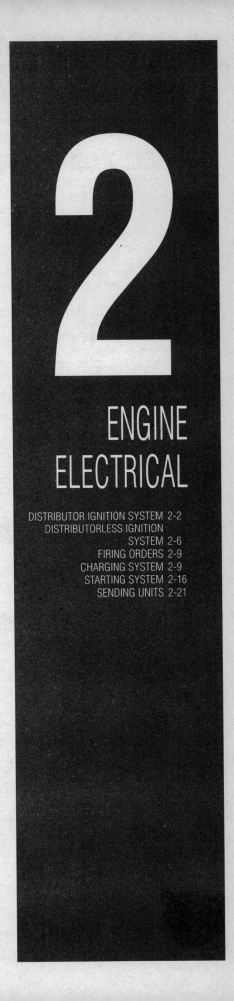

2

ENGINE ELECTRICAL

DISTRIBUTOR IGNITION SYSTEM

➡ **For information on understanding electricity and troubleshooting electrical circuits, please refer to Section 6 of this manual.**

General Information

The distributor ignition system differs from the conventional breaker points system in form only; its function is exactly the same: to supply a spark to the spark plugs at precisely the right moment to ignite the compressed air/fuel mixture in the cylinders and create mechanical movement.

Located in the distributor, in addition to the rotor, is a spoked reluctor which is pressed onto the distributor shaft. The reluctor revolves with the rotor; as it passes a pickup coil inside the distributor body, it breaks a high flux field, which occurs in the space between the reluctor and the pickup coil. The breaking of the field allows current to flow to the pickup coil. Primary ignition current is then cut off by the Powertrain Control Module (PCM), allowing the magnetic field in the ignition coil to collapse, creating the spark which the distributor passes on to the spark plugs.

The distributor ignition system has timing controlled by the Powertrain Control Module (PCM). The standard reference ignition timing data for the engine operating conditions are programmed in the memory of the PCM. The engine conditions (rpm, load and temperature) are detected by various sensors. Based on these sensor signals and the ignition timing data, a signal is sent to interrupt the primary current at the power transistor. The ignition coil is activated and a spark sent through the distributor, down the spark plug wires to the spark plugs. Ignition timing is controlled by the PCM for optimum performance.

The distributor ignition system can be identified by looking for the presence of a distributor (with spark plug wires connecting the distributor cap to the spark plugs). If no distributor is found, it can be assumed that the engine uses a distributorless ignition system. Coverage of the distributorless ignition system is found later in this section.

Diagnosis and Testing

SPARK PLUG CABLE TEST

▶ See Figure 1

✳✳ WARNING

Before beginning this test, be sure to wear rubber gloves and rubber-soled shoes for safety.

1. One at a time, disengage each spark plug wire with the engine idling to check whether the engine's performance changes or not.
2. If the performance does not change, check the resistance of each spark plug and wire. Refer to Section 1 for checking the resistance of the spark plug wires.

SECONDARY SPARK TEST

▶ **See Figures 2 and 3**

1. Remove a spark plug from the engine. Examine the spark plug for cracks in its insulation and replace if necessary.
2. Connect the spark plug to its spark plug wire.
3. Ground the spark plug's outer electrode to the engine (touch the spark plug's metal body to the engine block or other piece of metal on the car).
4. Crank the engine and look for spark across the electrodes of the spark plug.
5. If a strong blue spark exists across the plug electrode, the ignition system is functioning properly.

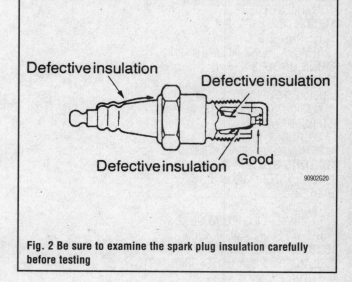

Fig. 2 Be sure to examine the spark plug insulation carefully before testing

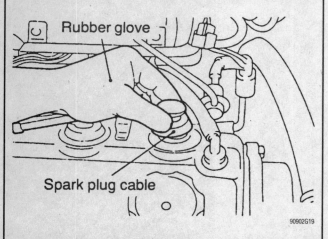

Fig. 1 Pull off the spark plug wires (cables) one at a time while wearing rubber gloves

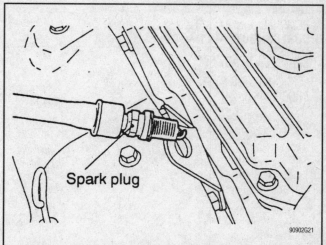

Fig. 3 The spark plug must be grounded to a metal part of the vehicle, such as the engine block

6. Repeat the test for the remaining cylinders. If one or more tests indicate irregular, weak or no spark, refer to the coil test.

7. If spark does not exist, remove the distributor cap and ensure that the rotor is turning when the engine is cranked.

DISTRIBUTOR CAP RESISTANCE TEST

▶ **See Figure 4**

The distributor cap has a resistor built into it.
1. Remove the distributor cap. Refer to Section 1.
2. Using an ohmmeter, connect one lead to the center button of the distributor cap.
3. Connect the other lead to the ignition coil terminal.
4. The ohmmeter should read approximately 5000 ohms.
5. Replace the distributor cap if the reading is incorrect; otherwise, reinstall the cap.

Fig. 4 Testing the distributor cap for correct resistance

Adjustments

All adjustments of the ignition system are controlled by the Powertrain Control Module (PCM) for optimum performance. No manual adjustments are possible.

Ignition Coil

TESTING

▶ **See Figures 5, 6 and 7**

The ignition coil is an integral component of the distributor assembly.

➡ **Prior to testing the coil, perform a secondary spark test. If spark occurs at the spark plug, the coil is functioning properly.**

1. Turn the ignition **OFF**.
2. Disconnect the negative battery cable. On the Cirrus, Stratus and Sebring convertible models, disconnect the remote negative battery cable connection on the left strut tower.

3. Disconnect the 2-pin electrical harness from the distributor.
4. Inspect the harness connector and ignition coil terminals for dirt, corrosion or damage. Repair as necessary.

➡ **It may be necessary to use jumper wires for testing access to the terminals.**

5. Using an ohmmeter, measure coil primary resistance between the terminals of the 2-pin connector on the distributor. Resistance should be 0.6–0.8 ohms.
6. Measure coil secondary resistance between the ignition coil tower and one terminal of the 2-pin connector on the distributor. Then, measure coil secondary resistance between the ignition coil tower and the other terminal of the 2-pin connector on the distributor. Resistance should be 12–18 kilohms.
7. If resistance is not within specifications, the coil may be faulty.

Fig. 5 The ignition coil is an integral component of the distributor housing. Note the location of the ignition coil tower (arrow)

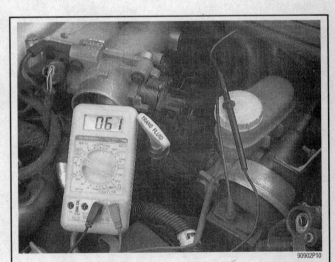

Fig. 6 Using a DVOM connected to jumper wires to test the ignition coil on the distributor housing

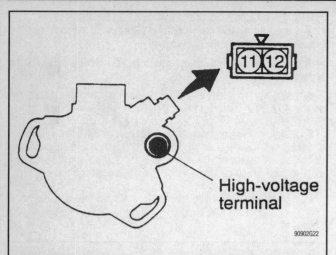

Fig. 7 Measure the secondary coil resistance between the coil tower and each 2-pin terminal

High-voltage terminal

90902G22

REMOVAL & INSTALLATION

The ignition coil for the 2.5L engine is located in the distributor housing. If the ignition coil is defective, the distributor assembly must be replaced. Refer to Distributor removal and installation.

Distributor

REMOVAL & INSTALLATION

2.5L Engine

▶ See Figures 8 thru 14

The 2.5L engine is equipped with a camshaft driven mechanical distributor. This engine uses a fixed ignition timing system, in which the basic ignition timing is not adjustable. The Powertrain Control Module (PCM) determines spark advance. The crankshaft position sensor and camshaft position sensor are Hall effect devices. The crankshaft sensor is mounted remotely from the distributor, while the camshaft position sensor is mounted inside the distributor housing. Both sensors generate pulses which serve as inputs to the PCM; the PCM determines crankshaft position from these sensors, then calculates injector sequence and ignition timing, based on the data.

1. Disconnect the negative battery cable. On vehicles other than Sebring coupe or Avenger, there is a remote connection at the left strut tower, which is equipped with an insulator grommet; be sure to place this grommet on the stud to prevent the negative battery cable from accidentally grounding.

2. If necessary for access, perform the following:

   a. Remove the bolt attaching the air inlet resonator to the intake manifold.

   b. Loosen the clamps holding the air cleaner cover to the air cleaner housing.

   c. Remove the PCV make-up air hose from the air inlet tube.

   d. Loosen the hose clamp at the throttle body.

   e. Remove the air cleaner cover, resonator and inlet tube.

   f. Remove the EGR tube.

3. Mark for identification, if necessary, and remove the spark plug wires from the distributor cap.

4. Remove the distributor cap.

5. Mark the rotor position with a scribe mark to indicate where to position the rotor when reinstalling the distributor. Remove the rotor.

6. Unfasten the 2 electrical harness connections from the distributor.

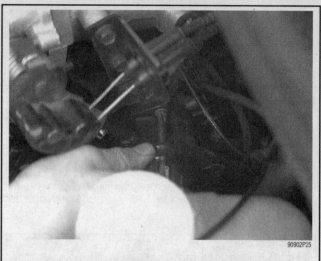

Fig. 8 Loosen the distributor cap hold-down screws

90902P25

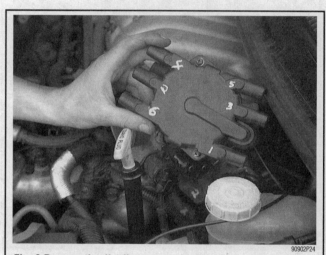

Fig. 9 Remove the distributor cap with the wires and terminals numbered for correct installation

90902P24

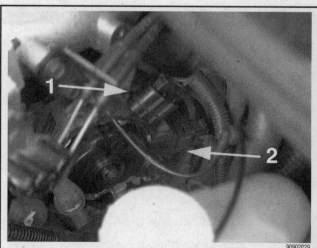

Fig. 10 After removing the distributor rotor, detach the 6-pin connector (1) and the 2-pin connector (2)

90902P29

Fig. 11 Remove the distributor assembly hold-down nuts and washers

Fig. 12 Locate, then remove the transaxle fluid dipstick retaining bolt

Fig. 13 For easier access to the distributor assembly, remove the transaxle fluid level dipstick and tube assembly by pulling up and out

Fig. 14 Grasp and remove the distributor assembly; it may have to be turned in order to pass through the space

7. Remove the 2 distributor hold-down nuts and washers.
8. If necessary, remove the spark plug cable mounting bracket.
9. Remove the transaxle dipstick tube.
10. Carefully remove the distributor from the engine.

INSTALLATION

Timing Not Disturbed

▶ **See Figure 15**

1. Inspect the rotor for cracks or burned electrodes, and replace if defective. Install the rotor onto the distributor.
2. Inspect the O-ring seal. If nicked or cracked, replace with a new one. Make sure the O-ring is properly seated on the distributor.
3. Carefully engage the distributor drive with the slotted end of the camshaft. When the distributor is installed properly, the rotor will be in line with the previously made mark.
4. Verify proper rotor alignment with the mark made at disassembly.
5. Reinstall the distributor hold-down nuts and washers. Tighten the nuts to 9 ft. lbs. (13 Nm).
6. Reinstall the spark plug cable bracket.

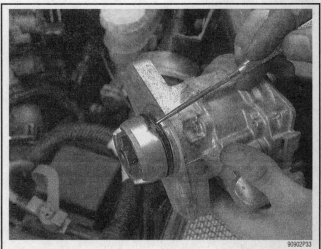

Fig. 15 Inspecting the distributor shaft rubber O-ring seal for nicks or cracks

7. Reconnect the 2 distributor wiring connectors.

8. Reinstall the distributor cap.

9. Reinstall the spark plug cables, following the identification marks made at disassembly.

10. Reinstall the transaxle dipstick tube.

11. If removed earlier, install the following:

a. Install the EGR tube and tighten the mounting bolts to 95 inch lbs. (11 Nm).

b. Install the air cleaner cover, resonator and inlet tube.

c. Tighten the hose clamp at the throttle body.

d. Install the PCV hose.

e. Tighten the clamps holding the air cleaner cover to the air cleaner housing.

f. Install the bolt attaching the air inlet resonator to the intake manifold.

12. Reconnect the negative battery cable.

Timing Disturbed

1. Rotate the crankshaft until the No. 1 piston is at Top Dead Center (TDC) of the compression stroke.

2. Rotate the rotor to the No. 1 terminal position on the distributor cap.

3. Lower the distributor into place, engaging the distributor drive with the drive on the camshaft. With the distributor fully seated on the engine, the rotor should be under the No. 1 terminal.

4. Verify proper rotor alignment with the mark made at disassembly.

5. Reinstall the distributor hold-down nuts and washers. Tighten the nuts to 9 ft. lbs. (13 Nm).

DISTRIBUTORLESS IGNITION SYSTEM

General Information

▶ See Figures 16, 17 and 18

The distributorless ignition system is referred to as the Direct Ignition System (DIS). This system's three main components are the coil pack, crankshaft sensor, and camshaft sensor. The crankshaft and camshaft sensors are Hall effect devices.

The ignition system is regulated by the Powertrain Control Module (PCM). The PCM supplies battery voltage to the ignition coil through the Auto Shutdown (ASD) relay. The PCM also controls the ground circuit for the ignition coil. By switching the ground path for the coil on and off, the PCM adjusts the ignition timing to meet changing engine operating conditions.

During the crank/start, period the PCM advances ignition timing a set amount. During engine operation, the amount of spark advance provided by the PCM is determined by these input factors:

- Intake air temperature
- Coolant temperature
- Engine RPM
- Available manifold vacuum
- Knock sensor

The PCM also regulates the fuel injection system.

The camshaft position sensor provides fuel injection synchronization and cylinder identification information. The sensor generates pulses that serve as input to the PCM. The PCM interprets the camshaft position sensor input (along with the crankshaft position sensor input) to determine crankshaft position. The PCM uses the crankshaft position sensor input to determine injector sequence and ignition timing.

The camshaft position sensor is mounted to the rear of the cylinder head. A target magnet attaches to the rear of the camshaft and indexes to the correct position. The target magnet has four different poles arranged in an asymmetrical pattern. As the target magnet rotates, the camshaft position sensor recognizes the change in polarity. The sensor switches from high (5 volts) to low (0.3 volts) as the target magnet rotates. When the north pole of the target magnet passes under the sensor, the output switches high. The sensor output switches low when the south pole of the target magnet passes underneath.

6. Reinstall the spark plug cable bracket.

7. Reconnect the 2 distributor wiring connectors.

8. Reinstall the distributor cap.

9. Reinstall the spark plug cables, following the identification marks made at disassembly.

10. Reinstall the transaxle dipstick tube.

11. If removed earlier, install the following:

a. Install the EGR tube and tighten the mounting bolts to 95 inch lbs. (11 Nm).

b. Install the air cleaner cover, resonator and inlet tube.

c. Tighten the hose clamp at the throttle body.

d. Install the PCV hose.

e. Tighten the clamps holding the air cleaner cover to the air cleaner housing.

f. Install the bolt attaching the air inlet resonator to the intake manifold.

12. Reconnect the negative battery cable.

Crankshaft Position Sensor

Refer to Electronic Engine Controls in Section 4 for information on servicing the crankshaft position sensor.

Camshaft Position Sensor

Refer to Electronic Engine Controls in Section 4 for information on servicing the camshaft position sensor.

The PCM uses the camshaft position sensor to determine injector sequence. The PCM determines ignition timing from the crankshaft position sensor. Once the crankshaft position has been determined, the PCM begins energizing the injectors in sequence.

The crankshaft position sensor is mounted to the engine block behind the alternator, just above the oil filter. The second crankshaft counterweight has machined into it two sets of four timing reference notches, including a 60 degree signature notch. From the crankshaft position sensor input, the PCM determines engine speed and crankshaft angle (position). The notches generate pulses front high to low in the crankshaft position sensor output voltage. When a metal portion of the counterweight aligns with the crankshaft position sensor, the sensor output voltage goes low (less than 0.5 volts). When a notch aligns with the sensor, voltage goes high (5.0 volts). As a group of notches pass under

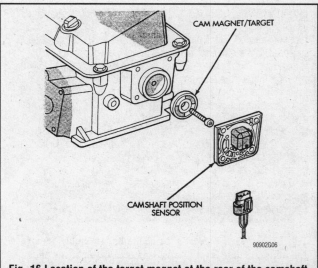

Fig. 16 Location of the target magnet at the rear of the camshaft

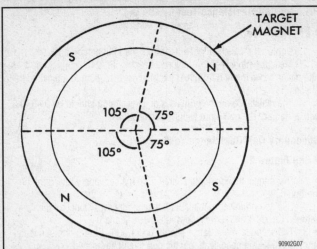

Fig. 17 Polarity of the target magnet of the camshaft position sensor

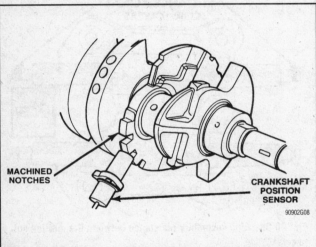

Fig. 18 Timing reference notches for the crankshaft position sensor

the sensor, the output voltage switches from low (metal) to high (notch), then back to low.

From the frequency of the output voltage pulses, the PCM calculates engine speed. The width of the pulses represent the amount of time the output voltage stays high before switching back to low. The period of time the voltage stays high before returning to low is called a pulse width. The faster the engine is operating, the smaller the pulse width.

By counting the pulses and referencing the pulse from the 60 degree signature notch, the PCM calculates crankshaft angle (position). In each group of timing reference notches, the first notch represents 69 degrees Before Top Dead Center (BTDC). The second notch represents 49 degrees BTDC. The third notch represents 29 degrees. The last notch in each set represents 9 degrees BTDC.

The timing reference notches are machined at 20 degree increments. From the voltage pulse-width, the PCM tells the difference between the timing reference notches and the 60 degree reference notches. The 60 degree signature notch produces a longer pulse-width than the smaller timing reference notches. If the camshaft position sensor input switches from high to low when the 60 degree signature notch passes under the crankshaft position sensor, the PCM knows cylinder No. 1 is the next cylinder at TDC.

The ignition coil assembly consists of 2 coils molded together. The assembly is mounted on top of the engine. The number of each coil appears on the front of the coil pack.

High tension leads route to each cylinder from the coil. The coil fires two spark plugs every power stroke; one plug is the cylinder under compression, the other cylinder fires on the exhaust stroke. The PCM determines which of the coils to charge and fire at the correct time. The coil's low primary resistance allows the PCM to fully charge the coil for each firing.

Diagnosis and Testing

To test the ignition system, perform the test procedures in a particular sequence. Start with the secondary spark test, commence to the coil test (located under the coil procedures later in this section) and, finally, perform the failure-to-start test. Performing the tests in this order will narrow down the ignition system problem in the easiest manner.

SECONDARY SPARK TEST

▶ **See Figure 3**

※ CAUTION

The Direct Ignition System generates approximately 40,000 volts. Personal injury could result from contact with this system.

Since there are 2 independent coils in the assembly, each coil must be checked individually. Cylinders 1 and 4, and 2 and 3 are grouped together.

1. Remove the cable from the No. 1 spark plug, then insert a clean spark plug into the spark plug boot.

➡ **Due to the high secondary voltage and risk of electrical shock, it is advisable to wrap a thick, dry cloth around the boot before grasping it.**

※ WARNING

Spark plug wire damage may occur if the spark plug is moved more than ¼ in. (6mm) away from the engine ground.

2. Ground the plug to the engine (touch the spark plug metal body to the engine block or other piece of metal on the car).
3. Crank the engine and look for a strong, blue spark across the electrodes of the spark plug.
4. Repeat the test for the three remaining cylinders. If there is no spark during all cylinder tests, refer to the failure-to-start test. If one or more tests indicate irregular, weak or no spark, refer to the coil test.

FAILURE-TO-START TEST

▶ **See Figure 19**

Before proceeding with this test, refer to the testing procedures for the ignition coil, later in this section.

1. Using a Digital Volt/Ohmmeter (DVOM) measure the voltage from the negative (-) battery terminal to the positive (+) battery terminal. The voltage should be at least 12.66 volts. This amount of voltage is necessary for an accurate inspection of the system.
2. Detach the ignition coil harness connector.
3. Connect a suitable test light to the B+ (battery voltage) terminal of the ignition coil electrical connector and ground. The center terminal of the connector supplies battery voltage.
4. Turn the ignition key to the **ON** position. The test light should flash ON and then OFF. Leave the ignition key **ON**.
   a. If the test light flashes momentarily, the PCM grounded the ASD relay. Proceed to the next step.
   b. If the test light did not flash, the ASD relay did not energize. This is caused by either the relay or one of the relay circuits.

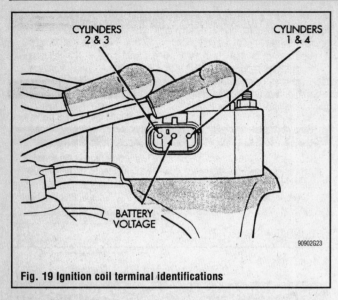

Fig. 19 Ignition coil terminal identifications

5. Crank the engine. (If the key was placed in the **OFF** position in Step 4, turn the key to the **ON** position before cranking. Wait for the test light to flash once, then crank the engine).

a. On 1995 vehicles, if the test light momentarily flashes during cranking, the PCM is not receiving a camshaft position sensor signal. On 1996–98 vehicles, if the test light momentarily flashes during cranking, the PCM is not receiving a crankshaft position sensor signal. Use a DRB or equivalent scan tool to test the sensor and related circuitry.

b. For 1995 vehicles, if the test light did not flash during cranking, unplug the camshaft position sensor connector. Turn the ignition key to the **OFF** position. Turn the key to the **ON** position, wait for the test light to momentarily flash once, then crank the engine. If the test light momentarily flashes, the camshaft position sensor is shorted and must be replaced. If the light did not flash when the engine was cranked, the cause of the no-start condition is in either the crankshaft or camshaft position sensor 8-volt supply circuit, or the crankshaft position sensor 5-volt output or ground circuits. Use a DRB or equivalent scan tool to test the crankshaft position sensor and related circuitry.

c. For 1996–98 vehicles, if the test light did not flash during cranking, unplug the crankshaft position sensor connector. Turn the ignition key to the **OFF** position. Turn the key to the **ON** position, wait for the test light to momentarily flash once, then crank the engine. If the test light momentarily flashes, the crankshaft position sensor is shorted and must be replaced. If the light did not flash when the engine was cranked, the cause of the no-start condition is in either the crankshaft or camshaft position sensor 8-volt supply circuit, or the camshaft position sensor output or ground circuits. Use a DRB or equivalent scan tool to test the camshaft position sensor and related circuitry.

Adjustments

All adjustments in the ignition system are controlled by the Powertrain Control Module (PCM) for optimum performance. No adjustments are possible.

Ignition Coil Pack

TESTING

➥ **Coil one fires cylinders 1 and 4, coil two fires cylinders 2 and 3. Each coil tower is labeled with the number of the corresponding cylinder.**

Primary Coil Resistance Test

▶ **See Figure 19**

1. Unplug the electrical connector from the ignition coil pack.
2. Measure the primary resistance of each coil. At the coil, connect an ohmmeter between the B+ pin and the pin corresponding to the cylinders in question.
3. The resistance on the primary side of each coil should be 0.45–0.65 ohms. Replace the coil if not within specifications.

Secondary Coil Resistance Test

▶ **See Figure 20**

1. Disconnect the spark plug wires from the secondary towers of the ignition coil.
2. Use an ohmmeter to measure the secondary resistance of the coil between towers 1 and 4, then between towers 2 and 3.
3. The secondary resistance should be 11,000–14,000 ohms. If resistance is not within specifications, the coil must be replaced.

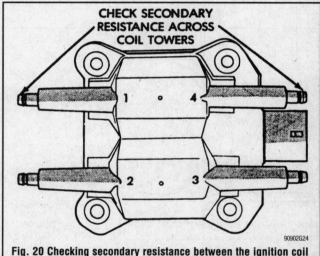

Fig. 20 Checking secondary resistance between the ignition coil towers

REMOVAL & INSTALLATION

1. Disconnect the negative battery cable.
2. Disengage the electrical connector from the ignition coil pack.
3. Label and disconnect the spark plug wires from each of the coil pack towers.
4. Remove the coil pack mounting fasteners.
5. Remove the coil pack from the vehicle. If equipped, remove the coil pack from the mounting bracket.

To install:

6. Place the coil pack into position on top of the engine valve cover, or mounting bracket, if equipped.
7. Install and tighten the coil pack mounting fasteners to 9 ft. lbs. (12 Nm).
8. Plug in the electrical connector to the ignition coil pack.
9. Connect each spark plug wire to each corresponding coil pack tower. The coil pack towers are numbered with the correct cylinder identification. Be sure that the spark plug wires snap firmly onto each coil tower.
10. Connect the negative battery cable.

Crankshaft Position Sensor

Refer to Electronic Engine Controls in Section 4 for information on servicing the crankshaft position sensor.

Camshaft Position Sensor

Refer to Electronic Engine Controls in Section 4 for information on servicing the camshaft position sensor.

FIRING ORDERS

▶ **See Figures 21 and 22**

➡ **To avoid confusion, remove and tag the spark plug wires one at a time, for replacement.**

If a distributor is not keyed for installation with only one orientation, it could have been removed previously and rewired. The resultant wiring would hold the correct firing order, but could change the relative placement of the plug towers in relation to the engine. For this reason, it is imperative that you label all wires before disconnecting any of them. Also, before removal, compare the current wiring with the accompanying illustrations. If the current wiring does not match, make notes in your book to reflect how your engine is wired.

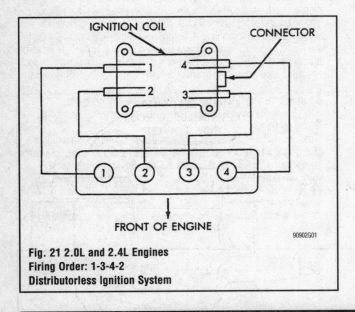

Fig. 21 2.0L and 2.4L Engines
Firing Order: 1-3-4-2
Distributorless Ignition System

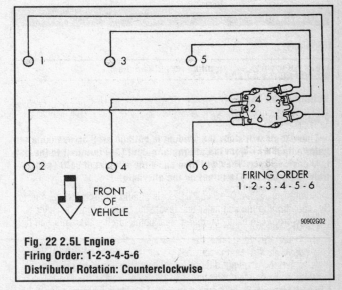

Fig. 22 2.5L Engine
Firing Order: 1-2-3-4-5-6
Distributor Rotation: Counterclockwise

CHARGING SYSTEM

General Information

The charging system is a negative (-) ground system which consists of an alternator, a regulator within the Powertrain Control Module (PCM), ignition switch, charge indicator lamp, battery, circuit protection and wiring connecting the components.

The alternator is belt-driven from the engine. Energy is supplied from the alternator to the rotating field through brushes to slip-rings. The slip-rings are mounted on the rotor shaft and are connected to the field coil. This energy supplied to the rotating field from the battery is called excitation current and is used to initially energize the field to begin the generation of electricity. Once the alternator starts to generate electricity, the excitation current comes from its own output, rather than from the battery.

The alternator produces power in the form of alternating current. The alternating current is rectified by diodes into direct current. The direct current is used to charge the battery and power the rest of the electrical system. When the ignition key is turned **ON**, current flows from the battery, through the charging system indicator light on the instrument panel, to the voltage regulator in the PCM, and to the alternator. Since the alternator is not producing any current, the alternator warning light comes on. When the engine is started, the alternator begins to produce current and turns the alternator light off.

As the alternator turns and produces current, the current is divided in two ways: charging the battery and powering the electrical components of the vehicle. Part of the current is returned to the alternator to enable it to increase its output. In this situation, the alternator is receiving current from the battery and from itself. A voltage regulator is wired into the current supply to the alternator to prevent it from receiving too much current, which would cause it to overproduce current. Conversely, if the voltage regulator does not allow the alternator to receive enough current, the battery will not be fully charged and will eventually go dead.

The battery is connected to the alternator at all times, whether the ignition key is turned **ON** or **OFF**. If the battery were shorted to ground, the alternator would also be shorted. This would damage the alternator. To prevent this, circuit protection (usually in the form of a fuse link) is installed in the wiring between the battery and the alternator. If the battery is shorted, the circuit protection will protect the alternator.

ALTERNATOR PRECAUTIONS

Several precautions must be observed with alternator equipped vehicles to avoid damage to the unit.

• ALWAYS observe proper polarity of the battery connections; be especially careful when jump starting the car. Reversing the battery connections may result in damage to the one-way rectifiers.

• ALWAYS remove the battery or, at least, disconnect the cables while charging.

• ALWAYS match and/or consider the polarity of the battery, alternator and regulator before making any electrical connections within the system.

• ALWAYS disconnect the battery ground terminal while repairing or replacing any electrical components.

• NEVER use a fast battery charger to jump start a dead battery.

- NEVER attempt to polarize an alternator.
- NEVER use test lights of more than 12 volts when checking diode continuity.
- NEVER ground or short out the alternator or regulator terminals.
- NEVER separate the alternator on an open circuit. Make sure all connections within the circuit are clean and tight.
- NEVER use arc welding equipment on the car with the alternator connected.
- NEVER operate the alternator with any of its or the battery's lead wires disconnected.
- NEVER subject the alternator to excessive heat or dampness (for instance, steam cleaning the engine).
- When utilizing a booster battery as a starting aid, always connect the positive to positive terminals and the negative terminal from the booster battery to a good engine ground on the vehicle being started.

Alternator

TESTING

♦ **See Figures 23 and 24**

Voltage Drop Test

♦ **See Figures 25 and 26**

➡**These tests will show the amount of voltage drop across the alternator output wire from the alternator output (B+) terminal to the battery positive post. They will also show the amount of voltage drop from the ground (-) terminal on the alternator.**

A voltmeter with a 0–18 volt DC scale should be used for these tests. By repositioning the voltmeter test leads, the point of high resistance (voltage drop) can easily be found. Test points on the alternator can be reached by either removing the air cleaner housing or below by raising the vehicle.

1. Before starting the test, make sure the battery is in good condition and is fully charged. Check the conditions of the battery cables.
2. Start the engine, let it warm up to normal operating temperatures, then turn the engine **OFF**.
3. Connect an engine tachometer, following the manufacturer's directions.
4. Make sure the parking brake is fully engaged.
5. Start the engine, then place the blower on HIGH, and turn on the high beam headlamps and interior lamps.
6. Bring the engine speed up to 2,400 rpm and hold it there.
7. To test the ground (-) circuitry, perform the following:
   a. Touch the negative lead of the voltmeter directly to the positive battery terminal.
   b. Touch the positive lead of the voltmeter to the B+ output terminal stud on the alternator (NOT the terminal mounting nut). The voltage should be no higher than 0.6 volts. If the voltage is higher than 0.6 volts, touch the test lead to the terminal mounting stud nut, and then to the wiring connector. If the voltage is now below 0.6 volts, look for dirty, loose or poor connections at this point. A voltage drop test may be performed at each ground (-) connection in the circuit to locate the excessive resistance.
8. To test the positive (+) circuitry, perform the following:
   a. Touch the positive lead of the voltmeter directly to the negative battery terminal.
   b. Touch the negative lead of the voltmeter to the ground terminal stud on the alternator case (NOT the terminal mounting nut). The voltage should be no higher than 0.3 volts. If the voltage is higher than 0.3 volts, touch the test lead to the terminal mounting stud nut, and then to the wiring connector. If the voltage is now below 0.3 volts, look for dirty, loose or poor connections at this point. A voltage drop test may be performed at each positive (+) connection in the circuit to locate the excessive resistance.

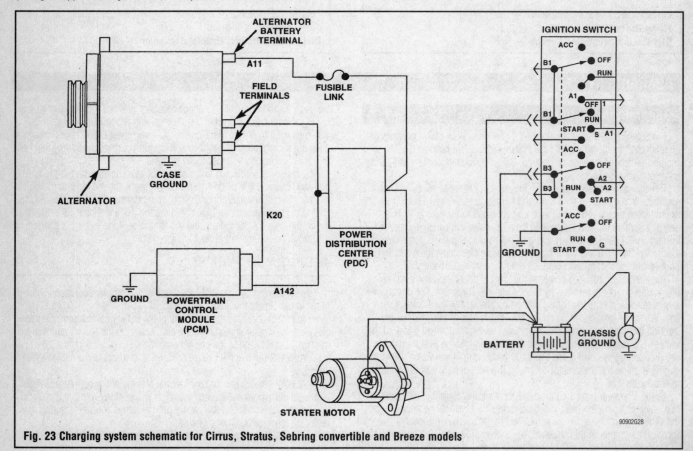

Fig. 23 Charging system schematic for Cirrus, Stratus, Sebring convertible and Breeze models

90902G28

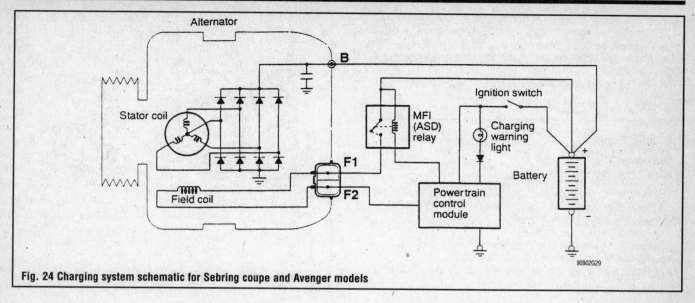

Fig. 24 Charging system schematic for Sebring coupe and Avenger models

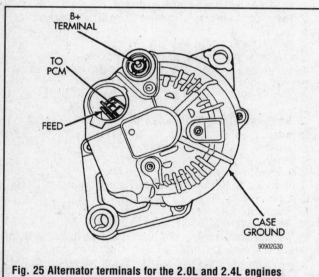

Fig. 25 Alternator terminals for the 2.0L and 2.4L engines

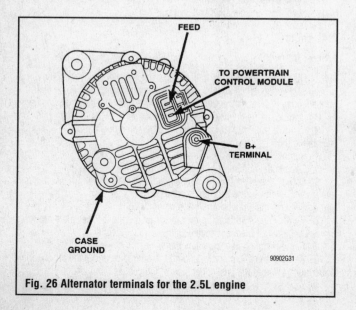

Fig. 26 Alternator terminals for the 2.5L engine

9. This test can also be performed between the alternator case and the engine. If the test voltage is higher than 0.3 volts, check for corrosion at the alternator mounting points or loose alternator mounting.

Output Voltage Test

1. Determine if any Diagnostic Trouble Codes (DTC'S) exist, as outlined in Section 4.

2. Before starting the test, make sure the battery is in good condition and is fully charged. Check the conditions of the battery cables.

3. Perform the voltage drop test to ensure clean and tight alternator/battery electrical connections.

4. Be sure the alternator drive belt is properly tensioned, as outlined in Section 1.

5. A volt/amp tester equipped with both a battery load control (carbon pile rheostat) and an inductive-type pickup clamp (ammeter probe) will be used for this test. Make sure to follows all directions supplied with the tester. If you are using a tester equipped with an inductive-type clamp, you don't have to remove the wiring from the alternator.

6. Start the engine and let it run until it reaches normal operating temperature, then shut the engine **OFF**.

7. Make sure all electrical accessories and lights are turned **OFF**.

8. Connect the volt/amp tester leads to the battery. Be sure the carbon pile rheostat control is in the OPEN or OFF position before connecting the leads.

9. Connect the inductive clamp (ammeter probe), following the instructions supplied with the test equipment.

10. If a volt/amp tester is not equipped with an engine tachometer, connect a separate tachometer to the engine.

11. Fully engage the parking brake.

12. Start the engine, then bring the engine speed up to 2,500 rpm.

❊❊ WARNING

This load test must be performed within 15 seconds to prevent damage to the test equipment!

13. With the engine speed held at 2,500 rpm, slowly adjust the rheostat control (load) on the tester to get the highest amperage reading. Do not let the voltage drop below 12 volts. Record the reading.

➡ **On certain brands of test equipment, this load will be applied automatically. Be sure to read the operating manual supplied with the test equipment before performing the test.**

14. The ammeter reading must meet the minimum test amps specification of 75 amps.

15. Rotate the load control to the OFF position.

16. Continue holding the engine speed at 2,500 rpm. If the EVR circuitry is OK, the amperage should drop below 15–20 amps. With all of the electrical accessories and vehicle lighting off, this could take several minutes of engine operation.

17. After the procedure is complete, remove the volt/amp tester.

REMOVAL & INSTALLATION

2.0L DOHC Engine

▶ See Figure 27

1. Disconnect the negative battery cable.
2. Remove the right side under cover.
3. Remove the speed control vacuum reservoir and related components, as required for alternator access.
4. Remove the alternator drive belt.
5. Remove the alternator mounting bolts.
6. Remove the alternator top brace from the engine.
7. Disconnect the alternator wiring and remove the alternator from the vehicle.

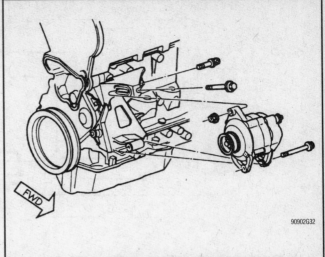

Fig. 28 Alternator assembly installation—2.0L SOHC engine

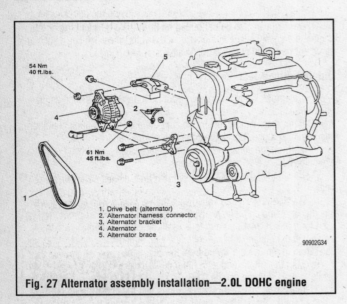

1. Drive belt (alternator)
2. Alternator harness connector
3. Alternator bracket
4. Alternator
5. Alternator brace

Fig. 27 Alternator assembly installation—2.0L DOHC engine

To install:

8. Install the alternator in position and connect the electrical harness.
9. Install the alternator top brace to the engine.
10. Install the alternator mounting bolts loosely.
11. Install the drive belt and adjust until the proper tension is achieved. Secure the lower alternator through-bolt nut to 45 ft. lbs. (61 Nm) and the alternator's upper lockbolt to 40 ft. lbs. (54 Nm).
12. Install the speed control vacuum reservoir and whatever related components were removed for alternator access.
13. Install the right side undercover.
14. Connect the negative battery cable. Start the engine and check the alternator for proper operation.

2.0L SOHC Engine

▶ See Figure 28

1. Disconnect the negative battery cable from the left strut tower. The ground cable is equipped with an insulator grommet, which should be placed on the stud to prevent the negative battery cable from accidentally grounding.

2. Unplug the field circuit from the alternator.
3. Remove the B+ terminal cover by spreading the cover with a small, flat bladed tool.
4. Remove the B+ nut and wire.
5. Loosen the adjusting bolt, but do not remove.
6. Loosen the pivot bolt and the adjusting bolt until the drive belt can be removed.
7. Remove the adjusting bolt and pivot bolt, but do not drop the spacer.
8. Remove the alternator by moving it toward the headlight bucket.

To install:

9. Install the alternator into the bracket on the engine.
10. Reinstall the pivot bolt, but do not tighten.
11. Reinstall the adjusting bolt, but do not tighten.
12. Reconnect the B+ wire and install the retaining nut. Tighten the nut to 75 inch lbs. (9 Nm).
13. Reinstall the B+ terminal cover.
14. Reconnect the field circuit to the alternator.
15. Reinstall the drive belt, making sure it is correctly routed and seated on the alternator pulley. Do not tension the drive belt at this time.
16. Adjust the drive belt and tighten the adjusting bolt to 40 ft. lbs. (54 Nm).
17. Tighten the pivot bolt to 40 ft. lbs. (54 Nm).
18. Reconnect the negative battery cable.

2.4L Engine

▶ See Figure 29

1. Disconnect the negative battery cable from the left strut tower. The ground cable is equipped with an insulator grommet, which should be placed on the stud to prevent the negative battery cable from accidentally grounding.
2. Unplug the field circuit from the alternator.
3. Remove the B+ terminal cover from by spreading the cover with a flat bladed tool.
4. Remove the B+ nut and wire.
5. Loosen the adjusting bolt, but do not remove.
6. Loosen the pivot bolt and the adjusting bolt until the drive belt can be removed. Remove the accessory drive belt.
7. Remove the adjusting bolt and pivot bolt.
8. Remove the ABS braking unit by removing the 2 lower plate mounting bolts. Leave all lines connected.
9. Remove the coolant overflow bottle.
10. Remove the alternator by sliding the alternator under the air conditioner lines towards the passenger side of the vehicle.

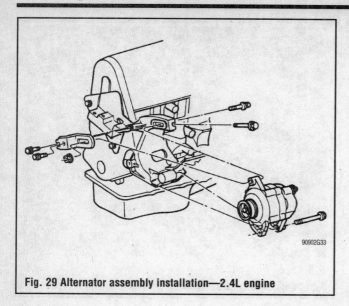

Fig. 29 Alternator assembly installation—2.4L engine

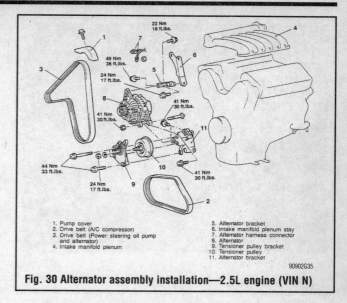

1. Pump cover
2. Drive belt (A/C compressor)
3. Drive belt (Power steering oil pump and alternator)
4. Intake manifold plenum
5. Alternator bracket
6. Intake manifold plenum stay
7. Alternator harness connector
8. Alternator
9. Tensioner pulley bracket
10. Tensioner pulley
11. Alternator bracket

Fig. 30 Alternator assembly installation—2.5L engine (VIN N)

To install:

11. Install the alternator into the bracket on the engine.
12. Install the adjusting and pivot bolts, but do not tighten at this time.
13. Connect the B+ wire and tighten the nut to 75 inch lbs. (9 Nm).
14. Reinstall the B+ terminal cover.
15. Reconnect the field circuit to the alternator.
16. Install the accessory drive belt. Be sure the drive belt is correctly routed on the engine and correctly seated on the alternator pulley.
17. Adjust the drive belt and tighten the adjusting bolt to 40 ft. lbs. (54 Nm).
18. Tighten the pivot bolt to 40 ft. lbs. (54 Nm).
19. Reinstall the ABS braking unit. Install and tighten the 2 lower plate mounting bolts.
20. Reinstall the coolant overflow bottle.
21. Reconnect the negative battery cable.

2.5L (VIN N) Engine

▶ See Figure 30

1. Disconnect the negative battery cable.
2. Remove the right side under cover.
3. Remove the speed control vacuum reservoir and related components as required for alternator access.
4. Remove the power steering pump cover.
5. Remove the A/C compressor drive belt.
6. Remove the alternator/power steering pump drive belt.
7. Remove the intake manifold plenum.
8. Remove the upper alternator bracket.
9. Remove the intake manifold plenum stay.
10. Detach the electrical connections at the alternator.
11. Unfasten the upper and lower bolts and remove the alternator. Be very careful not to damage neighboring components while removing the alternator.

To install:

12. Connect the wiring to the alternator.
13. Place the alternator on its lower bracket and install the upper and lower bolts finger-tight.
14. Install the upper alternator bracket.
15. Install the alternator/power steering pump belt, making sure it is properly seated.

16. Adjust the drive belt to the correct tension using the belt adjuster, then tighten the upper mounting bolt to 16 ft. lbs. (22 Nm) and the lower mounting bolt to 30 ft. lbs. (41 Nm).
17. Install the intake manifold plenum.
18. Install the intake manifold plenum stay.
19. Install the A/C compressor drive belt.
20. Install the power steering pump cover.
21. Connect the negative battery cable.
22. Check the charging system operation.

2.5L (VIN H) Engine

▶ See Figures 31 thru 41

1. Disconnect the negative battery cable from the left strut tower. The ground cable is equipped with an insulator grommet, which should be placed on the stud to prevent the negative battery cable from accidentally grounding.

Fig. 31 Disconnect the field coil terminal from the back of the alternator, then the B+ terminal nut and wire

Fig. 32 Loosen the top mounting ear bolt

Fig. 35 Removing the alternator drive belt

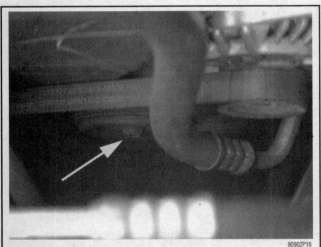

Fig. 33 Location of the idler pulley locknut—the adjuster screw is to the side

Fig. 36 Loosen the lower pivot bolt while securing the nut with a wrench

Fig. 34 Loosening the adjuster bolt from below the vehicle, to remove the drive belt

2. Unplug the field circuit from the alternator.
3. Remove the B+ terminal nut and wire.
4. Loosen the top mounting ear bolt.

➡ **It may be necessary to remove the drive belt and lower alternator pivot bolt from under the vehicle.**

5. Loosen the adjusting bolt on the idler to allow removal of the alternator drive belt.
6. Loosen, but do not remove, the pivot bolt. Use care not to lose the nut.
7. Remove the pivot bolt, using care not to lose the spacer.
8. Remove the top mounting ear bolt.
9. For easier access, disconnect and move all wiring harnesses out of the way.
10. Remove the alternator upper bracket.
11. Remove the alternator from the vehicle.

To install:
12. Install the alternator into the bracket on the engine.
13. Reinstall the alternator's upper mounting bracket and tighten the bolts.
14. Reinstall the pivot bolt, but do not tighten at this time.

Fig. 37 It may be easier to remove the alternator lower pivot bolt from below the vehicle

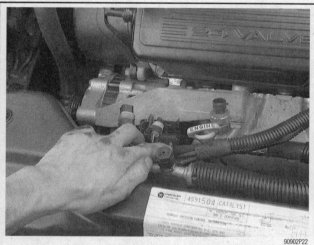

Fig. 38 Disconnect and move all wiring harnesses out of the way

Fig. 39 Remove the alternator's upper mounting bracket bolts . . .

Fig. 40 . . . then remove the upper mounting bracket

Fig. 41 Remove the alternator from the vehicle

15. Install the top mounting ear bolt, but do not tighten at this time.

16. Reconnect the B+ terminal wire and tighten the nut to 75 inch lbs. (9 Nm). Connect all wiring harnesses which were disconnected during removal.

17. Reconnect the field circuit to the alternator.

18. Reinstall the drive belt. Be sure the accessory drive belt is correctly routed on the engine and properly seated on the alternator pulley.

19. Adjust the drive belt and tighten the idler pulley bolt to 40 ft. lbs. (54 Nm).

20. Tighten the pivot bolt and top mounting ear bolt to 40 ft. lbs. (54 Nm).

21. Reconnect the negative battery cable.

STARTING SYSTEM

General Information

The battery and starting motor are linked by very heavy electrical cables designed to minimize resistance to the flow of current. Generally, the major power supply cable that leaves the battery goes directly to the starter, while other electrical system needs are supplied by a smaller cable. During starter operation, power flows from the battery to the starter and is grounded through the vehicle's frame/body or engine and the battery's negative ground strap.

The starter is a specially designed, direct current electric motor capable of producing a great amount of power for its size. One thing that allows the motor to produce a great deal of power is its tremendous rotating speed. It drives the engine through a tiny pinion gear (attached to the starter's armature), which drives the very large flywheel ring gear at a greatly reduced speed. Another factor allowing it to produce so much power is that only intermittent operation is required of it. Thus, little allowance for air circulation is necessary, and the windings can be built into a very small space.

The starter solenoid is a magnetic device which employs the small current supplied by the start circuit of the ignition switch. This magnetic action moves a plunger which mechanically engages the starter and closes the heavy switch connecting it to the battery. The starting switch circuit usually consists of the starting switch contained within the ignition switch, a neutral safety switch or clutch pedal switch, and the wiring necessary to connect these in series with the starter solenoid or relay.

The pinion, a small gear, is mounted to a one-way drive clutch. This clutch is splined to the starter armature shaft. When the ignition switch is moved to the **START** position, the solenoid plunger slides the pinion toward the flywheel ring gear via a collar and spring. If the teeth on the pinion and flywheel match properly, the pinion will engage the flywheel immediately. If the gear teeth butt one another, the spring will be compressed and will force the gears to mesh as soon as the starter turns far enough to allow them to do so. As the solenoid plunger reaches the end of its travel, it closes the contacts that connect the battery and starter, then the engine is cranked.

As soon as the engine starts, the flywheel ring gear begins turning fast enough to drive the pinion at an extremely high rate of speed. At this point, the one-way clutch begins allowing the pinion to spin faster than the starter shaft so that the starter will not operate at excessive speed. When the ignition switch is released from the starter position, the solenoid is de-energized, and a spring pulls the gear out of mesh, interrupting the current flow to the starter.

Some starters employ a separate relay, mounted away from the starter, to switch the motor and solenoid current on and off. The relay replaces the solenoid electrical switch, but does not eliminate the need for a solenoid mounted on the starter used to mechanically engage the starter drive gears. The relay is used to reduce the amount of current the starting switch must carry.

Starter

TESTING

Testing Preparation

Before commencing with the starting system diagnostics, verify:
- The battery posts/terminals are clean.
- The alternator drive belt tension and condition is correct.
- The battery state-of-charge is correct.
- The battery cable connections at the starter and engine block are clean and free from corrosion.

- The wiring harness connectors and terminals are clean and free from corrosion.
- The circuit is properly grounded.

Starter Feed Circuit

▶ See Figure 42

✳✳ CAUTION

The ignition and fuel systems must be disabled to prevent engine start while performing the tests.

1. Connect a volt-ampere tester (multimeter) to the battery terminals.
2. Disable the ignition and fuel systems by disconnecting the Automatic Shutdown (ASD) relay, located in the Power Distribution Center (PDC) in the engine compartment.
3. Verify that all lights and accessories are OFF, and the transaxle shift selector is in Park (automatic) or Neutral (manual). Set the parking brake.
4. Rotate and hold the ignition switch in the **START** position. Observe the volt-ampere tester:

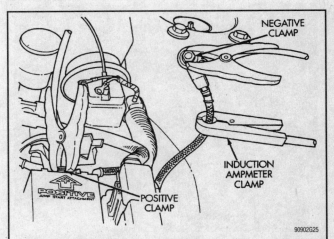

Fig. 42 Volt-Amp tester connections for Cirrus, Stratus, Sebring convertible and Breeze models. (Sebring and Avenger coupe models utilize a conventional hook-up method)

- If the voltage reads above 9.6 volts, and the amperage draw reads above 250 amps, go to the starter feed circuit resistance test (following this test).
- If the voltage reads 12.4 volts or greater and the amperage reads 0–10 amps, refer to the starter control circuit test.
- If the voltage reads below 9.6 volts and the amperage draw reads above 300 amps, the trouble is within the starter.

✳✳ WARNING

Do not overheat the starter motor or draw the battery voltage below 9.6 volts during cranking operations.

5. After the starting system problems have been corrected, verify the battery's state of charge, and charge the battery if necessary. Disconnect all of the testing equipment and connect the ignition coil cable or ignition coil connector. Start the vehicle several times to assure the problem was corrected.

Starter Feed Circuit Resistance

▶ **See Figures 43 and 44**

Before proceeding with this test, refer to the battery tests and starter feed circuit test. The following test will require a voltmeter, which is capable of accuracy to within 0.1 volt.

❊❊ CAUTION

The ignition and fuel systems must be disabled to prevent engine start while performing the tests.

1. Disable the ignition and fuel systems by disconnecting the Automatic Shutdown (ASD) relay, located in the Power Distribution Center (PDC) in the engine compartment.
2. With all wiring harnesses and components properly connected, perform the following:

a. Connect the negative (-) lead of the voltmeter to the negative battery terminal, and the positive (+) lead to a point on the engine block near the battery cable attaching point. Rotate and hold the ignition switch in the **START** position. Observe the voltmeter. If the voltage reads above 0.2 volt, correct the poor contact at the ground cable mounting points.

b. Connect the positive (+) lead of the voltmeter to the positive battery terminal, and the negative (-) lead to the positive battery cable terminal on the starter solenoid. Rotate and hold the ignition switch key in the **START** position while observing the voltmeter. If voltage reads above 0.2 volt, correct the poor contact between the cable end and battery terminal.

c. Connect the negative lead of the voltmeter to the negative (-) battery terminal, and the positive lead to the engine block near the battery cable attaching point. Rotate and hold the ignition switch in the **START** position. If the voltage reads above 0.2 volt, correct the poor contact at the ground cable attaching point. If the voltage reading is still above 0.2 volt after correcting the poor contact, replace the negative ground cable with a new one.

3. Refer to removal and installation procedures to gain access to the starter motor and solenoid connections. Perform the following steps:

a. Connect the positive (+) voltmeter lead to the starter motor housing and the negative (-) lead to the negative battery terminal. Hold the ignition switch key in the **START** position. If the voltage reads above 0.2 volt, correct the poor starter to engine ground.

b. Connect the positive (+) voltmeter lead to the positive battery terminal, and the negative lead to the battery cable terminal on the starter solenoid. Rotate and hold the ignition key in the **START** position. If the voltage reads above 0.2 volt, correct the poor contact at the battery cable to the solenoid connection. If the reading is still above 0.2 volt after correcting the poor contact, replace the positive battery cable with a new one.

c. If the resistance tests did not detect feed circuit failures, replace the starter motor.

REMOVAL & INSTALLATION

2.0L DOHC Engine

▶ **See Figure 45**

1. Disconnect the negative battery cable.
2. Disconnect the starter motor electrical connections.
3. Remove the starter motor mounting bolts and remove the starter.

To install:

4. Clean both surfaces of the starter motor flange and the rear plate. This is important since the starter grounds through its case and the transaxle flange to which it attached. Some remanufactured starters may have paint on these areas which should be cleaned off before installation. Install the starter motor onto the transaxle and secure with the retaining bolts. Tighten the bolts to 40 ft. lbs. (54 Nm).
5. Attach the electrical harness connectors to the starter.
6. Connect the negative battery cable and check the starter for proper operation.

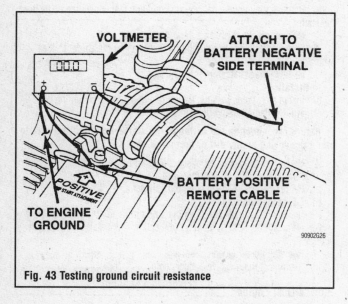

Fig. 43 Testing ground circuit resistance

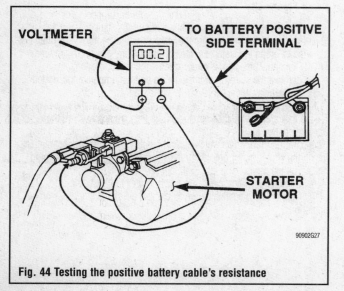

Fig. 44 Testing the positive battery cable's resistance

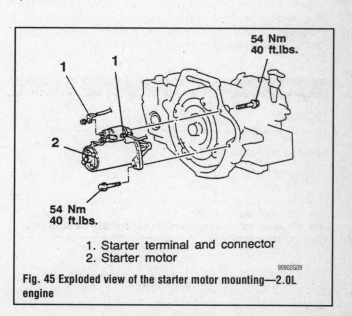

1. Starter terminal and connector
2. Starter motor

Fig. 45 Exploded view of the starter motor mounting—2.0L engine

2.0L SOHC Engine With Manual Transaxle

▶ **See Figures 45 and 46**

1. Disconnect the negative battery cable from the left strut tower. The ground cable is equipped with a insulator grommet which should be placed on the stud to prevent the negative battery cable from accidentally grounding.

2. Remove the air cleaner resonator.

3. Remove the positive battery cable retaining nut from the starter.

4. Disconnect the positive battery cable and alternator output wire from the starter.

5. Disconnect the push-on solenoid connector from the starter.

6. Remove the 2 bolts that attach the starter to the transaxle.

7. Remove the starter from the vehicle.

To install:

8. Install the starter and the attaching bolts to the transaxle assembly.

9. Tighten the attaching bolts to 40 ft. lbs. (54 Nm).

➡ **Clean all dirt and/or corrosion from the wire terminals before reconnecting the wiring to the solenoid.**

10. Reconnect the push-on solenoid connector to the starter.

11. Reconnect the alternator output wire and positive battery cable to the starter and tighten the retaining nut to 90 inch lbs. (10 Nm).

12. Install the air cleaner resonator.

13. Reconnect the negative battery cable.

2.0L SOHC Engine With Automatic Transaxle; 2.4L Engine

▶ **See Figures 45, 46 and 47**

1. Disconnect the negative battery cable from the left strut tower. The ground cable is equipped with a insulator grommet which should be placed on the stud to prevent the negative battery cable from accidentally grounding.

2. Remove the air cleaner resonator.

3. Remove the 3 bolts attaching the Transmission Control Module (TCM). Do not disconnect the TCM wiring. Move the TCM to gain access to the upper starter mounting bolt.

4. Remove the upper starter mounting bolt.

5. Raise and safely support the vehicle.

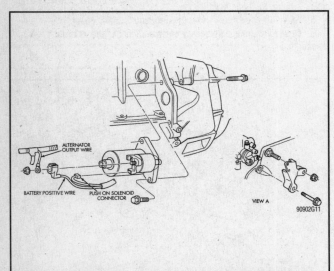

Fig. 46 Starter motor wiring terminal connections—2.0L engine

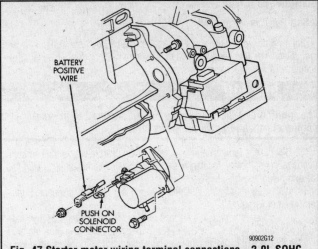

Fig. 47 Starter motor wiring terminal connections—2.0L SOHC engine with A/T; 2.4L engine

6. Remove the positive battery cable nut and disconnect the cable from the starter.

7. Disconnect the push-on solenoid connector.

8. Remove the lower mounting bolt that attaches the starter to the transaxle.

9. Remove the starter from the vehicle.

To install:

10. Install the starter onto the transaxle and the lower mounting bolt.

11. Tighten the mounting bolts to 40 ft. lbs. (54 Nm).

➡ **Before reconnecting the wiring to the starter solenoid, be sure to clean the wiring of any dirt or corrosion.**

12. Reconnect the positive battery cable to the solenoid post and tighten the retaining nut to 90 inch lbs. (10 Nm).

13. Reconnect the push-on solenoid connector.

14. Lower the vehicle.

15. Reinstall the upper attaching bolt and torque to 40 ft. lbs. (54 Nm).

16. Reinstall the TCM to its original location and install the mounting screws.

17. Reinstall the air cleaner resonator.

18. Reconnect the negative battery cable.

2.5L (VIN N) Engine

▶ **See Figure 48**

1. Disconnect the negative battery cable.

2. Most vehicles will require the removal of the front exhaust pipe. Use penetrating oil on the fasteners to ease removal.

3. Disconnect the starter motor electrical connections.

4. Remove the starter motor mounting bolts and remove the starter.

To install:

5. Clean both surfaces of the starter motor flange and the rear plate. This is important since the starter grounds through its case and the transaxle flange to which it attached. Some remanufactured starters may have paint on these areas which should be cleaned off before installation. Install the starter motor onto the transaxle and secure with the retaining bolts. Tighten the bolts to 20–25 ft. lbs. (26–33 Nm).

6. Connect the electrical harness connectors to the starter.

7. Connect the negative battery cable and check the starter for proper operation.

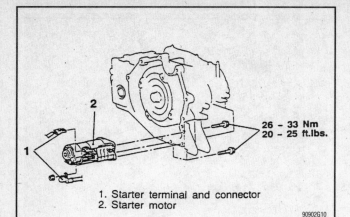

Fig. 48 Exploded view of the starter motor mounting—2.5L engine

1. Starter terminal and connector
2. Starter motor

90902G10

Fig. 50 Location of the positive battery cable nut (1) and the push-on solenoid connector (2)

90902P02

2.5L (VIN H) Engine

♦ **See Figures 49 thru 55**

1. Disconnect the negative battery cable from the left strut tower. The ground cable is equipped with an insulator grommet which should be placed on the stud to prevent the negative battery cable from accidentally grounding.

2. Raise and safely support the vehicle.

3. Loosen, but do not remove, the exhaust pipe-to-manifold retaining nuts.

4. Place a drain pan under the oil filter to prevent oil spillage, then remove the oil filter. For additional details, refer to Section 1.

5. Remove the positive battery cable retaining nut and battery cable from the starter.

6. Disconnect the push-on solenoid connector.

7. Remove the 3 bolts that attach the starter unit to the transaxle.

8. Pull the exhaust pipe down just enough to provide clearance for the starter motor. The exhaust pipe does not have to be separated from the pipe-to-manifold threaded studs.

9. Remove the starter unit from the vehicle.

To install:

10. Install the starter unit onto the transaxle and install the 3 mounting bolts.

Fig. 51 After removing the oil filter for access, unfasten the retaining nut and disconnect the positive battery cable

90902P03

Fig. 49 Loosen the exhaust pipe-to-manifold retaining nuts to provide removal clearance for the starter

90902P01

Fig. 52 Disengage the push-on starter solenoid connector

90902P04

11. Tighten the mounting bolts to 40 ft. lbs. (54 Nm).

➡ **Before reconnecting any wiring to the starter solenoid, clean the wire terminals of any dirt or corrosion.**

12. Reconnect the positive battery terminal and retaining nut to the starter solenoid post. Tighten the retaining nut to 90 inch lbs. (10 Nm).
13. Reconnect the push-on solenoid connector.
14. Reinstall the oil filter.
15. Lower the vehicle.
16. Reconnect the negative battery cable.

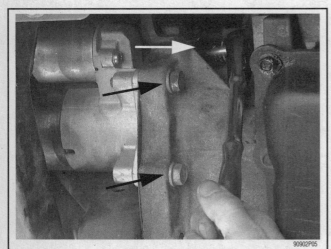

Fig. 53 Remove the 3 starter motor-to-transaxle housing attaching bolts

Fig. 54 Pull the exhaust pipe down just enough to provide removal clearance for the starter

Fig. 55 Carefully remove the starter motor from the vehicle

RELAY REPLACEMENT

◆ **See Figure 56**

On Cirrus, Stratus, Sebring convertible and Breeze models, the starter relay is located in the Power Distribution Center (PDC) in the engine compartment. Refer to the underside of the PDC cover for starter relay location.

On Sebring and Avenger coupes, the starter relay is located under the instrument panel, behind the instrument panel/center console panel. It may only be necessary to remove the center console panel to access the starter relay. However, if the entire console requires removal, refer to Section 10.

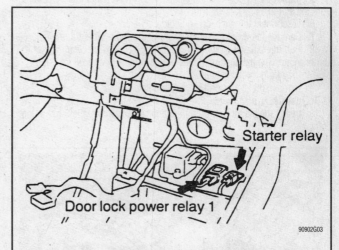

Fig. 56 Location of the starter relay on Sebring and Avenger coupes

SENDING UNITS

➡ **This section describes the operating principles of sending units, warning lights and gauges. Sensors which provide information to the Electronic Control Module (ECM) are covered in Section 4 of this manual.**

Instrument panels contain a number of indicating devices (gauges and warning lights). These devices are composed of two separate components. One is the sending unit, mounted on the engine or other remote part of the vehicle, and the other is the actual gauge or light in the instrument panel.

Several types of sending units exist, however most can be characterized as being either a pressure type or a resistance type. Pressure type sending units convert liquid pressure into an electrical signal which is sent to the gauge or warning light. Resistance type sending units are most often used to measure temperature and use variable resistance to control the current flow back to the indicating device. Both types of sending units are connected in series by a wire to the battery (through the ignition switch). When the ignition is turned **ON**, current flows from the battery through the indicating device and on to the sending unit.

Coolant Temperature Sender

The coolant temperature information is conveyed to the instrument panel, through the PCM, from the Engine Coolant Temperature (ECT) sensor. To test and remove the sensor, refer to Section 4. To test the gauge, perform the following testing procedure.

TESTING

Cirrus, Stratus, Sebring Convertible and Breeze

1. Initiate the instrument cluster self-diagnostics by pressing the odometer/trip reset button while turning the ignition key through the **OFF/RUN/START** positions. This will cycle an electronic display segment check and illumination of all the instrument cluster warning indicators and gauges.
2. If all of the gauges fail to move, replace the instrument cluster circuit board.
3. If any separate gauge fails to move, replace that gauge.
4. If any gauge is not positioned properly, replace the printed circuit board

Sebring Coupe and Avenger

▶ **See Figure 57**

1. Detach the coolant temperature sensor electrical connector.

2. Connect a 12 volt test light between the harness side connector and ground.
3. Turn the ignition switch to the **ON** position. The temperature gauge should be at its lowest position.
4. Replace the coolant temperature gauge if the test light illuminates but the gauge needle does not move.
5. If the test light illuminates and the gauge needle moves, replace the coolant temperature sensor.
6. If the test light does not illuminate and the gauge needle does not move repair the wiring harness.

Oil Pressure Sender

▶ **See Figures 58 and 59**

On all 2.0L and 2.4L engines, the oil pressure sending unit switch is located on the engine block, below the exhaust manifold, on the firewall side. On all 2.5L engines, the oil pressure sending unit switch is located on the engine block, below the front exhaust manifold on the radiator side.

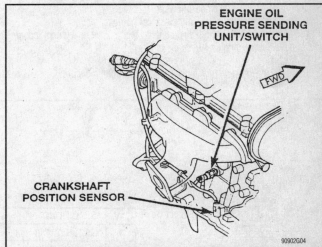

Fig. 58 Location of the oil pressure sending unit switch on all 2.0L and 2.4L engines

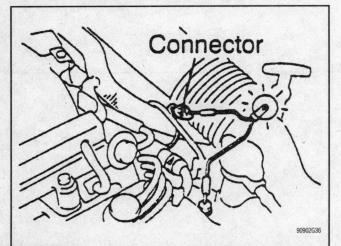

Fig. 57 Connect a 12 volt test light between the harness side connector and ground

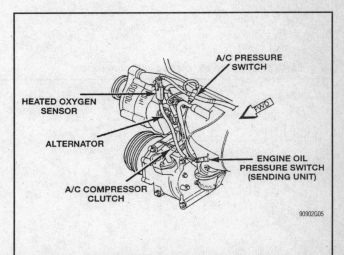

Fig. 59 Location of the oil pressure sending unit switch on all 2.5L engines

TESTING

▶ **See Figures 60 and 61**

The low oil pressure warning lamp will illuminate when the ignition switch is turned to the **ON** position without the engine running. The lamp also illuminates if the engine oil pressure drops below a safe oil pressure level. To test the system, perform the following:

1. Turn the ignition switch to the **ON** position.
2. If the lamp does not light, check for a broken or disconnected wire around the engine and oil pressure sending unit switch.
3. If the wire at the connector checks out OK, pull the connector loose from the switch and, with a jumper wire, ground the connector to the engine.
4. With the ignition switch turned to the **ON** position, check the warning lamp. If the lamp still fails to light, check for a burned out lamp or disconnected socket in the instrument cluster.

REMOVAL & INSTALLATION

1. Locate the oil pressure sending unit on the engine.
2. Disconnect the negative battery cable. On Cirrus, Stratus, Sebring convertible and Breeze models, disconnect the remote negative battery cable connection on the left strut tower.
3. Disconnect the sending unit electrical harness.
4. Using a pressure switch socket, deep-well socket or wrench, loosen and remove the sending unit from the engine.

To install:

5. Install the sending unit in the vehicle and tighten securely.

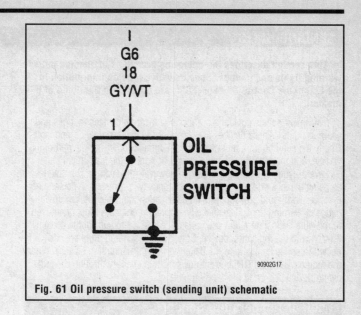

Fig. 61 Oil pressure switch (sending unit) schematic

6. Attach the electrical connector to the sending unit.
7. Connect the negative battery cable.
8. Start the engine, allow it to reach operating temperature and check for leaks.
9. Check for proper sending unit operation.

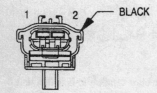

CAV	CIRCUIT	FUNCTION
1	G6 18GY/VT	OIL PRESSURE SWITCH SENSE
2		

Fig. 60 Oil pressure switch (sending unit) connector

Troubleshooting Basic Starting System Problems

Problem	Cause	Solution
Starter motor rotates engine slowly	• Battery charge low or battery defective	• Charge or replace battery
	• Defective circuit between battery and starter motor	• Clean and tighten, or replace cables
	• Low load current	• Bench-test starter motor. Inspect for worn brushes and weak brush springs.
	• High load current	• Bench-test starter motor. Check engine for friction, drag or coolant in cylinders. Check ring gear-to-pinion gear clearance.
Starter motor will not rotate engine	• Battery charge low or battery defective	• Charge or replace battery
	• Faulty solenoid	• Check solenoid ground. Repair or replace as necessary.
	• Damaged drive pinion gear or ring gear	• Replace damaged gear(s)
	• Starter motor engagement weak	• Bench-test starter motor
	• Starter motor rotates slowly with high load current	• Inspect drive yoke pull-down and point gap, check for worn end bushings, check ring gear clearance
	• Engine seized	• Repair engine
Starter motor drive will not engage (solenoid known to be good)	• Defective contact point assembly	• Repair or replace contact point assembly
	• Inadequate contact point assembly ground	• Repair connection at ground screw
	• Defective hold-in coil	• Replace field winding assembly
Starter motor drive will not disengage	• Starter motor loose on flywheel housing	• Tighten mounting bolts
	• Worn drive end busing	• Replace bushing
	• Damaged ring gear teeth	• Replace ring gear or driveplate
	• Drive yoke return spring broken or missing	• Replace spring
Starter motor drive disengages prematurely	• Weak drive assembly thrust spring	• Replace drive mechanism
	• Hold-in coil defective	• Replace field winding assembly
Low load current	• Worn brushes	• Replace brushes
	• Weak brush springs	• Replace springs

TCCS2C01

Troubleshooting Basic Charging System Problems

Problem	Cause	Solution
Noisy alternator	• Loose mountings • Loose drive pulley • Worn bearings • Brush noise • Internal circuits shorted (High pitched whine)	• Tighten mounting bolts • Tighten pulley • Replace alternator • Replace alternator • Replace alternator
Squeal when starting engine or accelerating	• Glazed or loose belt	• Replace or adjust belt
Indicator light remains on or ammeter indicates discharge (engine running)	• Broken belt • Broken or disconnected wires • Internal alternator problems • Defective voltage regulator	• Install belt • Repair or connect wiring • Replace alternator • Replace voltage regulator/alternator
Car light bulbs continually burn out— battery needs water continually	• Alternator/regulator overcharging	• Replace voltage regulator/alternator
Car lights flare on acceleration	• Battery low • Internal alternator/regulator problems	• Charge or replace battery • Replace alternator/regulator
Low voltage output (alternator light flickers continually or ammeter needle wanders)	• Loose or worn belt • Dirty or corroded connections • Internal alternator/regulator problems	• Replace or adjust belt • Clean or replace connections • Replace alternator/regulator

TCCS2C02

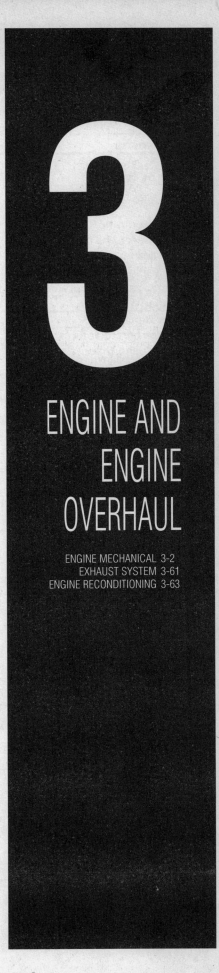

3

ENGINE AND ENGINE OVERHAUL

ENGINE MECHANICAL

2.0L SOHC ENGINE MECHANICAL SPECIFICATIONS

Description	English Specifications	Metric Specifications
Engine	In-line OHV, SOHC	
Number of cylinders	4	
Bore	3.445 in.	87.5mm
Stroke	3.268 in.	83.0mm
Compression ratio	9.8:1	
Displacement	122 cubic inches	2.0 liters
Firing order	1-3-4-2	
Compression pressure	170-225 psi	1172-1551 kPa
Maximum variation between cylinders	25%	
Lubrication	Pressure feed-full flow filtration (crank driven pump)	
Cylinder Block		
Cylinder bore diameter	3.4446-3.4452 in.	87.4924-87.5076mm
Out-of-round (max.)	0.002 in.	0.051mm
Taper (max.)	0.002 in.	0.051mm
Pistons		
Clearance 11/16 in. (17.5mm) from bottom of skirt	0.0004-0.0017 in.	0.012-0.044mm
Weight	11.47-11.82 oz.	325-335 grams
Land clearance (diametrical)	0.029-0.031 in.	0.734-0.797mm
Piston length	2.520 in.	64mm
Piston ring groove depth		
No. 1	0.157-0.165 in.	3.989-4.188mm
No. 2	0.176-0.184 in.	4.462-4.661mm
No. 3	0.151-0.163 in.	3.847-4.131mm
Piston pins		
Clearance in piston	0.0003-0.0008 in.	0.008-0.020mm
In rod (interference)	0.0007-0.0017 in.	0.018-0.043mm
Diameter	0.8267-0.8269 in.	20.998-21.003mm
End-play	None	
Length	2.943-2.963 in.	74.75-75.25mm
Piston rings		
Ring gap		
Top compression ring	0.009-0.020 in.	0.23-0.52mm
2nd compression ring	0.019-0.031 in.	0.49-0.78mm
Oil control (steel rails)	0.009-0.026 in.	0.23-0.66mm
Ring side clearance		
Compression rings	0.0010-0.0026 in.	0.025-0.065mm
Oil ring (pack)	0.0002-0.0070 in.	0.004-0.178mm
Ring width		
Compression rings	0.046-0.047 in.	1.17-1.19mm
Oil ring (pack)	0.1124-0.1184 in.	2.854-3.008mm
Connecting rod		
Bearing clearance	0.001-0.0023 in.	0.026-0.059mm
Piston pin bore diameter	0.8252-0.8260 in.	20.96-20.98mm
Large end bore diameter	2.0075-2.0081 in.	50.991-51.005mm
Side clearance	0.005-0.015 in.	0.13-0.38mm
Total weight (less bearing)	1.20 lbs.	0.543 grams

90903C01

2.0L SOHC ENGINE MECHANICAL SPECIFICATIONS

Description	English Specifications	Metric Specifications
Crankshaft		
Connecting rod journal diameter	1.8894-1.8900 in.	47.9924-48.0076mm
Out-of-round (max.)	0.0001 in.	0.0035mm
Taper (max.)	0.0001 in.	0.0038mm
Main bearing diametrical clearance		
Nos. 1-5	0.0008-0.0024 in.	0.022-0.062mm
End-play	0.0035-0.0094 in.	0.09-0.24mm
Main bearing journals		
Diameter	2.0469-2.0475 in.	51.9924-52.0076mm
Out-of-round (max.)	0.0001 in.	0.0035mm
Taper (max.)	0.0001 in.	0.0038mm
Rocker arm shaft		
Rocker arm shaft diameter	0.786-0.7867 in.	19.996-19.984mm
Rocker arm shaft retainers (width)		
Intake (all)	1.12 in.	28.46mm
Exhaust		
1 and 5	1.14 in.	29.20mm
2, 3 and 4	1.59 in.	40.45mm
Rocker arm/Hydraulic lash adjuster ①		
Rocker arm inside diameter	0.787-0.788 in.	20.00-20.02mm
Rocker arm shaft clearance	0.0006-0.0021 in.	0.016-0.054mm
Body diameter	0.9035-0.9040 in.	22.949-22.962mm
Plunger travel minimum (dry)	0.087 in.	2.2mm
Rocker arm ratio	1.4:1	
Cylinder head camshaft bearing diameter		
No. 1	1.622-1.6228 in.	41.20-41.221mm
No. 2	1.637-1.638 in.	41.6-41.621mm
No. 3	1.653-1.654 in.	42.0-42.021mm
No. 4	1.669-1.670 in.	42.4-42.421mm
No. 5	1.685-1.6858 in.	42.8-42.821mm
Camshaft journal diameter		
No. 1	1.619-1.6199 in.	41.128-41.147mm
No. 2	1.634-1.635 in.	41.528-41.547mm
No. 3	1.650-1.651 in.	41.928-41.947mm
No. 4	1.666-1.668 in.	42.328-42.374mm
No. 5	1.682-1.6829 in.	42.728-42.747mm
Diametrical bearing clearance	0.0027-0.003 in.	0.053-0.093mm
Max. allowable	0.0047 in.	0.12mm
End-play	0.0059 in.	0.05-0.39mm
Lift (Zero lash)		
Intake	0.283 in.	7.2mm
Exhaust	0.277 in.	7.03mm
Valve timing ②		
Exhaust valve		
Closes (ATDC)	5.4°	
Opens (BBDC)	43.7°	
Duration	229.1°	
Intake valve		
Closes (ABDC)	41.1°	
Opens (ATDC)	13.9°	
Duration	207.2°	
Valve overlap	0°	

90903C02

2.0L SOHC ENGINE MECHANICAL SPECIFICATIONS

Description	English Specifications	Metric Specifications
Cylinder head		
Material	Cast aluminum	
Gasket thickness (compressed)	0.045 in.	1.15mm
Valve seat		
Angle	45°	
Run-out (max.)	0.002 in.	0.050mm
Width (finish)		
Intake and exhaust	0.030-0.049 in.	0.75-1.25mm
Valve guide finished		
Diameter (I.D.)	0.235-0.236 in.	5.975-6.000mm
Guide bore diameter (std.)	0.4330-0.4338 in.	11.0-11.02mm
Valves		
Face angle		
Intake and exhaust	45-45 1/2 °	
Head diameter		
Intake	1.303-1.313 in.	32.12-33.37mm
Exhaust	1.124-1.135 in.	28.57-28.83mm
Valve margin		
Intake	0.0452-0.0582 in.	1.15-1.48mm
Exhaust	0.058-0.071 in.	1.475-1.805mm
Valve length (overall)		
Intake	4.515-4.535 in.	114.69-115.19mm
Exhaust	4.603-4.623 in.	109.59-110.09mm
Valve stem tip height		
Intake	1.77-1.81 in.	45.01-46.07mm
Exhaust	1.71-1.75 in.	43.51-44.57mm
Stem diameter		
Intake	0.234-0.234 in.	5.934-5.952mm
Exhaust	0.233-0.233 in.	5.906-5.924mm
Stem-to-guide clearance		
Intake	0.0018-0.0025 in.	0.048-0.066mm
Exhaust	0.0029-0.0037 in.	0.0736-0.094mm
Maximum allowable intake	0.003 in.	0.076mm
Maximum allowable exhaust	0.004 in.	0.101mm
Valve Springs		
Free length (approx.)	1.747 in.	44.4mm
Nominal force (valve closed)	67 ft. lbs. @ 1.57 in.	91 Nm @ 39.8mm
Nominal force (valve open)	176 lbs. @ 1.28 in.	239 Nm @ 32.6mm
Installed height	1.580 in.	40.18mm

① Service as an assembly with the rocker arms

② All readings in crankshaft degrees, at 0.019 inch (0.5mm) of valve lift

ATDC: After Top Dead Center

BBDC: Before Bottom Dead Center

ABDC: After Bottom Dead Center

Std: Standard

Max: Maximum

Min: Minimum

ID: Inside Diameter

Approx: Approximately

90903C03

2.0L DOHC ENGINE MECHANICAL SPECIFICATIONS

Description	English Specifications	Metric Specifications
Engine	In-line OHV, DOHC	
Number of cylinders	4	
Bore	3.445 in.	87.5mm
Stroke	3.267 in.	83.0mm
Piston displacement	121.8 cu. in.	1,996 cm (cubed)
Compression ratio	9.6	
Firing order	1-3-4-2	
Valve timing ①		
Intake		
Opens	1.3° BTDC	
Closes	39.7° ABDC	
Exhaust	36° BBDC	
Opens	1.1° ATDC	
Closes	Pressure feed-full flow	
Lubrication system	Trachoid type	
Oil pump type		
Drive belt (alternator)		
Tension		
When checked	90-110 lbs.	400-490 N
When a new belt is installed	110-160 lbs.	490-712 N
When a used belt is installed	90-110 lbs.	400-490 N
Deflection		
When checked	0.35-0.47 in.	9.0-12.0mm
When a new belt is installed	0.30-0.41 in.	7.5-10.5mm
When a used belt is installed	0.35-0.47 in.	9.0-12.0mm
Drive belt (power steering pump without A/C)		
Tension		
When checked	90-110 lbs.	400-490 N
When a new belt is installed	110-160 lbs.	490-712 N
When a used belt is installed	90-110 lbs.	400-490 N
Deflection		
When checked	0.43-0.55 in.	11.0-14.0mm
When a new belt is installed	0.26-0.37 in.	6.5-9.5mm
When a used belt is installed	0.43-0.55 in.	11.0-14.0mm
Drive belt (power steering pump and A/C compressor)		
Tension		
When checked	92.6-114.6 lbs.	412-510 N
When a new belt is installed	136.7-158.7 lbs.	608-706 N
When a used belt is installed	92.6-114.6 lbs.	412-510 N
Deflection		
When checked	0.39-0.43 in.	10.0-11.0 mm
When a new belt is installed	0.32-0.35 in.	8.0-9.0mm
When a used belt is installed	0.39-0.43 in.	10.0-11.0mm
Curb idle speed	700-800 r/min	
Idle mixture		
CO content %	0.5 or less	
HC content ppm	100 or less	
Compression pressure ②	170-225 psi	1,172-1,551 kPa
Compression pressure difference of all cylinders	max. 25%	
Intake manifold vacuum	min. 18 psi (60 kPa)	

90903C05

2.0L DOHC ENGINE MECHANICAL SPECIFICATIONS

Description	English Specifications	Metric Specifications
Camshaft		
Camshaft cam wear amount	0.001 in. (limit 0.01 in.)	0.0254mm (limit 0.254mm)
Camshaft bearing bore diameter	1.024-1.025 in.	26.020-26.041mm
Camshaft diameter bearing clearance	0.0027-0.0028 in.	0.069-0.071mm
Camshaft end-play	0.006 in.	0.15mm
Camshaft bearing journal diameter	1.0217-1.0224 in.	25.951-25.970mm
Camshaft lift		
Intake	0.324 in.	8.22mm
Exhaust	0.276 in.	7.00mm
Hydraulic lash adjuster body diameter	0.9035-0.9040 in.	22.949-22.962mm
Hydraulic lash adjuster plunger minimum travel (dry)	0.167 in.	4.24mm
Valves		
Valve seat angle	45°—45 1/2°	
Valve seat run-out (max.)	0.002 in.	0.05mm
Valve seat width (finish)	0.035-0.051 in.	0.9-1.3mm
Valve seat guide bore diameter	0.4330-0.4338 in.	11.0-11.2mm
Valve seat diameter		
Intake	1.358 in.	34.50mm
Exhaust	1.161 in.	29.50mm
Valve face angle	44.5—45°	
Valve head diameter		
Intake	1.364-1.375 in.	34.67-34.93mm
Exhaust	1.195-1.205 in.	30.37-30.63mm
Valve margin		
Intake	0.050-0.063 in.	1.285-1.615mm
Exhaust	0.038-0.051 in.	0.985-1.315mm
Valve length (overall)		
Intake	4.389-4.409 in.	111.49-111.99mm
Exhaust	4.314-4.334 in.	109.59-110.09mm
Valve stem tip height		
Intake	1.891 in.	48.04mm
Exhaust	1.889 in.	47.99mm
Valve stem diameter		
Intake	0.233-0.234 in.	5.934-5.952mm
Exhaust	0.233-0.233 in.	5.906-5.924mm
Valve stem-to-guide clearance		
Intake	0.0009-0.010 in.	0.023-0.25mm
Exhaust	0.0020-0.010 in.	0.051-0.25mm
Valve guide inner diameter	0.2352-0.2362 in.	5.975-6.000mm
Valve spring free length	1.811 in.	46mm
Valve spring tension		
Valve closed	55-60 lbs./1.496 in.	246-270 N/38.0mm
Valve open	123-137 lbs./1.153 in.	549-611 N/29.3mm
Valve spring number of coils	7.35	
Valve spring wire diameter	0.148 in.	3.76mm
Valve spring installed spring height	1.496 in.	38.00mm

90903C06

2.0L DOHC ENGINE MECHANICAL SPECIFICATIONS

Description	English Specifications	Metric Specifications
Oil pump		
Oil pump clearance over rotors	limit 0.004 in.	limit 0.102mm
Oil pump cover out-of-flatness	limit 0.003 in.	limit 0.076mm
Oil pump inner rotor thickness	limit 0.301 in.	limit 7.64mm
Oil pump outer rotor clearance	limit 0.015mm	limit 0.39mm
Oil pump outer rotor diameter	limit 3.148 in.	limit 79.95mm
Oil pump outer rotor thickness	limit 0.301 in.	limit 7.64mm
Oil pump tip clearance between rotors	limit 0.008 in.	limit 0.203mm
Oil pressure at curb idle speed	4 psi	25 kPa
Piston		
Standard piston size	3.443-3.4441 in.	87.463-87.481mm
Piston clearance ③	0.0005-0.0017 in.	0.012-0.044mm
Piston land clearance (diametrical)	0.029-0.032 in.	0.740-0.803mm
Piston Length	2.513 in.	63.82mm
Piston ring groove depth		
Top compression ring	0.157-0.163 in.	3.983-4.132mm
Intermediate compression ring	0.175-0.181 in.	4.456-4.605mm
Oil control (steel) ring	0.151-0.160 in.	3.841-4.075mm
Piston pin clearance in piston	0.0003-0.0008 in.	0.008-0.020mm
Piston pin in rod (interference)	0.0007-0.0017 in.	0.018-0.043mm
Piston pin diameter	0.8267-0.8269 in.	20.998-21.003mm
Piston pin length	2.943-2.963 in.	74.75-75.25mm
Piston ring gap		
Top compression ring	0.009-0.031in.	0.23-0.8mm
Intermediate compression ring	0.019-0.039 in.	0.49-1.0mm
Oil control (steel) ring	0.009-0.039 in.	0.23-1.0mm
Piston ring side clearance		
Top and intermediate compression ring	0.0010-0.004 in.	0.025-0.10mm
Oil control (pack) ring	0.0002-0.0070 in.	0.004-0.178mm
Piston ring width		
Top and intermediate compression ring	0.046-0.047 in.	1.17-1.19mm
Oil control (pack) ring	0.1124-0.1184 in.	2.854-3.008mm
Cylinder block		
Cylinder block cylinder bore diameter	3.445 in.	87.5mm
Cylinder block cylinder bore out-of-roundness	limit 0.002 in.	limit 0.051mm
Cylinder block cylinder bore taper	limit 0.002 in.	limit 0.051mm
Connecting rod		
Connecting rod bearing oil clearance	0.0010-0.0030 in.	0.026-0.075mm
Connecting rod piston bore diameter	0.8252-0.8260 in.	20.96-20.98mm
Connecting rod large end bore diameter	2.0075-2.0081 in.	50.991-51.005mm
Connecting rod side clearance	0.005-0.015 in.	0.13-0.38mm
Main bearing journal diameter	2.0469-2.0475 in.	51.9924-52.0076mm
Main bearing journal out-of-roundness	limit 0.0001 in.	limit 0.0035mm
Main bearing journal taper	limit 0.0001 in.	limit 0.0038mm
Crankshaft connecting rod journal diameter	1.8894-1.8900 in.	47.9924-48.0076mm
Crankshaft connecting rod journal out-of-roundness	limit 0.0001 in.	limit 0.0035mm
Crankshaft connecting rod journal taper	limit 0.0001 in.	limit 0.0038mm
Crankshaft main bearing diameter clearance	0.0009-0.0024 in.	0.022-0.062mm
Crankshaft end-play	0.0035-0.015 in.	0.09-0.37mm
Flatness of cylinder head gasket surface	0.004 in.	0.1mm

① Measured at 0.02 inch (0.5mm) lift
② @ 250-400 rpm
③ @ 0.69 in. (17.5mm) from the bottom of the skirt
BTDC: Before Top Dead Center
BBDC: Before Bottom Dead Center
ABDC: After Bottom Dead Center
ATDC: After Top Dead center

Max: Maximum
Min: Minimum
HC: HydroCarbons
CO: Carbon monoxide
PPM: Parts Per Million

2.4L DOHC ENGINE MECHANICAL SPECIFICATIONS

Description	English Specifications	Metric Specifications
Engine		In-line OHV, DOHC
Number of cylinders		4
Bore	3.445 in.	87.5mm
Stroke	3.976 in.	101mm
Piston displacement	121.8 cu. in.	1,996 cm (cubed)
Compression ratio		9.4:1
Displacement	148 cubic inches	2.4 liters
Firing order		1-3-4-2
Compression pressure	170-225 psi	1172-1551 kPa
Maximum variation between cylinders		25%
Lubrication		Pressure feed-full flow filtration (crankshaft driven pump)
Cylinder block		
Cylinder bore diameter	3.4446-3.4452 in.	87.4924-87.5076mm
Out-of-round (max.)	0.002 in.	0.051mm
Taper (max.)	0.002 in.	0.051mm
Pistons		
Piston clearance ①	0.00009-0.0022 in.	0.024-0.057mm
Weight	11.85-12.20 oz.	332-346 grams
Top land clearance (diametrical)	0.024-0.026 in.	0.614-0.664mm
Piston length	2.374 in.	60.30mm
Piston ring groove depth		
No. 1	0.182-0.188 in.	4.640-4.784 in.
No. 2	0.180-0.185mm	4.575-4.719mm
No. 3	0.161-0.166mm	4.097-4.236mm
Piston pin clearance in piston	0.0001-0.0007 in.	0.005-0.018mm
Piston pin in rod (interference)	0.0007-0.0017 in.	0.018-0.043mm
Piston pin diameter	0.8660-0.8662 in.	21.998-22.003mm
Piston pin length	2.864-2.883 in.	72.75-73.25mm
End-play		None
Piston ring gap		
Top compression ring	0.0098-0.020 in.	0.25-0.51mm
2nd compression ring	0.009-0.018 in.	0.023-0.48mm
Oil control (steel) ring	0.0098-0.025 in.	0.25-0.64mm
Piston ring side clearance		
Top and 2nd compression ring	0.0011-0.0031 in.	0.030-0.080mm
Oil control (pack) ring	0.0004-0.0070 in.	0.012-0.178mm
Piston ring width		
Compression rings	0.057-0.059 in.	1.47-1.50mm
Oil control (pack) ring	0.107-0.1133 in.	2.72-2.88mm
Connecting rod		
Connecting rod bearing clearance	0.0009-0.0027 in.	0.025-0.071mm
Connecting rod piston pin bore diameter	0.8252-0.8260 in.	20.96-20.98mm
Connecting rod large end bore diameter	2.0868-2.0863 in.	53.007-52.993mm
Connecting rod side clearance	0.0051-0.0150 in.	0.013-0.0150mm

90903C09

2.4L DOHC ENGINE MECHANICAL SPECIFICATIONS

Description	English Specifications	Metric Specifications
Crankshaft		
Connecting rod journal diameter	1.967-1.9685 in.	49.984-50.000mm
Out-of-round (max.)	0.0001 in.	0.0035mm
Taper (max.)	0.0001 in.	0.0038mm
Main bearing diametrical clearance		
No's. 1-5	0.0007-0.0023 in.	0.018-0.058mm
End-play	0.0035-0.0094 in.	0.09-0.24mm
Main bearing journals		
Diameter	2.361-2.3625 in.	59.992-60.008mm
Out-of-round (max.)	0.0001 in.	0.0035mm
Taper (max.)	0.0001 in.	0.0038mm
Hydraulic lash adjuster body diameter	0.626-0.6264 in.	15.901-15.913mm
Hydraulic lash adjuster plunger minimum travel (dry)	0.118 in.	3.0mm
Camshaft		
Bearing bore diameters		
No's. 1-6	1.024-1.025 in.	26.020-26.041mm
Diametrical bearing clearance	0.0027-0.003 in.	0.069-0.071mm
End-play	0.0019-0.0066 in.	0.050-0.170mm
Bearing journal diameter		
No's. 1-6	1.021-1.022 in.	25.951-25.970mm
Lift (zero lash)		
Intake	0.324 in.	8.25mm
Exhaust	0.256 in.	6.25mm
Valve timing		
Intake valve		
Closes (ABDC)		51°
Opens (BTDC)		1°
Duration		232°
Exhaust valve		
Close (ATDC)		8°
Opens (BBDC)		52°
Duration		240°
Valve overlap		9°
Cylinder head		
Material		Cast aluminum
Gasket thickness (compressed)	0.045 in.	1.15mm
Valve seat		
Angle		45°
Run-out (max.)	0.002 in.	0.050mm
Width (finish)		
Intake	0.035-0.051 in.	0.9-1.3mm
Exhaust	0.035-0.051 in.	0.91.3mm
Guide bore diameter (std.)	0.4330-0.4338 in.	11.0-11.02mm
Finish guide bore ID	0.235-0.236 in.	5.975-6.000mm

90903C10

2.4L DOHC ENGINE MECHANICAL SPECIFICATIONS

Description	English Specifications	Metric Specifications
Valves		
Face angle	44 1/2—45°	
Head diameter		
Intake	1.364-1.375 in.	34.67-34.93mm
Exhaust	1.195-1.205 in.	30.37-30.63mm
Length (overall)		
Intake	4.439-4.461 in.	112.76-113.32mm
Exhaust	4.314-4.334 in.	109.59-110.09mm
Valve margin		
Intake	0.050-0.063 in.	1.285-1.615mm
Exhaust	0.38-0.051 in.	0.985-1.315mm
Valve stem tip height		
Intake	1.891 in.	48.04mm
Exhaust	1.889 in.	47.99mm
Stem diameter		
Intake	0.234-0.234 in.	5.934-5.952mm
Exhaust	0.233-0.233 in.	5.906-5.924mm
Stem-to-guide clearance		
Intake	0.0018-0.0025 in.	0.048-0.066mm
Exhaust	0.0029-0.0037 in.	0.0736-0.094mm
Maximum stem-to-guide clearance		
Intake	0.010 in.	0.025mm
Exhaust	0.010 in.	0.025mm
Valve springs		
Free length (approx.)	1.905 in.	48.4mm
Spring tension		
Valve closed	71.48-80.48 lbs. @ 1.496 in.	318-358 N @ 38.0mm
Valve open	129-144 @ 1.172 in.	577-637 N @ 29.5mm
Number of coils	7.82	
Wire diameter	0.151 in.	3.86mm
Installed spring height	1.496 in.	38mm
Oil pump		
Oil pump clearance over rotors (max.)	0.004 in.	0.10mm
Oil pump cover out-of-flatness (max.)	0.001 in.	0.025mm
Oil pump inner rotor's thickness (min.)	0.370 in.	9.40mm
Oil pump outer rotor clearance (max.)	0.015 in.	0.39mm
Oil pump outer rotor diameter (min.)	3.148 in.	79.95mm
Oil pump outer rotor thickness (min.)	0.370 in.	9.40mm
Oil pump tip clearance between rotors (max.)	0.008 in.	0.20mm
Oil pressure		
At curb idle speed ②	4 psi	25 kPa
At 3000 rpm	25-80 psi	170-550 kPa

① Measured at 9/16 inch (14mm) from bottom of skirt

② If pressure reads zero at curb idle, do not run engine at 3000 rpm

BTDC: Before Top Dead Center

BBDC: Before Bottom Dead Center

ABDC: After Bottom Dead Center

ATDC: After Top Dead Center

Max: Maximum

Min: Minimum

2.5L SOHC ENGINE MECHANICAL SPECIFICATIONS

Description	English Specifications	Metric Specifications
Engine	V-block OHV, SOHC	
Number of cylinders	6	
Bore	3.29 in.	83.5mm
Stroke	2.992 in.	76.0mm
Compression ratio	9.4:1	
Displacement	152 cubic inches	2.5 liters
Firing order	1-2-3-4-5-6	
Lubrication	Pressure feed-full flow filtration	
Valve timing		
Intake valve		
Opens (BTDC)	19°	
Closes (ABDC)	45°	
Exhaust valve		
Opens (BBDC)	49°	
Closes (ATDC)	15°	
Compression pressure	178 psi @ 250 rpm	
Maximum variation between cylinders	14 psi	97 kPa
Service limit	25%	
Valve clearance—hot engine	Hydraulic lash adjuster	
Cylinder head		
Flatness of gasket surface	0.0012 in.	0.03mm
Service limit	0.008 in.	0.2mm
Grinding limit of gasket surface ①	0.08 in.	0.2mm
Manifold flatness		
Intake	0.004 in.	0.10mm
Service limit	0.008 in.	0.2mm
Exhaust	0.006 in.	0.15mm
Service limit	0.012 in.	0.3mm
Valves		
Thickness of valve head (margin)		
Intake	0.039 in.	1.0mm
Service limit	0.019 in.	0.5mm
Exhaust	0.047 in.	1.2mm
Service limit	0.028 in.	0.7mm
Valve stem-to-guide clearance		
Intake	0.0008-0.002 in.	0.02-0.05mm
Service limit	0.004 in.	0.10mm
Exhaust	0.0016-0.0028 in.	0.04-0.07mm
Service limit	0.006 in.	0.15mm
Valve face angle	45-45 1/2°	
Valve stem diameter		
Intake	0.236 in.	6.0mm
Exhaust	0.236 in.	6.0mm
Valve guide		
Height	0.551 in.	14.0mm
O.D.	0.443 in.	11.0mm
I.D.	0.236 in.	6.0mm
Valve seat		
Seat surface angle	44-44 1/2°	
Contact width	0.035-0.051 in.	0.9-1.3mm
Sinkage (service limit)	0.078 in.	0.2mm
Valve spring		
Free height	2.01 in.	51.0mm
Service limit	1.97 in.	50mm
Loaded height	1.74 in. @ 60 lbs.	44.2 N @ 267 N

90903C13

2.5L SOHC ENGINE MECHANICAL SPECIFICATIONS

Description	English Specifications	Metric Specifications
Valve spring (cont.)		
Perpendicularity		
Intake	2° maximum	
Service limit	4° maximum	
Exhaust	2° maximum	
Service limit	4° maximum	
Piston		
O.D.	3.29 in.	83.5mm
Piston-to-cylinder clearance	0.0008-0.0016 in.	0.02-0.04mm
Piston ring end-gap		
No. 1	0.010-0.016 in.	0.25-0.40mm
Service limit	0.031 in.	0.8mm
No. 2	0.016-0.022 in.	0.40-0.55mm
Service limit	0.031 in.	0.8mm
Oil	0.006-0.019 in.	0.15-0.50mm
Service limit	0.039 in.	1.0mm
Piston ring side clearance		
No. 1	0.0012-0.0028 in.	0.030-0.070mm
Service limit	0.004 in.	0.1mm
No. 2	0.0007-0.0024 in.	0.002-0.06mm
Service limit	0.004 in.	0.1mm
Connecting rod		
Length		
Center-to-center	5.547-5.551 in.	140.9-141.0mm
Parallelism		
Twist	0.0019 in.	0.05mm
Torsion	0.0039 in.	0.1mm
Big end thrust clearance	0.004-0.010 in.	0.10-0.25mm
Service limit	0.016 in.	0.4mm
Crankshaft		
End-play	0.002-0.010 in.	0.05-0.25mm
Service limit	0.016 in.	0.4mm
Main journal diameter	2.362 in.	60mm
Pin diameter	1.969 in.	50mm
Bearing surface (maximum out-of-round)	0.001 in.	0.03mm
Bearing surface taper (max.)	0.0002 in.	0.005mm
Bearing oil clearance	0.0008-0.0016 in.	0.02-0.04mm
Cylinder block		
I.D. (bore)	3.29 in.	83.50-83.53mm
Flatness of top surface	0.002 in.	0.05mm
Service limit	0.004 in.	0.1mm
Grinding limit of top surface ①	0.008 in.	0.2mm
Oil pump		
Relief valve opening pressure	71.45-85.75 psi	5.0-6.0 kg/cm2
Outer rotor-to-case clearance	0.004-0.007 in.	0.10-0.18mm
Service limit	0.0138 in.	0.35mm
Clearance over rotors (end clearance)	0.0015-0.0039 in.	0.04-0.10mm
Clearance between rotors		
Inner-to-outer rotor	0.003-0.007 in.	0.06-0.18mm
Minimum pressure		
At curb idle speed ②	6 psi	41 kPa
At 3000 rpm	35-75 psi	241-517 kPa

① Includes/combined with cylinder head and block top surface grinding
② If pressure reads zero at curb idle, do not run engine at 3000 rpm
BTDC: Before Top Dead Center
BBDC: Before Bottom Dead Center
O.D: Outside Diameter

ABDC: After Bottom Dead Center
ATDC: After Top Dead Center
Max: Maximum
Min: Minimum
I.D: Inside Diameter

90903C14

Engine

REMOVAL & INSTALLATION

In the process of removing the engine, you will come across a number of steps which call for the removal of a separate component or system, such as "disconnect the exhaust system" or "remove the radiator." In most instances, a detailed removal procedure can be found elsewhere in this manual.

It is virtually impossible to list each individual wire and hose which must be disconnected, simply because so many different model and engine combinations have been manufactured. Careful observation and common sense are the best possible approaches to any repair procedure.

Removal and installation of the engine can be made easier if you follow these basic points:

• If you have to drain any of the fluids, use a suitable container.
• Always tag any wires or hoses and, if possible, the components they came from before disconnecting them.
• Because there are so many bolts and fasteners involved, store and label the retainers from components separately in muffin pans, jars or coffee cans. This will prevent confusion during installation.
• After unbolting the transmission or transaxle, always make sure it is properly supported.
• If it is necessary to disconnect the air conditioning system, have this service performed by a qualified technician using a recovery/recycling station. If the system does not have to be disconnected, unbolt the compressor and set it aside.
• When unbolting the engine mounts, always make sure the engine is properly supported. When removing the engine, make sure that any lifting devices are properly attached to the engine. It is recommended that if your engine is supplied with lifting hooks, your lifting apparatus be attached to them.
• Lift the engine from its compartment slowly, checking that no hoses, wires or other components are still connected.
• After the engine is clear of the compartment, place it on an engine stand or workbench.
• After the engine has been removed, you can perform a partial or full teardown of the engine using the procedures outlined in this manual.

Cirrus, Stratus, Sebring Convertible and Breeze

◢ See Figures 1 and 2

➡**The following procedure requires the discharging/evacuation of the vehicle's air conditioning system. In many areas, it is illegal for anyone other than a MVAC-trained, EPA-certified, automotive technician to service the A/C system or its components. If the vehicle must be driven to and from such a facility, be sure to have this service performed *before* you begin the removal procedure.**

✳ CAUTION

Fuel injection systems remain under pressure, even after the engine has been turned OFF. The fuel system pressure MUST be relieved before disconnecting any fuel lines. Failure to do so may result in fire and/or personal injury.

1. Relieve the fuel system pressure. Disconnect the fuel line quick-connect fitting from the fuel rail by squeezing the retainer tabs together and pulling the fuel tube/quick-connect fitting assembly off the fuel tube nipple.
2. Remove the battery from the vehicle.
3. Remove the battery tray from the vehicle. Remove the battery blanket heater, if equipped.
4. Remove the complete air cleaner and inlet duct assembly.
5. Unbolt the Powertrain Control Module (PCM) and move it aside.
6. Drain and properly contain the coolant from the engine.
7. Remove the upper and lower radiator hoses, radiator and cooling fan.
8. Disconnect and plug the automatic transaxle cooler lines, if equipped.
9. Disconnect the clutch cable and transaxle shift linkage, if equipped.
10. Disconnect the throttle body linkage and the engine wiring harness.
11. Disconnect the heater hoses.
12. If not already done, have a qualified, trained technician recover and properly contain the refrigerant of the A/C system with an R-134a recovery unit.
13. Raise and safely support the vehicle. Remove the front wheels.
14. Drain the engine oil.
15. Remove the right side inner splash shield.
16. Remove the accessory drive belts.
17. Remove the right and left halfshaft assemblies.
18. Disconnect the exhaust pipe from the exhaust manifold.
19. Remove the front and rear engine mount brackets from the body.
20. Lower the vehicle.
21. Remove the power steering pump and reservoir.
22. Remove the A/C compressor as follows:
    a. Disconnect the compressor clutch wire lead.
    b. Disconnect and plug the refrigerant lines from the compressor.
    c. Remove the compressor mounting bolts.
    d. Remove the compressor unit from the vehicle. Be sure to plug all openings in the A/C system to prevent moisture contamination.
23. Disconnect the ground straps from the engine.
24. Raise the vehicle, then position an engine dolly under the vehicle to support the engine.

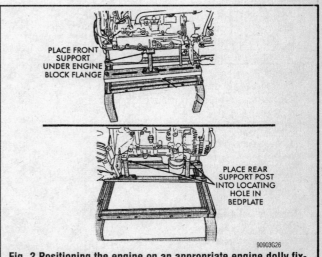

Fig. 1 Removal of the right inner splash shield

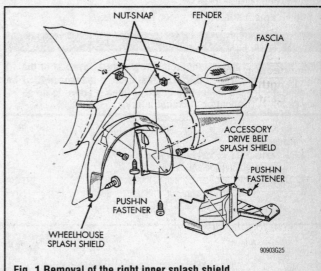

Fig. 2 Positioning the engine on an appropriate engine dolly fixture

25. Remove the transaxle and engine mount through-bolts.

26. Raise the vehicle slowly, allowing the engine and transaxle assembly to remain on the dolly.

To install:

27. Installation is the reverse of the removal procedure. Please note the following important steps.

28. Position the engine and the transaxle under the vehicle, then lower the vehicle onto the engine assembly.

29. Tighten the A/C compressor mounting bolts to 30 ft. lbs. (41 Nm).

30. Adjust the accessory drive belts.

31. Refill the cooling system with a 50/50 mixture of clean water and ethylene glycol or other suitable antifreeze.

32. Install fresh engine oil and a new oil filter.

33. Tighten the battery hold-down bracket bolt to 124 inch lbs. (14 Nm).

34. Tighten the battery cables to 150 inch lbs. (17 Nm).

35. Have a qualified, trained technician recharge the vehicle's air conditioning system.

36. Check to be sure all ducts, hoses, fuel lines and wiring harnesses have been properly reconnected.

37. Start and run the engine until it reaches operating temperature.

38. Check for leaks and proper operation.

Sebring Coupe and Avenger

▶ See Figures 3 and 4

※※ CAUTION

Fuel injection systems remain under pressure, even after the engine has been turned OFF. The fuel system pressure MUST be relieved before disconnecting any fuel lines. Failure to do so may result in fire and/or personal injury.

The transaxle must be removed before removing the engine. They will not come out as a unit.

1. Disconnect the negative battery cable.
2. Drain the engine coolant.
3. Drain the engine oil and the transmission oil.
4. Safely relieve the pressure within the fuel injection system.

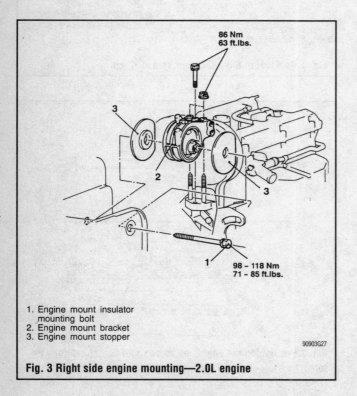

1. Engine mount insulator
   mounting bolt
2. Engine mount bracket
3. Engine mount stopper

90903G27

Fig. 3 Right side engine mounting—2.0L engine

1. Engine mount insulator mounting bolt
2. Engine mount bracket
3. Engine mount stopper
4. Dynamic damper

90903G28

Fig. 4 Right side engine mounting—2.5L engine

5. Matchmark the hood to the hinges and remove the hood. For further details, refer to Section 10.

6. Remove the engine undercover.

7. Remove the transaxle assembly, using the recommended procedure in Section 7.

8. Remove the radiator, after disconnecting the hoses at the engine.

9. Disconnect the accelerator cable and remove the bracket.

10. Disconnect the heater hoses.

11. Disconnect the brake booster vacuum hose at the engine.

12. Label and disconnect the vacuum hoses running to the bulkhead.

13. Disconnect the high pressure fuel line and discard the O-ring. It is not reusable.

14. Remove the fuel return hose.

15. Label and disengage the electrical connectors to the engine components. All wires and connectors should be labeled at the time of engine removal. This should save much time at assembly.

16. Remove the accessory drive belts. Remove the bolts holding the power steering pump to its bracket and hang the pump out of the way. Do not disconnect the hoses and do not allow the pump to hang by the hoses. Remove the power steering pump bracket.

17. Remove the air conditioning compressor from its mount and hang it from a stiff wire out of the way. Note that the hoses should be left attached. Do not loosen them or discharge the system.

18. Remove the bolts at the exhaust system joint just below the manifold. Separate the exhaust pipes. Discard the gasket and the two nuts.

19. Raise and safely support the vehicle. Install the engine hoist equipment and make certain the attaching points on the engine are secure. Draw tension on the hoist just enough to support the engine's weight, but no more. Do not disturb the placement of the vehicle on the stands.

20. Remove the through-bolt from the rear (firewall side) roll stopper. Remove the through-bolt from the front engine roll stopper.

21. Remove the nuts and bolts holding the upper (right side) engine mount to the engine. Remove the through-bolt and remove the mount assembly. Also remove the support bracket below the mount.

22. Double check for any remaining cables, wires or hoses running to the engine. Elevate the hoist and remove the engine from the vehicle. Immediately place the engine on an engine stand or support it with wooden blocks. Do not allow it to rest on the oil pan or lie on its side. Do not leave the engine hanging from the hoist.

To install:

After repairs, make certain the engine is fully reassembled before installation. All components removed with the engine out of the vehicle (or equivalent replacement parts) should be in place before reinstallation.

23. Installation is the reverse of the removal procedure. Please note the following important steps.

24. Connect the exhaust system to the manifold, using a new gasket. Tighten the bolts to 33 ft. lbs. (44 Nm).

25. Tighten the engine mount nuts and bolts. Correct torque values are:
- Nut and bolt holding the right side mount to engine: 63 ft. lbs. (86 Nm)
- Right side mount through-bolt: 71–85 ft. lbs. (98–118 Nm)
- Rear roll stopper through-bolt: 32 ft. lbs. (44 Nm)
- Front roll stopper through-bolt: 41 ft. lbs. (56 Nm)

➡Allow the mounts to support the engine weight before final tightening the front roll stopper through-bolt.

26. On the 2.0L engine, tighten the power steering pump bracket bolts to 16 ft. lbs. (22 Nm). On the 2.5L engine, tighten the power steering pump bracket bolts to 29 ft. lbs. (39 Nm).

27. Connect the wiring and harness connectors to the engine. Make certain each terminal is clean and the connector is firmly seated to its mate. Do not route wires near hot surfaces or moving parts.

28. Using a new O-ring lightly lubricated with clean engine oil, connect the high pressure fuel line and tighten the bolts to 22 inch lbs. (2.5 Nm).

29. Check the engine oil drain plug, and make sure that it is securely installed. Add the proper amount of clean engine oil.

30. Check the transaxle drain plug, tightening it if necessary, and install the proper amount of transmission oil.

31. Check the radiator and engine draincocks, making sure they are closed. Refill the cooling system with a 50/50 mixture of clean water and ethylene glycol or other suitable antifreeze.

32. Double check all installation items, paying particular attention to loose hoses or hanging wires, loosened nuts, poor routing of hoses and wires (too tight or rubbing) and tools left in the engine area.

33. Connect the negative battery cable. Start the engine and check for leaks.

34. Attend to all leaks immediately, remembering that fluids and metal surfaces may be hot. Adjust the drive belts to the correct tension. Adjust all cables (transmission, throttle, shift selector) and check the fluid levels. Check the operation of all gauges and dashboard lights.

35. In a safe location at low speed, road test the vehicle for correct operation of steering, brakes, transaxle, clutch and speedometer.

Rocker Arm (Valve) Cover

REMOVAL & INSTALLATION

2.0L SOHC Engine

▶ See Figure 5

1. Disconnect the negative battery cable.
2. Remove the air cleaner inlet duct.
3. Label and disconnect the spark plug wires. Remove the ignition coil pack, as described in Section 2.
4. Remove the valve cover retaining bolts.
5. Remove the valve cover from the engine.

To install:

➡Before installing the valve cover, clean the valve cover-to-cylinder head mating surfaces. Inspect the spark plug well seals for swelling or cracking and replace, if necessary.

6. Install the new valve cover gasket.
7. Place the valve cover into position on top of the cylinder head. Tighten the valve cover retaining bolts to 105 inch lbs. (12 Nm).
8. Install the coil pack assembly, as described in Section 2.

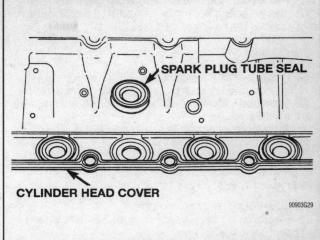

Fig. 5 Inspect the condition of the spark plug seals and replace if worn or cracked

9. Connect the spark plug wires. Follow the labels to assure correct plug wire connections.
10. Install the air cleaner inlet duct.
11. Connect the negative battery cable.

2.0L DOHC and 2.4L DOHC Engines

▶ See Figure 6

1. Disconnect the negative battery cable.
2. Label and disconnect the spark plug wires. Remove the ignition coil pack, as described in Section 2.
3. Remove the ground strap from the valve cover.
4. Disconnect the PCV and breather hoses.
5. Remove the valve cover retaining bolts.
6. Remove the valve cover from the engine.

To install:

➡Before installing the valve cover, clean the valve cover-to-cylinder head mating surfaces. Inspect the spark plug well seals for swelling or cracking, and replace if necessary.

7. Install the new valve cover gasket.
8. Apply MOPAR® Silicone Rubber Adhesive Sealant or equivalent at the camshaft cap corners and at the top edge of the ½ round seal.

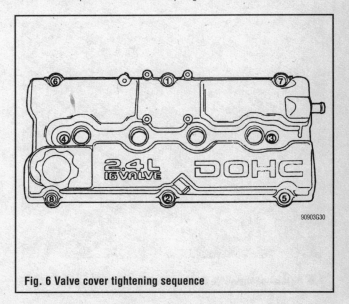

Fig. 6 Valve cover tightening sequence

9. Place the valve cover into position on top of the cylinder head. Tighten the valve cover retaining bolts in the correct sequence as illustrated. Use the 3-step tightening sequence as follows:

    a. 40 inch lbs. (4.5 Nm)
    b. 80 inch lbs. (9 Nm)
    c. 105 inch lbs. (12 Nm)

10. Connect the PCV and breather hoses.
11. Install the coil pack assembly, as described in Section 2.
12. Connect the spark plug wires. Follow the labels to assure correct plug wire connections.
13. Attach the ground strap to the valve cover.
14. Connect the negative battery cable.

2.5L Engine

▶ See Figures 7, 8, 9, 10 and 11

1. Disconnect the negative battery cable.
2. Remove the air intake plenum. Refer to the intake manifold procedure later in this section.
3. Cover the openings of the lower intake manifold to prevent any debris from entering the engine.
4. Label and disconnect the spark plug wires.

Fig. 9 Remove the valve cover from the engine

Fig. 7 After disconnecting the spark plug wires, unfasten the hose clamp and detach the breather hose

Fig. 10 Examine the spark plug tube gaskets and replace if worn or cracked

Fig. 8 Remove the valve cover mounting fasteners

Fig. 11 Replace the valve cover gasket

5. Disconnect the breather hoses. Disconnect the PCV hose, if necessary.

6. Remove the valve cover retaining bolts.

7. Remove the valve cover from the engine.

To install:

➡ **Before installing the valve cover, clean the valve cover-to-cylinder head mating surfaces.**

8. Install the new valve cover gasket.

9. Place the valve cover into position on top of the cylinder head. Tighten the valve cover retaining bolts to 88 inch lbs. (10 Nm).

10. Connect the breather hoses. Connect the PCV hose, if necessary.

11. Connect the spark plug wires. Follow the labels to assure correct plug wire connections.

12. Install the air intake plenum. Refer to the intake manifold procedure.

13. Connect the negative battery cable.

Rocker Arms/Shafts

REMOVAL & INSTALLATION

2.0L SOHC Engine

▶ **See Figure 12**

This engine uses a Single Overhead Camshaft (SOHC) running in an aluminum cylinder head. Rocker arm shafts mount directly to the cylinder head. Care must be taken to make sure that all valve timing marks align after cylinder head and valve train service. The hydraulic lash adjusters are located in the valve actuating end of the rocker arm and are serviced as an assembly.

✳✳ CAUTION

Fuel injection systems remain under pressure, even after the engine has been turned OFF. The fuel system pressure MUST be relieved before disconnecting any fuel lines. Failure to do so may result in fire and/or personal injury.

1. Disconnect the negative battery cable from the left strut tower. The ground cable is equipped with an insulator grommet, which should be placed on the stud to prevent the negative battery cable from accidentally grounding.

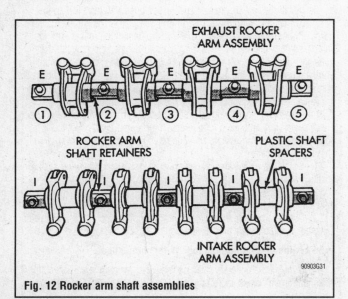

Fig. 12 Rocker arm shaft assemblies

2. Properly relieve the fuel system pressure, as described in Section 5.

3. Remove the rocker arm (valve) cover, as described earlier in this section.

4. Mark the rocker arm shaft assemblies to identify them for later installation.

5. Remove the rocker arm shaft bolts and remove the rocker arm assemblies from the cylinder head.

6. Mark the rocker arm spacers and retainers to identify them for correct installation. Disassemble the rocker arm/shaft assemblies by removing the attaching bolts from the rocker arm shaft.

7. Slide the rocker arm/hydraulic lash adjuster assembly and rocker arm spacers off the rocker arm shaft. Be sure the rocker arms and spacers are re-assembled in the same positions from which they are removed.

To install:

➡ **Inspect the rocker arms and shaft for scoring and/or wear on the rollers or damage to the rocker arm. If scoring, wear or damage is present, replace the rocker arm assemblies. The rocker arm shaft is hollow and, therefore, used as an oil lubrication duct. Inspect the oil holes for clogging, using a small wire, and clean if necessary. Inspect the location where the rocker arms mount to the shaft and replace if damaged or worn.**

8. If the camshaft lobes show signs of wear, check the corresponding rocker arm roller for wear or damage. Replace the rocker arms/hydraulic lash adjuster if worn or damaged. If the camshaft lobes show signs of pitting on the nose, flank or base circle, replace the camshaft.

9. Thoroughly lubricate all rocker arm components and spacers, and reinstall on the rocker arm shaft in their original locations.

10. If the vehicle exhibited a tappet-like noise, the valve lash adjusters built into the rocker arms should be cleaned and checked. Lash adjusters removed from a rocker arm should be returned to their original locations. Replacement of worn or defective lash adjusters would require the replacement of the rocker arm/hydraulic lash adjusters as an assembly. To install a lash adjuster, use the following procedure.

a. Lubricate the lash adjuster thoroughly with clean engine oil.

b. Reinstall the adjuster into the rocker arm, making sure the adjuster is at least partially filled with oil.

c. Place the rocker arm in clean engine oil and pump the plunger until the lash adjuster travel is taken up. If travel is not reduced, replace the adjuster with the rocker arm as an assembly.

d. Reinstall the rocker arm back on the rocker arm shaft.

11. Before installing the rocker arm and shaft assemblies, set the crankshaft to 3 notches before TDC on the crankshaft sprocket.

➡ **When installing the intake rocker arm/shaft assembly, be sure the plastic rocker arm spacers do not interfere with the spark plug tubes. If there is interference, rotate the plastic spacers until they are at the proper angle. Do not rotate the spacers by forcing down on the shaft assembly, or damage to the spark plug tubes will occur.**

12. Reinstall the rocker arm and shaft assemblies with the small notches in the rocker shafts pointing up and toward the timing belt side of the engine. Install the retainers in their original positions on the exhaust and intake shafts. Tighten the bolts in proper sequence to 200–250 inch lbs. (23–28 Nm).

13. Install a new gasket and valve cover, as described in the rocker arm cover procedure, earlier in this section.

14. Check to be sure that all electrical, vacuum and fluid connections are securely fastened.

➡ **An engine oil and filter change is recommended.**

15. Reconnect the negative battery cable.

16. Start the engine and check for leaks. Test drive vehicle to check for proper operation.

2.5L Engine

▶ See Figures 13, 14 and 15

Fuel injection systems remain under pressure, even after the engine has been turned OFF. The fuel system pressure MUST be relieved before disconnecting any fuel lines. Failure to do so may result in fire and/or personal injury.

1. Disconnect the negative battery cable. On Cirrus, Stratus, Breeze or Sebring convertible models, disconnect the negative battery cable from the left strut tower. The ground cable is equipped with an insulator grommet which should be placed on the stud to prevent the negative battery cable from accidentally grounding.

2. Relieve the fuel system pressure using the recommended procedure. Refer to Section 5.

3. If removing the right (firewall) side rocker arm/shaft assembly, remove the upper intake manifold (air intake plenum), which is a 2-piece

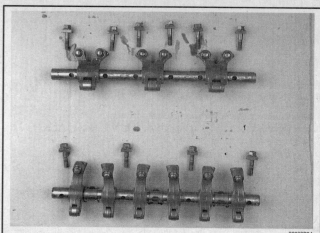

Fig. 15 Lay the rocker arm shaft assemblies upside down on a clean flat surface, keeping all the mounting bolts and components in correct order, and the lash adjusters in the rocker arms

unit of aluminum alloy. Refer to the intake manifold removal procedure, later in this section.

4. Remove the rocker arm (valve) cover(s), as described earlier in this section.

5. Identify the rocker arm shaft assemblies before removal.

6. Install the auto lash adjuster retainers, Special Tool MD 998443 or equivalent, to keep the auto lash adjusters from falling out of the rocker arms when the rocker arm assembly is removed.

7. Loosen the attaching fasteners and remove the rocker arm shaft assemblies from the cylinder head.

➡The hydraulic automatic lash adjusters are precision units installed in the machined openings in the rocker arm units. Do not disassemble the auto lash adjusters from the rocker arms.

To install:

8. The rocker arm shafts are hollow and used as a lubrication oil duct. Make sure all valve train parts are clean. Check the rocker arm mounting portion of the shafts for wear or damage. Replace if necessary. Check all oil holes for clogging with a small wire, and clean as required. If any rocker arms were removed, lubricate and install them on the shafts in their original positions.

9. Install the rocker arm and shaft assemblies with the FLAT in the rocker arm shafts facing toward the timing belt side of the engine for the right cylinder head. For the left cylinder head, install the rocker arm and shaft assembly with the FLAT in the rocker arm shaft facing toward the transaxle side of the engine. Install the retainers and spring clips in their original positions on the exhaust and intake shafts. Tighten the retainer bolts to 276 inch lbs. (31 Nm) working from the center, outward. Remove the valve lash retainer tools that were installed at disassembly.

10. Inspect the spark plug tube seals located on the ends of each tube. These seals slide onto each tube to seal the cylinder head cover to the spark plug tube. If these seals show signs of hardness and/or cracks, they should be replaced.

11. Install the rocker arm (valve) cover(s), as described earlier in this section.

12. Install the upper intake manifold (plenum), if necessary. Refer to intake manifold procedure.

13. Check to be sure that all remaining electrical connectors have been fastened. Tighten the air tube connections.

➡An engine oil and filter change is recommended.

14. Connect the negative battery cable. Start the engine and check for leaks, abnormal noises and vibrations.

Fig. 13 Remove the rocker arm/shaft assembly mounting bolts

Fig. 14 If lash adjuster retainers are not available, carefully turn the rocker arm/shaft assemblies upside down, so the lash adjusters will not fall out

Thermostat

REMOVAL & INSTALLATION

2.0L DOHC Engine

▶ See Figure 16

1. Disconnect the negative battery cable.
2. Drain the cooling system.
3. Disconnect the upper radiator hose from the water outlet.
4. Remove the thermostat housing.
5. Remove the thermostat, taking note of its original position in the housing.

To install:

6. Thoroughly clean the thermostat housing and cylinder head mating surfaces.
7. Install the thermostat so its flange seats tightly in the machined recess in the thermostat housing. Refer to its position prior to removal.
8. Clean the bolt threads well. Bolts that thread into openings exposed to the coolant may have a build-up of rust and corrosion. Clean threads are necessary to effectively tighten bolts. Install the water outlet to the thermostat housing with a new gasket. Tighten the housing mounting bolts to 16 ft. lbs. (22 Nm). Do not overtighten, or the thermostat housing and/or water outlet may crack.
9. Connect the lower hose and fill the system with coolant.
10. Connect the negative battery cable. With the radiator cap off, start the engine and allow it to run until the thermostat opens. Add coolant as necessary to fill the radiator completely. Watch the coolant temperature gauge (if equipped) for signs of overheating.
11. Once the vehicle has cooled, recheck the coolant level in the radiator and the coolant overflow tank.

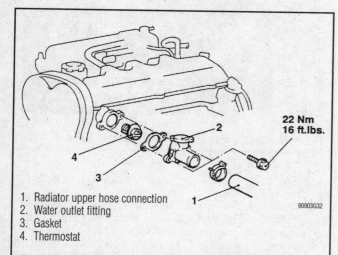

1. Radiator upper hose connection
2. Water outlet fitting
3. Gasket
4. Thermostat

90903G32

Fig. 16 Exploded view of the thermostat installation—2.0L DOHC engine

2.0L SOHC and 2.4L DOHC Engines

▶ See Figures 17 and 18

1. Disconnect the negative battery cable from the left strut tower. The ground cable is equipped with an insulator grommet, which should be placed on the stud to prevent the negative battery cable from accidentally grounding.
2. Place a large drain pan under the radiator drain plug. Allow the cooling system to sufficiently cool down before opening the drain plug to avoid personal injury. Drain the coolant level below that of the thermostat.

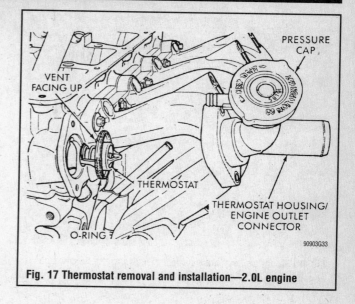

Fig. 17 Thermostat removal and installation—2.0L engine

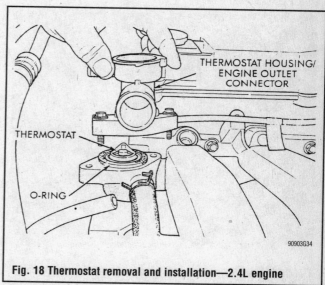

Fig. 18 Thermostat removal and installation—2.4L engine

3. Disconnect the coolant recovery hose and radiator hose.
4. Remove the thermostat housing bolts.
5. Remove the thermostat assembly from the vehicle.

To install:

6. Thoroughly clean all sealing surfaces.
7. Install the replacement thermostat and align the air bleed opening with the notch on the cylinder head. Install the thermostat housing using a new gasket.
8. Reinstall the thermostat housing bolts and tighten to 110 inch lbs. (12.5 Nm).
9. Reconnect the coolant recovery hose and radiator hose. Tighten the radiator hose clamp.
10. Reconnect the negative battery cable to the remote terminal at the shock tower.
11. Refill and bleed the engine cooling system.
12. Pressure test for leaks.

2.5L Engine

▶ See Figures 19 thru 25

1. Disconnect the negative battery cable from the left strut tower. The ground cable is equipped with an insulator grommet which should be

Fig. 19 Move the hose clamp down away from the thermostat housing

Fig. 22 Pull out the thermostat housing from the engine

Fig. 20 Pull the lower coolant hose off of the thermostat housing

Fig. 23 Remove the thermostat from the engine

Fig. 21 Remove the 3 thermostat housing fasteners

placed on the stud to prevent the negative battery cable from accidentally grounding.

2. Place a large drain pan under the radiator drain plug. Allow the cooling system to sufficiently cool down before opening the drain plug to avoid personal injury. Drain the coolant to below the thermostat level.

3. Remove the inlet radiator hose hose and coolant elbow from the thermostat housing.

4. Remove the thermostat housing bolts.

5. Remove the thermostat assembly from the vehicle and discard.

To install:

6. Thoroughly clean all sealing surfaces.

7. Install the thermostat into the recess of the thermostat housing. Be sure to install the new thermostat with the bleed vent hole positioned upward.

8. Reinstall the thermostat housing using a new gasket. Reinstall the thermostat housing bolts and tighten to 133 inch lbs. (13 Nm).

9. Reconnect the inlet radiator hose to the thermostat housing and tighten the radiator hose clamp.

10. Reconnect the negative battery cable.

11. Refill and bleed the engine cooling system.

12. Pressure test the cooling system for leaks.

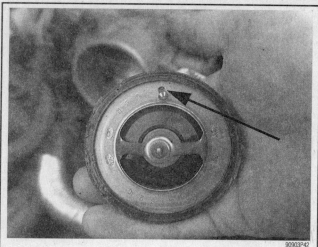

Fig. 24 When installing a new thermostat, make sure that the small bleed hole is positioned at the top

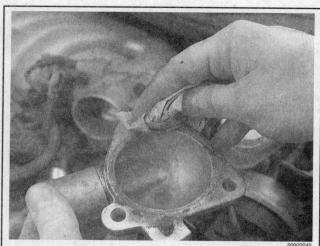

Fig. 25 Before installing a new thermostat, clean the flange surface of the housing

Intake Manifold

REMOVAL & INSTALLATION

2.0L SOHC and 2.4L DOHC Engines

▶ See Figures 26, 27 and 28

The intake manifold for the 2.0L SOHC engine is a long branch design made of a molded plastic composition. It is attached to the cylinder head with 10 fasteners. Please note that all seals are to be replaced with new seals and all fasteners are to be replaced with new fasteners. Obtain the necessary parts before beginning work.

The intake manifold for the 2.4L DOHC engine is a long branch design made of cast aluminum. It is attached to the cylinder head with 8 fasteners.

1. Disconnect the negative battery cable from the left strut tower. The ground cable is equipped with an insulator grommet, which should be placed on the stud to prevent the negative battery cable from accidentally grounding.

✳✳ CAUTION

Fuel injection systems remain under pressure after the engine has been turned OFF. The fuel system pressure MUST be relieved before disconnecting any fuel lines. Failure to do so may result in fire and/or personal injury.

2. Properly relieve the fuel system pressure using the procedure outlined in Section 5.

3. Remove the air inlet resonator as follows:

a. On the 2.4L DOHC engine only, remove the 2 mounting bolts that secure the air inlet resonator to the intake manifold.

b. Loosen the screw securing the air inlet resonator to the throttle body.

c. Loosen the clamp securing the air inlet resonator to the air inlet tube. Remove the resonator.

4. Disconnect the fuel supply line quick-connect fitting from the fuel rail by squeezing the retainer tabs together and pulling the fuel tube/quick-connect fitting from the fuel tube nipple. The retainer will remain on the fuel tube. Wrap shop towels around the fuel line openings to catch any spilling fuel.

5. Remove the fuel rail attaching screws and remove the fuel rail. Use care when handling the fuel injectors. Do not set them on their tips. Cover the fuel injector openings after fuel rail removal.

6. Remove the accelerator, kickdown and speed control cables from the throttle lever and bracket.

7. Disengage the Throttle Position Sensor (TPS) and the Idle Air Control (IAC) motor electrical connections.

8. Disconnect the vacuum hoses from the throttle body.

9. Disengage the connectors from the Manifold Absolute Pressure (MAP) sensor and the intake air temperature sensors.

10. Disconnect the vapor and brake booster hoses.

11. Disengage the knock sensor electrical connector, starter relay connector (if necessary), and the wiring harness from the tab located on the intake manifold.

12. Remove the transaxle to throttle body support bracket fasteners at the throttle body and loosen the fastener at the transaxle end.

13. Remove the throttle body assembly as outlined in Section 5.

14. Remove the EGR tube bolts at the valve and at the intake manifold. Remove the tube from the engine.

15. Remove the intake manifold-to-inlet water tube support fastener (2.0L) or intake manifold support bracket (2.4L).

16. Remove the intake manifold fasteners and washer assemblies. On the 2.0L engine, discard the fasteners and, during assembly, replace them with new fasteners.

17. Remove the intake manifold from the vehicle.

To install:

18. Clean all gasket sealing surfaces. Check the upper and lower manifold gasket surfaces for cracks or distortion.

19. For the 2.0L engine, install the intake manifold with new O-ring seals. For the 2.4L engine, install a new intake manifold gasket and position the manifold on the cylinder head. Tighten the fasteners to 105 inch lbs. (12 Nm) in correct sequence, starting from the center and working outward.

20. Remove the covers from the fuel injector openings and install the fuel injectors into the engine. Seat the injectors in place and tighten the fuel rail bolts to 200 inch lbs. (23 Nm).

21. Connect the PCV and brake booster hoses.

22. Inspect the quick-connect fittings for damage and repair as required. Lubricate the fuel line with clean 30W engine oil. Reconnect the fuel supply line hose to the fuel rail assembly. Check the connection by pulling on the connector to insure it is locked in position.

23. Engage the electrical connectors to the fuel injectors.

24. Install the throttle body and tighten to 200 inch lbs. (23 Nm). Reinstall the transaxle to throttle body support bracket and tighten to 105 inch lbs. (12 Nm) at the throttle body first. Next, tighten the bracket at the transaxle.

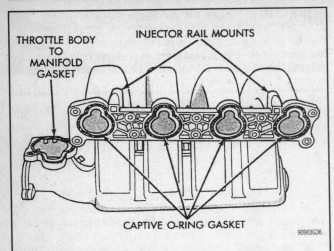

Fig. 26 Make sure that the intake manifold O-ring gaskets are properly seated—2.0L SOHC engine

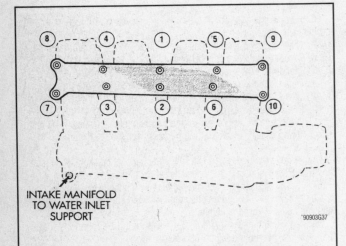

Fig. 27 Intake manifold tightening sequence—2.0L SOHC engine

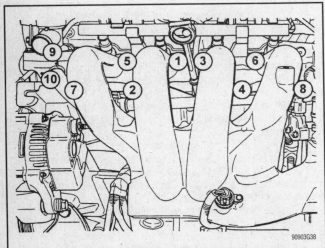

Fig. 28 Intake manifold tightening sequence—2.4L DOHC engine

25. Engage the MAP sensor and the air temperature sensor wiring connectors.

26. Engage the knock sensor electrical and starter relay connectors. Reconnect the wiring harness to the intake manifold tab.

27. Engage the IAC and TPS wiring connectors.

28. Reconnect the throttle body vacuum hoses.

29. Install the accelerator, kickdown and speed control cables to their bracket, then connect them to the throttle lever.

30. Loosely assemble the EGR tube onto the valve and intake manifold finger-tight. Tighten the tube fasteners at the EGR valve first to 95 inch lbs. (11 Nm), then tighten the intake manifold side fasteners to 95 inch lbs. (11 Nm).

31. Install the air inlet resonator to the throttle body. Connect the air inlet tube to the resonator and tighten the clamps to 20–30 inch lbs. (2–3 Nm).

32. Connect the negative battery cable. Pressurize the fuel system using the DRB Scan Tool, or equivalent. Perform the ASD Fuel System Test and check for leaks.

2.0L DOHC Engine

▶ See Figure 29

This engine uses a two-piece aluminum intake manifold. The upper half of the manifold (also called a plenum) mounts the throttle body. The lower half of the manifold contains the fuel rail and injectors. A non-reusable gasket joins the two halves. Use care when working with light alloy parts.

> **✳✳ CAUTION**
>
> **Fuel injection systems remain under pressure, even after the engine has been turned OFF. The fuel system pressure must be relieved before disconnecting any fuel lines. Failure to do so may result in fire and/or personal injury.**

1. Relieve the fuel system pressure.

2. Disconnect the negative battery cable and drain the cooling system.

3. Disconnect the accelerator cable, breather hose and air intake hose.

4. Disengage the vacuum connection at the power brake booster and the PCV valve. Disconnect all remaining vacuum hoses and pipes, as necessary. Tag for identification, if necessary, to save time at assembly.

5. Disconnect the fuel line(s), then remove the throttle control cable and brackets.

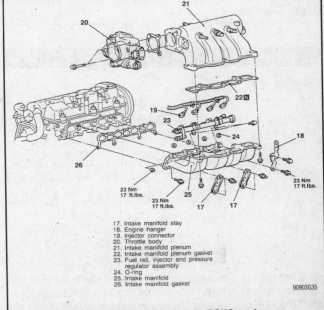

Fig. 29 Intake manifold assembly—2.0L DOHC engine

6. Unplug the alternator wiring harness connection.

7. Disengage the MAP sensor and the intake air temperature sensor connectors.

8. Disengage the TPS connector and position the engine wiring harness aside.

9. Disengage the EGR pipe connection.

10. Remove the intake manifold stay and the engine hanger. Disengage the fuel injector connectors.

11. Remove the throttle body assembly as outlined in Section 5.

12. Unfasten the mounting bolts and remove the intake manifold plenum and gasket.

13. Remove the complete fuel rail assembly. Use care since the fuel injectors can drop out of the fuel rail as it is being removed.

14. Remove the mounting bolts, then remove the intake manifold and gasket from the engine.

To install:

15. Clean all gasket material from the cylinder head and intake manifold assembly. Check both surfaces for cracks or other damage. Check the intake manifold water passages and air passages for clogging. Clean if necessary. Check the gasket surface of the intake manifold for flatness using a straightedge and feeler gauge. It should be 0.006 inch (0.152mm) or less. The limit is 0.008 inch (0.203mm).

16. Install a new intake manifold gasket to the cylinder head and install the manifold. Tighten the manifold in a crisscross pattern, starting from the inside and working outwards to 17 ft. lbs. (23 Nm).

17. Apply a thin coat of clean engine oil to the fuel injector O-rings. Install the fuel rail, injector and pressure regulator assembly to the lower intake manifold.

18. Thoroughly clean the mating surfaces and install the intake manifold plenum with a new gasket.

19. Install the throttle body assembly.

20. Install the intake manifold stay and the engine hanger. Plug in the fuel injector connectors.

21. Attach the EGR pipe connection.

22. Engage the engine control electrical connectors.

23. Engage the alternator wiring harness connection.

24. Connect the fuel line(s) and the throttle control cable brackets.

25. Connect the vacuum hose at the power brake booster and the PCV valve. Connect all remaining vacuum hoses and pipes.

26. Connect the accelerator cable, breather hose and air intake hose.

27. Connect the negative battery cable.

28. Start the engine and check for proper operation.

2.5L Engine

▶ **See Figures 30 thru 42**

1. Disconnect the negative battery cable. On Sebring convertible, Cirrus, Stratus and Breeze models, disconnect the negative battery cable from the left strut tower. The ground cable is equipped with an insulator grommet, which should be placed on the stud to prevent the negative battery cable from accidentally grounding.

2. Properly relieve the fuel system pressure using the procedure outlined in Section 5.

3. Disconnect the fuel line(s) from the fuel rail assembly. On quick-connect fittings, squeeze the fitting retainer tabs together and separate the connection.

4. Loosen the throttle body air inlet hose clamp, then release the snaps holding the air cleaner housing cover to the housing. Remove the air cleaner cover and inlet hose from the engine.

5. Unplug the vacuum connection at the power brake booster and the PCV valve. Disconnect all remaining vacuum hoses and pipes, as necessary. Tag for identification, if necessary, to save time at assembly.

➡**It may be helpful to identify and tag each sensor connector and vacuum connection as it is being removed or disengaged. This may save time at assembly.**

6. Disengage the connectors from the Manifold Absolute Pressure (MAP) sensor and the intake air temperature sensors.

7. If necessary, disengage the power steering pressure switch and oxygen sensor connectors.

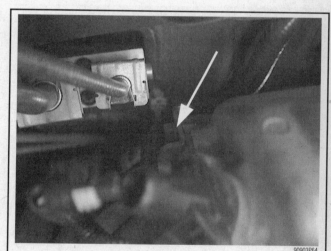

Fig. 30 Remove the right side intake manifold plenum support bracket bolt

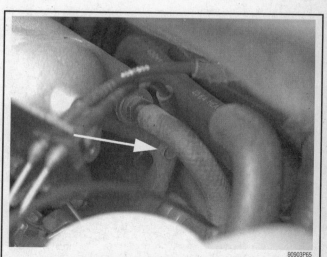

Fig. 31 Remove the left side intake manifold plenum support bracket bolt

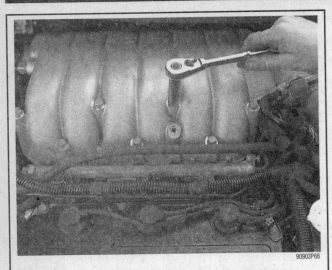

Fig. 32 Remove the intake manifold plenum mounting bolts

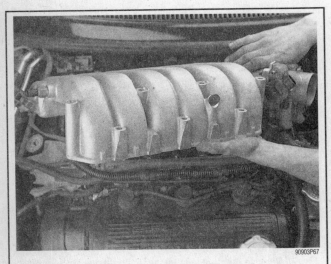

Fig. 33 Remove the intake manifold plenum from the engine

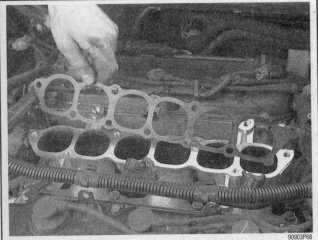

Fig. 34 Remove the intake plenum-to-lower intake manifold gasket

8. Remove the plenum support bracket located to the rear of the MAP sensor.

9. On all models except Sebring and Avenger coupes, loosen the attaching bolt, then remove the air inlet resonator. This is located on top of the engine intake manifold plenum.

10. On Sebring and Avenger coupes, remove the control wiring harness mounting fasteners located on top of the upper plenum near the valve cover.

11. Disconnect the Throttle Position Sensor (TPS) and the Idle Air Control (IAC) motor electrical connections.

12. Remove the throttle body assembly as outlined in Section 5.

13. Remove the throttle cable bracket.

14. Remove the EGR tube from the engine intake manifold.

15. On Sebring and Avenger coupes, remove the EGR valve and transducer assembly.

16. Remove the plenum support bracket located to the rear of the EGR tube.

17. Remove the 7 bolts attaching the upper intake plenum to the lower manifold, and remove the plenum. Remove the intake plenum-to-lower manifold gasket.

18. Detach the fuel injector electrical connectors.

19. Remove the 4 bolts attaching the fuel rail to the intake manifold.

Fig. 35 Loosen the power steering fluid reservoir mounting bracket bolts . . .

Fig. 36 . . . then remove the reservoir bracket from the engine

➡**There are spacers under each fuel rail bolt.**

20. Remove the fuel rail, using care not to lose the spacers.

➡**It may be necessary to remove the power steering fluid reservoir and mounting bracket to access all of the lower intake manifold fasteners.**

21. Remove the lower intake manifold attaching bolts.
22. Remove the intake manifold and discard the old gaskets.

To install:

23. Clean all gasket sealing surfaces. Check both surfaces for cracks or other damage. Check the intake manifold air passages for clogging. Clean if necessary.

24. Check the upper and lower manifold gasket surfaces for flatness using a straightedge and feeler gauge.

25. Surface must be flat within 0.006 inch (0.152mm) per 12 inches (30.48cm) of manifold length. The limit is 0.008 inch (0.203mm).

26. Properly position the new gaskets to the heads and install the lower intake manifold. Tighten the manifold in correct sequence, as illustrated following this procedure.

    a. Tighten the nuts in the front bank to 5 ft. lbs. (7 Nm).
    b. Tighten the nuts in the rear bank to 14 to 17 ft. lbs. (20 to 23 Nm).

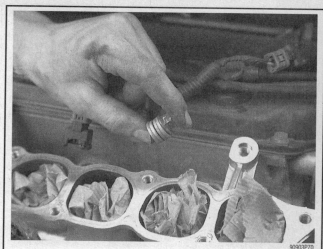

Fig. 39 Be careful not to lose the mounting fasteners and washers

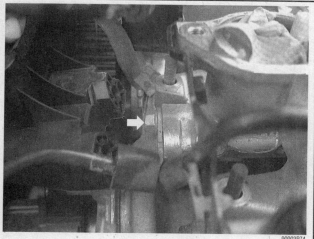

Fig. 37 There is a "hidden" intake manifold mounting bolt on the timing belt side that must be removed

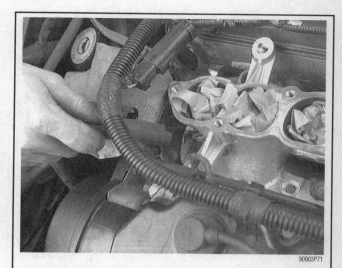

Fig. 40 Disconnect the vacuum hose from the intake manifold

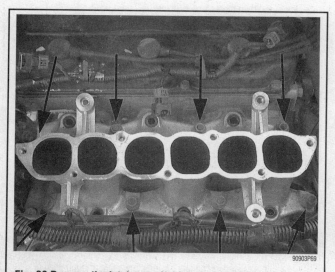

Fig. 38 Remove the intake manifold mounting fasteners

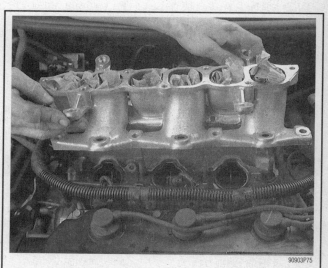

Fig. 41 Lift the intake manifold up and off of the engine

Fig. 42 Remove the intake manifold gaskets from the engine

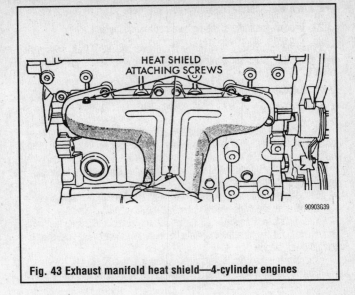

Fig. 43 Exhaust manifold heat shield—4-cylinder engines

  c. Tighten the nuts in the front bank to 14 to 17 ft. lbs. (20 to 23 Nm).
  d. Repeat Steps **b** and **c** again.
  27. Apply a light coating of engine oil to the fuel injector O-rings.
  28. Reinstall the fuel injectors into the engine.
  29. Seat the injectors in place and tighten the fuel rail bolts to 8 ft. lbs. (12 Nm).
  30. Engage the electrical connectors to the fuel injectors.
  31. Reconnect the fuel line(s) to the fuel rail assembly. Exert a slight tug on the fuel line away from the fuel rail to verify positive engagement.
  32. Install the upper intake plenum with new gaskets.
  33. Tighten the plenum bolts to 13 ft. lbs. (18 Nm).
  34. Reinstall the plenum support brackets and tighten to 13 ft. lbs. (18 Nm).
  35. On Sebring and Avenger coupes, install the EGR valve and transducer assembly.
  36. Install the EGR tube and tighten the screws to 95 inch lbs. (11 Nm).
  37. Install the throttle cable bracket.
  38. Install the throttle body assembly as outlined in Section 5.
  39. Reconnect the TPS and IAC electrical connections.
  40. On all models except Sebring and Avenger coupes, install the air inlet resonator and tighten the attaching bolt.
  41. On Sebring and Avenger coupes, place the control wiring harness into correct position on the engine and tighten the mounting fasteners.
  42. Engage the power steering pressure switch and oxygen sensor connectors, if previously disconnected.
  43. Engage the MAP sensor and the intake air temperature sensor connectors.
  44. Connect the vacuum hose at the power brake booster and the PCV valve. Connect all remaining vacuum hoses and pipes.
  45. Connect the remaining engine control system electrical connectors.
  46. Reinstall the air cleaner cover and air inlet hose. Tighten the intake hose-to-throttle body hose clamp.
  47. Reconnect the negative battery cable.
  48. Start the engine and check for leaks.

Exhaust Manifold

REMOVAL & INSTALLATION

2.0L DOHC Engine

◆ **See Figures 43 and 44**

  1. Disconnect the negative battery cable.
  2. Remove the air intake hose and the small air hose connection.

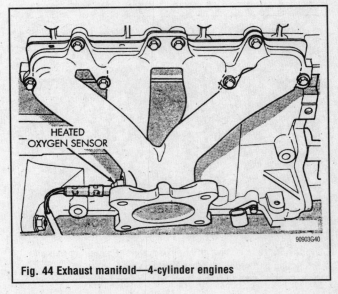

Fig. 44 Exhaust manifold—4-cylinder engines

  3. Properly drain the engine coolant.
  4. Disconnect the upper radiator hose from the thermostat housing.
  5. Disengage the control wiring harness connection.
  6. Remove the water pipe assembly and the engine oil level dipstick.
  7. Remove the heat shield and the engine hanger.
  8. Remove the pulsed secondary air injection valve, if equipped.
  9. Raise and safely support the vehicle.
  10. Remove the exhaust pipe-to-exhaust manifold locknuts and separate the exhaust pipe. Discard the gasket.
  11. Lower the vehicle.
  12. Loosen the mounting fasteners, and remove the exhaust manifold.
To install:
  13. Clean all gasket material from the mating surfaces and check the manifold for cracks or warpage.
  14. Install a new gasket and install the manifold. Tighten the fasteners, in a crisscross pattern to 17 ft. lbs. (23 Nm).
  15. Raise and safely support the vehicle.
  16. Install the exhaust pipe to the exhaust manifold with a new gasket and new locknuts. Tighten the nuts to 33 ft. lbs. (44 Nm).
  17. Lower the vehicle.
  18. Install the pulsed secondary air injection valve, if equipped.
  19. Install the heat shield and the engine hanger.

20. Engage the control wiring harness connection.
21. Connect the upper radiator hose to the thermostat housing.
22. Properly refill the engine cooling system.
23. Install the air intake hose and the small air hose connection.
24. Connect the negative battery cable, then start the engine and check for exhaust leaks.

2.0L SOHC and 2.4L DOHC Engines

♦ See Figures 43 and 44

1. Disconnect the negative battery cable from the left strut tower. The ground cable is equipped with an insulator grommet, which should be placed on the stud to prevent the negative battery cable from accidentally grounding.
2. Disconnect the exhaust pipe from the exhaust manifold. Apply penetrating oil on the exhaust manifold-to-exhaust pipe flange bolts to aid in removal. It may be necessary to remove the entire exhaust system.
3. Remove the exhaust manifold heat shield.
4. Disconnect the heated oxygen sensor, if necessary.
5. Remove the 8 manifold attaching bolts and remove the manifold from the vehicle.
To install:
6. Thoroughly clean all parts. Discard the gasket and clean all sealing surfaces of the manifold and cylinder head. Check the manifold gasket sur-

face for flatness with a straightedge and feeler gauge. The surface must be flat within 0.006 inches per foot (0.152mm per 30.48cm) of manifold length. Inspect the manifold for cracks or distortion. Replace if necessary.
7. Install the manifold into the vehicle with a new gasket. DO NOT APPLY SEALER.
8. Reinstall the 8 manifold bolts and tighten, starting at the center and working outward in both directions. Tighten to 200 inch lbs. (23 Nm).
9. Reconnect the heated oxygen sensor.
10. Reinstall the heat shield.
11. Reinstall the exhaust pipe and tighten the fasteners to 250 inch lbs. (28 Nm).
12. Reconnect the negative battery cable. Start the engine and allow it to idle while inspecting the manifold for exhaust leaks.

2.5L (VIN N) Engine

FRONT BANK SIDE

♦ See Figure 45

1. Disconnect the negative battery cable.
2. Remove the cooling fan motor assembly. Refer to the procedure later in this section.
3. Remove the engine oil level dipstick and tube.

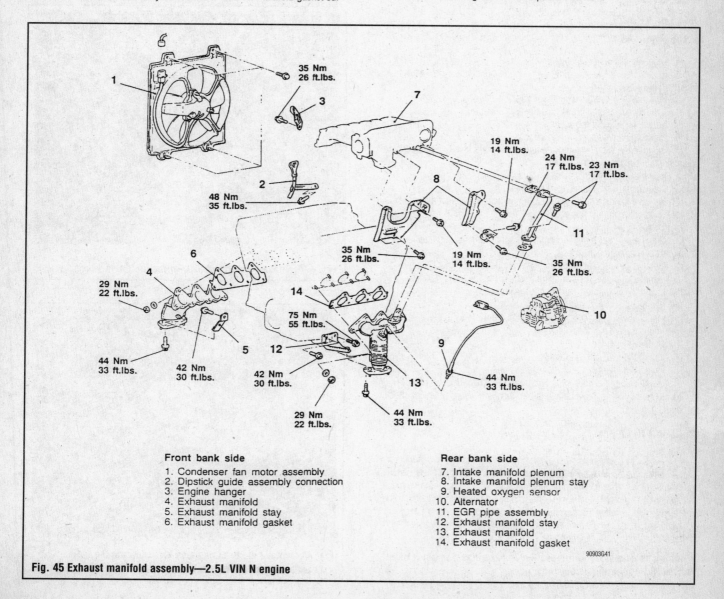

Front bank side
1. Condenser fan motor assembly
2. Dipstick guide assembly connection
3. Engine hanger
4. Exhaust manifold
5. Exhaust manifold stay
6. Exhaust manifold gasket

Rear bank side
7. Intake manifold plenum
8. Intake manifold plenum stay
9. Heated oxygen sensor
10. Alternator
11. EGR pipe assembly
12. Exhaust manifold stay
13. Exhaust manifold
14. Exhaust manifold gasket

Fig. 45 Exhaust manifold assembly—2.5L VIN N engine

4. Remove the engine hanger or lower heat shield, if equipped.

5. Raise and safely support the vehicle.

6. Remove the exhaust pipe-to-exhaust manifold locknuts and separate the exhaust pipe. Discard the gasket.

7. Lower the vehicle.

8. Remove the exhaust manifold mounting fasteners, exhaust manifold stay (brace), exhaust manifold and gasket.

To install:

9. Clean all gasket material from the mating surfaces and check the manifold for cracks or warpage.

10. Install a new gasket, then install the manifold and manifold stay (brace). Tighten the fasteners, in a crisscross pattern to 22 ft. lbs. (29 Nm).

11. Raise and safely support the vehicle.

12. Install the exhaust pipe to the exhaust manifold with a new gasket. Tighten the nuts to 33 ft. lbs. (44 Nm).

13. Lower the vehicle.

14. Install the engine hanger or lower heat shield, if equipped. Tighten the lower heat shield fasteners to 10 ft. lbs. (13 Nm).

15. Install the engine oil level dipstick and tube.

16. Install the cooling fan motor assembly, as outlined later in this section.

17. Connect the negative battery cable, then start the engine and check for exhaust leaks.

REAR BANK SIDE

▶ **See Figure 45**

1. Disconnect the negative battery cable.

2. Remove the intake manifold plenum and the plenum stay, as outlined earlier in this section.

3. Remove the heated oxygen sensor.

4. Remove the alternator, as described in Section 2.

5. Remove the EGR pipe assembly.

6. Raise and safely support the vehicle.

7. Remove the exhaust pipe-to-exhaust manifold locknuts and separate the exhaust pipe. Discard the gasket.

8. Lower the vehicle.

9. If equipped, remove the manifold heat shield.

10. Remove the exhaust manifold mounting bolts, exhaust manifold stay (brace), exhaust manifold and gasket.

To install:

11. Clean all gasket material from the mating surfaces and check the manifold for cracks or warpage.

12. Install a new gasket and install the manifold and manifold stay (brace). Tighten the nuts, in a crisscross pattern to 22 ft. lbs. (30 Nm).

13. Install the manifold heat shield, if equipped.

14. Raise and safely support the vehicle.

15. Install the exhaust pipe to the exhaust manifold with a new gasket. Tighten the nuts to 33 ft. lbs. (44 Nm).

16. Lower the vehicle.

17. Install the EGR pipe assembly.

18. Install the alternator and the oxygen sensor.

19. Install the intake manifold plenum and the plenum stay (brace).

20. Connect the negative battery cable, then start the engine and check for exhaust leaks.

2.5L (VIN H) Engine

▶ **See Figures 46 thru 54**

1. Disconnect the negative battery cable from the left strut tower. The ground cable is equipped with an insulator grommet, which should be placed on the stud to prevent the negative battery cable from accidentally grounding.

2. Raise and safely support the vehicle.

3. Disconnect the exhaust pipe connection to the rear (cowl side) exhaust manifold at the flex joint.

➡️It may be necessary to remove the whole exhaust system. Refer to procedure later in this section.

Fig. 46 The crossunder pipe can be separated from the rear exhaust manifold extension pipe (1) or the exhaust manifold flange (2)

Fig. 47 Remove the exhaust pipe-to-manifold flange gasket

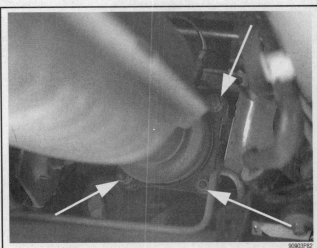

Fig. 48 Remove the retaining nuts and separate the main exhaust pipe from the rear exhaust manifold

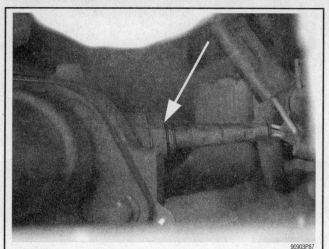

Fig. 49 Using a crow's foot wrench or O₂ sensor socket, remove the oxygen sensor from the exhaust manifold

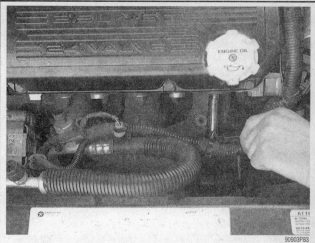

Fig. 52 Remove the exhaust manifold-to-cylinder head mounting bolts . . .

Fig. 50 Remove the exhaust manifold heat shield retainers . . .

Fig. 53 . . . then remove the front exhaust manifold from the vehicle

Fig. 51 . . . then pull out the front exhaust manifold heat shield

Fig. 54 Remove the exhaust manifold-to-cylinder head gasket

4. Remove the bolts attaching the cross-over pipe to the manifolds and remove the assembly.

5. Disconnect the oxygen sensor lead wire at the rear manifold. Remove the oxygen sensor at the rear exhaust manifold.

6. Remove the power steering bracket.

7. Remove the rear exhaust manifold heat shield.

8. Remove the rear manifold attaching nuts and remove the rear manifold.

9. Lower the vehicle and detach the front heated oxygen sensor wiring connector. Remove the front heated oxygen sensor.

10. Remove the front manifold heat shield.

➡**If necessary, remove the EGR transducer mounting bracket and oil level dipstick tube for easier removal.**

11. Remove the front manifold securing nuts, then remove the front manifold.

To install:

12. Thoroughly clean all parts. Inspect the exhaust manifolds for damage or cracks and check for distortion of the cylinder head sealing surface and exhaust crossover sealing surface with a straightedge and thickness gauge.

13. Install a new front manifold gasket.

14. Install the front manifold and tighten the nuts to 22 ft. lbs. (30 Nm).

15. Install the front exhaust manifold heat shield and tighten the mounting screws to 130 inch lbs. (15 Nm).

16. Install the front heated oxygen sensor. Engage the oxygen sensor wiring connector.

17. Raise and safely support the vehicle.

18. Install a new rear exhaust manifold gasket. Install the rear exhaust manifold.

19. Tighten the manifold nuts to 22 ft. lbs. (30 Nm).

20. Install the rear exhaust manifold heat shield and tighten the mounting screws to 115 inch lbs. (13 Nm).

21. Install the power steering bracket.

22. Install the crossover pipe and tighten the nuts to 22 ft. lbs. (30 Nm).

23. Install the rear heated oxygen sensor. Connect the rear heated oxygen sensor lead.

24. Connect the exhaust pipe to the rear manifold. Tighten the exhaust pipe-to-rear exhaust manifold flange mounting bolts to 21 ft. lbs. (28 Nm).

25. Lower the vehicle. Reconnect the negative battery cable. Start the engine and allow the engine to idle while inspecting the vehicle for exhaust leaks at the manifold.

Radiator

REMOVAL & INSTALLATION

Sebring Coupe and Avenger

▶ **See Figure 55**

The radiator is the corrugated fin, downflow type, and is cooled by electric radiator fans. Service the cooling system with high quality ethylene glycol or other aluminum compatible antifreeze coolant.

1. Disconnect the negative battery cable.

2. Loosen the radiator drain plug and, using a large capacity container, drain the cooling system.

3. Remove the radiator cap.

4. If necessary for clearance, remove the bracket and plastic branch tube running from the air cleaner.

5. Disconnect the overflow tube and remove the coolant reserve tank.

6. Disconnect the upper radiator hose.

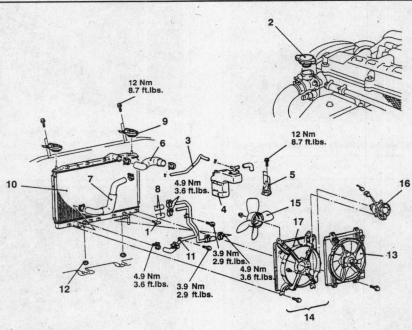

1. Drain plug
2. Radiator cap
3. Overflow hose
4. Reserve tank
5. Reserve tank bracket
6. Radiator upper hose
7. Radiator lower hose
8. Transaxle fluid cooler hose connection <Vehicles with A/T>
9. Upper insulator
10. Radiator assembly
11. Transaxle fluid cooler hose and pipe assembly <Vehicles with A/T>
12. Lower insulator
13. Condenser fan motor assembly <Vehicles with A/C>
14. Radiator fan motor assembly
15. Fan
16. Radiator fan motor
17. Shroud

90903G21

Fig. 55 Typical cooling system assembly—Sebring coupe and Avenger

➡️It is recommended that each clamp be matchmarked to the hose. Observe the marks and reinstall the clamps in exactly the same position when reinstalling the radiator.

7. Label and disengage the wiring to the thermosensors and the electric fan assemblies.

8. For vehicles with automatic transaxles, disconnect the oil cooler lines at the radiator. Plug the transaxle ports and the hose ends to contain the fluid and prevent contamination.

9. Remove the lower radiator hose.

10. Remove the bolts holding the upper mounting brackets to the support member. Remove the radiator, with the cooling fans as an assembly.

To install:

11. If the fan and shroud assemblies were removed with the radiator, they must be reinstalled before installing the radiator. The mounting bolts for the fans should be tightened to 10 ft. lbs. (14 Nm). If the thermosensors were removed, they should be reinstalled and tightened to 10 ft. lbs. (14 Nm).

12. Reinstall the radiator, making certain all the mounts and bushings are correctly positioned. Tighten the mounting bolts to 10 ft. lbs. (14 Nm). Double check the drain plug to make sure it is closed.

13. Connect the oil cooler lines and attach the brackets.

14. Connect the wiring to the electrical components, making sure each is correctly located and securely fastened.

15. Connect the upper and lower radiator hoses and the overflow hose. Install the coolant reserve tank.

16. Install the branch tube and its bracket.

17. Fill the system with coolant.

18. Connect the negative battery cable, run the vehicle until the thermostat opens, fill the radiator completely and check the automatic transaxle fluid level, if equipped.

19. Allow the engine to warm up fully and check that the fans cycle on and off correctly. Watch the coolant level carefully in the overflow tank.

20. Once the vehicle has cooled, recheck the coolant level.

Cirrus, Sebring Convertible, Stratus and Breeze

▶ **See Figures 56 thru 69**

✳✳ CAUTION

Do not open the radiator draincock or remove the radiator cap when the cooling system is hot and under pressure. This can cause serious burns from hot, pressurized coolant. Allow a sufficient amount of time for the cooling system to cool down before opening up the system.

➡️The radiator uses plastic tanks. Plastic tanks, while stronger than brass, are subject to damage by impact, such as slipped wrenches. Use care when working around these radiators.

1. Disconnect the negative battery cable from the left strut tower. The ground cable is equipped with an insulator grommet, which should be placed on the stud to prevent the negative battery cable from accidentally grounding.

2. Remove the air inlet resonator.

3. Place a large drain pan under the radiator drain plug. Drain and properly contain engine coolant.

➡️To open the drain plug on models equipped with a 2.5L engine, use a ⅜ inch drive extension 3 inches (7.6cm) long and a 19mm socket with universal joint. The drain plug can also be accessed by removing the right front fog light in the front lower bumper fascia.

4. Remove the upper radiator crossmember as follows:

   a. Remove the push-in mounting fasteners securing the front fascia/grille unit to the radiator support crossmember.

   b. Remove the mounting bolts securing the support braces to the bottom of the crossmember.

   c. Remove the bolts securing the crossmember to the radiator closure panel.

Fig. 56 Using a small flat bladed tool, pry up the center portion of the plastic front grille/fascia retainers, then pull them out

Fig. 57 To aid in a straight reassembly, matchmark the washer screws to the radiator crossmember using a marker

Fig. 58 Remove the radiator crossmember mounting fasteners

Fig. 59 Remove the mounting bolts for the hood lock latch mechanism

Fig. 61 Relieve the tension from the hose clamp, then disconnect the upper coolant hose at the radiator

Fig. 60 Remove the radiator support crossmember

Fig. 62 If equipped with an automatic transaxle, loosen the hose clamp and disconnect the transmission fluid cooler hose

  d. Remove the mounting nuts attaching the hood latch to the radiator crossmember. Remove the crossmember from the vehicle.

➡The following step and associated photos describe original type hose clamps. Some vehicles may instead have a worm gear type clamp, which can be loosened with a screwdriver.

  5. Using pliers, compress the tabs on each hose clamp, then slide the clamp a few inches away from the hose end. Carefully twist and pull the hoses from the radiator.

  6. Disconnect the engine block heater wire, if equipped.

  7. Disconnect and plug the transaxle cooler lines, if equipped.

  8. Remove screw attaching support bracket for external transaxle cooler lines to the left side of the radiator, if equipped.

  9. Remove the screw attaching the support bracket for air conditioning lines from the right side of the radiator. Remove the support bracket.

  10. Unplug the cooling fan wiring.

  11. Remove the air conditioning condenser mounting screws. Use care when working around the air conditioning condenser. Avoid bending the condenser inlet tube. Care should be taken not to damage the radiator or condenser cooling fins or water tubes during removal. It is not necessary to discharge the air conditioning system to remove the radiator.

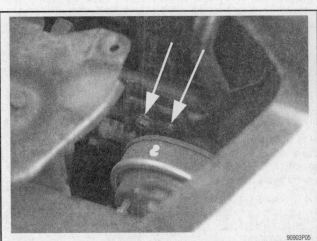

Fig. 63 Remove the mounting fasteners that retain the fluid and refrigerant line support brackets to each side of the radiator/condenser assembly

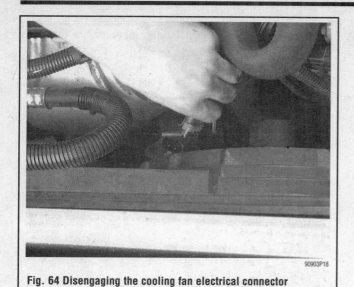

Fig. 64 Disengaging the cooling fan electrical connector

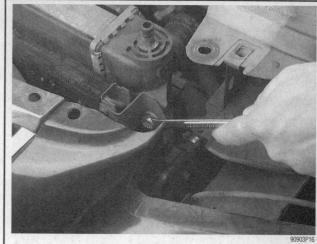

Fig. 67 Remove the A/C condenser-to-radiator mounting fasteners

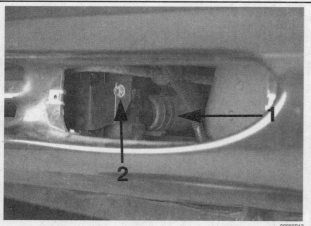

Fig. 65 Access to the lower radiator cooling hose (1) and lower left side A/C condenser-to-radiator mounting fasteners (2) is possible after removal of the left fog light

Fig. 68 Unclip the A/C line from the cooling fan module

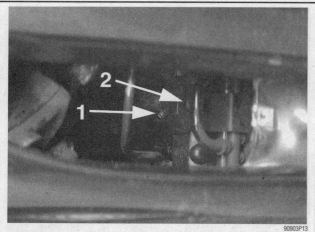

Fig. 66 Access to the lower transmission fluid cooler line (1) and lower right side A/C condenser-to-radiator mounting fasteners (2) is possible after removal of the right fog light

Fig. 69 Remove the radiator assembly from the vehicle

Fig. 70 Remove the cooling fan module-to-radiator mounting fasteners . . .

12. Carefully remove the radiator from the vehicle. The cooling fan/shroud assembly can be separated from the radiator at this time.

To install:

13. If separated, install the cooling fan/shroud assembly to the radiator unit.

14. Lower the radiator and fan module (assembly) into position. Seat the radiator assembly lower isolators in the mount holes provided.

15. Install the air conditioning condenser mounting screws and tighten to 45 inch lbs. (5 Nm).

16. Connect the radiator hoses and tighten the hose clamps to 22 inch lbs. (2.5 Nm). Be sure the hoses do not interfere with the accessory drive belt, and be sure the upper hose clamp does not interfere with the hood liner.

17. Connect the cooling fan wiring.

18. Connect the transaxle cooler lines to the radiator, if equipped.

19. Install the upper radiator crossmember as follows:

a. Place the radiator crossmember into the vehicle in proper position.

b. Install the hood latch to the radiator crossmember. Install and tighten the hood latch mounting nuts.

c. Install and tighten the crossmember-to-radiator closure panel mounting bolts.

d. Install and tighten the mounting bolts that secure the support braces to bottom of the radiator crossmember.

e. Install the push-in mounting fasteners holding the front fascia/grille unit to the radiator crossmember.

20. Connect the engine block heater, if equipped.

21. Install the air inlet resonator.

22. Fill the cooling system with the correct type and amount of engine coolant.

23. Reconnect the negative battery cable. Start the engine and allow it to idle until it reaches full operating temperature. Check the cooling system for correct fluid level and top off if necessary.

Electric Cooling Fan

REMOVAL & INSTALLATION

Sebring Coupe and Avenger

▶ See Figure 55

1. Disconnect the negative battery cable.

2. Loosen the radiator drain plug and drain the cooling system beneath the level of the upper radiator hose.

3. Disconnect the upper radiator hose to allow clearance for removal of the fan and shroud assembly.

➡It is recommended that each clamp be matchmarked to the hose. Observe the marks and reinstall the clamps in exactly the same position when reinstalling the radiator hose.

4. Unfasten the electrical connector from the cooling fan motor.

5. Remove the mounting bolts, fan and shroud assembly from the vehicle.

6. Remove the fan blade retainer nut from the shaft on the fan motor and separate the fan from the motor.

7. Remove the motor-to-shroud attaching screws and remove the motor from the shroud.

To install:

8. Install the motor to the shroud and secure it with the mounting bolts.

9. Install the fan to the motor shaft and secure it with the retainer nut.

10. Install the fan and shroud assembly into the engine compartment and secure the assembly to the radiator. Reattach the fan motor's electrical connector.

11. Install the upper radiator hose and properly fill the cooling system.

12. Connect the negative battery cable and check the cooling fan for proper operation.

Cirrus, Stratus, Sebring Convertible and Breeze

▶ See Figures 70 and 71

1. Disconnect the negative battery cable from the left strut tower. The ground cable is equipped with an insulator grommet, which should be placed on the stud to prevent the negative battery cable from accidentally grounding.

2. Unfasten the cooling fan electrical connections.

3. Remove the 4 cooling fan/shroud assembly mounting bolts.

4. Remove the cooling fan/shroud assembly.

5. To remove the fan blade from the fan motor on the shroud assembly, first support the motor on a bench, then remove the fan retaining clip from the motor shaft. Slide the fan off the motor shaft.

6. To remove the fan motor from the shroud unit, remove the mounting screws, then remove the motor from the fan shroud.

To install:

7. Install the motor onto the fan shroud assembly and tighten the mounting screws.

8. Install the fan blade onto the motor shaft and install the retaining clip.

9. Reinstall the cooling fan/shroud assembly into the vehicle.

10. Reinstall the cooling fan mounting bolts.

11. Tighten the fan mounting bolts to 65 inch lbs. (7.5 Nm).

12. Fasten the fan's electrical connections.

13. Reconnect the negative battery cable.

Fig. 71 . . . then remove the cooling fan module

TESTING

▶ **See Figure 72**

1. Detach the fan motor electrical connector.
2. Check to be sure that the radiator fan rotates when battery voltage is applied between the connector terminals.
3. Check that abnormal noises are not produced while the fan motor is turning.
4. If the fan runs normally, the motor is functioning properly.
5. If not, replace the fan module using the procedure earlier in this section.

➡ **If the motor is noticeably overheated, the system voltage may be too high.**

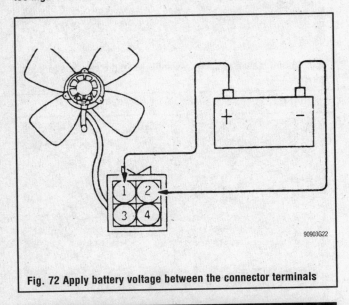

Fig. 72 Apply battery voltage between the connector terminals

Water Pump

REMOVAL & INSTALLATION

The water pump is driven by the timing belt from the crankshaft. It is good practice to turn the engine crankshaft by hand (clockwise) to set the engine to Top Dead Center (TDC) for the No. 1 cylinder compression stroke (firing position) before starting work. This should align all timing marks and serve as a reference point for later work.

2.0L and 2.4L Engines

▶ **See Figures 73 and 74**

1. Disconnect the negative battery cable.

➡ **This procedure requires removing the engine timing belt and the auto tensioner. The factory specifies that the timing marks should always be aligned before removing the timing belt. Set the engine at TDC on No. 1 compression stroke. This should align all timing marks on the crankshaft sprocket and both camshaft sprockets.**

2. Raise and safely support the vehicle to a level that allows access from above and below.
3. Remove the right inner splash shield.
4. Remove the accessory drive belts.
5. Place a drain pan under the radiator drain plug. Drain and properly contain the cooling system.
6. Support the engine using a floor jack and block of wood, then remove the right motor mount.
7. Remove the timing belt, tensioner and camshaft sprockets.

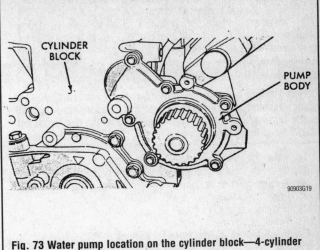

Fig. 73 Water pump location on the cylinder block—4-cylinder engines

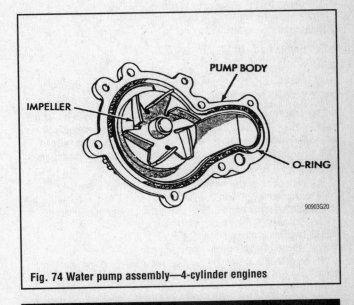

Fig. 74 Water pump assembly—4-cylinder engines

✳✳ **WARNING**

With the timing belt removed, DO NOT rotate the camshaft or crankshaft, or damage to the engine could occur.

8. Remove the rear timing belt cover to access the water pump.
9. Remove the water pump attaching bolts.
10. Remove the water pump.

To install:

11. Thoroughly clean all sealing surfaces. Replace the water pump if there are any cracks, signs of coolant leakage from the shaft seal, loose or rough turning bearings, a damaged impeller or sprocket, or a loose or damaged sprocket flange.
12. Install a new rubber O-ring into the water pump.

➡ **Make sure the O-ring is properly seated in the water pump groove before tightening the screws. An improperly located O-ring may cause damage to the O-ring and cause a coolant leak.**

13. Install the water pump and tighten the bolts to 105 inch lbs. (12 Nm).
14. Using a cooling system pressure tester, pressurize the cooling system to 15 psi and check for leaks. If okay, release the pressure and continue the engine assembly process.

15. Rotate the water pump by hand to check for freedom of movement.
16. Install the rear timing belt cover.
17. Install the camshaft sprocket(s), timing belt and tensioner. DO NOT allow the camshafts to turn while the sprocket bolts are being tightened, in order to maintain timing mark alignment.

✴✴ WARNING

Do not attempt to compress the tensioner plunger with the tensioner assembly installed in the engine. This will cause damage to the tensioner and other related components. The tensioner MUST be compressed in a vise.

18. Install the timing belt covers.
19. Install the right engine mount bracket and engine mount.
20. Remove the floor jack and wood block from underneath the engine.
21. Install the crankshaft damper.
22. Install the right inner splash shield.
23. Lower the vehicle.
24. Install and tension the accessory drive belts.
25. Refill the cooling system using the correct quantity and type of coolant. Bleed the cooling system.
26. Start the engine and check for proper operation.
27. Check and top off the cooling system, if necessary.

2.5L Engine

▶ See Figures 75, 76, 77, 78 and 79

1. Disconnect the negative battery cable.
2. Place a large drain pan under the radiator drain plug. Drain and properly contain the engine coolant.

➡This procedure requires removing the engine timing belt and the auto tensioner. To help assure proper alignment at assembly, it may be helpful to set the engine at TDC on No. 1 compression stroke. This should align all timing marks on the crankshaft sprocket and both camshaft sprockets.

3. Remove the accessory drive belts and crankshaft damper.
4. Remove the right engine mount. This requires safely supporting the engine with a floor jack and wood block so the mount can be removed.
5. Remove the timing belt covers.
6. Remove the timing belt and tensioner.
7. Remove the water pump mounting bolts.
8. Separate the water pump from the water inlet pipe and remove the pump.

Fig. 76 Pull the water pump assembly off of the engine and inlet pipe

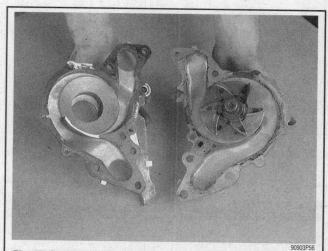
Fig. 77 Open the water pump housing and examine for cracks or damage

Fig. 75 Remove the water pump mounting bolts

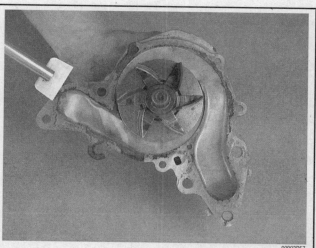
Fig. 78 Replace the water pump housing gasket using a scraper tool

Fig. 79 Always keep the water pump's mounting bolts lined up with their correct mounting holes

To install:

9. Thoroughly clean all sealing surfaces. Inspect the pump for damage or cracks, signs of coolant leakage at the vent, and excessive looseness or rough turning bearings. Any problems require a new pump.

10. Install a new O-ring on the water inlet pipe. Wet the O-ring with water to make installation easier. DO NOT use oil or grease on the O-ring.

11. Install a new gasket on the water pump and fit the pump inlet opening over the water pipe. Press the assembly together to force the pipe into the water pump.

12. Install the water pump-to-engine bolts and tighten to 20 ft. lbs. (27 Nm).

13. Install the timing belt and timing belt tensioner. Set the timing belt tension.

14. Install the timing belt covers. Install the right engine mount. Remove the floor jack and engine block from underneath the engine.

15. Install the crankshaft damper.

16. Install the accessory drive belts and set to the proper tension.

17. Connect the negative battery cable.

18. Fill and bleed the engine cooling system.

19. Start the engine and verify proper operation, with no leaks.

Cylinder Head

REMOVAL & INSTALLATION

4-Cylinder Engines

♦ See Figures 80 and 81

❈❈ CAUTION

Fuel injection systems remain under pressure, even after the engine has been turned OFF. The fuel system pressure MUST be relieved before disconnecting any fuel lines. Failure to do so may result in fire and/or personal injury.

1. Disconnect the negative battery cable from the left strut tower. The ground cable is equipped with an insulator grommet, which should be placed on the stud to prevent the negative battery cable from accidentally grounding.

2. Properly relieve the fuel system pressure using the procedure in Section 5.

3. Remove the air cleaner assembly.

4. Drain and properly contain the engine coolant.

5. Label and disengage all vacuum hoses, lines and wiring harness connections that are required for cylinder head removal.

6. Disconnect the fuel line.

7. Disconnect the throttle linkage.

8. Remove the accessory drive belt(s).

9. Detach the power steering pump and position it aside.

10. Disconnect the the coil pack wiring connector. Disconnect the spark plug wires from the spark plugs. Remove the ignition coil pack unit from the engine.

11. Remove the cylinder head cover.

12. Remove the intake and exhaust manifolds, if necessary.

13. Remove the timing belt cover, timing belt, camshaft sprocket and rear timing belt cover, using the procedures later in this section.

14. Remove the rocker arm/rocker arm shaft assemblies.

15. Unfasten the cylinder head bolts in the reverse order of their tightening sequence, then remove the cylinder head.

To install:

➥The cylinder head bolts should be checked for stretching before reuse. If the thread area of the bolt is "necked down," the bolts must be replaced with new ones. In any case, new head bolts are recommended.

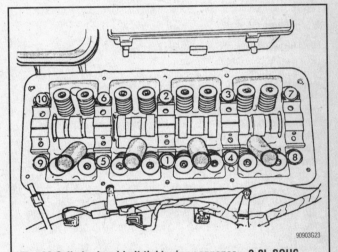

Fig. 80 Cylinder head bolt tightening sequence—2.0L SOHC engine

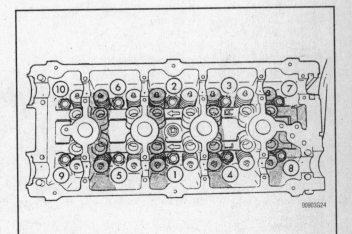

Fig. 81 Cylinder head bolt tightening sequence—2.0L and 2.4L DOHC engines

16. Thoroughly clean all parts. Clean all sealing surfaces. Use care not to scratch the aluminum cylinder head sealing surface. Check the cylinder head for flatness using a feeler gauge and a straightedge. The cylinder head must be flat within 0.004 inch (0.1mm).

17. Check the cylinder head for cracks or other damage.

18. Install a new gasket and the cylinder head to the engine block.

19. Be sure to oil the cylinder head bolt threads with clean engine oil. Install the cylinder head bolts, and be sure to place the four short 4.330 in. (110mm) bolts in positions 7, 8, 9 and 10. Tighten the bolts in proper sequence, as illustrated.

20. Tighten the bolts in 4 steps as follows:
   a. First: all bolts to 25 ft. lbs. (34 Nm).
   b. Second: all bolts to 50 ft. lbs. (68 Nm).
   c. Third: all bolts again to 50 ft. lbs. (68 Nm).
   d. Fourth: all bolts an additional ¼ turn.

➡ **Do not use a torque wrench for the fourth step.**

21. Install the rocker arm/rocker arm shaft assemblies.

22. Install the cylinder head cover.

23. Install the timing belt rear cover and camshaft sprocket. Install the timing belt.

24. Install the timing belt cover.

25. Install the intake and exhaust manifolds, if removed.

26. Install the ignition coil pack onto the engine. Reconnect the coil pack wiring connector and the spark plug wires to the correct spark plugs.

27. Install the power steering pump.

28. Install and adjust the accessory drive belts.

29. Connect the throttle linkage.

30. Check to be sure all ducts, hoses, fuel lines and wiring harness connectors have been properly engaged.

31. Install the air cleaner assembly.

32. Fill the cooling system with a 50/50 mixture of clean ethylene glycol or other suitable antifreeze and water. A complete engine oil and filter change is also recommended.

33. Connect the negative battery cable.

34. Start the engine and check for leaks. Run the engine with the radiator cap off, so as the engine warms and the thermostat opens, coolant can be added to the radiator. When satisfied that the cooling system is full, shut the engine **OFF**, install the radiator cap and allow the engine to cool.

35. With the engine cool, check all fluid levels. Add coolant and oil as required. Restart the engine and test drive the vehicle to check for proper operation.

6-Cylinder Engine

▶ **See Figures 82 thru 88**

1. Properly relieve the fuel system pressure, as described in Section 5.

2. Disconnect the negative battery cable.

3. Drain the engine cooling system.

4. Remove the timing belt and camshaft sprockets.

5. Label and disengage any wiring harnesses, vacuum hoses and lines that would inhibit removal of the cylinder head.

6. Remove the intake manifold assembly.

7. Remove the water pump inlet pipe retaining bolt on the inner rear part of the front cylinder head.

8. Remove the rocker arm (valve) covers and rocker arm assemblies.

9. Remove the distributor assembly.

10. On the front cylinder head, remove the ground strap on the left end of the head.

11. Remove the exhaust manifolds and crossunder pipe.

12. Remove the cylinder head mounting bolts in the reverse order of their tightening sequence, and place them in numbered order through holes made in a piece of cardboard.

13. Remove the cylinder head and gasket.

To install:

14. Thoroughly clean and dry the mating surfaces of the head and block. Check the cylinder head for cracks, damage or engine coolant leakage. Remove scale, sealing compound and carbon. Clean the oil passages

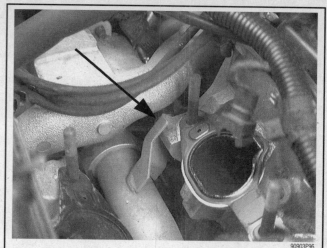

Fig. 82 Location of the water pump inlet pipe retaining bolt on the inner rear part of the front cylinder head

Fig. 83 On the front cylinder head, remove the grounding strap

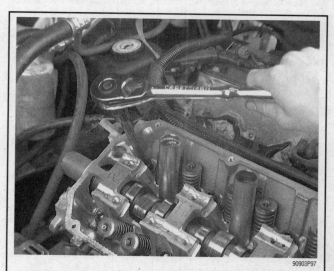

Fig. 84 Loosen each cylinder head mounting bolt

Fig. 85 After removing each bolt, examine the threads for stretching, and replace if necessary

Fig. 86 To insure correct installation, keep the cylinder head bolts in a piece of cardboard

Fig. 87 With an assistant, carefully lift the cylinder head off of the engine block

Fig. 88 Remove the cylinder head gasket

thoroughly. Check the cylinder head for flatness. End to end, the head should be no more than 0.008 inch (0.2mm) out-of-true. If the service limit is exceeded, correct to meet specifications. Note that the maximum amount of stock allowed to be removed from the cylinder head and mating cylinder block is 0.0079 inch (0.2mm). If the cylinder head cannot be made serviceable by removing this amount, replace the head.

15. Check that the new head gasket(s) have the proper identification marks for the engine. Position a new head gasket with the identification mark at the front top.

➡**Do not apply sealant to the cylinder head gasket or mating surfaces.**

16. Inspect the cylinder head bolts prior to installation. If the threads are "necked down" (stretched), the bolts should be replaced. Necking can be checked by holding a straightedge against the threads. If all of the threads do not contact the straightedge, the bolt should be replaced. In any case, all new head bolts are recommended.

17. Install the cylinder head straight down onto the block. Try to eliminate most of the side-to-side adjustments, as this may move the gasket out of position or damage the gasket. Before installing the bolts, the threads should be oiled with clean engine oil. Install the bolts and the special washers by hand and just start each bolt 1 or 2 turns on the threads.

➡**The washers must be installed correctly. The rounded shoulder of the washer denotes the face in contact with the bolt. The flat face contacts the head.**

18. Correct tightening of the cylinder head bolts requires 3 steps:
 a. Follow the tightening sequence and tighten each bolt to 62 ft. lbs. (84 Nm).
 b. Follow the tightening sequence and tighten each bolt to 70 ft. lbs. (95 Nm).
 c. Follow the tightening sequence and tighten each bolt to 80 ft. lbs. (108 Nm).

19. Install the valve cover and gasket.
20. Install the exhaust manifolds and crossunder pipe.
21. Install the distributor assembly.
22. Install the intake manifold assembly.
23. Check to make sure that all wiring harnesses, vacuum hoses and lines are all properly connected.

➡**Before proceeding, double check all installation items, paying particular attention to loose hoses or hanging wires, nuts not properly tightened, poor routing of hoses and wires (too tight or rubbing) and tools left in the engine area.**

24. Fill the cooling system with coolant. Changing the engine oil and filter is recommended to eliminate pollutants such as coolant in the oil.

25. Connect the negative battery cable. With the radiator cap off, start the engine and check for leaks of fuel, vacuum, oil or coolant. Check the operation of all engine electrical systems, as well as dashboard gauges and lights. Add coolant as the engine warms.

26. Perform necessary adjustments to the accelerator cable and drive belts. Allow the engine to cool and once again check and adjust the coolant level.

Oil Pan

REMOVAL & INSTALLATION

2.0L DOHC Engine

▶ **See Figures 89 and 90**

1. Disconnect the negative battery cable.
2. Raise and safely support the vehicle.
3. Remove the oil pan drain plug and drain the engine oil.
4. Remove the oil dipstick and tube.
5. Remove the front plate.
6. Remove the front exhaust pipe.
7. Remove the oil pan retaining bolts and carefully remove the oil pan.

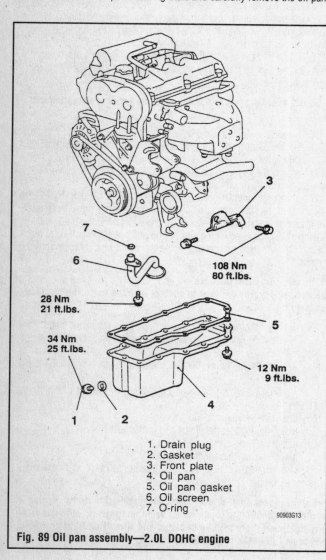

1. Drain plug
2. Gasket
3. Front plate
4. Oil pan
5. Oil pan gasket
6. Oil screen
7. O-ring

90903G13

Fig. 89 Oil pan assembly—2.0L DOHC engine

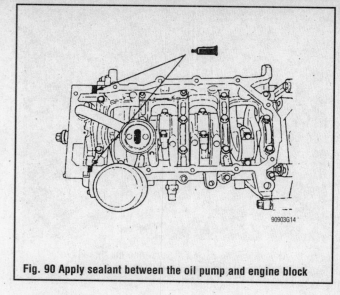

90903G14

Fig. 90 Apply sealant between the oil pump and engine block

To install:

8. Inspect the oil pan for damage and cracks; replace if faulty. While the pan is removed, inspect the oil screen for clogging, damage and cracks. Clean and/or replace if faulty.

9. Thoroughly clean the mating surfaces of the cylinder block and oil pan.

10. Apply sealant to the seams between the oil pump and the engine block.

11. Install the oil pan onto the cylinder block and tighten the retaining bolts to 9 ft. lbs. (12 Nm).

➡**Although no torque sequence is available, it is recommended that you begin at the center of each side and progress outward, in an alternating pattern.**

12. Install the front exhaust pipe.
13. Install the oil dipstick and tube.
14. Install the oil drain plug and tighten to 25 ft. lbs. (34 Nm). An oil filter change is recommended.
15. Lower the vehicle and fill the crankcase to the proper level with clean engine oil.
16. Connect the negative battery cable. Start the engine and check for leaks.

2.0L SOHC and 2.4L DOHC Engines

▶ **See Figures 91 and 92**

1. Disconnect the negative battery cable from the left strut tower. The ground cable is equipped with an insulator grommet which should be placed on the stud to prevent the negative battery cable from accidentally grounding.

2. Raise and safely support the vehicle.

3. Place a large oil pan under the oil pan drain plug. Drain the oil from the engine.

4. If necessary, remove the transaxle bending bracket.

5. Remove the front engine mount and bracket.

6. If necessary, remove the following:
• Transaxle inspection cover
• Oil filter and adapter

7. Remove the oil pan attaching bolts.

8. Remove the oil pan.

9. Clean the oil pan as well as the oil pan gasket sealing surfaces.

To install:

10. Using a suitable rubber adhesive gasket sealant, apply a ⅛ in. bead at the oil pump-to-engine block parting line.

11. Install the new oil pan gasket by positioning it properly onto the oil pan.

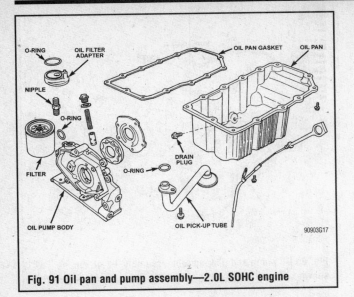

Fig. 91 Oil pan and pump assembly—2.0L SOHC engine

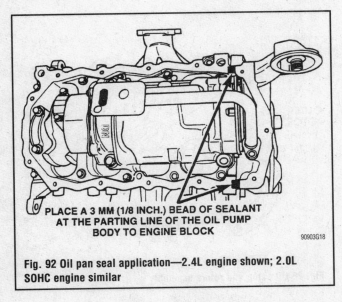

PLACE A 3 MM (1/8 INCH.) BEAD OF SEALANT AT THE PARTING LINE OF THE OIL PUMP BODY TO ENGINE BLOCK

Fig. 92 Oil pan seal application—2.4L engine shown; 2.0L SOHC engine similar

➡️**If a gasket is not available, use a ⅛ inch bead of silicone gasket maker.**

12. Install the oil pan onto the engine.
13. Tighten the oil pan attaching bolts to 105 inch lbs. (12 Nm).

➡️**Although no torque sequence is available, it is recommended that you begin at the center of each side and progress outward, in an alternating pattern.**

14. If removed, install the oil filter adapter as follows:
   a. Be sure the O-ring seal is seated in the groove on the adapter.
   b. Align the locating roll pin into the engine block.
   c. Tighten the retaining fastener to 60 ft. lbs. (80 Nm).
   d. Install a new oil filter.
15. Install the transaxle inspection cover, if removed.
16. Install the front engine mount and engine mount bracket.
17. Install the transaxle bending bracket.
18. Install the oil pan drain plug and gasket. Tighten the drain plug to 25 ft. lbs. (34 Nm).
19. Lower the vehicle.
20. Fill the engine with fresh oil to the proper level.
21. Connect the negative battery cable. Start the engine and check for leaks.

2.5L Engine

◆ See Figures 93 and 94

1. Disconnect the negative battery cable. On Cirrus, Stratus or Sebring convertible models, disconnect the remote negative battery connection at the left strut tower.
2. Raise and safely support the vehicle.
3. Place a large drain pan under the oil pan drain plug and drain the oil from the engine.
4. On Cirrus, Stratus and Sebring convertible models, it may be necessary to remove the engine support module. If necessary, remove the engine support module as follows:
   a. Place a suitable support jack underneath the engine/transaxle assembly at the transaxle to prevent it from rotating.
   b. Remove the through-bolt at the rear mount and remove the bolts securing the support module to the crossmember.
   c. Remove the upper mounting bolt from the rear support strut bracket.
   d. Remove the front mounting bolts from the support module to the lower radiator support member.
   e. Support the radiator/cooling fan assembly. Remove the lower radiator support member.

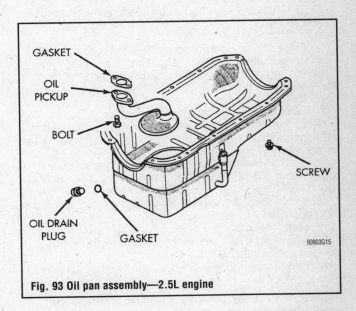

Fig. 93 Oil pan assembly—2.5L engine

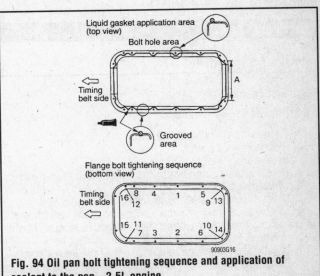

Fig. 94 Oil pan bolt tightening sequence and application of sealant to the pan—2.5L engine

f. Remove the through-bolt at the front engine mount and remove the engine support module.

5. On Sebring coupe and Avenger models, disconnect and lower the front exhaust pipe, then remove the center member.

6. Remove the engine oil dipstick tube and dipstick.

7. Remove the starter motor.

8. On Cirrus, Stratus and Sebring convertible models, remove the engine-to-transaxle struts.

9. On Sebring coupe and Avenger models, remove the front and rear plates.

10. Remove the transaxle inspection cover.

11. Remove the oil pan attaching bolts.

12. Remove the oil pan. If necessary, use a rubber faced mallet, or a hammer with a block of wood to separate the oil pan from the engine block.

To install:

13. Thoroughly clean and dry the oil pan, cylinder block, and cylinder block bolts and bolt holes.

14. Apply a continuous 0.157 inch (4mm) bead of MOPAR® Silicone Adhesive Sealant, or equivalent, to the oil pan gasket surface. Be sure to circle all mounting bolt holes, as well. Install the oil pan within a 10–15 minute period of applying the gasket material, to ensure proper sealing.

15. Install the oil pan to the engine.

16. Tighten the oil pan attaching bolts in the indicated sequence to 53 inch lbs. (6 Nm).

17. Install the transaxle inspection cover.

18. On Sebring coupe and Avenger models, install the front and rear plates and tighten the bolts to 80 ft. lbs. (108 Nm).

19. On Cirrus, Stratus and Sebring convertible models, install the engine-to-transaxle struts.

20. Install the starter motor.

21. Install the engine oil dipstick tube and dipstick.

22. On Sebring coupe and Avenger models, install the center member and tighten the mounting bolts to 65 ft. lbs. (88 Nm), then connect the front exhaust pipe.

23. On Cirrus, Stratus and Sebring convertible models, install the engine support module. Tighten the front and rear mount through-bolts to 45 ft. lbs. (61 Nm).

24. Reinstall the oil pan drain plug and gasket. Tighten the drain plug to 29 ft. lbs. (40 Nm).

25. Lower the vehicle.

26. Refill the engine with fresh oil to the proper level. An oil filter change is recommended.

27. Reconnect the negative battery cable. Start the engine and check for leaks.

➥Whenever the vehicle sub-frame is removed or lowered, the wheel alignment should be checked.

Oil Pump

REMOVAL & INSTALLATION

4-Cylinder Engines

▶ **See Figures 95, 96, 97 and 98**

1. Disconnect the negative battery cable.

2. Remove the timing belt.

3. Remove the oil pan.

4. Using a suitable puller, draw the crankshaft sprocket from the front of the crankshaft.

5. Remove the oil pump pickup tube and O-ring.

6. Remove the oil pump and front crankshaft seal. The front cover/oil pump mounting bolts may be different sizes and must be reinstalled in their original locations. Remove and tag the front cover mounting bolts.

7. Inspect the oil pump case for damage and remove the rear cover.

8. Remove the pump rotors and inspect the inside of the case for excessive wear.

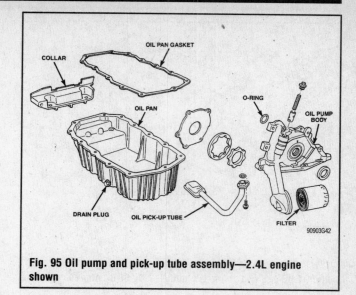

Fig. 95 Oil pump and pick-up tube assembly—2.4L engine shown

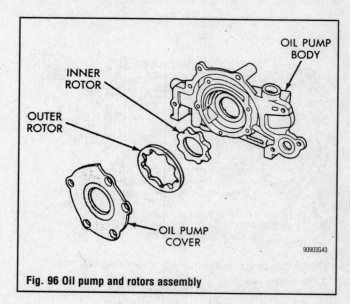

Fig. 96 Oil pump and rotors assembly

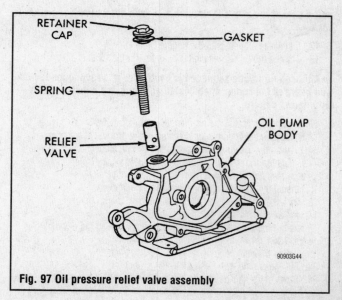

Fig. 97 Oil pressure relief valve assembly

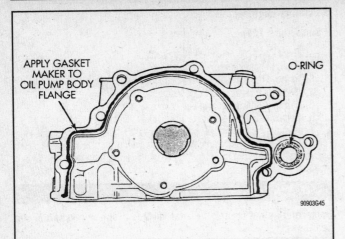

Fig. 98 Location of gasket maker sealant application—4-cylinder engines

9. Check that the oil relief plunger slides smoothly and check for a broken spring. Repair or replace components as necessary.

To install:

10. Clean all parts well. Make sure the block and pump surfaces are clean and free of old sealer.

11. Assemble the pump, using new parts as required, with clean oil. Align the marks on the inner and outer rotors when assembling.

12. Install the pump's rear cover and tighten the screws to 88 inch lbs. (10 Nm).

13. Reinstall the pump relief valve, spring, gasket and valve cap. Tighten the valve cap to 30–33 ft. lbs. (41–44 Nm).

14. Apply gasket maker sealant to the engine block mounting surface of the oil pump body.

15. Install the oil ring into the discharge passage of the pump body.

16. Prime the oil pump before installation by filling the rotor cavity with clean engine oil.

17. Align the flats of the oil pump rotor with the flats on the crankshaft as you install the pump to the engine block.

18. Install and tighten the oil pump-to-engine block mounting bolts to 17–21 ft. lbs. (23–28 Nm).

19. Install a new front oil seal.

20. Install the crankshaft sprocket.

21. Install the oil pump pickup tube and O-ring. Tighten the oil pump pickup tube mounting screw to 21 ft. lbs. (28 Nm).

22. Install the oil pan.

23. Install the timing belt and covers.

24. Install the crankshaft damper.

25. Install a new oil filter.

26. Refill the engine with new, clean engine oil and coolant.

27. Start the engine and check for leaks. An oil pressure gauge should be installed to verify proper engine oil pressure.

6-Cylinder Engines

▶ **See Figures 99 and 100**

1. Disconnect the negative battery cable.
2. Remove the drive belts and accessories.
3. Drain the engine coolant.
4. Raise and safely support the vehicle. Drain the engine oil.
5. Remove the crankshaft damper.
6. Remove the timing belt upper and lower covers.
7. Loosen the timing belt and crankshaft sprocket from the crankshaft.
8. Remove the 5 bolts that attach the oil pump to the block and remove the oil pump.
9. Inspect the oil pump case for damage and remove the rear cover.

10. Remove the pump rotors and inspect the inside of the case for excessive wear.

11. Check that the oil relief plunger slides smoothly and check for a broken spring. Repair or replace components as necessary.

To install:

12. Clean all parts well. Make sure the block and pump surfaces are clean and free of old sealer.

13. Assemble the pump, using new parts as required, with clean oil. Align the marks on the inner and outer rotors when assembling.

14. Install the pump's rear cover and tighten the screws to 88 inch lbs. (10 Nm).

15. Reinstall the pump relief valve, spring, gasket and valve cap. Tighten the valve cap to 30–33 ft. lbs. (41–44 Nm).

16. Prime the pump before installation by filling the rotor cavity with clean engine oil.

17. Apply gasket maker or equivalent sealer to the pump. Install the O-ring into the counter bore on the pump body discharge passage. Position the pump onto the crankshaft until seated on the block. Tighten the size M8 fasteners to 10 ft. lbs. (14 Nm) and size M10 fasteners to 30 ft. lbs. (41 Nm).

18. Install the timing belt and crankshaft sprocket.

19. Install the timing belt cover.

20. Install the crankshaft damper.

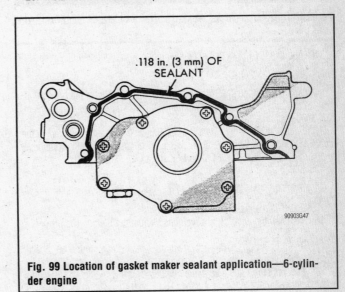

Fig. 99 Location of gasket maker sealant application—6-cylinder engine

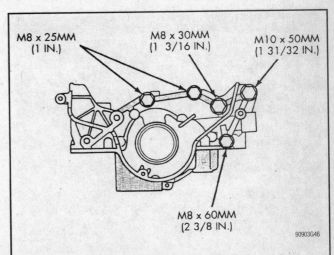

Fig. 100 Oil pump assembly mounting bolt identification and locations—6-cylinder engine

21. Install the drive belts and accessories.

22. Refill the cooling system. Install a new oil filter and refill the engine with oil.

23. Road test the vehicle. Check for proper operation as well as leaks.

Front Crankshaft Seal

REMOVAL & INSTALLATION

4-Cylinder Engines

▶ See Figure 101

1. Disconnect the negative battery cable.
2. Remove the accessory drive belts.
3. Raise and safely support the vehicle. Drain the engine oil.
4. Remove the crankshaft damper/pulley.
5. Remove the timing belt cover.
6. Remove the timing belt.
7. Remove the crankshaft sprocket.

❊❊ WARNING

Be careful as not to nick the seal surface of the crankshaft or the seal bore.

8. Remove the front crankshaft seal using a seal puller tool. Be careful not to damage the seal contact area of the crankshaft.

To install:

9. Apply a light coating of clean engine oil to the lip of the new oil seal. Install the new front crankshaft oil seal by using oil seal installer tool No. 6780-1 or an equivalent tool.

10. Place the new oil seal into the opening with the seal spring facing the inside of the engine. Be sure the oil seal is installed flush with the front cover.

11. Install the crankshaft timing belt sprocket.
12. Install the timing belt.
13. Install the timing belt cover.
14. Install the crankshaft damper/pulley.
15. Lower the vehicle.
16. Reinstall the accessory drive belts. Adjust the belts to the proper tension.
17. Refill the engine with the correct amount of clean engine oil. A filter change is recommended.
18. Reconnect the negative battery cable. Start the engine and check for leaks.

6-Cylinder Engines

▶ See Figure 101

1. Disconnect the negative battery cable.
2. Drain the engine oil.
3. Remove the accessory drive belts.
4. Remove the crankshaft damper/pulley.
5. Remove the front timing belt covers.
6. Remove the timing belt.
7. Remove the crankshaft sprocket and key.
8. Remove the front crankshaft seal by prying it out with a flat tipped prytool. Be sure to cover the end of the prytool tip with a shop towel.

❊❊ WARNING

Be careful as not to nick the seal surface of the crankshaft or the seal bore.

To install:

9. Apply a light coating of clean engine oil to the lip of the new oil seal. Install the new front crankshaft oil seal into the oil pump housing by using oil seal installer tool No. MD998717 or an equivalent tool. Be sure the oil seal is installed flush with the oil pump cover.

10. Install the crankshaft timing belt sprocket and key.
11. Install the timing belt.
12. Install the timing belt covers.
13. Install the crankshaft damper/pulley onto the crankshaft.
14. Install the accessory drive belts.
15. Fill the engine with the correct amount of clean engine oil.
16. Connect the negative battery cable. Start the engine and check for leaks.

Crankshaft Damper

REMOVAL & INSTALLATION

▶ See Figures 102, 103, 104, 105 and 106

1. Disconnect the negative battery cable.
2. Raise and safely support the vehicle. Remove the right side wheel and tire assembly.
3. Remove the right inner splash shield.
4. Remove the accessory drive belts.
5. Break the crankshaft damper bolt loose, but do not remove it.

Fig. 101 Use a seal puller tool to remove the front seal

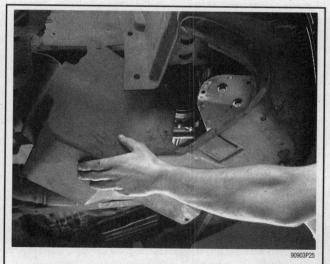

Fig. 102 Remove the right side inner fender splash shield

Fig. 103 From below the vehicle, remove the accessory drive belts

Fig. 104 If necessary, use a prying tool to wedge between the engine block and damper spoke hole, then loosen the center bolt

Fig. 105 Remove the crankshaft damper center bolt and washer

Fig. 106 Pull off the crankshaft damper, or remove using a 3-jawed puller tool

6. Remove the crankshaft damper. If necessary, attach a suitable 3-jawed puller to the crankshaft damper, then tighten the center bolt and remove the damper bolt and damper.

To install:

7. Install the crankshaft damper. It may be necessary to install the crankshaft damper using an M12-1.75 x 150mm bolt, washer, thrust bearing and nut from the crankshaft damper installation tool kit 6792 or equivalent.

8. Install the crankshaft damper bolt and tighten to the following specifications:

- 2.0L SOHC and DOHC engines—105 ft. lbs. (142 Nm).
- 2.4L engine—100 ft. lbs. (135 Nm)
- 2.5L engine—134 ft. lbs. (182 Nm)

9. Install the accessory drive belts.
10. Install the right inner splash shield. Install the right side wheel and tire assembly.
11. Carefully lower the vehicle, then connect the negative battery cable.

Timing Belt Covers

REMOVAL & INSTALLATION

2.0L SOHC Engine

♦ See Figure 107

1. Disconnect the negative battery cable.
2. Remove the accessory drive belts and accessories.
3. Remove the crankshaft damper.
4. Remove the right engine mount.
5. Place a floor jack and block of wood under the engine for support.
6. Remove the engine mount bracket.
7. Remove the front timing belt cover.

To install:

8. Install the front timing belt cover.
9. Install the engine mount bracket.
10. Install the right engine mount.
11. Remove the floor jack from under the vehicle.
12. Install the crankshaft damper.
13. Install the drive belts and accessories.
14. Install the right inner splash shield.
15. Connect the negative battery cable.
16. Check for leaks and proper engine operation.

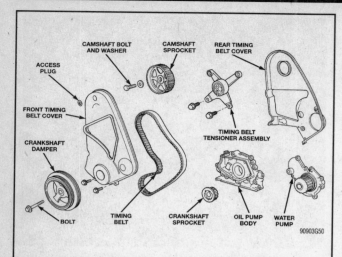

Fig. 107 Timing belt and cover assembly—shown with the mechanical belt tensioner

2.0L and 2.4L DOHC Engines

▶ See Figures 108 and 109

1. Disconnect the negative battery cable.
2. Remove the accessory drive belts.
3. Remove the crankshaft pulley.
4. Remove the power steering pump with the hose attached and position it aside.
5. Remove the power steering pump bracket, if necessary.
6. Place a floor jack under the engine oil pan, with a block of wood in between, and jack up the engine so that the weight of the engine is no longer being applied to the engine mount bracket.
7. Remove the upper engine mount and the engine mounting bracket.
8. Remove the front timing belt cover(s).

To install:

9. Install the front timing belt cover(s).
10. Lower the engine enough to install the engine mount bracket.
11. Install the bracket and remove the floor jack.
12. Install the power steering pump bracket and pump.
13. Install the crankshaft pulley.

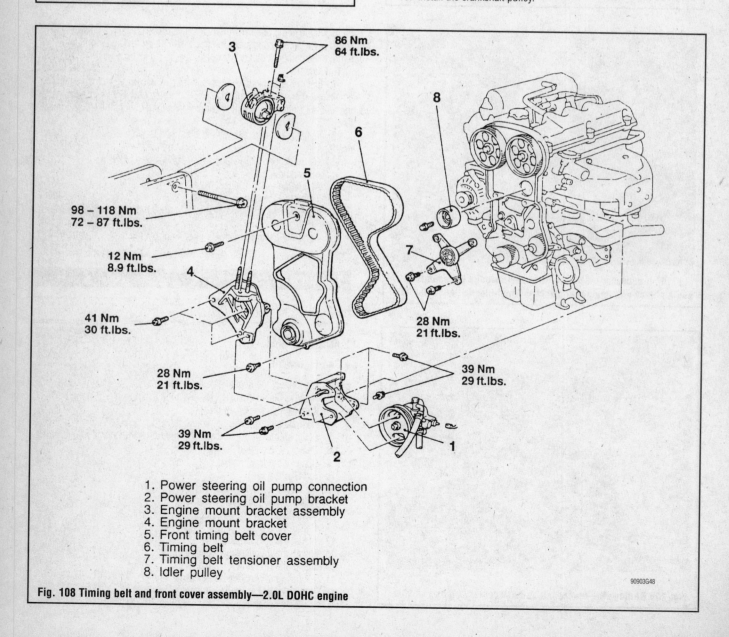

1. Power steering oil pump connection
2. Power steering oil pump bracket
3. Engine mount bracket assembly
4. Engine mount bracket
5. Front timing belt cover
6. Timing belt
7. Timing belt tensioner assembly
8. Idler pulley

Fig. 108 Timing belt and front cover assembly—2.0L DOHC engine

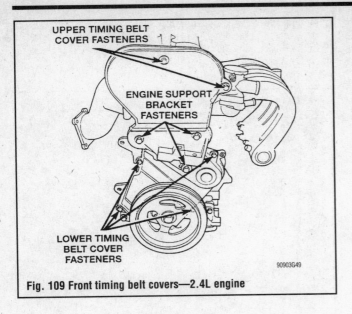

Fig. 109 Front timing belt covers—2.4L engine

Fig. 111 To access the upper right timing belt cover, remove the power steering fluid reservoir mounting bolts . . .

14. Install the accessory drive belts.
15. Connect the negative battery cable.
16. Start the engine, then check for leaks and proper engine operation.

2.5L Engine

▶ **See Figures 110 thru 122**

1. Disconnect the negative battery cable.
2. Remove the accessory drive belts.
3. Remove the crankshaft pulley.
4. Remove the power steering pump with the hose attached and position it aside.
5. Place a floor jack under the engine oil pan, with a block of wood in between, and jack up the engine so that the weight of the engine is no longer being applied to the engine support bracket.

➡ **The reamer (alignment) bolt may be heat-seized on the engine support bracket.**

6. Remove the upper engine mount. After spraying penetrating lubricant, slowly remove the reamer (alignment) bolt and remaining bolts, then remove the engine support bracket.

Fig. 112 . . . disengage the IAT and MAP sensor wiring connectors . . .

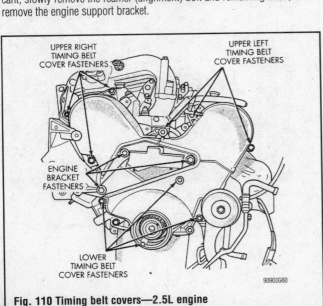

Fig. 110 Timing belt covers—2.5L engine

Fig. 113 . . . then lift up and position the power steering fluid reservoir out of the way

Fig. 114 Support the engine under the oil pan using a floor jack and a block of wood before removing the right side engine mount

Fig. 115 Remove the right side engine mount lower bolts from below the vehicle (arrows)

7. Remove the upper left timing belt cover (closest to the front of the vehicle), followed by the upper right cover and the lower cover.

➥Although the manufacturer claims that the upper right cover is removable from the top of the engine compartment, it may be easier to remove it from beneath.

To install:

8. Install the timing belt lower cover, followed by the upper right cover and the upper left cover.

9. Install the engine mounting bracket.

10. Lower the engine enough to install the engine mount onto bracket and remove the floor jack.

11. Install the power steering pump bracket and pump.

12. Install the crankshaft pulley and tighten the retaining bolt to 13 ft. lbs. (18 Nm).

13. Install the drive belts.

14. Properly fill the cooling system.

15. Connect the negative battery cable.

16. Start the engine and check for leaks. Verify proper engine and cooling system operation.

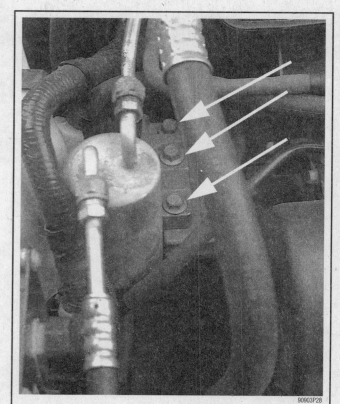

Fig. 116 Location of the right side engine mount-to-inner fender mounting bolts

Fig. 117 Location of the engine mount-to-engine attaching bolts

Fig. 118 When removing the right side engine mount assembly to access the timing belt, this mounting bolt is hidden by the lower timing belt cover

Fig. 121 Remove the upper left timing belt cover

Fig. 119 Location of the lower timing belt cover's mounting bolts (arrows)

Fig. 122 Removal of the upper right timing belt cover may be easier from underneath the vehicle

Timing Belt and Sprockets

➡For recommended timing belt replacement intervals, refer to Section 1.

REMOVAL & INSTALLATION

2.0L SOHC Engine

♦ See Figures 107 and 123

1. Disconnect the negative battery cable from the left strut tower. The ground cable is equipped with an insulator grommet, which should be placed on the stud to prevent the negative battery cable from accidentally grounding.
2. Remove the drive belts and accessories.
3. Remove the crankshaft damper.
4. Place a support under the engine and remove the right engine mount.
5. Remove the engine mount bracket
6. Remove the timing belt cover.

➡Align the camshaft and crankshaft timing marks before removing the timing belt by rotating the engine with the crankshaft.

Fig. 120 Location of the upper left timing belt cover mounting fasteners

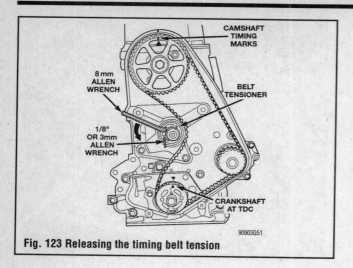

Fig. 123 Releasing the timing belt tension

7. Loosen the timing belt tensioner bolts.
8. Remove the timing belt and the tensioner.
9. Place the tensioner into a soft jawed vise to compress the tensioner.
10. If equipped with a hydraulic tensioner, after compressing the tensioner, place a pin (a ⁵⁄₆₄ in. Allen wrench will work) into the plunger side hole to retain the plunger until installation. If equipped with a mechanical tensioner, install an 8mm Allen wrench into the belt tensioner, then insert the long end of a ⅛ inch or 3mm Allen wrench into the pin hole on the front of the tensioner. Rotate the tensioner counterclockwise with the 8mm wrench, while pushing in lightly on the ⅛ inch or 3mm Allen wrench until it slides into the locking hole.
11. Remove the camshaft sprockets from the camshafts, if necessary, using a special camshaft sprocket holding tool.

To install:

12. If removed, reinstall the camshaft sprockets onto the camshaft. Install the sprocket retaining bolt and tighten to 85 ft. lbs. (115 Nm).
13. Set the crankshaft sprocket to Top Dead Center (TDC) by aligning the notch on the sprocket with the arrow on the oil pump housing, then back off the sprocket 3 notches before TDC.
14. Set the camshaft to align the timing marks.
15. Move the crankshaft to ½ notch before TDC.
16. Install the timing belt starting at the crankshaft, then around the water pump and around the camshaft last.
17. Move the crankshaft to TDC to take up the belt slack.
18. Reinstall the tensioner to the engine block, but do not tighten.
19. Tighten the tensioner fasteners as follows:
• Mechanical tensioner assembly—250 inch lbs. (28 Nm)
• Hydraulic tensioner assembly pulley bolt—50 ft. lbs. (68 Nm)
• Hydraulic tensioner assembly tensioner and pivot bracket bolt—23 ft. lbs. (31 Nm)
20. Remove the tensioner plunger pin(s). The tension is correct when the plunger pin can be removed and replaced easily.
21. Rotate the crankshaft 2 revolutions and recheck the timing marks.
22. Reinstall the timing belt cover.
23. Reinstall the engine mount bracket.
24. Reinstall the right engine mount.
25. Remove the engine support.
26. Reinstall the crankshaft damper and tighten to 105 ft. lbs. (142 Nm).
27. Reinstall the drive belts and accessories.
28. Reinstall the right inner splash shield.
29. Perform the crankshaft and camshaft "relearn" alignment procedure using the DRB scan tool or equivalent.

2.0L and 2.4L DOHC Engines

▶ **See Figures 124, 125 and 125a**

1. Disconnect the negative battery cable.
2. Remove the right inner splash shield.

3. Remove the accessory drive belts.
4. Remove the crankshaft damper.
5. Place a floor jack under the engine oil pan, with a block of wood in between, and jack up the engine slightly so that the weight of the engine is no longer on the engine mount bracket.
6. Remove the upper engine mount and the engine mounting bracket.
7. Remove the front timing belt cover(s).

✵✵ WARNING

Do not rotate the crankshaft or the camshafts after the timing belt has been removed. Damage to the valve components may occur. Before removing the timing belt, always align the timing marks.

8. Align the timing marks of the timing belt sprockets to the timing marks on the rear timing belt cover and oil pump cover.
9. If equipped with a mechanical tensioner, install a 6mm Allen wrench into the belt tensioner, then insert the long end of a ⅛ inch or 3mm Allen wrench into the pin hole on the front of the tensioner. Rotate the tensioner counterclockwise with the 6mm wrench, while pushing in lightly on the ⅛ inch or 3mm Allen wrench until it slides into the locking hole.
10. If equipped with a hydraulic tensioner, loosen the timing belt tensioner bolts
11. Remove the timing belt and, if applicable, hydraulic tensioner
12. Remove the camshaft sprockets, if necessary.
13. Remove the crankshaft sprocket, if necessary, using special removal tool No. 6793 or equivalent.
14. If equiped with a hydraulic tensioner, place the tensioner into a soft jawed vise to compress the tensioner. After compressing the tensioner, place a pin vise to compress the tensioner. After compressing the tensioner, place a pin (a ⁵⁄₆₄ in. Allen wrench will work) into the plunger side hole to retain the plunger until installation.

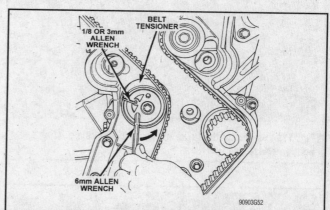

Fig. 124 Retracting and locking a mechanical timing belt tensioner

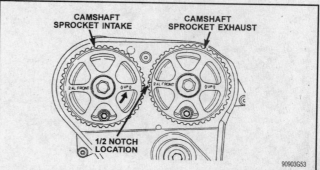

Fig. 125 Proper camshaft sprocket alignment for timing belt installation

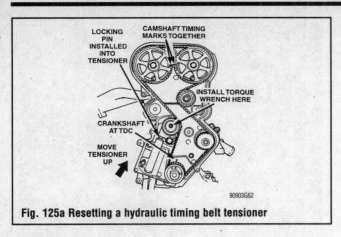

Fig. 125a Resetting a hydraulic timing belt tensioner

To install:

15. If applicable, use sprocket installation tool No. 6792 or equivalent to press the crankshaft sprocket onto the crankshaft.

16. If applicable, Install the crankshaft sprocket. Install and tighten the sprocket retaining bolts to 75 ft. lbs. (101 Nm).

17. Set the crankshaft sprocket to Top Dead Center (TDC) by aligning the notch on the sprocket with the arrow on the oil pump housing.

18. Set the camshafts timing marks so that the exhaust camshaft sprocket is ½ notch below the intake camshaft sprocket.

➡Ensure that the arrows on both camshaft sprockets are facing up.

19. Install the timing belt starting at the crankshaft, then around the water pump sprocket, idler pulley, camshaft sprockets, and then around the tensioner pulley.

20. Move the exhaust camshaft sprocket counterclockwise to align the camshaft timing marks and take up belt slack.

21. If equipped with a mechanical tensioner, remove the Allen wrench from the belt tensioner.

22. If equipped with a hydraulic tensioner, do the following:

   a. Install the tensioner to the engine block, but do not tighten.

   b. Using a torque wrech on the tensioner pulley, apply 250 inch lbs. (28 Nm) of torque to the tensioner pulley.

   c. With torque being applied to the tensioner pulley, move the tensioner up against the tensioner pulley bracket and tighten the fasteners to 275 inch lbs. (31 Nm).

   d. Remove the tensioner plunger pin. The tension is correct when the plunger pin can be removed and replaced easily.

23. Rotate the crankshaft 2 revolutions and recheck the timing marks.

24. If equipped with a hydraulic tensioner, wait a few minutes, then recheck that the plunger pin can easily be removed and installed.

25. Reinstall the front timing belt cover(s).

26. Reinstall the engine mount bracket.

27. Reinstall the right engine mount.

28. Remove the floor jack from under the vehicle.

29. Install the crankshaft damper and tighten to 105 ft. lbs. (142 Nm).

30. Install the accessory drive belts and adjust to the proper tension.

31. Install the right inner splash shield.

32. Reconnect the negative battery cable.

33. Check for leaks and proper engine operation.

2.5L Engine

▶ **See Figures 126 thru 138**

1. Disconnect the negative battery cable.

2. Raise and safely support the vehicle. Remove the right inner splash shield.

3. Remove the accessory drive belts.

4. Remove the crankshaft damper.

5. Place a suitable floor jack under the vehicle to support the engine.

6. Remove the right engine mount bracket.

7. Remove the timing belt upper left cover, followed by the upper right cover and lower cover.

8. Loosen the timing belt tensioner bolts.

➡Before removing the timing belt, be sure to align the sprocket timing marks to the timing marks on the rear timing belt cover.

Fig. 127 Timing belt and related components: timing belt (1), crankshaft sprocket (2), camshaft sprockets (3) and tensioner (4)

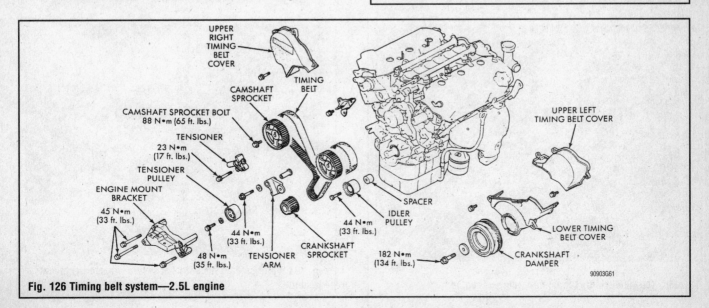

Fig. 126 Timing belt system—2.5L engine

Fig. 128 Remove the 2 timing belt tensioner mounting bolts

Fig. 131 If a sprocket holding tool is not available, one can be fabricated with a couple of nuts, long bolts and a thick, long piece of metal stock

Fig. 129 Mark the rotational direction of the timing belt if it is being removed and reused

Fig. 132 Hold the sprocket stationary with the special tool

Fig. 130 Remove the timing belt from the engine

Fig. 133 While holding the sprocket secure, loosen the mounting bolt

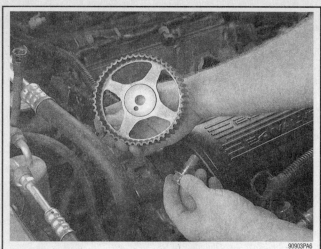

Fig. 134 Remove the sprocket and mounting bolt from the camshaft

Fig. 135 Remove the crankshaft sprocket and key

Fig. 136 After removing the timing belt tensioner, mount it in a bench vise and compress until the 2 holes of the tensioner align with each other . . .

Fig. 137 . . . then install a small diameter hex key to retain the compressed position

9. If the present timing belt is going to be reused, mark the running direction of the timing belt for installation. Remove the timing belt and the tensioner.

10. Remove the sprockets from the camshafts, if necessary, using a special camshaft sprocket holding tool.

11. Remove the crankshaft sprocket and key.

12. Place the tensioner into a soft jawed vise to compress the tensioner.

13. After compressing the tensioner, place a pin into the plunger side hole to retain the plunger until installation.

To install:

14. If removed, reinstall the sprockets onto the camshafts. Install the sprocket retaining bolts and tighten to 65 ft. lbs. (88 Nm).

15. If removed, reinstall the crankshaft sprocket and key onto the crankshaft.

16. Set the crankshaft sprocket to Top Dead Center (TDC) by aligning the notch on the sprocket with the arrow on the oil pump housing, then back off the sprocket 3 notches before TDC.

17. Set the camshafts so that their sprockets' timing marks align with those on the rear timing belt cover.

18. Install the timing belt on the right camshaft sprocket (the one closest to the firewall) first.

Fig. 138 Line up the crankshaft sprocket's timing mark with that on the oil pump housing

19. Install a binder clip on the belt to the sprocket so that it won't slip out of position.

20. Keeping the belt taut, install it under the water pump pulley and around the left camshaft sprocket.

21. Install a binder clip on the left camshaft sprocket and belt.

22. Rotate the crankshaft to TDC.

23. Continue routing the belt by the idler pulley and around the crankshaft sprocket to the tensioner pulley.

24. Remove the binder clips.

25. Move the crankshaft sprocket clockwise to TDC to take up the belt slack. Check that all timing marks are in alignment.

26. Reinstall the tensioner to the block, but do not tighten.

27. Using special tool No. MD998767 and a torque wrench on the tensioner pulley, apply 39 inch lbs. (4.4 Nm) of torque to the tensioner. Tighten the tensioner pulley bolt to 35 ft. lbs. (48 Nm).

28. With torque being applied to the tensioner pulley, move the tensioner up against the tensioner bracket and tighten the fasteners to 17 ft. lbs. (23 Nm).

29. Remove the tensioner plunger pin. The tension is correct when the plunger pin can be removed and replaced easily.

30. Rotate the crankshaft 2 revolutions clockwise and recheck the timing marks. Check to make sure the tensioner plunger pin can be easily installed and removed. If the pin does not remove and install easily, perform the procedure again.

31. Install the lower timing belt cover, followed by the upper right cover and upper left cover.

32. Install the engine mount bracket.

33. Install the right engine mount.

34. Remove the engine support.

35. Install the crankshaft damper and tighten to 134 ft. lbs. (182 Nm).

36. Install the accessory drive belts and adjust to proper tension.

37. Install the right inner splash shield.

Camshaft

REMOVAL & INSTALLATION

2.0L SOHC Engine

✳✳ CAUTION

Fuel injection systems remain under pressure, even after the engine has been turned OFF. The fuel system pressure MUST be relieved before disconnecting any fuel lines. Failure to do so may result in fire and/or personal injury.

1. Disconnect the negative battery cable from the left strut tower. The ground cable is equipped with an insulator grommet, which should be placed on the stud to prevent the negative battery cable from accidentally grounding.

2. Make sure the engine is cool before starting cylinder head removal.

3. Properly relieve the fuel system pressure, as described in Section 5.

4. Place a large drain pan under the vehicle's radiator drain plug. Open the drain plug and drain out the engine coolant.

5. Remove the complete air cleaner assembly.

6. Label the spark plug wires to the correct spark plugs. Disconnect the spark plug wires from each spark plug.

7. Remove the ignition coil pack.

8. Remove the rocker arm (valve) cover retaining bolts and remove the valve cover. Be sure to remove and discard the old gasket material. Clean the cylinder head and cover gasket mating surfaces. Inspect the gasket mating surfaces for flatness.

9. Mark the rocker arm shaft assemblies to identify them for later installation.

10. Remove the rocker arm shaft bolts and remove the rocker arm assemblies from the cylinder head.

11. Remove the timing belt and camshaft sprocket, using the procedure given earlier in this section.

12. Remove the cylinder head, following the procedure given earlier in this section.

13. Remove the camshaft position sensor, then remove the camshaft from the rear of the cylinder head.

To install:

➡**The cylinder head bolts should be checked for stretching before reuse. If the thread area of the bolt is "necked down," the bolts must be replaced with new ones. In any event, new head bolts are recommended.**

14. If the rocker arms and shaft are to be serviced, mark the rocker arms so any that are to be returned to service will be installed in their original locations.

15. Reinstall the rocker arm back on the rocker arm shaft.

16. To install the camshaft, lubricate the bearing journals thoroughly. Install the camshaft into the cylinder head carefully. Make sure it turns freely. If the camshaft installation is satisfactory, install the camshaft position sensor and tighten the screws to 85 inch lbs. (9.6 Nm).

17. Check camshaft end-play.

18. Install the camshaft seal. The camshaft must be installed before the camshaft seal is installed. The seal should be flush with the cylinder head after installation.

19. Reinstall the camshaft sprocket and tighten the bolt to 85 ft. lbs. (115 Nm).

20. Reinstall the cylinder head using the recommended procedure. Be sure to use new cylinder head mounting bolts.

21. Before installing the rocker arm and shaft assemblies, set the crankshaft to 3 notches before TDC on the crankshaft sprocket.

22. Reinstall the rocker arm and shaft assemblies.

23. Reinstall the camshaft sprocket and timing belt as described earlier in this section, taking care to align all valve timing marks.

24. Reinstall the valve cover, along with a new gasket. Tighten the retaining bolts to 105 inch lbs. (12 Nm).

25. Reinstall the ignition coil pack and tighten the retaining fasteners to 200 inch lbs. (23 Nm).

26. Reinstall the complete air cleaner assembly.

27. Reconnect the spark plug wires to the correct spark plugs.

28. Check to be sure all electrical, vacuum and fluid connections have been reconnected properly.

29. Refill the cooling system. An oil and filter change is recommended.

30. Reconnect the negative battery cable.

31. Start the engine and check for leaks. Run the engine with the radiator cap off, to allow the engine to warm up and the thermostat to open; if necessary, add coolant to the radiator.

32. Shut down the engine and allow it to cool. Verify the correct fluid levels. Test drive the vehicle to check for proper operation.

2.0L and 2.4L DOHC Engines

▶ **See Figures 139, 140, 141 and 142**

1. Disconnect the negative battery cable.

✳✳ CAUTION

Fuel injection systems remain under pressure, even after the engine has been turned OFF. The fuel system pressure MUST be relieved before disconnecting any fuel lines. Failure to do so may result in fire and/or personal injury.

2. Properly relieve the fuel system pressure, as described in Section 5.

3. Label and disconnect the spark plug wires from the spark plugs.

4. Remove the ignition coil pack and spark plug wires.

5. Remove the rocker arm (valve) cover retaining fasteners and remove the valve cover from the cylinder head. Discard the old valve cover gasket.

6. Detach the engine ground strap.

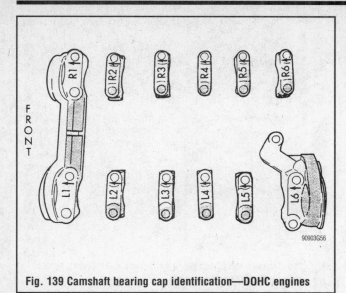

Fig. 139 Camshaft bearing cap identification—DOHC engines

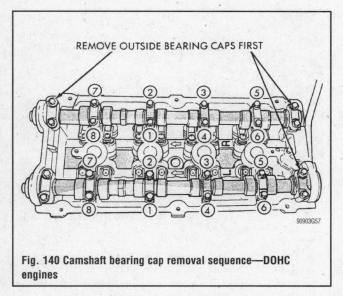

Fig. 140 Camshaft bearing cap removal sequence—DOHC engines

properly positioned. Install the camshaft followers in their original positions on the hydraulic adjuster and valve stem.

✷✷ WARNING

Make sure NONE of the pistons are at Top Dead Center (TDC) when installing the camshafts.

15. Lubricate the camshaft bearing journals and camshaft followers with clean engine oil and install the camshafts. Install the right and left camshaft bearing caps No. 2 through No. 5 and right side No. 6. Tighten the M6 fasteners to 105 inch lbs. (12 Nm) in the correct sequence.

16. Apply Mopar® Gasket Maker or equivalent sealer to the No. 1 and left side No. 6 bearing caps. Install the bearing caps and tighten the M8 fasteners to 250 inch lbs. (28 Nm). The end caps must be installed before the seals can be installed.

17. Install the camshaft end seals.

18. Reinstall the camshaft sprockets, if removed. Install the timing belt, taking care to make sure all timing marks are properly aligned, using the recommended procedure. Use care. DO NOT allow oil or solvents to contact the timing belt, as they can deteriorate the rubber and cause tooth skipping.

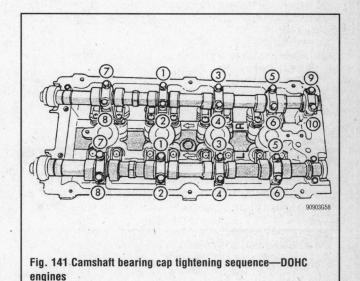

Fig. 141 Camshaft bearing cap tightening sequence—DOHC engines

7. Remove the timing belt covers, timing belt and camshaft sprockets, as described earlier in this section.

8. Remove the camshaft bearing caps, beginning with the outer ones. Take note that the caps are numbered for correct location during installation.

9. Loosen, but do not remove, the camshaft bearing cap retaining fasteners in the correct sequence, from the inside working outward. Perform this step on one camshaft at a time.

10. Identify the camshafts, if they are to be reused, for later installation. The camshafts are not interchangeable. Remove the camshaft bearing caps, then remove the camshafts.

11. Remove the camshaft followers. Any components that are to be reused must be installed in their original locations. Use care to identify and mark the positions of any removed valve train components, so they may be reinstalled correctly.

12. Inspect the camshaft bearing oil feed holes in the cylinder head for clogging. Inspect the camshaft bearing journals for wear or scoring. Check the camshaft surface for abnormal wear and damage. A visible worn groove in the roller path or on the camshaft lobes is cause for replacement.

To install:

13. Thoroughly clean the camshafts and related parts.

14. The hydraulic valve lash adjusters are inside the roller camshaft followers. Make sure they are clean, well lubricated with clean engine oil and

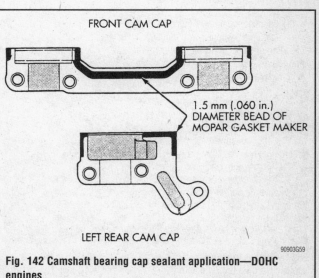

Fig. 142 Camshaft bearing cap sealant application—DOHC engines

Verify that all timing marks are correct. If the timing belt or sprockets are incorrectly installed, engine damage will occur. Take time to make sure all timing marks are correctly aligned.

19. Install the timing belt covers.
20. Clean all valve cover sealing surfaces. Make certain the rails are flat.
21. Install a new valve cover gasket. Apply Mopar Silicone Rubber Adhesive Sealant, or equivalent, at the camshaft cap corners and at the top edge of the ½ round seal.

➡Inspect the spark plug well seals for cracking and/or swelling, and replace if necessary.

22. Install the valve cover assembly to the cylinder head and tighten the fasteners in sequence, using the following 3 steps:
   a. First: tighten all valve cover fasteners to 40 inch lbs. (4.5 Nm).
   b. Second: tighten all fasteners to 80 inch lbs. (9 Nm).
   c. Third: tighten all fasteners to 105 inch lbs. (12 Nm).
23. Install the ignition coil pack and connect the spark plug wiring to the correct spark plugs. Tighten the coil pack retaining fasteners to 105 inch lbs. (12 Nm).
24. Reconnect the engine ground strap.
25. Check to be sure all vacuum lines and remaining wiring have been reconnected.
26. An oil and filter change is recommended.
27. Reconnect the negative battery cable and test run vehicle. Check for leaks and for proper operation.

2.5L Engine

◆ See Figures 143, 144, 145 and 146

➡For camshaft service, the cylinder head must be removed.

✳✳ **CAUTION**

Fuel injection systems remain under pressure, even after the engine has been turned OFF. The fuel system pressure MUST be relieved before disconnecting any fuel lines. Failure to do so may result in fire and/or personal injury.

1. Disconnect the negative battery cable.
2. Properly relieve the fuel system pressure, as described in Section 5.
3. Place a large drain pan under the radiator drain plug. Drain the cooling system.

Fig. 144 Remove the thrust plate and inspect the O-ring gasket for wear; replace if necessary

Fig. 145 Carefully pull the camshaft out of the rear of the cylinder head

Fig. 143 Remove the thrust plate mounting bolts from the left (front) cylinder head

Fig. 146 After removing the camshaft from the cylinder head, inspect it for wear

4. Remove the timing belt covers, timing belt and camshaft sprockets, as described earlier in this section.

5. The intake manifold is a two-piece unit. The upper part is a large air intake plenum of aluminum alloy. Use care working with light alloy parts. Remove the air intake plenum first, then remove the lower intake manifold.

6. Remove the valve cover(s).

7. Remove the cylinder head bolts and remove the cylinder head(s) from the vehicle.

8. If working on the left cylinder head, remove the thrust plate, then withdraw the camshaft from the rear of the head.

9. If working on the right cylinder head, and if not already done, remove the distributor, then withdraw the camshaft from the rear of the head.

To install:

10. Lubricate the camshaft journals and carefully install the camshaft into the cylinder head. Install the thrust plate and tighten the fasteners to 9 ft. lbs. (13 Nm).

11. Apply a light coating of engine oil to the camshaft oil seal lip and install the camshaft seal. The camshaft must be installed before installing the seal. Be sure the seal is installed flush with the cylinder head surface. Install the camshaft sprocket and tighten to 65 ft. lbs. (88 Nm).

12. Install the cylinder head(s).

13. Install the lower intake manifold, using new gaskets.

14. Install the rocker arm and shaft assemblies.

15. Install the timing belt.

16. Inspect the spark plug tube seals located on the ends of each tube. These seals slide onto each tube to seal the valve cover to the spark plug tube. If these seals show signs of hardness and/or cracks, they should be replaced.

17. Install the valve cover(s). Reconnect the spark plug wires.

18. Install the intake manifold plenum.

19. Connect the throttle and speed control cables.

20. Install the air inlet resonator, air inlet hose and air cleaner housing cover.

21. Check to be sure all remaining electrical connectors have been re-attached. Tighten the air tube connections.

22. Refill the cooling system. An oil and filter change is recommended whenever a cylinder head has been removed, since coolant can get into the lubrication system.

23. Reconnect the negative battery cable. Start the engine and check for leaks, abnormal noises and vibrations. Bleed the cooling system.

INSPECTION

4-Cylinder Engines

♦ **See Figures 147 and 148**

1. Thoroughly clean all parts. Inspect the camshaft journals for scoring. Check the oil feed holes in the cylinder head for blockage. Check the camshaft bearing journals for scoring. If light scratches are present, they may be removed with 400 grit abrasive paper. If deep scratches are present, replace the camshaft and check the cylinder head for damage. Replace the cylinder head if worn or damaged.

2. If the camshaft lobes show signs of wear, check the corresponding rocker arm roller for wear or damage. Replace any rocker arms/hydraulic lash adjusters which are worn or damaged. If the camshaft lobes show signs of pitting on the nose, flank or base circle, replace the camshaft.

3. Camshaft end-play should be checked using the following procedure:

a. On the DOHC engines, oil the camshaft journals and install the camshaft **WITHOUT** the camshaft follower assemblies. Install the rear camshaft bearing caps and tighten to 250 inch lbs. (28 Nm). On the SOHC engines, oil the camshaft journals and install the camshaft **WITHOUT** the rocker arm assemblies. Install the camshaft position sensor and tighten the screws to 85 inch lbs. (9.6 Nm).

b. Carefully push the camshaft as far rearward as it will go.

c. Set up a dial indicator to bear against the front of the camshaft (the sprocket end). Zero the indicator.

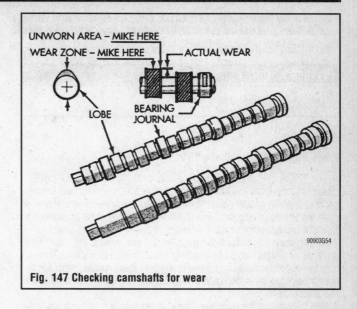

Fig. 147 Checking camshafts for wear

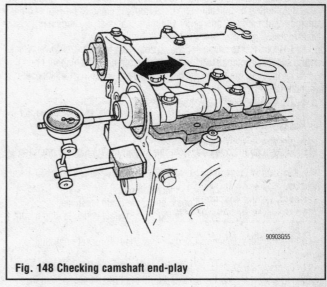

Fig. 148 Checking camshaft end-play

d. Move the camshaft forward as far as it will go. Read the dial indicator. End-play specification is 0.002–0.010 in. (0.05–0.15mm) for DOHC models, and 0.005–0.013 in. (0.13–0.33mm).

e. If excessive end-play is present, inspect the cylinder head and camshaft for wear; replace if necessary.

6-Cylinder Engines

♦ **See Figures 147 and 148**

1. Inspect the camshafts carefully for scratches or worn areas. If light scratches are seen, they may be removed with 400 grit sandpaper. If there are deep scratches, replace the camshaft.

2. Inspect the cylinder head for damage.

3. Check the oil feed holes to make sure they are open and free of debris.

4. If the camshaft lobes show signs of wear, check the corresponding rocker arm roller for wear or damage. Replace the rocker arm if worn or damaged. If the camshaft shows signs of wear on the lobes, replace it.

5. Check camshaft end-play. Oil the camshaft journals with clean engine oil and install the camshaft **WITHOUT** the rocker arm assemblies. Move the camshaft as far rearward as it will go. Mount a dial indicator to bear on

the front of the camshaft. Zero the indicator. Move the camshaft as far forward as it will go. End-play should be 0.004–0.008 in. (0.1–0.2mm). Maximum allowed end-play is 0.016 in. (0.4mm).

Balance Shaft

REMOVAL & INSTALLATION

2.4L Engine

▶ See Figures 149, 150 and 151

The 2.4L engine is equipped with 2 balance shafts installed in a carrier mounted to the lower crankcase. These balance shafts interconnect through gears to rotate in opposite directions. The gears are powered by a short, crankshaft-driven chain and rotate at 2 times the speed of the crankshaft. This will counterbalance certain reciprocating masses of the engine.

An oil passage from the No. 1 main bearing cap through the balance shaft carrier support leg provides lubrication to the balance shafts. This passage directly supplies engine oil to the front bearings and internal machined passages in the shafts that routes engine oil from the front to the rear shaft bearing journals.

Please note that this procedure requires removal of the timing belt. Valve train timing is critical to engine performance and to prevent engine damage. Work carefully and verify all timing marks as the engine is reassembled.

1. Disconnect the negative battery cable from the left strut tower. The ground cable is equipped with an insulator grommet, which should be placed on the stud to prevent the negative battery cable from accidentally grounding.
2. Remove the accessory drive belts. Refer to Section 1.
3. Remove the timing belt covers and timing belt, as outlined earlier in this section.
4. Raise and safely support the vehicle.
5. Place a large drain pan under the oil pan drain plug and drain the engine oil.
6. Remove the oil pump and oil pan.
7. Remove the balance shaft drive chain cover.
8. Remove the drive chain guide and drive chain tensioner.
9. Remove the gear cover retaining stud (double ended to also mount the drive chain guide).
10. Remove the balance shaft gear and chain sprocket retaining screws.
11. Remove the drive chain and chain sprocket assembly by using 2 prybars to work the sprocket back and forth until it is removed from the crankshaft.
12. Remove the gear cover and balance shafts.
13. Remove the 4 balance shaft carrier-to-crankcase mounting bolts, then separate the carrier from the engine bedplate.

To install:

14. Install the balance shafts into the carrier and place the carrier into proper position against the engine bedplate. Install and tighten the 4 mounting bolts to 40 ft. lbs. (54 Nm).
15. Rotate the balance shafts until both balance shaft keyways are pointed up parallel to the vertical centerline of the engine.
16. Reinstall the short hub drive gear onto the sprocket driven balance shaft and the long hub gear onto the chain driven shaft. Once the gears are installed onto the shafts, the gear and balance shaft keyways must be up, and gear alignment dots properly meshed.
17. Reinstall the gear cover and retaining stud fastener. Tighten the double ended retaining stud fastener to 105 inch lbs. (12 Nm).
18. Reinstall the drive chain's crankshaft sprocket. Be sure to align the flat on the sprocket to the flat on the crankshaft, with the sprocket facing front.
19. Rotate the crankshaft until the No. 1 cylinder is at Top Dead Center (TDC). The timing marks on the chain sprocket should align with the parting line on the left side of No. 1 main bearing cap.

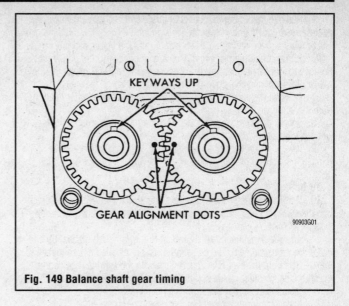

Fig. 149 Balance shaft gear timing

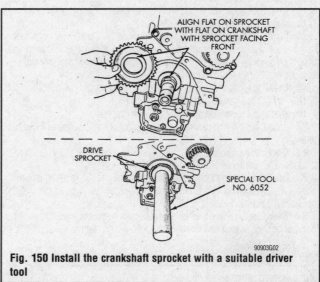

Fig. 150 Install the crankshaft sprocket with a suitable driver tool

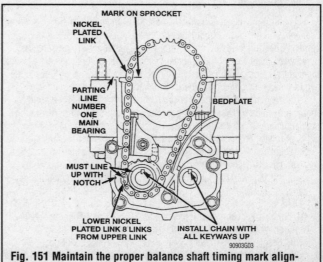

Fig. 151 Maintain the proper balance shaft timing mark alignment

20. Place the drive chain around the crankshaft sprocket so the nickel plated link of the chain is on the No. 1 cylinder timing mark of the crankshaft sprocket.

21. Reinstall the balance shaft sprocket into the drive chain. Be sure the timing mark on the balance shaft sprocket (yellow dot) lines up with lower nickel plated link on the chain.

22. With the keyways of the balance shaft pointing up in the 12 o'clock position, slide the balance shaft drive chain sprocket onto the end of the balance shaft. If necessary to allow for clearance, the balance shaft may be pushed in slightly.

➡**The lower nickel plated link, timing mark on the balance shaft sprocket, and arrow on the side of the gear cover should all line up when the balance shafts are properly timed.**

23. If the sprockets are timed correctly, install the balance shaft bolts and tighten to 250 inch lbs. (28 Nm). It may be necessary to place a wooden block between the crankcase and crankshaft counterbalance to prevent crankshaft and gear rotation.

24. Install the drive chain tensioner, but keep it loose at this point.

25. Position the drive chain guide onto the double ended stud fastener. Be sure the tab on the guide fits into the slot on the gear cover. Install the nut/washer assembly and tighten to 105 inch lbs. (12 Nm).

26. Place a shim 0.039 in. x 2.75 in. (1mm x 70mm) long between the tensioner and chain. Push the tensioner and shim up against the chain. Apply pressure of 5.5–6.6 lbs. directly behind the adjustment slot to take up the slack. Be sure the chain makes shoe radius contact.

27. With the pressure applied, tighten the top tensioner adjustment bolt first, then the lower pivot bolt. Tighten the bolts to 105 inch lbs. (12 Nm). Remove the shim after tightening the bolts.

28. Install the chain cover and tighten the screws to 105 inch lbs. (12 Nm).

29. Install oil pump and oil pan.

30. Install the oil pan drain plug and gasket. Tighten the drain plug to 25 ft. lbs. (34 Nm).

31. Lower the vehicle.

32. Install the timing belt and timing belt covers, as described earlier in this section. It is very important that all valve timing marks align properly, or engine damage will result.

33. Install the accessory drive belts, and adjust as necessary.

34. Refill the engine with new, clean engine oil to the proper level. An oil filter change is also recommended.

35. Reconnect the negative battery cable. Start the engine and check for leaks.

Rear Crankshaft Oil Seal

REMOVAL & INSTALLATION

4-Cylinder Engines

▶ **See Figures 152 and 153**

1. Disconnect the negative battery cable. On Cirrus, Stratus, Sebring convertible and Breeze models, disconnect the remote negative battery connection from the left strut tower.

2. Remove the transaxle and flexplate/flywheel. Refer to Section 7.

3. Remove the rear crankshaft oil seal from the oil seal housing, using a suitable flat bladed prying tool.

To install:

➡**When installing the seal, there is no need to lubricate the sealing surface.**

4. Install the seal into its housing using a suitable installation tool.

5. Install the transaxle and flexplate/flywheel assembly, as described in Section 7.

6. Reconnect the negative battery cable. Start the engine and check for leaks.

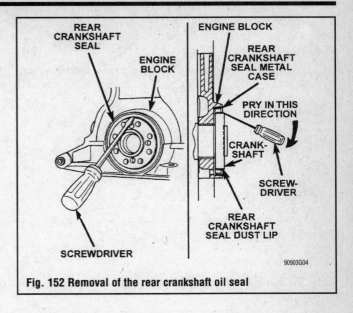

Fig. 152 Removal of the rear crankshaft oil seal

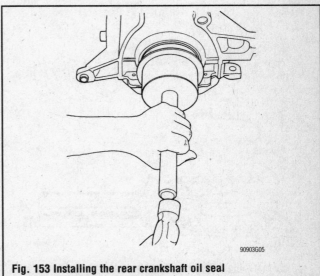

Fig. 153 Installing the rear crankshaft oil seal

6-Cylinder Engines

▶ **See Figures 154, 155 and 156**

1. Disconnect the negative battery cable. On Cirrus, Stratus, Sebring convertible and Breeze models, disconnect the remote negative battery connection from the left strut tower.

2. Remove the transaxle and flexplate/flywheel. Refer to Section 7.

3. Remove the 5 rear seal housing mounting bolts.

4. Remove the housing from the engine.

5. Remove the rear crankshaft oil seal from the oil seal housing, using a suitable flat bladed prying tool.

To install:

➡**When installing the seal, there is no need to lubricate the sealing surface.**

6. Install the seal into its housing using a suitable installation tool.

7. Apply silicone rubber adhesive sealant to the mating surface of the seal housing.

8. Apply a light coating of engine oil to the entire oil seal lip circumference.

9. Install the oil seal and housing to the engine cylinder block. Install and tighten the mounting bolts to 96 inch lbs. (11 Nm).

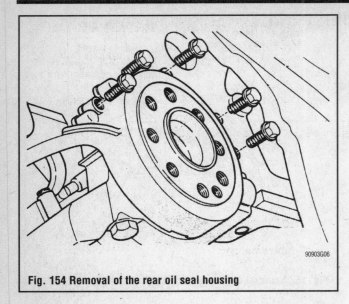
Fig. 154 Removal of the rear oil seal housing

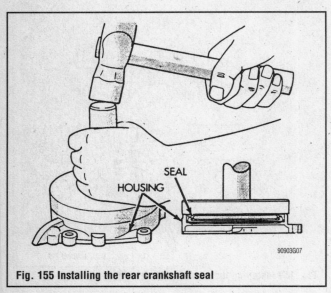
Fig. 155 Installing the rear crankshaft seal

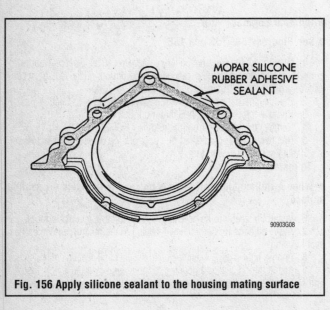
Fig. 156 Apply silicone sealant to the housing mating surface

10. Install the transaxle and flexplate/flywheel assembly, as described in Section 7.

11. Reconnect the negative battery cable. Start the engine and check for leaks.

Flywheel/Flexplate

REMOVAL & INSTALLATION

▶ **See Figure 157**

The flywheel on manual transaxle cars serves as the forward clutch engagement surface. It also serves as the ring gear with which the starter pinion engages to crank the engine. The most common reason to replace the flywheel is broken teeth on the starter ring gear.

On automatic transaxle cars, the torque converter actually forms part of the flywheel. It is bolted to a thin flexplate which, in turn, is bolted to the crankshaft. The flexplate also serves as the ring gear with which the starter pinion engages in engine cranking. The flexplate occasionally cracks; the teeth on the ring gear may also break, especially if the starter is often engaged while the pinion is still spinning. The torque converter and flexplate are separated, so the converter and transaxle can be removed together.

1. Remove the transaxle from the vehicle. For more information, refer to Section 7.

2. On vehicles equipped with a manual transaxle, remove the clutch assembly from the flywheel, as described in Section 7.

3. Support the flywheel in a secure manner (the flywheel on manual transaxle-equipped vehicles can be heavy).

4. Matchmark the flywheel/flexplate to the rear flange of the crankshaft.

5. Remove the attaching bolts and pull the flywheel/flexplate from the crankshaft.

To install:

6. Clean the flywheel/flexplate attaching bolts, the flywheel/flexplate and the rear crankshaft mounting flange.

7. Position the flywheel/flexplate onto the crankshaft flange so that the matchmarks align.

8. Coat the threads of the attaching bolts with Loctite® Thread Locker 271, or equivalent, to help ensure that the attaching bolts will not work loose. Install the bolts finger-tight.

9. Tighten the attaching bolts in a crisscross fashion in 3 even steps to 68–70 ft. lbs. (92–95 Nm).

10. For manual transaxle-equipped vehicles, install the clutch assembly. For more information, refer to Section 7.

11. Install the transaxle, as described in Section 7.

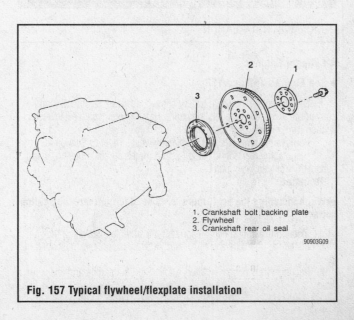
1. Crankshaft bolt backing plate
2. Flywheel
3. Crankshaft rear oil seal

Fig. 157 Typical flywheel/flexplate installation

EXHAUST SYSTEM

Inspection

▶ See Figures 158 thru 165

➡Safety glasses should be worn at all times when working on or near the exhaust system. Older exhaust systems will almost always be covered with loose rust particles which will shower you when disturbed. These particles are more than a nuisance and could injure your eye.

✳ CAUTION

DO NOT perform exhaust repairs or inspection with the engine or exhaust hot. Allow the system to cool completely before attempting any work. Exhaust systems are noted for sharp edges, flaking metal and rusted bolts. Gloves and eye protection are required. A healthy supply of penetrating oil and rags is highly recommended.

Your vehicle must be raised and supported safely to inspect the exhaust system properly. By placing 4 safety stands under the vehicle for support should provide enough room for you to slide under the vehicle and inspect the system completely. Start the inspection at the exhaust manifold or turbocharger pipe where the header pipe is attached and work

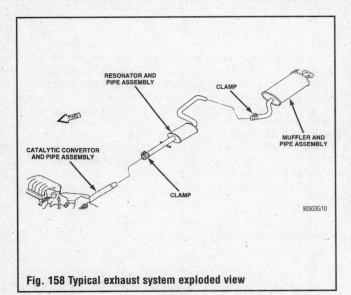

Fig. 158 Typical exhaust system exploded view

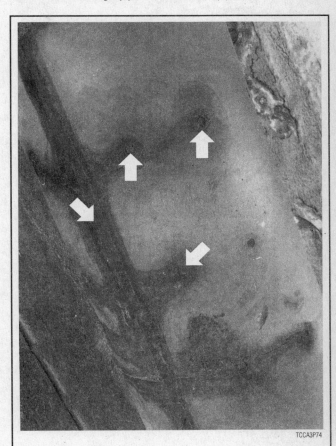

Fig. 160 Check the muffler for rotted spot welds and seams

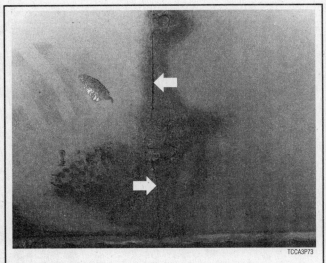

Fig. 159 Cracks in the muffler are guaranteed to cause a leak

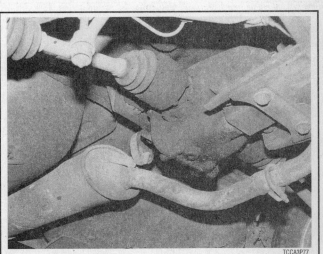

Fig. 161 Make sure the exhaust components are not contacting the body or suspension

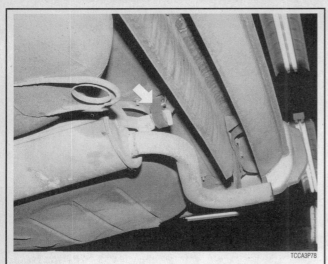
Fig. 162 Check for overstretched or torn exhaust hangers

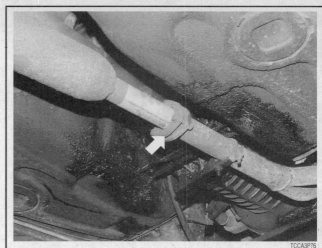
Fig. 165 Some systems, like this one, use large O-rings (donuts) in between the flanges

Fig. 163 Example of a badly deteriorated exhaust pipe

your way to the back of the vehicle. On dual exhaust systems, remember to inspect both sides of the vehicle. Check the complete exhaust system for open seams, holes loose connections, or other deterioration which could permit exhaust fumes to seep into the passenger compartment. Inspect all mounting brackets and hangers for deterioration, some models may have rubber O-rings that can be overstretched and non-supportive. These components will need to be replaced if found. It has always been a practice to use a pointed tool to poke up into the exhaust system where the deterioration spots are to see whether or not they crumble. Some models may have heat shield covering certain parts of the exhaust system, it will be necessary to remove these shields to have the exhaust visible for inspection also.

REPLACEMENT

◗ **See Figure 166**

There are basically two types of exhaust systems. One is the flange type where the component ends are attached with bolts and a gasket in-between. The other exhaust system is the slip joint type. These components slip into one another using clamps to retain them together.

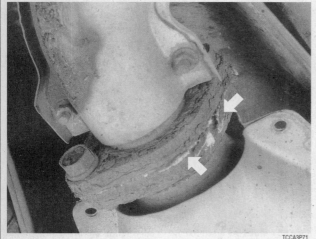
Fig. 164 Inspect flanges for gaskets that have deteriorated and need replacement

Fig. 166 Nuts and bolts will be extremely difficult to remove when deteriorated with rust

Allow the exhaust system to cool sufficiently before spraying a solvent exhaust fasteners. Some solvents are highly flammable and could ignite when sprayed on hot exhaust components.

Before removing any component of the exhaust system, ALWAYS squirt a liquid rust dissolving agent onto the fasteners for ease of removal. A lot of knuckle skin will be saved by following this rule. It may even be wise to spray the fasteners and allow them to sit overnight.

Flange Type

▶ **See Figure 167**

Do NOT perform exhaust repairs or inspection with the engine or exhaust hot. Allow the system to cool completely before attempting any work. Exhaust systems are noted for sharp edges, flaking metal and rusted bolts. Gloves and eye protection are required. A healthy supply of penetrating oil and rags is highly recommended. Never spray liquid rust dissolving agent onto a hot exhaust component.

Before removing any component on a flange type system, ALWAYS squirt a liquid rust dissolving agent onto the fasteners for ease of removal.

Start by unbolting the exhaust piece at both ends (if required). When unbolting the headpipe from the manifold, make sure that the bolts are free before trying to remove them. if you snap a stud in the exhaust manifold, the stud will have to be removed with a bolt extractor, which often means removal of the manifold itself. Next, disconnect the component from the mounting; slight twisting and turning may be required to remove the component completely from the vehicle. You may need to tap on the component with a rubber mallet to loosen the component. If all else fails, use a hacksaw to separate the parts. An oxy-acetylene cutting torch may be faster but the sparks are DANGEROUS near the fuel tank, and at the very least, accidents could happen, resulting in damage to the under-car parts, not to mention yourself.

Slip Joint Type

▶ **See Figure 168**

Before removing any component on the slip joint type exhaust system, ALWAYS squirt a liquid rust dissolving agent onto the fasteners for ease of removal. Start by unbolting the exhaust piece at both ends (if required). When unbolting the headpipe from the manifold, make sure that the bolts are free before trying to remove them. if you snap a stud in the exhaust manifold, the stud will have to be removed with a bolt extractor, which often means removal of the manifold itself. Next, remove the mounting U-bolts from around the exhaust pipe you are extracting from the vehicle. Don't be surprised if the U-bolts break while removing the nuts. Loosen the exhaust pipe from any mounting brackets retaining it to the floor pan and separate the components.

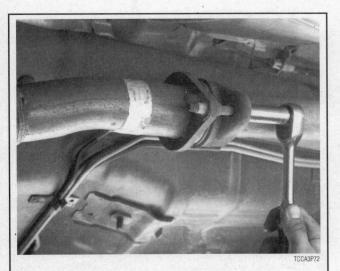

TCCA3P72

Fig. 167 Example of a flange type exhaust system joint

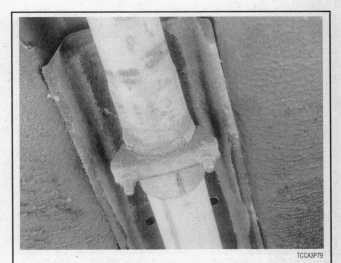

TCCA3P79

Fig. 168 Example of a common slip joint type system

ENGINE RECONDITIONING

Determining Engine Condition

Anything that generates heat and/or friction will eventually burn or wear out (ie. a light bulb generates heat, therefore its life span is limited). With this in mind, a running engine generates tremendous amounts of both; friction is encountered by the moving and rotating parts inside the engine and heat is created by friction and combustion of the fuel. However, the engine has systems designed to help reduce the effects of heat and friction and provide added longevity. The oiling system reduces the amount of friction encountered by the moving parts inside the engine, while the cooling system reduces heat created by friction and combustion. If either system is not maintained, a break-down will be inevitable. Therefore, you can see how regular maintenance can affect the service life of your vehicle. If you do not drain, flush and refill your cooling system at the proper intervals, deposits will begin to accumulate in the radiator, thereby reducing the amount of

heat it can extract from the coolant. The same applies to your oil and filter; if it is not changed often enough it becomes laden with contaminates and is unable to properly lubricate the engine. This increases friction and wear.

There are a number of methods for evaluating the condition of your engine. A compression test can reveal the condition of your pistons, piston rings, cylinder bores, head gasket(s), valves and valve seats. An oil pressure test can warn you of possible engine bearing, or oil pump failures. Excessive oil consumption, evidence of oil in the engine air intake area and/or bluish smoke from the tail pipe may indicate worn piston rings, worn valve guides and/or valve seals. As a general rule, an engine that uses no more than one quart of oil every 1000 miles is in good condition. Engines that use one quart of oil or more in less than 1000 miles should first be checked for oil leaks. If any oil leaks are present, have them fixed before determining how much oil is consumed by the engine, especially if blue smoke is not visible at the tail pipe.

COMPRESSION TEST

▶ See Figure 169

A noticeable lack of engine power, excessive oil consumption and/or poor fuel mileage measured over an extended period are all indicators of internal engine wear. Worn piston rings, scored or worn cylinder bores, blown head gaskets, sticking or burnt valves, and worn valve seats are all possible culprits. A check of each cylinder's compression will help locate the problem.

➡**A screw-in type compression gauge is more accurate than the type you simply hold against the spark plug hole. Although it takes slightly longer to use, it's worth the effort to obtain a more accurate reading.**

1. Make sure that the proper amount and viscosity of engine oil is in the crankcase, then ensure the battery is fully charged.
2. Warm-up the engine to normal operating temperature, then shut the engine **OFF**.
3. Disable the ignition system.
4. Label and disconnect all of the spark plug wires from the plugs.
5. Thoroughly clean the cylinder head area around the spark plug ports, then remove the spark plugs.
6. Set the throttle plate to the fully open (wide-open throttle) position. You can block the accelerator linkage open for this, or you can have an assistant fully depress the accelerator pedal.
7. Install a screw-in type compression gauge into the No. 1 spark plug hole until the fitting is snug.

❊❊ WARNING

Be careful not to crossthread the spark plug hole.

8. According to the tool manufacturer's instructions, connect a remote starting switch to the starting circuit.
9. With the ignition switch in the **OFF** position, use the remote starting switch to crank the engine through at least five compression strokes (approximately 5 seconds of cranking) and record the highest reading on the gauge.
10. Repeat the test on each cylinder, cranking the engine approximately the same number of compression strokes and/or time as the first.
11. Compare the highest readings from each cylinder to that of the others. The indicated compression pressures are considered within specifications if the lowest reading cylinder is within 75 percent of the pressure recorded for the highest reading cylinder. For example, if your highest reading cylinder pressure was 150 psi (1034 kPa), then 75 percent of that

would be 113 psi (779 kPa). So the lowest reading cylinder should be no less than 113 psi (779 kPa).

12. If a cylinder exhibits an unusually low compression reading, pour a tablespoon of clean engine oil into the cylinder through the spark plug hole and repeat the compression test. If the compression rises after adding oil, it means that the cylinder's piston rings and/or cylinder bore are damaged or worn. If the pressure remains low, the valves may not be seating properly (a valve job is needed), or the head gasket may be blown near that cylinder. If compression in any two adjacent cylinders is low, and if the addition of oil doesn't help raise compression, there is leakage past the head gasket. Oil and coolant in the combustion chamber, combined with blue or constant white smoke from the tail pipe, are symptoms of this problem. However, don't be alarmed by the normal white smoke emitted from the tail pipe during engine warm-up or from cold weather driving. There may be evidence of water droplets on the engine dipstick and/or oil droplets in the cooling system if a head gasket is blown.

OIL PRESSURE TEST

Check for proper oil pressure at the sending unit passage with an externally mounted mechanical oil pressure gauge (as opposed to relying on a factory installed dash-mounted gauge). A tachometer may also be needed, as some specifications may require running the engine at a specific rpm.

1. With the engine cold, locate and remove the oil pressure sending unit.
2. Following the manufacturer's instructions, connect a mechanical oil pressure gauge and, if necessary, a tachometer to the engine.
3. Start the engine and allow it to idle.
4. Check the oil pressure reading when cold and record the number. You may need to run the engine at a specified rpm, so check the specifications chart located earlier in this section.
5. Run the engine until normal operating temperature is reached (upper radiator hose will feel warm).
6. Check the oil pressure reading again with the engine hot and record the number. Turn the engine **OFF**.
7. Compare your hot oil pressure reading to that given in the chart. If the reading is low, check the cold pressure reading against the chart. If the cold pressure is well above the specification, and the hot reading was lower than the specification, you may have the wrong viscosity oil in the engine. Change the oil, making sure to use the proper grade and quantity, then repeat the test.

Low oil pressure readings could be attributed to internal component wear, pump related problems, a low oil level, or oil viscosity that is too low. High oil pressure readings could be caused by an overfilled crankcase, too high of an oil viscosity or a faulty pressure relief valve.

Buy or Rebuild?

Now that you have determined that your engine is worn out, you must make some decisions. The question of whether or not an engine is worth rebuilding is largely a subjective matter and one of personal worth. Is the engine a popular one, or is it an obsolete model? Are parts available? Will it get acceptable gas mileage once it is rebuilt? Is the car it's being put into worth keeping? Would it be less expensive to buy a new engine, have your engine rebuilt by a pro, rebuild it yourself or buy a used engine from a salvage yard? Or would it be simpler and less expensive to buy another car? If you have considered all these matters and more, and have still decided to rebuild the engine, then it is time to decide how you will rebuild it.

➡**The editors at Chilton feel that most engine machining should be performed by a professional machine shop. Don't think of it as wasting money, rather, as an assurance that the job has been done right the first time. There are many expensive and specialized tools required to perform such tasks as boring and honing an engine block or having a valve job done on a cylinder head. Even inspecting the parts requires expensive micrometers and gauges to properly measure wear and clearances. Also, a machine shop can deliver to you clean, and ready to assemble parts, saving you time**

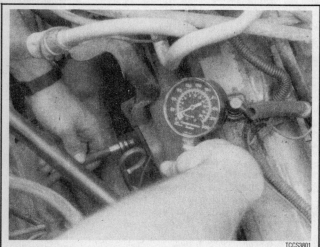

TCCS3801

Fig. 169 A screw-in type compression gauge is more accurate and easier to use without an assistant

and aggravation. **Your maximum savings will come from performing the removal, disassembly, assembly and installation of the engine and purchasing or renting only the tools required to perform the above tasks. Depending on the particular circumstances, you may save 40 to 60 percent of the cost doing these yourself.**

A complete rebuild or overhaul of an engine involves replacing all of the moving parts (pistons, rods, crankshaft, camshaft, etc.) with new ones and machining the non-moving wearing surfaces of the block and heads. Unfortunately, this may not be cost effective. For instance, your crankshaft may have been damaged or worn, but it can be machined undersize for a minimal fee.

So, as you can see, you can replace everything inside the engine, but, it is wiser to replace only those parts which are really needed, and, if possible, repair the more expensive ones. Later in this section, we will break the engine down into its two main components: the cylinder head and the engine block. We will discuss each component, and the recommended parts to replace during a rebuild on each.

Engine Overhaul Tips

Most engine overhaul procedures are fairly standard. In addition to specific parts replacement procedures and specifications for your individual engine, this section is also a guide to acceptable rebuilding procedures. Examples of standard rebuilding practice are given and should be used along with specific details concerning your particular engine.

Competent and accurate machine shop services will ensure maximum performance, reliability and engine life. In most instances it is more profitable for the do-it-yourself mechanic to remove, clean and inspect the component, buy the necessary parts and deliver these to a shop for actual machine work.

Much of the assembly work (crankshaft, bearings, piston rods, and other components) is well within the scope of the do-it-yourself mechanic's tools and abilities. You will have to decide for yourself the depth of involvement you desire in an engine repair or rebuild.

TOOLS

The tools required for an engine overhaul or parts replacement will depend on the depth of your involvement. With a few exceptions, they will be the tools found in a mechanic's tool kit (see Section 1 of this manual). More in-depth work will require some or all of the following:
- A dial indicator (reading in thousandths) mounted on a universal base
- Micrometers and telescope gauges
- Jaw and screw-type pullers
- Scraper
- Valve spring compressor
- Ring groove cleaner
- Piston ring expander and compressor
- Ridge reamer
- Cylinder hone or glaze breaker
- Plastigage®
- Engine stand

The use of most of these tools is illustrated in this section. Many can be rented for a one-time use from a local parts jobber or tool supply house specializing in automotive work.

Occasionally, the use of special tools is called for. See the information on Special Tools and the Safety Notice in the front of this book before substituting another tool.

OVERHAUL TIPS

Aluminum has become extremely popular for use in engines, due to its low weight. Observe the following precautions when handling aluminum parts:
- Never hot tank aluminum parts (the caustic hot tank solution will eat the aluminum.
- Remove all aluminum parts (identification tag, etc.) from engine parts prior to the tanking.

- Always coat threads lightly with engine oil or anti-seize compounds before installation, to prevent seizure.
- Never overtighten bolts or spark plugs especially in aluminum threads.

When assembling the engine, any parts that will be exposed to frictional contact must be prelubed to provide lubrication at initial start-up. Any product specifically formulated for this purpose can be used, but engine oil is not recommended as a prelube in most cases.

When semi-permanent (locked, but removable) installation of bolts or nuts is desired, threads should be cleaned and coated with Loctite® or another similar, commercial non-hardening sealant.

CLEANING

▶ **See Figures 170, 171, 172 and 173**

Before the engine and its components are inspected, they must be thoroughly cleaned. You will need to remove any engine varnish, oil sludge and/or carbon deposits from all of the components to insure an accurate inspection. A crack in the engine block or cylinder head can easily become overlooked if hidden by a layer of sludge or carbon.

Most of the cleaning process can be carried out with common hand tools and readily available solvents or solutions. Carbon deposits can be chipped away using a hammer and a hard wooden chisel. Old gasket material and varnish or sludge can usually be removed using a scraper and/or cleaning solvent. Extremely stubborn deposits may require the use of a power drill with a wire brush. If using a wire brush, use extreme care around any critical machined surfaces (such as the gasket surfaces, bearing saddles, cylinder bores, etc.). USE OF A WIRE BRUSH IS NOT RECOMMENDED ON ANY ALUMINUM COMPONENTS. Always follow any safety recommendations given by the manufacturer of the tool and/or solvent. You should always wear eye protection during any cleaning process involving scraping, chipping or spraying of solvents.

An alternative to the mess and hassle of cleaning the parts yourself is to drop them off at a local garage or machine shop. They will, more than likely, have the necessary equipment to properly clean all of the parts for a nominal fee.

❋❋ CAUTION

Always wear eye protection during any cleaning process involving scraping, chipping or spraying of solvents.

Remove any oil galley plugs, freeze plugs and/or pressed-in bearings and carefully wash and degrease all of the engine components including the fasteners and bolts. Small parts such as the valves, springs, etc., should be placed in a metal basket and allowed to soak. Use pipe cleaner type brushes,

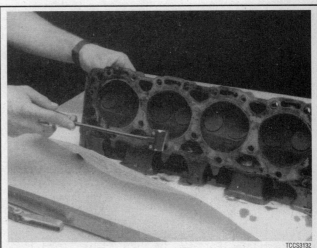

TCCS3132

Fig. 170 Use a gasket scraper to remove the old gasket material from the mating surfaces

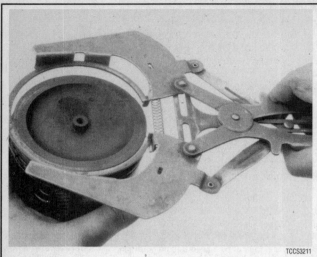

Fig. 171 Use a ring expander tool to remove the piston rings

Fig. 172 Clean the piston ring grooves using a ring groove cleaner tool, or . . .

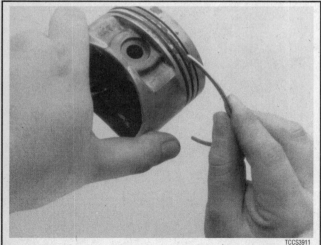

Fig. 173 . . . use a piece of an old ring to clean the grooves. Be careful, the ring can be quite sharp

and clean all passageways in the components. Use a ring expander and remove the rings from the pistons. Clean the piston ring grooves with a special tool or a piece of broken ring. Scrape the carbon off of the top of the piston. You should never use a wire brush on the pistons. After preparing all of the piston assemblies in this manner, wash and degrease them again.

❊❊ WARNING

Use extreme care when cleaning around the cylinder head valve seats. A mistake or slip may cost you a new seat.

When cleaning the cylinder head, remove carbon from the combustion chamber with the valves installed. This will avoid damaging the valve seats.

REPAIRING DAMAGED THREADS

▶ **See Figures 174, 175, 176, 177 and 178**

Several methods of repairing damaged threads are available. Heli-Coil® (shown here), Keenserts® and Microdot® are among the most widely used. All involve basically the same principle—drilling out stripped threads, tapping the hole and installing a prewound insert—making welding, plugging and oversize fasteners unnecessary.

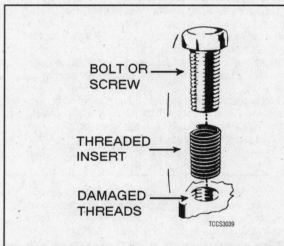

Fig. 174 Damaged bolt hole threads can be replaced with thread repair inserts

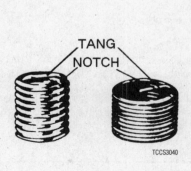

Fig. 175 Standard thread repair insert (left), and spark plug thread insert

Two types of thread repair inserts are usually supplied: a standard type for most inch coarse, inch fine, metric course and metric fine thread sizes and a spark lug type to fit most spark plug port sizes. Consult the individual tool manufacturer's catalog to determine exact applications. Typical thread repair kits will contain a selection of prewound threaded inserts, a tap (corresponding to the outside diameter threads of the insert) and an installation tool. Spark plug inserts usually differ because they require a tap equipped with pilot threads and a combined reamer/tap section. Most manufacturers also supply blister-packed thread repair inserts separately in addition to a master kit containing a variety of taps and inserts plus installation tools.

Before attempting to repair a threaded hole, remove any snapped, broken or damaged bolts or studs. Penetrating oil can be used to free frozen threads. The offending item can usually be removed with locking pliers or using a screw/stud extractor. After the hole is clear, the thread can be repaired, as shown in the series of accompanying illustrations and in the kit manufacturer's instructions.

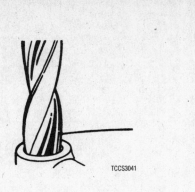

Fig. 176 Drill out the damaged threads with the specified size bit. Be sure to drill completely through the hole or to the bottom of a blind hole

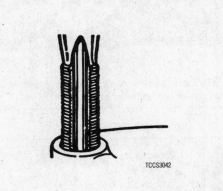

Fig. 177 Using the kit, tap the hole in order to receive the thread insert. Keep the tap well oiled and back it out frequently to avoid clogging the threads

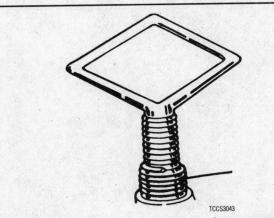

Fig. 178 Screw the insert onto the installer tool until the tang engages the slot. Thread the insert into the hole until it is ¼–½ turn below the top surface, then remove the tool and break off the tang using a punch

Engine Preparation

To properly rebuild an engine, you must first remove it from the vehicle, then disassemble and diagnose it. Ideally you should place your engine on an engine stand. This affords you the best access to the engine components. Follow the manufacturer's directions for using the stand with your particular engine. Remove the flywheel or flexplate before installing the engine to the stand.

Now that you have the engine on a stand, and assuming that you have drained the oil and coolant from the engine, it's time to strip it of all but the necessary components. Before you start disassembling the engine, you may want to take a moment to draw some pictures, or fabricate some labels or containers to mark the locations of various components and the bolts and/or studs which fasten them. Modern day engines use a lot of little brackets and clips which hold wiring harnesses and such, and these holders are often mounted on studs and/or bolts that can be easily mixed up. The manufacturer spent a lot of time and money designing your vehicle, and they wouldn't have wasted any of it by haphazardly placing brackets, clips or fasteners on the vehicle. If it's present when you disassemble it, put it back when you assemble, you will regret not remembering that little bracket which holds a wire harness out of the path of a rotating part.

You should begin by unbolting any accessories still attached to the engine, such as the water pump, power steering pump, alternator, etc. Then, unfasten any manifolds (intake or exhaust) which were not removed during the engine removal procedure. Finally, remove any covers remaining on the engine such as the rocker arm, front or timing cover and oil pan. Some front covers may require the vibration damper and/or crank pulley to be removed beforehand. The idea is to reduce the engine to the bare necessities (cylinder head(s), valve train, engine block, crankshaft, pistons and connecting rods), plus any other `in block' components such as oil pumps, balance shafts and auxiliary shafts.

Finally, remove the cylinder head(s) from the engine block and carefully place on a bench. Disassembly instructions for each component follow later in this section.

Cylinder Head

There are two basic types of cylinder heads used on today's automobiles: the Overhead Valve (OHV) and the Overhead Camshaft (OHC). The latter can also be broken down into two subgroups: the Single Overhead Camshaft (SOHC) and the Dual Overhead Camshaft (DOHC). Generally, if there is only a single camshaft on a head, it is just referred to as an OHC head. Also, an engine with an OHV cylinder head is also known as a pushrod engine.

Most cylinder heads these days are made of an aluminum alloy due to its light weight, durability and heat transfer qualities. However, cast iron was the material of choice in the past, and is still used on many vehicles today. Whether made from aluminum or iron, all cylinder heads have valves and seats. Some use two valves per cylinder, while the more hi-tech engines will utilize a multi-valve configuration using 3, 4 and even 5 valves per cylinder. When the valve contacts the seat, it does so on precision machined surfaces, which seals the combustion chamber. All cylinder heads have a valve guide for each valve. The guide centers the valve to the seat and allows it to move up and down within it. The clearance between the valve and guide can be critical. Too much clearance and the engine may consume oil, lose vacuum and/or damage the seat. Too little, and the valve can stick in the guide causing the engine to run poorly if at all, and possibly causing severe damage. The last component all cylinder heads have are valve springs. The spring holds the valve against its seat. It also returns the valve to this position when the valve has been opened by the valve train or camshaft. The spring is fastened to the valve by a retainer and valve locks (sometimes called keepers). Aluminum heads will also have a valve spring shim to keep the spring from wearing away the aluminum.

An ideal method of rebuilding the cylinder head would involve replacing all of the valves, guides, seats, springs, etc. with new ones. However, depending on how the engine was maintained, often this is not necessary. A major cause of valve, guide and seat wear is an improperly tuned engine. An engine that is running too rich, will often wash the lubricating oil out of the guide with gasoline, causing it to wear rapidly. Conversely, an engine which is running too lean will place higher combustion temperatures on the valves and seats allowing them to wear or even burn. Springs fall victim to the driving habits of the individual. A driver who often runs the engine rpm to the redline will wear out or break the springs faster then one that stays well below it. Unfortunately, mileage takes it toll on all of the parts. Generally, the valves, guides, springs and seats in a cylinder head can be machined and re-used, saving you money. However, if a valve is burnt, it may be wise to replace all of the valves, since they were all operating in the same environment. The same goes for any other component on the cylinder head. Think of it as an insurance policy against future problems related to that component.

Unfortunately, the only way to find out which components need replacing, is to disassemble and carefully check each piece. After the cylinder head(s) are disassembled, thoroughly clean all of the components.

DISASSEMBLY

▶ **See Figures 179 and 180**

Whether it is a single or dual overhead camshaft cylinder head, the disassembly procedure is relatively unchanged. One aspect to pay attention to is careful labeling of the parts on the dual camshaft cylinder head. There will be an intake camshaft and followers as well as an exhaust camshaft and followers and they must be labeled as such. In some cases, the components are identical and could easily be installed incorrectly. DO NOT MIX THEM UP! Determining which is which is very simple; the intake camshaft and components are on the same side of the head as was the intake manifold. Conversely, the exhaust camshaft and components are on the same side of the head as was the exhaust manifold.

Rocker Arm Type Camshaft Followers

▶ **See Figures 181 thru 189**

Most cylinder heads with rocker arm-type camshaft followers are easily disassembled using a standard valve spring compressor. However, certain models may not have enough open space around the spring for the standard tool and may require you to use a C-clamp style compressor tool instead.

1. If not already removed, remove the rocker arms and/or shafts and the camshaft. If applicable, also remove the hydraulic lash adjusters. Mark their positions for assembly.
2. Position the cylinder head to allow access to the valve spring.
3. Use a valve spring compressor tool to relieve the spring tension from the retainer.

➡**Due to engine varnish, the retainer may stick to the valve locks. A gentle tap with a hammer may help to break it loose.**

4. Remove the valve locks from the valve tip and/or retainer. A small magnet may help in removing the small locks.
5. Lift the valve spring, tool and all, off of the valve stem.

Fig. 179 Exploded view of a valve, seal, spring, retainer and locks from an OHC cylinder head

TCCA3P54

Fig. 180 Example of a multi-valve cylinder head. Note how it has 2 intake and 2 exhaust valve ports

TCCA3P62

Fig. 181 Example of the shaft mounted rocker arms on some OHC heads

Fig. 184 . . . then the camshaft can be removed by sliding it out (shown), or unbolting a bearing cap (not shown)

Fig. 182 Another example of the rocker arm type OHC head. This model uses a follower under the camshaft

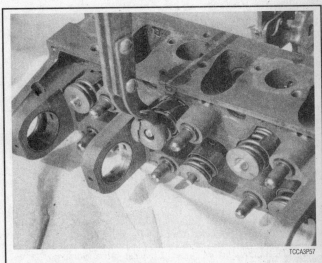

Fig. 185 Compress the valve spring . . .

Fig. 183 Before the camshaft can be removed, all of the followers must first be removed . . .

Fig. 186 . . . then remove the valve locks from the valve stem and spring retainer

Fig. 187 Remove the valve spring and retainer from the cylinder head

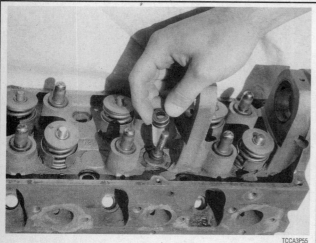

Fig. 188 Remove the valve seal from the guide. Some gentle prying or pliers may help to remove stubborn ones

Fig. 189 All aluminum and some cast iron heads will have these valve spring shims. Remove all of them as well

6. If equipped, remove the valve seal. If the seal is difficult to remove with the valve in place, try removing the valve first, then the seal. Follow the steps below for valve removal.

7. Position the head to allow access for withdrawing the valve.

➡**Cylinder heads that have seen a lot of miles and/or abuse may have mushroomed the valve lock grove and/or tip, causing difficulty in removal of the valve. If this has happened, use a metal file to carefully remove the high spots around the lock grooves and/or tip. Only file it enough to allow removal.**

8. Remove the valve from the cylinder head.

9. If equipped, remove the valve spring shim. A small magnetic tool or screwdriver will aid in removal.

10. Repeat Steps 3 though 9 until all of the valves have been removed.

INSPECTION

Now that all of the cylinder head components are clean, it's time to inspect them for wear and/or damage. To accurately inspect them, you will need some specialized tools:

- A 0–1 in. micrometer for the valves
- A dial indicator or inside diameter gauge for the valve guides
- A spring pressure test gauge

If you do not have access to the proper tools, you may want to bring the components to a shop that does.

Valves

▶ **See Figures 190 and 191**

The first thing to inspect are the valve heads. Look closely at the head, margin and face for any cracks, excessive wear or burning. The margin is the best place to look for burning. It should have a squared edge with an even width all around the diameter. When a valve burns, the margin will look melted and the edges rounded. Also inspect the valve head for any signs of tulipping. This will show as a lifting of the edges or dishing in the center of the head and will usually not occur to all of the valves. All of the heads should look the same, any that seem dished more than others are probably bad. Next, inspect the valve lock grooves and valve tips. Check for any burrs around the lock grooves, especially if you had to file them to remove the valve. Valve tips should appear flat, although slight rounding with high mileage engines is normal. Slightly worn valve tips will need to be machined flat. Last, measure the valve stem diameter with the micrometer. Measure the area that rides within the guide, especially towards the tip where most of the wear occurs. Take several measurements along its length and compare them to each other. Wear should be even along the length

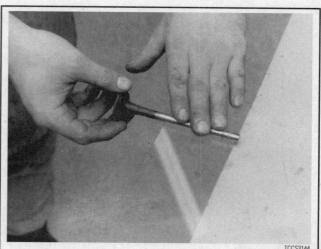

Fig. 190 Valve stems may be rolled on a flat surface to check for bends

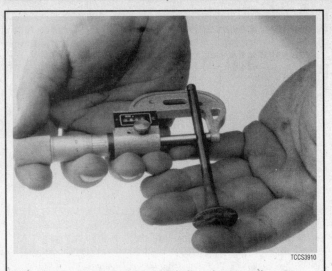

Fig. 191 Use a micrometer to check the valve stem diameter

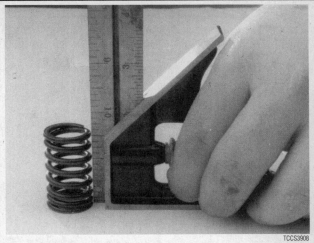

Fig. 193 Check the valve spring for squareness on a flat surface; a carpenter's square can be used

with little to no taper. If no minimum diameter is given in the specifications, then the stem should not read more than 0.001 in. (0.025mm) below the specification. Any valves that fail these inspections should be replaced.

Springs, Retainers and Valve Locks

▶ **See Figures 192 and 193**

The first thing to check is the most obvious, broken springs. Next check the free length and squareness of each spring. If applicable, insure to distinguish between intake and exhaust springs. Use a ruler and/or carpenters square to measure the length. A carpenters square should be used to check the springs for squareness. If a spring pressure test gauge is available, check each springs rating and compare to the specifications chart. Check the readings against the specifications given. Any springs that fail these inspections should be replaced.

The spring retainers rarely need replacing, however they should still be checked as a precaution. Inspect the spring mating surface and the valve lock retention area for any signs of excessive wear. Also check for any signs of cracking. Replace any retainers that are questionable.

Valve locks should be inspected for excessive wear on the outside contact area as well as on the inner notched surface. Any locks which appear worn or broken and its respective valve should be replaced.

Cylinder Head

There are several things to check on the cylinder head: valve guides, seats, cylinder head surface flatness, cracks and physical damage.

VALVE GUIDES

▶ **See Figure 194**

Now that you know the valves are good, you can use them to check the guides, although a new valve, if available, is preferred. Before you measure anything, look at the guides carefully and inspect them for any cracks, chips or breakage. Also if the guide is a removable style (as in most aluminum heads), check them for any looseness or evidence of movement. All of the guides should appear to be at the same height from the spring seat. If any seem lower (or higher) from another, the guide has moved. Mount a dial indicator onto the spring side of the cylinder head. Lightly oil the valve stem and insert it into the cylinder head. Position the dial indicator against the valve stem near the tip and zero the gauge. Grasp the valve stem and wiggle towards and away from the dial indicator and observe the readings. Mount the dial indicator 90 degrees from the initial point and zero the gauge and again take a reading. Compare the two readings for a out of round condition. Check the readings against the specifications given. An

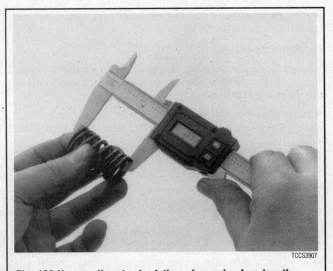

Fig. 192 Use a caliper to check the valve spring free-length

Fig. 194 A dial gauge may be used to check valve stem-to-guide clearance; read the gauge while moving the valve stem

Inside Diameter (I.D.) gauge designed for valve guides will give you an accurate valve guide bore measurement. If the I.D. gauge is used, compare the readings with the specifications given. Any guides that fail these inspections should be replaced or machined.

VALVE SEATS

A visual inspection of the valve seats should show a slightly worn and pitted surface where the valve face contacts the seat. Inspect the seat carefully for severe pitting or cracks. Also, a seat that is badly worn will be recessed into the cylinder head. A severely worn or recessed seat may need to be replaced. All cracked seats must be replaced. A seat concentricity gauge, if available, should be used to check the seat run-out. If run-out exceeds specifications the seat must be machined (if no specification is given use 0.002 in. or 0.051mm).

CYLINDER HEAD SURFACE FLATNESS

▶ See Figures 195 and 196

After you have cleaned the gasket surface of the cylinder head of any old gasket material, check the head for flatness.

Place a straightedge across the gasket surface. Using feeler gauges, determine the clearance at the center of the straightedge and across the

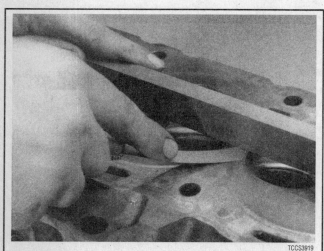

Fig. 195 Check the head for flatness across the center of the head surface using a straightedge and feeler gauge

TCCS3919

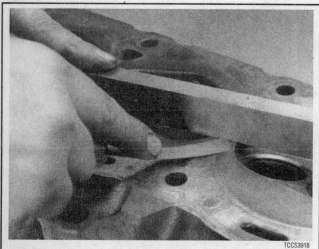

Fig. 196 Checks should also be made along both diagonals of the head surface

TCCS3918

cylinder head at several points. Check along the centerline and diagonally on the head surface. If the warpage exceeds 0.003 in. (0.076mm) within a 6.0 in. (15.2cm) span, or 0.006 in. (0.152mm) over the total length of the head, the cylinder head must be resurfaced. After resurfacing the heads of a V-type engine, the intake manifold flange surface should be checked, and if necessary, milled proportionally to allow for the change in its mounting position.

CRACKS AND PHYSICAL DAMAGE

Generally, cracks are limited to the combustion chamber, however, it is not uncommon for the head to crack in a spark plug hole, port, outside of the head or in the valve spring/rocker arm area. The first area to inspect is always the hottest: the exhaust seat/port area.

A visual inspection should be performed, but just because you don't see a crack does not mean it is not there. Some more reliable methods for inspecting for cracks include Magnaflux®, a magnetic process or Zyglo®, a dye penetrant. Magnaflux® is used only on ferrous metal (cast iron) heads. Zyglo® uses a spray on fluorescent mixture along with a black light to reveal the cracks. It is strongly recommended to have your cylinder head checked professionally for cracks, especially if the engine was known to have overheated and/or leaked or consumed coolant. Contact a local shop for availability and pricing of these services.

Physical damage is usually very evident. For example, a broken mounting ear from dropping the head or a bent or broken stud and/or bolt. All of these defects should be fixed or, if unrepairable, the head should be replaced.

Camshaft and Followers

Inspect the camshaft(s) and followers as described earlier in this section.

REFINISHING & REPAIRING

Many of the procedures given for refinishing and repairing the cylinder head components must be performed by a machine shop. Certain steps, if the inspected part is not worn, can be performed yourself inexpensively. However, you spent a lot of time and effort so far, why risk trying to save a couple bucks if you might have to do it all over again?

Valves

Any valves that were not replaced should be refaced and the tips ground flat. Unless you have access to a valve grinding machine, this should be done by a machine shop. If the valves are in extremely good condition, as well as the valve seats and guides, they may be lapped in without performing machine work.

It is a recommended practice to lap the valves even after machine work has been performed and/or new valves have been purchased. This insures a positive seal between the valve and seat.

LAPPING THE VALVES

➡Before lapping the valves to the seats, read the rest of the cylinder head section to insure that any related parts are in acceptable enough condition to continue.

➡Before any valve seat machining and/or lapping can be performed, the guides must be within factory recommended specifications.

1. Invert the cylinder head.
2. Lightly lubricate the valve stems and insert them into the cylinder head in their numbered order.
3. Raise the valve from the seat and apply a small amount of fine lapping compound to the seat.
4. Moisten the suction head of a hand-lapping tool and attach it to the head of the valve.
5. Rotate the tool between the palms of both hands, changing the position of the valve on the valve seat and lifting the tool often to prevent grooving.

6. Lap the valve until a smooth, polished circle is evident on the valve and seat.

7. Remove the tool and the valve. Wipe away all traces of the grinding compound and store the valve to maintain its lapped location.

✳✳ WARNING

Do not get the valves out of order after they have been lapped. They must be put back with the same valve seat with which they were lapped.

Springs, Retainers and Valve Locks

There is no repair or refinishing possible with the springs, retainers and valve locks. If they are found to be worn or defective, they must be replaced with new (or known good) parts.

Cylinder Head

Most refinishing procedures dealing with the cylinder head must be performed by a machine shop. Read the sections below and review your inspection data to determine whether or not machining is necessary.

VALVE GUIDES

➡**If any machining or replacements are made to the valve guides, the seats must be machined.**

Unless the valve guides need machining or replacing, the only service to perform is to thoroughly clean them of any dirt or oil residue.

There are only two types of valve guides used on automobile engines: the replaceable-type (all aluminum heads) and the cast-in integral-type (most cast iron heads). There are four recommended methods for repairing worn guides.

- Knurling
- Inserts
- Reaming oversize
- Replacing

Knurling is a process in which metal is displaced and raised, thereby reducing clearance, giving a true center, and providing oil control. It is the least expensive way of repairing the valve guides. However, it is not necessarily the best, and in some cases, a knurled valve guide will not stand up for more than a short time. It requires a special knurlizer and precision reaming tools to obtain proper clearances. It would not be cost effective to purchase these tools, unless you plan on rebuilding several of the same cylinder head.

Installing a guide insert involves machining the guide to accept a bronze insert. One style is the coil-type which is installed into a threaded guide. Another is the thin-walled insert where the guide is reamed oversize to accept a split-sleeve insert. After the insert is installed, a special tool is then run through the guide to expand the insert, locking it to the guide. The insert is then reamed to the standard size for proper valve clearance.

Reaming for oversize valves restores normal clearances and provides a true valve seat. Most cast-in type guides can be reamed to accept an valve with an oversize stem. The cost factor for this can become quite high as you will need to purchase the reamer and new, oversize stem valves for all guides which were reamed. Oversizes are generally 0.003 to 0.030 in. (0.076 to 0.762mm), with 0.015 in. (0.381mm) being the most common.

To replace cast-in type valve guides, they must be drilled out, then reamed to accept replacement guides. This must be done on a fixture which will allow centering and leveling off of the original valve seat or guide, otherwise a serious guide-to-seat misalignment may occur making it impossible to properly machine the seat.

Replaceable-type guides are pressed into the cylinder head. A hammer and a stepped drift or punch may be used to install and remove the guides. Before removing the guides, measure the protrusion on the spring side of the head and record it for installation. Use the stepped drift to hammer out the old guide from the combustion chamber side of the head. When installing, determine whether or not the guide also seals a water jacket in the head, and if it does, use the recommended sealing agent. If there is no water jacket, grease the valve guide and its bore. Use the stepped drift, and hammer the new guide into the cylinder head from the spring side of the cylinder head. A stack of washers the same thickness as the measured protrusion may help the installation process.

VALVE SEATS

➡**Before any valve seat machining can be performed, the guides must be within factory recommended specifications.**

➡**If any machining or replacements were made to the valve guides, the seats must be machined.**

If the seats are in good condition, the valves can be lapped to the seats, and the cylinder head assembled. See the valves section for instructions on lapping.

If the valve seats are worn, cracked or damaged, they must be serviced by a machine shop. The valve seat must be perfectly centered to the valve guide, which requires very accurate machining.

CYLINDER HEAD SURFACE

If the cylinder head is warped, it must be machined flat. If the warpage is extremely severe, the head may need to be replaced. In some instances, it may be possible to straighten a warped head enough to allow machining. In either case, contact a professional machine shop for service.

➡**Any OHC cylinder head that shows excessive warpage should have the camshaft bearing journals align bored after the cylinder head has been resurfaced.**

✳✳ WARNING

Failure to align bore the camshaft bearing journals could result in severe engine damage including but not limited to: valve and piston damage, connecting rod damage, camshaft and/or crankshaft breakage.

CRACKS AND PHYSICAL DAMAGE

Certain cracks can be repaired in both cast iron and aluminum heads. For cast iron, a tapered threaded insert is installed along the length of the crack. Aluminum can also use the tapered inserts, however welding is the preferred method. Some physical damage can be repaired through brazing or welding. Contact a machine shop to get expert advice for your particular dilemma.

ASSEMBLY

The first step for any assembly job is to have a clean area in which to work. Next, thoroughly clean all of the parts and components that are to be assembled. Finally, place all of the components onto a suitable work space and, if necessary, arrange the parts to their respective positions.

1. Lightly lubricate the valve stems and insert all of the valves into the cylinder head. If possible, maintain their original locations.

2. If equipped, install any valve spring shims which were removed.

3. If equipped, install the new valve seals, keeping the following in mind:

- If the valve seal presses over the guide, lightly lubricate the outer guide surfaces.
- If the seal is an O-ring type, it is installed just after compressing the spring but before the valve locks.

4. Place the valve spring and retainer over the stem.

5. Position the spring compressor tool and compress the spring.

6. Assemble the valve locks to the stem.

7. Relieve the spring pressure slowly and insure that neither valve lock becomes dislodged by the retainer.

8. Remove the spring compressor tool.

9. Repeat Steps 2 through 8 until all of the springs have been installed.

10. Install the camshaft(s), rockers, shafts and any other components that were removed for disassembly.

Engine Block

GENERAL INFORMATION

A thorough overhaul or rebuild of an engine block would include replacing the pistons, rings, bearings, timing belt/chain assembly and oil pump. For OHV engines also include a new camshaft and lifters. The block would then have the cylinders bored and honed oversize (or if using removable cylinder sleeves, new sleeves installed) and the crankshaft would be cut undersize to provide new wearing surfaces and perfect clearances. However, your particular engine may not have everything worn out. What if only the piston rings have worn out and the clearances on everything else are still within factory specifications? Well, you could just replace the rings and put it back together, but this would be a very rare example. Chances are, if one component in your engine is worn, other components are sure to follow, and soon. At the very least, you should always replace the rings, bearings and oil pump. This is what is commonly called a "freshen up".

Cylinder Ridge Removal

Because the top piston ring does not travel to the very top of the cylinder, a ridge is built up between the end of the travel and the top of the cylinder bore.

Pushing the piston and connecting rod assembly past the ridge can be difficult, and damage to the piston ring lands could occur. If the ridge is not removed before installing a new piston or not removed at all, piston ring breakage and piston damage may occur.

➡ It is always recommended that you remove any cylinder ridges before removing the piston and connecting rod assemblies. If you know that new pistons are going to be installed and the engine block will be bored oversize, you may be able to forego this step. However, some ridges may actually prevent the assemblies from being removed, necessitating its removal.

There are several different types of ridge reamers on the market, none of which are inexpensive. Unless a great deal of engine rebuilding is anticipated, borrow or rent a reamer.

1. Turn the crankshaft until the piston is at the bottom of its travel.
2. Cover the head of the piston with a rag.
3. Follow the tool manufacturers instructions and cut away the ridge, exercising extreme care to avoid cutting too deeply.
4. Remove the ridge reamer, the rag and as many of the cuttings as possible. Continue until all of the cylinder ridges have been removed.

DISASSEMBLY

▶ See Figures 197 and 198

The engine disassembly instructions following assume that you have the engine mounted on an engine stand. If not, it is easiest to disassemble the engine on a bench or the floor with it resting on the bellhousing or transmission mounting surface. You must be able to access the connecting rod fasteners and turn the crankshaft during disassembly. Also, all engine covers (timing, front, side, oil pan, whatever) should have already been removed. Engines which are seized or locked up may not be able to be completely disassembled, and a core (salvage yard) engine should be purchased.

If not done during the cylinder head removal, remove the timing belt and/or gear/sprocket assembly. Remove the oil pick-up and pump assembly and, if necessary, the pump drive. If equipped, remove any balance or auxiliary shafts. If necessary, remove the cylinder ridge from the top of the bore. See the cylinder ridge removal procedure earlier in this section.

Rotate the engine over so that the crankshaft is exposed. Use a number punch or scribe and mark each connecting rod with its respective cylinder number. The cylinder closest to the front of the engine is always number 1. However, depending on the engine placement, the front of the engine could either be the flywheel or damper/pulley end. Generally the front of the engine faces the front of the vehicle. Use a number punch or scribe and

Fig. 197 Place rubber hose over the connecting rod studs to protect the crankshaft and cylinder bores from damage

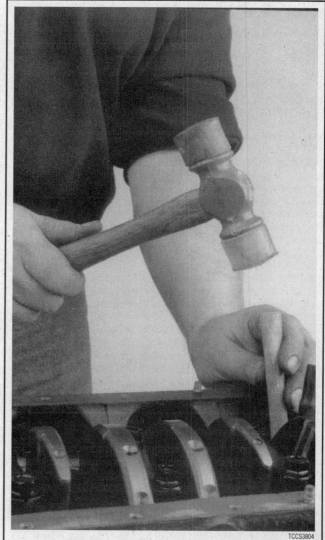

Fig. 198 Carefully tap the piston out of the bore using a wooden dowel

also mark the main bearing caps from front to rear with the front most cap being number 1 (if there are five caps, mark them 1 through 5, front to rear).

✺✺ WARNING

Take special care when pushing the connecting rod up from the crankshaft because the sharp threads of the rod bolts/studs will score the crankshaft journal. Insure that special plastic caps are installed over them, or cut two pieces of rubber hose to do the same.

Again, rotate the engine, this time to position the number one cylinder bore (head surface) up. Turn the crankshaft until the number one piston is at the bottom of its travel, this should allow the maximum access to its connecting rod. Remove the number one connecting rods fasteners and cap and place two lengths of rubber hose over the rod bolts/studs to protect the crankshaft from damage. Using a sturdy wooden dowel and a hammer, push the connecting rod up about 1 in. (25mm) from the crankshaft and remove the upper bearing insert. Continue pushing or tapping the connecting rod up until the piston rings are out of the cylinder bore. Remove the piston and rod by hand, put the upper half of the bearing insert back into the rod, install the cap with its bearing insert installed, and hand-tighten the cap fasteners. If the parts are kept in order in this manner, they will not get lost and you will be able to tell which bearings came form what cylinder if any problems are discovered and diagnosis is necessary. Remove all the other piston assemblies in the same manner. On V-style engines, remove all of the pistons from one bank, then reposition the engine with the other cylinder bank head surface up, and remove that banks piston assemblies.

The only remaining component in the engine block should now be the crankshaft. Loosen the main bearing caps evenly until the fasteners can be turned by hand, then remove them and the caps. Remove the crankshaft from the engine block. Thoroughly clean all of the components.

INSPECTION

Now that the engine block and all of its components are clean, it's time to inspect them for wear and/or damage. To accurately inspect them, you will need some specialized tools:

- Two or three separate micrometers to measure the pistons and crankshaft journals
- A dial indicator
- Telescoping gauges for the cylinder bores
- A rod alignment fixture to check for bent connecting rods

If you do not have access to the proper tools, you may want to bring the components to a shop that does.

Generally, you shouldn't expect cracks in the engine block or its components unless it was known to leak, consume or mix engine fluids, it was severely overheated, or there was evidence of bad bearings and/or crankshaft damage. A visual inspection should be performed on all of the components, but just because you don't see a crack does not mean it is not there. Some more reliable methods for inspecting for cracks include Magnaflux®, a magnetic process or Zyglo®, a dye penetrant. Magnaflux® is used only on ferrous metal (cast iron). Zyglo® uses a spray on fluorescent mixture along with a black light to reveal the cracks. It is strongly recommended to have your engine block checked professionally for cracks, especially if the engine was known to have overheated and/or leaked or consumed coolant. Contact a local shop for availability and pricing of these services.

Engine Block

ENGINE BLOCK BEARING ALIGNMENT

Remove the main bearing caps and, if still installed, the main bearing inserts. Inspect all of the main bearing saddles and caps for damage, burrs or high spots. If damage is found, and it is caused from a spun main bearing, the block will need to be align-bored or, if severe enough, replacement. Any burrs or high spots should be carefully removed with a metal file.

Place a straightedge on the bearing saddles, in the engine block, along the centerline of the crankshaft. If any clearance exists between the straightedge and the saddles, the block must be align-bored.

Align-boring consists of machining the main bearing saddles and caps by means of a flycutter that runs through the bearing saddles.

DECK FLATNESS

The top of the engine block where the cylinder head mounts is called the deck. Insure that the deck surface is clean of dirt, carbon deposits and old gasket material. Place a straightedge across the surface of the deck along its centerline and, using feeler gauges, check the clearance along several points. Repeat the checking procedure with the straightedge placed along both diagonals of the deck surface. If the reading exceeds 0.003 in. (0.076mm) within a 6.0 in. (15.2cm) span, or 0.006 in. (0.152mm) over the total length of the deck, it must be machined.

CYLINDER BORES

▶ See Figure 199

The cylinder bores house the pistons and are slightly larger than the pistons themselves. A common piston-to-bore clearance is 0.0015–0.0025 in. (0.0381mm–0.0635mm). Inspect and measure the cylinder bores. The bore should be checked for out-of-roundness, taper and size. The results of this inspection will determine whether the cylinder can be used in its existing size and condition, or a rebore to the next oversize is required (or in the case of removable sleeves, have replacements installed).

The amount of cylinder wall wear is always greater at the top of the cylinder than at the bottom. This wear is known as taper. Any cylinder that has a taper of 0.0012 in. (0.305mm) or more, must be rebored. Measurements are taken at a number of positions in each cylinder: at the top, middle and bottom and at two points at each position; that is, at a point 90 degrees from the crankshaft centerline, as well as a point parallel to the crankshaft centerline. The measurements are made with either a special dial indicator or a telescopic gauge and micrometer. If the necessary precision tools to check the bore are not available, take the block to a machine shop and have them mike it. Also if you don't have the tools to check the cylinder bores, chances are you will not have the necessary devices to check the pistons, connecting rods and crankshaft. Take these components with you and save yourself an extra trip.

For our procedures, we will use a telescopic gauge and a micrometer. You will need one of each, with a measuring range which covers your cylinder bore size.

1. Position the telescopic gauge in the cylinder bore, loosen the gauges lock and allow it to expand.

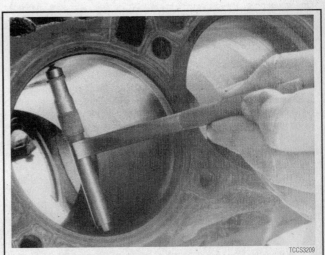

TCCS3209

Fig. 199 Use a telescoping gauge to measure the cylinder bore diameter—take several readings within the same bore

→ **Your first two readings will be at the top of the cylinder bore, then proceed to the middle and finally the bottom, making a total of six measurements.**

2. Hold the gauge square in the bore, 90 degrees from the crankshaft centerline, and gently tighten the lock. Tilt the gauge back to remove it from the bore.

3. Measure the gauge with the micrometer and record the reading.

4. Again, hold the gauge square in the bore, this time parallel to the crankshaft centerline, and gently tighten the lock. Again, you will tilt the gauge back to remove it from the bore.

5. Measure the gauge with the micrometer and record this reading. The difference between these two readings is the out-of-round measurement of the cylinder.

6. Repeat steps 1 through 5, each time going to the next lower position, until you reach the bottom of the cylinder. Then go to the next cylinder, and continue until all of the cylinders have been measured.

The difference between these measurements will tell you all about the wear in your cylinders. The measurements which were taken 90 degrees from the crankshaft centerline will always reflect the most wear. That is because at this position is where the engine power presses the piston against the cylinder bore the hardest. This is known as thrust wear. Take your top, 90 degree measurement and compare it to your bottom, 90 degree measurement. The difference between them is the taper. When you measure your pistons, you will compare these readings to your piston sizes and determine piston-to-wall clearance.

Crankshaft

Inspect the crankshaft for visible signs of wear or damage. All of the journals should be perfectly round and smooth. Slight scores are normal for a used crankshaft, but you should hardly feel them with your fingernail. When measuring the crankshaft with a micrometer, you will take readings at the front and rear of each journal, then turn the micrometer 90 degrees and take two more readings, front and rear. The difference between the front-to-rear readings is the journal taper and the first-to-90 degree reading is the out-of-round measurement. Generally, there should be no taper or out-of-roundness found, however, up to 0.0005 in. (0.0127mm) for either can be overlooked. Also, the readings should fall within the factory specifications for journal diameters.

If the crankshaft journals fall within specifications, it is recommended that it be polished before being returned to service. Polishing the crankshaft insures that any minor burrs or high spots are smoothed, thereby reducing the chance of scoring the new bearings.

Pistons and Connecting Rods

PISTONS

▶ **See Figure 200**

The piston should be visually inspected for any signs of cracking or burning (caused by hot spots or detonation), and scuffing or excessive wear on the skirts. The wristpin attaches the piston to the connecting rod. The piston should move freely on the wrist pin, both sliding and pivoting. Grasp the connecting rod securely, or mount it in a vise, and try to rock the piston back and forth along the centerline of the wristpin. There should not be any excessive play evident between the piston and the pin. If there are C-clips retaining the pin in the piston then you have wrist pin bushings in the rods. There should not be any excessive play between the wrist pin and the rod bushing. Normal clearance for the wrist pin is approx. 0.001–0.002 in. (0.025mm–0.051mm).

Use a micrometer and measure the diameter of the piston, perpendicular to the wrist pin, on the skirt. Compare the reading to its original cylinder measurement obtained earlier. The difference between the two readings is the piston-to-wall clearance. If the clearance is within specifications, the piston may be used as is. If the piston is out of specification, but the bore is not, you will need a new piston. If both are out of specification, you will need the cylinder rebored and oversize pistons installed. Generally if two or more pistons/bores are out of specification, it is best to rebore the entire block and purchase a complete set of oversize pistons.

Fig. 200 Measure the piston's outer diameter, perpendicular to the wrist pin, with a micrometer

CONNECTING ROD

You should have the connecting rod checked for straightness at a machine shop. If the connecting rod is bent, it will unevenly wear the bearing and piston, as well as place greater stress on these components. Any bent or twisted connecting rods must be replaced. If the rods are straight and the wrist pin clearance is within specifications, then only the bearing end of the rod need be checked. Place the connecting rod into a vice, with the bearing inserts in place, install the cap to the rod and tighten the fasteners to specifications. Use a telescoping gauge and carefully measure the inside diameter of the bearings. Compare this reading to the rods original crankshaft journal diameter measurement. The difference is the oil clearance. If the oil clearance is not within specifications, install new bearings in the rod and take another measurement. If the clearance is still out of specifications, and the crankshaft is not, the rod will need to be reconditioned by a machine shop.

→**You can also use Plastigage® to check the bearing clearances. The assembling section has complete instructions on its use.**

Camshaft

Inspect the camshaft and lifters/followers as described earlier in this section.

Bearings

All of the engine bearings should be visually inspected for wear and/or damage. The bearing should look evenly worn all around with no deep scores or pits. If the bearing is severely worn, scored, pitted or heat blued, then the bearing, and the components that use it, should be brought to a machine shop for inspection. Full-circle bearings (used on most camshafts, auxiliary shafts, balance shafts, etc.) require specialized tools for removal and installation, and should be brought to a machine shop for service.

Oil Pump

→**The oil pump is responsible for providing constant lubrication to the whole engine and so it is recommended that a new oil pump be installed when rebuilding the engine.**

Completely disassemble the oil pump and thoroughly clean all of the components. Inspect the oil pump gears and housing for wear and/or damage. Insure that the pressure relief valve operates properly and there is no binding or sticking due to varnish or debris. If all of the parts are in proper working condition, lubricate the gears and relief valve, and assemble the pump.

REFINISHING

▶ **See Figure 201**

Almost all engine block refinishing must be performed by a machine shop. If the cylinders are not to be rebored, then the cylinder glaze can be removed with a ball hone. When removing cylinder glaze with a ball hone, use a light or penetrating type oil to lubricate the hone. Do not allow the hone to run dry as this may cause excessive scoring of the cylinder bores and wear on the hone. If new pistons are required, they will need to be installed to the connecting rods. This should be performed by a machine shop as the pistons must be installed in the correct relationship to the rod or engine damage can occur.

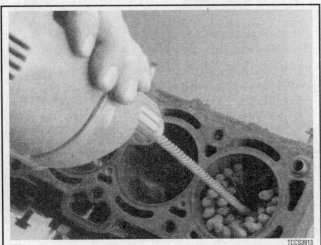

Fig. 201 Use a ball type cylinder hone to remove any glaze and provide a new surface for seating the piston rings

Pistons and Connecting Rods

▶ **See Figure 202**

Only pistons with the wrist pin retained by C-clips are serviceable by the home-mechanic. Press fit pistons require special presses and/or heaters to remove/install the connecting rod and should only be performed by a machine shop.

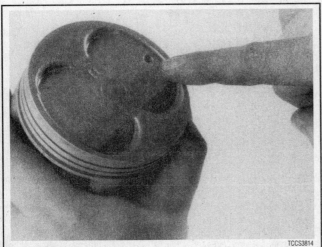

Fig. 202 Most pistons are marked to indicate positioning in the engine (usually a mark means the side facing the front)

All pistons will have a mark indicating the direction to the front of the engine and the must be installed into the engine in that manner. Usually it is a notch or arrow on the top of the piston, or it may be the letter F cast or stamped into the piston.

ASSEMBLY

Before you begin assembling the engine, first give yourself a clean, dirt free work area. Next, clean every engine component again. The key to a good assembly is cleanliness.

Mount the engine block into the engine stand and wash it one last time using water and detergent (dishwashing detergent works well). While washing it, scrub the cylinder bores with a soft bristle brush and thoroughly clean all of the oil passages. Completely dry the engine and spray the entire assembly down with an anti-rust solution such as WD-40® or similar product. Take a clean lint-free rag and wipe up any excess anti-rust solution from the bores, bearing saddles, etc. Repeat the final cleaning process on the crankshaft. Replace any freeze or oil galley plugs which were removed during disassembly.

Crankshaft

▶ **See Figures 203, 204, 205 and 206**

1. Remove the main bearing inserts from the block and bearing caps.
2. If the crankshaft main bearing journals have been refinished to a definite undersize, install the correct undersize bearing. Be sure that the bearing inserts and bearing bores are clean. Foreign material under inserts will distort bearing and cause failure.
3. Place the upper main bearing inserts in bores with tang in slot.

Fig. 203 Apply a strip of gauging material to the bearing journal, then install and tighten the cap

➥The oil holes in the bearing inserts must be aligned with the oil holes in the cylinder block.

4. Install the lower main bearing inserts in bearing caps.

5. Clean the mating surfaces of block and rear main bearing cap.

6. Carefully lower the crankshaft into place. Be careful not to damage bearing surfaces.

7. Check the clearance of each main bearing by using the following procedure:

a. Place a piece of Plastigage® or its equivalent, on bearing surface across full width of bearing cap and about ¼ in. off center.

b. Install cap and tighten bolts to specifications. Do not turn crankshaft while Plastigage® is in place.

c. Remove the cap. Using the supplied Plastigage® scale, check width of Plastigage® at widest point to get maximum clearance. Difference between readings is taper of journal.

d. If clearance exceeds specified limits, try a 0.001 in. or 0.002 in. undersize bearing in combination with the standard bearing. Bearing clearance must be within specified limits. If standard and 0.002 in. undersize bearing does not bring clearance within desired limits, refinish crankshaft journal, then install undersize bearings.

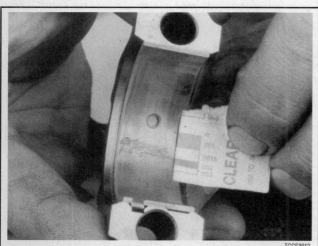

Fig. 204 After the cap is removed again, use the scale supplied with the gauging material to check the clearance

Fig. 205 A dial gauge may be used to check crankshaft end-play

Fig. 206 Carefully pry the crankshaft back and forth while reading the dial gauge for end-play

8. After the bearings have been fitted, apply a light coat of engine oil to the journals and bearings. Install the rear main bearing cap. Install all bearing caps except the thrust bearing cap. Be sure that main bearing caps are installed in original locations. Tighten the bearing cap bolts to specifications.

9. Install the thrust bearing cap with bolts finger-tight.

10. Pry the crankshaft forward against the thrust surface of upper half of bearing.

11. Hold the crankshaft forward and pry the thrust bearing cap to the rear. This aligns the thrust surfaces of both halves of the bearing.

12. Retain the forward pressure on the crankshaft. Tighten the cap bolts to specifications.

13. Measure the crankshaft end-play as follows:

a. Mount a dial gauge to the engine block and position the tip of the gauge to read from the crankshaft end.

b. Carefully pry the crankshaft toward the rear of the engine and hold it there while you zero the gauge.

c. Carefully pry the crankshaft toward the front of the engine and read the gauge.

d. Confirm that the reading is within specifications. If not, install a new thrust bearing and repeat the procedure. If the reading is still out of specifications with a new bearing, have a machine shop inspect the thrust surfaces of the crankshaft, and if possible, repair it.

14. Rotate the crankshaft so as to position the first rod journal to the bottom of its stroke.

15. Install the rear main seal.

Pistons and Connecting Rods

▶ See Figures 207, 208, 209 and 210

1. Before installing the piston/connecting rod assembly, oil the pistons, piston rings and the cylinder walls with light engine oil. Install connecting rod bolt protectors or rubber hose onto the connecting rod bolts/studs. Also perform the following:

a. Select the proper ring set for the size cylinder bore.

b. Position the ring in the bore in which it is going to be used.

c. Push the ring down into the bore area where normal ring wear is not encountered.

d. Use the head of the piston to position the ring in the bore so that the ring is square with the cylinder wall. Use caution to avoid damage to the ring or cylinder bore.

e. Measure the gap between the ends of the ring with a feeler gauge. Ring gap in a worn cylinder is normally greater than specification. If the ring gap is greater than the specified limits, try an oversize ring set.

f. Check the ring side clearance of the compression rings with a feeler gauge inserted between the ring and its lower land according to specification. The gauge should slide freely around the entire ring circumference without binding. Any wear that occurs will form a step at the inner portion of the lower land. If the lower lands have high steps, the piston should be replaced.

2. Unless new pistons are installed, be sure to install the pistons in the cylinders from which they were removed. The numbers on the connecting rod and bearing cap must be on the same side when installed in the cylinder bore. If a connecting rod is ever transposed from one engine or cylinder to another, new bearings should be fitted and the connecting rod

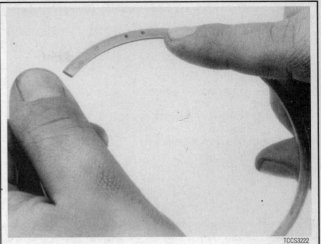

Fig. 209 Most rings are marked to show which side of the ring should face up when installed to the piston

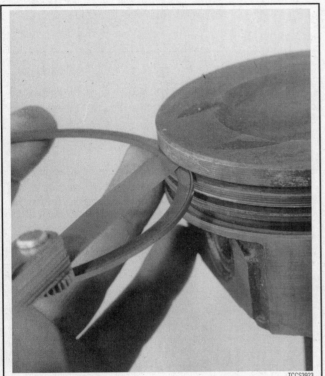

Fig. 207 Checking the piston ring-to-ring groove side clearance using the ring and a feeler gauge

Fig. 210 Install the piston and rod assembly into the block using a ring compressor and the handle of a hammer

Fig. 208 The notch on the side of the bearing cap matches the tang on the bearing insert

should be numbered to correspond with the new cylinder number. The notch on the piston head goes toward the front of the engine.

3. Install all of the rod bearing inserts into the rods and caps.

4. Install the rings to the pistons. Install the oil control ring first, then the second compression ring and finally the top compression ring. Use a piston ring expander tool to aid in installation and to help reduce the chance of breakage.

5. Make sure the ring gaps are properly spaced around the circumference of the piston. Fit a piston ring compressor around the piston and slide the piston and connecting rod assembly down into the cylinder bore, pushing it in with the wooden hammer handle. Push the piston down until it is only slightly below the top of the cylinder bore. Guide the connecting rod onto the crankshaft bearing journal carefully, to avoid damaging the crankshaft.

6. Check the bearing clearance of all the rod bearings, fitting them to the crankshaft bearing journals. Follow the procedure in the crankshaft installation above.

7. After the bearings have been fitted, apply a light coating of assembly oil to the journals and bearings.

8. Turn the crankshaft until the appropriate bearing journal is at the bottom of its stroke, then push the piston assembly all the way down until the connecting rod bearing seats on the crankshaft journal. Be careful not to

allow the bearing cap screws to strike the crankshaft bearing journals and damage them.

9. After the piston and connecting rod assemblies have been installed, check the connecting rod side clearance on each crankshaft journal.

10. Prime and install the oil pump and the oil pump intake tube.

Cylinder Head(s)

1. Install the cylinder head(s) using new gaskets.
2. Install the timing sprockets/gears and the belt/chain assemblies.

Engine Covers and Components

1. If equipped, install the auxiliary/balance shaft assembly.

Install the timing cover(s) and oil pan. Refer to your notes and drawings made prior to disassembly and install all of the components that were removed. Install the engine into the vehicle.

Engine Start-up and Break-in

STARTING THE ENGINE

Now that the engine is installed and every wire and hose is properly connected, go back and double check that all coolant and vacuum hoses are connected. Check that you oil drain plug is installed and properly tightened. If not already done, install a new oil filter onto the engine. Fill the crankcase with the proper amount and grade of engine oil. Fill the cooling system with a 50/50 mixture of coolant/water.

1. Connect the vehicle battery.
2. Start the engine. Keep your eye on your oil pressure indicator; if it does not indicate oil pressure within 10 seconds of starting, turn the vehicle off.

✴✴ WARNING

Damage to the engine can result if it is allowed to run with no oil pressure. Check the engine oil level to make sure that it is full. Check for any leaks and if found, repair the leaks before continuing. If there is still no indication of oil pressure, you may need to prime the system.

3. Confirm that there are no fluid leaks (oil or other).
4. Allow the engine to reach normal operating temperature (the upper radiator hose will be hot to the touch).
5. If necessary, set the ignition timing.
6. Install any remaining components such as the air cleaner (if removed for ignition timing) or body panels which were removed.

BREAKING IT IN

Make the first miles on the new engine, easy ones. Vary the speed but do not accelerate hard. Most importantly, do not lug the engine, and avoid sustained high speeds until at least 100 miles. Check the engine oil and coolant levels frequently. Expect the engine to use a little oil until the rings seat. Change the oil and filter at 500 miles, 1500 miles, then every 3000 miles past that.

KEEP IT MAINTAINED

Now that you have just gone through all of that hard work, keep yourself from doing it all over again by thoroughly maintaining it. Not that you may not have maintained it before, heck you could have had one to two hundred thousand miles on it before doing this. However, you may have bought the vehicle used, and the previous owner did not keep up on maintenance. Which is why you just went through all of that hard work. See?

2.0L SOHC ENGINE TORQUE SPECIFICATIONS

Components	Ft. Lbs.	Nm
Camshaft sensor pickup bolts	85 inch lbs.	9.6
Camshaft sprocket bolt	85	115
Connecting rod cap bolt	20 (plus a 1/4 turn)	24 (plus a 1/4 turn)
Collar—Oil pan-to-transaxle bolts		
Step 1: Collar-to-oil pan bolts	30 inch lbs.	3
Step 2: Collar-to-transaxle bolts	80	108
Step 3: Collar-to-oil pan bolts	40	54
Crankshaft main bearing cap/bedplate		
M8 bedplate bolts	22	30
M11 main bearing cap bolts	60	81
Crankshaft damper bolt	105	142
Cylinder head bolts	①	
Cylinder head cover bolts	105 inch lbs.	12
Drive plate-to-flywheel bolts	70	95
Engine mount bracket—right	45	61
Exhaust manifold-to-cylinder head bolts	200 inch lbs.	23
Exhaust manifold heat shield bolts	105 inch lbs.	12
Front mount torque bracket bolts	24	33
Front powertrain bending strut		
Long bolts	75	101
Short bolts	45	61
Intake manifold bolts	105 inch lbs.	12
Oil filter adapter		
Fastener	60	80
Oil filter	15	20
Oil pan		
Bolts	105 inch lbs.	12
Drain plug	20	27
Oil pump attaching		
Bolts	250 inch lbs.	28
Oil pump cover fastener	105 inch lbs.	12
Oil pump pick-up tube bolt	250 inch lbs.	28
Oil pump relief valve cap	30	41
Rear torque bracket		
Bolts with automatic transaxle	80	110
Bolts with manual transaxle	45	61
Rocker arm shaft		
Bolts	250 inch lbs.	28
Spark plugs	20	27
Thermostat housing bolts	200 inch lbs.	23
Timing belt cover bolts (M6)	105 inch lbs.	12
Timing belt tensioner assembly—mechanical		
Bolts	250 inch lbs.	28
Timing belt tensioner—hydraulic		
Pulley bolt	50	68
Pivot bracket bolt	23	31
Tensioner bolt	23	31
Water pump mounting bolts	105 inch lbs.	12

① Refer to the text for the tightening sequence

90903C04

2.0L DOHC ENGINE TORQUE SPECIFICATIONS

Components	Ft. Lbs.	Nm
Camshaft and cam follower		
Cylinder head cover	9	12-Jan
Bearing head covers No's. 2, 3, 4 and 5	9	12
Bearing head cover No's. 1 and 6	20	28
Cylinder head and valve		
Cylinder head bolts		
Long bolt	48 (plus a 1/4 turn)	67 (plus a 1/4 turn)
Short bolt	20 (plus a 1/4 turn)	28 (plus a 1/4 turn)
Oil pan and oil pump		
Oil filter	15	21
Adapter	40	55
Oil pan	9	12
Oil pick-up tube	20	28
Oil pump	17	23
Oil pump		
Relief valve retaining cap	39	54
Oil pump cover	9	12
Piston, connecting rod and cylinder block		
Connecting rod cap bolt	20 (plus a 1/4 turn)	28 (plus a 1/4 turn)
Crankshaft		
Knock sensor	7	10
Bedplate bolts	21	28
Main bearing cap bolts	55	75

90903C08

2.4L DOHC ENGINE TORQUE SPECIFICATIONS

Components	Ft. Lbs.	Nm
Balance shaft carrier-to-block bolts	40	54
Balance shaft gear cover fastener	105 inch lbs.	12
Balance shaft sprockets bolts	250 inch lbs.	28
Balance shaft chain tensioner bolts	105 inch lbs.	12
Balance shaft carrier cover bolts	105 inch lbs.	12
Camshaft sensor pickup bolts	20	27
Camshaft sprocket bolt	75	101
Connecting rod cap bolts	20 (plus a 1/4 turn)	27 (plus a 1/4 turn)
Crankshaft main bearing cap/bedplate		
M8 bedplate bolts	250 inch lbs.	34
Main cap bolts M11	30 (plus a 1/4 turn)	41 (plus a 1/4 turn)
Crankshaft damper bolt	100	135
Cylinder head bolts	①	
Cylinder head cover bolts	105 inch lbs.	12
Drive plate-to-crankshaft bolts	70	95
Engine mount bracket—right	45	61
Engine mount—front and rear	45	61
Exhaust manifold-to-cylinder head bolts	200 inch lbs.	23
Exhaust manifold heat shield bolts	105 inch lbs.	12
Front torque bracket bolts	24	33
Front powertrain bending strut		
Long bolts	75	101
Short bolts	45	61
Intake manifold bolts	20	27
Oil filter	15	20
Oil pan		
Bolts	105 inch lbs.	12
Drain plug	20	27
Oil pan collar		
Collar-to-pan bolts	①	
Collar-to-transaxle bolts	①	
Oil pump attaching		
Attaching bolts	250 inch lbs.	28
Pump cover fastener	105 inch lbs.	12
Pump pick-up tube bolt	250 inch lbs.	28
Relief valve cap	30	41
Rear torque bracket bolts	80	110
Spark plugs	20	28
Thermostat housing bolts	200 inch lbs.	23
Timing belt cover		
Bolts M6	40 inch lbs.	4.5
Inner cover to head/oil pump bolts M6	105 inch lbs.	12
Timing belt tensioner assembly bolts	45	61
Water pump mounting bolts	105 inch lbs.	12

① Refer to the text for the tightening sequence

2.5L SOHC ENGINE TORQUE SPECIFICATIONS

Components	Ft. Lbs.	Nm
Auto tensioner bolt	17	23
Camshaft sprocket bolt	65	88
Connecting rod cap nut	38	52
Crankshaft pulley bolt	134	182
Cylinder head bolts	80	108
Cylinder head cover bolts	31 inch lbs.	3.5
Distributor nut	115 inch lbs.	13
Drive plate-to-crankshaft bolts	70	95
Exhaust manifold nut	33	44
Engine support bracket bolt	33	44
Heater pipe assembly	168 inch lbs.	19
Idler pulley bolt	33	44
Intake manifold plenum bolt	160 inch lbs.	18
Intake manifold plenum support		
M8 bolt	160 inch lbs.	18
M10 bolt	26.5	36
Intake manifold nut	186 inch lbs.	21
Main bearing cap bolt	69	94
Oil filter	124 inch lbs.	14
Oil filter bracket bolt	17	23
Oil pan bolt	53 inch lbs.	6
Oil pickup tube bolt	168 inch lbs.	19
Oil pump case		
M8 bolt	124 inch lbs.	14
M10 bolt	30	41
Oil pump cover bolt	88.5 inch lbs.	10
Oil seal retainer bolt	97 inch lbs.	11
Rocker arm and shaft bolt	23	31
Spark plug	18	25
Tensioner pulley bolt	35	48
Tensioner arm assembly bolt	33	44
Thermostat housing bolt	168 inch lbs.	19
Thrust case bolt	115 inch lbs.	13
Water inlet pipe bolt	124 inch lbs.	14
Water pump bolt	17	24

90903C15

USING A VACUUM GAUGE

White needle = steady needle   *Dark needle = drifting needle*

The vacuum gauge is one of the most useful and easy-to-use diagnostic tools. It is inexpensive, easy to hook up, and provides valuable information about the condition of your engine.

Indication: Normal engine in good condition

Gauge reading: Steady, from 17–22 in./Hg.

Indication: Sticking valve or ignition miss

Gauge reading: Needle fluctuates from 15–20 in./Hg. at idle

Indication: Late ignition or valve timing, low compression, stuck throttle valve, leaking carburetor or manifold gasket.

Gauge reading: Low (15–20 in./Hg.) but steady

Indication: Improper carburetor adjustment, or minor intake leak at carburetor or manifold

NOTE: Bad fuel injector O-rings may also cause this reading.

Gauge reading: Drifting needle

Indication: Weak valve springs, worn valve stem guides, or leaky cylinder head gasket (vibrating excessively at all speeds).

NOTE: A plugged catalytic converter may also cause this reading.

Gauge reading: Needle fluctuates as engine speed increases

Indication: Burnt valve or improper valve clearance. The needle will drop when the defective valve operates.

Gauge reading: Steady needle, but drops regularly

Indication: Choked muffler or obstruction in system. Speed up the engine. Choked muffler will exhibit a slow drop of vacuum to zero.

Gauge reading: Gradual drop in reading at idle

Indication: Worn valve guides

Gauge reading: Needle vibrates excessively at idle, but steadies as engine speed increases

TCCS3C01

Troubleshooting Engine Mechanical Problems

Problem	Cause	Solution
External oil leaks	• Cylinder head cover RTV sealant broken or improperly seated	• Replace sealant; inspect cylinder head cover sealant flange and cylinder head sealant surface for distortion and cracks
	• Oil filler cap leaking or missing	• Replace cap
	• Oil filter gasket broken or improperly seated	• Replace oil filter
	• Oil pan side gasket broken, improperly seated or opening in RTV sealant	• Replace gasket or repair opening in sealant; inspect oil pan gasket flange for distortion
	• Oil pan front oil seal broken or improperly seated	• Replace seal; inspect timing case cover and oil pan seal flange for distortion
	• Oil pan rear oil seal broken or improperly seated	• Replace seal; inspect oil pan rear oil seal flange; inspect rear main bearing cap for cracks, plugged oil return channels, or distortion in seal groove
	• Timing case cover oil seal broken or improperly seated	• Replace seal
	• Excess oil pressure because of restricted PCV valve	• Replace PCV valve
	• Oil pan drain plug loose or has stripped threads	• Repair as necessary and tighten
	• Rear oil gallery plug loose	• Use appropriate sealant on gallery plug and tighten
	• Rear camshaft plug loose or improperly seated	• Seat camshaft plug or replace and seal, as necessary
Excessive oil consumption	• Oil level too high	• Drain oil to specified level
	• Oil with wrong viscosity being used	• Replace with specified oil
	• PCV valve stuck closed	• Replace PCV valve
	• Valve stem oil deflectors (or seals) are damaged, missing, or incorrect type	• Replace valve stem oil deflectors
	• Valve stems or valve guides worn	• Measure stem-to-guide clearance and repair as necessary
	• Poorly fitted or missing valve cover baffles	• Replace valve cover
	• Piston rings broken or missing	• Replace broken or missing rings
	• Scuffed piston	• Replace piston
	• Incorrect piston ring gap	• Measure ring gap, repair as necessary
	• Piston rings sticking or excessively loose in grooves	• Measure ring side clearance, repair as necessary
	• Compression rings installed upside down	• Repair as necessary
	• Cylinder walls worn, scored, or glazed	• Repair as necessary

TCCS3C02

Troubleshooting Engine Mechanical Problems

Problem	Cause	Solution
Excessive oil consumption (cont.)	• Piston ring gaps not properly staggered • Excessive main or connecting rod bearing clearance	• Repair as necessary • Measure bearing clearance, repair as necessary
No oil pressure	• Low oil level • Oil pressure gauge, warning lamp or sending unit inaccurate • Oil pump malfunction • Oil pressure relief valve sticking • Oil passages on pressure side of pump obstructed • Oil pickup screen or tube obstructed • Loose oil inlet tube	• Add oil to correct level • Replace oil pressure gauge or warning lamp • Replace oil pump • Remove and inspect oil pressure relief valve assembly • Inspect oil passages for obstruction • Inspect oil pickup for obstruction • Tighten or seal inlet tube
Low oil pressure	• Low oil level • Inaccurate gauge, warning lamp or sending unit • Oil excessively thin because of dilution, poor quality, or improper grade • Excessive oil temperature • Oil pressure relief spring weak or sticking • Oil inlet tube and screen assembly has restriction or air leak • Excessive oil pump clearance • Excessive main, rod, or camshaft bearing clearance	• Add oil to correct level • Replace oil pressure gauge or warning lamp • Drain and refill crankcase with recommended oil • Correct cause of overheating engine • Remove and inspect oil pressure relief valve assembly • Remove and inspect oil inlet tube and screen assembly. (Fill inlet tube with lacquer thinner to locate leaks.) • Measure clearances • Measure bearing clearances, repair as necessary
High oil pressure	• Improper oil viscosity • Oil pressure gauge or sending unit inaccurate • Oil pressure relief valve sticking closed	• Drain and refill crankcase with correct viscosity oil • Replace oil pressure gauge • Remove and inspect oil pressure relief valve assembly
Main bearing noise	• Insufficient oil supply • Main bearing clearance excessive • Bearing insert missing • Crankshaft end-play excessive • Improperly tightened main bearing cap bolts • Loose flywheel or drive plate • Loose or damaged vibration damper	• Inspect for low oil level and low oil pressure • Measure main bearing clearance, repair as necessary • Replace missing insert • Measure end-play, repair as necessary • Tighten bolts with specified torque • Tighten flywheel or drive plate attaching bolts • Repair as necessary

TCCS3C03

Troubleshooting Engine Mechanical Problems

Problem	Cause	Solution
Connecting rod bearing noise	• Insufficient oil supply	• Inspect for low oil level and low oil pressure
	• Carbon build-up on piston	• Remove carbon from piston crown
	• Bearing clearance excessive or bearing missing	• Measure clearance, repair as necessary
	• Crankshaft connecting rod journal out-of-round	• Measure journal dimensions, repair or replace as necessary
	• Misaligned connecting rod or cap	• Repair as necessary
	• Connecting rod bolts tightened improperly	• Tighten bolts with specified torque
Piston noise	• Piston-to-cylinder wall clearance excessive (scuffed piston)	• Measure clearance and examine piston
	• Cylinder walls excessively tapered or out-of-round	• Measure cylinder wall dimensions, rebore cylinder
	• Piston ring broken	• Replace all rings on piston
	• Loose or seized piston pin	• Measure piston-to-pin clearance, repair as necessary
	• Connecting rods misaligned	• Measure rod alignment, straighten or replace
	• Piston ring side clearance excessively loose or tight	• Measure ring side clearance, repair as necessary
	• Carbon build-up on piston is excessive	• Remove carbon from piston
Valve actuating component noise	• Insufficient oil supply	• Check for: (a) Low oil level (b) Low oil pressure (c) Wrong hydraulic tappets (d) Restricted oil gallery (e) Excessive tappet to bore clearance
	• Rocker arms or pivots worn	• Replace worn rocker arms or pivots
	• Foreign objects or chips in hydraulic tappets	• Clean tappets
	• Excessive tappet leak-down	• Replace valve tappet
	• Tappet face worn	• Replace tappet; inspect corresponding cam lobe for wear
	• Broken or cocked valve springs	• Properly seat cocked springs; replace broken springs
	• Stem-to-guide clearance excessive	• Measure stem-to-guide clearance, repair as required
	• Valve bent	• Replace valve
	• Loose rocker arms	• Check and repair as necessary
	• Valve seat runout excessive	• Regrind valve seat/valves
	• Missing valve lock	• Install valve lock
	• Excessive engine oil	• Correct oil level

TCCS3C04

Troubleshooting Engine Performance

Problem	Cause	Solution
Hard starting (engine cranks normally)	• Faulty engine control system component	• Repair or replace as necessary
	• Faulty fuel pump	• Replace fuel pump
	• Faulty fuel system component	• Repair or replace as necessary
	• Faulty ignition coil	• Test and replace as necessary
	• Improper spark plug gap	• Adjust gap
	• Incorrect ignition timing	• Adjust timing
	• Incorrect valve timing	• Check valve timing; repair as necessary
Rough idle or stalling	• Incorrect curb or fast idle speed	• Adjust curb or fast idle speed (If possible)
	• Incorrect ignition timing	• Adjust timing to specification
	• Improper feedback system operation	• Refer to Chapter 4
	• Faulty EGR valve operation	• Test EGR system and replace as necessary
	• Faulty PCV valve air flow	• Test PCV valve and replace as necessary
	• Faulty TAC vacuum motor or valve	• Repair as necessary
	• Air leak into manifold vacuum	• Inspect manifold vacuum connections and repair as necessary
	• Faulty distributor rotor or cap	• Replace rotor or cap (Distributor systems only)
	• Improperly seated valves	• Test cylinder compression, repair as necessary
	• Incorrect ignition wiring	• Inspect wiring and correct as necessary
	• Faulty ignition coil	• Test coil and replace as necessary
	• Restricted air vent or idle passages	• Clean passages
	• Restricted air cleaner	• Clean or replace air cleaner filter element
Faulty low-speed operation	• Restricted idle air vents and passages	• Clean air vents and passages
	• Restricted air cleaner	• Clean or replace air cleaner filter element
	• Faulty spark plugs	• Clean or replace spark plugs
	• Dirty, corroded, or loose ignition secondary circuit wire connections	• Clean or tighten secondary circuit wire connections
	• Improper feedback system operation	• Refer to Chapter 4
	• Faulty ignition coil high voltage wire	• Replace ignition coil high voltage wire (Distributor systems only)
	• Faulty distributor cap	• Replace cap (Distributor systems only)
Faulty acceleration	• Incorrect ignition timing	• Adjust timing
	• Faulty fuel system component	• Repair or replace as necessary
	• Faulty spark plug(s)	• Clean or replace spark plug(s)
	• Improperly seated valves	• Test cylinder compression, repair as necessary
	• Faulty ignition coil	• Test coil and replace as necessary

Troubleshooting Engine Performance

Problem	Cause	Solution
Faulty acceleration (cont.)	• Improper feedback system operation	• Refer to Chapter 4
Faulty high speed operation	• Incorrect ignition timing • Faulty advance mechanism • Low fuel pump volume • Wrong spark plug air gap or wrong plug • Partially restricted exhaust manifold, exhaust pipe, catalytic converter, muffler, or tailpipe • Restricted vacuum passages • Restricted air cleaner • Faulty distributor rotor or cap • Faulty ignition coil • Improperly seated valve(s) • Faulty valve spring(s) • Incorrect valve timing • Intake manifold restricted • Worn distributor shaft • Improper feedback system operation	• Adjust timing (if possible) • Check advance mechanism and repair as necessary (Distributor systems only) • Replace fuel pump • Adjust air gap or install correct plug • Eliminate restriction • Clean passages • Cleaner or replace filter element as necessary • Replace rotor or cap (Distributor systems only) • Test coil and replace as necessary • Test cylinder compression, repair as necessary • Inspect and test valve spring tension, replace as necessary • Check valve timing and repair as necessary • Remove restriction or replace manifold • Replace shaft (Distributor systems only) • Refer to Chapter 4
Misfire at all speeds	• Faulty spark plug(s) • Faulty spark plug wire(s) • Faulty distributor cap or rotor • Faulty ignition coil • Primary ignition circuit shorted or open intermittently • Improperly seated valve(s) • Faulty hydraulic tappet(s) • Improper feedback system operation • Faulty valve spring(s) • Worn camshaft lobes • Air leak into manifold • Fuel pump volume or pressure low • Blown cylinder head gasket • Intake or exhaust manifold passage(s) restricted	• Clean or relace spark plug(s) • Replace as necessary • Replace cap or rotor (Distributor systems only) • Test coil and replace as necessary • Troubleshoot primary circuit and repair as necessary • Test cylinder compression, repair as necessary • Clean or replace tappet(s) • Refer to Chapter 4 • Inspect and test valve spring tension, repair as necessary • Replace camshaft • Check manifold vacuum and repair as necessary • Replace fuel pump • Replace gasket • Pass chain through passage(s) and repair as necessary
Power not up to normal	• Incorrect ignition timing • Faulty distributor rotor	• Adjust timing • Replace rotor (Distributor systems only)

Troubleshooting Engine Performance

Problem	Cause	Solution
Power not up to normal (cont.)	• Incorrect spark plug gap	• Adjust gap
	• Faulty fuel pump	• Replace fuel pump
	• Faulty fuel pump	• Replace fuel pump
	• Incorrect valve timing	• Check valve timing and repair as necessary
	• Faulty ignition coil	• Test coil and replace as necessary
	• Faulty ignition wires	• Test wires and replace as necessary
	• Improperly seated valves	• Test cylinder compression and repair as necessary
	• Blown cylinder head gasket	• Replace gasket
	• Leaking piston rings	• Test compression and repair as necessary
	• Improper feedback system operation	• Refer to Chapter 4
Intake backfire	• Improper ignition timing	• Adjust timing
	• Defective EGR component	• Repair as necessary
	• Defective TAC vacuum motor or valve	• Repair as necessary
Exhaust backfire	• Air leak into manifold vacuum	• Check manifold vacuum and repair as necessary
	• Faulty air injection diverter valve	• Test diverter valve and replace as necessary
	• Exhaust leak	• Locate and eliminate leak
Ping or spark knock	• Incorrect ignition timing	• Adjust timing
	• Distributor advance malfunction	• Inspect advance mechanism and repair as necessary (Distributor systems only)
	• Excessive combustion chamber deposits	• Remove with combustion chamber cleaner
	• Air leak into manifold vacuum	• Check manifold vacuum and repair as necessary
	• Excessively high compression	• Test compression and repair as necessary
	• Fuel octane rating excessively low	• Try alternate fuel source
	• Sharp edges in combustion chamber	• Grind smooth
	• EGR valve not functioning properly	• Test EGR system and replace as necessary
Surging (at cruising to top speeds)	• Low fuel pump pressure or volume	• Replace fuel pump
	• Improper PCV valve air flow	• Test PCV valve and replace as necessary
	• Air leak into manifold vacuum	• Check manifold vacuum and repair as necessary
	• Incorrect spark advance	• Test and replace as necessary
	• Restricted fuel filter	• Replace fuel filter
	• Restricted air cleaner	• Clean or replace air cleaner filter element
	• EGR valve not functioning properly	• Test EGR system and replace as necessary
	• Improper feedback system operation	• Refer to Chapter 4

Troubleshooting the Serpentine Drive Belt

Problem	Cause	Solution
Tension sheeting fabric failure (woven fabric on outside circumference of belt has cracked or separated from body of belt)	• Grooved or backside idler pulley diameters are less than minimum recommended • Tension sheeting contacting (rubbing) stationary object • Excessive heat causing woven fabric to age • Tension sheeting splice has fractured	• Replace pulley(s) not conforming to specification • Correct rubbing condition • Replace belt • Replace belt
Noise (objectional squeal, squeak, or rumble is heard or felt while drive belt is in operation)	• Belt slippage • Bearing noise • Belt misalignment • Belt-to-pulley mismatch • Driven component inducing vibration • System resonant frequency inducing vibration	• Adjust belt • Locate and repair • Align belt/pulley(s) • Install correct belt • Locate defective driven component and repair • Vary belt tension within specifications. Replace belt.
Rib chunking (one or more ribs has separated from belt body)	• Foreign objects imbedded in pulley grooves • Installation damage • Drive loads in excess of design specifications • Insufficient internal belt adhesion	• Remove foreign objects from pulley grooves • Replace belt • Adjust belt tension • Replace belt
Rib or belt wear (belt ribs contact bottom of pulley grooves)	• Pulley(s) misaligned • Mismatch of belt and pulley groove widths • Abrasive environment • Rusted pulley(s) • Sharp or jagged pulley groove tips • Rubber deteriorated	• Align pulley(s) • Replace belt • Replace belt • Clean rust from pulley(s) • Replace pulley • Replace belt
Longitudinal belt cracking (cracks between two ribs)	• Belt has mistracked from pulley groove • Pulley groove tip has worn away rubber-to-tensile member	• Replace belt • Replace belt
Belt slips	• Belt slipping because of insufficient tension • Belt or pulley subjected to substance (belt dressing, oil, ethylene glycol) that has reduced friction • Driven component bearing failure • Belt glazed and hardened from heat and excessive slippage	• Adjust tension • Replace belt and clean pulleys • Replace faulty component bearing • Replace belt
"Groove jumping" (belt does not maintain correct position on pulley, or turns over and/or runs off pulleys)	• Insufficient belt tension • Pulley(s) not within design tolerance • Foreign object(s) in grooves	• Adjust belt tension • Replace pulley(s) • Remove foreign objects from grooves

TCCS3C09

Troubleshooting the Serpentine Drive Belt

Problem	Cause	Solution
"Groove jumping" (belt does not maintain correct position on pulley, or turns over and/or runs off pulleys)	• Excessive belt speed • Pulley misalignment • Belt-to-pulley profile mismatched • Belt cordline is distorted	• Avoid excessive engine acceleration • Align pulley(s) • Install correct belt • Replace belt
Belt broken (Note: identify and correct problem before replacement belt is installed)	• Excessive tension • Tensile members damaged during belt installation • Belt turnover • Severe pulley misalignment • Bracket, pulley, or bearing failure	• Replace belt and adjust tension to specification • Replace belt • Replace belt • Align pulley(s) • Replace defective component and belt
Cord edge failure (tensile member exposed at edges of belt or separated from belt body)	• Excessive tension • Drive pulley misalignment • Belt contacting stationary object • Pulley irregularities • Improper pulley construction • Insufficient adhesion between tensile member and rubber matrix	• Adjust belt tension • Align pulley • Correct as necessary • Replace pulley • Replace pulley • Replace belt and adjust tension to specifications
Sporadic rib cracking (multiple cracks in belt ribs at random intervals)	• Ribbed pulley(s) diameter less than minimum specification • Backside bend flat pulley(s) diameter less than minimum • Excessive heat condition causing rubber to harden • Excessive belt thickness • Belt overcured • Excessive tension	• Replace pulley(s) • Replace pulley(s) • Correct heat condition as necessary • Replace belt • Replace belt • Adjust belt tension

TCCS3C10

Troubleshooting the Cooling System

Problem	Cause	Solution
High temperature gauge indication— overheating	• Coolant level low • Improper fan operation • Radiator hose(s) collapsed • Radiator airflow blocked • Faulty pressure cap • Ignition timing incorrect • Air trapped in cooling system • Heavy traffic driving • Incorrect cooling system component(s) installed • Faulty thermostat • Water pump shaft broken or impeller loose • Radiator tubes clogged • Cooling system clogged • Casting flash in cooling passages • Brakes dragging • Excessive engine friction • Antifreeze concentration over 68% • Missing air seals • Faulty gauge or sending unit • Loss of coolant flow caused by leakage or foaming • Viscous fan drive failed	• Replenish coolant • Repair or replace as necessary • Replace hose(s) • Remove restriction (bug screen, fog lamps, etc.) • Replace pressure cap • Adjust ignition timing • Purge air • Operate at fast idle in neutral intermittently to cool engine • Install proper component(s) • Replace thermostat • Replace water pump • Flush radiator • Flush system • Repair or replace as necessary. Flash may be visible by removing cooling system components or removing core plugs. • Repair brakes • Repair engine • Lower antifreeze concentration percentage • Replace air seals • Repair or replace faulty component • Repair or replace leaking component, replace coolant • Replace unit
Low temperature indication— undercooling	• Thermostat stuck open • Faulty gauge or sending unit	• Replace thermostat • Repair or replace faulty component
Coolant loss—boilover	• Overfilled cooling system • Quick shutdown after hard (hot) run • Air in system resulting in occasional ''burping'' of coolant • Insufficient antifreeze allowing coolant boiling point to be too low • Antifreeze deteriorated because of age or contamination • Leaks due to loose hose clamps, loose nuts, bolts, drain plugs, faulty hoses, or defective radiator	• Reduce coolant level to proper specification • Allow engine to run at fast idle prior to shutdown • Purge system • Add antifreeze to raise boiling point • Replace coolant • Pressure test system to locate source of leak(s) then repair as necessary

TCCS3C11

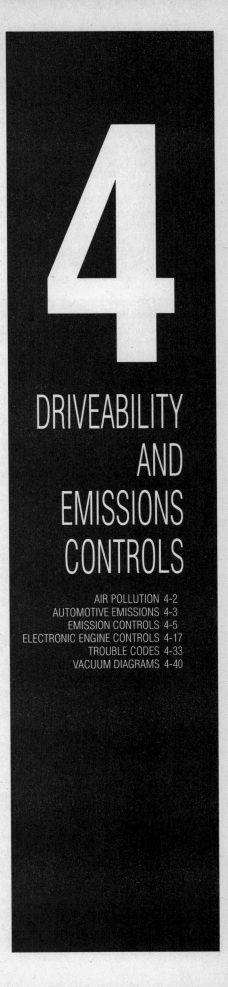

4

DRIVEABILITY AND EMISSIONS CONTROLS

AIR POLLUTION

The earth's atmosphere, at or near sea level, consists approximately of 78 percent nitrogen, 21 percent oxygen and 1 percent other gases. If it were possible to remain in this state, 100 percent clean air would result. However, many varied sources allow other gases and particulates to mix with the clean air, causing our atmosphere to become unclean or polluted.

Some of these pollutants are visible while others are invisible, with each having the capability of causing distress to the eyes, ears, throat, skin and respiratory system. Should these pollutants become concentrated in a specific area and under certain conditions, death could result due to the displacement or chemical change of the oxygen content in the air. These pollutants can also cause great damage to the environment and to the many man made objects that are exposed to the elements.

To better understand the causes of air pollution, the pollutants can be categorized into 3 separate types, natural, industrial and automotive.

Natural Pollutants

Natural pollution has been present on earth since before man appeared and continues to be a factor when discussing air pollution, although it causes only a small percentage of the overall pollution problem. It is the direct result of decaying organic matter, wind born smoke and particulates from such natural events as plain and forest fires (ignited by heat or lightning), volcanic ash, sand and dust which can spread over a large area of the countryside.

Such a phenomenon of natural pollution has been seen in the form of volcanic eruptions, with the resulting plume of smoke, steam and volcanic ash blotting out the sun's rays as it spreads and rises higher into the atmosphere. As it travels into the atmosphere the upper air currents catch and carry the smoke and ash, while condensing the steam back into water vapor. As the water vapor, smoke and ash travel on their journey, the smoke dissipates into the atmosphere while the ash and moisture settle back to earth in a trail hundreds of miles long. In some cases, lives are lost and millions of dollars of property damage result.

Industrial Pollutants

Industrial pollution is caused primarily by industrial processes, the burning of coal, oil and natural gas, which in turn produce smoke and fumes. Because the burning fuels contain large amounts of sulfur, the principal ingredients of smoke and fumes are sulfur dioxide and particulate matter. This type of pollutant occurs most severely during still, damp and cool weather, such as at night. Even in its less severe form, this pollutant is not confined to just cities. Because of air movements, the pollutants move for miles over the surrounding countryside, leaving in its path a barren and unhealthy environment for all living things.

Working with Federal, State and Local mandated regulations and by carefully monitoring emissions, big business has greatly reduced the amount of pollutant introduced from its industrial sources, striving to obtain an acceptable level. Because of the mandated industrial emission clean up, many land areas and streams in and around the cities that were formerly barren of vegetation and life, have now begun to move back in the direction of nature's intended balance.

Automotive Pollutants

The third major source of air pollution is automotive emissions. The emissions from the internal combustion engines were not an appreciable problem years ago because of the small number of registered vehicles and the nation's small highway system. However, during the early 1950's, the trend of the American people was to move from the cities to the surrounding suburbs. This caused an immediate problem in transportation because the majority of suburbs were not afforded mass transit conveniences. This lack of transportation created an attractive market for the automobile manufacturers, which resulted in a dramatic increase in the number of vehicles produced and sold, along with a marked increase in highway construction

between cities and the suburbs. Multi-vehicle families emerged with a growing emphasis placed on an individual vehicle per family member. As the increase in vehicle ownership and usage occurred, so did pollutant levels in and around the cities, as suburbanites drove daily to their businesses and employment, returning at the end of the day to their homes in the suburbs.

It was noted that a smoke and fog type haze was being formed and at times, remained in suspension over the cities, taking time to dissipate. At first this "smog," derived from the words "smoke" and "fog," was thought to result from industrial pollution but it was determined that automobile emissions shared the blame. It was discovered that when normal automobile emissions were exposed to sunlight for a period of time, complex chemical reactions would take place.

It is now known that smog is a photo chemical layer which develops when certain oxides of nitrogen (NOx) and unburned hydrocarbons (HC) from automobile emissions are exposed to sunlight. Pollution was more severe when smog would become stagnant over an area in which a warm layer of air settled over the top of the cooler air mass, trapping and holding the cooler mass at ground level. The trapped cooler air would keep the emissions from being dispersed and diluted through normal air flows. This type of air stagnation was given the name "Temperature Inversion."

TEMPERATURE INVERSION

In normal weather situations, surface air is warmed by heat radiating from the earth's surface and the sun's rays. This causes it to rise upward, into the atmosphere. Upon rising it will cool through a convection type heat exchange with the cooler upper air. As warm air rises, the surface pollutants are carried upward and dissipated into the atmosphere.

When a temperature inversion occurs, we find the higher air is no longer cooler, but is warmer than the surface air, causing the cooler surface air to become trapped. This warm air blanket can extend from above ground level to a few hundred or even a few thousand feet into the air. As the surface air is trapped, so are the pollutants, causing a severe smog condition. Should this stagnant air mass extend to a few thousand feet high, enough air movement with the inversion takes place to allow the smog layer to rise above ground level but the pollutants still cannot dissipate. This inversion can remain for days over an area, with the smog level only rising or lowering from ground level to a few hundred feet high. Meanwhile, the pollutant levels increase, causing eye irritation, respiratory problems, reduced visibility, plant damage and in some cases, even disease.

This inversion phenomenon was first noted in the Los Angeles, California area. The city lies in terrain resembling a basin and with certain weather conditions, a cold air mass is held in the basin while a warmer air mass covers it like a lid.

Because this type of condition was first documented as prevalent in the Los Angeles area, this type of trapped pollution was named Los Angeles Smog, although it occurs in other areas where a large concentration of automobiles are used and the air remains stagnant for any length of time.

HEAT TRANSFER

Consider the internal combustion engine as a machine in which raw materials must be placed so a finished product comes out. As in any machine operation, a certain amount of wasted material is formed. When we relate this to the internal combustion engine, we find that through the input of air and fuel, we obtain power during the combustion process to drive the vehicle. The by-product or waste of this power is, in part, heat and exhaust gases with which we must dispose.

The heat from the combustion process can rise to over 4000°F (2204°C). The dissipation of this heat is controlled by a ram air effect, the use of cooling fans to cause air flow and a liquid coolant solution surrounding the combustion area to transfer the heat of combustion through the cylinder walls and into the coolant. The coolant is then directed to a thin-finned, multi-tubed radiator, from which the excess heat is transferred to the atmosphere by 1 of the 3 heat transfer methods, conduction, convection or radiation.

The cooling of the combustion area is an important part in the control of exhaust emissions. To understand the behavior of the combustion and transfer of its heat, consider the air/fuel charge. It is ignited and the flame front burns progressively across the combustion chamber until the burning charge reaches the cylinder walls. Some of the fuel in contact with the walls is not hot enough to burn, thereby snuffing out or quenching the combustion process. This leaves unburned fuel in the combustion chamber. This unburned fuel is then forced out of the cylinder and into the exhaust system, along with the exhaust gases.

Many attempts have been made to minimize the amount of unburned fuel in the combustion chambers due to quenching, by increasing the coolant temperature and lessening the contact area of the coolant around the combustion area. However, design limitations within the combustion chambers prevent the complete burning of the air/fuel charge, so a certain amount of the unburned fuel is still expelled into the exhaust system, regardless of modifications to the engine.

AUTOMOTIVE EMISSIONS

Before emission controls were mandated on internal combustion engines, other sources of engine pollutants were discovered along with the exhaust emissions. It was determined that engine combustion exhaust produced approximately 60 percent of the total emission pollutants, fuel evaporation from the fuel tank and carburetor vents produced 20 percent, with the final 20 percent being produced through the crankcase as a by-product of the combustion process.

Exhaust Gases

The exhaust gases emitted into the atmosphere are a combination of burned and unburned fuel. To understand the exhaust emission and its composition, we must review some basic chemistry.

When the air/fuel mixture is introduced into the engine, we are mixing air, composed of nitrogen (78 percent), oxygen (21 percent) and other gases (1 percent) with the fuel, which is 100 percent hydrocarbons (HC), in a semi-controlled ratio. As the combustion process is accomplished, power is produced to move the vehicle while the heat of combustion is transferred to the cooling system. The exhaust gases are then composed of nitrogen, a diatomic gas (N_2), the same as was introduced in the engine, carbon dioxide (CO_2), the same gas that is used in beverage carbonation, and water vapor (H_2O). The nitrogen (N_2), for the most part, passes through the engine unchanged, while the oxygen (O_2) reacts (burns) with the hydrocarbons (HC) and produces the carbon dioxide (CO_2) and the water vapors (H_2O). If this chemical process would be the only process to take place, the exhaust emissions would be harmless. However, during the combustion process, other compounds are formed which are considered dangerous. These pollutants are hydrocarbons (HC), carbon monoxide (CO), oxides of nitrogen (NOx) oxides of sulfur (SOx) and engine particulates.

HYDROCARBONS

Hydrocarbons (HC) are essentially fuel which was not burned during the combustion process or which has escaped into the atmosphere through fuel evaporation. The main sources of incomplete combustion are rich air/fuel mixtures, low engine temperatures and improper spark timing. The main sources of hydrocarbon emission through fuel evaporation on most vehicles used to be the vehicle's fuel tank and carburetor float bowl.

To reduce combustion hydrocarbon emission, engine modifications were made to minimize dead space and surface area in the combustion chamber. In addition, the air/fuel mixture was made more lean through the improved control which feedback carburetion and fuel injection offers and by the addition of external controls to aid in further combustion of the hydrocarbons outside the engine. Two such methods were the addition of air injection systems, to inject fresh air into the exhaust manifolds and the installation of catalytic converters, units that are able to burn traces of hydrocarbons without affecting the internal combustion process or fuel economy.

To control hydrocarbon emissions through fuel evaporation, modifications were made to the fuel tank to allow storage of the fuel vapors during periods of engine shut-down. Modifications were also made to the air intake system so that at specific times during engine operation, these vapors may be purged and burned by blending them with the air/fuel mixture.

CARBON MONOXIDE

Carbon monoxide is formed when not enough oxygen is present during the combustion process to convert carbon (C) to carbon dioxide (CO_2). An increase in the carbon monoxide (CO) emission is normally accompanied by an increase in the hydrocarbon (HC) emission because of the lack of oxygen to completely burn all of the fuel mixture.

Carbon monoxide (CO) also increases the rate at which the photo chemical smog is formed by speeding up the conversion of nitric oxide (NO) to nitrogen dioxide (NO_2). To accomplish this, carbon monoxide (CO) combines with oxygen (O_2) and nitric oxide (NO) to produce carbon dioxide (CO_2) and nitrogen dioxide (NO_2). ($CO + O_2 + NO = CO_2 + NO_2$).

The dangers of carbon monoxide, which is an odorless and colorless toxic gas are many. When carbon monoxide is inhaled into the lungs and passed into the blood stream, oxygen is replaced by the carbon monoxide in the red blood cells, causing a reduction in the amount of oxygen supplied to the many parts of the body. This lack of oxygen causes headaches, lack of coordination, reduced mental alertness and, should the carbon monoxide concentration be high enough, death could result.

NITROGEN

Normally, nitrogen is an inert gas. When heated to approximately 2500°F (1371°C) through the combustion process, this gas becomes active and causes an increase in the nitric oxide (NO) emission.

Oxides of nitrogen (NOx) are composed of approximately 97–98 percent nitric oxide (NO). Nitric oxide is a colorless gas but when it is passed into the atmosphere, it combines with oxygen and forms nitrogen dioxide (NO_2). The nitrogen dioxide then combines with chemically active hydrocarbons (HC) and when in the presence of sunlight, causes the formation of photochemical smog.

Ozone

To further complicate matters, some of the nitrogen dioxide (NO_2) is broken apart by the sunlight to form nitric oxide and oxygen. ($NO_2 +$ sunlight $= NO + O$). This single atom of oxygen then combines with diatomic (meaning 2 atoms) oxygen (O_2) to form ozone (O_3). Ozone is one of the smells associated with smog. It has a pungent and offensive odor, irritates the eyes and lung tissues, affects the growth of plant life and causes rapid deterioration of rubber products. Ozone can be formed by sunlight as well as electrical discharge into the air.

The most common discharge area on the automobile engine is the secondary ignition electrical system, especially when inferior quality spark plug cables are used. As the surge of high voltage is routed through the secondary cable, the circuit builds up an electrical field around the wire, which acts upon the oxygen in the surrounding air to form the ozone. The faint glow along the cable with the engine running that may be visible on a dark night, is called the "corona discharge." It is the result of the electrical field passing from a high along the cable, to a low in the surrounding air, which forms the ozone gas. The combination of corona and ozone has been a major cause of cable deterioration. Recently, different and better quality insulating materials have lengthened the life of the electrical cables.

Although ozone at ground level can be harmful, ozone is beneficial to the earth's inhabitants. By having a concentrated ozone layer called the "ozonosphere," between 10 and 20 miles (16–32 km) up in the atmosphere, much of the ultra violet radiation from the sun's rays are absorbed and screened. If this ozone layer were not present, much of the earth's surface would be burned, dried and unfit for human life.

OXIDES OF SULFUR

Oxides of sulfur (SOx) were initially ignored in the exhaust system emissions, since the sulfur content of gasoline as a fuel is less than 1/10 of 1 percent. Because of this small amount, it was felt that it contributed very little to the overall pollution problem. However, because of the difficulty in solving the sulfur emissions in industrial pollutions and the introduction of catalytic converter to the automobile exhaust systems, a change was mandated. The automobile exhaust system, when equipped with a catalytic converter, changes the sulfur dioxide (SO_2) into sulfur trioxide (SO_3).

When this combines with water vapors (H_2O), a sulfuric acid mist (H_2SO_4) is formed and is a very difficult pollutant to handle since it is extremely corrosive. This sulfuric acid mist that is formed, is the same mist that rises from the vents of an automobile battery when an active chemical reaction takes place within the battery cells.

When a large concentration of vehicles equipped with catalytic converters are operating in an area, this acid mist may rise and be distributed over a large ground area causing land, plant, crop, paint and building damage.

PARTICULATE MATTER

A certain amount of particulate matter is present in the burning of any fuel, with carbon constituting the largest percentage of the particulates. In gasoline, the remaining particulates are the burned remains of the various other compounds used in its manufacture. When a gasoline engine is in good internal condition, the particulate emissions are low but as the engine wears internally, the particulate emissions increase. By visually inspecting the tail-pipe emissions, a determination can be made as to where an engine defect may exist. An engine with light gray or blue smoke emitting from the tail pipe normally indicates an increase in the oil consumption through burning due to internal engine wear. Black smoke would indicate a defective fuel delivery system, causing the engine to operate in a rich mode. Regardless of the color of the smoke, the internal part of the engine or the fuel delivery system should be repaired to prevent excess particulate emissions.

Diesel and turbine engines emit a darkened plume of smoke from the exhaust system because of the type of fuel used. Emission control regulations are mandated for this type of emission and more stringent measures are being used to prevent excess emission of the particulate matter. Electronic components have been introduced to control the injection of the fuel at precisely the proper time of piston travel, to achieve the optimum in fuel ignition and fuel usage. Other particulate after-burning components are being tested to achieve a cleaner emission.

Good grades of engine lubricating oils should be used, which meet the manufacturers specification. Cut-rate oils can contribute to the particulate emission problem because of their low flash or ignition temperature point. Such oils burn prematurely during the combustion process causing emission of particulate matter.

The cooling system is an important factor in the reduction of particulate matter. The optimum combustion will occur, with the cooling system operating at a temperature specified by the manufacturer. The cooling system must be maintained in the same manner as the engine oiling system, as each system is required to perform properly in order for the engine to operate efficiently for a long time.

Crankcase Emissions

Crankcase emissions are made up of water, acids, unburned fuel, oil fumes and particulates. These emissions are classified as hydrocarbons (HC) and are formed by the small amount of unburned, compressed air/fuel mixture entering the crankcase from the combustion area (between the cylinder walls and piston rings) during the compression and power strokes. The head of the compression and combustion help to form the remaining crankcase emissions.

Since the first engines, crankcase emissions were allowed into the atmosphere through a road draft tube, mounted on the lower side of the engine block. Fresh air came in through an open oil filler cap or breather. The air passed through the crankcase mixing with blow-by gases. The motion of the vehicle and the air blowing past the open end of the road draft tube caused a low pressure area (vacuum) at the end of the tube. Crankcase emissions were simply drawn out of the road draft tube into the air.

To control the crankcase emission, the road draft tube was deleted. A hose and/or tubing was routed from the crankcase to the intake manifold so the blow-by emission could be burned with the air/fuel mixture. However, it was found that intake manifold vacuum, used to draw the crankcase emissions into the manifold, would vary in strength at the wrong time and not allow the proper emission flow. A regulating valve was needed to control the flow of air through the crankcase.

Testing, showed the removal of the blow-by gases from the crankcase as quickly as possible, was most important to the longevity of the engine. Should large accumulations of blow-by gases remain and condense, dilution of the engine oil would occur to form water, soots, resins, acids and lead salts, resulting in the formation of sludge and varnishes. This condensation of the blow-by gases occurs more frequently on vehicles used in numerous starting and stopping conditions, excessive idling and when the engine is not allowed to attain normal operating temperature through short runs.

Evaporative Emissions

Gasoline fuel is a major source of pollution, before and after it is burned in the automobile engine. From the time the fuel is refined, stored, pumped and transported, again stored until it is pumped into the fuel tank of the vehicle, the gasoline gives off unburned hydrocarbons (HC) into the atmosphere. Through the redesign of storage areas and venting systems, the pollution factor was diminished, but not eliminated, from the refinery standpoint. However, the automobile still remained the primary source of vaporized, unburned hydrocarbon (HC) emissions.

Fuel pumped from an underground storage tank is cool but when exposed to a warmer ambient temperature, will expand. Before controls were mandated, an owner might fill the fuel tank with fuel from an underground storage tank and park the vehicle for some time in warm area, such as a parking lot. As the fuel would warm, it would expand and should no provisions or area be provided for the expansion, the fuel would spill out of the filler neck and onto the ground, causing hydrocarbon (HC) pollution and creating a severe fire hazard. To correct this condition, the vehicle manufacturers added overflow plumbing and/or gasoline tanks with built-in expansion areas or domes.

However, this did not control the fuel vapor emission from the fuel tank. It was determined that most of the fuel evaporation occurred when the vehicle was stationary and the engine not operating. Most vehicles carry 5–25 gallons (19–95 liters) of gasoline. Should a large concentration of vehicles be parked in one area, such as a large parking lot, excessive fuel vapor emissions would take place, increasing as the temperature increases.

To prevent the vapor emission from escaping into the atmosphere, the fuel systems were designed to trap the vapors while the vehicle is stationary, by sealing the system from the atmosphere. A storage system is used to collect and hold the fuel vapors from the carburetor (if equipped) and the fuel tank when the engine is not operating. When the engine is started, the storage system is then purged of the fuel vapors, which are drawn into the engine and burned with the air/fuel mixture.

EMISSION CONTROLS

Crankcase Ventilation System

OPERATION

▶ See Figures 1, 2, 3 and 4

All vehicles are equipped with a Positive Crankcase Ventilation (PCV) system. In this system, the intake manifold vacuum removes crankcase vapors and piston blow-by from the engine. The emissions pass through the PCV valve into the intake manifold where they become part of the set air/fuel ratio. They are burned and released with the exhaust gases. The air cleaner provides replacement air when the engine does not have enough vapor or blow-by gases. In this system, fresh air does not enter the crankcase. The PCV system is composed of a PCV valve, oil separator (1995 2.0L SOHC engines only) and connecting hoses.

The PCV valve has a spring loaded plunger. The plunger meters the amount of crankcase vapors routed into the combustion chamber, depending upon intake manifold vacuum. When the engine is not operating or during engine backfire, the spring forces the plunger back against the seat, preventing vapors from flowing through the valve. When the engine is at idle or cruising, high manifold vacuum is present. At these times, manifold vacuum is able to completely compress the spring and pull the plunger to the top of the valve. There is minimal vapor flow through the valve in this position. During periods of moderate manifold vacuum, the plunger is only pulled part of the way back from the inlet, resulting in maximum vapor flow.

On 1995 2.0L SOHC engines only, the PCV system also includes an oil separator. The crankcase vapors enter the bottom of the separator, then oil accumulated in the separator drains back into the crankcase from an outlet in the bottom of the separator. The PCV valve on these engines connects to the separator and to intake manifold vacuum. Replacement air is provided to the separator by a hose attached to the air cleaner air tube.

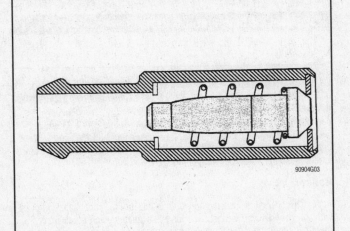

Fig. 1 Location of the oil separator, behind the intake manifold on the 1995 2.0L SOHC engine

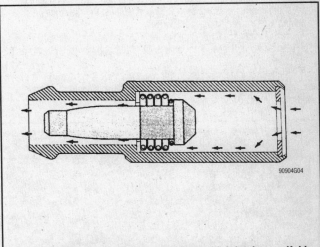

Fig. 3 Cutaway view of a PCV valve during high intake manifold vacuum, when there is minimal vapor flow

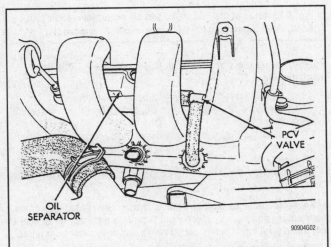

Fig. 2 Cutaway view of a PCV valve with the engine off or during engine backfire, when there is no vapor flow

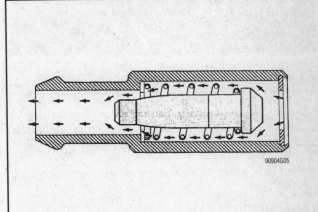

Fig. 4 Cutaway view of a PCV valve during moderate intake manifold vacuum, when there is maximum vapor flow

COMPONENT TESTING

▶ **See Figure 5**

> ✳✳ **CAUTION**
>
> **ALWAYS block the drive wheels and apply the parking brake any time you are performing a test or adjustment in which the engine must be running!**

1. With the engine idling, remove the PCV valve from its attaching point. If the valve is not obstructed, a hissing noise will be heard as air passes through the valve. Also, a strong vacuum should be felt when you place your finger over the valve inlet.

2. Attach the hose to the PCV valve. Disconnect the replacement air hose from the air plenum at the rear of the engine. Hold a piece of rigid paper loosely over the end of the replacement air hose.

3. After allowing about one minute for the crankcase pressure to decrease, the paper should draw up against the hose with a noticeable force. If the engine does not draw the paper against the grommet after installing a new valve, replace the valve hose.

4. Turn the engine **OFF**. Remove the PCV valve from the intake manifold, then shake the valve. The valve is OK if a rattling noise is heard as the valve is shaken.

5. If any of the previous tests fail, replace the PCV valve and/or hose and retest the system. Do not try to clean and reuse the old PCV valve. It should be replaced with a new one.

Fig. 5 Checking the PCV valve for clogging

REMOVAL & INSTALLATION

PCV Valve

For PCV valve removal and installation procedures, refer to Section 1 of this manual.

Oil Separator

▶ **See Figure 6**

➡ **An oil separator is only used on 1995 2.0L SOHC engines.**

1. Disconnect the negative battery cable.

2. Remove the intake manifold from the vehicle, as outlined in Section 3 of this manual.

➡ **Constant tension hose clamps are used on the separator hoses. During removal and installation, you should use the**

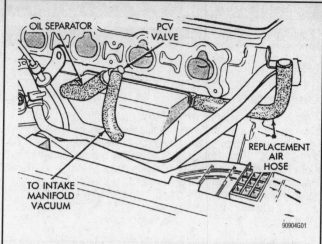

Fig. 6 Location of the PCV valve and oil separator—1995 2.0L SOHC engine (shown with the intake manifold removed)

special clamp tools available for this purpose (No. 6094 or equivalent).

3. Disconnect the PCV valve hose from the oil separator.

4. Unfasten the hose clamps, then detach the 2 hoses from the bottom of the separator.

5. Remove the 2 separator-to-block retaining bolts, then remove the separator from the vehicle.

To install:

6. Position the separator in the vehicle, and secure with the 2 retaining bolt.

➡ **An identification number or letter is stamped into the tongue of the constant tension clamps. If you need to replace a clamp, make sure to get an original replacement clamp with a matching number or letter.**

7. Connect the 2 hoses to the bottom of the separator, then secure the hoses with the clamps.

8. Attach the PCV valve hose to the oil separator.

9. Install the intake manifold, as outlined in Section 3 of this manual.

10. Connect the negative battery cable.

Evaporative Emission Controls

OPERATION

The evaporation control system prevents the emission of fuel tank vapors into the atmosphere. When fuel evaporates in the fuel tank, the vapors pass through vent hoses or tubes to a charcoal filled evaporative canister. This canister holds the vapors temporarily. The Powertrain Control Module (PCM) allows intake manifold vacuum to draw vapors into the combustion chambers during certain operating conditions. The evaporation control system is made up of the following components:

Rollover Valve

All Cirrus, Stratus, Sebring convertible and Breeze models are equipped with rollover valve(s). The rollover valve is a safety device which prevents fuel flow through the fuel tank vent valve hoses, should the vehicle roll over in an accident. The rollover valve is located on top of the fuel tank. In order to access the rollover valve, the fuel tank must be removed; however, the valve is not a serviceable component.

EVAP Canister

All vehicles use a sealed, maintenance-free evaporative (EVAP) canister. Fuel tank pressure vents into the canister. The canister temporarily holds the fuel vapors until intake manifold vacuum draws them into the combustion chamber. The PCM purges the canister through the duty cycle EVAP purge solenoid. The canister is purged at intervals and engine conditions which are predetermined by the PCM.

On all 1995–97 vehicles, as well as the 1998 Sebring convertible, the canister mounts to a bracket located behind the front passenger side fascia. On 1998 vehicles, except Sebring convertible, the canister is mounted to the rear of the vehicle, on top of the fuel tank. The vacuum and vapor tubes connect to the top of the canister. There is no scheduled maintenance interval for the charcoal canister.

Duty Cycle Evap Purge Solenoid Valve

▶ See Figure 7

Sebring and Avenger coupes with the 2.5L engine and all 1995–97 Cirrus, Stratus, Sebring convertible and Breeze models are equipped with a Duty Cycle EVAP Purge solenoid. The Duty Cycle EVAP Purge solenoid regulates the rate of vapor flow from the EVAP canister to the throttle body. The PCM operates the solenoid. During the cold start warm-up period and the hot start time delay, the PCM does not energize the solenoid. When de-energized, no vapors are purged.

When purging, the PCM energizes and de-energizes the solenoid about 5–10 times per second, depending upon operating conditions. The PCM varies the vapor flow rate by changing the solenoid pulse width. Pulse width is the amount of time the solenoid energizes.

The solenoid will not operate properly unless it is installed with the electrical connector at the top.

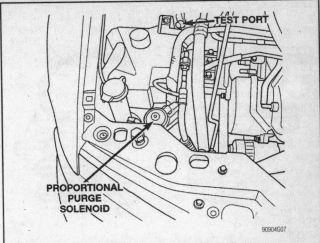

Fig. 8 Location of the Proportional Purge solenoid on Cirrus, Stratus, Sebring convertible and Breeze models

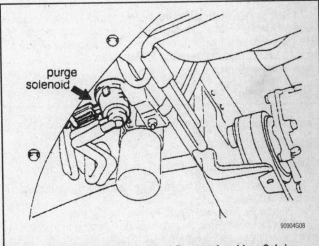

Fig. 9 Location of the Proportional Purge solenoid on Sebring and Avenger coupe models

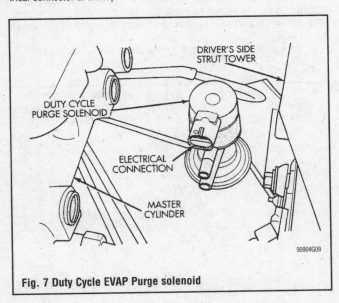

Fig. 7 Duty Cycle EVAP Purge solenoid

Proportional Purge Solenoid

▶ See Figures 8 and 9

All Sebring and Avenger coupes with the 2.0L DOHC engine, as well as all 1998 Cirrus, Stratus, Sebring convertible and Breeze models come equipped with a Proportional Purge solenoid. The solenoid regulates the rate of vapor flow from the EVAP canister to the throttle body. The PCM operates the solenoid. During the cold start warm-up period and the hot start time delay, the PCM does not energize the solenoid. When de-energized, no vapors are purged.

The solenoid operates at a frequency of 200 Hz and is controlled by an engine controller circuit that senses the current being applied to the solenoid, then adjusts that same current to achieve the desired purge flow. The proportional purge solenoid controls the purge rate of the fuel vapors from the EVAP canister and fuel tank to the engine intake manifold.

Pressure Vacuum Filler Cap

▶ See Figure 10

A pressure vacuum relief cap is used to seal the fuel tank. Tightening the cap on the fuel filler tube creates a seal between them. The relief valves in the cap are a safety feature which prevent possible excessive pressure or vacuum in the fuel tank. Excessive fuel tank pressure could be caused by a malfunction in the system or damage to the vent lines.

When the cap is removed, the seal is broken and fuel tank pressure is relieved. If the filler cap ever needs to be replaced, make sure to get the correct part.

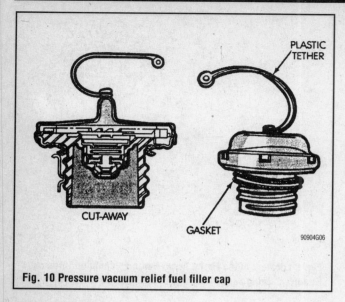

Fig. 10 Pressure vacuum relief fuel filler cap

Leak Detection Pump

All vehicles except the Sebring and Avenger coupes use a leak detection pump, which is a device used to find leaks in the evaporative emission system. The pump has a 3-port solenoid, a pump that contains a switch, a spring loaded canister vent valve seal, 2 check valves and a spring/diaphragm.

COMPONENT TESTING

Purge Control System Check

1995–97 VEHICLES

▶ See Figure 11

1. Disconnect the vacuum hose from the throttle body, then connect it to a hand-held vacuum pump.
2. Plug the nipple where the vacuum hose was disconnected.
3. Start the engine. When the engine reaches operating temperature, that is, a coolant temperature of 176°F (80°C) or higher, apply 15.7 in. Hg

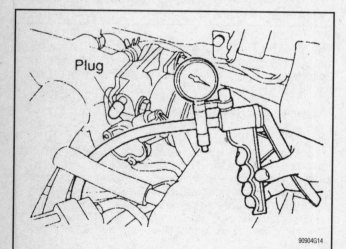

Fig. 11 Be sure to plug the vacuum hose nipple on the throttle body before checking the system

(53 kPa) of vacuum at idle to check the condition of the engine and vacuum as follows:

    a. Right after the engine is started, the vacuum should be maintained.

    b. After ten or more seconds, the vacuum should leak.

4. If any of the test results differ from the specifications, there is a fault in the operation of the system and further diagnosis is required.

1998 VEHICLES

▶ See Figure 12

➡ This test requires the use of a special purge flow indicator tool, MB995061 or equivalent.

1. Disconnect the purge hose from the EVAP canister, then connect Purge Flow Indicator MB995061, or equivalent, between the canister and the purge hose.
2. The engine should be warmed up to operating temperature, that is, a coolant temperature of 170–203°F (80–95°C) or higher, with all lights, fans and accessories off. The transaxle should be in Park for automatics or Neutral for manuals. Headlights and tail lights on Canadian vehicles will stay on even after the light switch is turned off, but this is okay.
3. Run the engine at idle for at least 3–4 minutes.
4. Check the purge flow volume when the brake is depressed suddenly a few times. The reading should be 2.5 SCFH (20cm/sec.) or more.
5. If the volume is less than the standard value, check it again with the vacuum hose disconnected from the canister. If the purge flow volume is less than the standard, check for blockages in the vacuum port and vacuum hose, and also inspect the evaporative emission purge solenoid and purge control valve.
6. If the purge flow volume is at the standard value, replace the EVAP canister.

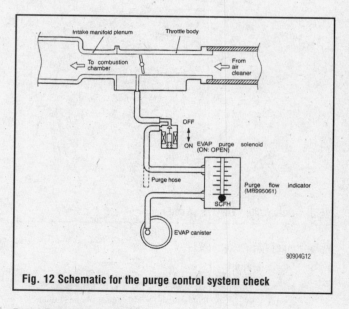

Fig. 12 Schematic for the purge control system check

Purge Port Vacuum Check

▶ See Figure 13

1. Disconnect the hose from the throttle body purge vacuum nipple.
2. Connect a hand-held vacuum pump to the nipple.
3. Start the engine and raise the idle. Regardless of the increase in engine RPM, vacuum should remain constant.
4. If no engine vacuum registers on the pump, inspect the throttle body purge port for clogging.

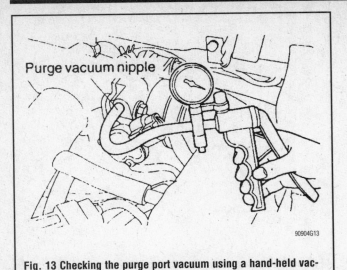

Fig. 13 Checking the purge port vacuum using a hand-held vacuum pump

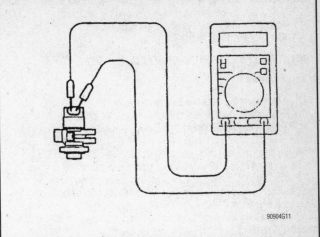

Fig. 15 Measure the resistance between the solenoid valve connector terminals

Evaporative Emission Purge Solenoid

▶ **See Figures 14 and 15**

1. Tag and disconnect the vacuum hoses from the Duty Cycle Evap Purge Solenoid or Proportional Purge Solenoid.
2. Detach the harness connector.
3. Attach a hand-held vacuum pump to the nipple (A) of the solenoid valve, as shown in the accompanying figures.
4. Check air tightness by applying vacuum with voltage applied directly from the battery to the Evaporative Emission Purge solenoid, and then without applying voltage. The desired results are as follows:
   • With battery voltage applied—vacuum should leak
   • With battery voltage not applied—vacuum should be maintained
5. Measure the resistance across the terminals of the solenoid. The standard values are as follows:
   a. 1995–97 2.0L and 2.4L engines: 25–35 ohms when at 68°F (20°C).
   b. 1995–97 2.5L engine: 31–45 ohms when at 68°F (20°C).
   c. All 1998 engines: 27–37 ohms when at 68°F (20°C).
6. If the test results differ from the specifications, replace the Evaporative Emission Purge solenoid.

REMOVAL & INSTALLATION

Evaporative Canister

ALL 1995–97 VEHICLES AND 1998 SEBRING CONVERTIBLE

▶ **See Figure 16**

1. Disconnect the negative battery cable.
2. Raise and safely support the vehicle. Remove the front passenger's side wheel.
3. Remove the retainers, then remove the splash shield.
4. Tag and disconnect the vacuum lines from the evaporative canister.
5. Push the locking tab on the electrical connector to unlock and disengage the connector.
6. Unfasten the retaining nuts, then remove the canister from the mounting bracket.

To install:

7. Install the evaporative canister to the bracket, then secure with the retaining nuts. Tighten to 50 inch lbs. (5.6 Nm).
8. Attach the electrical connector to the pump, then push the locking tab to lock the connector in place.

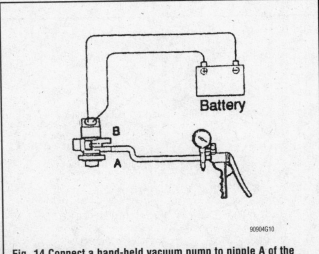

Fig. 14 Connect a hand-held vacuum pump to nipple A of the solenoid valve

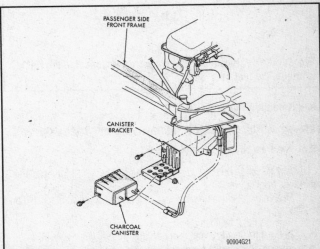

Fig. 16 Typical EVAP canister location behind the right lower front bumper fascia

9. Connect the vacuum lines to the canister, as tagged during removal.
10. Install the splash shield, securing it with the retainers.
11. Install the wheel, then carefully lower the vehicle.
12. Connect the negative battery cable.

1998 VEHICLES EXCEPT SEBRING CONVERTIBLE

▶ See Figure 17

1. Disconnect the negative battery cable.
2. Properly relieve the fuel system pressure, as described in Section 5.
3. Raise and safely support the rear of the vehicle securely on jackstands.
4. Remove the fuel tank assembly, as described in Section 5.
5. Disconnect and label the hoses from the evaporative canister.
6. On Cirrus, Stratus and Breeze models, perform the following:
   a. Disengage the electrical harness to the leak detection pump.
   b. Remove the canister-to-mounting bracket push pin.
7. On Sebring and Avenger coupes, remove the canister-to-fuel tank mounting fasteners.
8. Remove the evaporative canister from the fuel tank.

To install:

9. Place the canister into correct position on top of the fuel tank.
10. If necessary, raise and safely support the vehicle, remove the front passenger's side wheel, then remove the splash shield.
11. If necessary, remove the battery from the vehicle.
12. Tag and disconnect all necessary vacuum lines.
13. Unfasten all retaining bolts and/or straps, then remove the canister from the vehicle.
14. Installation is the reverse of the removal procedure.

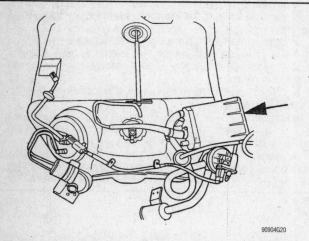

Fig. 17 The EVAP canister is the square component to the right, on top of the fuel tank

Leak Detection Pump (LDP)

1995–97 VEHICLES EXCEPT SEBRING AND AVENGER COUPES

▶ See Figures 18, 19, 20 and 21

The leak detection pump is located underneath the right front headlamp, behind the front fascia.

1. Disconnect the negative battery cable remote connection located on the left strut tower.
2. Remove the 2 headlamp unit mounting screws.
3. Pull the headlamp assembly out of the vehicle and unplug the wiring harness. Remove the headlamp assembly.
4. Disconnect the vacuum hose from the leak detection pump.
5. Label and disconnect the EVAP canister hoses.
6. Remove the 3 EVAP canister-to-pump bracket retaining nuts.

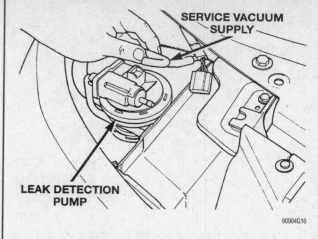

Fig. 18 Disconnect the vacuum line from the leak detection pump

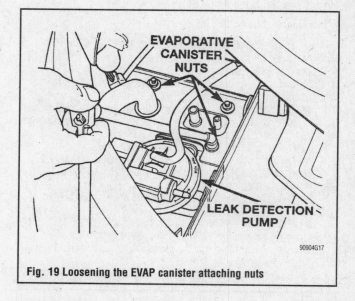

Fig. 19 Loosening the EVAP canister attaching nuts

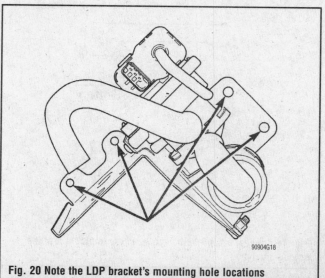

Fig. 20 Note the LDP bracket's mounting hole locations

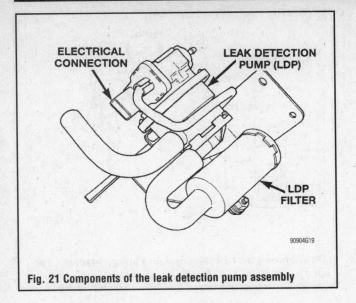

Fig. 21 Components of the leak detection pump assembly

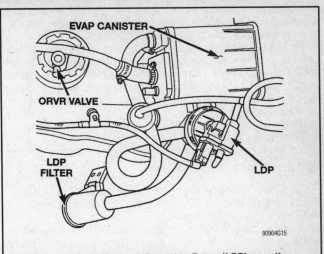

Fig. 22 Location of the Leak Detection Pump (LDP) near the EVAP canister, on top of the fuel tank

7. Allow the canister to sit on the lower fascia.
8. Remove the 4 leak detection pump bracket bolts.
9. Remove the pump and bracket, as an assembly.
10. Remove the EVAP canister from the vehicle.
11. Remove the pump from the bracket.

To install:

12. Set the EVAP canister on the lower front fascia.
13. Install the pump and bracket assembly to the body, then tighten the 4 retaining bolts.
14. Insert the EVAP canister into its bracket. Install and tighten the 3 retaining nuts.
15. Connect the vacuum hoses to the EVAP canister and leak detection pump.
16. Plug in the headlamp wiring harness. Install the headlamp assembly into position and tighten the 2 mounting screws.
17. Connect the negative battery cable.
18. Test the system using a DRB scan tool, or equivalent.

1998 VEHICLES EXCEPT SEBRING AND AVENGER COUPES

♦ See Figure 22

The leak detection pump is located at the rear of the vehicle, on top of the fuel tank assembly.

1. Properly relieve the fuel system pressure, as described in Section 5.
2. Disconnect the negative battery cable remote connection located on the left strut tower.
3. Safely raise and support the vehicle.
4. Remove the fuel tank assembly, as described in Section 5.
5. Disconnect the purge and vent lines.
6. Disconnect the EVAP canister hoses.
7. Disengage the electrical connector at the leak detection pump.
8. Remove the push pin fastener from the EVAP canister bracket.
9. Remove the bracket and LDP.
10. Separate the LDP from the bracket.

To install:

11. Install the leak detection pump onto the bracket.
12. Install the LDP and bracket assembly onto the fuel tank.
13. Install the EVAP canister onto the bracket and secure with the push pin.
14. Connect the LDP and canister vacuum lines.
15. Install the fuel tank assembly, as outlined in Section 5. Connect the purge and vent lines.
16. Fasten the LDP and fuel pump wiring connectors.
17. Lower the vehicle.
18. Connect the negative battery cable.

19. Fill up the fuel tank and pressurize the system using a DRB scan tool or equivalent. Inspect for leaks.

Evaporative Emission/Duty Cycle EVAP/Proportional Purge Solenoid Valve

♦ See Figures 7, 8 and 9

The Duty Cycle EVAP Purge solenoid is located in a bracket on the left side strut tower of all 1995–97 vehicles except the Sebring and Avenger coupes. The Proportional Purge solenoid is located behind the right headlamp assembly on all 1998 vehicles except Sebring and Avenger coupes. The Evaporative Emission Purge solenoid is located behind the right front fascia on the Sebring and Avenger coupes.

1. Disconnect the negative battery cable.
2. Label and remove the vacuum and electrical harness connections from the purge solenoid valve.
3. Remove the solenoid and mounting bracket from the engine compartment.
4. Installation is the reverse of the removal procedure.

Exhaust Gas Recirculation System

OPERATION

The Exhaust Gas Recirculation (EGR) system reduces oxides of Nitrogen (NOx) in the engine exhaust and helps prevent detonation (engine knock). Under normal operating conditions, engine cylinder temperature can reach over 3000°F (1649°C). The formation of NOx increases proportionally with combustion temperature. To reduce the emission of these oxides, cylinder temperature must be lowered. The system allows a predetermined amount of hot exhaust gas to recirculate and dilute the incoming air/fuel mixture. The diluted mixture lowers temperatures during combustion. The EGR system consists of the following components:

- EGR tube
- EGR valve
- Electric EGR Transducer (EET)
- Connecting hoses

The electric EGR transducer container an electrically operated solenoid and a backpressure transducer. The Powertrain Control Module (PCM) operated the solenoid, determining when to energize the solenoid. Exhaust system backpressure controls the transducer.

When the PCM energizes the solenoid, vacuum doesn't reach the transducer. Vacuum flows to the transducer when the PCM de-energizes the solenoid. When exhaust system backpressure becomes high enough, it fully closes a bleed valve in the transducer. When the PCM de-energizes the solenoid and backpressure closes the transducer bleed valve, vacuum flows through the transducer to operate the EGR valve.

De-engergizing the solenoid, but not fully closing the transducer bleed hole (because of low backpressure), varies the strength of vacuum applied to the EGR valve. Varying the strength of the vacuum changes the amount of EGR supplied to the engine. This provides the correct amount of exhaust gas recirculation for different operating conditions. This system does not allow EGR at idle.

COMPONENT TESTING

EGR System On-Board Diagnostics

The PCM performs an on-board diagnostic check of the EGR system. The diagnostic system uses the electric EGR transducer for the system tests.

The check activates only during certain conditions. When the conditions are met, the PCM energizes the transducer solenoid to disable the EGR system. The PCM checks for a change in the heated oxygen sensor signal. If the air/fuel ratio goes lean, the PCM will try to enrich the mixture. The PCM records a Diagnostic Trouble Code (DTC) if the EGR system is not operating properly. After registering a DTC, the PCM turns on the Check Engine lamp (malfunction indicator) after 2 consecutive trips. There are 2 types of failures sensed by the PCM; a short or open in the circuit, or a mechanical failure or loss of vacuum. The Malfunction Indicator Lamp (MIL) denotes the need for service.

If you find a problem indicated by the MIL and a DTC is set, first check for proper operation of the EGR system. If the system tests properly, check the system using Chrysler's DRB® or equivalent scan tool. Make sure to follow all of the instructions included with the scan tool.

EGR System Test

> ❊❊ **CAUTION**

ALWAYS block the drive wheels and apply the parking brake anytime you are performing a test or adjustment in which the engine must be running.

1995–96 VEHICLES

▶ **See Figure 23**

A failed or malfunctioning EGR system can cause engine spark knock, hesitation or sags, rough idle, stalling and/or increased emissions. To make sure the EGR system is operating properly, all passages and moving parts must be clean of deposits that could cause plugging or sticking. Make sure the hoses don't leak and replace any components that do leak.

Check the hose connections between the intake manifold, EGR solenoid and transducer, and the EGR valve. Replace any hardened, cracked, melted or leaking hoses. Repair or replace faulty connectors.

1. Check the EGR control system and EGR valve with the engine fully warmed up and running with the engine coolant temperature at 170°F (77°C) or over. With the transmission in Neutral and the throttle closed, allow the engine to idle for about 70 seconds.

2. Abruptly accelerate the engine to about 2,000 rpm, but NOT over 3,000 rpm. The EGR valve stem should move when accelerating the engine.

3. Repeat the test a few times to confirm movement. If the valve stem moves, the EGR system is operating properly. If the stem doesn't move, then the EGR system is not operating properly.

4. Disconnect and plug the vacuum hose from the EGR valve.

5. Connect a suitable hand-held vacuum pump to the EGR valve.

6. With the engine running at idle speed, slowly apply vacuum. Engine speed should begin to drop when the applied vacuum reaches 2.0–3.5 in. Hg. Engine speed may drop quickly or the engine may even stall. This indicates that EGR gas is flowing through the system.

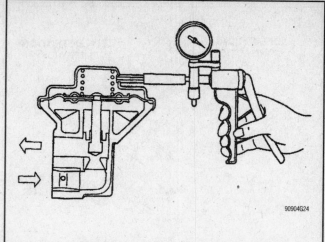

Fig. 23 Testing the EGR valve operation using a hand-held vacuum pump

7. If the engine speed doesn't drop when applying the vacuum, remove both the EGR valve and EGR tube, and check for plugged passages; clean or replace as necessary.

1997–98 VEHICLES

1. Check the condition of all EGR system hoses and tubes for leaks, blockage, cracks, kinks or hardening. Repair or replace them as necessary before beginning the test.

2. Make sure the hoses at both the EGR valve and EGR valve control are connected properly, and that the electrical connector is firmly attached at the valve control.

3. To check EGR system operation, connect a DRB® or equivalent scan tool to the 16-way data link connector. (The data link connector is located on the lower edge of the instrument panel, near the steering column.) Make sure to follow all of the manufacturer's instructions when connecting the scan tool and testing the EGR system.

4. After checking the system with the scan tool, proceed to the remaining EGR valve control tests.

EGR Gas Flow Test

▶ **See Figures 23 and 24**

Use this test to see if exhaust gas is flowing through the EGR system.

➡**The engine must be started, running and at normal operating temperature for this test. This test is not to be used as a complete test of the EGR system, but in conjunction with the other system tests.**

1. All engines are equipped with 2 fittings on the EGR valve, as shown in the accompanying figure. The upper fitting (located on the vacuum motor) supplies engine vacuum to a diaphragm within the EGR valve for valve operation. The lower fitting (located on the base of the EGR valve) is used to supply exhaust backpressure to the EGR valve control.

2. Disconnect the rubber hose from the vacuum motor fitting on top of the EGR valve vacuum motor.

3. Start the engine. Use a hand-held vacuum gauge to apply about 5 in. (17 kPa) of vacuum to the fitting on the EGR valve motor.

4. While applying a minimum 3 in. (10 kPa) of vacuum, and with the engine running at idle speed, the idle speed should drop or the engine may even stall, if the vacuum is applied quickly. This indicates that exhaust gas is flowing through the EGR tube between the intake and exhaust manifolds.

5. If the engine speed did not change, the EGR valve may be defective or the EGR tube may be plugged with carbon, or the passages in the intake and/or exhaust manifold may be plugged with carbon. Perform the following to see if the components are plugged:

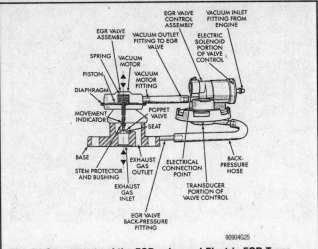

Fig. 24 Components of the EGR valve and Electric EGR Transducer Solenoid assembly

a. Remove the EGR valve from the engine, as outlined later in this section.

b. Apply vacuum to the vacuum motor fitting and check the stem on the valve. If it's moving, the EGR valve is working properly and the problem is either a plugged EGR tube or plugged passages at the intake or exhaust manifolds (refer to the next step).

c. Remove the EGR tube between the intake and exhaust manifolds. Check and clean the EGR tube and its related openings on the manifolds.

6. Do not try to clean the EGR valve. If the valve shows evidence of heavy carbon build-up near the base, replace it.

EGR Valve Leakage Test

▶ **See Figures 23 and 24**

If the engine will not idle, stalls while idling or the idle is rough or slow, the poppet valve, located at the base of the EGR valve, may be leaking in the closed position.

1. The engine should be **OFF** for the following test.

2. Disconnect the rubber hose from the fitting at the top (vacuum motor) side of the EGR valve, and perform the following:

a. Connect a hand-held vacuum pump to this fitting.

b. Apply 15 in. (51 kPa) of vacuum to the pump, then observe the gauge reading on the pump.

c. If the vacuum falls off, the diaphragm in the EGR valve has ruptured.

d. Replace the EGR valve, as outlined later in this section.

➡ **The EGR valve, valve control and attaching hoses are replaced as an assembly.**

e. Go on to the next step.

3. A small metal fitting (backpressure fitting) is located at the base of the EGR valve. A rubber backpressure hose connects it to the backpressure fitting on the EGR valve control. Disconnect this hose from the EGR valve fitting.

4. Remove the air cleaner inlet tube from the throttle body.

5. Using compressed air from an air nozzle with a rubber tip, apply about 50 psi (345 kPa) of regulated air to the metal backpressure fitting on the EGR valve.

6. By hand, open the throttle to the wide open position. Air should NOT be heard coming from the intake manifold while applying air pressure to the fitting.

7. If air CAN be heard coming from the intake manifold, the poppet valve is leaking at the bottom of the EGR valve. Replace the EGR valve.

Electric EGR Transducer Solenoid Test

▶ **See Figures 25 and 26**

➡ **Before disconnecting any vacuum hoses, place an identification mark on each of them for correct installation.**

1. Label, then disconnect each vacuum hose from the electric EGR transducer solenoid.

2. Disengage the wiring harness connector from the transducer solenoid.

3. Plug vacuum hose nipple A.

4. Connect a hand-held vacuum pump to hose nipple B.

5. Connect a positive pressure-type hand pump to hose nipple C.

6. Using 2 jumper wires, connect one between the transducer solenoid terminal and positive battery terminal, and the second wire to the remaining solenoid terminal.

7. Connect and disconnect the second jumper wire to the negative battery terminal side, while applying vacuum and positive pressure to check airtightness. With vacuum applied, this test should produce the following results:

• Jumper wire disconnected and positive pressure not applied should produce a vacuum leak.

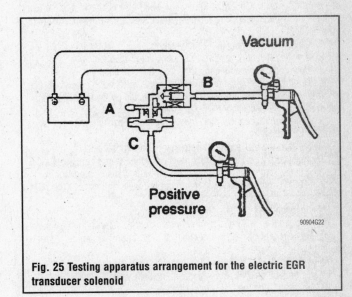

Fig. 25 Testing apparatus arrangement for the electric EGR transducer solenoid

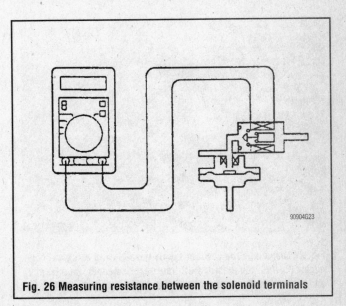

Fig. 26 Measuring resistance between the solenoid terminals

• Jumper wire disconnected and positive pressure applied should maintain vacuum.

• Jumper wire connected and positive pressure not applied should maintain vacuum.

8. Using an ohmmeter, measure resistance between the transducer solenoid terminals.

9. On 2.0L and 2.4L engines, the ohmmeter should read 25–35 ohms at approximately 68°F (20°C). On 2.5L engines, the ohmmeter should read 31–41 ohms at approximately 68°F (20°C).

10. If the resistance measures out of specifications, replace the electric EGR transducer solenoid.

REMOVAL & INSTALLATION

EGR Valve and Electric Transducer

▶ **See Figures 24 and 27 thru 34**

➡**Although the EGR valve and Electric EGR Transducer (EET) can be removed separately, they must be replaced as a pair, since they are calibrated together.**

On the 2.0L and 2.4L engines, the EGR valve and EET attach to the rear of the cylinder head. On 2.5L engines, the EGR valve is attached to the rear of the front cylinder head, and the EET is attached to the front exhaust manifold.

1. Disconnect the negative battery cable.
2. If necessary, remove the air cleaner/inlet duct assembly.
3. Detach the vacuum supply tube from the EET solenoid.
4. Unplug the electrical connector from the solenoid. If necessary, use a pair of wire cutters to remove the wire tie installed by the factory. Once removed, it is not necessary to install a new one.
5. Label and disconnect the vacuum outlet and backpressure hoses from the EET solenoid.
6. Remove the EET solenoid from the mounting bracket.
7. If necessary on the 2.5L engine, loosen the 60-way connector retaining screw and detach the connector from the Transmission Control Module (TCM), then unscrew the mounting fasteners and remove the TCM from the engine compartment.
8. Unfasten the EGR tube-to-EGR valve screws.
9. Remove the EGR valve mounting screws, then remove the EGR valve.
10. Remove and discard the old gaskets. Thoroughly clean the gasket mating surfaces and/or passages.
   To install:
11. Using new gaskets, loosely install the EGR valve.
12. Finger-tighten the EGR tube fasteners.

Fig. 28 If necessary, use a pair of wire cutters to cut the wire tie installed by the factory. It is not necessary to install a new one

Fig. 29 If equipped with a 2.5L engine, disengage the Transmission Control Module (TCM) electrical connector after loosening the center retaining fastener . . .

Fig. 27 Disengage the vacuum supply hose (1) and electrical connector (2) from the electric EGR transducer solenoid, then label and disconnect the vacuum outlet and backpressure hoses (3)

Fig. 30 . . . then remove the TCM's mounting fasteners

Fig. 31 Removing the TCM from the vehicle will allow better access to the EGR valve

Fig. 32 After removing the EGR-to-EGR valve mounting screws, loosen and remove the EGR valve mounting bolts

Fig. 33 Remove the EGR valve and mounting gasket from the vehicle

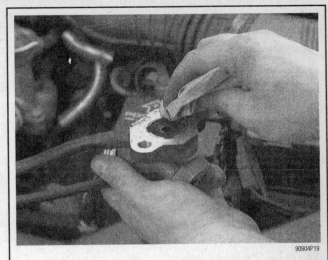

Fig. 34 Clean the mounting surface of the EGR valve with a rag

13. Tighten the EGR tube fasteners to 95 inch lbs. (11 Nm).

14. Tighten the EGR valve mounting screws to 200 inch lbs. (22 Nm).

15. If removed, install the TCM into the engine compartment and tighten the mounting fasteners. Secure the TCM 60-way connector and tighten the retaining screw.

16. Install the EET solenoid onto the mounting bracket.

17. Connect the vacuum outlet and backpressure hoses between the EGR valve and the EET solenoid.

18. Attach the vacuum supply tube and electrical connector to the solenoid.

19. If removed, install the air cleaner/inlet duct assembly.

20. Connect the negative battery cable.

EGR Tube

◆ See Figures 35 thru 42

The EGR tube attaches to the intake manifold plenum near the throttle body and EGR valve.

1. Disconnect the negative battery cable.

2. For easier access to the EGR tube, it may be necessary to remove the air cleaner/inlet hose assembly.

Fig. 35 Slide the throttle cable from the lever

Fig. 36 Hold the throttle lever in the wide open position to release the cruise control cable

Fig. 37 Remove the throttle cable bracket mounting bolts

Fig. 38 Place the throttle cable bracket out of the way for access to the upper EGR tube bolts

Fig. 39 Loosen the upper EGR tube-to-intake manifold plenum screws

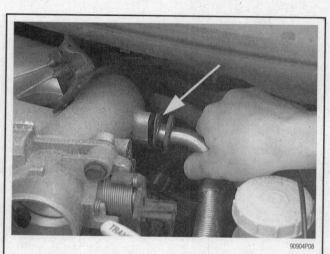

Fig. 40 When removing the EGR tube from the plenum, be sure not to lose the mounting gasket

Fig. 41 Loosen the EGR tube-to-EGR valve mounting screws . . .

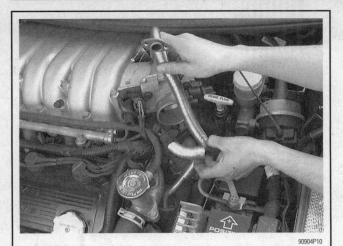

Fig. 42 . . . then remove the EGR tube from the engine compartment

3. If equipped with a 2.5L engine, it may be necessary to remove the throttle cable/bracket assembly for easier access to the EGR tube. Remove the throttle cable/bracket assembly as follows:

a. Pull on the throttle cable and slide it out of the throttle lever.

b. If equipped with cruise control, move the throttle lever to the wide open position, pull on the cruise control cable and slide it out of the lever.

c. Remove the throttle cable bracket mounting fasteners and move the cable/bracket assembly out of the way.

4. Remove the screws attaching the EGR tube to the intake manifold. Be careful not to lose the gasket.

5. Unfasten the EGR tube-to-EGR valve screws. Again, be careful not to lose the gasket.

6. Remove the EGR tube from the vehicle. Make sure to clean the gasket surface on the EGR valve and wipe the grommet on the intake manifold clean.

To install:

➡**The rubber grommet that seals the EGR tube-to-intake manifold connection is reusable.**

7. Loosely install the EGR tube and fasteners.

8. Tighten the EGR tube-to-intake manifold plenum and EGR tube-to-EGR valve screws to 95 inch lbs. (11 Nm).

9. If equipped with a 2.5L engine, install the throttle bracket/cable assembly.

10. If removed, install the air cleaner/inlet hose assembly.

11. Connect the negative battery cable.

ELECTRONIC ENGINE CONTROLS

Powertrain Control Module (PCM)

OPERATION

The Powertrain Control Module (PCM) is a digital computer containing a microprocessor. The PCM recieves input signals from various switches and sensors that are referred to as PCM inputs. Based on these inputs, the PCM adjusts various engine and vehicle operations through devices that are referred to as PCM outputs.

Based on inputs it receives, the PCM adjusts fuel injector pulse width, idle speed, ignition spark advance, ignition coil dwell and EVAP canister purge operation. The PCM regulates the cooling fan, air conditioning and speed control systems. The PCM changes the alternator charge rate by adjusting the alternator field. The PCM also performs diagnostic functions.

✳✳ WARNING

To prevent the possibility of permanent control module damage, the ignition switch MUST always be OFF when disconnecting power from or reconnecting power to the module. This includes unplugging the module connector, disconnecting the negative battery cable, removing the module fuse or even attempting to jump start your dead battery using jumper cables.

REMOVAL & INSTALLATION

▶ **See Figures 43 and 44**

The PCM is located in the left side of the engine compartment, beside the Power Distribution Center (PDC).

1. Disconnect the negative battery cable. On Cirrus, Stratus, Sebring convertible and Breeze models, disconnect the negative battery cable from the auxiliary jumper terminal.

2. Disengage the two 40-way connectors from the PCM.

3. Remove the fasteners that secure the PCM to the mounting bracket.

4. Lift up the PCM and remove it from the vehicle.

To install:

5. Position the PCM in the vehicle, then install the mounting fasteners and tighten to 35 inch lbs. (4 Nm).

6. Attach the two 40-way connectors to the PCM.

7. Connect the negative battery cable.

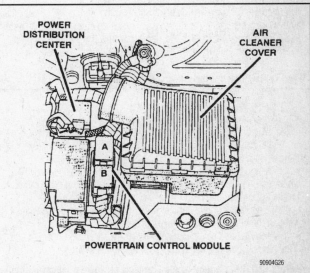

Fig. 43 Location of the PCM on the Cirrus, Stratus, Sebring convertible and Breeze models

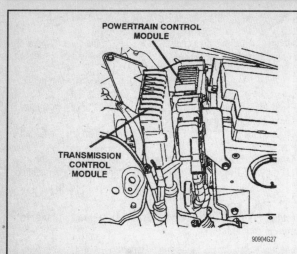

Fig. 44 Location of the PCM on the Sebring coupe and Avenger models

Heated Oxygen Sensor

OPERATION

As a vehicle accrues mileage, the catalytic converter deteriorates. The deterioration results in a less effective catalyst. To monitor catalytic converter deterioration, the fuel injection system uses two heated oxygen sensors: one which is upstream of the catalytic converter and one downstream of the converter.

The PCM compares the reading from the sensors to calculate the catalytic converter oxygen storage capacity and storage efficiency. The PCM also uses the upstream heated oxygen sensor input when adjusting the injector pulse width. When the catalytic converter efficiency drops below preset emission criteria, the PCM stores a Diagnostic Trouble Code (DTC) and illuminates the Malfunction Indicator Lamp (MIL).

The automatic shutdown relay supplies battery voltage to both of the heated oxygen sensors. The sensors have heating elements which reduce the amount of time it takes for the sensors to reach operating temperature.

TESTING

1. Visually check the connector, making sure it is properly attached, and that all of the terminals are straight, tight and free of corrosion.
2. Allow the heated oxygen sensor to cool to room temperature.
3. Use an ohmmeter to test the heating element of the heated oxygen sensors:

    a. Detach the electrical connector from each oxygen sensor. The white wires in the sensor connector are the power and ground circuits for the heater elements.

    b. Connect the ohmmeter test leads to the terminals of the white wires in the heated oxygen sensor connector.

4. Replace the heated oxygen sensor if the resistance is not 5–7 ohms for 1995 vehicles or 4–7 ohms for 1996–98 vehicles.

➥Before installing a new oxygen sensor, perform a visual inspection. Black, sooty deposits on the sensor tip may indicate a rich air/fuel mixture. White, gritty deposits could result from an internal antifreeze leak. Brown deposits indicate oil consumption. All of these contaminants can damage a new sensor.

REMOVAL & INSTALLATION

▶ **See Figures 45 and 46**

1. Disconnect the negative battery cable. On Cirrus, Stratus, Sebring convertible and Breeze models, disconnect the negative battery cable at the remote location on the left strut tower.
2. Raise and safely support the vehicle.
3. Unplug the upstream oxygen sensor connector.
4. If removing the downstream oxygen sensor, detach the sensor electrical harness from the clips along the body.
5. Remove the sensor using a suitable oxygen sensor crow's foot wrench. After removing the sensor, the exhaust manifold must be cleaned with an 18mm x 1.5 + 6E tap.

To install:

6. New oxygen sensors will be packaged with a special anti-seize compound already applied to the threads. If you are reinstalling the old sensor,

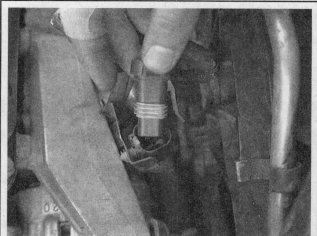

Fig. 45 Disconnecting the oxygen sensor connector

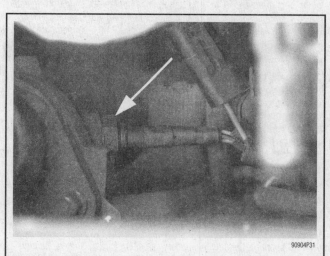

Fig. 46 Using an oxygen sensor crow's foot wrench or open end wrench, remove the sensor from the exhaust manifold

the sensor threads must be coated with fresh anti-seize compound. You must use the correct type of anti-seize compound containing liquid graphite and glass beads. This is not a conventional anti-seize paste; the graphite will tend to burn away, but the glass beads will remain. The use of a regular compound may electrically insulate the sensor, rendering it inoperative. You must coat the threads with an electrically conductive anti-seize compound.

7. Carefully thread the sensor into the bore, then tighten to 20 ft. lbs. (28 Nm) on Cirrus, Stratus, Sebring convertible and Breeze models, or 33 ft. lbs. (44 Nm) on Sebring and Avenger coupes.

8. If installing the downstream oxygen sensor, route the sensor electrical harness through the clips along the body.

9. Attach the oxygen sensor electrical connector.

10. Carefully lower the vehicle, then connect the negative battery cable.

Idle Air Control Motor

OPERATION

▶ **See Figure 47**

The Idle Air Control (IAC) motor, attached to the side of the throttle body, is operated by the PCM. The PCM adjusts engine idle speed through the idle air control motor to compensate for load on the engine, or changes in coolant temperature or barometric pressure.

The throttle body has an air passage that provides air for the engine during closed throttle idle. The idle air control motor pintle protrudes into the air bypass passage and regulates the air flow through it. The PCM adjusts the idle speed by moving the IAC motor pintle in and out of the bypass passage. The adjustments are based on various sensor and switch inputs received by the PCM.

Fig. 47 Location of the TPS (1) and the IAC motor (2) on the throttle body assembly—shown with the air cleaner assembly removed

TESTING

▶ **See Figures 48 and 49**

Visually check the connector, making sure it is properly attached, and that all of the terminals are straight, tight and free of corrosion.

You need to have access to a DRB® or equivalent scan tool to test the Idle Air Control (IAC) motor and related circuits. Make sure to carefully follow all of the scan tool manufacturer's directions when testing the IAC motor. However, a resistance test of the idle air control motor can be performed with the following steps.

1. Disconnect the negative battery cable. On Cirrus, Stratus, Sebring convertible and Breeze models, disconnect the negative battery cable at the remote location on the left strut tower.

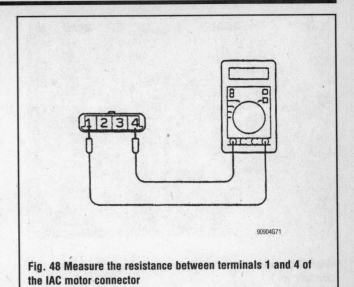

Fig. 48 Measure the resistance between terminals 1 and 4 of the IAC motor connector

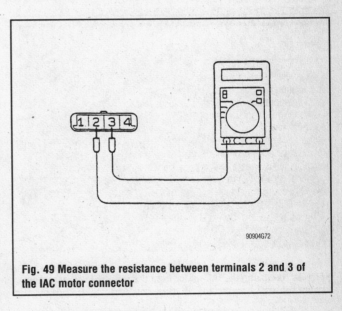

Fig. 49 Measure the resistance between terminals 2 and 3 of the IAC motor connector

2. Disengage the IAC motor connector.

3. Using an ohmmeter, measure the resistance between terminals 1 and 4 of the connector at the IAC motor side. Then, measure the resistance between terminals 2 and 3 of the connector at the IAC motor side. Resistance value should measure 38–52 ohms at 68°F (20°C).

4. Replace the IAC motor if the resistance measures outside the standard value.

REMOVAL & INSTALLATION

▶ **See Figures 50 and 51**

➡ **You will need to have access to a DRB® or equivalent scan tool when installing the IAC motor, as the IAC motor pintle must be properly retracted if extends more than 1 in. (25mm).**

1. Disconnect the negative battery cable. On Cirrus, Stratus, Sebring convertible and Breeze models, disconnect the negative battery cable at the remote location on the left strut tower.

2. Disconnect the EVAP purge hose from the throttle body.

3. Remove the throttle body from the vehicle, as outlined in

4. Detach the electrical connectors from the IAC motor and Throttle Position (TP) sensor.

Fig. 50 Loosen the IAC mounting screws using a Torx® head screwdriver

Fig. 51 Removing the IAC motor from the throttle body assembly

5. Unfasten the IAC motor mounting screws from the throttle body, then remove the motor from the throttle body. Make sure the O-ring is removed with the motor. Remove and discard the O-ring.

When servicing throttle body components, always install the components with new O-rings and seals, when applicable. Do NOT use any lubricants on the O-rings or seals, as damage may result. If you're having trouble, use a little water to help ease installation.

To install:

6. The new IAC motor has a new O-ring installed on it. Measure the pintle on the new IAC valve. If it is longer than 1 in. (25mm), it must be retracted using the Idle Air Control Motor Open/Close test on the DRB® or equivalent scan tool. Note that the battery must be connected for this test.

7. If the old IAC motor is being installed, place a new O-ring on the motor.

8. Carefully plate the IAC motor into the throttle body and install the retaining screws. Tighten the screws to 25 inch lbs. (3 Nm).

9. Attach the electrical connectors to the IAC motor and TP sensor.

10. Install the throttle body. Connect the EVAP purge hose to the throttle body nipple.

11. Connect the negative battery cable.

Coolant Temperature Sensor

OPERATION

The PCM determines engine coolant temperature from the coolant temperature sensor. The combination coolant temperature sensor has two elements. One supplies a coolant temperature signal to the PCM, and the other element provides a coolant temperature signal to the instrument panel gauge cluster. As coolant temperature changes, the coolant temperature sensor's resistance changes, resulting in a different input voltage to the PCM and gauge. When the air is cold, the PCM provides a slightly richer air/fuel ratio and higher idle speed until the proper normal operating temperature is reached.

TESTING

▶ **See Figures 52 and 53**

1. Turn the ignition switch to the **OFF** position.
2. Detach the coolant temperature sensor electrical connector.
3. Using a DVOM set to the ohms scale, connect one lead to one terminal of the coolant temperature sensor.

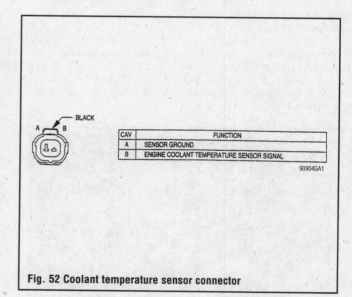

CAV	FUNCTION
A	SENSOR GROUND
B	ENGINE COOLANT TEMPERATURE SENSOR SIGNAL

Fig. 52 Coolant temperature sensor connector

Fig. 53 Testing the engine coolant temperature sensor

4. Connect the other ohmmeter lead to the remaining sensor connector terminal.

5. With the engine at normal operating temperature, approximaterly 200°F (93°C), the ohmmeter should read approximately 700–1000 ohms.

6. With the engine at room temperature, approximately 70°F (21°C), the ohmmeter should read approximately 7000–13,000 ohms.

7. If not within specifications, replace the engine coolant temperature sensor.

REMOVAL & INSTALLATION

♦ **See Figures 54, 55 and 56**

On the 2.0L SOHC engine, the coolant temperature sensor threads into the rear of the cylinder head. On the 2.0L and 2.4L DOHC engines, the coolant temperature sensor threads into the front of the cylinder head, below the coolant filler neck. On all 2.5L engines, the coolant temperature sensor is located next to the coolant filler neck.

1. Locate the engine coolant temperature sensor on the engine.
2. Disconnect the negative battery cable. On Cirrus, Stratus, Sebring

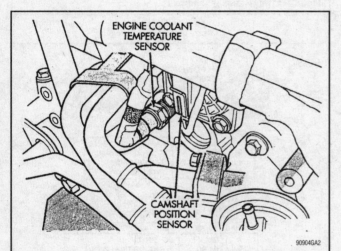

Fig. 54 Engine coolant temperature sensor location on the 2.0L SOHC engine

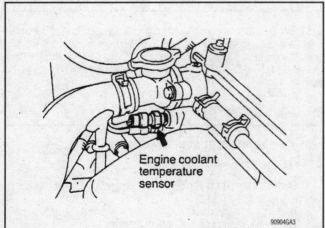

Fig. 55 Engine coolant temperature sensor location on the 2.0L and 2.4L DOHC engines

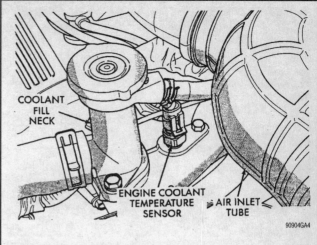

Fig. 56 Engine coolant temperature sensor location on the 2.5L engine

convertible and Breeze models, disconnect the remote negative battery cable connection on the left strut tower.

3. Drain the engine coolant below the level of the sensor.
4. Disconnect the sensor electrical harness.
5. Using a deep-well socket or wrench, loosen and remove the sensor from the engine.

To install:

6. Install the sensor in the vehicle and tighten securely. On the 2.0L SOHC and 2.5L engines, tighten the sensor to 60 inch lbs. (7 Nm). On the 2.0L and 2.4L DOHC engines, tighten the sensor to 20 ft. lbs. (27 Nm).

7. Attach the electrical connector to the sensor.
8. Refill the cooling system.
9. Connect the negative battery cable.
10. Start the engine, allow it to reach operating temperature and check for leaks.
11. Check for proper sensor operation.

Intake Air Temperature Sensor

OPERATION

The Intake Air Temperature (IAT) sensor measures the temperature of the intake air as it enters the engine. The sensor supplies one of the inputs the PCM uses to determine injector pulse width and spark advance. As the intake air temperature varies, the IAT sensor's resistance changes, resulting in a different input voltage to the PCM.

On all vehicles except 1996–98 models with the 2.0L SOHC engine, the IAT sensor threads into the intake manifold. On 1996–98 vehicles equipped with a 2.0L SOHC engine, the IAT and Manifold Absolute Pressure (MAP) sensors are combined into a single sensor which is attached to the intake manifold.

TESTING

Except 1996–98 Vehicles With 2.0L SOHC Engine

♦ **See Figures 57 and 58**

1. Visually check the connector, making sure it is attached properly and all of the terminals are straight, tight and free of corrosion.
2. With the ignition key **OFF**, detach the wire harness connector from the IAT sensor.

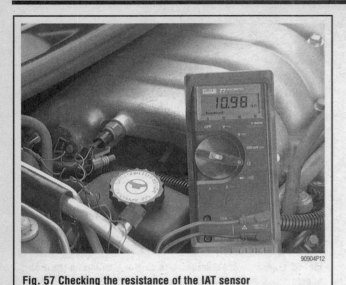

Fig. 57 Checking the resistance of the IAT sensor

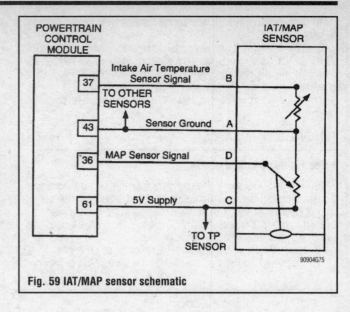

Fig. 59 IAT/MAP sensor schematic

Fig. 58 Testing the Intake Air Temperature (IAT) sensor. Use a hair dryer to produce a temperature change

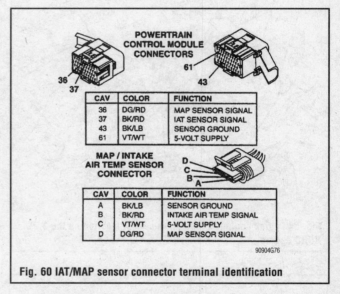

Fig. 60 IAT/MAP sensor connector terminal identification

3. Connect a digital ohmmeter (DVOM) to the sensor terminals. The ohmmeter should read as follows:

a. With the engine and sensor at normal operating temperature, about 200°F, the DVOM should read about 700–1,000 ohms.

b. With the engine and sensor at room temperature, about 70°F, the DVOM should read about 7,000–13,000 ohms.

1996–98 Vehicles With 2.0L SOHC Engine

▶ See Figures 59 and 60

1. Test the MAP/IAT sensor output voltage at the sensor connector, between terminals A and B.

2. With the ignition **ON**, but the engine NOT running, the output voltage should be 4–5 volts. The voltage should drop to 1.5–2.1 volts with a hot, neutral idle speed condition. If OK, go to next step. If not OK, go to Step 4.

3. Test the PCM terminal 37 for the same voltage described in the previous step to check wiring harness condition. Repair as necessary.

4. Test the IAT sensor ground circuit at the sensor connector terminal A and the PCM terminal 43. If OK, go to the next step. If not, repair as necessary.

5. Test the IAT sensor supply voltage between sensor connector terminal C and A with the ignition key **ON**. The voltage should be about 3.5–4.5 volts. There should also be 3.5–4.5 volts at terminal 61 of the PCM. If OK, replace the MAP/IAT sensor. If not, repair or replace the wire harness as required.

REMOVAL & INSTALLATION

1995 Vehicles With 2.0L SOHC Engines

▶ See Figure 61

1. Disengage the remote negative battery connection located on the left side strut tower.

2. Remove the engine cover.

3. Detach the electrical connector from the sensor.

4. Remove the sensor from the intake manifold.

To install:

5. Thread the sensor into the intake manifold and tighten to 90 inch lbs. (10 Nm).

6. Attach the electrical connector to the sensor.

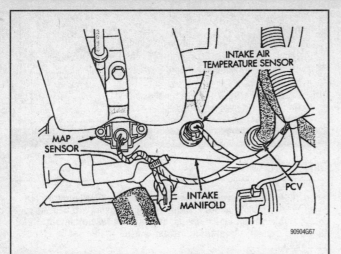

Fig. 61 IAT and MAP sensor location on the 2.0L SOHC engine (1995 models only)

7. Install the engine cover.
8. Connect the negative battery cable.

1996–98 Vehicles With 2.0L SOHC Engine

▶ **See Figure 62**

On 1996–98 vehicles equipped with a 2.0L SOHC engine, the IAT and Manifold Absolute Pressure (MAP) sensors are combined into a single sensor, which is attached to the intake manifold.

1. Disengage the remote negative battery connection located on the left side strut tower.
2. Detach the electrical connector from the MAP/IAT sensor.
3. Unfasten the mounting screws, then remove the MAP/IAT sensor from the vehicle.

To install:

4. Insert the sensor into the intake manifold, but be careful not to damage the sensor's O-ring seal.
5. Tighten the sensor mounting screws to 20 inch lbs. (2 Nm) on a plastic manifold, or 30 inch lbs. (3 Nm) on an aluminum manifold.
6. Attach the sensor electrical connector.
7. Connect the negative battery cable.

Vehicles With 2.4L Engines

▶ **See Figure 63**

1. Disengage the remote negative battery connection located on the left side strut tower.
2. Remove the air cleaner/inlet duct assembly from the intake manifold.
3. Reaching through the intake manifold from the throttle body side, detach the electrical connector from the IAT sensor.
4. Remove the sensor from the vehicle.

To install:

5. Install the sensor into the intake manifold. Tighten the sensor to 20 ft. lbs. (28 Nm).
6. Attach the sensor electrical connector.
7. Install the air cleaner/inlet duct assembly to the intake manifold. Make sure the duct doesn't interfere with the spark plug wires.
8. Connect the negative battery cable.

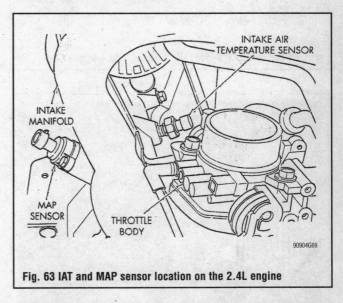

Fig. 63 IAT and MAP sensor location on the 2.4L engine

Vehicles With 2.0L DOHC, 2.5L (VIN H) and 2.5L (VIN N) Engines

▶ **See Figures 64, 65, 66 and 67**

1. Disconnect the negative battery cable.
2. Detach the electrical connector from the IAT sensor.

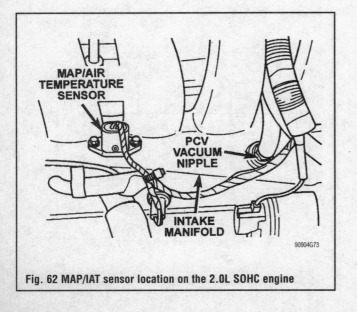

Fig. 62 MAP/IAT sensor location on the 2.0L SOHC engine

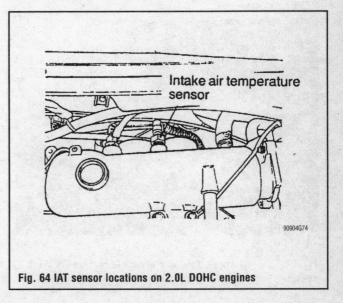

Fig. 64 IAT sensor locations on 2.0L DOHC engines

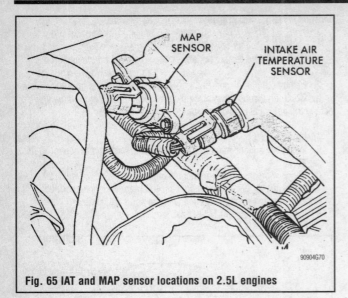

Fig. 65 IAT and MAP sensor locations on 2.5L engines

Fig. 66 Unplug the IAT sensor connector . . .

Fig. 67 . . . and use an open end wrench to remove the IAT sensor

3. Remove the sensor from the vehicle.

To install:

4. Insert the sensor into the intake manifold.

5. Tighten the sensor to 60 inch lbs. (7 Nm) on 2.0L DOHC and 2.5L (VIN N) engines. Tighten the sensor to 20 ft. lbs. (28 Nm) on 2.5L (VIN H) engines.

6. Attach the electrical connector to the sensor.

7. Connect the negative battery cable.

Manifold Absolute Pressure Sensor

OPERATION

➡ On 1996–98 vehicles equipped with the 2.0L SOHC engine, the IAT and Manifold Absolute Pressure (MAP) sensors are combined into a single sensor which is attached to the intake manifold. Refer to the IAT sensor information, located earlier in this section for operation.

The PCM supplies 5 volts of direct current to the Manifold Absolute Pressure (MAP) sensor. The MAP sensor then converts the intake manifold pressure into voltage. The PCM monitors the MAP sensor output voltage. As vacuum increases, the MAP sensor voltage decreases proportionately. Also, as vacuum decreases, the MAP sensor voltage increases proportionally.

With the ignition key **ON**, before the engine is started, the PCM determines atmospheric air pressure from the MAP sensor voltage. While the engine operates, the PCM figures out intake manifold pressure from the MAP sensor voltage. Based on the MAP sensor voltage and inputs from other sensors, the PCM adjusts spark advance and the air/fuel ratio. The MAP sensor is mounted to the intake manifold.

TESTING

▶ **See Figures 68, 69, 70 and 71**

➡ On 1996–98 vehicles equipped with the 2.0L SOHC engine, the IAT and Manifold Absolute Pressure (MAP) sensors are combined into a single sensor which is attached to the intake manifold. For those vehicles, refer to the IAT sensor information, located earlier in this section for testing.

✳✳ WARNING

When testing the MAP sensor, make sure the harness wires do not become damaged by the test meter probes.

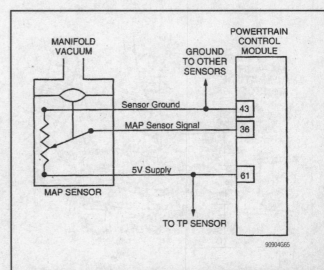

Fig. 68 Manifold Absolute Pressure (MAP) sensor schematic

Fig. 69 Disconnecting the MAP sensor's electrical lead

Fig. 70 Testing for reference voltage to the MAP sensor

1. Visually check the connector, making sure it is attached properly and that all of the terminals are straight, tight and free of corrosion.

2. Test the MAP sensor output voltage at the sensor connector between terminals 1 and 3, as illustrated.

3. With the ignition switch **ON** and the engine not running, the output voltage should be 4–5 volts. The voltage should fall to 1.5–2.1 volts with a hot, neutral idle speed condition. If OK, go to Step 4 or 5. If not OK, go to Step 6 or 7.

4. On all vehicles except 1995 Sebring coupe and Avenger models with 2.0L DOHC engines, test the PCM terminal 36 for the same voltage described in the previous step to make sure the wire harness is OK. Repair as necessary.

5. On 1995 Sebring coupe and Avenger models with the 2.0L DOHC engines, test the PCM terminal 29 for the same voltage described in Step 3 to make sure the wire harness is OK. Repair as necessary.

6. On all vehicles except 1995 Sebring coupe and Avenger models, test the MAP sensor ground circuit at the sensor connector terminal 1 and PCM terminal 43. If OK, go to Step 8. If not OK, repair as necessary.

7. On 1995 Sebring coupe and Avenger models, test the MAP sensor ground circuit at the sensor connector terminal 1 and PCM terminal 11. If OK, go to the next step. If not OK, repair as necessary.

8. Test the MAP sensor supply voltage between the sensor connector terminals 2 and 1 with the ignition key in the **ON** position. The voltage should be about 4.5–5.5 volts.

9. On all vehicles except 1995 Sebring coupe and Avenger models with 2.0L DOHC engines, there should also be 4.5–5.5 volts at terminal 61 of the PCM.

10. On 1995 Sebring coupe and Avenger models with 2.0L DOHC engines, there should also be 4.5–5.5 volts at terminal 3 of the PCM. If OK, replace the MAP sensor.

11. If not, repair or replace the wire harness as required.

REMOVAL & INSTALLATION

▶ **See Figures 61, 63, 65 and 72**

➡ **On 1996–98 vehicles equipped with the 2.0L SOHC engine, the IAT and Manifold Absolute Pressure (MAP) sensors are combined into a single sensor which is attached to the intake manifold. For these vehicles, refer to the IAT sensor information, located earlier in this section, for removal and installation.**

1. Disconnect the negative battery cable.
2. Detach the electrical connector from the MAP sensor.
3. Unfasten the mounting screws, then remove the MAP sensor from the vehicle.

POWERTRAIN
CONTROL MODULE
CONNECTORS

36

61

43

CAV	COLOR	FUNCTION
36	YL/BK	Map Sensor Signal
43	BK/DG	Sensor Ground
61	DG/YL	5-Volt Supply

MAP SENSOR
CONNECTOR

1
2
3

CAV	COLOR	FUNCTION
1	DG/YL	5-Volt Supply
2	BK/DG	Sensor Ground
3	YL/BK	Map Sensor Signal

Fig. 71 MAP sensor and PCM terminal identifications

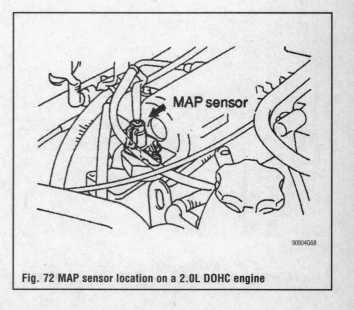

MAP sensor

Fig. 72 MAP sensor location on a 2.0L DOHC engine

To install:

4. Insert the sensor into the intake manifold, but be careful not to damage the sensor's O-ring seal.

5. For 2.0L DOHC and 2.4L engines, tighten the sensor mounting screws to 20 inch lbs. (2 Nm). For 2.5L engines, tighten the sensor mounting screws to 30 inch lbs. (3.4 Nm).

6. Attach the sensor electrical connector.

7. Connect the negative battery cable.

Throttle Position Sensor

OPERATION

The Throttle Position Sensor (TPS) is mounted to the side of the throttle body and connects to the throttle blade shaft. The TPS is a variable resistor that provides the PCM with an input signal (voltage). The signal represents throttle blade position. As the position of the throttle blade changes, the resistance of the TPS changes.

The PCM supplies about 5 volts of DC current to the TPS. The TPS output voltage (input signal to the PCM) represents throttle blade position. For 1995 vehicles, the TPS output voltage to the PCM varies from about 0.5 volt at idle to a maximum of 3.7 volts at wide open throttle. For 1996–98 vehicles, the TPS output voltage to the PCM varies from about 0.35–1.03 volts at idle to a maximum of 3.1–4.0 volts at wide open throttle.

Along with inputs from other sensors, the PCM uses the TPS input to determine current engine operating conditions. The PCM also adjusts fuel injector pulse width and ignition timing based on these inputs.

TESTING

▶ **See Figures 73, 74 and 75**

In order to perform a complete test of the TPS and related circuits, you must use a DRB® or equivalent scan tool, and follow the manufacturer's directions. To check the Throttle Position Sensor (TPS) only, proceed with the following tests.

➥**Visually check the connector, making sure it is attached properly and that all of the terminals are straight, tight and free of corrosion.**

1. The TPS can be tested using a digital ohmmeter. The center terminal of the sensor supplies the output voltage.

2. Connect the DVOM between the center terminal and sensor ground.

3. With the ignition key to the **ON** position and the engine **OFF**, check the output voltage at the center terminal wire of the connector.

4. Check the output voltage at idle and at Wide Open Throttle (WOT):

• For 1995 vehicles at idle, the TPS output voltage should be about 0.5 volts. At WOT, the output voltage should be about 3.7 volts. The output voltage should gradually increase as the throttle plate moves slowly from idle to WOT.

• For 1996–98 vehicles at idle, the TPS output voltage should be about 0.38–1.20 volts. At WOT, the output voltage should be greater than 0.6 volts. At WOT, the output voltage should be less than 4.5 volts. The output voltage should gradually increase as the throttle plate moves slowly from idle to WOT.

5. Check the resistance of the TPS as follows:

a. Unplug the TPS connector.

b. Using an ohmmeter, or a DVOM set to the ohms scale, measure the resistance between terminals 1 and 3 of the connector on the TPS side.

c. Resistance should measure 3.5–6.5K ohms.

d. Measure the resistance between terminals 2 and 3 of the connector on the TPS side.

e. Measure the resistance with the throttle closed, with the throttle about halfway open and at wide open throttle.

f. The resistance should increase smoothly as the throttle plate is opened.

g. If resistance measures outside these values, replace the TPS.

6. Before replacing the TPS, check for spread terminals and also inspect the PCM connections.

Fig. 74 Checking resistance of the TPS, which reads 4.51K ohms with the throttle lever closed

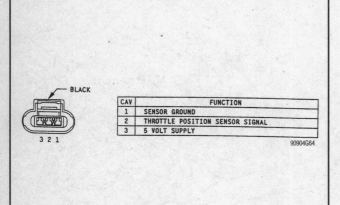

CAV	FUNCTION
1	SENSOR GROUND
2	THROTTLE POSITION SENSOR SIGNAL
3	5 VOLT SUPPLY

90904G64

Fig. 73 Throttle position sensor connector terminal identification

Fig. 75 While checking resistance of the TPS, readings should change smoothly in proportion to the opening angle of the throttle lever

REMOVAL & INSTALLATION

▶ **See Figures 76, 77 and 78**

1. Disconnect the negative battery cable.
2. Disconnect the EVAP purge hose from the throttle body.
3. Detach the electrical connector from the IAC motor and the TPS.
4. Remove the throttle body from the vehicle, as outlined in Section 5 of this manual.
5. Unfasten the mounting screws, then remove the TPS from the throttle body.

To install:

6. The throttle shaft end of the throttle body slides into a socket in the TPS. The socket has 2 tabs inside it. The throttle shaft rests against the tabs. When indexed correctly, the TPS can rotate clockwise a few degrees to line up the mounting screw holes with the screw holes in the throttle body. The TPS has slight tension when rotated into position. If it is difficult to rotate the TPS into position, install the sensor with the throttle shaft on the other side of the tabs in the socket.
7. Install the sensor mounting screws and tighten to 17 inch lbs. (2 Nm).
8. After installing the TPS, the throttle plate should be closed. If the throttle plate is open, install the sensor on the other side of the tabs in the socket.

Fig. 78 Remove the TPS from the throttle body. Note how the throttle shaft rests against the tabs in the TPS

9. Install the throttle body, as outlined in Section 5.
10. Attach the electrical connectors to the IAC motor and TPS.
11. Connect the EVAP purge hose to the throttle body nipple.
12. Connect the negative battery cable.

Camshaft Position Sensor

OPERATION

▶ **See Figures 79 and 80**

The camshaft position sensor (along with the crankshaft position sensor) provides inputs to the PCM to determine fuel injection synchronization and cylinder identification. From these inputs, the PCM determines crankshaft position.

On 4-cylinder engines, the camshaft position sensor mounts to the rear of the cylinder head. The sensor also serves as a thrust plate to control end-play of the camshaft.

The 6-cylinder engines are equipped with a camshaft driven mechanical distributor, which is equipped with an internal camshaft position (fuel sync) sensor.

Fig. 76 Disconnect the TPS wiring harness

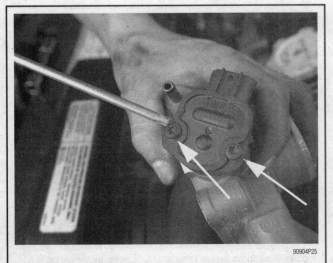

Fig. 77 Loosen the TPS screws using a Torx® head screwdriver

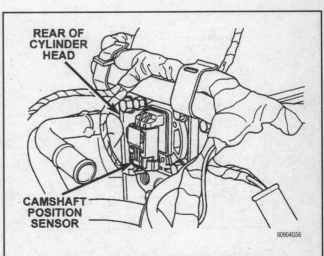

Fig. 79 Camshaft position sensor location on 2.0L SOHC engines

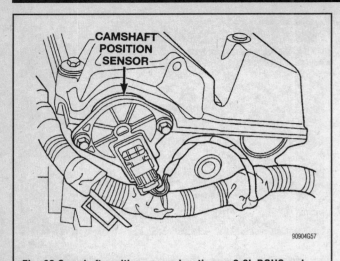

Fig. 80 Camshaft position sensor location on 2.0L DOHC and 2.4L engines

TESTING

▶ **See Figures 81, 82, 83 and 84**

➡ To test this sensor, you will need the use of an oscilloscope.

Visually check the connector, making sure it is attached properly and that all of the terminals are straight, tight and free of corrosion.

The output voltage of a properly operating camshaft position sensor switches from high (5.0 volts) to low (0.3 volts). By connecting an oscilloscope to the sensor output circuit, you can view the square wave pattern produced by the voltage swing.

REMOVAL & INSTALLATION

4-Cylinder Engines

▶ **See Figures 79, 80, 85 and 86**

1. Disconnect the negative battery cable.
2. Remove the air cleaner/inlet duct assembly from the vehicle.
3. For SOHC engines, detach the electrical connectors from the engine coolant sensor and the camshaft position sensor.

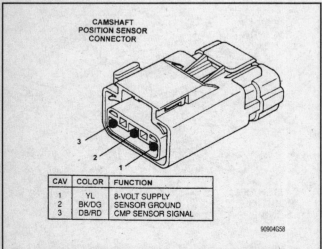

Fig. 81 Camshaft position sensor connector terminal identification for 2.0L DOHC engine

CAV	COLOR	FUNCTION
1	YL	8-VOLT SUPPLY
2	BK/DG	SENSOR GROUND
3	DB/RD	CMP SENSOR SIGNAL

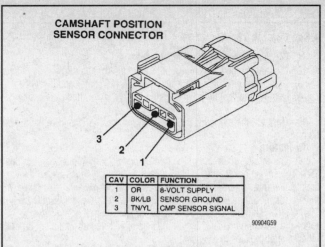

Fig. 82 Camshaft position sensor connector terminal identification for 2.0L SOHC and 2.4L engines

CAV	COLOR	FUNCTION
1	OR	8-VOLT SUPPLY
2	BK/LB	SENSOR GROUND
3	TN/YL	CMP SENSOR SIGNAL

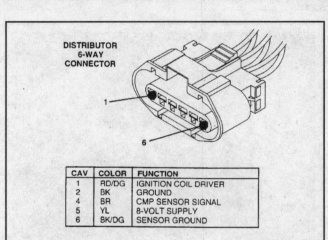

Fig. 83 Distributor 6-way connector terminal identification for 2.5L (VIN N) engine

CAV	COLOR	FUNCTION
1	RD/DG	IGNITION COIL DRIVER
2	BK	GROUND
4	BR	CMP SENSOR SIGNAL
5	YL	8-VOLT SUPPLY
6	BK/DG	SENSOR GROUND

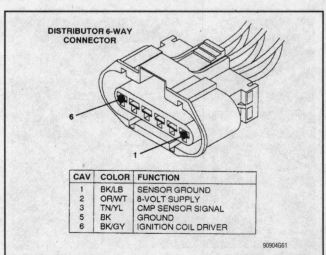

Fig. 84 Distributor 6-way connector terminal identification for 2.5L (VIN H) engine

CAV	COLOR	FUNCTION
1	BK/LB	SENSOR GROUND
2	OR/WT	8-VOLT SUPPLY
3	TN/YL	CMP SENSOR SIGNAL
5	BK	GROUND
6	BK/GY	IGNITION COIL DRIVER

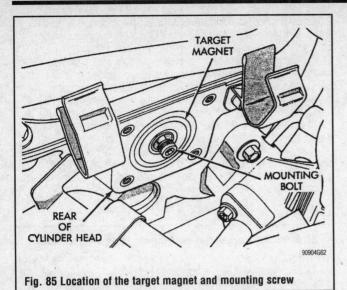

Fig. 85 Location of the target magnet and mounting screw

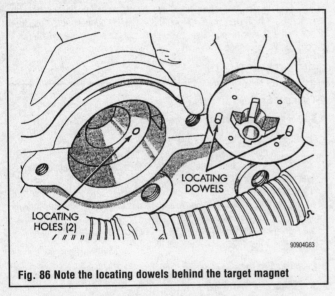

Fig. 86 Note the locating dowels behind the target magnet

4. For DOHC engines, unplug the electrical connector from the camshaft position sensor.

5. For SOHC engines, remove the brake booster hose and the electrical connectors form the holders on the end of the cylinder head cover.

6. Unfasten the camshaft position sensor mounting screws, then remove the sensor.

7. Loosen the screw/bolt attaching the target magnet to the rear of the camshaft.

To install:

➡ The target magnet has 2 locating dowels which fit into the machined locating holes in the end of the camshaft.

8. Install the target magnet in the end of the camshaft. Tighten the retainer to 30 inch lbs. (3.4 Nm).

9. Install the camshaft position sensor. Tighten the sensor mounting screws to 80 inch lbs. (9 Nm).

10. For SOHC engines, place the brake booster hose and electrical harness in the holders on the end of the valve cover.

11. Carefully attach the electrical connector(s) to the camshaft position sensor and coolant temperature sensor (if necessary). Be careful, since installation at any angle may damage the pins.

12. Install the air cleaner/inlet duct assembly.

13. Connect the negative battery cable.

6-Cylinder Engines

➡ The 2.5L engines are equipped with a distributor unit containing an integral camshaft position sensor. If the camshaft position sensor fails, the distributor assembly must be replaced. For distributor service, refer to Section 2.

Crankshaft Position Sensor

OPERATION

▶ **See Figures 87, 88, 89, 90 and 91**

The PCM determines what cylinder to fire from the crankshaft position sensor input and the camshaft position sensor input. On 4-cylinder engines, the second crankshaft counterweight has two sets of four timing reference notches, including a 60° signature notch. From the crankshaft position sensor input, the PCM determines engine speed and crankshaft angle (position). On 6-cylinder engines, this sensor is a Hall effect device that detects notches in the flexplate.

The notches generate pulses from high to low in the crankshaft position sensor output voltage. When a metal portion of the notches line up with the crankshaft position sensor, the sensor output voltage goes low (less than

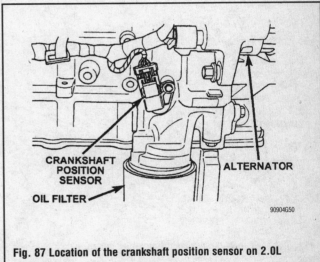

Fig. 87 Location of the crankshaft position sensor on 2.0L engines

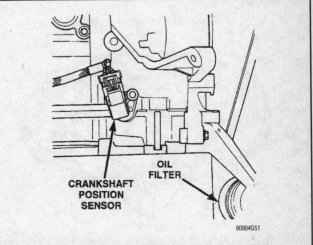

Fig. 88 Location of the crankshaft position sensor on 2.4L engines

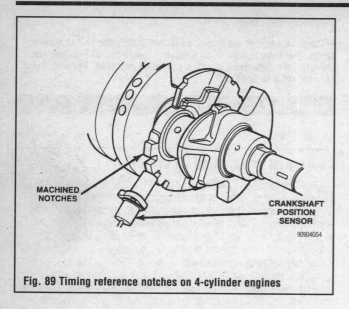

Fig. 89 Timing reference notches on 4-cylinder engines

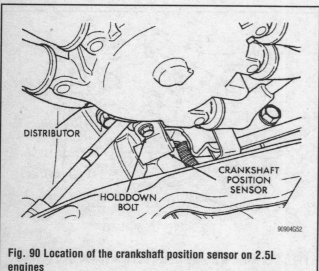

Fig. 90 Location of the crankshaft position sensor on 2.5L engines

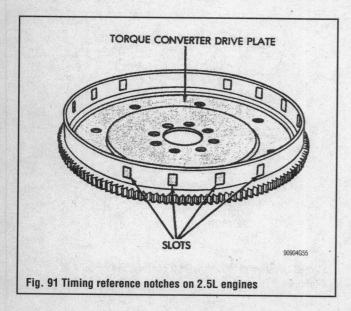

Fig. 91 Timing reference notches on 2.5L engines

0.5 volts). When a notch aligns with the sensor, voltage goes high (5.0 volts). As a group of notches pass under the sensor, the output voltage switches from low (metal) to high (notch), then back to low.

If available, an oscilloscope can display the square wave patterns of each voltage pulse. From the width of the output voltage pulses, the PCM calculates engine speed. The width of the pulses represent the amount of time the output voltage stays high before switching back to low. The period of time the sensor output voltage stays high before switching back to low is referred to as pulse width. The faster the engine is operating, the smaller the pulse width on the oscilloscope.

On 4-cylinder engines, the crankshaft position sensor is mounted to the engine block behind the alternator, just above the oil filter. On 6-cylinder engines, the crankshaft position sensor is mounted on the transaxle housing, above the vehicle speed sensor.

TESTING

➡️**To test this sensor, you will need the use of an oscilloscope.**

Visually check the connector, making sure it is attached properly and that all of the terminals are straight, tight and free of corrosion. Also inspect the notches in the crankshaft (4-cylinder) or flywheel (6-cylinder) for damage, and replace if necessary.

The output voltage of a properly operating crankshaft position sensor switches from high (5.0 volts) to low (0.3 volts). By connecting an oscilloscope to the sensor output circuit, you can view the square wave pattern produced by the voltage swing.

REMOVAL & INSTALLATION

4-Cylinder Engines

▶ **See Figures 87 and 88**

1. Disconnect the negative battery cable.
2. Detach the crankshaft position sensor electrical connector.
3. Unfasten the sensor mounting screw, then remove the sensor from the vehicle.

To install:

4. Install the sensor in the vehicle and secure with the retaining screw. Tighten the retaining screw to 105 inch lbs. (12 Nm).
5. Attach the crankshaft position sensor electrical connector.
6. Connect the negative battery cable.

6-Cylinder Engines

▶ **See Figures 91 and 92**

1. Disconnect the negative battery cable.
2. If necessary for access, remove the speed control servo unit from the left side strut tower.
3. Unfasten the sensor mounting screw, then pull the sensor straight up and out of the transaxle housing.

➡️**The sensor connector may be attached to the heater tube bracket with a push-on clip. If so, pull the connector from the bracket to free it.**

4. Detach the crankshaft position sensor electrical connector and remove it from the vehicle.

To install:

➡️**The crankshaft position sensor should be adjustable, which is identifiable by the presence of an elongated mounting hole on the sensor itself. If the sensor removed is being re-installed, clean off the old paper spacer from the sensor face. A new spacer must be mounted on the face before installation. However, if a new crankshaft position sensor is being installed, confirm that a paper spacer is already present.**

5. Install the sensor into the transaxle and push down until it contacts the flexplate. Hold the sensor in position and install the mounting screw. Tighten the sensor mounting screw to 105 inch lbs. (12 Nm).
6. Attach the crankshaft position sensor's electrical connector.

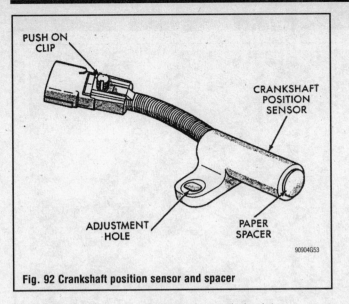

Fig. 92 Crankshaft position sensor and spacer

7. Attach the electrical connector to the heater tube bracket.

8. If removed, install the speed control servo unit back into position and tighten the mounting nuts to 80 inch lbs. (9 Nm).

9. Connect the negative battery cable.

Knock Sensor

OPERATION

All the vehicles with 4-cylinder engines are equipped with a knock sensor, which is threaded into the side of the cylinder block, in front of the starter. When the knock sensor detects a knock in one of the cylinders, it sends an input signal to the PCM. In response, the PCM retards ignition timing for all cylinders by a scheduled amount.

Knock sensors contain a piezoelectric material which sends an input voltage (signal) to the PCM. As the intensity of the engine knock vibration increases, the knock sensor output voltage also increases.

TESTING

▶ See Figures 93 and 94

Visually check the connector, making sure it is attached properly and that all of the terminals are straight, tight and free of corrosion.

A number of factors affect the engine knock sensor. A few of these are: ignition timing, cylinder pressure, fuel octane, etc. The knock sensor produces an AC voltage whose amplitude increases with the amount of engine knock. The knock sensor can be tested with a digital voltmeter. The RMS voltage is produced at about 20mVac (at about 700 rpm) and increases to about 600mVac (5000 rpm). If the output falls outside of this range, a Diagnostic Trouble Code (DTC) will set.

REMOVAL & INSTALLATION

▶ See Figure 95

1. Disconnect the negative battery cable.

2. Unplug the electrical connector from the knock sensor, which is located on the engine block, in front of the starter.

3. Use a crow's foot wrench to remove the knock sensor from the vehicle.

To install:

4. Install the sensor in the vehicle and tighten to 7 ft. lbs. (10 Nm). Make sure not to over or under-tighten the sensor, as is could adversely affect knock sensor performance, causing improper spark control.

5. Attach the knock sensor electrical connector.

6. Connect the negative battery cable.

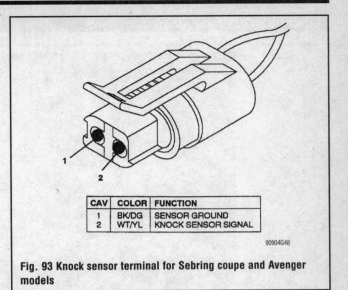

CAV	COLOR	FUNCTION
1	BK/DG	SENSOR GROUND
2	WT/YL	KNOCK SENSOR SIGNAL

Fig. 93 Knock sensor terminal for Sebring coupe and Avenger models

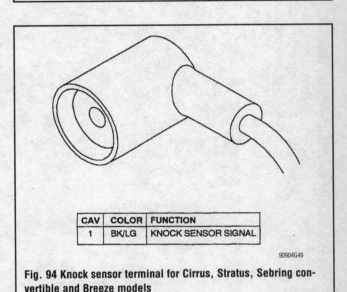

CAV	COLOR	FUNCTION
1	BK/LG	KNOCK SENSOR SIGNAL

Fig. 94 Knock sensor terminal for Cirrus, Stratus, Sebring convertible and Breeze models

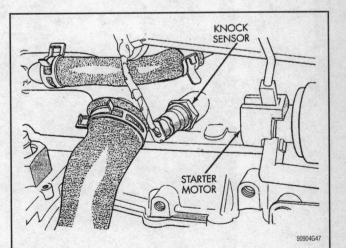

Fig. 95 The knock sensor is located on the side of the engine block, in front of the starter motor

COMPONENT LOCATIONS

EMISSION AND ELECTRONIC ENGINE CONTROL COMPONENT LOCATIONS

1. PCV valve
2. EGR valve
3. Electronic EGR transducer solenoid
4. Powertrain Control Module (PCM)
5. Heated oxygen sensor (front bank)
6. Idle air control motor
7. Intake air temperature sensor
8. Manifold absolute pressure sensor
9. Throttle position sensor
10. Vehicle Emission Control Information (VECI) label

9090P35

TROUBLE CODES

General Information

The Powertrain Control Module (PCM) monitors many different circuits in the fuel injection, ignition, emissions and engine systems. If the PCM senses a problem with a monitored circuit often enough to indicate an actual problem, it will store a Diagnostic Trouble Code (DTC) in the PCM's memory. If the code is applicable to a non-emission related component or system, and the problem is repaired or ceases to exist, the PCM will cancel the code after 40 engine warm-up cycles. A DTC that affects emissions will light up the Malfunction Indicator Lamp (MIL).

Certain guidelines must be met before the PCM will store a code in its memory. The criteria might be a certain range of the engine rpm, engine temperature and/or input voltage to the PCM. The PCM may not store a DTC for a monitored circuit, even though a malfunction has occurred. This may happen because one of the DTC criteria for the circuit has not been met. For example, the DTC criteria may require the PCM to monitor the circuit only when the engine operates between 750–2,000 rpm. If the sensor's output circuit shorted to ground when the engine operated above 2,400 rpm, (with a result of 0 volt input to the PCM), then no DTC would be stored, since the engine condition occurred at an engine speed above the maximum threshold of 2,000 rpm. There are various operating conditions for which the PCM monitors and sets DTC's.

➡**Various diagnostic procedures may actually cause a diagnostic monitor to set a DTC. For example, disconnecting a spark plug wire to perform a spark test may set the misfire code. When a repair is completed and verified, use Chryslers DRB® or equivalent scan tool to erase all DTC's, thereby shutting off the MIL.**

As a functional test, the Malfunction Indicator Lamp (MIL) lights up at the ignition key **ON** position before engine cranking. Whenever the PCM sets a DTC that affects emissions, it lights up the MIL. If a problem is detected, the PCM sends a message to the instrument cluster, illuminating the lamp. The PCM will light up the MIL only for codes that affect vehicle emissions. The MIL stays on constantly when the PCM has entered Limp-In mode or has found a failed emission component or system. The MIL stays on until the DTC is erased.

The MIL will either flash or light up constantly when the PCM detects active engine misfire. Also, the PCM may reset (turn off) the MIL when one of the following conditions occur:

• PCM does not detect the malfunction for 3 successive trips (except misfire and fuel system monitors).

• PCM does not detect a malfunction while performing three consecutive engine misfire or fuel system tests. The PCM performs these tests while the engine is operating within 375 rpm of and within 10% of the load of the operating condition at which the problem was first detected.

• The MIL will reset at the next ignition key **ON** setting, if the fault is not present (1995 Cirrus/Stratus models with the 2.5L engine only).

Diagnostic Connector

▶ **See Figures 96 and 97**

The Data Link Connector (diagnostic connector), is a 16-pin connector located inside the vehicle, under the instrument panel and to the left of the steering column. On Sebring coupe and Avenger models only, there are 2 data link connectors: the regular 16-pin connector, along with an additional 12-pin connector. The diagnostic connector is used as a link between the DRB® or equivalent scan tool and the PCM. The PCM communicates with the scan tool through the data link receive and transmit circuits. You can attach the scan tool to the data link connector to access any stored DTC's.

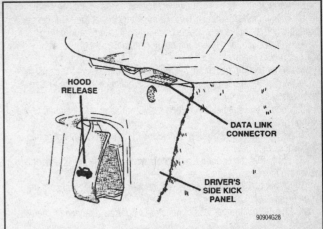

Fig. 96 On Cirrus, Stratus, Sebring convertible and Breeze models, the data link connector can be found under the dashboard panel, to the left of the steering wheel

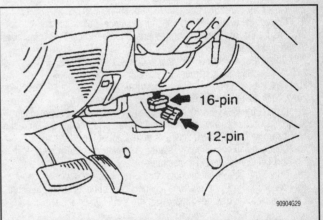

Fig. 97 On Sebring coupe and Avenger models, the data link connectors (16-pin and 12-pin) can be found under the dashboard panel, to the right of the steering wheel, near the center console

Visual Inspection

➡**This is a general procedure and the specific steps may differ from vehicle-to-vehicle; adjust the procedure as necessary.**

When a fault code is exhibited by the engine computer, it is a good idea to perform this general inspection to make sure that the cause is not a loose wire or a dirty connection.

Perform a visual inspection for loose, disconnected or misrouted wires and hoses before diagnosing or servicing the fuel injection system. A visual check saves unnecessary test and diagnostic time. A thorough visual inspection includes the following:

1. Check for correct spark plug cable routing. Ensure that the cables are completely connected to the spark plugs and distributor.

2. Check the ignition coil electrical connections.

3. Verify that the electrical connector is attached to the purge solenoid.

4. Verify that the vacuum connection at the purge solenoid is secure and not leaking.

5. Verify that the electrical connector is attached to the MAP sensor.

6. Check the MAP sensor hose (if so equipped) at the MAP sensor assembly and at the vacuum connection at the intake plenum fitting.

7. Check the alternator wiring connections. Ensure the accessory drive belt has proper tension.

8. Verify that the hoses are securely attached to the vapor canister.

9. Verify that the engine ground strap is attached at the engine and dash panel.

10. Ensure that the heated oxygen sensor connector is attached to the wiring harness.

11. Verify that the distributor connector (if so equipped) is attached to the harness connector.

12. Verify that the coolant temperature sensor connector is attached to the wiring harness.

13. Check that the vacuum hose connection at the fuel pressure regulator and intake plenum.

14. Ensure that the harness connector is securely attached to each fuel injector.

15. Check the oil pressure sending unit electrical connection.

16. Check the hose connections at the throttle body.

17. Check the throttle body electrical connections.

18. Check the PCV system hose connections.

19. Check the EGR system vacuum hose connections.

20. Check the EGR tube to intake plenum connections.

21. Inspect the electrical EGR transducer solenoid electrical connector.

22. Ensure that the vacuum connections at the electrical EGR transducer is secure and not leaking.

23. Check the power brake booster and speed connections.

24. Inspect the engine harness to main harness connections.

25. Check all automatic transaxle electrical connections, if so equipped.

26. Check the vehicle speed sensor electrical connector.

27. Inspect the PCM electrical connector(s) for damage or spread terminals. Verify that the 60-way connector is fully inserted into the socket of the PCM. Ensure wires are not stretched or pulled out of the connector.

28. Check the air conditioning, starter, automatic shutdown relay, fuel pump, and radiator fan relay connections.

29. Check the battery cable connections.

30. Check the hose and electrical connections at the fuel pump. Ensure that the connector is making contact with the terminals on the pump.

Reading Codes

♦ **See Figure 98**

On all 1995–97 vehicles, as well as the 1998 Sebring coupe and Avenger models with a 2.0L engine, you can access the DTC's in the following two ways:

• The preferred and most accurate way of reading a DTC is by using Chrysler's DRB® or equivalent scan tool. The scan tool supplies detailed diagnostic information, which can be used for more accurate and specific diagnosis of the code.

• The second way of reading DTC's is by observing the 2-digit number displayed by the Malfunction Indicator Lamp (MIL). The MIL is shown on the instrument panel as the Check Engine lamp. This method should be used as a "quick test" only. You should always use a scan tool to get the most detailed information.

On all 1998 vehicles except the Sebring coupe and Avenger with the 2.0L DOHC engine, the only way to retrieve DTC's is by using a DRB® or equivalent scan tool.

➡**Keep in mind that DTC's are the result of a system or circuit failure, but may not directly identify the failed component(s).**

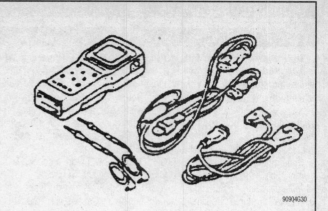

90904G30

Fig. 98 Use of the Chrysler Diagnostic Readout Box (DRB) or equivalent scan tool will give more accurate and specific code diagnosis

READING DTC'S USING A SCAN TOOL

♦ **See Figure 99**

1. Connect Chrysler's Diagnostic Readout Box (DRB) or equivalent scan tool to the data link (diagnostic) connector. On Sebring coupe and Avenger models, there is also an additional 12-pin connector. The connector is located at the lower edge of the instrument panel, near the steering column.

➡**Always make sure to follow the manufacturer's instructions when using a scan tool.**

2. Turn the ignition switch **ON**, and access the "Read Fault" screen with the scan tool.

3. Record all of the DTC's and "freeze frame" information shown on the scan tool.

4. Once the repairs have been completed, erase the trouble codes. Once the codes have been erased, check that the scan tool displays "normal".

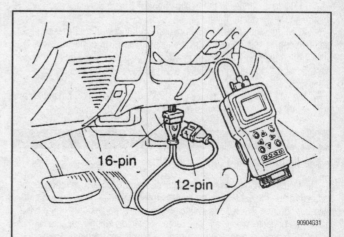

16-pin

12-pin

90904G31

Fig. 99 Connect the DRB, or equivalent scan tool, to the data link conector under the dashboard. Sebring coupe and Avenger models utilize an additional 12-pin connector

READING CODES USING MIL (CHECK ENGINE) LAMP

▶ **See Figures 100 thru 109**

➡️**Be advised that the MIL or CHECK ENGINE light can only perform a limited number of functions, and it is a good idea to have the system checked with a scan tool to double check the circuit function.**

1. Within a period of 5 seconds, cycle the ignition key **ON–OFF–ON–OFF–ON**.

2. Count the number of times the MIL (check engine lamp) on the instrument panel flashes on and off. The number of flashes represents the trouble code. There is a short pause between the flashes representing the 1st and 2nd digits of the code. Longer pauses are used to separate individual 2-digit trouble codes.

An example of a flashed DTC is as follows:

- Lamp flashes 4 times, pauses, then flashes 6 more times. This denotes a DTC number 46.

- Lamp flashes 5 times, pauses, then flashes 5 more times. This indicates a DTC number 55. DTC 55 will always be the last code to be displayed.

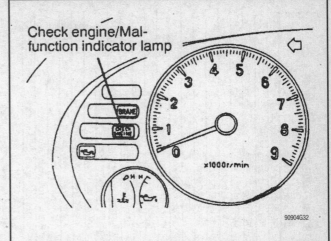

90904G32

Fig. 100 Typical location of a CHECK ENGINE or MIL light on the instrument cluster

1995-97 DIAGNOSTIC TROUBLE CODE (DTC) APPLICATIONS

MIL Code	Scan Tool Code	DRB Scan Tool Display
11	P0335	No crank reference signal at PCM
11	P1390	Timing belt skipped 1 tooth or more
11	P1391	Intermittent loss of CMP or CKP
11	P1398	Misfire adaptive numerator at limit
12		Battery disconnect
13		Slow change in idle MAP sensor signal (VIN N engine)
13	P1297	No change in MAP from from start to run
14	P0107	MAP sensor voltage too low
14	P0108	MAP sensor voltage too high
14	P1296	No 5 volts to MAP sensor
14	P1496	5 volt supply output too low
15	P0500	No vehicle speed sensor signal
16	P0325	Knock sensor signal
17		Engine cold too long
17	P0125	Closed loop temperature not reached
21		Front O2S shorted to voltage
21		Front O2S stays at center
21		Rear O2S shorted to voltage
21		Rear O2S stays at center
21	P0131	Upstream O2S shorted to ground
21	P0132	Upstream O2S shorted to voltage
21	P0133	Upstream O2S response
21	P0134	Upstream O2S stays at center
21	P0135	Upstream O2S heater failure
21	P0137	Downstream O2S shorted to ground
21	P0138	Downstream O2S shorted to voltage
21	P0139	Downstream O2S response
21	P0140	Downstream O2S signal inactive
21	P0141	Downstream O2S heater failure
21	P0151	Front bank upstream O2S shorted to ground (6 cylinder)
21	P0152	Front bank upstream O2S shorted to voltage (6 cylinder)
21	P0153	Front bank upstream O2S slow response (6 cylinder)
21	P0154	Front bank upstream O2S stays at center (6 cylinder)
21	P0155	Front bank upstream O2S heater failure (6 cylinder)
21	P0157	Front bank downstream O2S shorted to ground (6 cylinder)
21	P0158	Front bank downstream O2S shorted to voltage (6 cylinder)
21	P0160	Front bank downstream O2S stays at center (6 cylinder)
21	P0161	Front bank downstream O2S heater failure (6cylinder)
22	P0117	ECT sensor voltage too low
22	P0118	ECT sensor voltage too high
23	P0112	Intake air temperature voltage low
23	P0113	Intake air temperature voltage high

90904C01

Fig. 101 Diagnostic trouble code chart (1 of 3)—all 1995–97 vehicles

1995-97 DIAGNOSTIC TROUBLE CODE (DTC) APPLICATIONS

MIL Code	Scan Tool Code	DRB Scan Tool Display
24	P0121	TPS voltage does not agree with MAP
24	P0122	Throttle position sensor voltage low
24	P0123	Throttle position sensor voltage high
24	P1295	No 5 volts to TPS
25	P0505	Idle air control motor circuits
25	P1294	Target idle not reached
25	P1299	Vacuum leak found (IAC fully seated)
27	P0201	Injector #1 control circuit
27	P0202	Injector #2 control circuit
27	P0203	Injector #3 control circuit
27	P0204	Injector #4 control circuit
27	P0205	Injector #5 control circuit (6 cylinder)
27	P0206	Injector #6 control circuit (6 cylinder)
31	P0441	Evap purge flow monitor failure
31	P0442	EVAP system small leak
31	P0443	EVAP solenoid circuit
31	P0455	Evap system large leak
31	P1486	EVAP leak monitor pinched hose
31	P1494	Leak detection pump pressure switch
31		EVAP emission vent solenoid switch or mechanical failure
31	P1495	Leak detection pump solenoid circuit
31	P1495	EVAP emission vent solenoid circuit
31	P1498	High speed radiator fan ground control relay circuit
32	P0401	EGR system failure
32	P0403	EGR solenoid circuit
33		A/C pressure sensor volts too high
33		A/C pressure sensor volts too low
33		A/C clutch relay circuit
34		Speed control switch always low
34		Speed control switch always high
34		Speed control solenoid circuits
35		High speed condenser fan control relay circuit
35		High fan and high fan ground control relay circuit
35	P1487	High speed radiator fan control relay circuit
35	P1489	High speed fan control relay circuit
35	P1490	Low speed fan control relay circuit
37	P1899	Park/Neutral switch failure
41		Alternator field not switching properly
42		Auto shutdown relay control circuit
42		No ASD relay output voltage at PCM
42		Fuel level sending unit volts too low
42		Fuel level sending unit volts too high

Fig. 102 Diagnostic trouble code chart (2 of 3)—all 1995-97 vehicles

1995-97 DIAGNOSTIC TROUBLE CODE (DTC) APPLICATIONS

MIL Code	Scan Tool Code	DRB Scan Tool Display
42		Fuel level unit no change over miles
42	P0220	Fuel pump relay control circuit
43	P0300	Multiple cylinder misfire
43	P0301	Cylinder #1 misfire
43	P0302	Cylinder #2 misfire
43	P0303	Cylinder #3 misfire
43	P0304	Cylinder #4 misfire
43	P0305	Cylinder #5 misfire
43	P0306	Cylinder #6 misfire
43	P0351	Ignition coil #1 primary circuit
43	P0352	Ignition coil #2 primary circuit
44		Ambient temperature sensor
44		Battery temperature sensor volts out of limit
44	P1492	Battery temperature sensor voltage too high
44	P1493	Battery temperature sensor voltage too low
45	P0700	Transaxle fault present
46		Charging system voltage too high
47		Charging system voltage too low
51	P0171	Fuel system lean (4 cylinder)
51	P0171	Rear bank fuel system lean (6 cylinder)
51	P0174	Front bank fuel system lean (6 cylinder)
52	P0172	Fuel system rich (4 cylinder)
52	P0172	Rear bank fuel system rich (6 cylinder)
52	P0175	Front bank fuel system rich (6 cylinder)
53	P0601	Internal controller failure
53	P0600	PCM failure SPI communications
53	P0605	Internal controller failure
53	P0605	PCM failure SPI communications
54	P0340	No cam signal at PCM
55		Completion of fault code display on Check Engine Lamp
62	P1697	PCM failure SRI mile not stored
63	P1696	PCM failure EEPROM write denied
64	P0420	Catalytic converter efficiency failure
64	P0422	Rear bank catalytic converter efficiency failure
65	P0551	Power steering switch failure
65	P0703	Brake switch performance circuit
66		No CCD message from body controller
66		No CCD message from TCM
71	P1698	5 volt output low speed control power circuit
72	P1496	Catalytic converter efficiency failure
72	P0420	Front bank catalytic converter efficiency failure
77	P0432	Malfunction detected with power feed to speed control servo

Fig. 103 Diagnostic trouble code chart (3 of 3)—all 1995-97 vehicles

1998 DIAGNOSTIC TROUBLE CODE (DTC) APPLICATIONS
Cirrus, Stratus, Sebring Convertible and Breeze

Hex Code	Scan Tool Code	DRB Scan Tool Display
1	P0340	No cam signal at PCM
2	P0601	Internal controller failure
5	P1682	Charging system voltage too low
6	P1594	Charging system voltage too high
0A	P1388	Auto shutdown relay control circuit
0B	P0622	Alternator field not switching properly
0F	P1595	Speed control solenoid circuits
10	P0645	A/C clutch relay circuit
11	P0403	EGR solenoid circuit
12	P0443	EVAP purge solenoid circuit
13	P0203	Injector #3 control circuit
14	P0202	Injector #2 control circuit
15	P0201	Injector #1 control circuit
19	P0605	Idle air control motor circuits
1A	P0122	Throttle position sensor voltage low
1B	P0123	Throttle position sensor voltage high
1E	P0117	ECT sensor voltage too low
1F	P0118	ECT sensor voltage too high
20	P0134	Right rear upstream O2S stays at center
21	P1281	Engine is cold too long
23	P0500	No vehicle speed sensor signal
24	P0107	MAP sensor voltage too low
25	P0108	MAP sensor voltage too high
27	P1297	No change in MAP from start to run
28	P0320	No crank reference signal at PCM
2A	P0352	Ignition coil #2 primary circuit
2B	P0351	Ignition coil #1 primary circuit
2C	P1389	No ASD relay output voltage at PCM
2E	P0401	EGR system failure
30	P1697	PCM failure SRI miles not stored
31	P1696	PCM failure, EEPROM write denied
39	P0112	Intake air temperature sensor voltage low
3A	P0113	Intake air temperature sensor voltage high
3B	P0325	Knock sensor #1 circuit
3C	P0106	Barometric pressure out of range
3D	P0204	Injector #4 control circuit
3E	P0132	Right rear upstream O2S shorted to voltage
44	P0600	PCM failure, SPI communications
45	P0205	Injector #5 control circuit
46	P0206	Injector #6 control circuit
52	P1683	S/C power relay circuit or S/C 12V driver circuit

Fig. 104 Diagnostic trouble code chart (1 of 3)—1998 Cirrus, Stratus, Sebring convertible and Breeze

90904C04

1998 DIAGNOSTIC TROUBLE CODE (DTC) APPLICATIONS
Cirrus, Stratus, Sebring Convertible and Breeze

Hex Code	Scan Tool Code	DRB Scan Tool Display
56	P1596	Speed control switch always high
57	P1597	Speed control switch always low
5A	P1598	A/C pressure sensor volts too high
5B	P1599	A/C pressure sensor volts too low
5C	P1490	Low speed fan control relay circuit
5D	P1489	High speed fan relay circuit
60	P1698	No CCD messages from TCM
61	P1695	No CCD message from body control module
65	P1282	Fuel pump relay control circuit
66	P0133	Right bank upstream O2S slow response
67	P0135	Right rear upstream O2S heater failure
69	P0141	Right rear downstream O2S heater failure
6A	P0300	Multiple cylinder misfire
6B	P0301	Cylinder #1 misfire
6C	P0302	Cylinder #2 misfire
6D	P0303	Cylinder #3 misfire
6E	P0304	Cylinder #4 misfire
70	P0420	Right rear catalyst efficiency failure
71	P0441	Incorrect purge flow monitor failure
72	P1899	P/N switch stuck in park or in gear
73	P0551	Power steering switch failure
76	P0172	Right rear fuel system rich
77	P0171	Right rear fuel system lean
7E	P0138	Right rear downstream O2S shorted to voltage
80	P0125	Closed loop temperature not reached
81	P0140	Right rear downstream O2S stays at center
84	P0121	TPS voltage does not agree with MAP
85	P1390	Timing belt skipped 1 tooth or more
89	P0700	EATX controller DTC present
8A	P1294	Target idle not reached
91	P1299	Vacuum leak found (IAC fully seated)
92	P1496	5 volt supply output too low
95	P0462	Fuel level sending unit voltage too low
96	P0463	Fuel level sending unit voltage too high
97	P0460	Fuel level unit no change over miles
98	P0703	Brake switch stuck, pressed or released
99	P1493	Ambient battery temperature sensor voltage too low
9A	P1492	Ambient battery temperature sensor voltage too high
9B	P0131	Right rear upstream O2S shorted to ground
9C	P0137	Right rear downstream O2S shorted to ground
9D	P1391	Intermittent loss of CMP or CKP

Fig. 105 Diagnostic trouble code chart (2 of 3)—1998 Cirrus, Stratus, Sebring convertible and Breeze

90904C05

1998 DIAGNOSTIC TROUBLE CODE (DTC) APPLICATIONS
Sebring Coupe and Avenger models

Key On-Off Code*	Scan Tool Code	DRB Scan Tool Display
11	P0335	No crank reference signal at PCM
11	P1390	Timing belt skipped 1 tooth or more
11	P1391	Intermittent loss of CMP or CKP
11	P1398	Misfire adaptive numerator at limit
13	P1297	No change in MAP from start to run
14	P0107	MAP sensor voltage too low
14	P0108	MAP sensor voltage too high
14	P1296	No 5 volts to MAP sensor
14	P1496	5 volt supply output too low
15	P0500	No vehicle speed sensor signal
16	P0325	Knock sensor #1 circuit
17	P0125	Closed loop temperature not reached
17	P1281	Engine is cold too long
21	P0131	(Left bank) Upstream O2S shorted to ground
21	P0132	(Right rear) Upstream O2S shorted to voltage
21	P0133	Slow (left bank) upstream O2S circuit during catalyst monitor
21	P0133	(Left bank) Upstream O2S slow response
21	P0134	(Right rear) Upstream O2S slow response
21	P0135	(Left bank) Upstream O2S heater failure
21	P0137	(Left bank) Downstream O2S shorted to ground
21	P0138	(Left bank) Downstream O2S shorted to voltage
21	P0140	(Left bank) Downstream O2S stays at center
21	P0141	(Left bank) Downstream O2S heater failure
22	P0117	ECT sensor voltage too low
22	P0118	ECT sensor voltage too high
23	P0112	Intake air temperature sensor voltage low
23	P0113	Intake air temperature sensor voltage high
24	P0121	TPS voltage does not agree with MAP
24	P0122	Throttle position sensor voltage low
24	P0123	Throttle position sensor voltage high
24	P1295	No 5 volts to TPS
25	P0505	Idle air control motor circuits
25	P1294	Target idle not reached
27	P0201	Injector #1 control circuit
27	P0202	Injector #2 control circuit
27	P0203	Injector #3 control circuit
27	P0204	Injector #4 control circuit
31	P0441	Incorrect purge flow monitor failure
31	P0442	Evap leak monitor; small leak detected
31	P0443	EVAP purge solenoid circuit
31	P0455	Evap leak monitor; large leak detected

90994C07

Fig. 107 Diagnostic trouble code chart (1 of 3)—1998 Sebring coupe and Avenger

1998 DIAGNOSTIC TROUBLE CODE (DTC) APPLICATIONS
Cirrus, Stratus, Sebring Convertible and Breeze

Hex Code	Scan Tool Code	DRB Scan Tool Display
A0	P0442	Evap leak monitor; small leak detected
A1	P0455	Evap leak monitor; large leak detected
AE	P0305	Cylinder #5 misfire
AF	P0306	Cylinder #6 misfire
B7	P1495	Leak detection pump solenoid circuit
B8	P1494	Leak detect pump switch or mechanical fault
BA	P1398	Misfire adaptive numerator at limit
BB	P1486	Evap hose pinched
C0	P1195	Catalyst monitor slow O2 upstream
E2	P1686	No skim bus message

90994C06

Fig. 106 Diagnostic trouble code chart (3 of 3)—1998 Cirrus, Stratus, Sebring convertible and Breeze

1998 DIAGNOSTIC TROUBLE CODE (DTC) APPLICATIONS

Sebring Coupe and Avenger models

Key On-Off Code*	Scan Tool Code	DRB Scan Tool Display
31	P1486	Evap hose pinched
31	P1494	Leak detection pump solenoid switch or mechanical fault
31	P1495	Leak detection pump solenoid circuit
32	P0401	EGR system failure
32	P0403	EGR solenoid circuit
33	P0645	A/C clutch relay circuit
35	P1487	High speed radiator fan control relay circuit
35	P1489	High speed fan relay circuit
35	P1490	Low speed fan control relay circuit
37	P1899	P/N switch stuck in park or in gear
41	P0622	Alternator field not switching properly
42	P0220	Fuel pump relay control circuit
42	P0460	Fuel level unit no change over miles
42	P0462	Fuel level sending unit voltage too low
42	P0463	Fuel level sending unit voltage too high
42	P1388	Auto shutdown relay control circuit
42	P1389	No ASD relay output voltage at PCM
43	P0300	Multiple cylinder misfire
43	P0301	Cylinder #1 misfire
43	P0302	Cylinder #2 misfire
43	P0303	Cylinder #3 misfire
43	P0304	Cylinder #4 misfire
43	P0351	Ignition coil #1 primary circuit
43	P0352	Ignition coil #2 primary circuit
44	P1492	Battery temperature sensor volts out of limit
44	P1493	Ambient battery temperature sensor voltage too high
44	P0700	Ambient battery temperature sensor voltage too low
45	P1594	EATX controller DTC present
46	P1682	Charging system voltage too high
47	P0171	Charging system voltage too low
51	P0172	(Left bank) Fuel system lean
52	P0600	(Left bank) Fuel system rich
53	P0601	PCM failure, SPI communications
53	P0340	Internal controller failure
54	P0106	No cam signal at PCM
61	P1697	Barometric pressure out of range
62	P1696	PCM failure SRI miles not stored
63	P0422	PCM failure, EEPROM write denied
64	P0551	(Left bank) Catalytic converter efficiency failure
65	P1698	Power steering switch failure
66		No CCD messages from TCM

Fig. 108 Diagnostic trouble code chart (2 of 3)—1998 Sebring coupe and Avenger

90904C08

1998 DIAGNOSTIC TROUBLE CODE (DTC) APPLICATIONS

Sebring Coupe and Avenger models

Key On-Off Code*	Scan Tool Code	DRB Scan Tool Display
NA	P0151	Right bank upstream O2S shorted to ground
NA	P0152	Right bank upstream O2S shorted to voltage
NA	P0153	Right bank upstream O2S slow response
NA	P0153	Slow right bank upstream O2S circuit during catalyst monitor
NA	P0154	Right bank upstream O2S stays at center
NA	P0155	Right bank upstream O2S heater failure
NA	P0157	Right bank downstream O2S shorted to ground
NA	P0158	Right bank downstream O2S shorted to voltage
NA	P0160	Right bank downstream O2S stays at center
NA	P0161	Right bank downstream O2S heater failure
NA	P0174	Right bank fuel system lean
NA	P0175	Right bank fuel system rich
NA	P0205	Injector #5 control circuit
NA	P0206	Injector #6 control circuit
NA	P0305	Cylinder #5 misfire
NA	P0306	Cylinder #6 misfire
NA	P0432	Right bank catalytic converter efficiency failure
NA	P1494	Evaporative emission ventilation solenoid switch or mechanical fault
NA	P1495	Evaporative emission ventilation solenoid circuit
NA	P1498	High speed radiator fan ground control relay circuit

NA - Not applicable
* 2.0L DOHC engine only

Fig. 109 Diagnostic trouble code chart (3 of 3)—1998 Sebring coupe and Avenger

90904C09

Clearing Codes

Erase the DTC's with Chrysler's DRB® or equivalent scan tool, using the "Erase Trouble Code" data screen on the scan tool. Do NOT erase any DTC's until the malfunctions have been checked and repairs performed.

VACUUM DIAGRAMS

Following are vacuum diagrams for most of the engine and emissions package combinations covered by this manual. Because vacuum circuits will vary based on various engine and vehicle options, always refer first to the vehicle emission control information label, if present. Should the label be missing, or should the vehicle be equipped with a different engine than the vehicle's original equipment, refer to the diagrams below for the same or similar configuration.

If you wish to obtain a replacement emissions label, most manufacturers make the labels available for purchase. The labels can usually be ordered from a local dealer.

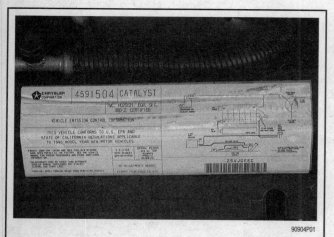

Fig. 110 The Vehicle Emission Control Information (VECI) label, located in the engine compartment, contains important emissions information

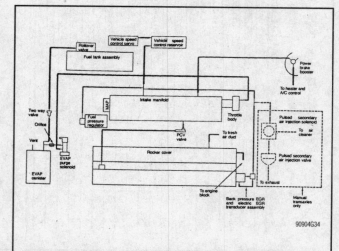

Fig. 112 Emission control system vacuum hose routing—1995 Sebring coupe/Avenger with 2.0L DOHC engine

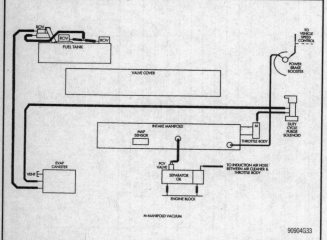

Fig. 111 Emission control system vacuum hose routing—1995 Cirrus/Stratus with 2.0L SOHC engine

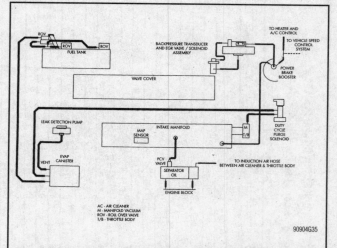

Fig. 113 Emission control system vacuum hose routing—1995 Cirrus/Stratus with 2.4L engine

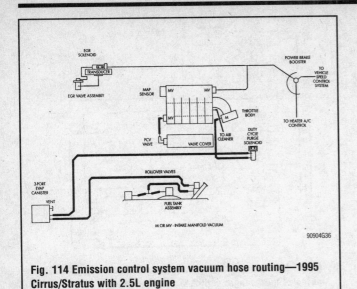

Fig. 114 Emission control system vacuum hose routing—1995 Cirrus/Stratus with 2.5L engine

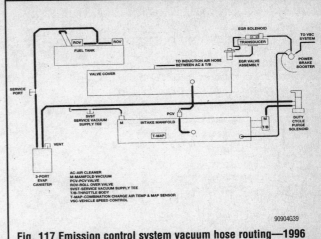

Fig. 117 Emission control system vacuum hose routing—1996 Cirrus/Stratus/Sebring convertible/Breeze with 2.0L SOHC engine and automatic transaxle

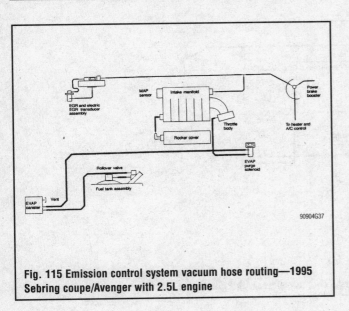

Fig. 115 Emission control system vacuum hose routing—1995 Sebring coupe/Avenger with 2.5L engine

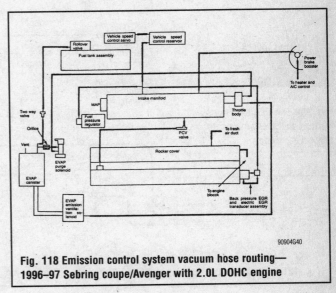

Fig. 118 Emission control system vacuum hose routing—1996–97 Sebring coupe/Avenger with 2.0L DOHC engine

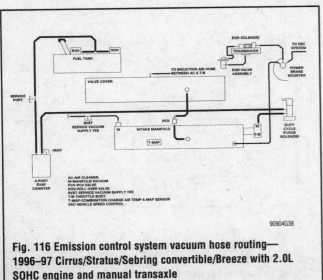

Fig. 116 Emission control system vacuum hose routing—1996–97 Cirrus/Stratus/Sebring convertible/Breeze with 2.0L SOHC engine and manual transaxle

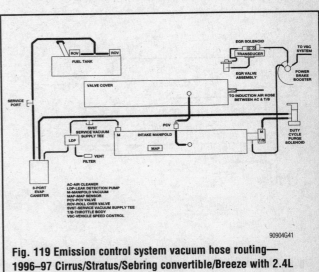

Fig. 119 Emission control system vacuum hose routing—1996–97 Cirrus/Stratus/Sebring convertible/Breeze with 2.4L engine

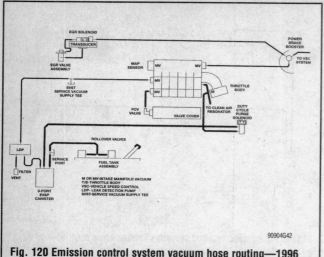

90904G42

Fig. 120 Emission control system vacuum hose routing—1996 Cirrus/Stratus/Sebring convertible/Breeze with 2.5L engine

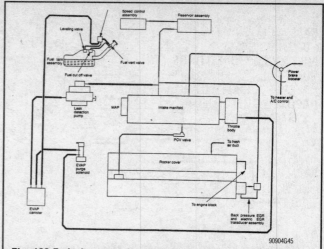

90904G45

Fig. 123 Emission control system vacuum hose routing—1998 Sebring coupe/Avenger with 2.0L DOHC engine

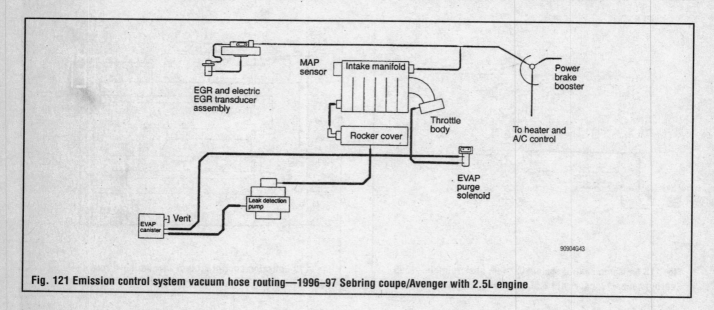

90904G43

Fig. 121 Emission control system vacuum hose routing—1996–97 Sebring coupe/Avenger with 2.5L engine

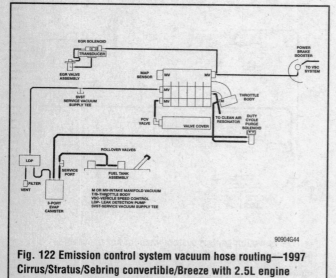

90904G44

Fig. 122 Emission control system vacuum hose routing—1997 Cirrus/Stratus/Sebring convertible/Breeze with 2.5L engine

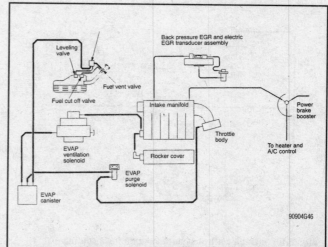

90904G46

Fig. 124 Emission control system vacuum hose routing—1998 Sebring coupe/Avenger with 2.5L engine

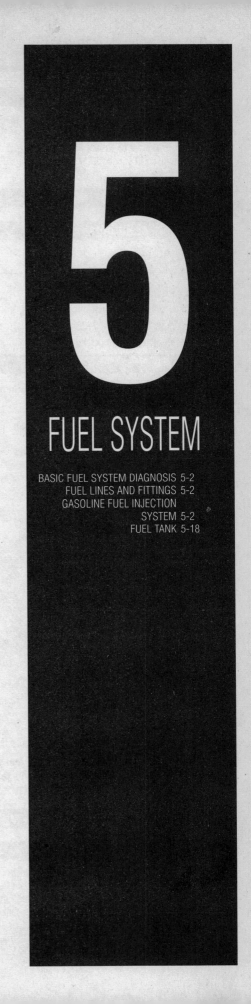

5

FUEL SYSTEM

BASIC FUEL SYSTEM DIAGNOSIS

When there is a problem starting or driving a vehicle, two of the most important checks involve the ignition and the fuel systems. The questions most mechanics attempt to answer first, "is there spark?" and "is there fuel?" will often lead to solving most basic problems. For ignition system diagnosis and testing, please refer to the information on engine electrical components and ignition systems found earlier in this manual. If the ignition system checks out (there is spark), then you must determine if the fuel system is operating properly (is there fuel?).

FUEL LINES AND FITTINGS

Quick-Connect Fittings

REMOVAL & INSTALLATION

◗ See Figures 1 and 2

➡When disconnecting a quick-connect fitting, the retainer will remain on the fuel tube nipple.

1. Disconnect the negative battery cable.

✳✳ CAUTION

You MUST relieve the fuel system pressure before disconnecting any quick-connect fittings.

2. Properly relieve the fuel system pressure, as outlined later in this section.
3. Squeeze the retainer tabs together and pull the fuel tube/quick-connect fitting assembly off of the fuel tube nipple. The retainer will remain on the tube.

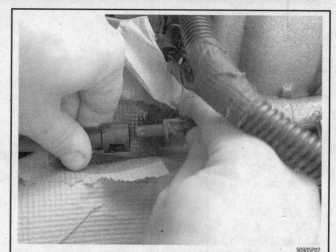

Fig. 2 . . . then pull the fuel tube/quick-connect fitting assembly off of the nipple

To install:

✳✳ WARNING

Never install a quick-connect fitting without the retainer being either on the fuel tube or already in the quick-connect fitting. In either case, make sure the retainer locks securely into the quick-connect fitting by firmly pulling on the fuel tube and fitting to ensure that it is fastened.

4. Using a clean, lint-free cloth, clean the fuel tube nipple and retainer.
5. Before connecting the fitting to the fuel tube, coat the tube nipple with clean 30-weight engine oil.
6. Push the quick-connect fitting over the fuel tube until the retainer seats and a click is heard.
7. The plastic quick-connect fitting has windows in the sides of the casing. When the fitting completely attaches to the fuel tube, the retainer locking ears and the fuel tube shoulder are visible in the windows. If they are not visible, the retainer was not installed properly. Do NOT count on the audible click to confirm a secure connection.
8. Use a DRB or equivalent scan tool to pressurize the fuel system and check for leaks.

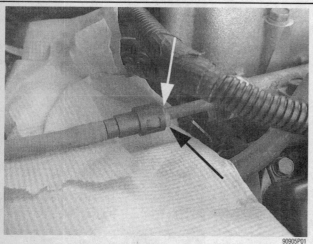

Fig. 1 Position a rag or towel to absorb any fuel spillage, then squeeze the quick-connect fitting retainer tabs (at arrows) . . .

GASOLINE FUEL INJECTION SYSTEM

General Information

The Multi-port Fuel Injection (MFI) system is electronically controlled by the Powertrain Control Module (PCM), based on data from various sensors. The PCM controls the fuel flow, idle speed and ignition timing.

Fuel is supplied to the injectors by an electric in-tank fuel pump and is distributed to the respective injectors via the main fuel pipe. The fuel pressure applied to the injector is constant and higher than the pressure in the intake manifold. The pressure is controlled by the fuel pressure regulator.

All vehicles covered in this manual are equipped with a returnless fuel injection system, except for 1995 Sebring and Avenger coupes, in which the excess fuel is returned to the tank through a fuel return pipe.

When an electric current flows in the injector, the injector valve is fully opened to supply fuel. Since the fuel pressure is constant, the amount of the fuel injected from the injector into the manifold is increased or decreased in proportion to the time the electric current flows. Based on PCM signals, the injectors inject fuel to the cylinder manifold ports in firing order.

Air enters the air intake plenum or manifold through the throttle body. In the intake manifold, the air is mixed with the fuel from the injectors and is drawn into the cylinder. The air flow rate is controlled according to the degree of the throttle valve and the servo motor openings.

The system is monitored through a number of sensors which feed information on engine conditions and requirements to the PCM. The PCM calculates the injection time and rate according to the signals from the sensors.

Fuel System Service Precaution

Safety is an important factor when servicing the fuel system. Failure to conduct maintenance and repairs in a safe manner may result in serious personal injury. Maintenance and testing of the vehicle's fuel system components can be accomplished safely and effectively by adhering to the following rules and guidelines.

• To avoid the possibility of fire and personal injury, always disconnect the negative battery cable unless the repair or test procedure requires that battery voltage be applied.

• Always relieve the fuel system pressure prior to disconnecting any fuel system component (injector, fuel rail, pressure regulator, etc.), fitting or fuel line connection. Exercise extreme caution whenever relieving fuel system pressure to avoid exposing skin, face and eyes to fuel spray. Please be advised that fuel under pressure may penetrate the skin or any part of the body that it contacts.

• Always place a shop towel or cloth around the fitting or connection prior to loosening to absorb any excess fuel due to spillage. Ensure that all fuel spillage is quickly removed from engine surfaces. Ensure that all fuel soaked cloths or towels are deposited into a suitable waste container.

• Always keep a dry chemical (Class B) fire extinguisher near the work area.

• Do not allow fuel spray or fuel vapors to come into contact with a spark or open flame.

• Always use a backup wrench when loosening and tightening fuel line connection fittings. This will prevent unnecessary stress and torsion to fuel line piping. Always follow the proper torque specifications.

• Always replace worn fuel fitting O-rings. Do not substitute fuel hose where fuel pipe is installed.

Relieving Fuel System Pressure

CIRRUS, STRATUS, SEBRING CONVERTIBLE & BREEZE

2.0L and 2.4L Engines

▶ See Figures 3 and 4

✳✳ CAUTION

Fuel injection systems remain under pressure, even after the engine has been turned OFF. The fuel system pressure MUST be relieved before disconnecting any fuel lines. Failure to do so may result in fire and/or personal injury.

1. Disconnect the remote negative battery cable from the left strut tower. The ground cable is equipped with an insulator grommet which should be placed on the stud to prevent the negative battery cable from accidentally grounding.
2. Remove the fuel filler cap.
3. Remove the cap on the fuel pressure test port on the fuel rail.
4. Place the open end of a fuel pressure release hose (special tool number C-4799-1 or equivalent) into an approved gasoline container. Connect the other end of the hose to the fuel pressure test port. Fuel pressure will bleed off through the hose, and into the gasoline container.

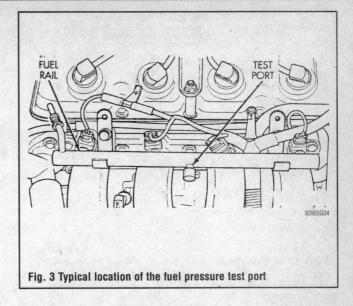

Fig. 3 Typical location of the fuel pressure test port

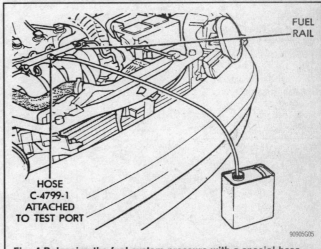

Fig. 4 Releasing the fuel system pressure with a special hose and gasoline container

2.5L Engine

▶ See Figures 5 and 6

✳✳ CAUTION

Fuel injection systems remain under pressure, even after the engine has been turned OFF. The fuel system pressure MUST be relieved before disconnecting any fuel lines. Failure to do so may result in fire and/or personal injury.

1. Disconnect the fuel rail electrical harness from the engine harness. This is connector C165, a black plastic connector located at the right rear of the intake manifold.
2. Circuit A142 supplies voltage for the fuel injectors while the Powertrain Control Module (PCM) controls the ground for each injector. Connect a jumper wire to the terminal for Circuit A142 (terminating an 18 gauge dark green wire with an orange tracer, from the ASD relay).
3. Connect the other end of the jumper wire to a 12 volt power source.
4. Connect one end of a second jumper wire to a ground source.

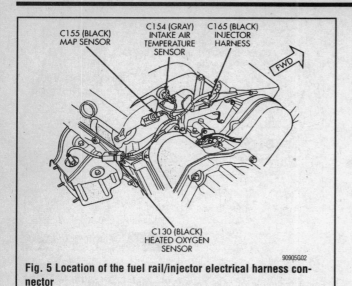

Fig. 5 Location of the fuel rail/injector electrical harness connector

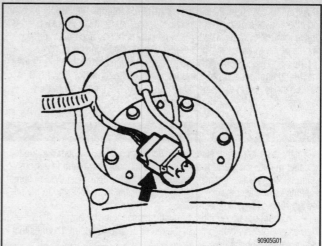

Fig. 7 Disengage the fuel pump harness connector at the fuel pump

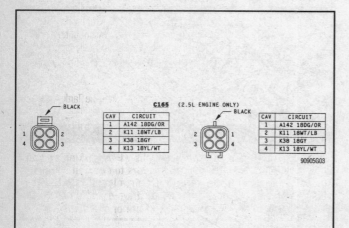

Fig. 6 Fuel rail/injector harness connector terminal identification

5. Momentarily ground each of the injectors by connecting the other end of the jumper wire to the injector terminal in the harness connector. Repeat this procedure for 2 or 3 injectors.

✷✷ WARNING

Do not attempt to start the engine for several minutes to avoid hydrostatic lock.

SEBRING COUPE & AVENGER

▶ See Figure 7

✷✷ CAUTION

Fuel injection systems remain under pressure even after the engine has been turned OFF. The fuel system pressure must be relieved before disconnecting any fuel lines. Failure to do so may result in fire and/or personal injury.

1. Remove the fuel filler cap to release fuel tank pressure.
2. Remove the rear seat cushion, as described in Section 10, then remove the fuel pump access cover.

➡There are two access covers underneath the seat. The panel on the far right side is for the fuel pump.

3. At the top of the fuel pump, disengage the fuel pump harness connector.
4. Start the vehicle and allow it to run until it stalls from lack of fuel. Turn the key to the **OFF** position.
5. Disconnect the negative battery cable, then plug in the fuel pump connector.
6. Install the fuel filler cap and rear seat cushion (unless other work, such as fuel pump service, requires its removal).

✷✷ CAUTION

Always wrap shop towels around a fitting that is being disconnected to absorb residual fuel in the lines.

Fuel Pump

REMOVAL & INSTALLATION

Sebring Coupe and Avenger

▶ See Figures 8 and 9

✷✷ CAUTION

Fuel injection systems remain under pressure, even after the engine has been turned OFF. The fuel system pressure must be relieved before disconnecting any fuel lines. Failure to do so may result in fire and/or personal injury.

Do not use conventional fuel filters, hoses or clamps when servicing fuel injection systems. They are not compatible with the injection system and could fail, causing personal injury or damage to the vehicle. Use only hoses and clamps specifically designed for fuel injection.

1. Remove the fuel pump's access cover and relieve fuel system pressure, using the proper procedure as previously outlined. Be sure to leave both the negative battery cable and fuel pump harness disconnected.

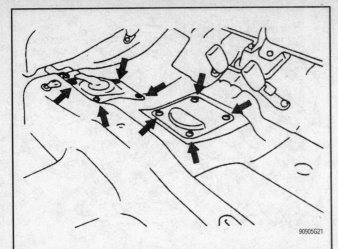

Fig. 8 The fuel pump is under the far right access cover, while the fuel gauge unit is below the far left cover

➡The rear seat cushion must be removed in order to gain access to the fuel pump.

2. Disconnect the return hose and the high pressure fuel hose.

❋❋ CAUTION

Observe all applicable safety precautions when working around fuel. Do not allow fuel spray or fuel vapors to come into contact with a spark or open flame. Keep a dry chemical (Class B) fire extinguisher near the work area. Never drain or store fuel in an open container due to the possibility of fire or explosion. Cover all fuel hose connections with a shop towel, prior to disconnecting, to prevent a splash of fuel that could be caused by residual pressure remaining in the fuel line.

3. Remove the fuel pump mounting nuts and withdraw the pump assembly.

To install:

4. Align the seal position projections with the holes in the fuel pump assembly and install the assembly in the tank. Tighten the retaining nuts to 22 inch lbs. (2.5 Nm).

5. Connect the high pressure hose, return hose and fuel pump wiring.

6. Connect the negative battery cable.

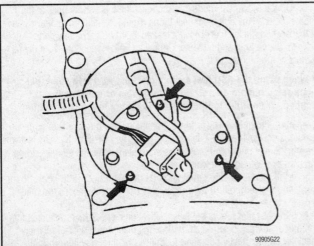

Fig. 9 The seal position projections must be aligned with the holes in the fuel pump assembly

7. Check the fuel pump for proper pressure and inspect the entire system for leaks.

8. Apply sealant to the access cover and install the cover.

9. Install the rear seat cushion.

10. Pressurize the fuel system by turning the ignition key to the **ON** position. Check for leaks. Start the engine to verify proper fuel pump performance.

Cirrus, Stratus, Sebring Convertible and Breeze

▶ **See Figures 10 and 11**

The fuel pump is serviced as part of the fuel pump module. The fuel pump module is installed in the top of the fuel tank and contains the electric fuel pump, fuel pump reservoir, inlet strainer fuel gauge sending unit, fuel supply and return line connections and the pressure regulator. The inlet strainer, fuel pressure regulator and level sensor are the only serviceable items. If the fuel pump requires service, replace the fuel pump module.

❋❋ CAUTION

Fuel injection systems remain under pressure, even after the engine has been turned OFF. The fuel system pressure MUST be relieved before disconnecting any fuel lines. Failure to do so may result in fire and/or personal injury.

1. Disconnect the negative battery cable from the left strut tower. The ground cable is equipped with an insulator grommet which should be placed on the stud to prevent the negative battery cable from accidentally grounding.

2. Remove the fuel filler cap and relieve the fuel system pressure, as outlined earlier in this procedure.

3. Raise and safely support the vehicle.

4. Drain and remove the fuel tank, as outlined under the Tank Assembly removal and installation procedure, later in this section.

❋❋ CAUTION

Observe all applicable safety precautions when working around fuel. Do not allow fuel spray or fuel vapors to come in contact with a spark or open flame. Keep a dry chemical (Class B) fire extinguisher near the work area. Never drain or store fuel in an open container due to the possibility of fire or explosion.

5. Clean the top of the tank to remove any loose dirt.

6. Disconnect the fuel lines from the fuel pump module by depressing the quick-connect retainers with your thumb and forefinger.

7. Using special tool 6856 (Fuel Pump Module Ring Spanner) or equivalent, remove the fuel pump lock ring.

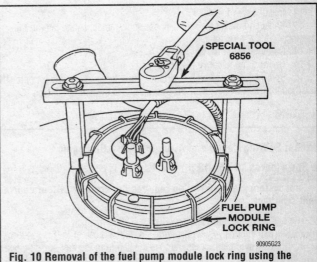

Fig. 10 Removal of the fuel pump module lock ring using the special tool

✲✲ WARNING

The fuel reservoir of the fuel pump module does not empty out when the tank is drained. The fuel in the reservoir may spill out when the module is removed.

8. Remove the fuel pump and O-ring seal from the tank. Discard the old O-ring seal.

To install:

9. Thoroughly clean all parts. Wipe the seal area of the tank clean. Place a new O-ring on the ledge between the tank threads and the pump module opening.

10. Position the fuel pump module in the tank. Make sure the alignment tab on the underside of the pump module flange sits in the corresponding notch in the fuel tank.

11. While holding the fuel pump module in place, install the locking ring and tighten to 45 ft. lbs. (61 Nm), using special tool 6856 or an equivalent spanner-type tool.

✲✲ WARNING

Do not overtighten the pump lock ring, as this may cause a fuel leak.

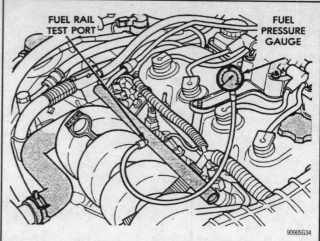

Fig. 12 Checking the fuel pressure at the intake manifold—4-cylinder models

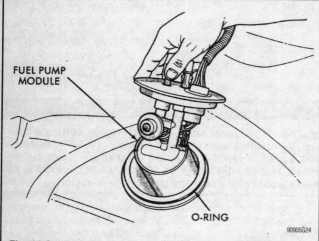

Fig. 11 Carefully remove the fuel pump module from the fuel tank

12. Install a new fuel filter.

13. Raise and install the fuel tank assembly, as described later in this section.

14. Carefully lower the vehicle.

15. Connect the negative battery cable.

16. Refill the fuel tank with clean fuel. Turn the ignition switch to the **ON** position to pressurize the system. Check the fuel system for leaks.

TESTING

Except Sebring Coupe and Avenger With 2.5L Engine

◆ **See Figures 12 and 13**

➥**Fuel system pressure testing requires the use of a DRB or equivalent scan tool.**

The fuel pump operates at about 49 psi (338 kPa).

1. Release the fuel system pressure, as outlined earlier in this section.

2. On all 4-cylinder models, remove the cap from the fuel pressure test port on the fuel rail and connect a suitable fuel pressure gauge.

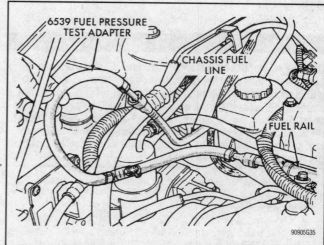

Fig. 13 Install the fuel pressure test adapter—6-cylinder models, except Sebring coupe and Avenger

3. On the 6-cylinder models, disconnect the fuel supply hose at the engine. Refer to the quick-connect fitting disengagement procedure earlier in this section. Install fuel pressure test adapter 6539, or equivalent, between the fuel rail and fuel line. Connect a suitable fuel pressure gauge to the test port on the adapter.

➥**When using the ASD fuel system test, the ASD relay and fuel pump relay remain energized for 7 minutes or until the test is stopped, or until the ignition switch is turned to the OFF position.**

4. Turn the ignition key to the **ON** position. Using the DRB or equivalent scan tool, access the ASD Fuel System Test. The ASD Fuel System Test will activate the fuel pump and pressurize the system. Note the gauge reading and compare with the following:

• If the gauge reading equals approximately 49 psi (338 kPa), no further testing is required. If the pressure is not correct, record the reading.

• If the fuel pressure is below specifications, check for a restricted fuel pump inlet strainer. If restricted, replace the inlet strainer. If not restricted, check for an incorrectly operating fuel filter, pressure regulator or fuel pump, and replace as necessary.

- If the fuel pressure is above specifications (54 psi or higher), check for a kinked or restricted fuel supply line. If the line is not kinked or restricted, check for a restriction in the chassis fuel supply line or for a kinked or plugged fuel supply line. If none of the lines are restricted, replace the fuel pressure regulator.

Sebring Coupe and Avenger With 2.5L Engine

▶ See Figures 14 thru 20

➡Fuel system pressure testing requires the use of a DRB or equivalent scan tool.

1. Release fuel system pressure as outlined earlier in this section.
2. On 1995 models, disconnect the high pressure fuel hose at the fuel rail side. On 1996–98 models, remove the fuel plate from the fuel rail.

✳✳ CAUTION

Cover the fuel plate or hose connection with a shop towel to absorb any fuel splash that could be caused by any residual pressure remaining in the fuel line.

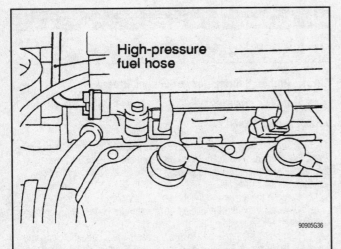

Fig. 14 Disconnect the high pressure fuel hose at the fuel rail—1995 models

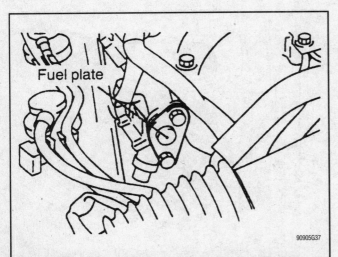

Fig. 15 Remove the fuel plate from the fuel rail—1996–98 models

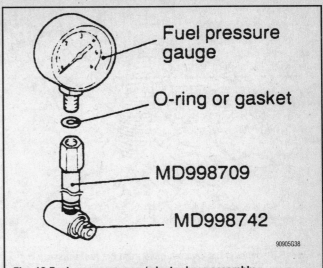

Fig. 16 Fuel pressure gauge/adapter hose assembly

3. Remove the union joint and bolt from the adapter hose tool MD998709 or equivalent and connect special hose adapter tool MD998742 or equivalent to the adapter hose.
4. Install a fuel pressure gauge to the adapter hose. Be sure to install a suitable O-ring or gasket between the fuel pressure gauge and adapter fitting to prevent any fuel leakage.
5. On 1995 models, install the fuel gauge/adapter hose assembly between the fuel rail and high pressure hose. On 1996–98 models, install the fuel gauge/adapter hose assembly between the fuel rail and fuel plate.
6. Using the DRB, or equivalent scan tool, access the "Fuel System Test" to operate the fuel pump. Check for leaks in the fuel gauge and adapter hose assembly connections.
7. Start the engine and allow it to run at idle.
8. Measure the fuel pressure while the engine is running at idle. The pressure should read as follows:
- On 1995 models, the pressure should read 38 psi (265 kPa) with the fuel pressure regulator vacuum hose connected. With the vacuum hose disconnected and hose end blocked, the pressure should read 47–50 psi (324–343 kPa).
- On 1996–98 models, the pressure should read 47–50 psi (324–343 kPa).

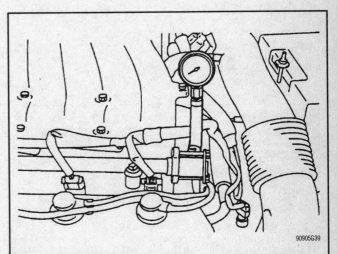

Fig. 17 Installation of the fuel pressure gauge/adapter hose assembly

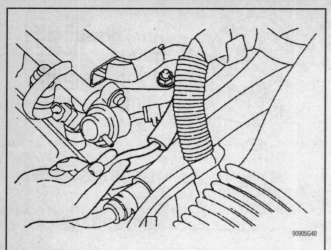

Fig. 18 Disconnect the vacuum hose from the fuel pressure regulator and plug with a finger—1995 models

Fig. 19 Fuel pressure out-of-range troubleshooting chart

Symptom	Probable cause	Remedy
• Fuel pressure too low • Fuel pressure drops after racing • No fuel pressure in fuel return hose	Clogged fuel filter	Replace fuel filter
	Fuel leaking to return side due to poor fuel regulator valve seating or settled spring	Replace fuel pressure regulator
	Low fuel pump delivery pressure	Replace fuel pump
Fuel pressure too high	Binding valve in fuel pressure regulator	Replace fuel pressure regulator
	Clogged fuel return hose or pipe	Clean or replace hose or pipe
Same fuel pressure when vacuum hose is connected and when disconnected	Damaged vacuum hose or clogged nipple	Replace vacuum hose or clean nipple

Fig. 20 Fuel pressure drop troubleshooting chart

Symptom	Probable cause	Remedy
Fuel pressure drops gradually after engine is stopped	Leaky injector	Replace injector
	Leaky fuel regulator valve seat	Replace fuel pressure regulator
Fuel pressure drops sharply immediately after engine is stopped	Check valve in fuel pump is held open	Replace fuel pump

9. Race the engine several times and check that the fuel pressure at idle does not stop. On 1995 models, while racing the engine, hold the fuel return hose lightly with fingers to feel the presence of pressure in the return hose.

➡**If the fuel flow rate is low, there will be no pressure in the return hose.**

10. If any of the fuel pressure readings are out of specifications, refer to the troubleshooting chart.

11. Stop the engine and observe the fuel pressure gauge reading. It is normal if the reading does not drop within 2 minutes. If it does drop, observe the rate at which it does and refer to the troubleshooting chart.

12. Release the residual pressure from the system and remove the fuel pressure gauge/adapter hose assembly.

✳✳ CAUTION

Cover the fuel plate or hose connection with a shop towel to absorb any fuel splash that could be caused by residual pressure remaining in the fuel line.

13. On 1995 models, install the O-ring seal and connect the high pressure fuel hose. On 1996–98 models, install the fuel plate to the fuel rail. Install the retaining bolts and tighten to 43 inch lbs. (5 Nm).

Throttle Body

REMOVAL & INSTALLATION

Cirrus, Stratus, Sebring Convertible and Breeze

2.0L AND 2.4L ENGINES

◗ **See Figures 21 and 22**

1. Disconnect the remote negative battery cable from the left strut tower. The ground cable is equipped with an insulator grommet which should be placed on the stud to prevent the negative battery cable from accidentally grounding.

2. Remove the air cleaner/inlet resonator assembly.

3. Disengage the throttle cable from the throttle lever by relieving tension on the cable and sliding out the cable clasp.

4. Compress the retaining tabs on the cable, then slide the cable end out of the bracket.

5. If equipped with cruise control, also remove the speed control cable from the throttle lever by sliding the clasp out of the hole used for the throttle cable.

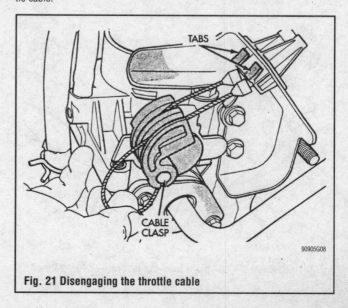

Fig. 21 Disengaging the throttle cable

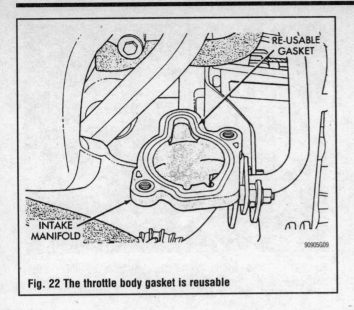

Fig. 22 The throttle body gasket is reusable

RE-USABLE GASKET

INTAKE MANIFOLD

90905G09

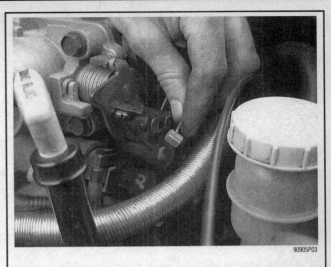

Fig. 23 Disengage the throttle cable from the throttle lever

90905P03

6. Disconnect the EVAP purge hose from the base of the throttle body.

7. Remove the 2 screws holding the cable mounting bracket and support bracket.

8. Remove the throttle body mounting bolts.

9. Partially lift the throttle body, detach the IAC motor and TPS electrical connectors, then remove the throttle body from the vehicle.

10. The rubber O-ring gasket is reusable, so wipe it clean and inspect it. If it's in good condition, you can reinstall it. If not, replace it with a new one.

To install:

11. Attach the IAC motor and TPS electrical connections to the throttle body.

12. Position the throttle body on the intake manifold. Do not tighten the mounting bolts at this time.

13. Attach the cable mounting bracket and support bracket. Secure with the 2 mounting screws, but do not tighten at this time.

14. Tighten the throttle body mounting bolts to 175–225 inch lbs. (19.5–25.5 Nm).

15. Tighten the throttle cable bracket mounting bolts to 85–125 inch lbs. (9.5–14 Nm).

16. Connect the EVAP purge hose to the throttle body.

17. Install the cable housing retainer tabs into the bracket.

18. If equipped with cruise control, rotate the throttle lever forward to the wide open throttle position and slide the speed control cable all the way into the lever.

19. Rotate the throttle lever forward to the wide open position and install the throttle cable.

20. Install the air cleaner/inlet resonator assembly.

21. Connect the negative battery cable.

2.5L ENGINE

▶ **See Figures 23 thru 30**

1. Disconnect the remote negative battery cable from the left strut tower. The ground cable is equipped with an insulator grommet which should be placed on the stud to prevent the negative battery cable from accidentally grounding.

2. Remove the air cleaner/inlet resonator assembly.

3. Disengage the throttle cable from the throttle lever by relieving tension on the cable and sliding out the cable clasp.

4. If equipped with cruise control, remove the speed control cable from the throttle lever by rotating the lever to the wide open throttle position and sliding the cable clasp out of the hole.

5. Disconnect the EVAP purge hose from the base of the throttle body.

6. Disengage the IAC motor and TPS electrical connectors.

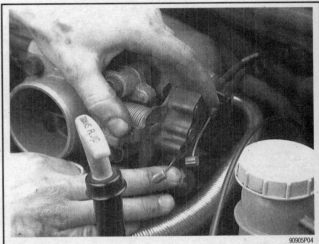

Fig. 24 Hold the throttle lever to the wide open throttle position, then disengage the cruise control cable, if equipped

90905P04

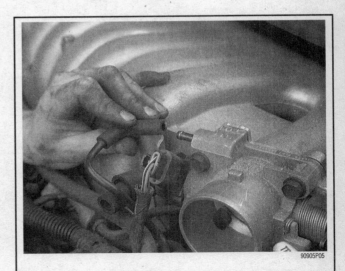

Fig. 25 Disconnect the EVAP purge hose from the throttle body

90905P05

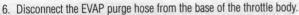

Fig. 26 Disengage the wiring connector to the TPS . . .

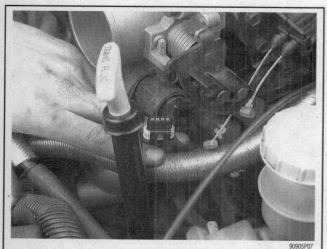

Fig. 27 . . . then disengage the wiring connector to the IAC motor

Fig. 28 Loosen the 4 throttle body mounting bolts . . .

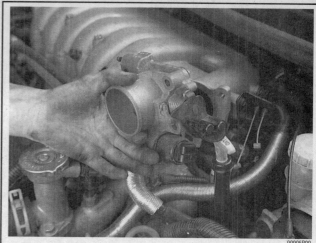

Fig. 29 . . . then remove the throttle body from the intake manifold plenum

Fig. 30 Remove and inspect the throttle body gasket. If it is in good condition, you can reuse it

7. Unfasten the throttle body mounting bolts.
8. Remove the throttle body from the vehicle. Remove the throttle body gasket and clean the gasket mating surfaces.

To install:

9. Install a new throttle body gasket, then position the throttle body onto the intake manifold and install the mounting bolts. Tighten the throttle body mounting bolts to 250 inch lbs. (28 Nm).
10. Fasten the IAC motor and TPS electrical connections to the throttle body.
11. Install the cruise control cable first (if equipped), then the throttle cable into the throttle lever.
12. Connect the EVAP purge hose to the throttle body.
13. Install the air cleaner/inlet resonator assembly.
14. Connect the negative battery cable.

Sebring Coupe and Avenger

▶ See Figures 31 thru 40

1. Disconnect the negative battery cable.
2. Remove the air intake hose to the throttle body. It may be necessary to first remove the battery.

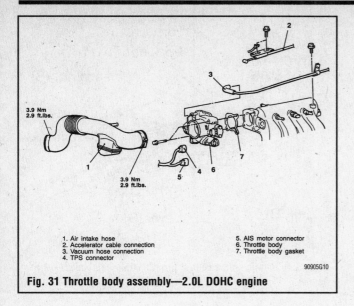

1. Air intake hose
2. Accelerator cable connection
3. Vacuum hose connection
4. TPS connector
5. AIS motor connector
6. Throttle body
7. Throttle body gasket

90905G10

Fig. 31 Throttle body assembly—2.0L DOHC engine

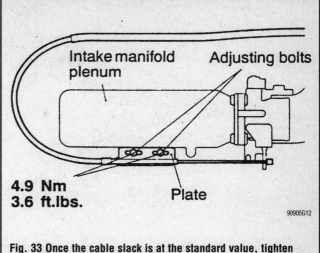

4.9 Nm
3.6 ft.lbs.

90905G12

Fig. 33 Once the cable slack is at the standard value, tighten the adjusting bolts to the specified torque

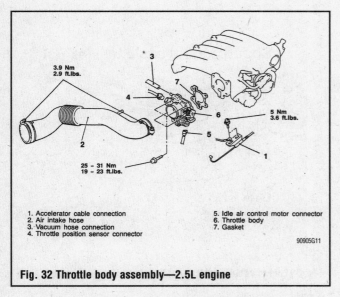
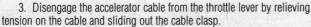

1. Accelerator cable connection
2. Air intake hose
3. Vacuum hose connection
4. Throttle position sensor connector
5. Idle air control motor connector
6. Throttle body
7. Gasket

90905G11

Fig. 32 Throttle body assembly—2.5L engine

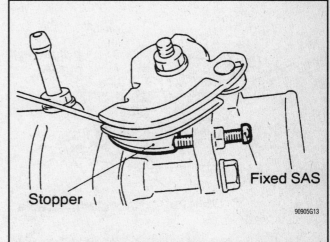

90905G13

Fig. 34 Confirm that the throttle lever stopper contacts the fixed SAS

3. Disengage the accelerator cable from the throttle lever by relieving tension on the cable and sliding out the cable clasp.

4. Disconnect the EVAP purge hose from the base of the throttle body.

5. Disengage the IAC motor and TPS electrical connectors.

6. Unfasten the throttle body mounting bolts.

7. Remove the throttle body from the vehicle. Remove the throttle body gasket and clean the gasket mating surfaces.

To install:

8. Install a new throttle body gasket, then position the throttle body onto the intake manifold and install the mounting bolts. Tighten the throttle body mounting bolts to 19–23 ft. lbs. (25–31 Nm).

9. Fasten the IAC motor and TPS electrical connections to the throttle body.

10. Install the accelerator cable into the throttle lever.

11. Connect the EVAP purge hose to the throttle body.

12. Install the air intake hose to the throttle body.

13. If a new throttle body is being installed, the accelerator cable must be adjusted.

14. If not equipped with cruise control, adjust the accelerator cable as follows:

   a. Turn **OFF** the air conditioning and all lights.

   b. Start the engine and allow it to idle until it reaches normal operating temperature.

   c. After confirming the idle speed is at the prescribed engine RPM, turn the engine **OFF**.

   d. Check to make sure that the accelerator cable has no sharp kinks in it, then check the inner cable for correct slack. If too much slack exists, loosen the cable adjusting bolts.

   e. Move the plate to a position immediately before the throttle lever begins to move, then slightly push the plate toward the throttle body in order to bring the cable slack to the standard value of 0.04–0.08 inches (1–2mm).

   f. Tighten the adjusting bolts to 43 inch lbs. (5 Nm).

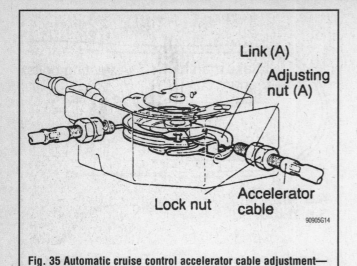

Fig. 35 Automatic cruise control accelerator cable adjustment—2.0L DOHC engine

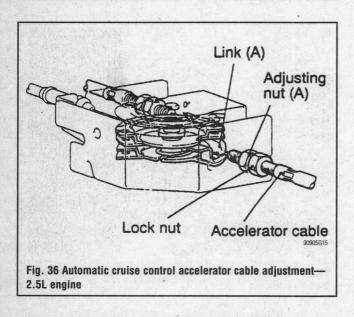

Fig. 36 Automatic cruise control accelerator cable adjustment—2.5L engine

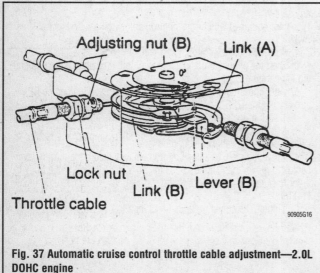

Fig. 37 Automatic cruise control throttle cable adjustment—2.0L DOHC engine

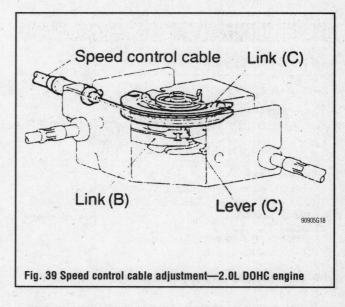

Fig. 38 Automatic cruise control throttle cable adjustment—2.5L engine

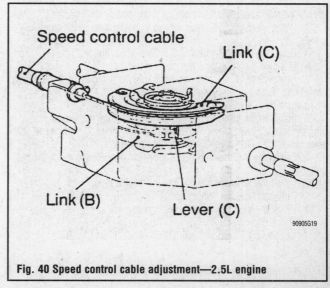

Fig. 39 Speed control cable adjustment—2.0L DOHC engine

Fig. 40 Speed control cable adjustment—2.5L engine

g. Confirm that the throttle lever stopper touches the fixed SAS.
15. If equipped with cruise control, adjust the accelerator cable as follows:

a. Remove the link cover and inspect the slack of the accelerator, speed control and throttle cables.

b. If there is excessive slack or none at all in any of the cables, loosen, but do not remove, the adjusting bolts and nuts in the throttle lever and each link to release.

c. Adjust with nut A so that when link A contacts the stopper, accelerator (inner) cable play reaches the standard value:

- Manual transaxle—0–0.04 inches (0–1mm)
- Automatic transaxle—0.08–0.12 inches (2–3mm)

d. Secure the accelerator cable with the locknut.

e. Adjust with nut B so that when lever B contacts link A, the throttle (inner) cable play reaches the standard value of 0.04–0.08 inches (1–2mm).

f. Secure the throttle cable with the locknut.

g. Tighten the throttle lever-side adjusting bolt.

h. Hold link C at the position where lever C contacts link B. Secure the speed control cable.

i. Install the link cover.
16. Connect the negative battery cable.
17. Road test the vehicle for proper operation.

Fuel Injectors

REMOVAL & INSTALLATION

▶ **See Figures 41, 42 and 43**

1. Disconnect the negative battery cable.
2. Properly relieve the fuel system pressure, as described earlier in this section.
3. Remove the fuel rail, as outlined later in this section.
4. Unfasten the fuel injector-to-rail retaining clip, then pull the fuel injector out of the rail.
5. Use a small awl or equivalent tool to carefully remove the O-rings from each end of the injector. Discard the O-rings and replace with new ones during installation.

To install:

6. Install new O-rings on each end of the injector.
7. Lightly coat the upper and lower O-ring gaskets of the injector with clean engine oil.
8. Install the injector in the cup on the fuel rail, then secure with the retaining clip.

Fig. 41 Remove the fuel injector-to-fuel rail retaining clip

Fig. 42 Carefully pull the fuel injector out of the fuel rail

Fig. 43 Use a small awl, or equivalent, to remove the fuel injector O-ring gaskets

9. Install the fuel rail, as outlined later in this section.
10. Connect the negative battery cable.

TESTING

▶ **See Figure 44**

1. Unplug the injector electrical connector.
2. Using an ohmmeter, test the injector resistance across the injector terminals. The reading should be approximately 12–15 ohms at 68°F (20°C).

a. If the resistance falls outside specifications, replace the faulty injector.

b. If the resistance is within specifications, proceed with the testing.
3. Place a 12 volt test lamp across the injector's electrical connector terminals. Watch the test lamp while cranking the engine and compare with the following:

a. If the test lamp does not flash, check the power feed and ground circuits between the PCM and the injector connector. Refer to the wiring diagrams in Section 6 for wire colors. If the circuits are faulty, repair them. If the circuits are OK, test the engine control system.

b. If the test lamp flashes, proceed with the testing.

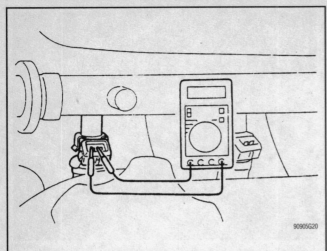

Fig. 44 Connect an ohmmeter to the fuel injector terminals and measure the resistance

4. Check for fuel delivery at the suspect injector by removing the injector from the fuel rail and check for fuel and/or restrictions in the rail or injector fuel inlet. Compare your results with the following:

   a. If there is no fuel present at the injector, replace the plugged injector, or clean the restricted passage, as necessary.

   b. If there is fuel present at the injector, proceed with the testing.

5. With the injector removed from the fuel rail, connect a 12 volt source to one terminal on the injector connector and a ground wire to the other terminal. The injector should "click" each time the ground wire is connected and disconnected to and from the terminal.

6. If the injector "clicks," it is OK. If it does not "click," it must be replaced.

Fuel Rail

REMOVAL & INSTALLATION

2.0L and 2.4L Engines

❋❋ CAUTION

Fuel injection systems remain under pressure, even after the engine has been turned OFF. The fuel system pressure must be relieved before disconnecting any fuel lines. Failure to do so may result in fire and/or personal injury.

1. Properly relieve the fuel system pressure, as described earlier in this section.

2. Disconnect the negative battery cable. On Cirrus, Stratus, Sebring convertible and Breeze models, disconnect the remote negative battery connection from the left strut tower. The ground cable is equipped with an insulator grommet which should be placed on the stud to prevent the negative battery cable from accidentally grounding.

3. On Sebring coupe and Avenger models, remove the bolts holding the high pressure fuel line to the fuel rail and disconnect the line. On Cirrus, Stratus, Sebring convertible and Breeze models, disconnect the fuel supply line quick-connect fitting from the fuel rail. Refer to the procedure outlined earlier in this section. Plug the line to keep out dirt and debris.

❋❋ CAUTION

Wrap shop towels around the hose connection to catch any gasoline spillage.

4. On 1995 Sebring coupe and Avenger models only, remove the fuel pressure regulator, as outlined later in this section.

5. Label and disengage the electrical connector from each injector.

6. Remove the bolts holding the fuel rail to the manifold. Carefully lift the rail up and remove it with the injectors attached. Take care not to drop an injector. Place the rail and injectors in a safe location on the workbench. Cover the fuel injector openings in the intake manifold. Protect the tips of the injectors from dirt and/or impact.

7. Remove and discard the injector insulators from the intake manifold. The insulators are not reusable.

8. If the fuel injectors are being removed, refer to the procedure earlier in this section.

To install:

9. Install a new insulator in each injector port in the manifold.

10. Install the fuel injector(s) into the fuel rail assembly, as outlined earlier in this section.

11. Install the injector into the fuel rail, constantly turning the injector left and right during installation. When fully installed, the injector should still turn freely in the rail. If it does not, remove the injector and inspect the O-ring for deformation or damage.

12. Install the delivery pipe and injectors to the engine. Make certain that each injector fits correctly into its port and that the rubber insulators for the fuel rail mounts are in position.

13. Install the fuel rail retaining bolts.

14. Connect the wiring harnesses to the appropriate injectors.

15. Connect the vacuum hose to the pressure regulator.

16. Replace the O-ring on the high pressure fuel line, coat the O-ring lightly with clean, thin oil and install the line to the fuel rail. Tighten the mounting bolts to 22 inch lbs. (2.5 Nm).

17. Connect the negative battery cable. Pressurize the fuel system and inspect all connections for leaks.

2.5L Engine

▶ See Figures 45 thru 51

The intake manifold assembly is composed of an upper plenum and lower manifold. This aluminum alloy manifold has long runners to improve airflow inertia. The plenum chamber absorbs air pulsations created during the suction phase of each cylinder. The lower intake manifold is machined for 6 injectors and the fuel rail mounts. The fuel injectors are mounted in 2 fuel rails which bolt to the lower half of the two-piece intake manifold assembly. The upper half (plenum) of the intake manifold must be removed to access the fuel rails for fuel injector removal.

1. Disconnect the negative battery cable from the left strut tower. The ground cable is equipped with an insulator grommet which should be placed on the stud to prevent the negative battery cable from accidentally grounding.

2. Properly relieve the fuel system pressure, as described earlier in this section.

❋❋ CAUTION

Fuel injection systems remain under pressure, even after the engine has been turned OFF. The fuel system pressure MUST be relieved before disconnecting any fuel lines. Failure to do so may result in fire and/or personal injury.

3. Disconnect the fuel supply line from the fuel rail. This is a quick-connect fitting. Squeeze the fitting retainer tabs together and separate the connection.

❋❋ WARNING

Wrap shop towels around the connection to catch any gasoline spillage.

➡ It may be helpful to identify and tag each sensor connector as it is being removed. This may save time at assembly.

4. Unfasten the connectors from the Manifold Absolute Pressure (MAP) sensor and the intake air temperature sensor.

5. Remove the plenum support bracket located to the rear of the MAP sensor.

6. Remove the air inlet resonator attaching bolt.

7. Loosen the throttle body air inlet hose clamp.

8. Release the snaps holding the air cleaner housing cover to the housing. Remove the air cleaner cover and inlet hoses from the engine.

9. Detach the Throttle Position Sensor (TPS) and the Idle Air Control (IAC) motor electrical connections.

10. Squeeze the retainer tab on the throttle cable and slide the cable out of the bracket.

11. If equipped with speed control, slide the speed control cable out of the bracket.

12. Remove the EGR tube from the engine.

13. Remove the plenum support bracket located to the rear of the EGR tube.

14. Remove the 7 bolts attaching the upper intake plenum to the intake manifold and remove the plenum.

15. Unfasten the fuel injector electrical connectors.

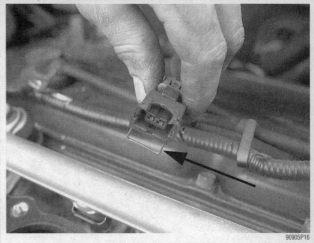

Fig. 47 Some of the connectors have small wire retainers (arrow)

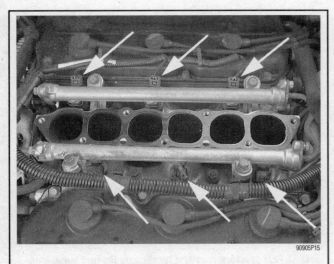

Fig. 45 Locations of the fuel injector wiring connectors (arrows)

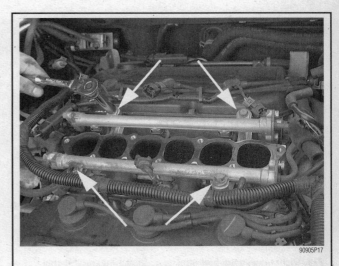

Fig. 48 Remove the 4 fuel rail mounting fasteners (arrow)

Fig. 46 Disconnect the fuel injector connectors

Fig. 49 Carefully lift off the fuel rail assembly

Fig. 50 Remove the fuel rail-to-intake manifold mounting grommets

Fig. 51 Removing the fuel injector-to-intake manifold O-ring gasket

16. Remove the 4 bolts attaching the fuel rails to the lower intake manifold and carefully lift the fuel rails off the engine. There are spacers under each fuel rail bolt.

17. Remove the fuel injector clip.

18. Pull the fuel injector out of the fuel rail.

To install:

19. Using new O-rings, apply a light coating of engine oil to the fuel injector O-rings on the nozzle end of each injector.

20. Install the fuel injectors into the fuel rail and secure with the fuel injector clips. Install the fuel injector/fuel rail assembly into the engine.

21. Seat the injectors in place, making sure the spacers are properly located under each fuel rail mounting position, and tighten the fuel rail bolts to 96 inch lbs. (11 Nm).

22. Reattach the electrical connectors to the fuel injectors.

23. Reconnect the fuel supply line to the fuel rail. Be sure the quick-connect fittings are fully engaged.

24. Reinstall the upper intake plenum with new gaskets.

25. Tighten the plenum bolts to 13 ft. lbs. (18 Nm).

26. Install the plenum support brackets and tighten to 13 ft. lbs. (18 Nm).

27. Install the EGR tube and tighten the screws to 95 inch lbs. (11 Nm).

28. Reinstall the throttle cables.

29. Secure the TPS and IAC electrical connections.

30. Reconnect the MAP sensor and the intake air temperature sensor.

31. Reinstall the air cleaner assembly and tighten the hose clamps to 25 inch lbs. (3 Nm).

32. Reinstall the air inlet resonator attaching bolt.

33. Reconnect the negative battery cable. Start the engine and check for fuel leaks.

Fuel Pressure Regulator

REMOVAL & INSTALLATION

Cirrus, Stratus, Sebring Convertible and Breeze

▶ **See Figures 52 and 53**

The fuel pressure regulator is part of the fuel pump module. Remove the module from the fuel tank for access to the regulator.

1. Disconnect the negative battery cable.

2. Properly relieve the fuel system pressure, as described earlier in this section.

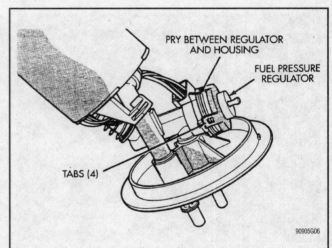

Fig. 52 Fuel pressure regulator location on the fuel pump module assembly

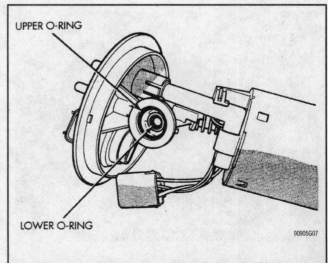

Fig. 53 Remember to remove the upper and lower O-rings

3. Remove the fuel pump module, as outlined earlier in this section.

4. Spread the tabs on the pressure regulator retainer.

5. Using a suitable prytool, carefully pry the regulator out of the housing.

➡**Make sure both the upper and lower O-rings were removed with the regulator.**

To install:

6. Lightly lubricate the O-rings with clean engine oil, then place them into the fuel pump module opening.

7. Push the regulator into the opening in the pump module.

8. Fold the tabs on the regulator retainer over the tabs on the housing.

9. Install the fuel pump module, as outlined earlier in this section.

10. Connect the negative battery cable.

Sebring Coupe and Avenger

1995 MODELS WITH 2.0L ENGINE

▸ **See Figure 54**

➡**The fuel pressure regulator is mounted on the right end of the fuel rail.**

1. Properly relieve the fuel system pressure, as outlined earlier in this section.

2. If not done already, disconnect the negative battery cable.

3. If necessary, remove the air intake hose.

4. Disconnect the vacuum hose to the fuel pressure regulator.

5. Using snapring pliers, or equivalent, remove the pressure regulator retaining snapring.

6. Remove the fuel pressure regulator assembly. Make sure the upper and lower O-rings are still on the pressure regulator.

To install:

7. Lightly coat the pressure regulator O-rings with clean engine oil. Be careful not to allow engine oil to enter the fuel rail opening.

8. Insert the fuel pressure regulator into the opening of the fuel rail assembly. If the regulator assembly does not insert smoothly, it may be a binding O-ring seal. Pull out the regulator and inspect the O-ring seal(s) for damage.

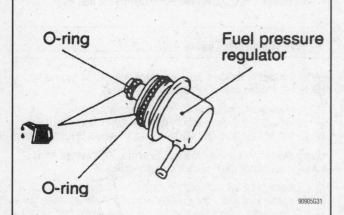

Fig. 54 Apply a small amount of clean engine oil to each O-ring before installation

9. Install the pressure regulator snapring.

10. Attach the fuel pressure regulator vacuum hose.

11. If removed, install the air intake hose.

12. Connect the negative battery cable.

1995 MODELS WITH 2.5L ENGINE

▸ **See Figure 55**

➡**The fuel pressure regulator is mounted on the left end of the front fuel rail.**

1. Properly relieve the fuel system pressure, as outlined earlier in this section.

2. If necessary for access to the regulator, remove the air cleaner/inlet duct assembly.

3. Remove the vacuum hose from the fuel pressure regulator.

4. Disconnect the fuel return hose from the pressure regulator.

5. Remove the fuel regulator retainer bolts, then remove the fuel regulator from the fuel rail.

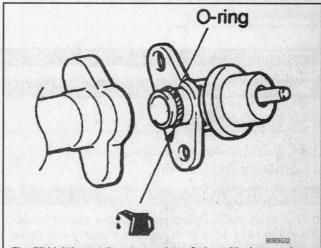

Fig. 55 Lightly coat the new regulator O-ring with clean engine oil before installing it to the fuel rail

To install:

6. Replace the O-ring on the fuel pressure regulator with a new one and coat it lightly with clean, thin oil.

7. Insert the regulator straight into the rail, then check that it can be rotated freely.

➡**If it does not rotate smoothly, remove it and inspect the O-ring for deformation or damage.**

8. When properly installed, align the mounting holes. Install and tighten the retaining bolts to 78 inch lbs. (9 Nm).

9. Connect the fuel return hose to the pressure regulator.

10. Install the vacuum hose to the fuel pressure regulator.

11. If removed, install the air cleaner/inlet duct assembly.

12. Connect the negative battery cable and pressurize the fuel system. Inspect for leaks.

1996–98 MODELS

▸ **See Figure 56**

➡**The fuel pressure regulator on these vehicles is located next to the fuel filter, which is mounted near the fuel tank.**

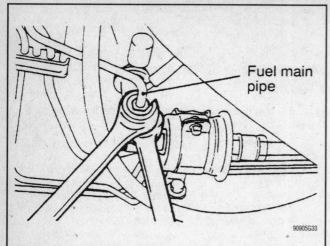

Fuel main pipe

90905G33

Fig. 56 Disconnect the fuel main pipe using a flare nut wrench and a backup wrench

1. Properly relieve the fuel system pressure, as outlined earlier in this section.
2. If not done already, disconnect the negative battery cable.
3. Raise and safely support the vehicle.
4. Using flare nut and backup wrenches, disconnect the fuel main pipe from the fuel filter/pressure regulator joint connector.
5. Disconnect the fuel return hose from the pressure regulator.
6. Using an open end wrench, unscrew the fuel pressure regulator and remove it from the vehicle.

To install:

7. Screw the fuel pressure regulator onto the filter/pressure regulator joint connector. Tighten the fuel pressure regulator to 22 ft. lbs. (29 Nm).
8. Connect the fuel return hose to the pressure regulator.
9. Connect the fuel main pipe to the fuel filter/pressure regulator joint connector. Tighten the fitting to 27 ft. lbs. (36 Nm).
10. Carefully lower the vehicle, then connect the negative battery cable.

FUEL TANK

Tank Assembly

REMOVAL & INSTALLATION

Cirrus, Stratus, Sebring Convertible and Breeze

▶ See Figures 57, 58, 59 and 60

❊❊ CAUTION

Observe all applicable safety precautions when working around fuel. Whenever servicing the fuel system, always work in a well ventilated area. Do not allow fuel spray or vapors to come in contact with a spark or open flame. Keep a dry chemical fire extinguisher near the work area. Always keep fuel in a container specifically designed for fuel storage; also, always properly seal fuel containers to avoid the possibility of fire or explosion.

1. Properly relieve the fuel system pressure, as outlined earlier in this section.
2. Disconnect the remote negative battery cable from the left strut tower. The ground cable is equipped with an insulator grommet, which should be placed on the stud to prevent the negative battery cable from accidentally grounding.
3. On all of these models, except the 1998 Sebring convertible, disengage the fuel pump wiring jumper from the main body harness, located in the trunk. The 4-pin connector is located under the trunk compartment floor mat to the left side, near the base of the shock tower. Locate the body grommet for the jumper near the base of the rear seat.
4. On the 1998 Sebring convertible, remove the rear seat. Refer to Section 10. Disengage the fuel pump module wiring connector from the main body harness.
5. Push the body grommet out and pass the wiring completely through the hole.
6. Release the pressure in the fuel tank, by slowly removing the fuel filler cap.
7. Raise and safely support the vehicle.
8. Place a transmission jack or equivalent support fixture under the fuel tank.
9. Place an approved fuel storage container, with at least a 16 gallon capacity, under the drain plug located on the bottom left edge of the fuel tank. Remove the drain plug and allow the fuel to empty into the container.

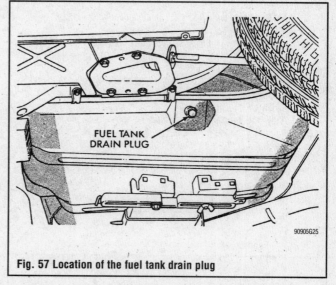

FUEL TANK DRAIN PLUG

90905G25

Fig. 57 Location of the fuel tank drain plug

➡**After the tank is finished draining, there will still be approximately 1–2 gallons of fuel remaining.**

10. Install the drain plug and tighten to 32 inch lbs. (4 Nm).
11. To reduce fuel splash, carefully disconnect the rubber filler hose from the fuel tank, as there may still be some residual fuel in the filler hose.

➡**Wrap shop towels around the fuel hoses to catch any gasoline that may spill when the lines are disconnected.**

12. Disengage the quick-connect fuel tubes from the fuel pump module. If necessary, refer to the quick-connect fitting information earlier in this section.
13. Disconnect the vapor line from the fuel tank-mounted rollover valve. The rollover valve is located at the rear of the fuel tank and connects to the vapor line with a rubber hose.
14. With the tank supported by a transmission jack, or equivalent, remove the bolts and fuel tank mounting straps. Start with the passenger side mounting strap first.
15. On 1998 Cirrus, Stratus and Breeze models only, perform the following steps:
    a. Lower the fuel tank just enough to disconnect the purge and vent hoses.

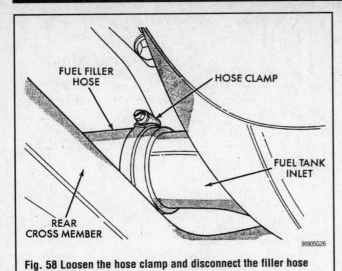

FUEL FILLER HOSE

HOSE CLAMP

FUEL TANK INLET

REAR CROSS MEMBER

90905G26

Fig. 58 Loosen the hose clamp and disconnect the filler hose from the fuel tank

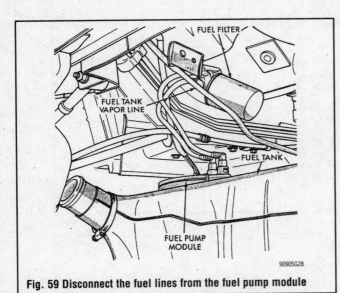

FUEL FILTER

FUEL TANK VAPOR LINE

FUEL TANK

FUEL PUMP MODULE

90905G28

Fig. 59 Disconnect the fuel lines from the fuel pump module

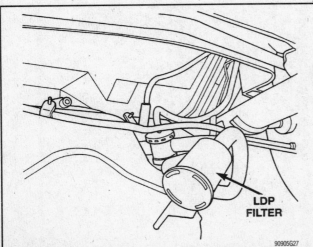

LDP FILTER

90905G27

Fig. 60 Disengage the electrical connector from the leak detection pump

b. Disconnect the hoses from the EVAP canister.

c. Unplug the electrical connector from the Leak Detection Pump (LDP).

16. Remove the fuel tank from the vehicle. Slide the fuel tank forward during removal to enable the filler neck to clear the rear suspension cross-member.

To install:

17. Position the fuel tank onto the transmission jack.

18. Raise the tank into position. Connect the vapor line to the rollover valve.

19. On 1998 Cirrus, Stratus and Breeze models only, perform the following steps:

a. Connect the wiring harness to the LDP.

b. Connect the hoses to the EVAP canister.

c. Connect the purge and vent hoses.

20. Connect the chassis fuel tube to the fuel filter. If necessary, refer to the quick-connect fitting information earlier in this section.

21. Connect the filler hose to the fuel tank inlet. Tighten the hose clamp to 25–31 inch lbs. (3–3.5 Nm).

22. Install the fuel pump module wiring harness grommet into the body.

23. Position the fuel filter and tank straps. Install the front bolts first, then the rear bolts. Tighten the fuel tank strap bolts to 21 ft. lbs. (28 Nm). Check to make sure that the tank straps are not twisted or bent. Remove the transmission jack.

24. Carefully lower the vehicle.

25. Attach the fuel pump module electrical connector.

26. On 1998 Sebring convertible models, install the rear seat.

27. Fill the fuel tank, install the filler cap, then connect the negative battery cable.

✳✳ CAUTION

When performing the ASD fuel system test, the ASD relay will remain energized for either 7 minutes, until the test is completed, or until the ignition switch is turned to the OFF position.

28. Pressurize the fuel system using the Chrysler DRB, or equivalent scan tool, to perform the ASD fuel system test. Check the fuel system for leaks.

Sebring Coupe and Avenger

◆ **See Figures 61 and 62**

1. Properly relieve the fuel system pressure, as outlined earlier in this section.

2. Drain the fuel from the fuel tank into an approved container.

3. Raise the vehicle and support it safely.

4. Disconnect the return hose and high pressure hose from the fuel pump assembly.

5. Detach the electrical connectors at the pump module and fuel gauge sending unit.

✳✳ CAUTION

Cover all fuel hose connections with a shop towel, prior to disconnecting, to prevent a splash of fuel which could be caused by residual pressure remaining in the fuel line.

6. Disconnect the filler and vent hoses.

7. On 1998 models only, disconnect the liquid separator and leveling valve assembly hoses.

8. Remove the fuel tank filler tube protector.

9. Place a transmission jack, or equivalent support fixture, under the center of the fuel tank and apply a slight upward pressure. Remove the fuel tank strap retaining nut or tank retaining nuts, as applicable.

10. Lower the tank slightly and disconnect any remaining electrical or hose connectors at the fuel tank.

11. Remove the fuel tank from the vehicle.

To install:

12. Install the fuel tank onto the transmission jack. Raise the tank in position under the vehicle. Leave enough clearance to attach the electrical and hose connections to the top of the fuel pump.

13. Connect the return hose and high pressure hose to the fuel pump.

14. Attach all other connections to the top of the tank.

15. Raise the tank completely and position the retainer straps around the fuel tank, if equipped. Install new fuel tank self-locking nuts and tighten to 19–22 ft. lbs. (25–30 Nm).

16. On 1998 models only, connect the liquid separator and leveling valve assembly hoses.

17. Install the vent hose and filler hose.

18. Install the fuel tank filler tube protector and install the retainers.

19. Carefully lower the vehicle and fill the fuel tank.

20. Install the filler cap, then connect the negative battery cable.

21. Check the fuel pump for proper pressure and inspect the entire system for leaks.

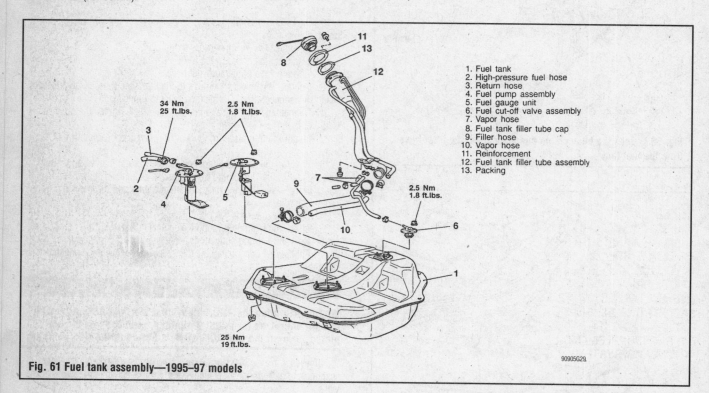

1. Fuel tank
2. High-pressure fuel hose
3. Return hose
4. Fuel pump assembly
5. Fuel gauge unit
6. Fuel cut-off valve assembly
7. Vapor hose
8. Fuel tank filler tube cap
9. Filler hose
10. Vapor hose
11. Reinforcement
12. Fuel tank filler tube assembly
13. Packing

90905G29

Fig. 61 Fuel tank assembly—1995–97 models

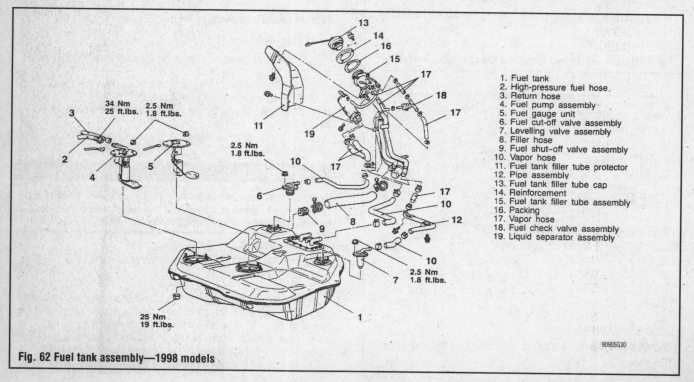

1. Fuel tank
2. High-pressure fuel hose
3. Return hose
4. Fuel pump assembly
5. Fuel gauge unit
6. Fuel cut-off valve assembly
7. Levelling valve assembly
8. Filler hose
9. Fuel shut-off valve assembly
10. Vapor hose
11. Fuel tank filler tube protector
12. Pipe assembly
13. Fuel tank filler tube cap
14. Reinforcement
15. Fuel tank filler tube assembly
16. Packing
17. Vapor hose
18. Fuel check valve assembly
19. Liquid separator assembly

90905G30

Fig. 62 Fuel tank assembly—1998 models

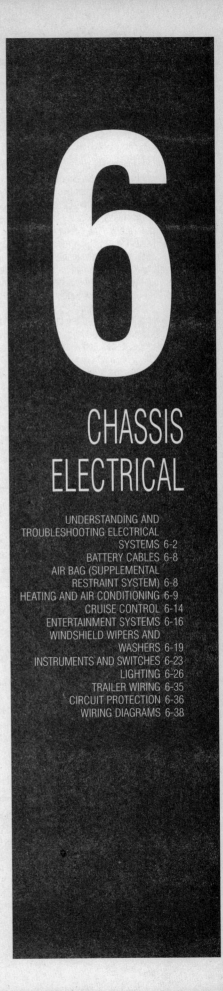

6

CHASSIS ELECTRICAL

UNDERSTANDING AND TROUBLESHOOTING ELECTRICAL SYSTEMS

Basic Electrical Theory

▶ See Figure 1

For any 12 volt, negative ground, electrical system to operate, the electricity must travel in a complete circuit. This simply means that current (power) from the positive (+) terminal of the battery must eventually return to the negative (-) terminal of the battery. Along the way, this current will travel through wires, fuses, switches and components. If, for any reason, the flow of current through the circuit is interrupted, the component fed by that circuit will cease to function properly.

Perhaps the easiest way to visualize a circuit is to think of connecting a light bulb (with two wires attached to it) to the battery—one wire attached to the negative (-) terminal of the battery and the other wire to the positive (+) terminal. With the two wires touching the battery terminals, the circuit would be complete and the light bulb would illuminate. Electricity would follow a path from the battery to the bulb and back to the battery. It's easy to see that with longer wires on our light bulb, it could be mounted anywhere. Further, one wire could be fitted with a switch so that the light could be turned on and off.

The normal automotive circuit differs from this simple example in two ways. First, instead of having a return wire from the bulb to the battery, the current travels through the frame of the vehicle. Since the negative (-) battery cable is attached to the frame (made of electrically conductive metal), the frame of the vehicle can serve as a ground wire to complete the circuit. Secondly, most automotive circuits contain multiple components which receive power from a single circuit. This lessens the amount of wire needed to power components on the vehicle.

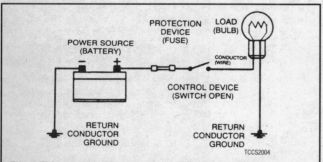

Fig. 1 This example illustrates a simple circuit. When the switch is closed, power from the positive (+) battery terminal flows through the fuse and the switch, and then to the light bulb. The light illuminates and the circuit is completed through the ground wire back to the negative (-) battery terminal. In reality, the two ground points shown in the illustration are attached to the metal frame of the vehicle, which completes the circuit back to the battery

HOW DOES ELECTRICITY WORK: THE WATER ANALOGY

Electricity is the flow of electrons—the subatomic particles that constitute the outer shell of an atom. Electr/ons spin in an orbit around the center core of an atom. The center core is comprised of protons (positive charge) and neutrons (neutral charge). Electrons have a negative charge and balance out the positive charge of the protons. When an outside force causes the number of electrons to unbalance the charge of the protons, the electrons will split off the atom and look for another atom to balance out. If this imbalance is kept up, electrons will continue to move and an electrical flow will exist.

Many people have been taught electrical theory using an analogy with water. In a comparison with water flowing through a pipe, the electrons would be the water and the wire is the pipe.

The flow of electricity can be measured much like the flow of water through a pipe. The unit of measurement used is amperes, frequently abbreviated as amps (a). You can compare amperage to the volume of water flowing through a pipe. When connected to a circuit, an ammeter will measure the actual amount of current flowing through the circuit. When relatively few electrons flow through a circuit, the amperage is low. When many electrons flow, the amperage is high.

Water pressure is measured in units such as pounds per square inch (psi); The electrical pressure is measured in units called volts (v). When a voltmeter is connected to a circuit, it is measuring the electrical pressure.

The actual flow of electricity depends not only on voltage and amperage, but also on the resistance of the circuit. The higher the resistance, the higher the force necessary to push the current through the circuit. The standard unit for measuring resistance is an ohm Ω. Resistance in a circuit varies depending on the amount and type of components used in the circuit. The main factors which determine resistance are:

• Material—some materials have more resistance than others. Those with high resistance are said to be insulators. Rubber materials (or rubber-like plastics) are some of the most common insulators used in vehicles as they have a very high resistance to electricity. Very low resistance materials are said to be conductors. Copper wire is among the best conductors. Silver is actually a superior conductor to copper and is used in some relay contacts, but its high cost prohibits its use as common wiring. Most automotive wiring is made of copper.

• Size—the larger the wire size being used, the less resistance the wire will have. This is why components which use large amounts of electricity usually have large wires supplying current to them.

• Length—for a given thickness of wire, the longer the wire, the greater the resistance. The shorter the wire, the less the resistance. When determining the proper wire for a circuit, both size and length must be considered to design a circuit that can handle the current needs of the component.

• Temperature—with many materials, the higher the temperature, the greater the resistance (positive temperature coefficient). Some materials exhibt the opposite trait of lower resistance with higher temperatures (negative temperature coefficient). These principles are used in many of the sensors on the engine.

OHM'S LAW

There is a direct relationship between current, voltage and resistance. The relationship between current, voltage and resistance can be summed up by a statement known as Ohm's law. Voltage (E) is equal to amperage (I) times resistance (R): E=I x R

Other forms of the formula are R=E/I and I=E/R

In each of these formulas, E is the voltage in volts, I is the current in amps and R is the resistance in ohms. The basic point to remember is that as the resistance of a circuit goes up, the amount of current that flows in the circuit will go down, if voltage remains the same.

The amount of work that the electricity can perform is expressed as power. The unit of power is the watt (w). The relationship between power, voltage and current is expressed as:

Power (w) is equal to amperage (I) times voltage (E): W=I x E

This is only true for direct current (DC) circuits; The alternating current formula is a tad different, but since the electrical circuits in most vehicles are DC type, we need not get into AC circuit theory.

Electrical Components

POWER SOURCE

Power is supplied to the vehicle by two devices: The battery and the alternator. The battery supplies electrical power during starting or during periods when the current demand of the vehicle's electrical system exceeds the output capacity of the alternator. The alternator supplies electrical current when the engine is running. Just not does the alternator supply the current needs of the vehicle, but it recharges the battery.

The Battery

In most modern vehicles, the battery is a lead/acid electrochemical device consisting of six 2 volt subsections (cells) connected in series, so that the unit is capable of producing approximately 12 volts of electrical pressure. Each subsection consists of a series of positive and negative plates held a short distance apart in a solution of sulfuric acid and water.

The two types of plates are of dissimilar metals. This sets up a chemical reaction, and it is this reaction which produces current flow from the battery when its positive and negative terminals are connected to an electrical load. The power removed from the battery is replaced by the alternator, restoring the battery to its original chemical state.

The Alternator

On some vehicles there isn't an alternator, but a generator. The difference is that an alternator supplies alternating current which is then changed to direct current for use on the vehicle, while a generator produces direct current. Alternators tend to be more efficient and that is why they are used.

Alternators and generators are devices that consist of coils of wires wound together making big electromagnets. One group of coils spins within another set and the interaction of the magnetic fields causes a current to flow. This current is then drawn off the coils and fed into the vehicles electrical system.

GROUND

Two types of grounds are used in automotive electric circuits. Direct ground components are grounded to the frame through their mounting points. All other components use some sort of ground wire which is attached to the frame or chassis of the vehicle. The electrical current runs through the chassis of the vehicle and returns to the battery through the ground (-) cable; if you look, you'll see that the battery ground cable connects between the battery and the frame or chassis of the vehicle.

➡ It should be noted that a good percentage of electrical problems can be traced to bad grounds.

PROTECTIVE DEVICES

▶ See Figure 2

It is possible for large surges of current to pass through the electrical system of your vehicle. If this surge of current were to reach the load in the circuit, the surge could burn it out or severely damage it. It can also overload the wiring, causing the harness to get hot and melt the insulation. To prevent this, fuses, circuit breakers and/or fusible links are connected into the supply wires of the electrical system. These items are nothing more than a built-in weak spot in the system. When an abnormal amount of current flows through the system, these protective devices work as follows to protect the circuit:

• Fuse—when an excessive electrical current passes through a fuse, the fuse "blows" (the conductor melts) and opens the circuit, preventing the passage of current.

• Circuit Breaker—a circuit breaker is basically a self-repairing fuse. It will open the circuit in the same fashion as a fuse, but when the surge subsides, the circuit breaker can be reset and does not need replacement.

• Fusible Link—a fusible link (fuse link or main link) is a short length of special, high temperature insulated wire that acts as a fuse. When an excessive electrical current passes through a fusible link, the thin gauge wire inside the link melts, creating an intentional open to protect the circuit. To repair the circuit, the link must be replaced. Some newer type fusible links are housed in plug-in modules, which are simply replaced like a fuse, while older type fusible links must be cut and spliced if they melt. Since this link is very early in the electrical path, it's the first place to look if nothing on the vehicle works, yet the battery seems to be charged and is properly connected.

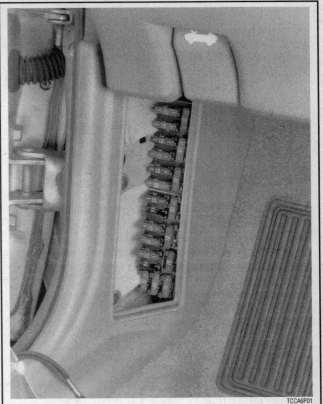

Fig. 2 Most vehicles use one or more fuse panels. This one is located on the driver's side kick panel

TCCA6P01

✳✳ CAUTION

Always replace fuses, circuit breakers and fusible links with identically rated components. Under no circumstances should a component of higher or lower amperage rating be substituted.

SWITCHES & RELAYS

▶ See Figures 3 and 4

Switches are used in electrical circuits to control the passage of current. The most common use is to open and close circuits between the battery and the various electric devices in the system. Switches are rated according to the amount of amperage they can handle. If a sufficient amperage rated switch is not used in a circuit, the switch could overload and cause damage.

Some electrical components which require a large amount of current to operate use a special switch called a relay. Since these circuits carry a large amount of current, the thickness of the wire in the circuit is also greater. If this large wire were connected from the load to the control switch, the switch would have to carry the high amperage load and the fairing or dash would be twice as large to accommodate the increased size of the wiring harness. To prevent these problems, a relay is used.

Relays are composed of a coil and a set of contacts. When the coil has a current passed though it, a magnetic field is formed and this field causes the contacts to move together, completing the circuit. Most relays are normally open, preventing current from passing through the circuit, but they can take any electrical form depending on the job they are intended to do. Relays can be considered "remote control switches." They allow a smaller current to operate devices that require higher amperages. When a small current operates the coil, a larger current is allowed to pass by the contacts. Some common circuits which may use relays are the horn, headlights, starter, electric fuel pump and other high draw ciruits.

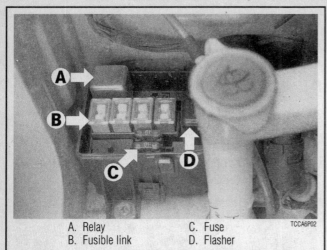

A. Relay   C. Fuse
B. Fusible link   D. Flasher

TCCA6P02

Fig. 3 The underhood fuse and relay panel usually contains fuses, relays, flashers and fusible links

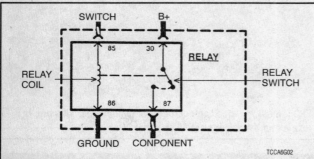

TCCA6G02

Fig. 4 Relays are composed of a coil and a switch. These two components are linked together so that when one operates, the other operates at the same time. The large wires in the circuit are connected from the battery to one side of the relay switch (B+) and from the opposite side of the relay switch to the load (component). Smaller wires are connected from the relay coil to the control switch for the circuit and from the opposite side of the relay coil to ground

LOAD

Every electrical circuit must include a "load" (something to use the electricity coming from the source). Without this load, the battery would attempt to deliver its entire power supply from one pole to another. This is called a "short circuit."All this electricity would take a short cut to ground and cause a great amount of damage to other components in the circuit by developing a tremendous amount of heat. This condition could develop sufficient heat to melt the insulation on all the surrounding wires and reduce a multiple wire cable to a lump of plastic and copper.

WIRING & HARNESSES

The average vehicle contains meters and meters of wiring, with hundreds of individual connections. To protect the many wires from damage and to keep them from becoming a confusing tangle, they are organized into bundles, enclosed in plastic or taped together and called wiring harnesses. Different harnesses serve different parts of the vehicle. Individual wires are color coded to help trace them through a harness where sections are hidden from view.

Automotive wiring or circuit conductors can be either single strand wire, multi-strand wire or printed circuitry. Single strand wire has a solid metal core and is usually used inside such components as alternators, motors, relays and other devices. Multi-strand wire has a core made of many small strands of wire twisted together into a single conductor. Most of the wiring in an automotive electrical system is made up of multi-strand wire, either as a single conductor or grouped together in a harness. All wiring is color coded on the insulator, either as a solid color or as a colored wire with an identification stripe. A printed circuit is a thin film of copper or other conductor that is printed on an insulator backing. Occasionally, a printed circuit is sandwiched between two sheets of plastic for more protection and flexibility. A complete printed circuit, consisting of conductors, insulating material and connectors for lamps or other components is called a printed circuit board. Printed circuitry is used in place of individual wires or harnesses in places where space is limited, such as behind instrument panels.

Since automotive electrical systems are very sensitive to changes in resistance, the selection of properly sized wires is critical when systems are repaired. A loose or corroded connection or a replacement wire that is too small for the circuit will add extra resistance and an additional voltage drop to the circuit.

The wire gauge number is an expression of the cross-section area of the conductor. Vehicles from countries that use the metric system will typically describe the wire size as its cross-sectional area in square millimeters. In this method, the larger the wire, the greater the number. Another common system for expressing wire size is the American Wire Gauge (AWG) system. As gauge number increases, area decreases and the wire becomes smaller. An 18 gauge wire is smaller than a 4 gauge wire. A wire with a higher gauge number will carry less current than a wire with a lower gauge number. Gauge wire size refers to the size of the strands of the conductor, not the size of the complete wire with insulator. It is possible, therefore, to have two wires of the same gauge with different diameters because one may have thicker insulation than the other.

It is essential to understand how a circuit works before trying to figure out why it doesn't. An electrical schematic shows the electrical current paths when a circuit is operating properly. Schematics break the entire electrical system down into individual circuits. In a schematic, usually no attempt is made to represent wiring and components as they physically appear on the vehicle; switches and other components are shown as simply as possible. Face views of harness connectors show the cavity or terminal locations in all multi-pin connectors to help locate test points.

CONNECTORS

▶ **See Figures 5 and 6**

Three types of connectors are commonly used in automotive applications—weatherproof, molded and hard shell.

• Weatherproof—these connectors are most commonly used where the connector is exposed to the elements. Terminals are protected against moisture and dirt by sealing rings which provide a weathertight seal. All repairs require the use of a special terminal and the tool required to service it. Unlike standard blade type terminals, these weatherproof terminals cannot be straightened once they are bent. Make certain that the connectors are properly seated and all of the sealing rings are in place when connecting leads.

• Molded—these connectors require complete replacement of the connector if found to be defective. This means splicing a new connector assembly into the harness. All splices should be soldered to insure proper contact. Use care when probing the connections or replacing terminals in them, as it is possible to create a short circuit between opposite terminals. If this happens to the wrong terminal pair, it is possible to damage certain components. Always use jumper wires between connectors for circuit checking and NEVER probe through weatherproof seals.

• Hard Shell—unlike molded connectors, the terminal contacts in hard-shell connectors can be replaced. Replacement usually involves the use of a special terminal removal tool that depresses the locking tangs (barbs) on the connector terminal and allows the connector to be removed from the

Fig. 5 Hard shell (left) and weatherproof (right) connectors have replaceable terminals

Fig. 6 Weatherproof connectors are most commonly used in the engine compartment or where the connector is exposed to the elements

rear of the shell. The connector shell should be replaced if it shows any evidence of burning, melting, cracks, or breaks. Replace individual terminals that are burnt, corroded, distorted or loose.

Test Equipment

Pinpointing the exact cause of trouble in an electrical circuit is most times accomplished by the use of special test equipment. The following describes different types of commonly used test equipment and briefly explains how to use them in diagnosis. In addition to the information covered below, the tool manufacturer's instructions booklet (provided with the tester) should be read and clearly understood before attempting any test procedures.

JUMPER WIRES

✳✳ CAUTION

Never use jumper wires made from a thinner gauge wire than the circuit being tested. If the jumper wire is of too small a gauge, it may overheat and possibly melt. Never use jumpers to bypass high resistance loads in a circuit. Bypassing resis-

tances, in effect, creates a short circuit. This may, in turn, cause damage and fire. Jumper wires should only be used to bypass lengths of wire or to simulate switches.

Jumper wires are simple, yet extremely valuable, pieces of test equipment. They are basically test wires which are used to bypass sections of a circuit. Although jumper wires can be purchased, they are usually fabricated from lengths of standard automotive wire and whatever type of connector (alligator clip, spade connector or pin connector) that is required for the particular application being tested. In cramped, hard-to-reach areas, it is advisable to have insulated boots over the jumper wire terminals in order to prevent accidental grounding. It is also advisable to include a standard automotive fuse in any jumper wire. This is commonly referred to as a "fused jumper". By inserting an in-line fuse holder between a set of test leads, a fused jumper wire can be used for bypassing open circuits. Use a 5 amp fuse to provide protection against voltage spikes.

Jumper wires are used primarily to locate open electrical circuits, on either the ground (-) side of the circuit or on the power (+) side. If an electrical component fails to operate, connect the jumper wire between the component and a good ground. If the component operates only with the jumper installed, the ground circuit is open. If the ground circuit is good, but the component does not operate, the circuit between the power feed and component may be open. By moving the jumper wire successively back from the component toward the power source, you can isolate the area of the circuit where the open is located. When the component stops functioning, or the power is cut off, the open is in the segment of wire between the jumper and the point previously tested.

You can sometimes connect the jumper wire directly from the battery to the "hot" terminal of the component, but first make sure the component uses 12 volts in operation. Some electrical components, such as fuel injectors or sensors, are designed to operate on about 4 to 5 volts, and running 12 volts directly to these components will cause damage.

TEST LIGHTS

◆ **See Figure 7**

The test light is used to check circuits and components while electrical current is flowing through them. It is used for voltage and ground tests. To use a 12 volt test light, connect the ground clip to a good ground and probe wherever necessary with the pick. The test light will illuminate when voltage is detected. This does not necessarily mean that 12 volts (or any particular amount of voltage) is present; it only means that some voltage is present. It is advisable before using the test light to touch its ground clip and probe across the battery posts or terminals to make sure the light is operating properly.

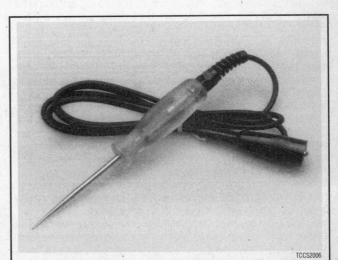

Fig. 7 A 12 volt test light is used to detect the presence of voltage in a circuit

✳✳ WARNING

Do not use a test light to probe electronic ignition, spark plug or coil wires. Never use a pick-type test light to probe wiring on computer controlled systems unless specifically instructed to do so. Any wire insulation that is pierced by the test light probe should be taped and sealed with silicone after testing.

Like the jumper wire, the 12 volt test light is used to isolate opens in circuits. But, whereas the jumper wire is used to bypass the open to operate the load, the 12 volt test light is used to locate the presence of voltage in a circuit. If the test light illuminates, there is power up to that point in the circuit; if the test light does not illuminate, there is an open circuit (no power). Move the test light in successive steps back toward the power source until the light in the handle illuminates. The open is between the probe and a point which was previously probed.

The self-powered test light is similar in design to the 12 volt test light, but contains a 1.5 volt penlight battery in the handle. It is most often used in place of a multimeter to check for open or short circuits when power is isolated from the circuit (continuity test).

The battery in a self-powered test light does not provide much current. A weak battery may not provide enough power to illuminate the test light even when a complete circuit is made (especially if there is high resistance in the circuit). Always make sure that the test battery is strong. To check the battery, briefly touch the ground clip to the probe; if the light glows brightly, the battery is strong enough for testing.

➡ **A self-powered test light should not be used on any computer controlled system or component. The small amount of electricity transmitted by the test light is enough to damage many electronic automotive components.**

MULTIMETERS

Multimeters are an extremely useful tool for troubleshooting electrical problems. They can be purchased in either analog or digital form and have a price range to suit any budget. A multimeter is a voltmeter, ammeter and ohmmeter (along with other features) combined into one instrument. It is often used when testing solid state circuits because of its high input impedance (usually 10 megaohms or more). A brief description of the multimeter main test functions follows:

• Voltmeter—the voltmeter is used to measure voltage at any point in a circuit, or to measure the voltage drop across any part of a circuit. Voltmeters usually have various scales and a selector switch to allow the reading of different voltage ranges. The voltmeter has a positive and a negative lead. To avoid damage to the meter, always connect the negative lead to the negative (-) side of the circuit (to ground or nearest the ground side of the circuit) and connect the positive lead to the positive (+) side of the circuit (to the power source or the nearest power source). Note that the negative voltmeter lead will always be black and that the positive voltmeter will always be some color other than black (usually red).

• Ohmmeter—the ohmmeter is designed to read resistance (measured in ohms) in a circuit or component. Most ohmmeters will have a selector switch which permits the measurement of different ranges of resistance (usually the selector switch allows the multiplication of the meter reading by 10, 100, 1,000 and 10,000). Some ohmmeters are "auto-ranging" which means the meter itself will determine which scale to use. Since the meters are powered by an internal battery, the ohmmeter can be used like a self-powered test light. When the ohmmeter is connected, current from the ohmmeter flows through the circuit or component being tested. Since the ohmmeter's internal resistance and voltage are known values, the amount of current flow through the meter depends on the resistance of the circuit or component being tested. The ohmmeter can also be used to perform a continuity test for suspected open circuits. In using the meter for making continuity checks, do not be concerned with the actual resistance readings. Zero resistance, or any ohm reading, indicates continuity in the circuit. Infinite resistance indicates an opening in the circuit. A high resistance reading where there should be none indicates a problem in the circuit. Checks for short circuits are made in

the same manner as checks for open circuits, except that the circuit must be isolated from both power and normal ground. Infinite resistance indicates no continuity, while zero resistance indicates a dead short.

✳✳ WARNING

Never use an ohmmeter to check the resistance of a component or wire while there is voltage applied to the circuit.

• Ammeter—an ammeter measures the amount of current flowing through a circuit in units called amperes or amps. At normal operating voltage, most circuits have a characteristic amount of amperes, called "current draw" which can be measured using an ammeter. By referring to a specified current draw rating, then measuring the amperes and comparing the two values, one can determine what is happening within the circuit to aid in diagnosis. An open circuit, for example, will not allow any current to flow, so the ammeter reading will be zero. A damaged component or circuit will have an increased current draw, so the reading will be high. The ammeter is always connected in series with the circuit being tested. All of the current that normally flows through the circuit must also flow through the ammeter; if there is any other path for the current to follow, the ammeter reading will not be accurate. The ammeter itself has very little resistance to current flow and, therefore, will not affect the circuit, but it will measure current draw only when the circuit is closed and electricity is flowing. Excessive current draw can blow fuses and drain the battery, while a reduced current draw can cause motors to run slowly, lights to dim and other components to not operate properly.

Troubleshooting Electrical Systems

When diagnosing a specific problem, organized troubleshooting is a must. The complexity of a modern automotive vehicle demands that you approach any problem in a logical, organized manner. There are certain troubleshooting techniques, however, which are standard:

• Establish when the problem occurs. Does the problem appear only under certain conditions? Were there any noises, odors or other unusual symptoms? Isolate the problem area. To do this, make some simple tests and observations, then eliminate the systems that are working properly. Check for obvious problems, such as broken wires and loose or dirty connections. Always check the obvious before assuming something complicated is the cause.

• Test for problems systematically to determine the cause once the problem area is isolated. Are all the components functioning properly? Is there power going to electrical switches and motors. Performing careful, systematic checks will often turn up most causes on the first inspection, without wasting time checking components that have little or no relationship to the problem.

• Test all repairs after the work is done to make sure that the problem is fixed. Some causes can be traced to more than one component, so a careful verification of repair work is important in order to pick up additional malfunctions that may cause a problem to reappear or a different problem to arise. A blown fuse, for example, is a simple problem that may require more than another fuse to repair. If you don't look for a problem that caused a fuse to blow, a shorted wire (for example) may go undetected.

Experience has shown that most problems tend to be the result of a fairly simple and obvious cause, such as loose or corroded connectors, bad grounds or damaged wire insulation which causes a short. This makes careful visual inspection of components during testing essential to quick and accurate troubleshooting.

Testing

OPEN CIRCUITS

▸ **See Figure 8**

This test already assumes the existance of an open in the circuit and it is used to help locate the open portion.

1. Isolate the circuit from power and ground.
2. Connect the self-powered test light or ohmmeter ground clip to the ground side of the circuit and probe sections of the circuit sequentially.

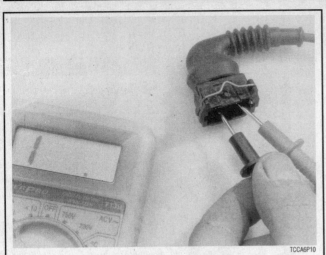

Fig. 8 The infinite reading on this multimeter (1 .) indicates that the circuit is open

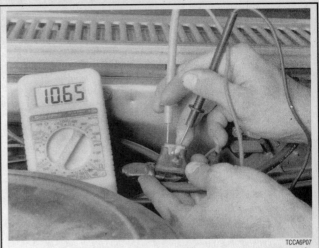

Fig. 9 This voltage drop test revealed high resistance (low voltage) in the circuit

3. If the light is out or there is infinite resistance, the open is between the probe and the circuit ground.

4. If the light is on or the meter shows continuity, the open is between the probe and the end of the circuit toward the power source.

SHORT CIRCUITS

➡**Never use a self-powered test light to perform checks for opens or shorts when power is applied to the circuit under test. The test light can be damaged by outside power.**

1. Isolate the circuit from power and ground.

2. Connect the self-powered test light or ohmmeter ground clip to a good ground and probe any easy-to-reach point in the circuit.

3. If the light comes on or there is continuity, there is a short somewhere in the circuit.

4. To isolate the short, probe a test point at either end of the isolated circuit (the light should be on or the meter should indicate continuity).

5. Leave the test light probe engaged and sequentially open connectors or switches, remove parts, etc. until the light goes out or continuity is broken.

6. When the light goes out, the short is between the last two circuit components which were opened.

VOLTAGE

This test determines voltage available from the battery and should be the first step in any electrical troubleshooting procedure after visual inspection. Many electrical problems, especially on computer controlled systems, can be caused by a low state of charge in the battery. Excessive corrosion at the battery cable terminals can cause poor contact that will prevent proper charging and full battery current flow.

1. Set the voltmeter selector switch to the 20V position.

2. Connect the multimeter negative lead to the battery's negative (-) post or terminal and the positive lead to the battery's positive (+) post or terminal.

3. Turn the ignition switch **ON** to provide a load.

4. A well charged battery should register over 12 volts. If the meter reads below 11.5 volts, the battery power may be insufficient to operate the electrical system properly.

VOLTAGE DROP

▶ **See Figure 9**

When current flows through a load, the voltage beyond the load drops. This voltage drop is due to the resistance created by the load and also by small resistances created by corrosion at the connectors and damaged insulation on the wires. The maximum allowable voltage drop under load is critical, especially if there is more than one load in the circuit, since all voltage drops are cumulative.

1. Set the voltmeter selector switch to the 20 volt position.

2. Connect the multimeter negative lead to a good ground.

3. Operate the circuit and check the voltage prior to the first component (load).

4. There should be little or no voltage drop in the circuit prior to the first component. If a voltage drop exists, the wire or connectors in the circuit are suspect.

5. While operating the first component in the circuit, probe the ground side of the component with the positive meter lead and observe the voltage readings. A small voltage drop should be noticed. This voltage drop is caused by the resistance of the component.

6. Repeat the test for each component (load) down the circuit.

7. If a large voltage drop is noticed, the preceding component, wire or connector is suspect.

RESISTANCE

▶ **See Figures 10 and 11**

✳✳ WARNING

Never use an ohmmeter with power applied to the circuit. The ohmmeter is designed to operate on its own power supply. The normal 12 volt electrical system voltage could damage the meter!

1. Isolate the circuit from the vehicle's power source.

2. Ensure that the ignition key is **OFF** when disconnecting any components or the battery.

3. Where necessary, also isolate at least one side of the circuit to be checked, in order to avoid reading parallel resistances. Parallel circuit resistances will always give a lower reading than the actual resistance of either of the branches.

4. Connect the meter leads to both sides of the circuit (wire or component) and read the actual measured ohms on the meter scale. Make sure the selector switch is set to the proper ohm scale for the circuit being tested, to avoid misreading the ohmmeter test value.

Wire and Connector Repair

Almost anyone can replace damaged wires, as long as the proper tools and parts are available. Wire and terminals are available to fit almost any

Fig. 10 Checking the resistance of a coolant temperature sensor with an ohmmeter. Reading is 1.04 kilohms

need. Even the specialized weatherproof, molded and hard shell connectors are now available from aftermarket suppliers.

Be sure the ends of all the wires are fitted with the proper terminal hardware and connectors. Wrapping a wire around a stud is never a permanent solution and will only cause trouble later. Replace wires one at a time to avoid confusion. Always route wires exactly the same as the factory.

➡**If connector repair is necessary, only attempt it if you have the proper tools. Weatherproof and hard shell connectors require special tools to release the pins inside the connector. Attempting to repair these connectors with conventional hand tools will damage them.**

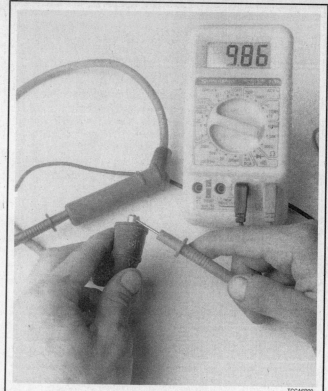

Fig. 11 Spark plug wires can be checked for excessive resistance using an ohmmeter

BATTERY CABLES

Disconnecting the Cables

When working on any electrical component on the vehicle, it is always a good idea to disconnect the negative (-) battery cable. This will prevent potential damage to many sensitive electrical components such as the Engine Control Module (ECM), radio, alternator, etc.

➡**Any time you disengage the battery cables, it is recommended that you disconnect the negative (-) battery cable first. This will prevent your accidentally grounding the positive (+) terminal to the body of the vehicle when disconnecting it, thereby preventing damage to the above mentioned components.**

Before you disconnect the cable(s), first turn the ignition to the **OFF** position. This will prevent a draw on the battery which could cause arcing (electricity trying to ground itself to the body of a vehicle, just like a spark plug jumping the gap) and, of course, damaging some components such as the alternator diodes.

When the battery cable(s) are reconnected (negative cable last), be sure to check that your lights, windshield wipers and other electrically operated safety components are all working correctly. If your vehicle contains an Electronically Tuned Radio (ETR), don't forget to also reset your radio stations: Ditto for the clock.

AIR BAGS (SUPPLEMENTAL RESTRAINT SYSTEM)

General Information

The Supplemental Restraint System (SRS), found on all vehicles covered by this manual, is designed to be used along with the front seat belts to reduce the risk or amount of injury by deploying one or both air bags during certain frontal collisions.

The air bag system is made up of left and right front impact sensors, air bag modules for the driver (in the steering wheel) and front passenger (right side instrument panel above the glove compartment), SRS diagnosis unit (with a safing sensor) and a SRS warning lamp in the instrument cluster.

The SRS system is designed to deploy when the safing sensor, along with either or both of the impact sensors, simultaneously activate while the ignition is **ON**. The sensors will activate during frontal or near-frontal impacts of moderate to severe force.

SERVICE PRECAUTIONS

▶ **See Figure 12**

When working on the SRS or any components which require the removal of the air bag, adhere to all of these precautions to minimize the risks of personal injury or component damage:

• Before attempting to diagnose, remove or install the air bag system components, you must first detach and isolate the negative (-) battery cable. Failure to do so could result in accidental deployment and possible personal injury.

• SRS components should not be subjected to heat over 200°F (93°C), so remove the SRS control unit, air bag modules and clock spring before drying or baking the vehicle after painting:

• When an undeployed air bag assembly is to be removed, after detaching the negative battery cable, allow the system capacitor to discharge for

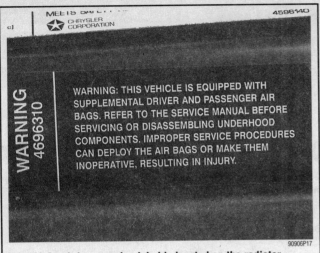

Fig. 12 An air bag warning label is located on the radiator crossmember in the engine compartment

two minutes before commencing with the air bag system component removal.

• Replace the air bag system components only with Mopar® specified replacement parts, or equivalent. Substitute parts may visually appear interchangeable, but internal differences may result in inferior occupant protection.

• Never use an analog ohmmeter to test SRS components.

• The fasteners, screws, and bolts originally used for the SRS have special coatings and are specifically designed for the SRS. They must never be replaced with any substitutes. Anytime a new fastener is needed, replace with the correct fasteners provided in the service package or fasteners listed in the parts books.

Handling a Live Air Bag Module

At no time should any source of electricity be permitted near the inflator on the back of the module. When carrying a live module, the trim cover should be pointed away from the body to minimize injury in the event of accidental deployment. In addition, if the module is placed on a bench or other surface, the plastic trim cover should be face up to minimize movement in case of accidental deployment.

When handling a steering column with an air bag module attached, never place the column on the floor or other surface with the steering wheel or module face down.

Handling a Deployed Air Bag Module

The vehicle interior may contain a very small amount of sodium hydroxide powder, a by-product of air bag deployment. Since this powder can irritate the skin, eyes, nose or throat, be sure to wear safety glasses, rubber gloves and long sleeves during cleanup.

If you find that the cleanup is irritating your skin, run cool water over the affected area. Also, if you experience nasal or throat irritation, exit the vehicle for fresh air until the irritation ceases. If irritation continues, see a physician.

Begin the cleanup by putting tape over the two air bag exhaust vents so that no additional powder will find its way into the vehicle interior. Then, remove the air bag(s) and air bag module(s) from the vehicle.

Use a vacuum cleaner to remove any residual powder from the vehicle interior. Work from the outside in so that you avoid kneeling or sitting in an uncleaned area.

Be sure to vacuum the heater and A/C outlets as well. In fact, it's a good idea to run the blower on low and to vacuum up any powder expelled from the plenum. You may need to vacuum the interior of the car a second time to recover all of the powder.

Check with the local authorities before disposing of the deployed bag and module in your trash.

After an air bag has been deployed, the air bag module and clockspring must be replaced because they cannot be reused. Other air bag system components should be replaced with new ones if damaged.

DISARMING THE SYSTEM

1. Position the front wheels straight ahead.
2. Place the ignition switch in the **LOCK** position, then remove the ignition key.
3. Disconnect the negative battery cable. Isolate the battery cable by taping up any exposed metal areas of the cable. This will keep the cable from inadvertently contacting the battery and causing accidental deployment of the air bag.
4. Allow the system capacitor to discharge for at least 2 minutes, although 10 minutes is recommended to allow the dissipation of any residual energy.

ARMING THE SYSTEM

➡**A DRB or equivalent scan tool is necessary to test the SRS after the system has been rearmed. If no scan tool is available, arm the system by simply removing the tape and reconnecting the negative battery cable.**

If a scan tool is available, perform the following procedure:

1. Connect a DRB or equivalent scan tool to the Data Link Connector (DLC), located near the steering column and at the lower edge of the lower instrument panel.
2. Turn the ignition key to the **ON** position. Get out of the vehicle with the scan tool. Make sure you are using the latest version of the proper cartridge.
3. After making sure no one is in the vehicle, remove the tape, then reconnect the negative battery cable.
4. Read and record any stored Diagnostic Trouble Codes (DTCs). If any diagnostic trouble codes are recorded, take your vehicle to a reputable repair shop for diagnosis.
5. If there are no DTCs, and if the AIRBAG warning lamp either fails to light, with the ignition switch **ON**, or the light goes on and stays on, there is a system malfunction. If any of these conditions exist, you should take your vehicle to a reputable repair shop for diagnosis.

HEATING AND AIR CONDITIONING

Blower Motor

REMOVAL & INSTALLATION

♦ **See Figures 13, 14 and 15**

1. Disconnect the negative battery cable.
2. Remove the lower right underpanel silencer duct.
3. Disengage the blower motor wiring connector from the resistor block.

4. On Sebring coupe and Avenger models equipped with a 2.0L engine and A/C, remove the automatic compressor ECM.
5. Remove the blower motor mounting fasteners.
6. Lower the blower motor assembly from the unit housing.

To install:

7. Raise the blower motor into position in the unit housing and secure with the mounting fasteners.
8. Attach the blower motor electrical connector.
9. Install the automatic compressor ECM, if so equipped.
10. Install the lower right underpanel silencer duct.
11. Connect the negative battery cable.

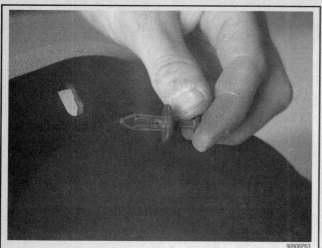

Fig. 13 Disengage the plastic push-in retainers securing the lower right underpanel silencer duct

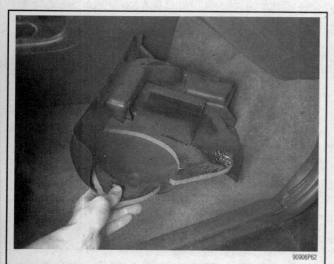

Fig. 14 Remove the lower right underpanel silencer duct

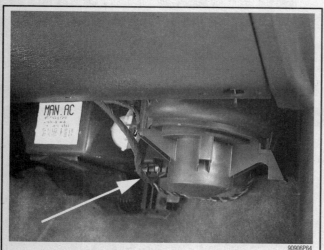

Fig. 15 Disengage the blower motor electrical connector from the resistor block

Heater Core

REMOVAL & INSTALLATION

Cirrus, Stratus, Sebring Convertible and Breeze
▶ See Figures 16 and 17

1. Disconnect the negative battery cable.
2. Remove the radio/HVAC control module bezel.

✳✳ CAUTION

The vehicles covered by this manual are equipped with a Supplemental Restraint System (SRS), which uses air bags. Whenever working near any of the SRS components, such as the impact sensors, air bag modules, steering column and instrument panel, disable the SRS, as described earlier in this section.

3. Remove the right instrument panel side trim.
4. Remove the two retaining screws at the lower right side support beam.

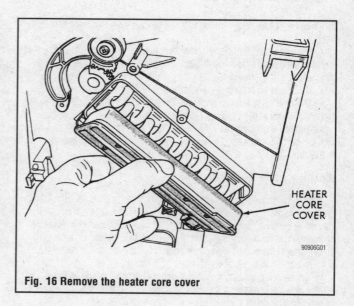

Fig. 16 Remove the heater core cover

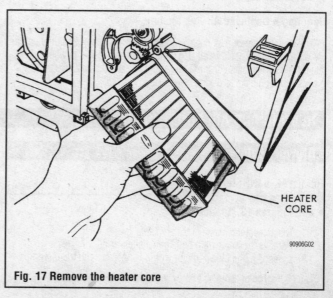

Fig. 17 Remove the heater core

5. Remove the instrument panel support bolt at the A-pillar.

6. Remove the left instrument panel side trim and upper instrument panel bezel.

7. Remove the lower knee bolster and console screws at the instrument panel.

8. Remove the gearshift knob and shifter bezel.

9. Remove the mounting screws at the front and rear of the floor console. Remove the front and rear console halves.

10. Remove the right side instrument panel support strut.

11. Drain the cooling system into a suitable container, then disconnect the heater hoses at the cowl panel. Plug the heater core outlets to prevent coolant from spilling during unit housing removal.

12. Remove the mounting screws and heater core cover.

13. Remove the heater core from the vehicle.

To install:

14. Carefully position the heater core unit into the heater housing.

15. Install the heater core cover onto the heater housing and tighten the mounting screws.

16. Install the right side instrument panel support strut.

17. Install the front and rear console halves.

18. Install the shifter bezel and gearshift knob.

19. Install the lower knee bolster and console screws at the instrument panel.

20. Install the upper instrument panel bezel and left instrument panel side trim.

21. Install the instrument panel support bolt at the A-pillar.

22. Install the two retaining screws at the lower right side support beam.

23. Install the right instrument panel side trim.

24. Install the radio/HVAC control module bezel.

25. Fill the cooling system to the proper level.

26. Connect the negative battery cable.

Sebring Coupe and Avenger

♦ **See Figure 18**

1. Disconnect the negative battery cable.

✳✳ CAUTION

The vehicles covered by this manual are equipped with a Supplemental Restraint System (SRS), which uses air bags. Whenever working near any of the SRS components, such as the impact sensors, air bag modules, steering column and instrument panel, disable the SRS, as described earlier in this section.

2. Remove the instrument panel from the vehicle, as outlined in Section 10 of this manual.

3. Drain the cooling system into a suitable container, then disconnect the heater hoses from the dashboard panel. Plug the heater core outlets to prevent coolant from spilling during unit housing removal.

4. Remove the center stay.

5. Remove the lap cooler duct mounting screw. Remove the center duct.

6. Remove the left and right rear heater ducts.

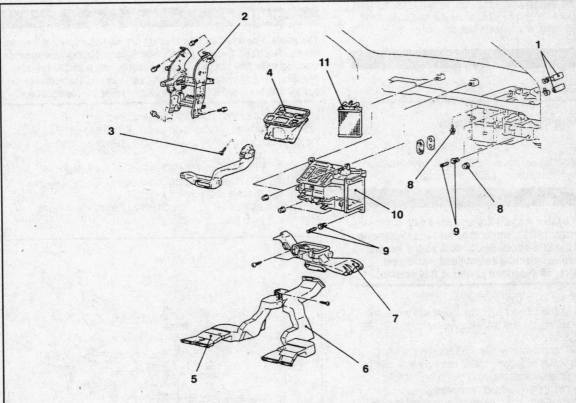

1. Heater hose connection
2. Center stay
3. Lap cooler duct mounting screw
4. Center duct
5. Rear heater duct (L.H.)
6. Rear heater duct (R.H.)
7. Foot distribution duct
8. Cooling unit mounting bolt and nut <Vehicles with A/C>
9. Clip
10. Heater unit
11. Heater core

90906G03

Fig. 18 Exploded view of heater unit and core assembly

7. Remove the foot distribution duct.

8. If equipped with A/C, remove the cooling unit mounting nut and bolt.

9. Remove the retainer clip, then the heater unit.

10. Remove the heater core.

To install:

11. Install the heater core into the heater housing.

12. Install the heater housing and retainer clip into the vehicle.

13. If equipped with A/C, install the cooling unit mounting bolt and nut.

14. Install the foot distribution duct. Install the left and right rear heater ducts.

15. Install the center duct, then install the lap cooler duct mounting screw.

16. Install the center stay and connect the heater hoses to the heater core at the dashboard panel.

17. Install the instrument panel.

18. Fill the cooling system to the proper level.

19. Connect the negative battery cable.

Air Conditioning Components

REMOVAL & INSTALLATION

Repair or service of air conditioning components is not covered by this manual, because of the risk of personal injury or death, and because of the legal ramifications of servicing these components without the proper EPA certification and experience. Cost, personal injury or death, environmental damage, and legal considerations (such as the fact that it is a federal crime to vent refrigerant into the atmosphere), dictate that the A/C components on your vehicle should be serviced only by a Motor Vehicle Air Conditioning (MVAC) trained, and EPA certified automotive technician.

Control Cables

REMOVAL & INSTALLATION

Cirrus, Stratus, Sebring Convertible and Breeze

▶ **See Figure 19**

The following procedure can be used to remove either the recirculation door control cable or temperature control cable, as necessary.

❋❋ CAUTION

The models covered by this manual are equipped with a Supplemental Restraint System (SRS), which uses air bags. Whenever working near any of the SRS components, such as the impact sensors, air bag modules, steering column and instrument panel, disable the SRS, as described earlier in this section.

1. Place the ignition key in the **OFF** position.

2. Disconnect the negative battery cable. You should wait a minimum of 2 minutes before proceeding, to allow the SRS system capacitor ample time to discharge.

3. Remove the HVAC control module from the instrument panel.

4. Release the recirculation door control cable or temperature control cable retaining clip, as necessary, from the top of the control module. Retain the clip for future use, then disconnect the control cable.

5. If removing the recirculation door control cable, remove the right underpanel silencer duct and disconnect the cable at the right of the recirculation housing.

6. If removing the temperature control cable, disconnect the cable at the A/C housing.

7. Remove the cable core end from the actuator lever.

8. Remove the recirculation door or temperature control cable from the vehicle, as applicable.

9. Installation is the reverse of the removal procedure.

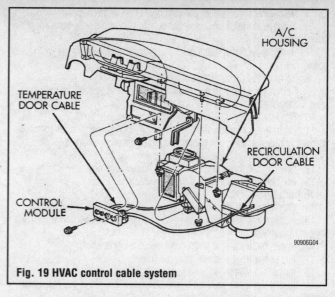

Fig. 19 HVAC control cable system

10. After installation, check for interference and make sure to adjust the cable, as outlined later in this section.

Sebring Coupe and Avenger

▶ **See Figures 20 and 21**

❋❋ CAUTION

The models covered by this manual are equipped with a Supplemental Restraint System (SRS), which uses air bags. Whenever working near any of the SRS components, such as the impact sensors, air bag modules, steering column and instrument panel, disable the SRS, as described earlier in this section.

1. Place the ignition key in the **OFF** position.

2. Disconnect the negative battery cable. You should wait a minimum of 2 minutes before proceeding to allow the SRS system capacitor ample time to discharge.

3. Remove the HVAC control module from the instrument panel.

4. Using a flat bladed prying tool, disengage the claws, then remove the cable(s) from the back of the control module.

5. Compress the lever pin, then disengage the cable(s) from the heater/cooling unit housing actuator lever(s).

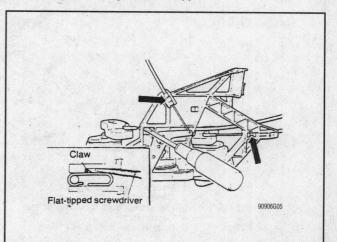

Fig. 20 Use a prying tool to disengage the cables from the control module

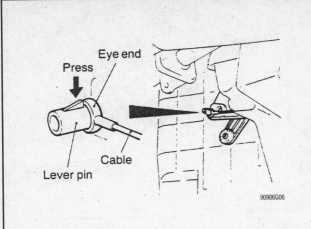

Fig. 21 Compress the lever pin to disengage the control cables from the heater/blower unit

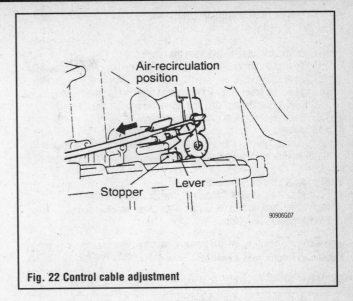

Fig. 22 Control cable adjustment

6. Remove the control cable(s) from the vehicle, as applicable.
7. Turn the applicable knob, lever or actuator to the maximum hot, air recirculation or defrost positions. Install the control cables.
8. After installation, check for interference and adjust the cable, as outlined in the following procedure.

ADJUSTMENT

Cirrus, Stratus, Sebring Convertible and Breeze

1. Attach the cable(s) to the actuator arm(s) of the heater/cooling unit housing.
2. Fasten the other end of the cable(s) to the instrument control panel.
3. Turn the applicable knob completely counterclockwise.
4. While holding the knob in the counterclockwise position, pull on the black casing of the cable until it is taut. This will take up any free-play in the cable and index the recirculation/temperature door to the knob.
5. Clip the cable jacket to the control module.
6. Once the cable is properly adjusted, the knob should travel a full 180 degrees.

Sebring Coupe and Avenger

▶ See Figure 22

1. Attach the cable(s) to the actuator arm(s) of the heater/cooling unit housing.
2. Fasten the other end of the cable(s) to the instrument control panel.
3. Turn the applicable knob or lever to the maximum hot, air recirculation or defrost positions.
4. Pull on the black casing of the cable, at the heater/blower unit, until it is taut. This will take up any free-play in the cable.
5. Secure the cable with the clip.

Control Panel

REMOVAL & INSTALLATION

Cirrus, Stratus, Sebring Convertible and Breeze

▶ See Figures 23 and 24

1. Place the ignition key in the **OFF** position.
2. Disconnect and isolate the negative battery cable.
3. Using a suitable trim panel removal tool, carefully pry out and remove the radio/HVAC control module bezel.

Fig. 23 Remove the radio/HVAC control trim panel by disengaging the clips and pulling away

Fig. 24 Location of the radio and HVAC control panel mounting fasteners

4. Remove the cluster hood bezel retaining screws in the trim bezel opening.

5. Pry up the cluster hood bezel a few inches to expose the cubby bin/cigar lighter bezel and wiring.

6. Unfasten the mounting screws from around the control module.

7. Lower the control module into the cigar lighter/cubby bin bezel opening and disengage the wiring harness from behind the control module.

8. Disconnect the control cables from behind the control module.

9. Remove the control module assembly.

To install:

10. Connect the control cables and wiring harnesses to the back of the control module assembly. Make sure the cables are securely retained by the clips.

11. Install the control module assembly.

12. Install and tighten the control module mounting screws.

13. Install and tighten the cluster hood bezel retaining screws.

14. Install the trim bezel.

15. Connect the negative battery cable.

Sebring Coupe and Avenger

▶ See Figure 25

1. Disconnect the negative battery cable.

✳✳ CAUTION

The models covered by this manual are equipped with a Supplemental Restraint System (SRS), which uses air bags. Whenever working near any of the SRS components, such as the impact sensors, air bag modules, steering column and instrument panel, disable the SRS, as described earlier in this section.

2. Using a suitable trim panel removal tool, carefully pry out and remove the radio/HVAC control module bezel.

3. Remove the floor console.

4. Remove the radio.

5. Remove the glove box stoppers.

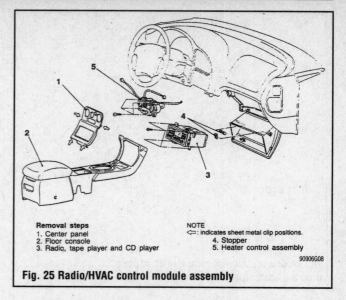

Removal steps
1. Center panel
2. Floor console
3. Radio, tape player and CD player

NOTE
⟸: indicates sheet metal clip positions.
4. Stopper
5. Heater control assembly

90906G08

Fig. 25 Radio/HVAC control module assembly

6. Remove the control module retaining screws and pull the module out of the instrument panel.

7. Disengage the control cables and wiring harness from behind the module.

To install:

8. Connect the control cables and wiring harnesses to the back of the control module assembly. Make sure the cables are securely retained by the clips.

9. Install the control module assembly and tighten the mounting screws.

10. Install the glove box stoppers.

11. Install the radio.

12. Install the floor console.

13. Install the trim bezel.

14. Connect the negative battery cable.

CRUISE CONTROL

▶ See Figures 26, 27, 28 and 29

Cruise control is a speed control system that maintains a desired vehicle speed under normal driving conditions. However, ascending or descending steep grades may cause variations in the selected speeds. On these vehicles, the speed control system is electrically controlled and vacuum operated. The electronic control is integrated in the Powertrain Control Module (PCM), located in the engine compartment.

The main parts of the cruise control system are the functional control switches, speed control servo, servo cable, PCM, vacuum reservoir and the release switches, including the dual function brake light switch.

The cruise control module assembly contains a low speed limit, which will prevent system engagement below 30 mph (50 km/h). The module is controlled by the functional switches, which are located on a lever on the steering column or steering wheel, and on the instrument panel.

The release switches are mounted on the brake/clutch/accelerator pedal bracket. When the brake or clutch pedal is depressed, the cruise control system is electrically disengaged and the throttle is returned to the idle position.

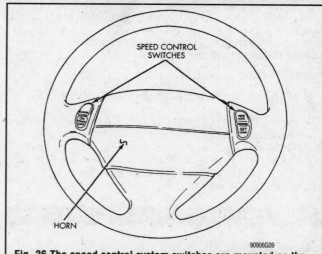

90906G09

Fig. 26 The speed control system switches are mounted on the steering wheel

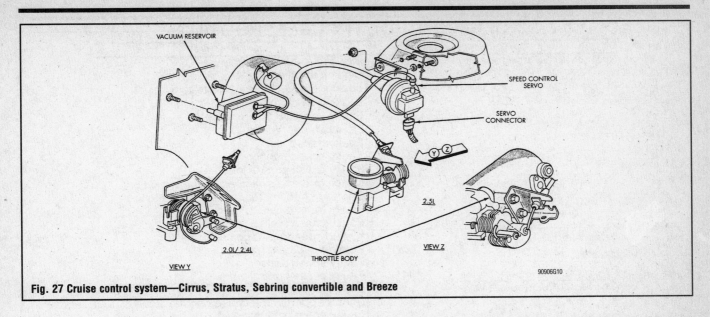

Fig. 27 Cruise control system—Cirrus, Stratus, Sebring convertible and Breeze

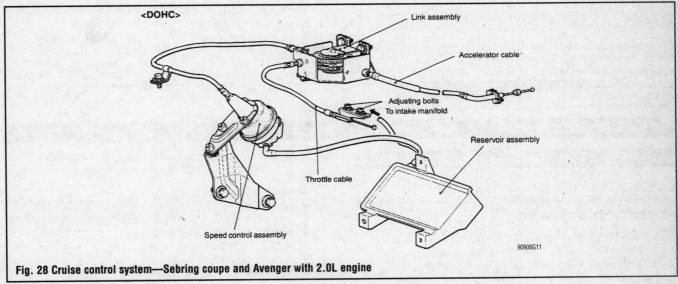

Fig. 28 Cruise control system—Sebring coupe and Avenger with 2.0L engine

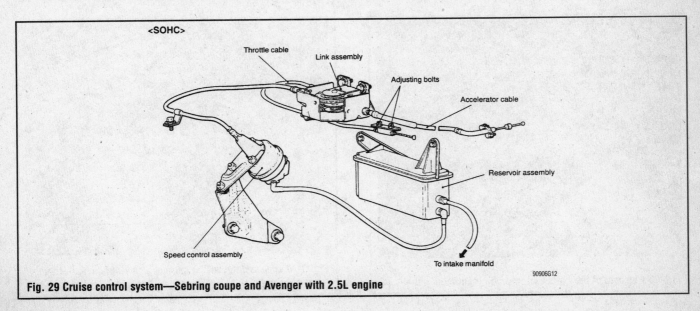

Fig. 29 Cruise control system—Sebring coupe and Avenger with 2.5L engine

CRUISE CONTROL TROUBLESHOOTING

Problem	Possible Cause
Will not hold proper speed	Incorrect cable adjustment
	Binding throttle linkage
	Leaking vacuum servo diaphragm
	Leaking vacuum tank
	Faulty vacuum or vent valve
	Faulty stepper motor
	Faulty transducer
	Faulty speed sensor
	Faulty cruise control module
Cruise intermittently cuts out	Clutch or brake switch adjustment too tight
	Short or open in the cruise control circuit
	Faulty transducer
	Faulty cruise control module
Vehicle surges	Kinked speedometer cable or casing
	Binding throttle linkage
	Faulty speed sensor
	Faulty cruise control module
Cruise control inoperative	Blown fuse
	Short or open in the cruise control circuit
	Faulty brake or clutch switch
	Leaking vacuum circuit
	Faulty cruise control switch
	Faulty stepper motor
	Faulty transducer
	Faulty speed sensor
	Faulty cruise control module

Note: Use this chart as a guide. Not all systems will use the components listed.

TCCA6C01

ENTERTAINMENT SYSTEMS

Radio Receiver/Amplifier/Tape Player/CD Player

REMOVAL & INSTALLATION

▶ **See Figures 23, 24, 30 and 31**

1. Place the ignition key in the **OFF** position.
2. Disconnect and isolate the negative battery cable.
3. Using a suitable trim panel removal tool, carefully pry out and remove the radio/HVAC control module bezel.
4. Unfasten the mounting screws from around the radio unit.
5. Disconnect the wiring harness and antenna lead from behind the radio.
6. Remove the radio from the vehicle.

To install:

7. Connect the antenna lead and wiring harness to the back of the radio.
8. Install the radio into the instrument panel.
9. Install and tighten the radio mounting screws.
10. Install the trim bezel.
11. Connect the negative battery cable.

Fig. 30 Removal of the radio unit from the instrument panel

90906P40

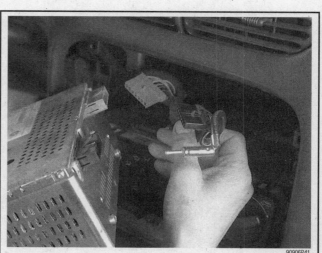

Fig. 31 Disconnect the wiring harness and antenna lead from behind the radio unit

90906P41

Speakers

REMOVAL & INSTALLATION

Instrument Panel Speakers

CIRRUS, STRATUS, SEBRING CONVERTIBLE AND BREEZE

◆ **See Figures 32 and 33**

1. Disconnect the negative battery cable.
2. Remove the instrument panel top cover as follows:
   a. Remove the screw from the right side of the top cover.
   b. Carefully pry up on each end of the top cover to disengage the retaining clips.
   c. Lift up the rear edge of the top cover, using a trim stick along the rear edge.
   d. While lifting up on the rear edge, slide the top cover rearward to disengage the front clips and remove the top cover.
3. Unfasten the speaker retaining screws.
4. Partially lift the speaker up, detach the electrical connector, then remove the speaker from the vehicle.

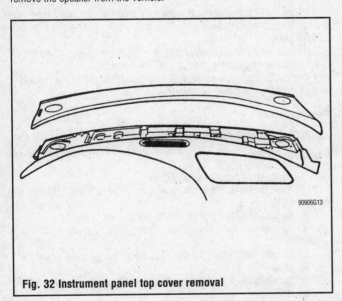

Fig. 32 Instrument panel top cover removal

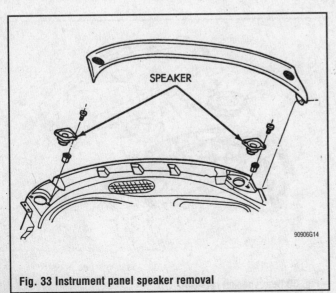

Fig. 33 Instrument panel speaker removal

To install:

5. Attach the electrical connector to the speaker, then position the speaker in the instrument panel.
6. Install the speaker retaining screws.
7. Install the instrument panel top cover.
8. Connect the negative battery cable.

SEBRING COUPE AND AVENGER

◆ **See Figure 34**

1. Disconnect the negative battery cable.
2. Using a small, flat bladed prying tool, carefully pry upward on the left or right side speaker.
3. Partially lift the speaker up, detach the electrical connector, then remove the speaker from the vehicle.

To install:

4. Attach the electrical connector to the speaker, then position the speaker in the instrument panel.
5. Apply slight downward pressure on the speaker to engage the retaining clips.
6. Connect the negative battery cable.

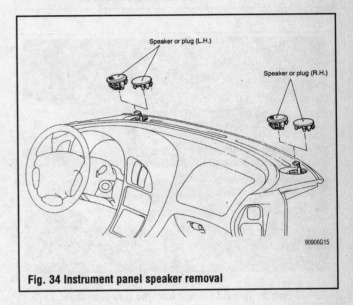

Fig. 34 Instrument panel speaker removal

Front Door Speakers

CIRRUS, STRATUS, SEBRING CONVERTIBLE AND BREEZE

◆ **See Figures 35, 36 and 37**

1. Disconnect the negative battery cable.
2. Using a small, prying tool, remove the door panel speaker grille.
3. Remove the 3 speaker mounting screws.
4. Partially pull the speaker up out of its mounting position, then unplug the connector and remove the speaker from the vehicle.

To install:

5. Attach the electrical connector, then position the speaker in the door.
6. Install and tighten the 3 speaker retaining screws.
7. Install the door panel speaker grille.
8. Connect the negative battery cable.

SEBRING COUPE AND AVENGER

◆ **See Figure 38**

1. Disconnect the negative battery cable.
2. Remove the door trim panel, as outlined in Section 10 of this manual.
3. Remove the speaker retaining screws.

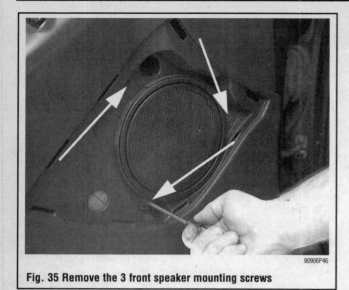

Fig. 35 Remove the 3 front speaker mounting screws

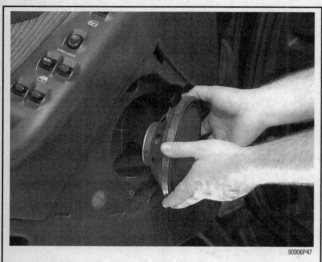

Fig. 36 Pull the speaker unit out from the side door panel . . .

Fig. 37 . . . then disengage the speaker wiring connector

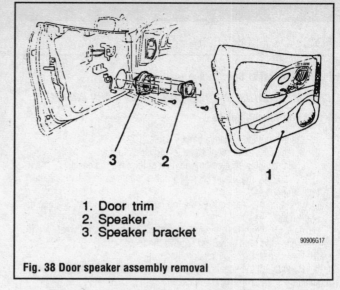

1. Door trim
2. Speaker
3. Speaker bracket

Fig. 38 Door speaker assembly removal

4. Partially lift the speaker out, detach the electrical connector, then remove the speaker from the door.
   To install:
5. Attach the electrical connector, then position the speaker in the door.
6. Install and tighten the speaker retaining screws.
7. Install the door trim panel, as outlined in Section 10 of this manual.
8. Connect the negative battery cable.

Rear Speakers

CIRRUS, STRATUS AND BREEZE

▶ See Figure 39

1. Disconnect the negative battery cable.
2. Remove the parcel shelf trim panel from the vehicle using the following procedure:
   a. Remove the interior upper quarter trim panels.
   b. Remove the rear seat cushion and seat back, or quarter extension panels.
   c. Remove the push-in fastener securing the parcel shelf trim to the shelf panel.
   d. Pull the trim forward to disengage the clip holding the trim to the shelf panel.

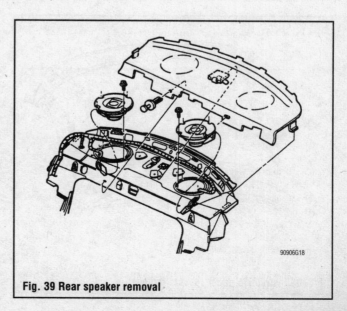

Fig. 39 Rear speaker removal

e. Remove the parcel shelf trim panel from the vehicle.

3. Remove the 4 speaker retaining screws.

4. Partially pull the speaker up and out of its mounting position, then unplug the connector and remove the speaker from the vehicle.

To install:

5. Attach the electrical connector, then position the speaker in the rear shelf panel.

➡**Be sure that the wiring connectors are facing outward in the vehicle.**

6. Install and tighten the 4 speaker retaining screws.

7. Install the parcel shelf panel into the vehicle.

8. Connect the negative battery cable.

SEBRING COUPE AND AVENGER

▶ **See Figure 40**

1. Disconnect the negative battery cable.

2. From inside the trunk area, remove the speaker grille retaining fasteners. Remove the speaker grille from the vehicle. If accessible from the trunk area, unplug the speaker connector.

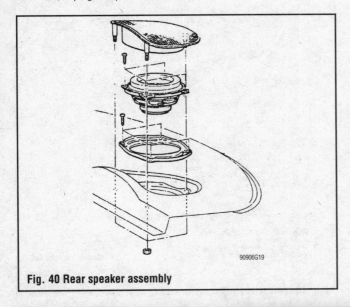

Fig. 40 Rear speaker assembly

3. Remove the speaker retaining screws.

4. Partially pull the speaker up and out of its mounting position, then unplug the wiring connector, if not done earlier, and remove the speaker from the vehicle.

5. Installation is the reverse of the removal procedure.

6. Connect the negative battery cable.

Rear Quarter Panel Speaker

SEBRING CONVERTIBLE

▶ **See Figure 41**

1. Disconnect the negative battery cable.

2. Using a small, prying tool, remove the rear quarter panel speaker grille.

3. Remove the 4 speaker retaining screws.

4. Partially pull the speaker up and out of its mounting position, then unplug the connector and remove the speaker from the vehicle.

5. Installation is the reverse of the removal procedure.

6. Connect the negative battery cable.

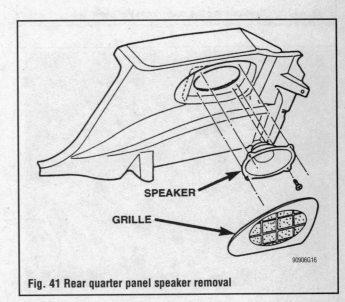

SPEAKER

GRILLE

Fig. 41 Rear quarter panel speaker removal

WINDSHIELD WIPERS AND WASHERS

Windshield Wiper Blade and Arm

REMOVAL & INSTALLATION

▶ **See Figures 42, 43, 44 and 45**

1. Place the wipers are in the PARK position, then turn the ignition **OFF**.

2. Disconnect the negative battery cable.

3. Unsnap the plastic retaining nut cover and remove it from the wiper arm.

4. Remove the wiper arm retaining nut.

5. Remove the wiper arm by using a universal puller tool, or by hand using a rocking motion, to pull the wiper blade and arm from the pivot shaft.

To install:

6. Position the wiper blade and arm on the pivot, making sure it is proper seated. Position the wiper arms so that the heel of the blade is on the PARK line of the windshield.

7. Start the retaining nut.

8. Raise the blade off of the windshield while tightening the retaining nut. Tighten the retaining nut to 23–29 ft. lbs. (33–40 Nm) for Cirrus, Stra-

Fig. 42 Lift up the wiper arm pivot nut cover . . .

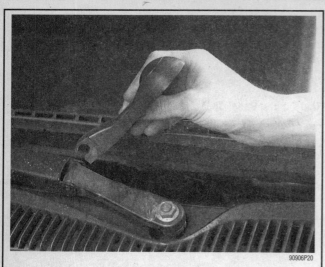

Fig. 43 . . . then remove the cover from the wiper arm

Fig. 44 Use a wrench to unfasten the wiper arm pivot nut

Fig. 45 Removing the wiper arm assembly with a puller tool

tus, Sebring convertible and Breeze. Tighten the retaining nut to 9 ft. lbs. (13 Nm) on Sebring coupe and Avenger models.

9. Install the plastic retaining nut cover.
10. Connect the negative battery cable.

Windshield Wiper Motor

REMOVAL & INSTALLATION

▶ **See Figures 46 thru 58**

1. Disconnect the negative battery cable.
2. Remove the wiper arm and blade assemblies, as outlined earlier in this section.

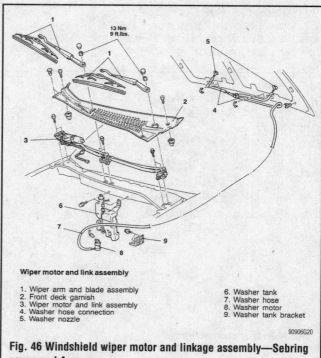

Wiper motor and link assembly

1. Wiper arm and blade assembly
2. Front deck garnish
3. Wiper motor and link assembly
4. Washer hose connection
5. Washer nozzle
6. Washer tank
7. Washer hose
8. Washer motor
9. Washer tank bracket

Fig. 46 Windshield wiper motor and linkage assembly—Sebring coupe and Avenger

Fig. 47 Remove the Torx head screws from the cowl panel

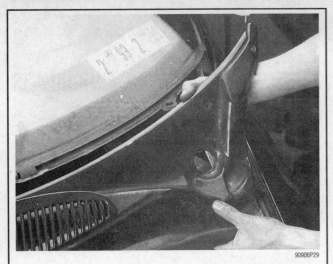

Fig. 48 Pull up to remove the plastic cowl panel from the vehicle

Fig. 51 Disconnect the wiring harness clip from the forward mounting leg with a small pair of pliers

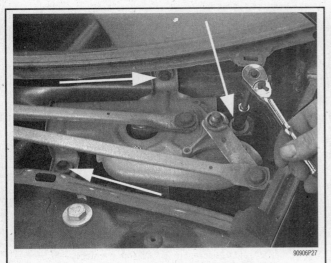

Fig. 49 Remove the wiper motor assembly mounting bolts

Fig. 52 Disconnect the wiper motor wiring harness

Fig. 50 Remove the wiper linkage mounting bolt to the far right

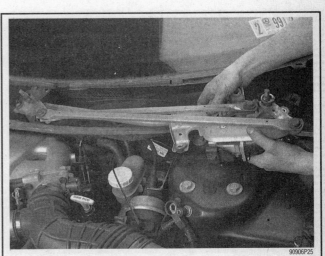

Fig. 53 Remove the wiper motor/linkage assembly from the vehicle

Fig. 54 Using a flat bladed prying tool, disconnect the drive linkage from the motor output crank arm

Fig. 57 To ease installation, mark the location of the wiper motor arm to the shaft before pulling it off

Fig. 55 When removing the wiper motor mounting nuts, a backup wrench can be used to keep the bolts from turning

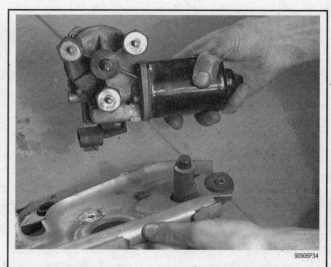

Fig. 58 Remove the wiper motor from the linkage assembly

3. Remove the cowl screen.

4. Remove the wiper motor/linkage assembly mounting screws.

5. Lift up the assembly slightly and disconnect the wiring harness clip from the forward mounting leg.

6. Unplug the wiring harness connector from the wiper motor, and lift the entire assembly from the vehicle.

7. Disconnect the drive linkage from the motor output crank arm. Using a prying tool or a tie rod/ball joint separator, separate the ball cap from the ball.

8. If necessary, mark the position of the output crank arm to the wiper motor shaft. Remove the crank arm from the motor shaft.

9. Use an open end wrench as a backup, if necessary, and remove the wiper motor-to-linkage assembly mounting fasteners. Remove the wiper motor.

To install:

10. Install the wiper motor to the linkage assembly. Install and tighten the mounting fasteners.

11. Install the crank arm onto the wiper motor shaft and tighten the center nut. Be sure that the marks line up.

12. Connect the drive linkage to the wiper motor output crank arm by popping the ball cap onto the ball.

13. Place the wiper motor/linkage assembly in the vehicle. Connect the wiring harness to the wiper motor.

Fig. 56 Remove the wiper motor arm center nut

14. Install and tighten the wiper motor/linkage assembly mounting screws.
15. Install the cowl screen.
16. Install the wiper arm and blade assemblies.
17. Connect the negative battery cable.

Windshield Washer Pump

REMOVAL & INSTALLATION

Cirrus, Stratus, Sebring Convertible and Breeze

▶ See Figures 59 and 60

1. Disconnect the negative battery cable.
2. Raise and safely support the vehicle.
3. Remove the front right inner fender splash shield.
4. Partially remove the bumper fascia, as necessary, to gain access to the washer pump by first removing the plastic push-in fasteners.
5. Detach the electrical connector from the reservoir pump.
6. Place a suitable drain pan under the reservoir, then disconnect the washer hose from the pump and allow the reservoir to drain into the pan.
7. Carefully pry the pump away from the reservoir and out of the retaining grommet. Be careful not to puncture the reservoir when removing the pump.
8. Remove and discard the rubber grommet.
To install:
9. Place a new rubber grommet in the reservoir.
10. Place the pump into position, then push it onto the grommet until it is fully seated.
11. Attach the pump's electrical connector.
12. Position the bumper fascia back into its correct position and secure with the plastic push-in fasteners.
13. Install the inner fender splash shield.
14. Carefully lower the vehicle.
15. Fill the windshield washer reservoir with the proper type and amount of fluid.
16. Connect the negative battery cable, then check the system for proper operation.

Sebring Coupe and Avenger

▶ See Figure 46

1. Disconnect the negative battery cable.
2. Remove the brake fluid reservoir mounting bolt.
3. Loosen the mounting fasteners and remove the washer fluid reservoir.
4. Disconnect the rubber washer fluid hose from the washer pump motor.
5. Detach the electrical connector from the washer pump.
6. Carefully remove the washer pump from the reservoir.
To install:
7. Install the washer pump onto the reservoir.
8. Attach the electrical connector to the washer pump.
9. Connect the washer fluid hose to the washer pump motor.

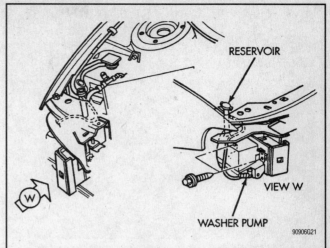

Fig. 59 Location of the windshield washer pump and fluid reservoir on the vehicle

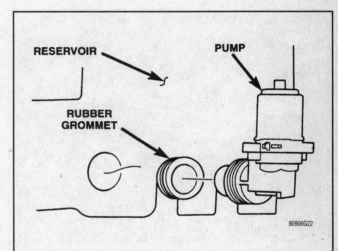

Fig. 60 The washer pump is mounted at the base of the reservoir

10. Place the washer fluid reservoir in correct position and tighten the mounting fasteners.
11. Install and tighten the brake fluid reservoir mounting bolt.
12. Fill the windshield washer reservoir with the proper type and amount of fluid.
13. Connect the negative battery cable, then check the system for proper operation.

INSTRUMENTS AND SWITCHES

Instrument Cluster

REMOVAL & INSTALLATION

Cirrus, Stratus, Sebring Convertible and Breeze

▶ See Figures 61 thru 68

➥When handling or storing the instrument cluster, make sure that the overlays are not damaged. If you put the cluster down, make sure it is in the face-up position, or the gauge operation will be damaged.

1. Disconnect the negative battery cable.
2. Remove the instrument panel left end cap.
3. Tilt the steering column down to its furthest position.
4. Remove the instrument panel center bezel by disengaging the 4 retaining clips.
5. Remove the 3 cluster hood mounting screws under the center bezel.
6. Remove the retaining screw at the left end of the instrument panel.
7. Pull the cluster hood straight back to disengage the 8 retaining clips. If equipped with a mini trip computer, pull the hood back approximately 3 inches (7.6cm), then stop. Reach through the radio opening in the cluster hood and disconnect the minitrip computer wiring harness.

Fig. 61 Remove the center bezel by disengaging the retaining clips

Fig. 62 Remove the 3 attaching screws under the center trim bezel

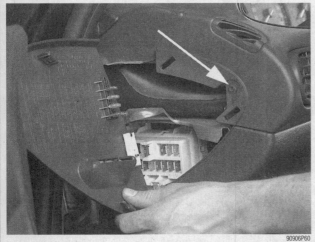

Fig. 63 Remove the screw at the left end of the cluster hood panel

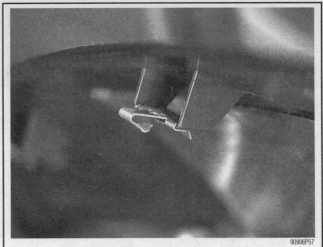

Fig. 64 When removing the cluster hood, these clips must be carefully disengaged

Fig. 65 Carefully remove the cluster hood panel

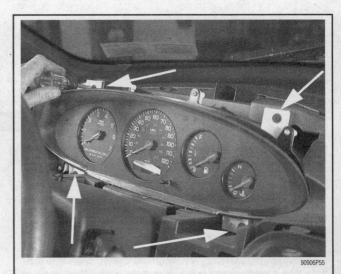

Fig. 66 Remove the 4 instrument cluster mounting screws

Fig. 67 Carefully pull the cluster assembly out of the instrument panel

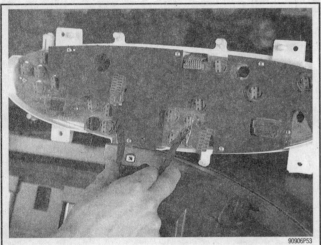

Fig. 68 Disconnect the wiring harnesses behind the instrument cluster assembly

8. Remove the cluster hood panel.

9. Remove the 4 instrument cluster mounting screws.

10. Remove the instrument cluster and unplug the wiring harness connectors from behind the cluster assembly. Remove the cluster from the vehicle.

To install:

11. Plug in the wiring harness connectors to the back of the instrument cluster assembly.

12. Place the instrument cluster assembly into correct position on the instrument panel. Install and tighten the 4 cluster mounting screws.

13. Place the cluster hood panel over the instrument panel and connect the wiring harness to the mini trip computer, if equipped. Keep the forward edge of the cluster hood down on the instrument panel, while sliding the hood forward to engage the 8 retaining clips.

14. Tighten the cluster hood panel mounting screws behind the center bezel and left end of the panel.

15. Install the center bezel into the instrument panel by engaging the 4 retaining clips.

16. Install the instrument panel left end cap.

17. Connect the negative battery cable.

Sebring Coupe and Avenger

▶ See Figure 69

➡ When handling or storing the instrument cluster, make sure that the overlays are not damaged. If you put the cluster down, make sure it is in the face-up position, or the gauge operation will be damaged.

1. Disconnect the negative battery cable.

2. If equipped, tilt the steering column down to its furthest position. If necessary for access, remove the steering wheel.

3. Loosen the mounting screws and remove the instrument cluster bezel.

4. Remove the 4 instrument cluster mounting screws.

5. Remove the instrument cluster and unplug the wiring harness connectors from behind the cluster assembly. Remove the cluster from the vehicle.

To install:

6. Plug in the wiring harness connectors to the back of the instrument cluster assembly.

7. Place the instrument cluster assembly into correct position on the instrument panel. Install and tighten the 4 cluster mounting screws.

8. Install the instrument cluster bezel and tighten the mounting screws.

9. If removed, install the steering wheel.

10. Connect the negative battery cable.

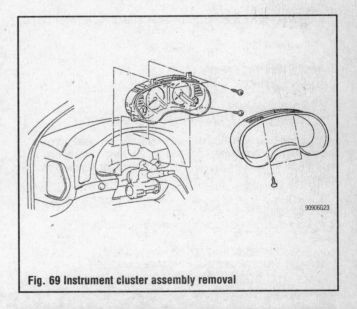

Fig. 69 Instrument cluster assembly removal

Gauges

REMOVAL & INSTALLATION

Cirrus, Stratus, Sebring Convertible and Breeze

▶ See Figure 70

1. Disconnect the negative battery cable.

2. Remove the instrument cluster from the vehicle.

➡ When handling or storing the instrument cluster, make sure that the overlays are not damaged. If you put the cluster down, make sure it is in the face-up position, or the gauge operation will be damaged.

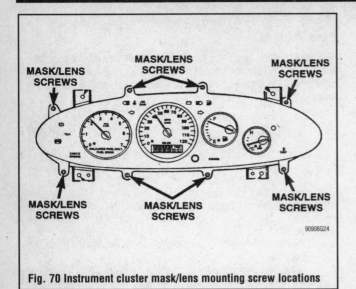

Fig. 70 Instrument cluster mask/lens mounting screw locations

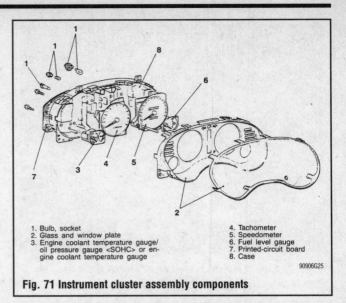

1. Bulb, socket
2. Glass and window plate
3. Engine coolant temperature gauge/
   oil pressure gauge <SOHC> or engine coolant temperature gauge

4. Tachometer
5. Speedometer
6. Fuel level gauge
7. Printed-circuit board
8. Case

Fig. 71 Instrument cluster assembly components

3. Loosen the retaining screws and remove the mask/lens from the instrument cluster assembly.

4. Disengage the odometer/transaxle range indicator connector from the printed circuit board.

5. Remove the applicable gauge mounting screws and remove from the housing.

6. Installation is the reverse of the removal procedure.

Sebring Coupe and Avenger

▶ **See Figure 71**

1. Disconnect the negative battery cable.
2. Remove the instrument cluster from the vehicle.

➡**When handling or storing the instrument cluster, make sure that the overlays are not damaged. If you put the cluster down, make sure it is in the face-up position, or the gauge operation will be damaged.**

3. Carefully disengage the plastic clips and remove the cluster glass and window plate from the cluster housing.

4. Disconnect the applicable gauge from the printed circuit board.

5. Remove the applicable gauge from the housing.

6. Installation is the reverse of the removal procedure.

LIGHTING

Headlights

REMOVAL & INSTALLATION

❊❊ CAUTION

Halogen bulbs contain gas which is under pressure. Handling the bulbs incorrectly could cause it to shatter into flying glass fragments. Do NOT leave the light switch ON. Always allow the bulb to cool before removal. Handle the bulb only by the base; avoid touching the glass itself. Whenever handling a halogen bulb, ALWAYS follow these precautions:

• Turn the headlight switch **OFF** and allow the bulb to cool before changing it. Leave the switch **OFF** until the change is complete.

Windshield Wiper Switch

REMOVAL & INSTALLATION

The windshield wiper switch and intermittent wiper relay are built into a multi-function combination switch, which is mounted on the steering column. Refer to Section 8 for removal and installation procedures.

Headlight Switch

REMOVAL & INSTALLATION

The headlight switch is built into a multi-function combination switch, which is mounted on the steering column. Refer to Section 8 for removal and installation procedures.

Ignition Switch

REMOVAL & INSTALLATION

The ignition switch is mounted in the steering column. Refer to Section 8 for removal and installation procedures.

• ALWAYS wear eye protection when changing a halogen bulb.
• Handle the bulb only by its base. Avoid touching the glass.
• DO NOT drop or scratch the bulb.
• Keep dirt and moisture away from the bulb.
• Place the used bulb in the new bulb's package and dispose of it properly.

Cirrus, Stratus, Sebring Convertible and Breeze

▶ **See Figures 72, 73, 74, 75 and 76**

1. Open the vehicle's hood and secure it in an upright position.
2. Disconnect the negative battery cable.
3. Remove the 2 screws securing the headlight module to the radiator closure panel.
4. Pull out the headlight module from the vehicle.
5. Detach the headlight electrical connector.

Fig. 72 Using a Torx® head screwdriver, remove the 2 headlight module retaining screws

Fig. 75 Turn the light bulb retaining ring counterclockwise, and remove it from the back of the module

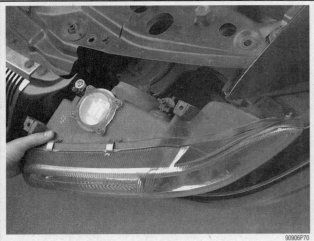

Fig. 73 Pull the headlight module straight out of the front of the vehicle to remove the bulbs

Fig. 76 Pull the light bulb out from behind the module. Never touch the glass of the light bulb

6. Remove the retaining ring holding the bulb to the back of the headlight module.

7. Pull the bulb from the back of the headlight module. Hold the bulb by its base only; try not to touch the glass itself.

To install:

8. Holding the bulb by the base, place it in the headlight module, then secure with the retaining ring.

9. Attach the electrical connector to the bulb.

10. Install the headlight module into the vehicle and tighten the 2 retaining screws.

11. Connect the negative battery cable and check the headlight operation.

Sebring Coupe and Avenger

▶ **See Figures 77 and 78**

1. Open the vehicle's hood and secure it in an upright position.
2. Disconnect the negative battery cable.
3. Remove the sealing cover by rotating it counterclockwise.
4. Remove the bulb attaching spring and pull out the light bulb.

To install:

5. Install the bulb into the headlight module.
6. Install the bulb attaching spring.

Fig. 74 Disconnect the wiring harness for the headlight bulb

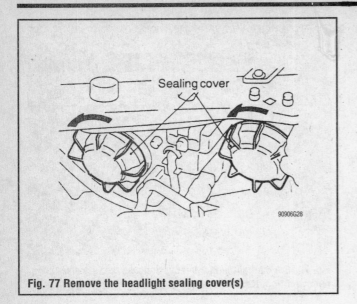

Fig. 77 Remove the headlight sealing cover(s)

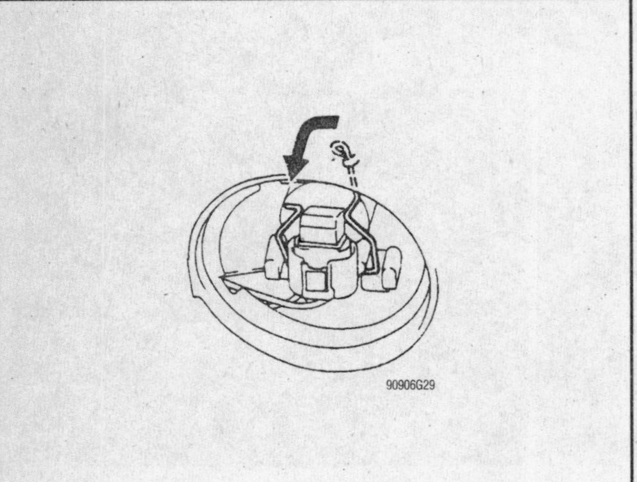

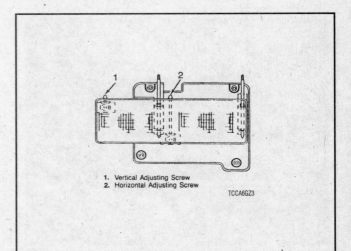

Fig. 78 Remove the attaching spring and pull out the bulb

Headlight adjustment may be temporarily made using a wall, as described below, or on the rear of another vehicle. When adjusted, the lights should not glare in oncoming car or truck windshields, nor should they illuminate the passenger compartment of vehicles driving in front of you. These adjustments are rough and should always be fine-tuned by a repair shop which is equipped with headlight aiming tools. Improper adjustments may be both dangerous and illegal.

For most of the vehicles covered by this manual, horizontal and vertical aiming of each sealed beam unit is provided by one or two adjusting screws which move the retaining ring and adjusting plate against the tension of a coil spring. There is no adjustment for focus; this is done during headlight manufacturing.

➡**Because the composite headlight assembly is bolted into position, no adjustment should be necessary or possible. Some applications, however, may be bolted to an adjuster plate or may be retained by adjusting screws. If so, follow this procedure when adjusting the lights, BUT always have the adjustment checked by a reputable shop.**

Before removing the headlight bulb or disturbing the headlamp in any way, note the current settings in order to ease headlight adjustment upon reassembly. If the high or low beam setting of the old lamp still works, this can be done using the wall of a garage or a building:

1. Vertical Adjusting Screw
2. Horizontal Adjusting Screw

Fig. 79 Example of headlight adjustment screw location for composite headlamps

7. Install the sealing cover.
8. Connect the negative battery cable and check the headlight operation.

AIMING THE HEADLIGHTS

▶ **See Figures 79, 80, 81 and 82**

The headlights must be properly aimed to provide the best, safest road illumination. The lights should be checked for proper aim and adjusted as necessary. Certain state and local authorities have requirements for headlight aiming; these should be checked before adjustment is made.

⁘ CAUTION

About once a year, when the headlights are replaced or any time front end work is performed on your vehicle, the headlight should be accurately aimed by a reputable repair shop using the proper equipment. Headlights not properly aimed can make it virtually impossible to see and may blind other drivers on the road, possibly causing an accident. Note that the following procedure is a temporary fix, until you can take your vehicle to a repair shop for a proper adjustment.

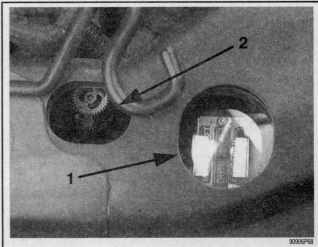

Fig. 80 A level (1) for headlight aiming is on top of each headlamp module; adjustment screws (2) are next to it

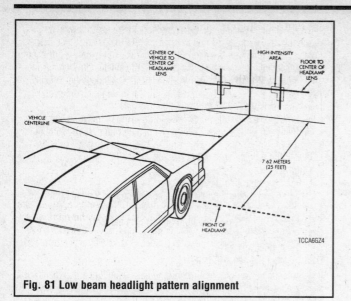

Fig. 81 Low beam headlight pattern alignment

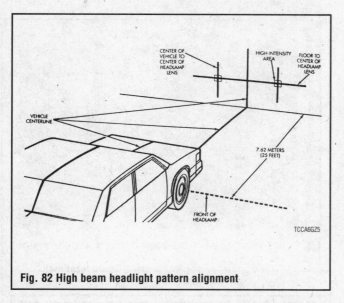

Fig. 82 High beam headlight pattern alignment

1. Park the vehicle on a level surface, with the fuel tank about ½ full and with the vehicle empty of all extra cargo (unless normally carried). The vehicle should be facing a wall which is no less than 6 feet (1.8m) high and 12 feet (3.7m) wide. The front of the vehicle should be about 25 feet (7.6m) from the wall.

2. If aiming is to be performed outdoors, it is advisable to wait until dusk in order to properly see the headlight beams on the wall. If done in a garage, darken the area around the wall as much as possible by closing shades or hanging cloth over the windows.

3. Turn the headlights **ON** and mark the wall at the center of each light's low beam, then switch on the brights and mark the center of each light's high beam. A short length of masking tape which is visible from the front of the vehicle may be used. Although marking all four positions is advisable, marking one position from each light should be sufficient.

4. If neither beam on one side is working, and if another like-sized vehicle is available, park the second one in the exact spot where the vehicle was and mark the beams using the same-side light. Then, switch the vehicles so the one to be aimed is back in the original spot. It must be parked no closer to or farther away from the wall than the second vehicle.

5. Perform any necessary repairs, but make sure the vehicle is not moved, or is returned to the exact spot from which the lights were marked. Turn the headlights **ON** and adjust the beams to match the marks on the wall.

6. Have the headlight adjustment checked as soon as possible by a reputable repair shop.

Signal and Marker Lights

REMOVAL & INSTALLATION

Front Turn Signal and Parking Lights

▶ **See Figures 83, 84 and 85**

1. Open the vehicle's hood and secure it in an upright position.
2. Disconnect the negative battery cable.
3. Remove the headlight module (Cirrus, Stratus, Sebring convertible and Breeze) or the turn signal lens module (Sebring coupe and Avenger).
4. Disengage the bulb socket connector (Cirrus, Stratus, Sebring convertible and Breeze).
5. Twist the bulb and socket counterclockwise to unlock, then pull the assembly from the housing. Pull the bulb straight from the socket.

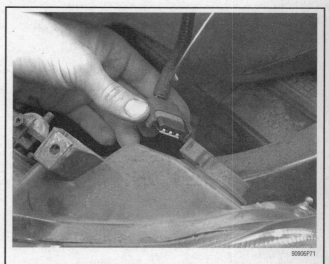

Fig. 83 Disengage the side marker/turn signal bulb connector

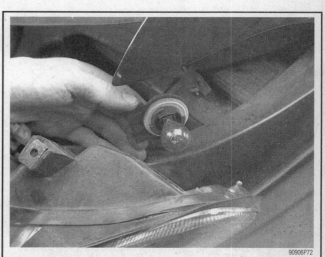

Fig. 84 Turn the side marker bulb socket counterclockwise and pull it out of the module

Fig. 85 After removing the socket, pull the side marker bulb straight out of the socket

To install:

6. Push the bulb into the socket. Position the bulb and socket in the housing, then turn the assembly clockwise to lock it into place.

7. Engage the bulb socket connector (Cirrus, Stratus, Sebring convertible and Breeze).

8. Position and install the headlight module or turn signal module, and secure with the retaining screws.

9. Connect the negative battery cable, then check the light operation.

Side Marker Light

SEBRING COUPE AND AVENGER

▶ **See Figure 86**

1. Disconnect the negative battery cable.

2. In the engine compartment, from behind the outer corner of the headlight module, turn the light socket counterclockwise and pull it out of the module.

3. Carefully pull the bulb straight out of the socket.

4. Installation is the reverse of removal.

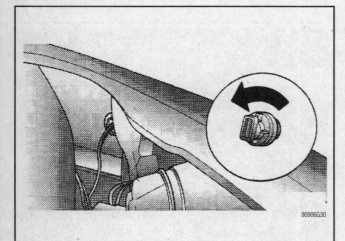

Fig. 86 Turn the front side marker light socket counterclockwise and pull it out

Rear Turn Signal, Brake and Parking Lights

▶ **See Figures 87 thru 92**

1. Disconnect the negative battery cable, then open the trunk.

2. Remove the fasteners securing the tail lamp assembly to the rear closure panel.

3. Pull the assembly away from the closure panel.

4. If necessary, disengage the light bulb wiring harness.

5. Rotate the bulb socket counterclockwise and pull it out of the housing.

6. Pull the bulb straight out of the socket.

To install:

7. Push the bulb into the socket.

8. Install and rotate the bulb socket clockwise into the tail light housing.

9. If necessary, connect the light bulb wiring harness.

10. Install the tail light housing onto the vehicle.

11. Close the trunk lid.

12. Connect the negative battery cable.

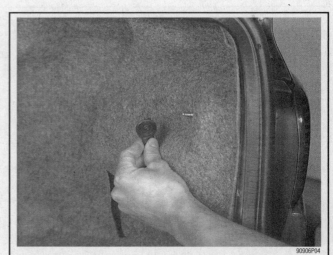

Fig. 87 Removing the tail light module fasteners from inside the trunk

Fig. 88 Remove the tail light module from the vehicle

Fig. 89 Unplug the tail light bulb wiring harness connector

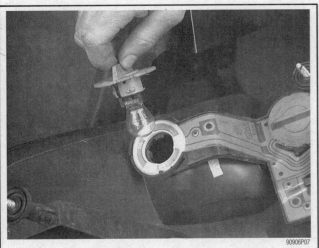

Fig. 90 Twist the tail light bulb socket counterclockwise and pull it out

Fig. 91 Pull the light bulb straight out of the socket

Fig. 92 Note the rotational directions on the back of the socket when replacing a light bulb

High-Mount Brake Light

▶ **See Figures 93 and 94**

1. Disconnect the negative battery cable, then open the trunk.
2. Rotate the bulb socket counterclockwise and remove it from the high-mount brake light housing.
3. Pull the bulb straight from the socket.

To install:

4. Push the bulb into the socket.
5. Position the bulb socket in the housing, then rotate it clockwise to lock into place.
6. Close the trunk, connect the negative battery cable, then check the light's operation.

Dome Light

▶ **See Figures 95 thru 100**

1. Disconnect the negative battery cable.
2. Insert a small prytool between the headliner and dome lamp lens.
3. Carefully pry downward on the four corners of the lamp lens.
4. Separate the lens from the lamp.
5. Pull the bulb from the lamp socket.

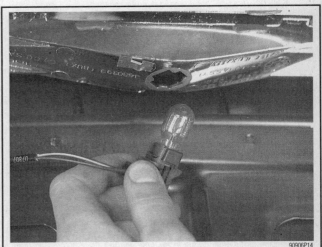

Fig. 93 Twist and pull the high-mount center brake light socket from its light module

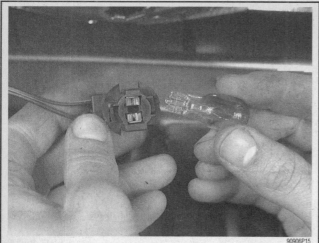

Fig. 94 Pull the light bulb out of the high-mount brake light bulb socket

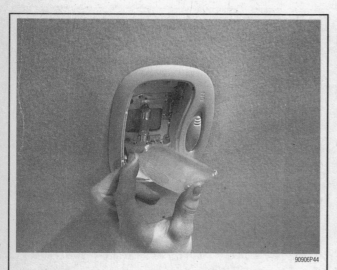

Fig. 95 Removal of the middle interior dome light lens

Fig. 96 Pull out the middle dome light bulb from the socket's clips

Fig. 97 Remove the front interior dome light lens

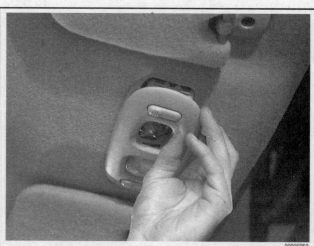

Fig. 98 Pull the front dome light fixture down from the headliner by disengaging the retaining clips

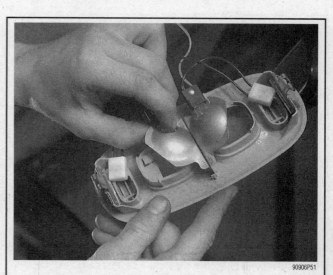

Fig. 99 Push out the bulb from its socket assembly . . .

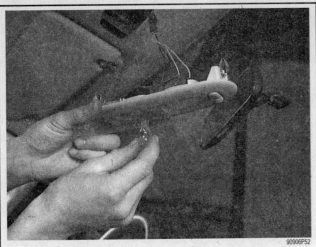

Fig. 100 . . . then withdraw the bulb through the bottom of the lamp assembly

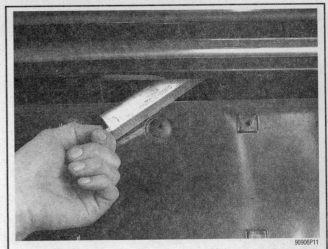

Fig. 102 Carefully pull out the license plate light module from inside the trunk lid

To install:

6. Install the bulb into the socket.
7. Position the lens onto the lamp and snap it securely into place.
8. Connect the negative battery cable.

License Plate Lights

▶ **See Figures 101, 102, 103 and 104**

1. Disconnect the negative battery cable.
2. Remove the screws holding the license plate lamp to the rear bumper fascia or trunk lid.
3. Separate the lamp from the bumper or trunk lid.
4. Twist the bulb socket counterclockwise, then pull it from the lamp.
5. Pull the bulb straight from the socket.

To install:

6. Push the bulb into the socket.
7. Insert the bulb socket into the lamp assembly, then turn it clockwise.
8. Position the lamp into the bumper or trunk lid, then install the mounting screws.
9. Connect the negative battery cable.

Fig. 103 Twist the light bulb socket counterclockwise and pull it out of the license plate lamp module

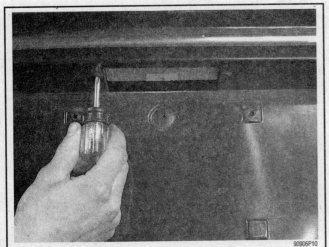

Fig. 101 Removal of the license plate light lens mounting screws

Fig. 104 Carefully pull the license plate light bulb straight out of the socket

Fog/Driving Lights

REMOVAL & INSTALLATION

▶ **See Figures 105, 106, 107 and 108**

1. Disconnect the negative battery cable.
2. Remove the fog lamp module from the bumper fascia.

3. Pull the fog lamp module out of the opening in the fascia.
4. Detach the electrical connector from the fog lamp bulb base.
5. Remove the bulb from the lamp.

To install:

6. Install the bulb in the lamp.
7. Attach the electrical connector to the fog lamp bulb base.
8. Place the fog lamp in position on the front fascia and tighten the mounting screws.
9. Connect the negative battery cable.

Fig. 105 Remove the fog light module mounting screws

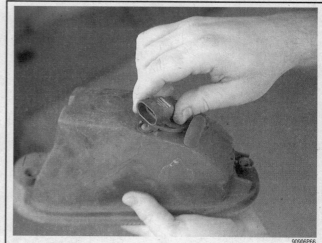

Fig. 107 Hold the fog light module and turn the light bulb counterclockwise, . . .

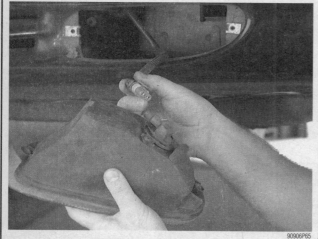

Fig. 106 Pull the fog lamp out of the front fascia panel and disengage the wiring connector

Fig. 108 . . . then withdraw the light bulb from the module

Bulb Specifications—Cirrus, Stratus, Sebring Convertible and Breeze

INTERIOR LIGHT BULBS

Type	Bulb No.
Instrument Cluster	PC 194
Fog Light Indicator	PC 161
Dome Light	578
Front Reading/Map Lights	906
Trunk Light	906
Cup Holder Light	37
Climate Control Light	37

EXTERIOR LIGHT BULBS

Type	Bulb No.
Headlight	9007
Park/Turn Signal	3157NA
Fog Light	9006
Tail/Stop/Turn Signal	3057
Back Up Light	921
Center Stop Light	921
License Light	168

90906C31

Bulb Specifications—Sebring Coupe and Avenger

Outside

Description	Wattage	SAE Trade No.
1 - Headlights (inside)	60W	HB3
2 - Headlights (outside)	51W	HB4
3 - Parking and front side-marker light	3cp	168
4 - Front turn-signal light	32cp	1156
5 - Front fog light	55W	–
6 - High-mounted stop light	21cp	921
7 - Back up light	32cp	1156
8 - Stop and tail light/Rear turn signal light	32/2cp	2057
9 - Rear side-marker light	3cp	168
10 - License plate light	3cp	168

Inside

Description	Wattage	SAE Trade No.
Reading light	10W	–
Reading lamp	6cp	–
Luggage compartment light	5W	–
Foot light (front)	1.4W	74
Foot light (rear)	5W	–

90906C32

TRAILER WIRING

➡**Trailer towing is absolutely NOT recommended for the Sebring coupe or Avenger models. However, it is okay for any Cirrus, Stratus, Sebring convertible or Breeze models to tow a trailer, provided that certain rules and criteria are met. Before proceeding to wire your vehicle for trailer towing use, refer to "Trailer Towing" in Section 1.**

Wiring the vehicle for towing is fairly easy. There are a number of good wiring kits available and these should be used, rather than trying to design your own.

All trailers will need brake lights and turn signals, as well as tail lights and side marker lights. Most areas require extra marker lights for overwide trailers. Also, most areas have recently required back-up lights for trailers, and most trailer manufacturers have been building trailers with back-up lights for several years.

Additionally, some Class I, most Class II and just about all Class III and IV trailers will have electric brakes. Add to this number an accessories wire, to operate trailer internal equipment or to charge the trailer's battery, and you can have as many as seven wires in the harness.

Determine the equipment on your trailer and buy the wiring kit necessary. The kit will contain all the necessary wires, plus a plug adapter set which includes the female plug, mounted on the bumper or hitch, and the male plug, wired into, or plugged into the trailer harness.

When installing the kit, follow the manufacturer's instructions. The color coding of the wires is usually standard throughout the industry. One point to note: some domestic vehicles, and most imported vehicles, have separate turn signals. On most domestic vehicles, the brake lights and rear turn signals operate with the same bulb. For those vehicles without separate turn signals, you can purchase an isolation unit so that the brake lights won't blink whenever the turn signals are operated.

One final point, the best kits are those with a spring loaded cover on the vehicle mounted socket. This cover prevents dirt and moisture from corroding the terminals. Never let the vehicle socket hang loosely; always mount it securely to the bumper or hitch.

CIRCUIT PROTECTION

Fuses

The main fuse block on these vehicles is located at the left side of the dashboard, behind an access panel. These is also a Power Distribution Center (PDC) which can be found under the hood.

Each fuse block uses miniature fuses which are designed for increased circuit protection and greater reliability. The compact fuse is a blade terminal design which allows easy pull-out/push-in removal and replacement.

Although the fuses are interchangeable, the amperage values are not. The values are usually molded in bold, color coded, easy to read numbers on the fuse body. Use only fuses of equal replacement valve.

REPLACEMENT

▶ **See Figures 109, 110, 111 and 112**

1. Remove the fuse block access panel or cover.
2. Locate the fuse for the circuit in question.

Fig. 109 Location of the Power Distribution Center (PDC)

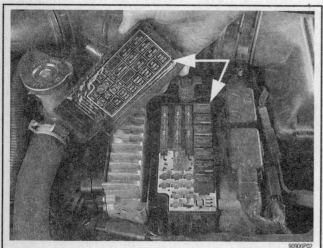

Fig. 110 Location and fuse amperage ratings for fuses and relays can be found on the underside of the PDC lid

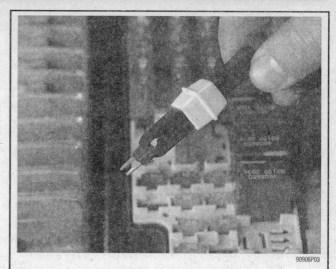

Fig. 111 Use a fuse puller tool to ease fuse removal

Fig. 112 The interior fuse box is located at the left side of the dashboard. Fuse locations and spare fuses are on the inside of the cover

➡ **When replacing the fuse, DO NOT use one with a higher amperage rating.**

3. Check the fuse by pulling it from the fuse block and observing the element. If it is broken, install a replacement fuse of the same amperage rating. If the fuse blows again, check the circuit for a short to ground or faulty device in the circuit protected by the fuse.

4. Continuity can also be checked with the fuse installed in the fuse block with the use of a test light connected across the 2 test points on the end of the fuse. If the test light lights, replace the fuse. Check the circuit for a short to ground or faulty device in the circuit which is protected by the fuse.

Fusible Links

In addition to circuit breakers and fuses, the wiring harness incorporates fusible links to protect the wiring. Links are used rather than a fuse, in wiring circuits that are not normally fused, such as the ignition circuit. The fusible links are color coded red in the charging and load circuits to match the color coding of the circuits they protect. Each link is four gauges smaller than the cable it protects, and is marked on the insulation with the gauge size because the insulation makes it appear heavier than it really is. The engine compartment wiring harness has several fusible links. The same size wire with a special Hypalon insulation must be used when replacing a fusible link.

➡**For more details, see the information on fusible links at the beginning of this section.**

On these vehicles, there is a fusible link placed between the output terminal of the alternator and the engine starter motor terminal.

Circuit Breakers

OPERATION

Circuit breakers differ from fuses in that they are reusable. Circuit breakers open when the flow of current exceeds a specified value and close after a few seconds when current flow returns to normal. Some of the circuits protected by circuit breakers include electric windows and power accessories. Circuit breakers are used in these applications due to the fact that they must operate at times under prolonged high current flow due to demand, even though there is not a malfunction in the circuit.

There are 2 types of circuit breakers. The first type opens when high current flow is detected. A few seconds after the excessive current flow has been removed, the circuit breaker will close. If the high current flow is experienced again, the circuit will open again.

The second type is referred to as the Positive Temperature Coefficient (PTC) circuit breaker. When excessive current flow passes through the PTC circuit breaker, the circuit is not opened, but its resistance increases. As the device heats up with the increase in current flow, the resistance increases to the point where the circuit is effectively open. Unlike other circuit breakers, the PTC circuit breaker will not reset until the circuit is opened and voltage is removed from the terminals. Once the voltage is removed, the circuit breaker will not reset until the circuit is opened and voltage is removed from the terminals. Once the voltage is removed, the circuit breaker will re-close within a few seconds.

Various circuit breakers are located under the instrument panel. In order to gain access to these components, it may be necessary to first remove the underdash padding. Most of the circuit breakers are located in the power distribution center or the fuse panel. Replace the circuit breaker by unplugging the old one and plugging in the new one. Confirm proper circuit operation.

Flashers

REPLACEMENT

Flashers are located either on the bottom of the fuse block or on a module under the dashboard. They are replaced by simply pulling them straight out. Note that the prongs are arranged in such a way that the flasher must be properly oriented before attempting to install it. Turn the flasher until the orientation of the prongs is correct and simply push it firmly in until the prongs are fully engaged.

INDEX OF WIRING DIAGRAMS

SAMPLE DIAGRAM: HOW TO READ & INTERPRET WIRING DIAGRAMS

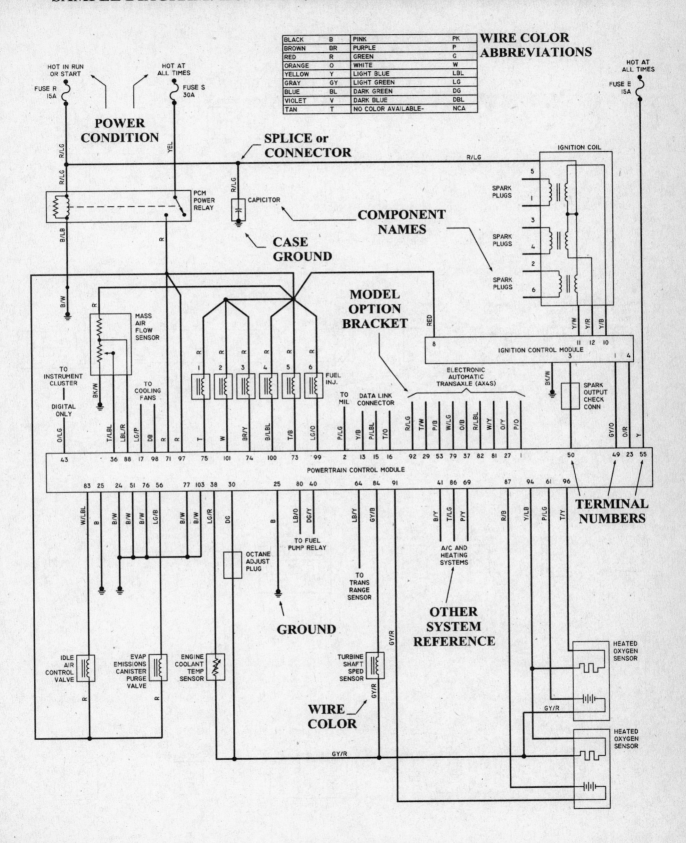

DIAGRAM 1

TCCA6W01

WIRING DIAGRAM SYMBOLS

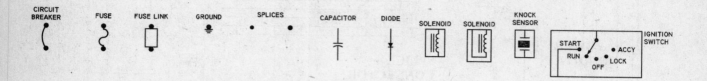

CIRCUIT BREAKER   FUSE   FUSE LINK   GROUND   SPLICES   CAPACITOR   DIODE   SOLENOID   SOLENOID   KNOCK SENSOR   IGNITION SWITCH

START RUN ACCY OFF LOCK

NORMALLY OPEN SWITCH   NORMALLY CLOSED SWITCH   NORMALLY OPEN SWITCH   NORMALLY CLOSED SWITCH   3 POSITION SWITCH   BATTERY   RELAY   RELAY

RESISTOR   RESISTOR   VARIABLE RESISTOR   VARIABLE RESISTOR   SPEED SENSOR   CHOICE BRACKET   MOTOR

BULB   BULB   LED   OXYGEN SENSOR   OXYGEN SENSOR   HEATING ELEMENT   HEATING ELEMENT

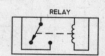

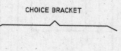

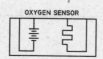

DIAGRAM 2

TCCA6W02

1995 Sebring/Avenger 2.0L Engine Schematic

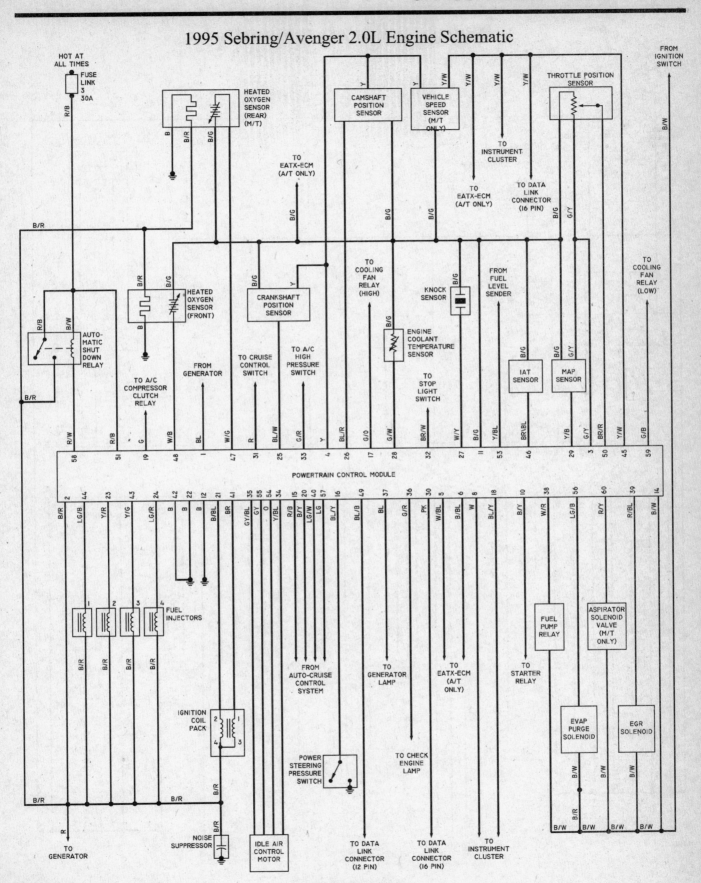

DIAGRAM 3

90906E01

1995 Sebring/Avenger 2.5L Engine Schematic

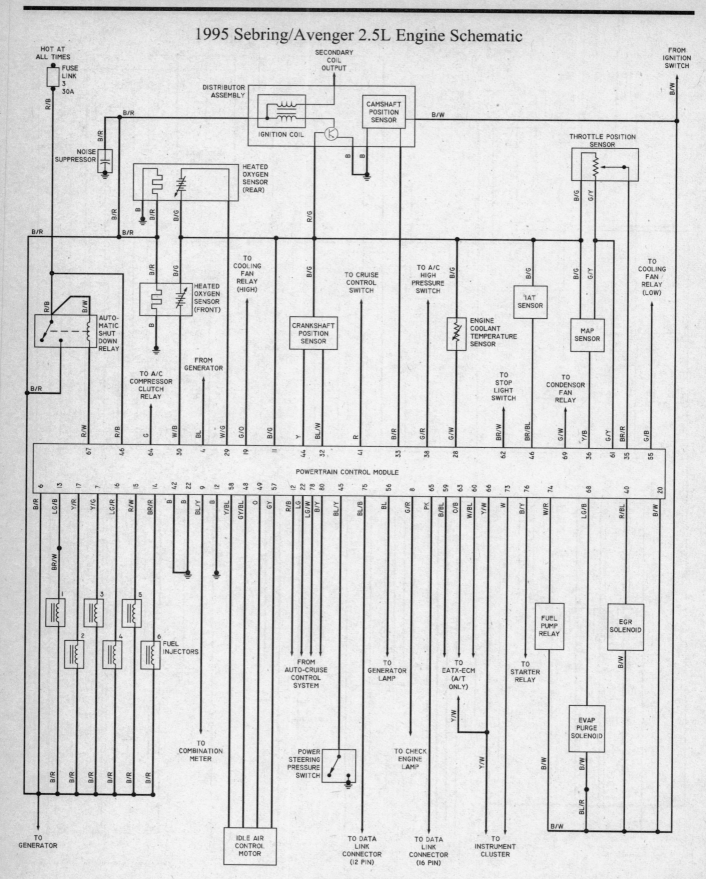

DIAGRAM 4

90906E02

1996-98 Sebring/Avenger 2.0L Engine Schematic

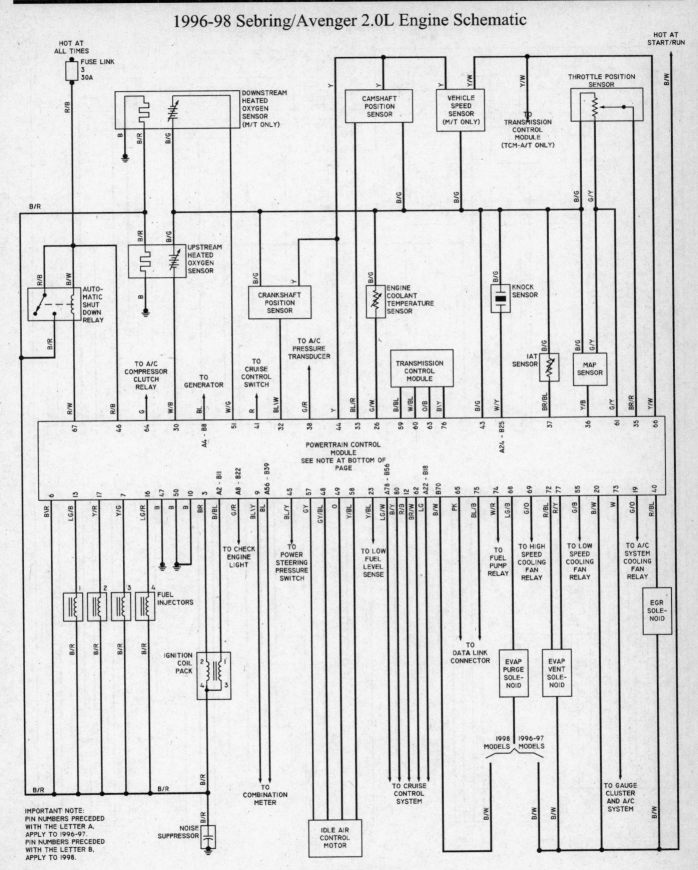

DIAGRAM 5

90906E03

1996-98 Sebring/Avenger 2.5L Engine Schematic

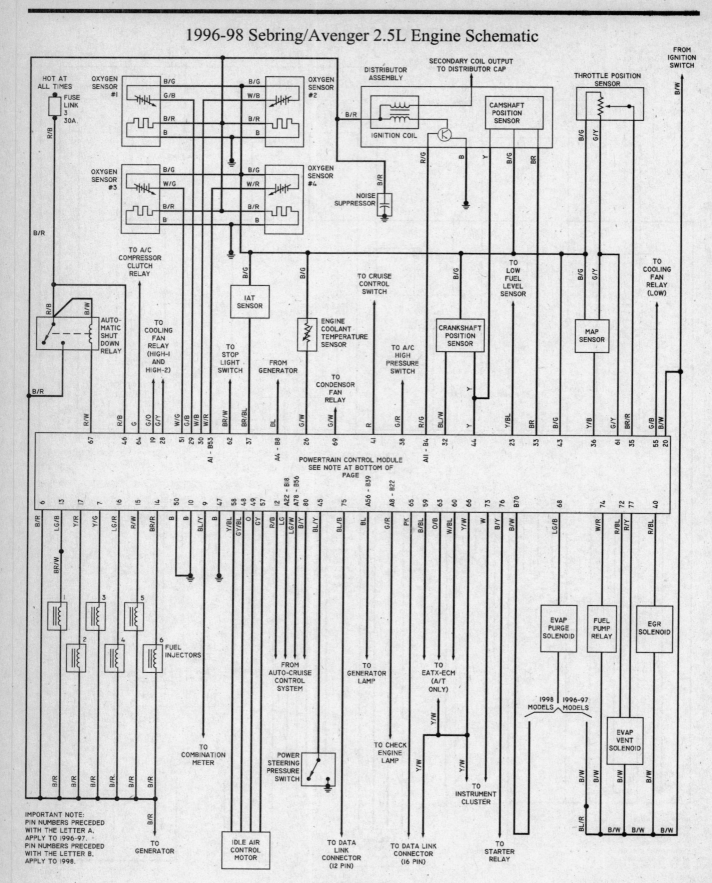

DIAGRAM 6

90906E04

1995-98 Cirrus/Stratus/Breeze 2.0L & 2.4L Engine Schematics

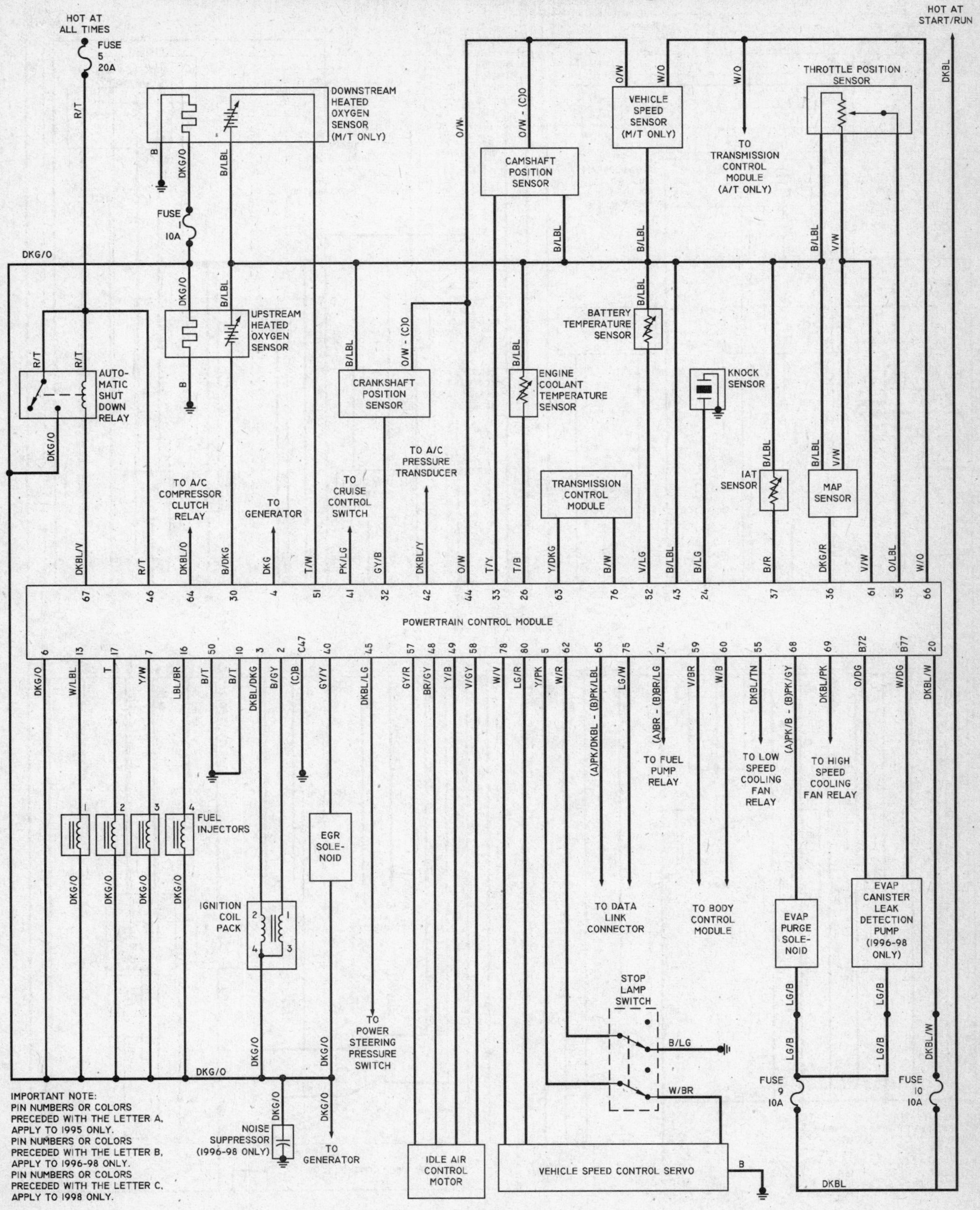

IMPORTANT NOTE:
PIN NUMBERS OR COLORS PRECEDED WITH THE LETTER A, APPLY TO 1995 ONLY.
PIN NUMBERS OR COLORS PRECEDED WITH THE LETTER B, APPLY TO 1996-98 ONLY.
PIN NUMBERS OR COLORS PRECEDED WITH THE LETTER C, APPLY TO 1998 ONLY.

DIAGRAM 7

90906E05

1995-98 Cirrus/Stratus/Breeze 2.5L Engine Schematic

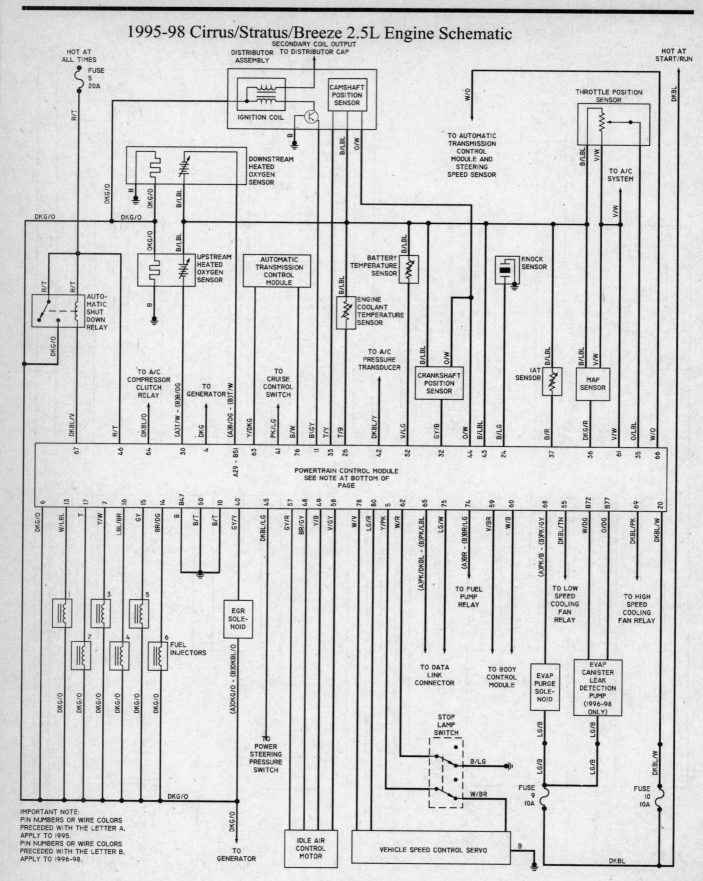

DIAGRAM 8

90906E06

1995-98 Cirrus/Stratus/Breeze/Sebring Convertible Chassis Schematics

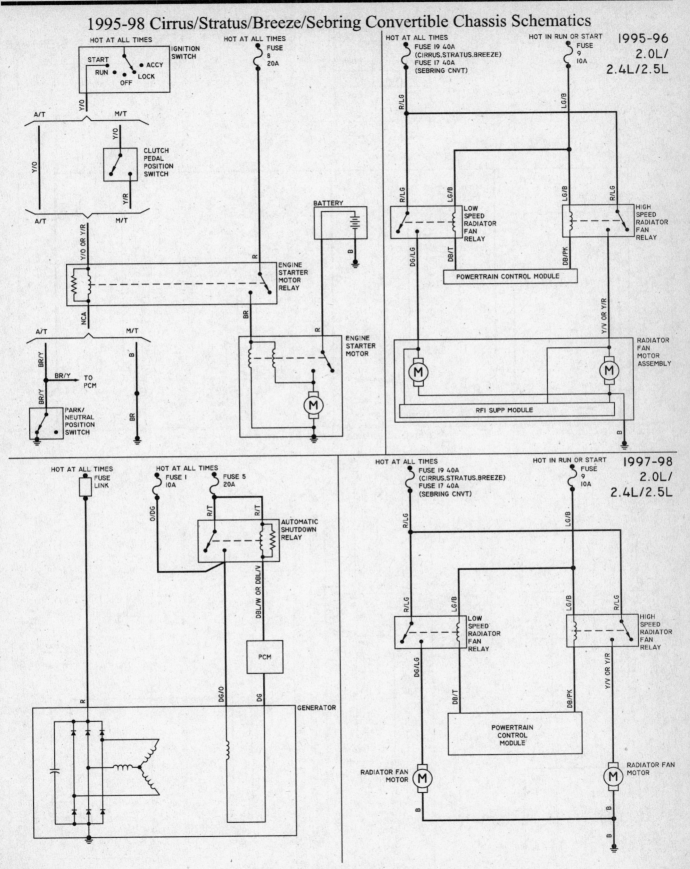

DIAGRAM 9

90906B01

1995-98 Cirrus/Stratus/Breeze/Sebring Convertible Chassis Schematics

CIRRUS/STRATUS/BREEZE

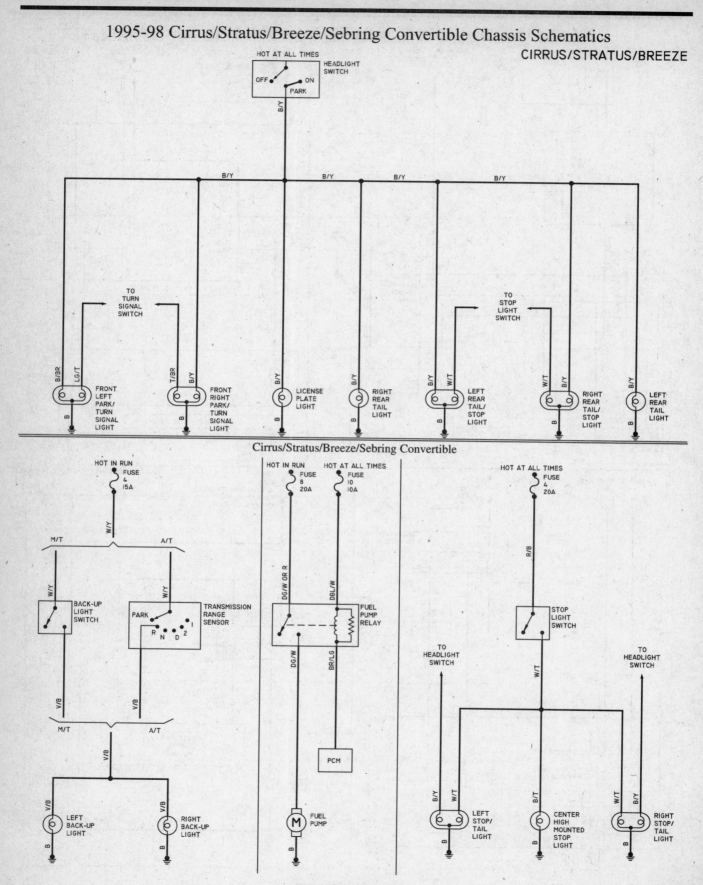

Cirrus/Stratus/Breeze/Sebring Convertible

DIAGRAM 10

90906B02

1995-98 Cirrus/Stratus/Breeze/Sebring Convertible Chassis Schematics

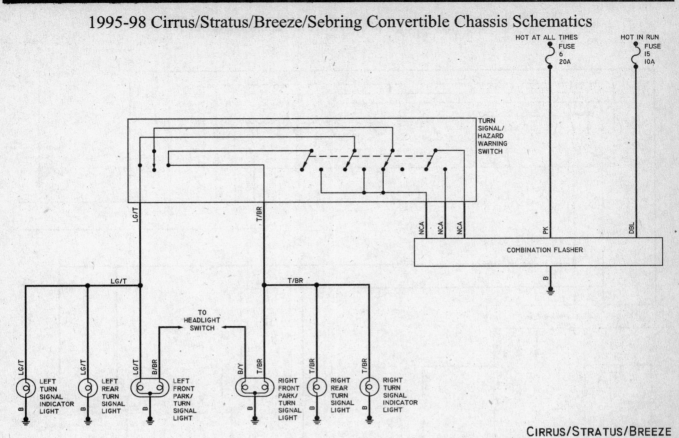

CIRRUS/STRATUS/BREEZE

CIRRUS/STRATUS/BREEZE/SEBRING CONVERTIBLE

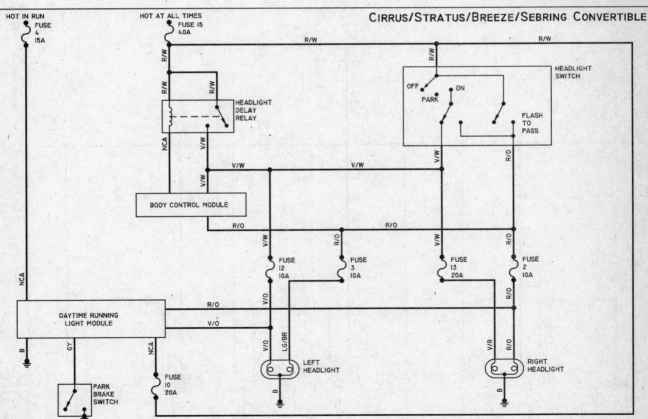

DIAGRAM 11

90906B03

1995-98 Sebring Convertible Chassis Schematics

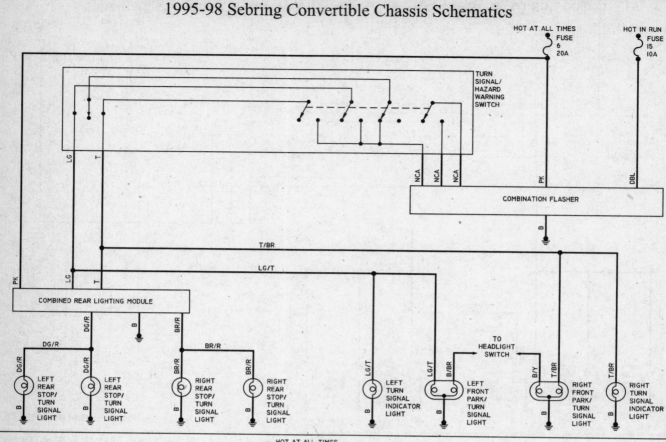

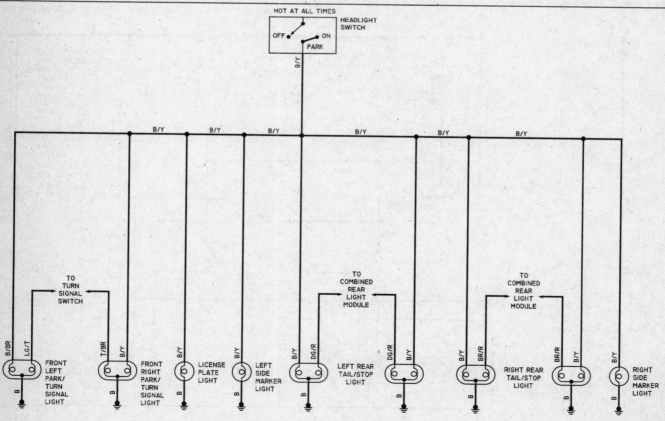

DIAGRAM 12

90906B08

1995-98 Avenger/Sebring Chassis Schematics

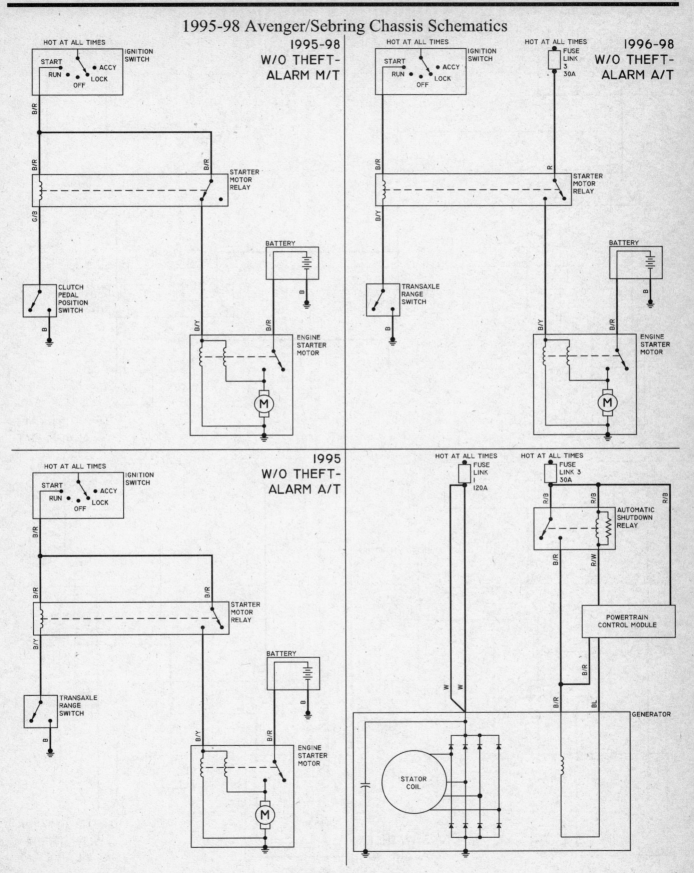

DIAGRAM 13

90906B09

1995-98 Avenger/Sebring Chassis Schematics

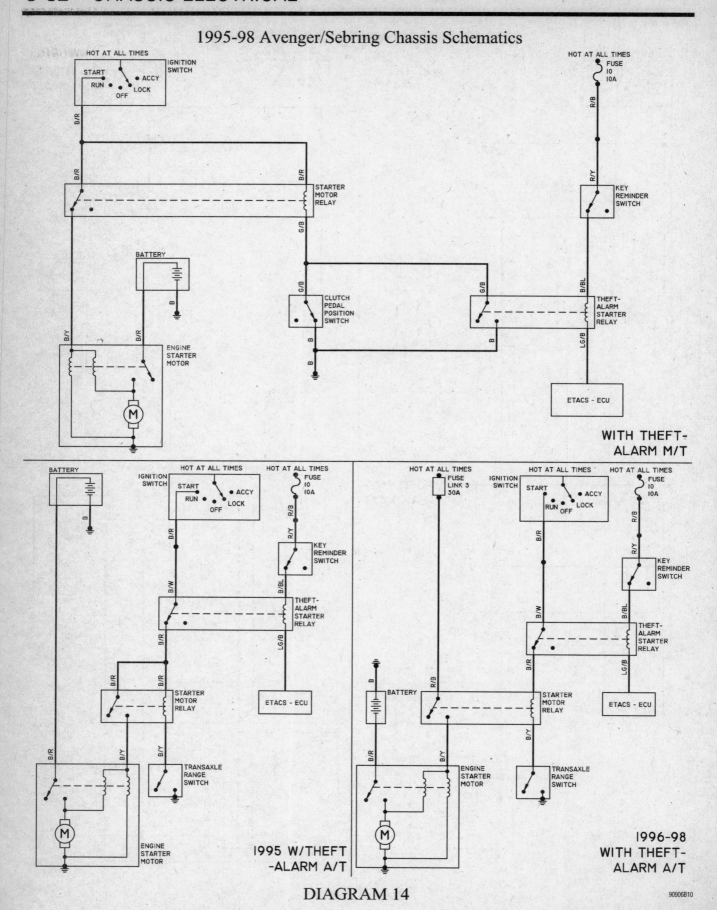

DIAGRAM 14

90906B10

1995-98 Avenger/Sebring Chassis Schematics

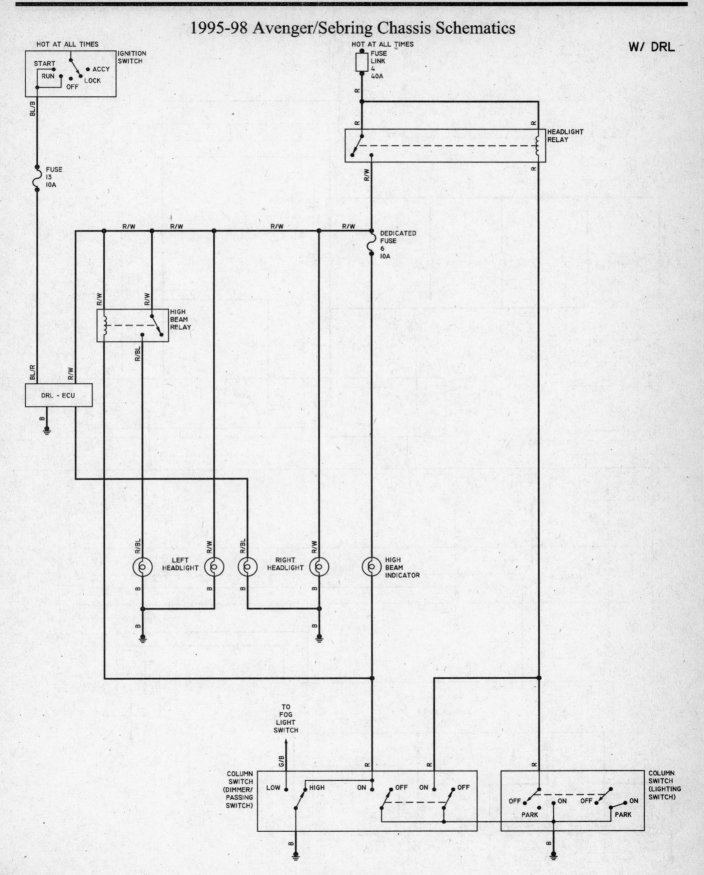

DIAGRAM 15

90906B06

1995-98 Avenger/Sebring Chassis Schematics

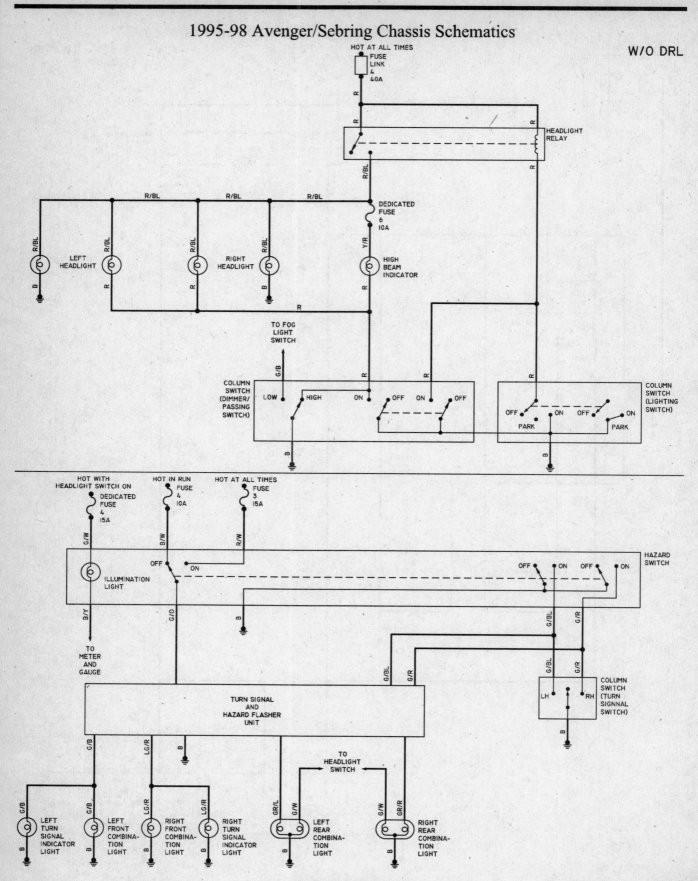

DIAGRAM 16

90906B07

1995-98 Avenger/Sebring Chassis Schematics

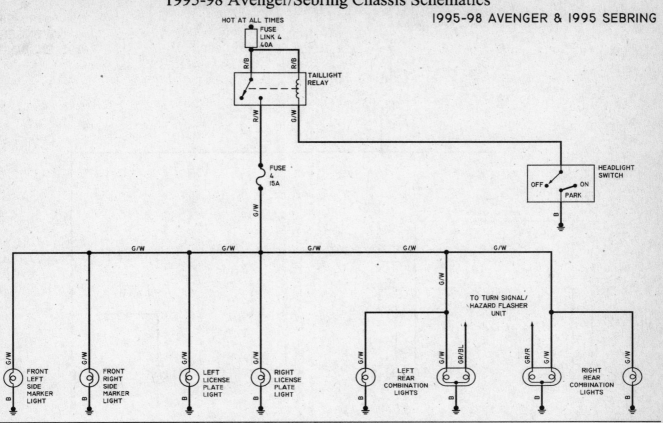

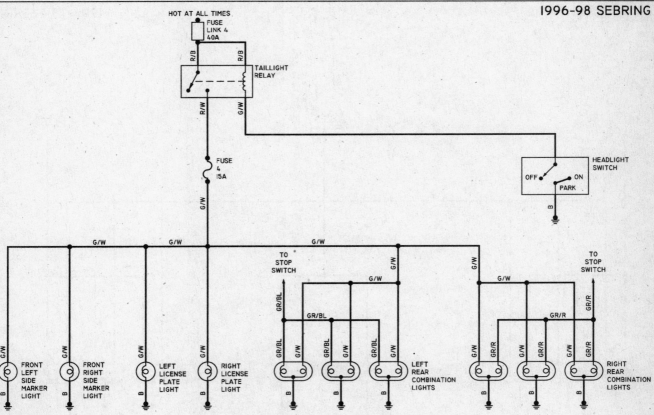

DIAGRAM 17

90906B11

1995-98 Avenger/Sebring Chassis Schematics

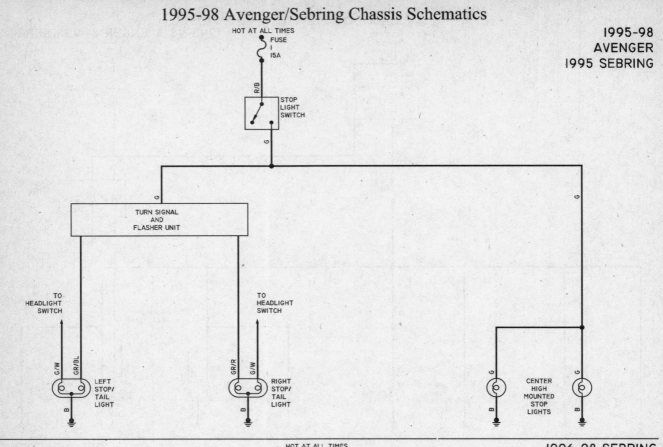

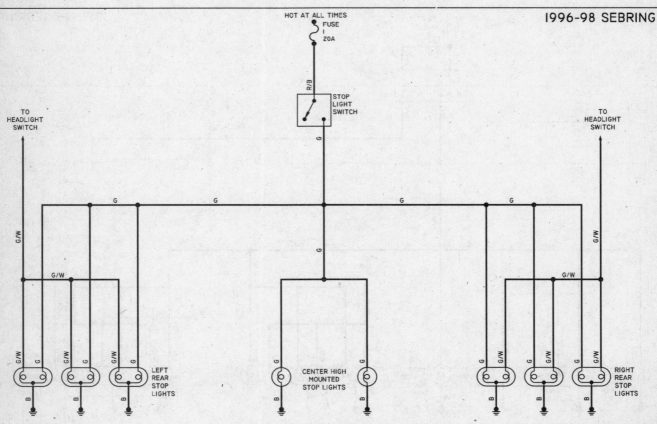

DIAGRAM 18

90906B12

1995-98 Avenger/Sebring Chassis Schematics

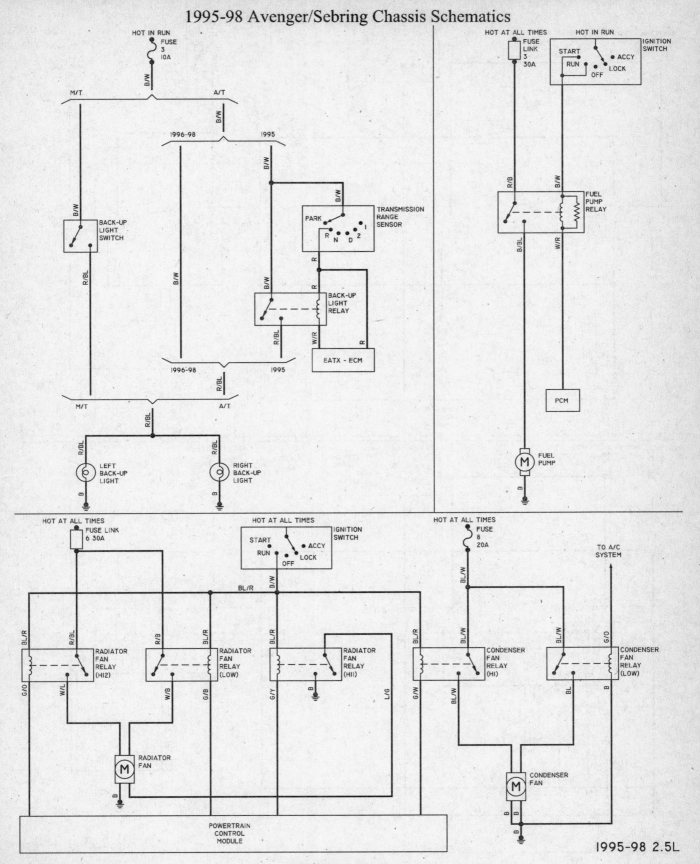

1995-98 2.5L

DIAGRAM 19

90906B04

1995-98 Avenger/Sebring Chassis Schematics

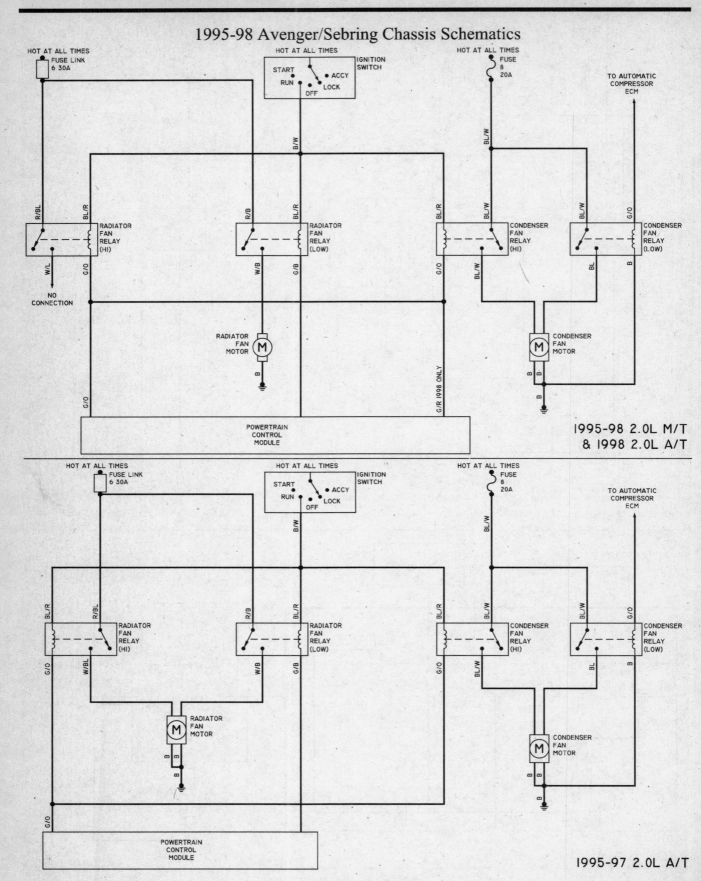

DIAGRAM 20

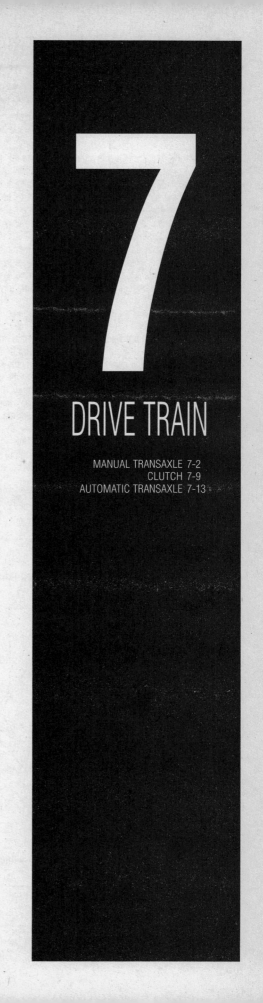

7

DRIVE TRAIN

MANUAL TRANSAXLE

Understanding the Manual Transaxle

Because of the way an internal combustion engine breathes, it can produce torque, or twisting force, only within a narrow speed range. Most modern, overhead valve pushrod engines must turn at about 2500 rpm to produce their peak torque. By 4500 rpm they are producing so little torque that continued increases in engine speed produce no power increases. The torque peak on overhead camshaft engines is generally much higher, but much narrower.

The manual transaxle and clutch are employed to vary the relationship between engine speed and the speed of the wheels so that adequate engine power can be produced under all circumstances. The clutch allows engine torque to be applied to the transaxle input shaft gradually, due to mechanical slippage. Consequently, the vehicle may be started smoothly from a full stop. The transaxle changes the ratio between the rotating speeds of the engine and the wheels by the use of gears. The gear ratios allow full engine power to be applied to the wheels during acceleration at low speeds and at highway/passing speeds.

In a front wheel drive transaxle, power is usually transmitted from the input shaft to a mainshaft or output shaft located slightly beneath and to the side of the input shaft. The gears of the mainshaft mesh with gears on the input shaft, allowing power to be carried from one to the other. All forward gears are in constant mesh and are free from rotating with the shaft unless the synchronizer and clutch is engaged. Shifting from one gear to the next causes one of the gears to be freed from rotating with the shaft and locks another to it. Gears are locked and unlocked by internal dog clutches which slide between the center of the gear and the shaft. The forward gears employ synchronizers; friction members which smoothly bring gear and shaft to the same speed before the toothed dog clutches are engaged.

Back-up Light Switch

REMOVAL & INSTALLATION

▶ See Figure 1

➡The back-up light switch is located on the top left front side of the transaxle case.

1. Disconnect the negative battery cable.
2. Raise and safely support the vehicle.
3. From the bottom side of the vehicle, detach the wiring connector from the switch.
4. Unscrew the switch from the transaxle case.
5. Installation is the reverse of the removal procedure. You must use Teflon® tape or equivalent sealant on the switch threads.

✻✻ WARNING

Do NOT overtighten the switch.

6. After installation, make sure the back-up lamps are working properly.

Manual Transaxle Assembly

REMOVAL & INSTALLATION

▶ See Figures 2 thru 7

1. Disconnect both battery cables, negative side first. Remove the battery, battery tray and, on the Sebring coupe and Avenger, the stay brace.
2. Remove the air cleaner and intake hoses.
3. Drain the transaxle into a suitable waste container.
4. Remove the select and shift cables from the transaxle.
5. Disconnect the back-up light switch harness and position it aside.
6. Disengage the speedometer electrical harness from the transaxle assembly.
7. Remove the starter motor.
8. Using engine assembly support tool 7137 or C-4852, or equivalent, secure the engine assembly.
9. Remove the rear roll stopper mounting bracket.
10. Remove the transaxle mount bracket.
11. Remove the upper transaxle mounting bolts.

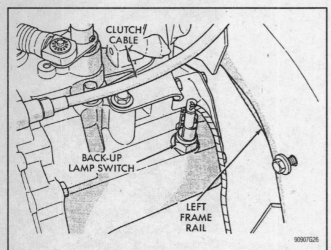

Fig. 1 Location of the back-up lamp switch—vehicles with manual transaxles

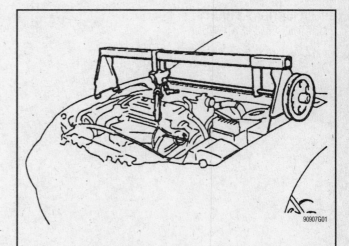

Fig. 2 Secure the engine assembly with an appropriate support fixture

12. Raise and safely support the vehicle.

13. Remove the front wheel assemblies.

14. Remove the undercover.

15. Remove the halfshaft assemblies. Plug the halfshaft openings in the transaxle assembly to prevent foreign material from entering.

16. On Sebring coupe and Avenger, remove the clutch release cylinder and, without disconnecting the hydraulic line, secure it to the chassis.

17. Remove the cover from the transaxle bell housing.

18. Remove the engine front roll stopper through-bolt.

19. Remove the centermember.

20. Support the transaxle, using a transaxle jack.

21. Rotate the engine clockwise to gain access to the flexplate clutch bolts. Remove the flexplate clutch bolts.

22. Remove the lower engine-to-transaxle mounting bolts.

23. Slide the transaxle rearward and carefully lower it from the vehicle.

To install:

24. Installation is the reverse of the removal procedure. Please note the following important steps.

25. The following items must be tightened to the specifications listed.

• Tighten the transaxle-to-engine mounting bolts to 70 ft. lbs (95 Nm).

• Tighten the transaxle bellhousing cover bolts to 7 ft. lbs. (9 Nm).

• Tighten the centermember front mounting bolts to 65 ft. lbs. (88 Nm) and the rear bolt to 54 ft. lbs. (73 Nm). Install the front engine roll stopper through-bolt and lightly tighten. Once the full weight of the engine is on the mounts, tighten the bolt to 42 ft. lbs. (57 Nm).

• Tighten the damper fork-to-lower control arm through-bolt to 65 ft. lbs. (88 Nm).

• Tighten the stabilizer link-to-damper fork nut to 29 ft. lbs. (39 Nm).

• Install the transaxle mount bracket to the transaxle, and tighten the mounting nuts to 32 ft. lbs. (43 Nm).

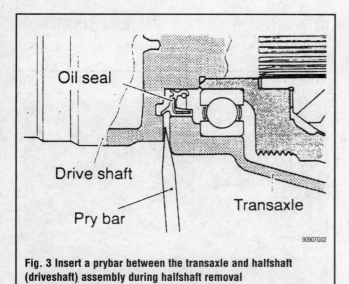

Fig. 3 Insert a prybar between the transaxle and halfshaft (driveshaft) assembly during halfshaft removal

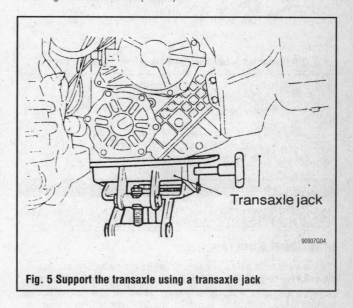

Fig. 5 Support the transaxle using a transaxle jack

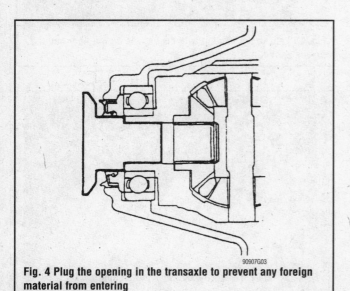

Fig. 4 Plug the opening in the transaxle to prevent any foreign material from entering

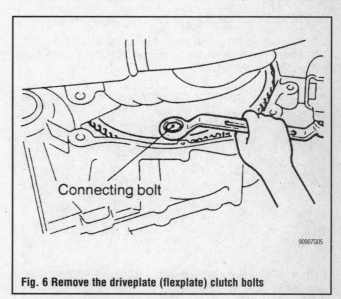

Fig. 6 Remove the driveplate (flexplate) clutch bolts

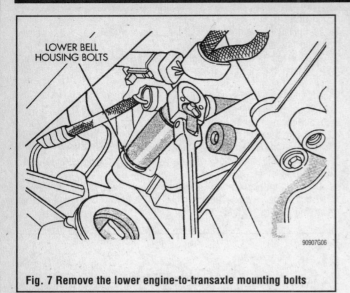

Fig. 7 Remove the lower engine-to-transaxle mounting bolts

Fig. 9 Remove the nut lock and spring washer from the CV-joint stub shaft

- Tighten the transaxle mount through-bolt to 51 ft. lbs. (69 Nm).

26. Check to make sure that all fasteners are tightened and connections made.

27. Make sure the vehicle is level, and refill the transaxle.

28. Check the transaxle for proper operation. Make sure the reverse lights come on when the gear selector is in Reverse.

Halfshafts

REMOVAL & INSTALLATION

▶ **See Figures 8 thru 14**

➡️If the vehicle is going to be rolled while the halfshafts are out of the vehicle, obtain 2 outer CV-joints or proper equivalent tools and install to the hubs. If the vehicle is rolled without the proper torque applied to the front wheel bearings, the bearings will no longer be usable.

1. Disconnect the negative battery cable.
2. Remove the cotter pin, nut lock and spring washer.
3. Loosen, but do not remove, the halfshaft nut while the vehicle is on the floor with the brakes applied.

Fig. 10 Loosen the hub nut with the vehicle on the floor and the brakes applied

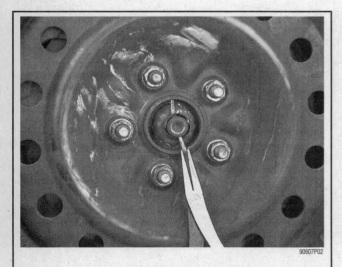

Fig. 8 Remove the cotter pin from the outer CV-joint stub shaft

Fig. 11 After removing the wheel and brake hardware, remove the axle shaft nut and washer

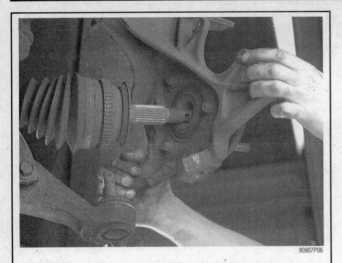

Fig. 12 Pulling the steering knuckle away from the stub shaft

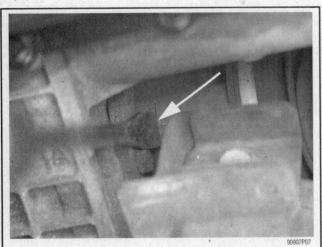

Fig. 13 Place a prybar between the tripod joint housing and transaxle and pry outward

Fig. 14 Support the halfshaft assembly and slide it out of the vehicle

4. Raise and safely support the vehicle.
5. Remove the wheel.
6. Remove the brake caliper assembly and support it from the strut coil using a strong piece of wire.
7. Remove the brake rotor.
8. Remove the halfshaft nut and washer.
9. Using joint separation tool MB991113 or equivalent, disconnect the tie rod end from the steering knuckle.

✳✳ WARNING

Use of improper methods of joint separation can result in damage to the joint, leading to possible failure.

10. If equipped with an Anti-lock Brake System (ABS), remove the speed sensor cable routing bracket.
11. If necessary, disconnect the sway bar link from the damper fork.
12. Remove the damper fork lower through-bolts and upper pinch bolt. Remove the damper fork assembly.
13. Using a joint separation tool, disconnect the steering knuckle from the lower control arm.
14. Remove the halfshaft from the hub/knuckle by setting up a puller on the outside wheel hub, if necessary, and pressing the halfshaft from the front hub. After pressing the outer shaft, insert a prybar between the transaxle case and the halfshaft and pry the shaft from the transaxle.

➡**Do not pull on the shaft. Doing so damages the inboard joint. Do not insert the prybar too far, or the oil seal in the case may be damaged.**

To install:

15. Inspect the halfshaft boot for damage or deterioration. Check the ball joints and splines for wear.
16. Replace the circlips on the ends of the halfshaft(s).
17. Insert the halfshaft into the transaxle. Make sure it is fully seated.
18. Pull the knuckle assembly outward and install the other end of the halfshaft into the hub.
19. Install the washer so the chamfered edge faces outward. Install the halfshaft nut and tighten temporarily.
20. Connect the control arm to the steering knuckle. Tighten the self-locking nuts to 43–52 ft. lbs. (59–71 Nm).
21. Install the damper fork. Tighten the lower through-bolt/nut to 65 ft. lbs. (88 Nm) and the upper pinch bolt to 76 ft. lbs. (103 Nm).
22. Connect the tie rod end to the steering knuckle. Tighten the retaining nut to 17–25 ft. lbs. (24–33 Nm) and install a new cotter pin.
23. Connect the sway bar link to the damper fork and tighten the link nut to 29 ft. lbs. (39 Nm).
24. Install the lockwasher and axle nut. Tighten the axle nut to 145–188 ft. lbs. (200–260 Nm).

➡**Before securely tightening the axle nut, make sure there is no load on the wheel bearings.**

25. Install the brake rotor and caliper assembly.
26. Install a new cotter pin and bend to secure.
27. Install the wheel.
28. Check the transaxle fluid level, and top off if necessary.
29. Connect the negative battery cable.
30. Test drive the vehicle and check for proper operation.

CV-JOINT OVERHAUL

➡**The only service that can be performed on the halfshaft assemblies is to replace the driveshaft seal boots.**

If any failure to the internal halfshaft components is found, the halfshaft must be replaced as an assembly.

➡**The lubricant type and amount necessary for the inner joints is different than that for the outer joints. Use only the recommended lubricants in the specified amounts when servicing the halfshafts.**

Inner Tripod Joint Seal Boot

▶ **See Figures 15 thru 22**

The inner tripod joints do not use any internal retainers in the tripod housing to hold the spider assembly in the housing. Therefore, do not pull on the interconnecting shaft to detach the tripod housing from the transaxle stub shaft. Removing them in this way will damage the inboard joint sealing boots.

1. Remove the halfshaft requiring boot replacement from the vehicle, as outlined earlier in this section.

2. Remove the large boot clamp that holds the inner tripod joint sealing boot to the tripod joint housing. Discard the clamp. Then, remove the small clamp that holds the inner tripod joint sealing boot to the interconnecting shaft and discard. Remove the sealing boot from the tripod housing and slide it down the interconnecting shaft.

☀☀ WARNING

When removing the tripod joint housing from the spider joint, hold the rollers in place on the spider trunions to keep the roller and needle bearings from falling off.

3. Slide the interconnecting shaft and spider assembly out of the tripod joint housing.

4. Remove the snapring that holds the spider assembly to the interconnecting shaft. Remove the spider assembly from the interconnecting shaft. If the spider won't come off by hand, you can remove it by tapping the spider with a brass drift. Do NOT hit the outer tripod bearings trying to remove the spider assembly from the interconnecting shaft.

5. Slide the sealing boot off the interconnecting shaft.

6. Thoroughly clean and inspect the spider assembly, tripod joint housing, and interconnecting shaft for any signs of excessive wear. If any parts show extreme wear, the halfshaft must be replaced.

To install:

➡**The inner tripod joint sealing boots are made from two different types of material. High temperature applications use silicone rubber, whereas standard temperature applications use Hytrel® plastic. The silicone sealing boots are soft and pliable. The Hytrel® sealing boots are stiff and rigid. The replacement sealing boot MUST BE the same type of material as the sealing boot that was removed.**

7. Slide the inner tripod joint sealing boot retaining clamp onto the interconnecting shaft. Then, slide the replacement inner tripod joint sealing boot onto the interconnecting shaft. The inner tripod joint sealing boot MUST be positioned on the interconnecting shaft, so the raised bead on the inside of the seal boot is in the groove on the interconnecting shaft.

8. Install the spider assembly onto the interconnecting shaft with the chamfer on the spider assembly toward the interconnecting shaft. The spider must be positioned on the interconnecting shaft far enough to fully install the retaining snapring. If the spider assembly will not fully install by hand, you can tap the spider body with a brass drift. Do NOT hit the outer tripod bearings trying to install the spider on the interconnecting shaft.

9. Install the spider assembly-to-interconnecting shaft retaining snapring into the groove on the end of the interconnecting shaft. Be sure the snapring is fully seated in the groove on the interconnecting shaft.

10. Distribute ½ the amount of the grease provided in the seal boot service package (DO NOT USE ANY OTHER TYPE OF GREASE) into the tripod housing. Put the remaining amount into the sealing boot.

11. Align the tripod housing with the spider assembly, then slide the tripod housing over the spider assembly and interconnecting shaft.

12. Install the inner tripod joint seal boot-to-interconnecting shaft clamp evenly on the sealing boot.

13. Clamp the sealing boot onto the interconnecting shaft using a suitable crimper. Place the crimping tool over the bridge of the clamp. Tighten the nut on the tool until the jaws of the tool are closed completely together, face-to-face.

➡**The seal must not be dimpled, stretched or out-of-shape in any way. If the seal is NOT correctly shaped, equalize the pressure in the seal and shape it by hand.**

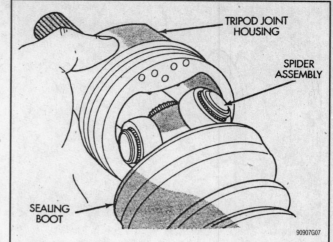

Fig. 15 After discarding the boot clamps, remove the tripod joint housing from the interconnecting shaft and spider assembly

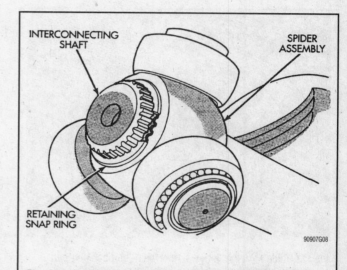

Fig. 16 Location of the spider assembly's retaining snapring

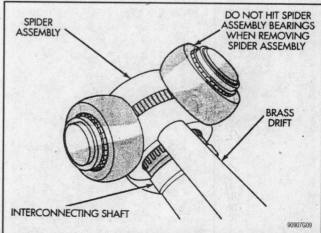

Fig. 17 If you encounter difficulty removing the spider assembly from the interconnecting shaft, use a brass drift to tap the spider

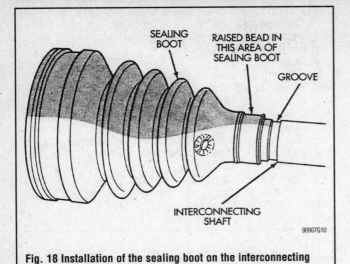

Fig. 18 Installation of the sealing boot on the interconnecting shaft

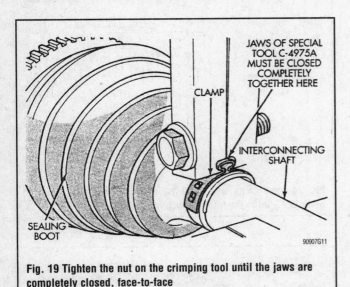

Fig. 19 Tighten the nut on the crimping tool until the jaws are completely closed, face-to-face

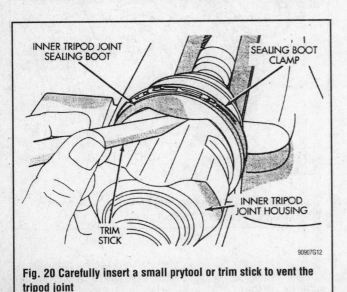

Fig. 20 Carefully insert a small prytool or trim stick to vent the tripod joint

14. Position the sealing boot into the tripod housing retaining groove. Install the seal boot retaining clamp evenly on the sealing boot.

✳✳ WARNING

The following positioning procedure determines the correct air pressure inside the inner tripod joint assembly before clamping the sealing boot to the inner tripod joint housing. If this procedure is not performed before clamping the sealing boot to the tripod joint housing, boot durability can be adversely affected. When venting the inner tripod joint, be careful so the inner tripod sealing boot does not get punctured or damaged in any other way. If the sealing boot is punctured or damaged while being vented, it cannot be used.

15. Insert a small prytool or equivalent tool between the tripod joint and sealing boot to vent the inner tripod joint assembly. When inserting the prytool between the tripod housing and the sealing boot, make sure the tool is held flat and firmly against the tripod housing. If this is not done, damage to the sealing boot can occur. If the inner tripod joint has a Hytrel® (hard plastic) boot, make sure the tool is placed between the soft rubber insert and the tripod housing, and not the hard plastic sealing boot and soft rubber insert.

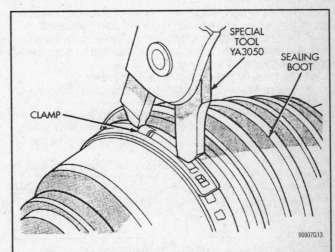

Fig. 21 When installing a latching-type boot clamp, position a suitable clamp locking tool on the clamp as shown . . .

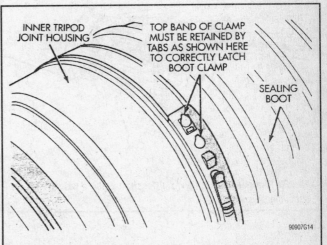

Fig. 22 . . . then squeeze the tool together in order to properly install the latching-type clamp

16. With the tool inserted between the sealing boot and the tripod joint housing, position the inner tripod joint on the driveshaft until the correct sealing boot edge-to-edge length is attained for the type of sealing boot material being used. Then remove the tool.

17. Clamp the tripod sealing boot to the tripod joint using the proper procedure for the type of boot clamp. If the boot uses a crimp-type boot clamp, clamp the sealing boot onto the tripod housing using crimping tool C-4975-A or equivalent. Place the tool over the bridge of the clamp, then tighten the nut on the tool until the jaws are closed completely together, face-to-face.

18. If the boot uses low profile, latching type boot clamps, clamp the sealing boot onto the tripod housing using clamp locking tool YA3050 or equivalent, as shown in the accompanying figure. Place the prongs of the clamp locking tool in the holes of the clamp. Squeeze the tool together until the top band of the clamp is latched behind the 2 tabs on the lower band of the clamp.

19. Install the halfshaft in the vehicle, as outlined earlier in this section.

Outer CV-Joint Seal Boot

♦ **See Figures 23, 24 and 25**

1. Remove the halfshaft requiring boot replacement from the vehicle, as outlined earlier in this section.

2. Remove the large boot clamp that holds the inner tripod joint sealing boot to the tripod joint housing. Discard the clamp. Then, remove the small clamp that holds the inner tripod joint sealing boot to the interconnecting shaft and discard. Remove the sealing boot from the tripod housing and slide it down the interconnecting shaft.

3. Wipe away the grease to expose the outer CV-joint.

4. Remove the outer CV-joint from the interconnecting shaft by performing the following:

   a. Place the interconnecting shaft in a soft jawed vise.

   b. Using a soft-faced hammer, sharply hit the end of the CV-joint housing to dislodge the housing from the internal circlip on the interconnecting shaft.

   c. Slide the outer CV-joint off the end of the interconnecting shaft; the joint may have to be tapped off using a soft-faced hammer.

5. Use a pair of snapring pliers to remove the large circlip from the interconnecting shaft before trying to remove the outer CV-joint sealing boot.

6. Slide the faulty boot off the interconnecting shaft.

7. Throughly clean and inspect the outer CV-joint and interconnecting joint for signs of excessive wear. If any parts show extreme wear, the half-shaft must be replaced.

To install:

8. Slide the new boot-to-interconnecting shaft retaining clamp onto the interconnecting shaft. Slide the outer CV-joint assembly boot onto the interconnecting shaft. The boot must be positioned on the interconnecting shaft so the raised bead of the inside of the seal boot is in the groove on the interconnecting shaft.

9. Align the splines on the interconnecting shaft with the splines on the cross of the outer CV-joint and start the outer CV-joint onto the inter-connecting shaft.

10. Install the outer CV-joint onto the interconnecting shaft by using a soft-faced hammer and tapping the end of the stub axle (with the nut installed) until the outer CV-joint is fully seated on the shaft.

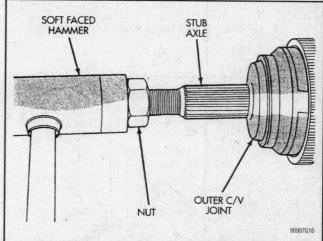

Fig. 24 If necessary, use a soft faced hammer to install the outer C/V joint to the interconnecting shaft

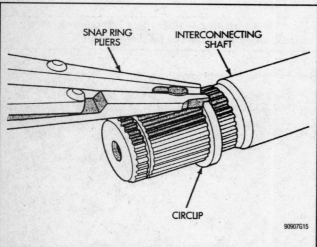

Fig. 23 Remove the circlip from the shaft using a pair of snapring pliers

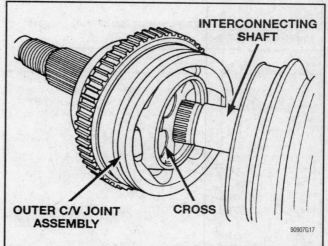

Fig. 25 The outer CV-joint must be installed until the cross of the joint is seated against the shaft circlip

11. The outer CV-joint must be installed on the interconnecting shaft until the cross of the CV-joint is seated against the circlip on the shaft.

12. Place ½ of the grease provided with the boot service package (DO NOT USE ANY OTHER TYPE OF GREASE) into the outer CV-joint housing. Place the remaining grease into the boot.

13. Install the outer CV-joint boot-to-interconnecting shaft clamp evenly on the sealing boot.

14. Clamp the boot onto the interconnecting shaft using C-4975-A or an equivalent crimping tool, as follows:

a. Place the crimping tool over the bridge of the clamp.

b. Tighten the nut on the crimping tool until the jaws on the tool are closed completely together, face-to-face.

15. Position the outer CV-joint boot into its retaining groove on the outer CV-joint housing. Install the boot-to-housing clamp evenly on the housing. Install the sealing boot-to-outer CV-joint retaining clamp evenly on the sealing boot.

16. Clamp the boot onto the outer CV-joint housing using a suitable crimping tool. Place the crimping tool over the bridge of the clamp, then tighten the nut on the crimping tool until the jaws on the tool are closed completely together, face-to-face.

17. Install the halfshaft in the vehicle, as outlined earlier in this section.

CLUTCH

Understanding the Clutch

✳✳ CAUTION

The clutch driven disc may contain asbestos, which has been determined to be a cancer causing agent. Never clean clutch surfaces with compressed air! Avoid inhaling any dust from any clutch surface! When cleaning clutch surfaces, use a commercially available brake cleaning fluid.

The purpose of the clutch is to Disengage and connect engine power at the transaxle. A vehicle at rest requires a lot of engine torque to get all that weight moving. An internal combustion engine does not develop a high starting torque (unlike steam engines) so it must be allowed to operate without any load until it builds up enough torque to move the vehicle. Torque increases with engine rpm. The clutch allows the engine to build up torque by physically Disengageing the engine from the transaxle, relieving the engine of any load or resistance.

The transfer of engine power to the transaxle (the load) must be smooth and gradual; if it weren't, drive line components would wear out or break quickly. This gradual power transfer is made possible by gradually releasing the clutch pedal. The clutch disc and pressure plate are the connecting link between the engine and transaxle. When the clutch pedal is released, the disc and plate contact each other (the clutch is engaged) physically joining the engine and transaxle. When the pedal is pushed inward, the disc and plate separate (the clutch is disengaged) disconnecting the engine from the transaxle.

Most clutches utilize a single plate, dry friction disc with a diaphragm-style spring pressure plate. The clutch disc has a splined hub which attaches the disc to the input shaft. The disc has friction material where it contacts the flywheel and pressure plate. Torsion springs on the disc help absorb engine torque pulses. The pressure plate applies pressure to the clutch disc, holding it tight against the surface of the flywheel. The clutch operating mechanism consists of a release bearing, fork and cylinder assembly.

The release fork and actuating linkage transfer pedal motion to the release bearing. In the engaged position (pedal released) the diaphragm spring holds the pressure plate against the clutch disc, so engine torque is transmitted to the input shaft. When the clutch pedal is depressed, the release bearing pushes the diaphragm spring center toward the flywheel. The diaphragm spring pivots on the fulcrum, relieving the load on the pressure plate. Steel spring straps riveted to the clutch cover lift the pressure plate from the clutch disc, disengaging the engine drive from the transaxle and enabling the gears to be changed.

The clutch is operating properly if:

1. It will stall the engine when released with the vehicle held stationary.

2. The shift lever can be moved freely between 1st and reverse gears when the vehicle is stationary and the clutch disengaged.

Driven Disc and Pressure Plate

REMOVAL & INSTALLATION

Stratus and Breeze

♦ See Figure 26

➡ The transaxle assembly must be removed to service the clutch assembly.

1. Disconnect the negative battery cable from the left strut tower. The ground cable is equipped with an insulator grommet, which should be placed on the stud to prevent the negative battery cable from accidentally grounding.

2. Raise and safely support the vehicle.

3. Disconnect the starter wiring and remove the starter assembly.

4. Remove the rear and front transaxle support brackets.

5. Remove the clutch inspection cover.

6. Remove the bolts attaching the modular clutch to the flywheel.

7. Remove the transaxle assembly with the clutch as an assembly.

8. Remove the clutch assembly from the input shaft of the transaxle.

To install:

9. Clean all parts well. Inspect for oil leakage through the engine rear crankshaft oil seal and transaxle input shaft seal. If leakage is noted, it should be corrected at this time.

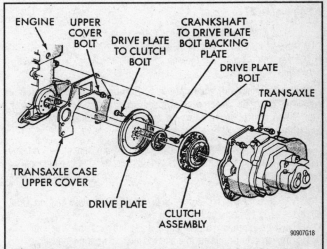

Fig. 26 Exploded view of the clutch assembly—Stratus and Breeze

10. Examine the throwout or clutch release bearing. It is prelubricated and sealed, and should not be washed in solvent. The bearing should turn smoothly when held in the hand with a light thrust load. A light drag caused by the lubricant fill is normal. If the bearing is noisy, rough or dry, replace the complete bearing assembly. In most cases where a clutch is being serviced, the complete clutch assembly and release bearing are usually replaced together.

11. Check the condition of the stud pivot spring clips on the back side of the clutch fork. If the clips are broken or distorted, replace the clutch fork. The pivot ball pocket in the fork is Teflon® coated and should be installed WITHOUT any lubricant, such as grease, which will break down the Teflon® coating. Make sure the ball stud and fork pocket are clean of contamination and dirt. When assembling the fork to the bearing, the small pegs on the bearing must go over the fork arms.

12. Check the flywheel for cracks, glazing or grooves. If any of these conditions exist, machine (reface) or replace the flywheel to prevent clutch chatter and premature clutch wear.

➡ **The manual transaxle is equipped with a Reverse brake. It functions as a synchronizer, but only if the vehicle is not moving. When the clutch pedal is depressed to the floor and held for 3 seconds, and the transaxle shifts to Reverse, no gear clash should be present. If there is, the input shaft should be checked. When the transaxle is removed for clutch service, check the input clutch shaft, clutch disc splines and release bearing for dry rust. If present, clean off the rust and apply a light coating of high temperature bearing grease to the input shaft splines. Apply grease on the input shaft splines only where the clutch disc slides. Verify that the clutch disc slides freely along the input shaft splines.**

13. Install the modular clutch assembly onto the input shaft of the transaxle.

14. Install the transaxle assembly, as described earlier in this section.

15. Install new clutch-to-driveplate (flywheel) bolts. Tighten the bolts to 55 ft. lbs. (75 Nm) in a crisscross pattern, a few turns at a time to prevent distortion of the flywheel.

16. Install the clutch inspection cover.

17. Install the transaxle lower support brackets.

18. Install the starter assembly.

19. Lower the vehicle. Connect the negative battery cable.

20. Road test the vehicle to check for proper clutch operation.

Sebring Coupe and Avenger

▶ **See Figure 27**

1. Disconnect the negative battery cable.
2. Raise and safely support the vehicle.
3. Remove the transaxle assembly from the vehicle, as described earlier in this section.

➡ **The modular clutch assembly used in these vehicles consists of a single, dry-type clutch disc and a diaphragm style clutch cover. The clutch unit is serviced as an assembly; no disassembly is possible.**

4. Remove the pressure plate attaching bolts, pressure plate and clutch disc. If the pressure plate is to be reused, loosen the bolts in a diagonal pattern, 1 or 2 turns at a time. This will prevent warping the clutch cover assembly.

5. Remove the return clip and the pressure plate release bearing. Do not use solvent to clean the bearing.

6. Inspect the clutch release fork and fulcrum for damage or wear. If necessary, remove the release fork and the fulcrum from the transaxle.

7. Carefully inspect the condition of the clutch components and replace any worn or damaged parts.

To install:

8. Inspect the flywheel for heat damage or cracks. Resurface or replace the flywheel as required. Install the flywheel using new bolts.

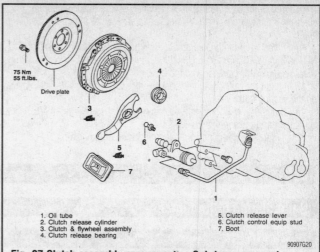

1. Oil tube
2. Clutch release cylinder
3. Clutch & flywheel assembly
4. Clutch release bearing
5. Clutch release lever
6. Clutch control equip stud
7. Boot

75 Nm
55 ft.lbs.
Drive plate

90907G20

Fig. 27 Clutch assembly components—Sebring coupe and Avenger

9. Install the fulcrum, if removed, and tighten. Install the release fork. Apply a coating of multi-purpose grease to the point of contact with the fulcrum and the point of contact with the release bearing. Apply a coating of multi-purpose grease to the end of the release cylinder's pushrod and to the pushrod hole in the release fork.

➡ **When installing the clutch, apply grease to each part, but be careful not to apply excessive grease. Excessive grease will cause clutch slippage and shudder.**

10. Apply multi-purpose grease to the clutch release bearing. Pack the bearing inner surface and the groove with grease. Do not apply grease to the resin portion of the bearing. Place the bearing in position and install the return clip.

11. Apply a coating of grease to the clutch disc splines and then use a brush to rub it in the grooves. Using a universal clutch disc alignment tool, position the clutch disc on the flywheel. Install the retainer bolts and tighten a little at a time, in a diagonal sequence to 55 ft. lbs. (75 Nm).

12. Install the transaxle assembly, as described earlier in this section, and check the fluid level.

13. Verify proper clutch operation.

ADJUSTMENTS

Free-Play

STRATUS AND BREEZE

▶ **See Figure 28**

The manual transaxle clutch release system has a unique self-adjusting mechanism to compensate for clutch disc wear. This adjuster mechanism is located with the clutch cable assembly. The preload spring maintains tension on the cable. This tension keeps the clutch release bearing continuously loaded against the fingers of the clutch cover assembly. No manual adjustment is obtainable.

When servicing this vehicle or if removing and installing the clutch cable, do not pull on the clutch cable housing to remove it from the dashboard panel. Damage to the cable self-adjuster may occur.

To check the function of the adjuster mechanism, use the following procedure:

1. With slight pressure, pull the clutch release lever end of the cable to draw the cable taut.

2. Push the clutch cable housing toward the dashboard panel. With less than 25 lbs. of effort, the cable housing should move 1.2–2.0 inches (30–50mm). This indicates proper adjuster mechanism function.

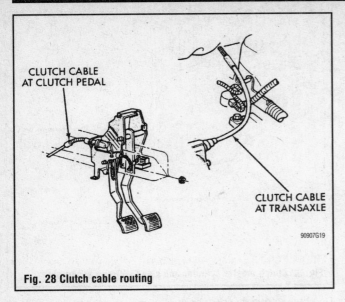

Fig. 28 Clutch cable routing

3. If the cable does not adjust, determine if the mechanism is properly seated on the bracket.

SEBRING COUPE AND AVENGER

▶ **See Figures 29, 30 and 31**

1. With the carpet under the clutch pedal turned back, measure the clutch pedal height from the face of the pedal pad to the firewall. Compare the measured value with the desired distance of 7.00–7.09 inches (175–180mm).

2. Measure the clutch pedal clevis pin play at the face of the pedal pad. Press the pedal lightly until resistance is met, and measure this distance. The clutch pedal clevis pin play should be within 0.040–0.120 inch (1–3mm).

3. If the clutch pedal height and/or clevis pin play are not within specifications, adjust as follows:

a. For vehicles without cruise control, turn and adjust the stop bolt so the pedal height is within specifications, then tighten the locknut.

b. For vehicles with an auto-cruise control system, unfasten the clutch switch connector and turn the switch to obtain the specified clutch pedal height. Hold this setting by tightening the locknut.

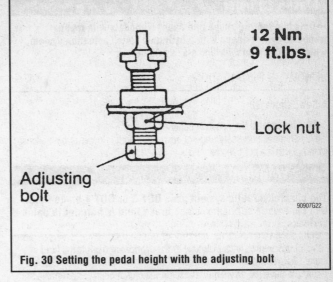

**12 Nm
9 ft.lbs.**

Lock nut

Adjusting bolt

Fig. 30 Setting the pedal height with the adjusting bolt

c. Turn the pushrod to adjust the clutch pedal clevis pin play within specifications, then secure the pushrod with the locknut.

➡ **When adjusting the clutch pedal height or the clutch pedal clevis pin play, be careful not to force the pushrod toward the master cylinder.**

d. Check that when the clutch pedal is depressed all the way, the interlock switch changes from **ON** to **OFF**.

4. Move the clutch pedal until the resistance begins to increase; measure between this point and the pedal resting point, to determine the clutch pedal free-play. The clutch pedal free-play measurement should be 0.240–0.510 inch (6–13mm). With the pedal fully disengaged, check the distance between the firewall and the top of the pedal pad. The measurement should be 2.760 inches (70mm) or more.

5. If the measurements are not within specification, bleed the clutch hydraulic system. If, after bleeding, the measurements are still not within the specified range, the master cylinder or clutch must be replaced.

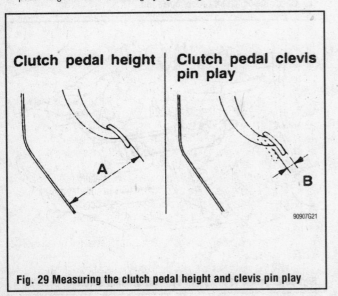

Clutch pedal height

Clutch pedal clevis pin play

A

B

Fig. 29 Measuring the clutch pedal height and clevis pin play

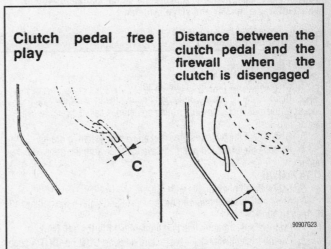

Clutch pedal free play

Distance between the clutch pedal and the firewall when the clutch is disengaged

C

D

Fig. 31 Clutch pedal free-play and distance-to-firewall adjustment

Master Cylinder

→Only the Sebring coupe and Avenger models with manual transaxle are equipped with a hydraulic clutch actuation system, which utilizes a master and slave cylinder.

REMOVAL & INSTALLATION

▶ See Figure 32

1. Disconnect the negative battery cable.
2. Remove necessary underhood components in order to gain access to the clutch master cylinder.

☀☀ WARNING

The clutch hydraulic system uses DOT 3 or DOT 4 brake fluid. Use care when servicing, since brake fluid is harmful to painted surfaces.

3. Loosen the clutch fluid line at the cylinder and allow the fluid to drain.
4. Remove the clevis pin retainer at the clutch pedal, and remove the washer and clevis pin.
5. From inside the passenger compartment, remove the nut securing the master cylinder to the firewall.
6. From under the hood, remove the nut and pull the master cylinder from the firewall. A seal should be between the mounting flange and firewall; this seal should be replaced.

To install:

7. Mount the master cylinder on the studs, using a new seal, and tighten both nuts to 10 ft. lbs. (13 Nm).
8. Lubricate all pivot points with grease and install the clevis pin.
9. Connect the hydraulic line. With an assistant pressing on the clutch pedal, bleed the system at the slave cylinder. Keep the reservoir filled with fresh DOT 3 or DOT 4 brake fluid.
10. Check the adjustment of the clutch pedal for proper free-play.
11. Connect the negative battery cable. Test drive the vehicle and verify correct shifting and transaxle operation.

Slave Cylinder

→Only the Sebring coupe and Avenger models with manual transaxle are equipped with a hydraulic clutch actuation system, which utilizes a master and slave cylinder.

REMOVAL & INSTALLATION

▶ See Figure 32

1. Disconnect the negative battery cable.
2. Remove the necessary underhood components in order to gain access to the clutch slave cylinder (also sometimes called a release cylinder or actuator).
3. Disconnect the hydraulic line and allow the system to drain.
4. Remove the bolts and pull the slave cylinder from the transaxle housing.

To install:

5. Lubricate all pivot points with grease.
6. Mount the slave cylinder to the transaxle and tighten the bolts to 13 ft. lbs. (18 Nm).
7. Connect the hydraulic line and tighten to 11 ft. lbs. (15 Nm).
8. Fill the system with clean brake fluid meeting DOT 3 or DOT 4 specifications.
9. Bleed the clutch hydraulic system.
10. Check and adjust the clutch pedal height, as necessary.

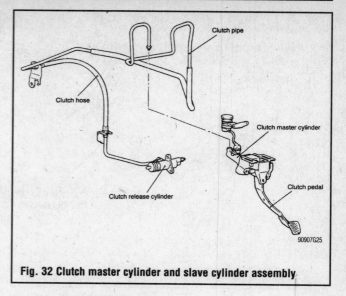

Fig. 32 Clutch master cylinder and slave cylinder assembly

HYDRAULIC SYSTEM BLEEDING

▶ See Figure 33

☀☀ WARNING

The clutch hydraulic system uses DOT 3 or DOT 4 brake fluid. Use care, since brake fluid is harmful to painted surfaces.

1. Fill the reservoir with clean DOT 3 or DOT 4 brake fluid.
2. Loosen the bleed screw, and have an assistant press the clutch pedal to the floor.
3. Tighten the bleed screw and release the clutch pedal.
4. Repeat the procedure until the fluid is free of air bubbles.

→It is suggested that a hose be attached to the bleeder with the other end immersed in a container at least half full of brake fluid during the bleeding operation. Do not allow the reservoir to run out of fluid during bleeding.

5. Refill the reservoir with clean brake fluid.
6. Check the clutch for proper operation.

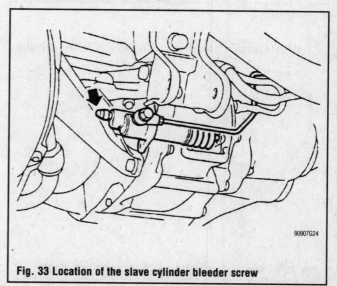

Fig. 33 Location of the slave cylinder bleeder screw

AUTOMATIC TRANSAXLE

Understanding the Automatic Transaxle

The automatic transaxle allows engine torque and power to be transmitted to the front wheels within a narrow range of engine operating speeds. It will allow the engine to turn fast enough to produce plenty of power and torque at very low speeds, while keeping it at a sensible rpm at high vehicle speeds (and it does this job without driver assistance). The transaxle uses a light fluid as the medium for the transmission of power. This fluid also works in the operation of various hydraulic control circuits and as a lubricant. Because the transaxle fluid performs all of these functions, trouble within the unit can easily travel from one part to another. For this reason, and because of the complexity and unusual operating principles of the transaxle, a very sound understanding of the basic principles of operation will simplify troubleshooting.

Fluid Pan

For automatic transaxle fluid pan removal and filter replacement, please refer to Section 1 of this manual.

Neutral Safety Switch

REMOVAL & INSTALLATION

1995 Cirrus and Stratus; 1995–96 Sebring Coupe and Avenger

▶ See Figure 34

➡On these vehicles, the neutral safety switch (Park/Neutral position switch) is located to the right of the transaxle range switch on the front of the transaxle, just above the fluid pan.

1. Disconnect the negative battery cable.
2. Safely raise and support the vehicle.
3. Disengage the electrical connector from the switch.
4. Unscrew the switch from the transaxle case.

To install:

5. Position a new seal washer, then screw the switch into the transaxle case.
6. Attach the electrical connector to the switch.
7. Lower the vehicle.
8. Connect the negative battery cable.

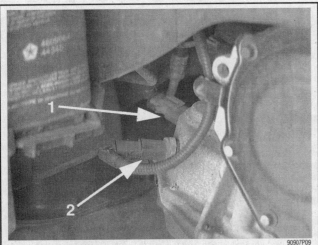

Fig. 34 Location of the transaxle range switch (1) and the Park/Neutral position switch (2)

1996–98 Cirrus, Stratus, Sebring Convertible and Breeze; 1997–98 Sebring Coupe and Avenger

▶ See Figures 35, 36 and 37

➡These vehicles are not equipped with a conventional neutral safety switch or back-up light switch. Instead, the automatic transaxle is equipped with a Transaxle Range Sensor (TRS), which is located on top of the valve body. This sensor performs the functions of the neutral safety and back-up light switches.

The TRS, if defective, must be removed with the transaxle's valve body as an assembly. The TRS is mounted on the top side of the valve body.

1. Disconnect the negative battery cable.
2. Remove the air cleaner assembly.
3. Disconnect the gear shift cable.
4. Remove the manual valve lever.
5. Unplug the transaxle range sensor's electrical connector.
6. Raise and safely support the vehicle.

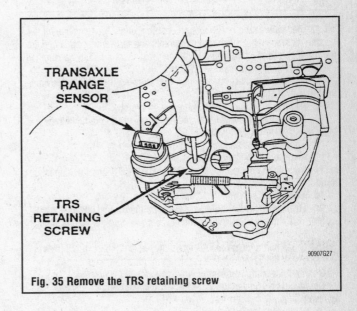

Fig. 35 Remove the TRS retaining screw

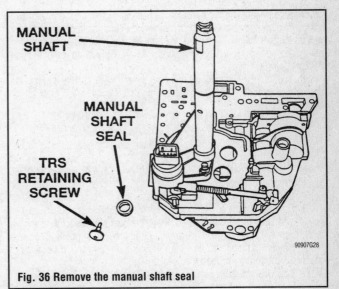

Fig. 36 Remove the manual shaft seal

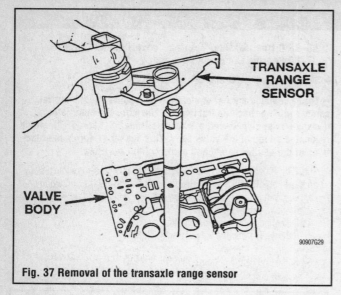

Fig. 37 Removal of the transaxle range sensor

7. Place a drain pan, with a large opening, under the transaxle oil pan. Loosen the transaxle oil pan mounting bolts and tap the oil pan at one corner to break it loose, allowing the fluid to drain. After the fluid has drained, remove the transaxle oil pan.

8. Remove the transaxle oil filter while allowing the residual transaxle fluid to fully drain.

9. Remove the mounting bolts for the valve body.

10. Separate the Park rod from the guide bracket and remove the valve body assembly from the transaxle.

11. Place the valve body assembly on a workbench.

12. Remove the TRS attaching screw.

13. Remove the manual shaft seal and slide the TRS up the manual shaft to remove it from the valve body.

To install:

14. Install the TRS by sliding it down onto the manual shaft.

15. Install the manual shaft seal halfway down onto the manual shaft, and seat it in the shaft seal groove.

16. Install and tighten the TRS retaining screw to 45 inch lbs. (5 Nm).

17. Install the valve body assembly up into the transaxle. Engage the Park rod into the guide bracket.

18. Install and tighten the valve body mounting bolts to 105 inch lbs. (12 Nm).

19. Install a new transaxle oil filter and O-ring.

20. Before installing the transaxle oil pan, be sure to thoroughly clean the gasket mating surfaces of the transaxle case and transaxle oil pan, as well as the pan magnet. Then, place a light bead of RTV sealer on the oil pan gasket surface. Properly position the new pan gasket on top of the pan gasket mating surface.

21. Position the transaxle oil pan onto the transaxle case and install the pan mounting bolts. Tighten the oil pan mounting bolts to 165 inch lbs. (19 Nm).

22. Lower the vehicle.

23. Plug in the transaxle range sensor's electrical connector.

24. Install the manual valve lever and reconnect the gear shift cable.

25. Install the air cleaner assembly.

26. Pour 4 quarts of MOPAR® ATF PLUS Type 7176 or equivalent ATF into the transaxle filler tube.

27. Connect the negative battery cable.

28. Start the engine and allow it to idle for at least one minute. Apply both the parking and service brakes. Move the gear shift selector momentarily through each gear position, ending up in the **P** or **N** position.

29. Check the fluid level, while the engine is running and, if necessary, add sufficient fluid to bring to the correct level.

30. Road test the vehicle.

ADJUSTMENTS

The neutral safety switch and the transaxle range sensor are both non-adjustable components.

Back-up Light Switch

REMOVAL & INSTALLATION

1995 Cirrus and Stratus; 1995–96 Sebring Coupe and Avenger

▶ See Figure 38

➡On these vehicles, the back-up light switch is referred to as the transmission range switch, and is located on the front of the transaxle, just above the fluid pan.

1. Disconnect the negative battery cable.
2. Place a suitable drain pan under the transaxle.
3. Disengage the electrical connector from the switch.
4. Unscrew the switch from the transaxle case, letting the fluid drain into the pan.

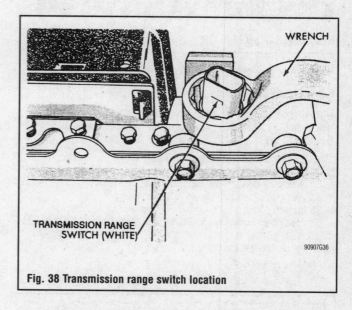

Fig. 38 Transmission range switch location

To install:

5. Position a new seal washer, then screw the switch into the transaxle case.

6. Attach the electrical connector to the switch.

7. Add fluid to the transaxle to bring it up to the proper level.

8. Connect the negative battery cable.

1996–98 Cirrus, Stratus, Sebring Convertible and Breeze; 1997–98 Sebring Coupe and Avenger

➡On these vehicles, neutral safety switch and back-up light switch functions are performed by a transaxle range sensor, which is located within the transaxle assembly. To remove the sensor, the transaxle fluid pan and valve body must be removed.

For transaxle range sensor removal and installation on 1996–98 Cirrus/Stratus/Sebring convertible/Breeze and 1997–98 Sebring coupe/Avenger models, refer to the Neutral Safety Switch procedure earlier in this section.

Automatic Transaxle Assembly

REMOVAL & INSTALLATION

▸ See Figures 39 thru 44

⁂ WARNING

If the vehicle is going to be rolled on its wheels while the transaxle is out of the vehicle, obtain 2 outer CV-joints to install to the hubs. If the vehicle is rolled without the proper torque applied to the front wheel bearings, the bearings will no longer be usable.

1. Disconnect both battery cables, negative side first.
2. On Sebring coupe/Avenger, remove the entire battery tray assembly.
3. If necessary, drain the coolant and remove the coolant return extension.
4. Remove the air cleaner/inlet duct assembly. Remove the upper bell housing bolts and water tube, where applicable.
5. Label and disengage all electrical connectors, cable linkages, hoses and mounting brackets required for removal of the transaxle assembly.
6. Remove the bolt securing the fluid dipstick tube to the transaxle. Remove the dipstick and tube from the transaxle.
7. Using engine support tool 7137 or C-4852, or equivalent, secure the engine assembly.
8. Remove the starter motor.
9. Drain the transaxle fluid into a suitable waste container.
10. Raise the vehicle and support it safely.
11. Remove the front tire and wheel assemblies.
12. Remove the splash shields.
13. Disconnect the exhaust pipe from the exhaust manifold.
14. Remove the halfshaft assemblies, as described earlier in this section. Position a drain pan under the transaxle where the shafts enter the differential or extension housing.
15. Unbolt the center bearing and remove the intermediate axle from the transaxle, if equipped.
16. Disconnect and tag the oil cooler lines at the transaxle.
17. If equipped with a distributorless Direct Ignition System (DIS), disconnect the harness connector and remove the crankshaft position sensor from the transaxle bell housing.

➡ Only 4-cylinder engines are equipped with DIS; the 6-cylinder engines utilize a distributor.

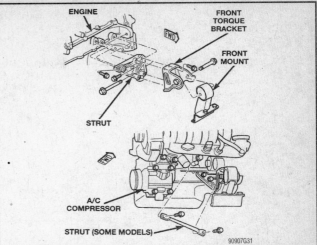

Fig. 40 Exploded view of the front engine mounts—Cirrus, Stratus, Sebring convertible and Breeze

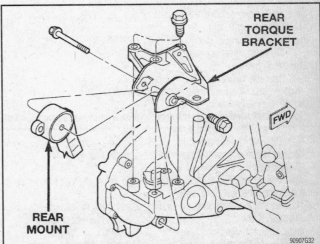

Fig. 41 Exploded view of the rear engine mounts—Cirrus, Stratus, Sebring convertible and Breeze

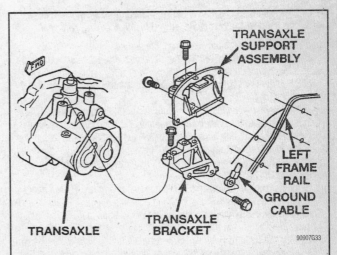

Fig. 42 Exploded view of the left side transaxle mounting components—Cirrus, Stratus, Sebring convertible and Breeze

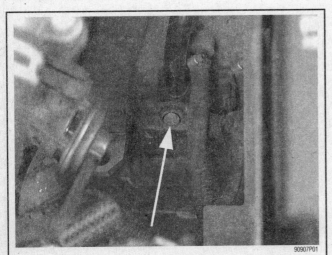

Fig. 39 Location of the transaxle solenoid assembly 8-way connector and retaining bolt

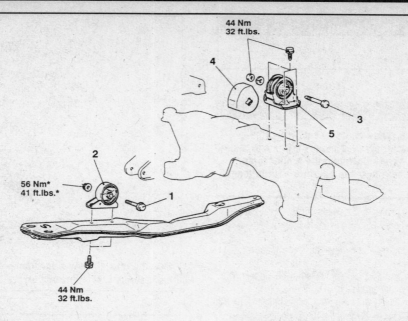

44 Nm
32 ft.lbs.

4

3

5

2

56 Nm*
41 ft.lbs.*

1

44 Nm
32 ft.lbs.

1. Front roll stopper bracket mounting bolt
2. Front roll stopper bracket assembly
3. Rear roll stopper bracket mounting bolt
4. Heat protector <Vehicles for California>
5. Rear roll stopper bracket assembly

Caution
* : Indicates parts which should be temporarily tightened, and then fully tightened with the vehicle in the unladen condition.

90907G34

Fig. 43 Exploded view of the front and rear engine mounts (roll stoppers)—Sebring coupe and Avenger

18. Remove the front and rear engine/transaxle mounts.

19. Remove the centermember.

20. Remove the torque converter inspection cover, then matchmark the torque converter to the flexplate.

21. Remove the bolts holding the flexplate to the torque converter with a box wrench. Rotate the crankshaft to bring the bolts into position for removal, one at a time.

22. Support the transaxle using a transaxle jack (at the side of the case, NOT at the pan).

23. Remove the lower bell housing bolts.

24. Remove the transaxle mount bolts.

➡**The torque converter can become disengaged from the transaxle. Keep the front of the transaxle slightly raised during removal.**

25. Carefully pry the transaxle from the engine.

26. Slide the transaxle rearward until dowels disengage from the mating holes in the transaxle case.

27. Pull the transaxle completely away from the engine and remove it from the vehicle.

28. To prepare the vehicle for rolling, secure the engine with a suitable support or reinstall the front engine mount to the engine. Then, reinstall the ball joints to the steering knuckle and install the retaining bolt. Install the outer CV-joints to the hubs, then install the washers and tighten the axle nuts to 180 ft. lbs. (244 Nm). The vehicle may now be safely rolled.

To install:

29. Installation is the reverse of the removal procedure. Please note the following important steps.

30. Tighten the transaxle-to-engine mounting bolts to 70 ft. lbs. (95 Nm).

31. Tighten the torque converter-to-flexplate bolts to 55 ft. lbs. (74 Nm).

32. On Sebring coupe and Avenger models, tighten the centermember front mounting bolts to 65 ft. lbs. (88 Nm) and rear bolts to 51–58 ft. lbs. (69–78 Nm).

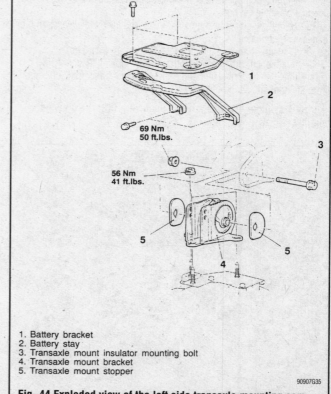

1

2

69 Nm
50 ft.lbs.

3

56 Nm
41 ft.lbs.

5

4

5

1. Battery bracket
2. Battery stay
3. Transaxle mount insulator mounting bolt
4. Transaxle mount bracket
5. Transaxle mount stopper

90907G35

Fig. 44 Exploded view of the left side transaxle mounting components—Sebring coupe and Avenger

33. Tighten the torque converter inspection cover mounting bolts to 108 inch lbs. (12 Nm).

34. On Cirrus, Stratus, Sebring convertible and Breeze models, tighten the engine mounts to the following specifications:

- Front mount-to-lower radiator support bolts—45 ft. lbs. (61 Nm)
- Rear mount-to-front suspension crossmember—45 ft. lbs. (61 Nm)
- Rear mount through-bolt—45 ft. lbs. (61 Nm)
- Left engine mount-to-frame rail—24 ft. lbs. (33 Nm)

35. On Sebring coupe and Avenger models, tighten the engine mounts (roll stoppers) to the following specifications:

- Lightly tighten the front engine roll stopper through-bolt. Once the full weight of the engine is on the mounts, tighten the bolt to 42 ft. lbs. (56 Nm).
- Tighten the rear engine roll stopper through-bolt to 32 ft. lbs. (44 Nm).
- Tighten the left transaxle mount fasteners to 41 ft. lbs. (56 Nm).
- Tighten the left transaxle mount through-bolt to 50 ft. lbs. (69 Nm).

36. Tighten the shifter lever retaining nut to 14 ft. lbs. (19 Nm).

37. Check to make sure that all wiring harness plugs, cable linkages and hoses have been properly connected during installation.

38. Adjust the gear shift and throttle cables.

39. Reconnect the negative battery cable.

40. Refill the transaxle with the suitable type and amount of automatic transaxle fluid. For more information, refer to Section 1 of this manual.

41. Perform the transaxle quick-learn procedure, as outlined in the following adjustments.

42. Check the transaxle for proper operation. Make sure the car's back-up lights and speedometer are working properly.

ADJUSTMENTS

Gear Shift Cable

CIRRUS, STRATUS, SEBRING CONVERTIBLE AND BREEZE

Normal operation of the Park/Neutral position switch provides a quick check to confirm proper linkage adjustment.

Move the gear selector lever slowly forward until it clicks into the Park position. The starter should operate when the ignition switch is turned to the **START** position.

After checking the Park position, move the selector slowly toward the Neutral position, until the lever drops into the **N** position. If the starter will also operate at this point, the gear shift linkage is properly adjusted. If the starter fails to operate in either position, linkage adjustment is necessary, as follows:

1. Set the parking brake.
2. Remove the gear shift knob setscrew and knob.
3. Remove the gear shift selector bezel and lamp wiring.
4. Install the gear shift knob.
5. Place the gear shift lever in the Park position.
6. Loosen the cable adjuster nut at the shifter assembly.
7. Move the gear shift lever on the transaxle case to the Park position.
8. Verify that both the shift lever and transaxle are in the Park position.
9. Tighten the cable adjuster nut at the shifter assembly. The gear shift linkage should now be correctly adjusted.
10. Check adjustment as follows:

a. Detent position for Neutral and Drive should be within the limits of the hand lever gate stops.

b. Key start must occur only when the shift lever is in the Park or Neutral position.

SEBRING COUPE AND AVENGER

▶ See Figure 45

Normal operation of the Park/Neutral position switch provides a quick check to confirm proper linkage adjustment.

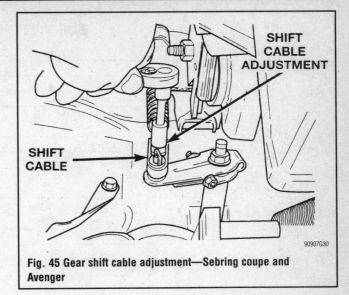

Fig. 45 Gear shift cable adjustment—Sebring coupe and Avenger

Move the gear selector lever slowly forward until it clicks into the Park position. The starter should operate.

After checking the Park position, move the selector slowly toward the Neutral position, until the lever drops into the **N** position. If the starter will operate also at this point, the gear shift linkage is properly adjusted. If the starter fails to operated in either position, linkage adjustment is necessary, as follows:

1. Park the vehicle on level ground and set the parking brake.
2. Place the gear shift lever in the Park (**P**) position and remove the key.
3. Loosen the cable adjustment screw at the transaxle operating lever.
4. Move the transaxle operating lever fully forward to the Park (**P**) position.
5. Release the parking brake, then rock the vehicle to assure that it is locked in Park. Reset the parking brake.
6. Tighten the cable adjustment screw to 70 inch lbs. (8 Nm). The gear shift cable should now be correctly adjusted.

Transaxle Quick-Learn Procedure

Whenever the transaxle assembly, transaxle control module, solenoid pack, valve body or seals are replaced, the transaxle quick-learn procedure must be performed with the use of a DRB, or equivalent scan tool. To perform this procedure, the following conditions must all be met:

- Brakes applied
- Engine speed over 500 rpm
- Throttle angle (TPS) must be less than 3°
- Shift lever position must stay until commanded to shift into overdrive
- Shift lever position must remain in overdrive after the "Shift To Overdrive" command, until the scan tool indicates completion
- Oil temperature must be above 605°F (320°C) and below 2005°F (1105°C).

1. Plug the scan tool into the data link connector, which is located under the instrument panel.
2. Go to the "Transmission" screen.
3. Then, go to the "Miscellaneous" screen.
4. Select the Quick-Learn Procedure. Follow the scan tool's instructions to correctly perform this procedure.

Halfshafts

For halfshaft removal, installation and overhaul, refer to the Halfshaft procedures in the manual transaxle portion of this section.

TORQUE SPECIFICATIONS

System	Component	Ft. Lbs.	Nm
MANUAL TRANSAXLE			
	Manual Transaxle Assembly		
	Transaxle-to-engine bolts	70	95
	Transaxle bellhousing cover bolts	7	9
	Centermember front bolts	65	88
	Centermember rear bolts	54	73
	Transaxle mount bracket nuts	32	43
	Transaxle mount through-bolt	51	69
HALFSHAFTS			
	Control arm-to-steering knuckle self-locking nuts	43-52	59-71
	Damper fork lower through-bolt/nut	65	88
	Damper fork upper pinch bolt	76	103
	Tie rod end-to-steering knuckle nut	17-25	24-33
	Sway bar link-to-damper fork nut	29	39
	Axle nut	145-188	200-260
CLUTCH			
	Driven Disc and Pressure Plate		
	Clutch-to-driveplate (flywheel) bolts	55	75
	Clutch Master Cylinder		
	Master cylinder nuts	10	13
	Clutch Slave Cylinder		
	Slave cylinder-to-transaxle bolts	13	18
	Hydraulic line fitting	11	15
AUTOMATIC TRANSAXLE			
	Transaxle range sensor retaining screw	45 inch lbs.	5
	Valve body mounting bolts	105 inch lbs.	12
	Transaxle oil pan mounting bolts	165 inch lbs.	19
	Torque converter inspection cover mounting bolts	9	12
	Shifter lever retaining nut	14	19
	Automatic Transaxle Assembly		
	Transaxle-to-engine mounting bolts	70	95
	Torque converter-to-flexplate bolts	55	74
	Centermember (Sebring coupe/Avenger)		
	Front mounting bolts	65	88
	Rear mounting bolts	51-58	69-78
	Engine mounts (Cirrus/Stratus/Sebring Conv./Breeze)		
	Front mount-to-lower radiator support bolts	45	61
	Rear mount-to-front suspension crossmember fasteners	45	61
	Rear mount through-bolt	45	61
	Left engine mount-to-frame rail fasteners	24	33
	Engine mounts (Sebring Coupe/Avenger)		
	Front engine roll stopper through-bolt	42	56
	Rear engine roll stopper through-bolt	32	44
	Left transaxle mount fasteners	42	56
	Left ransaxle mount through-bolt	50	69
	Gearshift cable (Sebring Coupe/Avenger)		
	Cable adjustment screw	70 inch lbs.	8

90907C01

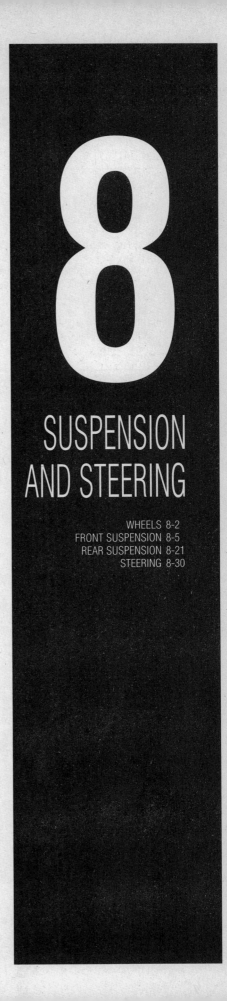

8

SUSPENSION AND STEERING

WHEELS

Wheels

REMOVAL & INSTALLATION

♦ **See Figures 1 thru 6**

1. Park the vehicle on a level surface.

2. Remove the jack, tire iron and, if necessary, the spare tire from their storage compartments.

3. Check the owner's manual or refer to Section 1 of this manual for the jacking points on your vehicle. Then, place the jack in the proper position.

4. If equipped with lug nut trim caps, remove them by either unscrewing or pulling them off the lug nuts, as appropriate. Consult the owner's manual, if necessary.

5. If equipped with a wheel cover or hub cap, insert the tapered or small end of the tire iron in the groove and pry off the cover.

6. Apply the parking brake and block the diagonally opposite wheel with a wheel chock or two.

➡Wheel chocks may be purchased at your local auto parts store, or a block of wood cut into wedges may be used. If possible, keep one or two of the chocks in your tire storage compartment, in case any of the tires has to be removed on the side of the road.

7. If equipped with an automatic transaxle, place the selector lever in **P** or Park; with a manual transaxle, place the shifter in Reverse.

8. With the tires still on the ground, use the tire iron/wrench to break the lug nuts loose.

➡If a nut is stuck, never use heat to loosen it or damage to the wheel and bearings may occur. If the nuts are seized, one or two heavy hammer blows directly on the end of the bolt usually loosens the rust. Be careful, as continued pounding will likely damage the brake drum or rotor.

9. Using the jack, raise the vehicle until the tire is clear of the ground. Support the vehicle safely using jackstands.

10. Remove the lug nuts, then remove the tire and wheel assembly.

Fig. 1 Always make sure that the vehicle is parked on a level surface with the emergency brake applied when utilizing the emergency jack

Fig. 3 When utilizing the vehicle's emergency jack, always make sure it is properly positioned under the pointed location at each corner pinch weld

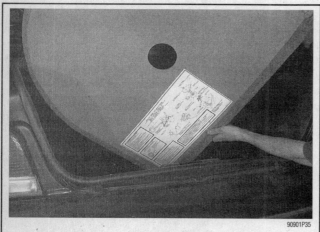

Fig. 2 Jacking instructions for the manufacturer-supplied jack, as well as the contact points, are explained and illustrated in the owner's manual and inside the spare tire cover

Fig. 4 To avoid scuffing or distorting the wheel cover, use the small prying end of the lug wrench for removal

To install:

11.   Make sure the wheel and hub mating surfaces, as well as the wheel lug studs, are clean and free of all foreign material. Always remove rust from the wheel mounting surface and the brake rotor or drum. Failure to do so may cause the lug nuts to loosen in service.

12.   Install the tire and wheel assembly and hand-tighten the lug nuts.

13.   Using the tire wrench, tighten all the lug nuts, in a crisscross pattern, until they are snug.

14.   Raise the vehicle and withdraw the jackstand, then lower the vehicle.

15.   Using a torque wrench, tighten the lug nuts in a crisscross pattern to 95 ft. lbs. (129 Nm). Check your owner's manual or refer to Section 1 of this manual for the proper tightening sequence.

✳✳ WARNING

Do not overtighten the lug nuts, as this may cause the wheel studs to stretch or the brake disc (rotor) to warp.

16.   If so equipped, install the wheel cover or hub cap. Make sure the valve stem protrudes through the proper opening before tapping the wheel cover into position.

Fig. 5 With the vehicle still on the ground, break the lug nuts loose using the wrench end of the tire iron

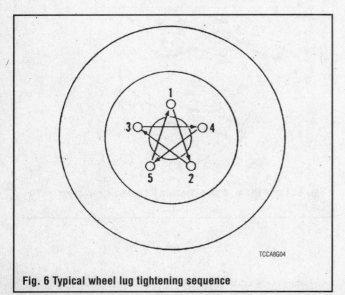

Fig. 6 Typical wheel lug tightening sequence

17.   If equipped, install the lug nut trim caps by pushing them or screwing them on, as applicable.

18.   Remove the jack from under the vehicle, and place the jack and tire iron/wrench in their storage compartments. Remove the wheel chock(s).

19.   If you have removed a flat or damaged tire, place it in the storage compartment of the vehicle and take it to your local repair station to have it fixed or replaced as soon as possible.

INSPECTION

Inspect the tires for lacerations, puncture marks, nails and other sharp objects. Repair or replace as necessary. Also check the tires for treadwear and air pressure as outlined in Check the wheel assemblies for dents, cracks, rust and metal fatigue. Repair or replace as necessary.

Wheel Lug Studs

REPLACEMENT

With Disc Brakes

◗ **See Figures 7 and 8**

1.   Raise and support the appropriate end of the vehicle safely using jackstands, then remove the wheel.

2.   Remove the brake pads and caliper. Support the caliper aside using wire or a coat hanger. For details, please refer to Section 9 of this manual.

3.   Remove the brake rotor. If equipped with rear disc brakes, remove the parking brake shoe assembly.

4.   Install a lug nut on the end of the stud to be removed from the hub/bearing assembly. Turn the hub so that the stud being removed is lined up with the notch cast into the front of the steering knuckle. Install special stud removal tool C-4150, or equivalent, on the hub/bearing flange and wheel stud.

5.   Tighten down on the special tool; this will push the stud out from behind the hub/bearing flange.

To install:

6.   Clean the stud hole with a wire brush.

7.   Install the new lug stud through the hole in the hub/bearing flange, then position about 4 flat washers over the stud and thread the lug nut. Hold the hub/rotor while tightening the lug nut, and the stud should be drawn into position. MAKE SURE THE STUD IS FULLY SEATED, then remove the lug nut and washers.

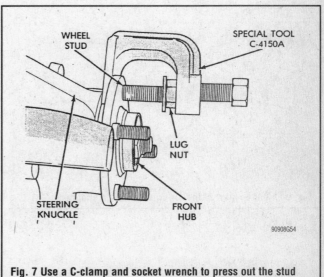

Fig. 7 Use a C-clamp and socket wrench to press out the stud

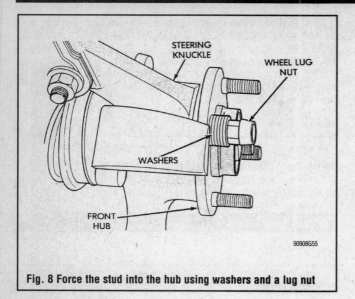

Fig. 8 Force the stud into the hub using washers and a lug nut

8. Install the brake rotor. If equipped with rear disc brakes, install the parking brake shoe assembly.

9. Install the brake caliper and pads.

10. Install the wheel, then remove the jackstands and carefully lower the vehicle.

11. Tighten the lug nuts to the proper torque.

With Drum Brakes

▶ **See Figures 9, 10 and 11**

1. Raise the vehicle and safely support it with jackstands, then remove the wheel.

2. Remove the brake drum.

3. If necessary to provide clearance, remove the brake shoes, as outlined in Section 9 of this manual.

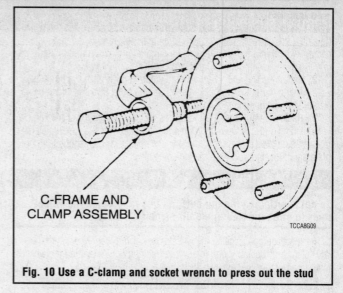

Fig. 10 Use a C-clamp and socket wrench to press out the stud

4. Using a large C-clamp and socket, press the stud from the axle flange.

5. Coat the serrated part of the stud with liquid soap and place it into the hole.

To install:

6. Position about 4 flat washers over the stud and thread the lug nut. Hold the flange while tightening the lug nut, and the stud should be drawn into position. MAKE SURE THE STUD IS FULLY SEATED, then remove the lug nut and washers.

7. If applicable, install the brake shoes.

8. Install the brake drum.

9. Install the wheel, then remove the jackstands and carefully lower the vehicle.

10. Tighten the lug nuts to the proper torque.

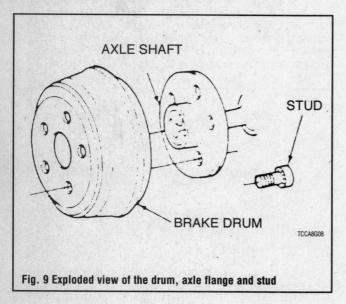

Fig. 9 Exploded view of the drum, axle flange and stud

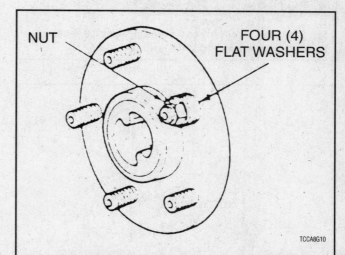

Fig. 11 Force the stud onto the axle flange using washers and a lug nut

FRONT SUSPENSION

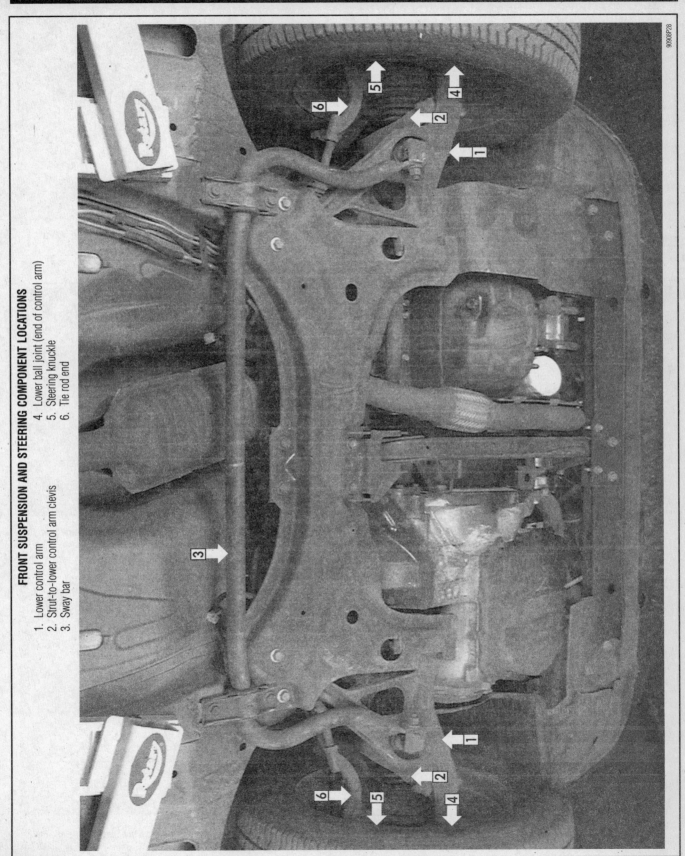

FRONT SUSPENSION AND STEERING COMPONENT LOCATIONS

1. Lower control arm
2. Strut-to-lower control arm clevis
3. Sway bar
4. Lower ball joint (end of control arm)
5. Steering knuckle
6. Tie rod end

Struts

REMOVAL & INSTALLATION

Cirrus, Stratus, Sebring Convertible and Breeze

▶ **See Figures 12 thru 23**

1. Disconnect the negative battery cable.
2. Raise and safely support the vehicle.
3. Remove the wheel and tire assembly.
4. If equipped with an Anti-lock Brake System (ABS), remove the wheel speed sensor cable routing bracket from the steering knuckle.
5. Remove the cotter pin and castle nut from the upper ball joint stud, then, using a puller tool, separate the upper control arm ball stud from the steering knuckle. Pull the steering knuckle out and position it rearward in the front wheel opening.
6. Remove the pinch bolt attaching the strut to the strut clevis.
7. Remove the through-bolt attaching the clevis to the lower control arm.
8. Tap the clevis with a brass drift to remove from the strut.

Fig. 14 Using a ball joint separator tool, separate the upper control arm ball joint from the steering knuckle

Fig. 12 Remove the upper ball joint stud cotter pin

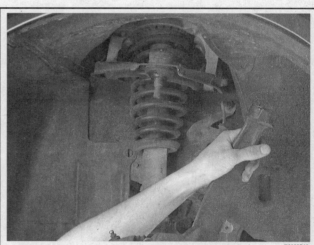

Fig. 15 After separating the upper control arm ball joint from the steering knuckle, position the knuckle rearward

Fig. 13 Loosen the upper control arm ball joint stud castle nut

Fig. 16 Loosen, then remove the clevis bracket-to-strut pinch bolt

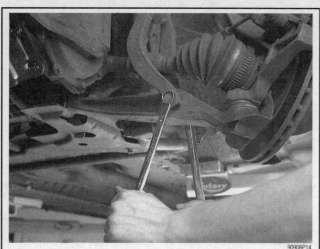

Fig. 17 Loosen the clevis bracket-to-lower control arm through-bolt . . .

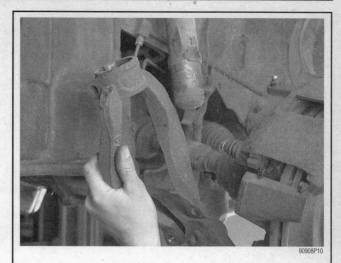

Fig. 20 Remove the clevis bracket from the vehicle

Fig. 18 . . . then pull the through-bolt out

Fig. 21 Remove the 4 strut mounting bracket-to-strut tower bolts

Fig. 19 Using a hammer and a drift, separate the clevis bracket from the strut

9. Remove the 4 bolts attaching the strut to the strut tower.
10. Remove the strut and upper control arm as an assembly.

To install:

11. Install the strut assembly into the strut tower.
12. Install the 4 upper strut mounting bolts.
13. Tighten the bolts to 68 ft. lbs. (90 Nm).
14. Install the clevis onto the strut with a brass drift until the clevis is fully seated against the locating tab.
15. Install the clevis pin bolt.
16. Install the clevis onto the lower control arm.
17. Install the clevis through-bolt.
18. Tighten the clevis-to-strut pin bolt to 70 ft. lbs. (95 Nm).
19. Install the upper control arm ball joint into the steering knuckle. Install the ball stud castle nut and tighten to 45 ft. lbs. (62 Nm). Install a new cotter pin.
20. If equipped with ABS, install the wheel speed sensor cable routing bracket to the steering knuckle.
21. Lower the vehicle onto a jackstand supporting the lower control arm.
22. Tighten the clevis-to-lower control arm mounting bolt to 68 ft. lbs. (90 Nm).
23. Install the wheel and tire assembly.

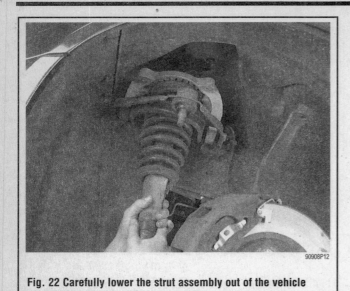

Fig. 22 Carefully lower the strut assembly out of the vehicle

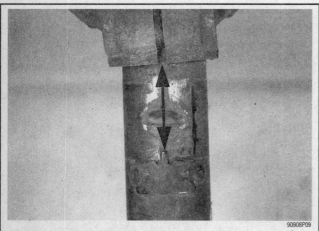

Fig. 23 When installing the clevis bracket (damper fork) onto the strut assembly, be sure that the locating tab on the strut fits into the slot in the bracket

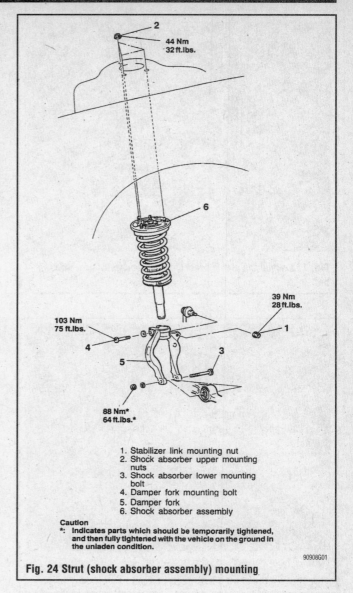

1. Stabilizer link mounting nut
2. Shock absorber upper mounting nuts
3. Shock absorber lower mounting bolt
4. Damper fork mounting bolt
5. Damper fork
6. Shock absorber assembly

Caution
*: Indicates parts which should be temporarily tightened, and then fully tightened with the vehicle on the ground in the unladen condition.

90908G01

Fig. 24 Strut (shock absorber assembly) mounting

24. Remove the jackstand and lower the vehicle.
25. Connect the negative battery cable.

Sebring Coupe and Avenger

♦ See Figure 24

1. Disconnect the negative battery cable.
2. Raise and safely support the vehicle.
3. Remove the appropriate wheel assembly.
4. Disconnect the sway bar link from the damper fork.
5. Remove the damper fork lower through-bolt and upper pinch bolt. Remove the damper fork assembly.
6. Remove the strut upper nuts and remove the strut assembly from the vehicle. Do NOT remove the large center nut.

To install:

7. Position the strut to the vehicle and tighten the upper mounting nuts to 32 ft. lbs. (44 Nm).
8. Align the strut to the damper fork and install the damper fork. Tighten the lower through-bolt/nut to 65 ft. lbs. (88 Nm) and the upper pinch bolt to 76 ft. lbs. (103 Nm).
9. Connect the sway bar link to the damper fork and tighten the link nut to 29 ft. lbs. (39 Nm).
10. Install the wheel and tire assembly.

11. Lower the vehicle.
12. Connect the negative battery cable.
13. Have the front end aligned by a trained technician at a properly equipped facility.

OVERHAUL

♦ See Figures 25 thru 31

➡Do not clamp the strut in a bench vise by the body of the strut. Instead, the clevis bracket (or damper fork) must be installed on the strut and then clamped in the vise using the bracket.

1. Install the clevis bracket (damper fork) onto the strut body, then secure in a bench vise at the bracket.

➡Due to the fact that the front strut upper mounting bracket also includes the upper control arm for the Cirrus, Stratus, Sebring convertible and Breeze models, it is important to use Spring Compressor Tool 7521-A, or an equivalent tool, equipped with special top and bottom attachment shoes.

2. Install a coil spring compressor tool so that it captures the full top and bottom coils of the spring. Tighten the compressor and slowly compress the spring. Make certain the compressor is properly engaged before tightening.

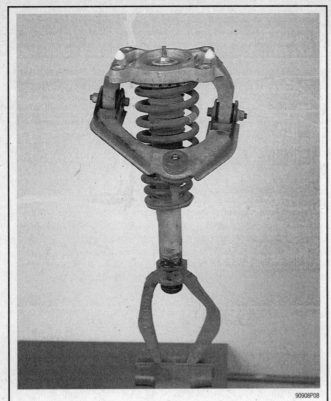

Fig. 25 Mount the strut assembly in a vise with the clevis bracket (damper fork) installed on the bottom of the strut assembly

3. After tension has been removed from the strut assembly and strut plate, remove the piston rod nut and washer from the top of the strut assembly.

4. If the spring is to be replaced, slowly release the tension on the spring compressor. Allow the spring to expand fully. If only the strut cartridge is being replaced, the spring may remain in the compressor assembly.

5. By hand, remove any bushings, washers, shields or other components below the mounting bracket/bearing plate. Take notice of each component's location for proper reassembly. Examine the condition of these components, and replace any if necessary.

Fig. 26 After securing the strut assembly in a vise, install a spring compressor tool onto the coil spring and begin to slowly compress the coil

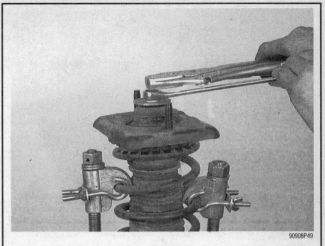

Fig. 27 After tension has been removed from the strut assembly and mounting plate, loosen the piston rod nut and washer . . .

Fig. 28 . . . then remove the piston rod nut and washer from the strut assembly

Fig. 29 Remove the strut mounting bracket from the top of the strut assembly

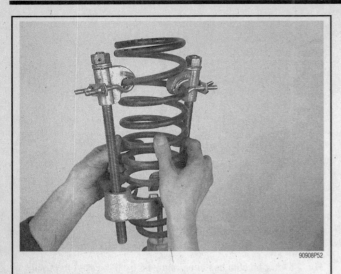

Fig. 30 Lift the compressed spring off of the strut assembly

To install:

6. Install the lower insulator, strut bumper and uncompressed spring. Install the upper spring insulator, strut shield, mount and washer.

7. Install or align the spring compressor. Make certain the spring is correctly positioned relative to the upper and lower insulator rings. Smoothly compress the spring.

8. Install the washer and piston rod nut. Tighten the nut to 18 ft. lbs. (25 Nm) on Sebring coupe/Avenger and 40 ft. lbs. (55 Nm) on Cirrus/Stratus/Sebring convertible/Breeze. Install the dust cap.

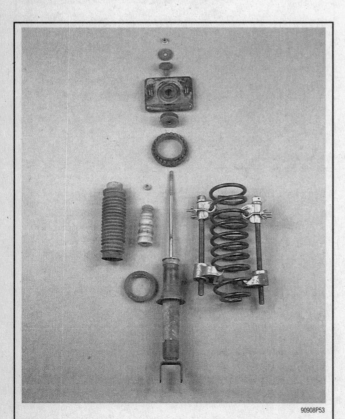

Fig. 31 Remove any bushings, washers, shields or other components below the mounting bracket. Note each component's location for proper reassembly

9. Carefully release the spring compressor, watching the spring position as it seats. When the spring is properly seated, release/remove the compressor tools.

10. Reinstall the strut assembly.

Upper Ball Joint

INSPECTION

Inspect the ball joint dust cover for cracks and damage by pushing on it with your finger. If the dust cover is cracked or damaged, the component must be replaced, or damage to the ball joint will result.

Except Sebring Coupe and Avenger

The front suspension ball joints operate with no free-play. The ball joints are replaceable ONLY as an assembly. Do not attempt any type of repair on the ball joint assembly. To check the ball joint with the weight of the vehicle resting on its tires, grasp the grease fitting and, without using any tools, attempt to move the grease fitting. If the ball joint is worn, the grease fitting will move easily. If movement is noted, replacement of the ball joint is recommended.

Sebring Coupe and Avenger

▶ **See Figure 32**

1. Ball joint breakaway torque can be checked using the following procedure.

   a. An adapter (MB 990326 or equivalent) is available that fits onto the ball joint stud and adapts to an inch pound torque wrench. If this tool is not available, a shop-made substitute can be fabricated.

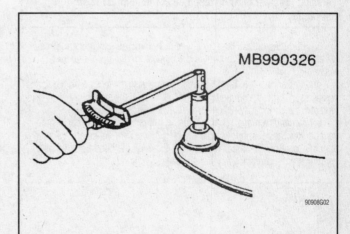

Fig. 32 Inspecting the ball joint breakaway torque—lower control arm and ball joint shown; similar procedure for upper ball joint

   b. Turn the ball joint stud with the torque wrench. The factory standard for breakaway torque is 3–13 inch lbs. (0.3–1.5 Nm).

   c. If the ball joint stud is out of specification (turns too easily or is too stiff), the upper control arm requires replacement.

REMOVAL & INSTALLATION

The upper ball joint is an integral part of the upper control arm assembly, and cannot be serviced separately. A worn or damaged ball joint requires replacement of the upper control arm assembly.

Lower Ball Joint

INSPECTION

Inspect the ball joint dust cover for cracks and damage by pushing on it with with your finger. If the dust cover is cracked or damaged, the component must be replaced, or damage to the ball joint will result.

1. Raise and support the vehicle safely.
2. Install a dial indicator on the vehicle, so that it contacts the top surface of the steering knuckle near the lower ball joint stud castle nut.
3. Firmly grasp the tire at the top and bottom. Push the tire up and down firmly.
4. Note the amount of up and down movement of the steering knuckle, as recorded on the dial indicator.
5. Replace the lower control arm if the movement in the lower control arm exceeds 0.059 inch (1.5mm).

Sebring Coupe and Avenger

▶ See Figure 32

1. Ball joint breakaway torque can be checked using the following procedure.

    a. An adapter (MB 990326) is available that fits onto the ball joint stud and adapts to an inch pound torque wrench. If this tool is not available, a shop-made substitute can be fabricated.

    b. Install a nut onto the ball joint stud.

    c. Turn the ball joint stud with the torque wrench. On the compression lower arm ball joint, the factory standard for breakaway torque is 4–22 inch lbs. (0.5–2.5 Nm).

    d. On the lateral lower arm ball joint, the factory standard for breakaway torque is 13 inch lbs. (1.5 Nm).

    e. If either ball joint stud is out of specification (turns too easily or is too stiff), the control arm requires replacement.

REMOVAL & INSTALLATION

On all vehicles, the lower ball joint cannot be serviced separately. Ball joints and lower arms are removed and replaced as an assembly. A front end alignment is required after these procedures.

Sway (Stabilizer) Bar

REMOVAL & INSTALLATION

Cirrus, Stratus, Sebring Convertible and Avenger

▶ See Figures 33 and 34

1. Disconnect the negative battery cable.
2. Raise and safely support the vehicle.
3. Remove the nuts and sway bar attaching link assemblies from the front lower control arms. When removing the attaching link nut, keep the stud from turning by installing an Allen wrench in the end of the stud.
4. Remove the 4 bolts attaching the sway bar bushing retainers to the crossmember and body.
5. Remove the sway bar bushings, bushing retainers, sway bar and attaching links from the vehicle as an assembly.

To install:

6. Inspect for broken or distorted sway bar bushings, bushing retainers and attaching links. If sway bar-to-front crossmember bushing replacement is required, use the following procedure for each bushing:

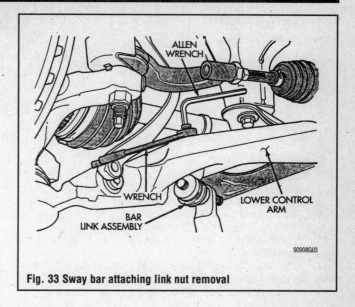

Fig. 33 Sway bar attaching link nut removal

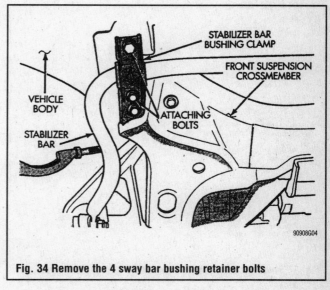

Fig. 34 Remove the 4 sway bar bushing retainer bolts

    a. Bend back the 4 crimp locations on the sway bar bushing retainer.

    b. Separate the sway bar bushing retainer.

    c. Open the slit and peel the bushing off the sway bar.

    d. Install the new sway bar bushings on the bar. The bushings must be installed on the sway bar so that the slit in the bushing faces the front of the vehicle when the sway bar is installed.

    e. Install new bushing retainers on the sway bar.

7. Install the sway bar and bushings as an assembly into the vehicle.

8. Align the sway bar attaching link and bushing assemblies with the attaching link mounting holes in the lower control arms. Install the attaching links into the control arms. Tighten the attaching link nuts to 78 ft. lbs. (105 Nm).

9. Install the 4 sway bar retainer bushing bolts into the crossmember and tighten the bolts to 45 ft. lbs. (61 Nm).

10. Lower the vehicle and connect the negative battery cable.

Sebring Coupe and Avenger

▶ **See Figures 35 and 36**

1. Disconnect the negative battery cable.
2. Raise and safely support the vehicle.
3. Disconnect the stabilizer bar links by removing the self-locking nuts.
4. Remove the stabilizer bar mounting brackets and bushings.
5. Remove the stabilizer bar from the vehicle.
6. Inspect all components for wear or damage, and replace parts as needed.

To install:

7. Install the stabilizer bar into the vehicle.
8. Loosely install the stabilizer bar brackets on the vehicle.
9. Align the side locating markings on the stabilizer bar so that the marking on each side of the bar extends approximately ⅜ inch (0.40 inch or 10mm) from the inner edge of each mounting bracket.
10. With the stabilizer bar properly aligned, tighten the mounting bracket bolts to 28 ft. lbs. (39 Nm).
11. Connect the links to the damper fork and the stabilizer bar. Tighten the locking nuts to 28 ft. lbs. (38 Nm).
12. Lower the vehicle and connect the negative battery cable.

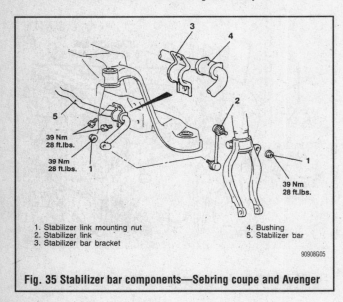

1. Stabilizer link mounting nut
2. Stabilizer link
3. Stabilizer bar bracket
4. Bushing
5. Stabilizer bar

90908G05

Fig. 35 Stabilizer bar components—Sebring coupe and Avenger

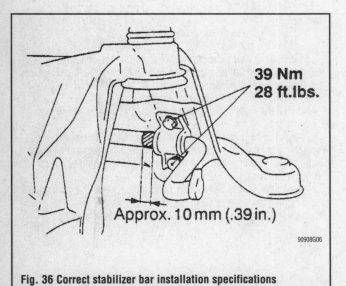

39 Nm
28 ft.lbs.

Approx. 10 mm (.39 in.)

90908G06

Fig. 36 Correct stabilizer bar installation specifications

Upper Control Arm

REMOVAL & INSTALLATION

Cirrus, Stratus, Sebring Convertible and Breeze

▶ **See Figure 37**

1. Disconnect the negative battery cable.
2. Remove the strut assembly.
3. Disassemble the strut assembly as outlined in the "Overhaul" portion of the strut removal procedure, earlier in this section.
4. Once the upper control arm/strut mounting bracket is separated from the strut assembly, remove the 2 bolts attaching the control arm to the bracket.
5. Remove the upper control arm from the mounting bracket.

To install:

6. Install the upper control arm to the mounting bracket.

➥ **The upper control arm bolts MUST be installed so that the bolt heads are facing the coil spring once the mounting bracket is installed on the strut.**

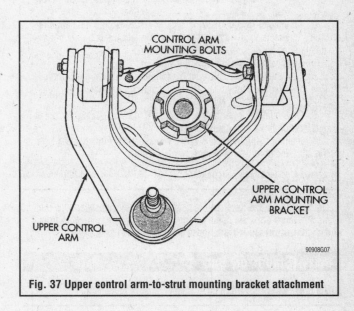

CONTROL ARM
MOUNTING BOLTS

UPPER CONTROL
ARM MOUNTING
BRACKET

UPPER CONTROL
ARM

90908G07

Fig. 37 Upper control arm-to-strut mounting bracket attachment

7. Install the 2 bolts attaching the control arm to the mounting bracket. Tighten the bolts to 67 ft. lbs. (90 Nm).

Sebring Coupe and Avenger

▶ **See Figure 38**

1. Disconnect the negative battery cable.
2. Raise and safely support the vehicle.
3. Remove the appropriate wheel.
4. Using ball joint separator tool MB991113 or equivalent, disconnect the upper ball joint stud from the steering knuckle.
5. Inspect the ball joint, as outlined in earlier in this section.
6. Inside the engine compartment, at the strut tower, locate the upper control arm mounting nuts. Remove the nuts and separate the upper arm shafts from the strut tower.
7. Remove the control arm assembly.

To install:

8. Align the upper control arm shafts to the strut tower and secure with the mounting nuts. Tighten the mounting nuts to 62 ft. lbs. (86 Nm).
9. Connect the ball joint to the knuckle and tighten the locking nut to 20 ft. lbs. (28 Nm).

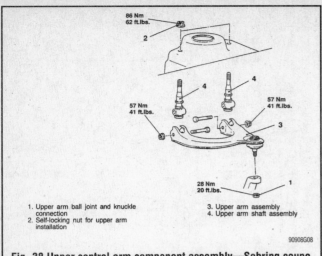

Fig. 38 Upper control arm component assembly—Sebring coupe and Avenger

1. Upper arm ball joint and knuckle connection
2. Self-locking nut for upper arm installation
3. Upper arm assembly
4. Upper arm shaft assembly

Fig. 40 Pull out the lower ball joint cotter pin

10. Install the wheel and lower the vehicle.
11. Connect the negative battery cable.
12. Check the wheel alignment, and adjust if necessary.

CONTROL ARM BUSHING REPLACEMENT

➡**Only the Cirrus, Stratus, Sebring Convertible and Breeze models utilize upper control arm bushings.**

The upper control arm bushings are not serviceable. If they are worn out or damaged, the control arm mounting bracket must be replaced.

Lower Control Arm

REMOVAL & INSTALLATION

Cirrus, Stratus, Sebring Convertible and Breeze

◗ See Figures 39 thru 45

1. Disconnect the negative battery cable.
2. Raise and safely support the vehicle.
3. Remove the front wheels and tires.

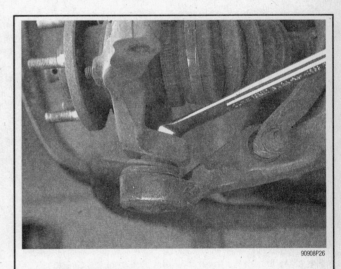

Fig. 41 Loosen the castle nut . . .

Fig. 39 If equipped with 15 inch wheels, remove the ball joint heat shield

Fig. 42 . . . then remove it from the ball stud

4. If equipped with 15 in. wheels, the heat shield will need to be removed before the lower control arm can be separated from the steering knuckle.

5. Remove the cotter pin and castle nut from the lower ball joint stud.

6. Remove the sway bar attaching bolts from both control arms.

7. Disconnect the strut clevis from the lower control arm.

8. Loosen the sway bar-to-crossmember attaching bolts and rotate the sway bar away from the control arm.

9. Using a hammer, strike the steering knuckle boss to separate the lower control arm from the knuckle.

10. Remove the 2 control arm attaching bolts (first the one at the rear, and then the one at the front of the control arm).

11. Remove the front of the control arm from the front crossmember, then remove the rear of the control arm. Keep the control arm as level as possible, so that the rear bushing will not bind on the crossmember.

To install:

12. Install the control arm into the vehicle, beginning with the rear portion.

13. Install the 2 control arm attaching bolts and nuts.

➡**Do not tighten the front attaching bolt at this time.**

14. Tighten the rear control arm attaching bolt to 85 ft. lbs. (115 Nm).

Fig. 43 To loosen the lower ball joint stud from the steering knuckle, strike the steering knuckle boss with a hammer

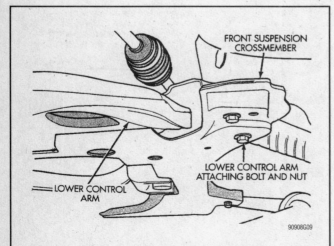

Fig. 44 Remove the lower control arm's rear attaching bolt and nut at the front crossmember

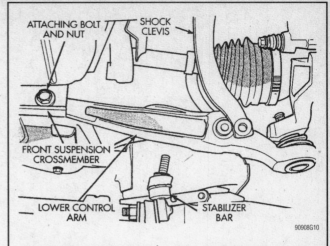

Fig. 45 Remove the lower control arm's front attaching bolt and nut at the front crossmember

15. Install the control arm to the steering knuckle and tighten to 55 ft. lbs. (74 Nm). Install the ball joint heat shield, if equipped.

16. Rotate the sway bar up to the control arms.

17. Install the sway bar attaching bolts.

18. Tighten the sway bar link bolts to 77 ft. lbs. (105 Nm).

19. Install the strut clevis bolt finger-tight.

20. Lower the vehicle and support the weight of the vehicle with jackstands placed underneath the lower control arms, but not under the ball joint.

21. Tighten the clevis-to-control arm bolt to 65 ft. lbs. (88 Nm).

22. Tighten the front lower control arm nut and bolt to 135 ft. lbs. (182 Nm).

23. Tighten the sway bar-to-crossmember attaching bolts 45 ft. lbs. (61 Nm).

24. Reinstall the wheels and tires.

25. Lower the vehicle.

26. Connect the negative battery cable.

Sebring Coupe and Avenger

LATERAL LOWER ARM

▶ **See Figure 46**

1. Disconnect the negative battery cable.

2. Raise and safely support the vehicle.

3. Remove the appropriate wheel assembly.

4. Remove the stay bracket from the crossmember.

5. Using ball joint separator MB991113, or equivalent, disconnect the ball joint stud from the steering knuckle.

6. Remove the through-bolt, connecting the damper fork to the lower control arm.

7. Remove the mounting bolt connecting the lower control arm to the suspension crossmember.

8. Remove the lower control arm from the vehicle.

To install:

9. When installing the control arm, temporarily tighten the nuts and/or bolts securing the control arm to the suspension crossmember. Tighten them fully only after the vehicle is sitting on its wheels.

10. Connect the damper fork to the lower control arm and tighten the through-bolt to 64 ft. lbs. (88 Nm).

11. Connect the ball joint stud to the knuckle and tighten the nut to 43–51 ft. lbs. (59–71 Nm). Install a new cotter pin.

12. Connect the stay bracket to the crossmember and tighten the mounting bolts to 51–58 ft. lbs. (69–78 Nm).

13. Install the wheels and lower the vehicle to the floor.

14. Once the full weight of the vehicle is on the suspension, tighten the inner lower arm mounting bolt nut to 71–85 ft. lbs. (98–118 Nm).

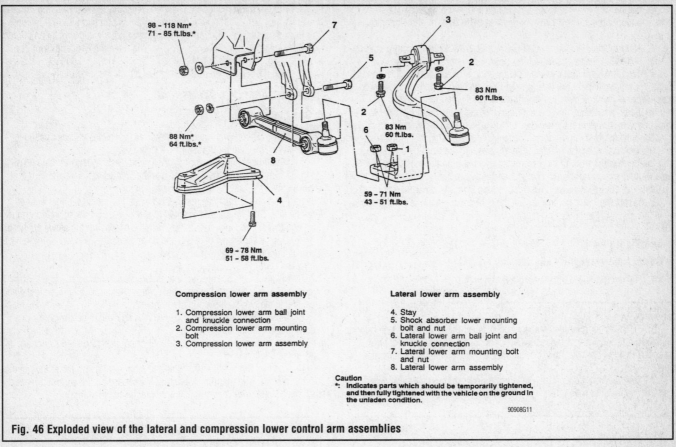

98 – 118 Nm*
71 – 85 ft.lbs.*

88 Nm*
64 ft.lbs.*

69 – 78 Nm
51 – 58 ft.lbs.

83 Nm
60 ft.lbs.

83 Nm
60 ft.lbs.

59 – 71 Nm
43 – 51 ft.lbs.

Compression lower arm assembly

1. Compression lower arm ball joint and knuckle connection
2. Compression lower arm mounting bolt
3. Compression lower arm assembly

Lateral lower arm assembly

4. Stay
5. Shock absorber lower mounting bolt and nut
6. Lateral lower arm ball joint and knuckle connection
7. Lateral lower arm mounting bolt and nut
8. Lateral lower arm assembly

Caution
*: Indicates parts which should be temporarily tightened, and then fully tightened with the vehicle on the ground in the unladen condition.

90908G11

Fig. 46 Exploded view of the lateral and compression lower control arm assemblies

15. Connect the negative battery cable.
16. Check the front end alignment and adjust as required.

COMPRESSION LOWER ARM

▶ See Figure 46

1. Disconnect the negative battery cable.
2. Raise and support the vehicle safely.
3. Remove the appropriate wheel assembly.
4. Using ball joint separator MB991113 or equivalent, disconnect the ball joint stud from the steering knuckle.
5. Remove the mounting bolts connecting the lower control arm to the suspension crossmember.

To install:

6. Connect the control arm to the suspension crossmember, and tighten the bolts to 60 ft. lbs. (83 Nm).
7. Connect the ball joint stud to the knuckle and tighten the nut to 43–51 ft. lbs. (59–71 Nm).
8. Install the wheels and lower the vehicle to the floor.
9. Connect the negative battery cable.
10. Check the front end alignment and adjust as required.

CONTROL ARM BUSHING REPLACEMENT

Cirrus, Stratus, Sebring Convertible and Breeze

FRONT ISOLATOR BUSHING

▶ See Figure 47

1. Remove the lower control arm from the vehicle, as previously outlined. If possible, mount the control arm in a vise.

2. Install bushing remover tool 6602-5 and bushing receiver tool MB-990799, or their equivalents, on a suitable C-clamp, such as part C-4212-F or equivalent.
3. Position the bushing remover and receiver tools on either side of the bushing. Be sure that the receiver tool is square on the lower control arm and that the remover tool is positioned correctly on the isolator bushing.
4. Tighten the screw on the C-clamp to press the front bushing out of the lower control arm.

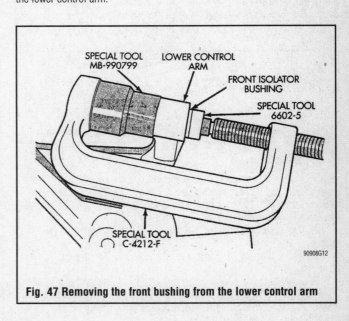

SPECIAL TOOL MB-990799   LOWER CONTROL ARM

FRONT ISOLATOR BUSHING

SPECIAL TOOL 6602-5

SPECIAL TOOL C-4212-F

90908G12

Fig. 47 Removing the front bushing from the lower control arm

To install:

5. Mount bushing installer tool 6876 or equivalent on the stationary part of the base of the C-clamp.

6. Mount bushing stopper tool 6758 or equivalent on the screw portion of the C-clamp.

7. Start the front bushing into the lower control arm by hand, making sure it is square with its mounting hole. The bushing is to be installed in the lower control arm from the machined surface side of the hole.

8. Position the bushing installer and stopper tools on either side of the bushing. Make sure that the stopper tool is square on the control arm, and that the installer tool is positioned correctly on the bushing.

9. Tighten the screw of the C-clamp, pressing the front bushing into the lower control arm until the installer tool is flush on the machined surface of the lower control arm. This will correctly position the front bushing in the lower control arm. Remove the C-clamp from the control arm.

10. Install the lower control arm in the vehicle, as previously outlined.

REAR ISOLATOR BUSHING

♦ **See Figure 48**

1. Remove the lower control arm from the vehicle, as previously outlined. If possible, mount the control arm in a vise.

2. Install bushing remover tool 6756 and bushing receiver tool C-4366-2, or their equivalents, on a suitable C-clamp, such as tool C-4212-F or equivalent.

3. Position the bushing remover and receiver tools on either side of the bushing. Be sure that the receiver tool is square on the lower control arm and that the remover tool is positioned correctly on the isolator bushing.

4. Tighten the screw on the C-clamp to press the rear bushing out of the lower control arm.

9. Tighten the screw of the C-clamp, pressing the rear bushing into the lower control arm. Continue to press until the bushing is sitting flush on the machined surface of the lower control arm. This will correctly position the rear bushing in the lower control arm. Remove the C-clamp from the control arm.

10. Install the lower control arm in the vehicle, as previously outlined.

CONTROL ARM CLEVIS BUSHING

♦ **See Figure 49**

1. Remove the lower control arm from the vehicle, as previously outlined. If possible, mount the control arm in a vise.

2. Install bushing remover tool 6877 and bushing receiver tool 6876, or their equivalents, on a suitable C-clamp, such as tool C-4212-F or equivalent.

3. Position the bushing remover and receiver tools on either side of the bushing. Be sure that the receiver tool is square on the lower control arm and that the remover tool is positioned correctly on the clevis bushing.

4. Tighten the screw on the C-clamp to press the clevis bushing out of the lower control arm.

To install:

5. Install the clevis bushing into the lower control arm by hand, making sure it is square with the mounting hole. The bushing is to be installed from the machined surface side of the hole.

6. Mount bushing installer tool 6877 or equivalent on the screw portion of the C-clamp.

7. Mount bushing stopper tool 6876 or equivalent on the stationary part of the C-clamp.

8. Position the bushing installer and stopper tools on either side of the bushing. Make sure that the stopper tool is square on the control arm, and that the installer tool is positioned correctly on the bushing.

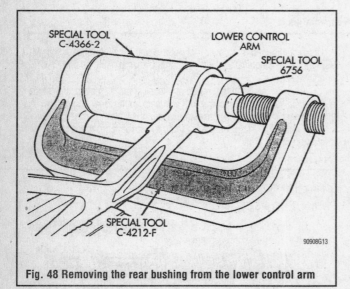

Fig. 48 Removing the rear bushing from the lower control arm

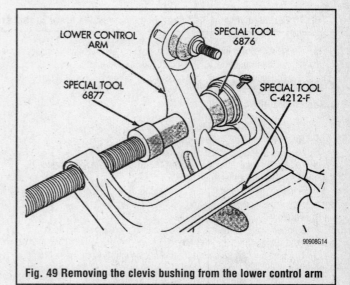

Fig. 49 Removing the clevis bushing from the lower control arm

To install:

5. Install the rear bushing into the lower control arm by hand, making sure it is square with the mounting hole. The bushing is to be installed from the machined surface side of the lower control arm bushing hole, with the void in the bushing pointing away from the ball joint.

6. Mount bushing installer tool 6760 on the screw portion of the C-clamp.

7. Mount bushing stopper tool 6756 or equivalent on the stationary part of the C-clamp.

8. Position the bushing installer and stopper tools on either side of the bushing. Make sure that the stopper tool is square on the control arm, and that the installer tool is positioned correctly on the bushing.

9. Tighten the screw of the C-clamp, pressing the clevis bushing into the lower control arm. Continue to press until the bushing is sitting flush on the machined surface of the lower control arm. This will correctly position the clevis bushing in the lower control arm. Remove the C-clamp from the control arm.

10. Install the lower control arm in the vehicle, as previously outlined.

Sebring Coupe and Avenger

The lower control arm bushings on the Sebring coupe and Avenger models are not serviceable. If they are worn out or damaged, the lateral and/or compression lower arm(s) must be replaced.

Knuckle

REMOVAL & INSTALLATION

Cirrus, Stratus, Sebring Convertible and Breeze

◆ See Figures 39, 40, 41, 42, 43, and 50

1. Remove the cotter pin, locknut and spring washer from the front stub axle. Discard the cotter pin.

> ※※ **WARNING**
>
> **The wheel bearing will be damaged if, after loosening the hub nut, the vehicle is rolled on the ground or the weight of the vehicle is allowed to be supported by the tires.**

2. With the vehicle still on the ground and the brakes applied, loosen the hub nut. The hub and halfshaft are splined together through the knuckle (bearing) and retained by the hub nut.
3. Raise and safely support the vehicle.
4. Remove the front wheel and tire assembly.
5. Unfasten the brake caliper-to-steering knuckle attaching bolts.
6. Remove the brake caliper from the steering knuckle. The caliper is removed by first lifting its bottom portion away from the knuckle, then moving the top portion out from under the steering knuckle.
7. Support the caliper from the strut using a suitable piece of wire. Do NOT allow the caliper to hang by the brake hose.
8. Remove the brake rotor from the front hub and bearing assembly.
9. If equipped with 15 inch wheels, remove the lower ball joint heat shield from the lower control arm.
10. Remove the nut attaching the tie rod end to the steering knuckle. The nut can be removed as follows:
   a. Hold the tie rod end stud with an $^{11}\!/_{32}$ in. socket while loosening and removing the nut with a wrench.
11. Separate the tie rod end from the steering knuckle with a tie rod end presser, such as MB-991113 or equivalent.
12. If equipped with an Anti-lock Brake System (ABS), remove the speed sensor cable routing bracket from the steering knuckle.
13. Remove the cotter pin and castle nut from the lower control arm ball joint.
14. Turn the steering knuckle to its furthest point, and separate the ball joint stud from the steering knuckle by striking the steering knuckle boss with a hammer. Continue to do this until the ball joint stud separates from the steering knuckle. Be careful to not strike the lower control arm or the ball joint grease seals.

Fig. 50 Lift the steering knuckle upward to separate it from the ball joint stud

➡ **Be sure not to separate the inner CV-joint during this operation. Do not let the halfshaft hang by the inner CV-joint; the halfshaft MUST be supported.**

15. Lift up on the steering knuckle to separate it from the lower ball joint stud.
16. Pull the steering knuckle out and away from the outer CV-joint.
17. Remove the cotter pin and castle nut from the upper ball joint stud-to-steering knuckle attachment.
18. Using a ball joint separator tool, detach the upper control arm ball joint stud from the steering knuckle.
19. Remove the steering knuckle from the vehicle.

To install:

20. If necessary, install a new hub and bearing assembly onto the steering knuckle.
21. Slide the halfshaft into the hub/bearing assembly, then install the steering knuckle onto the lower control arm ball joint stud.
22. Install the lower ball joint stud castle nut.
23. Install the upper control arm ball joint stud into the steering knuckle. Install the castle nut and tighten to 45 ft. lbs. (62 Nm). Then, using a crow's foot attachment and a torque wrench, tighten the lower ball joint castle nut to 55 ft. lbs. (75 Nm). Install new cotter pins to both ball joints.
24. If equipped with ABS, install the speed sensor cable routing bracket onto the steering knuckle and tighten the mounting bolt.
25. Insert the tie rod end into the steering knuckle, then install the attaching nut. Hold the stud of the tie rod end secure while tightening the attaching nut. Then, using a crow's foot attachment and $^{11}\!/_{32}$ inch socket, tighten the attaching nut to 45 ft. lbs. (61 Nm).
26. If equipped, install the lower ball joint heat shield to the lower control arm.
27. Install the brake rotor.
28. Install the brake caliper assembly.
29. Clean all dirt and/or foreign matter from the threads of the outer CV-joint stub axle. Install the washer and hub nut onto the threads of the stub axle and hand-tighten.
30. With the brakes applied (to keep the rotor from turning), tighten the hub nut to 180 ft. lbs. (244 Nm).
31. Install the front wheel and tire assembly. Tighten the lug nuts in a star pattern to 95 ft. lbs. (129 Nm).
32. Carefully lower the vehicle.
33. Install the spring washer, locknut and a new cotter pin. Wrap the cotter pin prongs tightly around the locknut.
34. Take the vehicle to a reputable front end alignment shop to have the toe checked, and adjusted if necessary.

Sebring Coupe and Avenger

◆ See Figure 51

1. Remove the cotter pin, locknut and spring washer from the front stub axle. Discard the cotter pin.

> ※※ **WARNING**
>
> **The wheel bearing will be damaged if, after loosening the hub nut, the vehicle is rolled on the ground or the weight of the vehicle is allowed to be supported by the tires.**

2. With the vehicle still on the ground and the brakes applied, loosen the hub nut. The hub and halfshaft are splined together through the knuckle (bearing) and retained by the hub nut.
3. Raise and safely support the vehicle.
4. Remove the front wheel and tire assembly.
5. Unfasten the brake caliper-to-steering knuckle attaching bolts.
6. Remove the caliper from the steering knuckle.
7. Support the caliper from the strut using a suitable piece of wire. Do NOT allow the caliper to hang by the brake hose.
8. Remove the brake rotor.
9. Remove the nut attaching the tie rod end to the steering knuckle.

90908P23

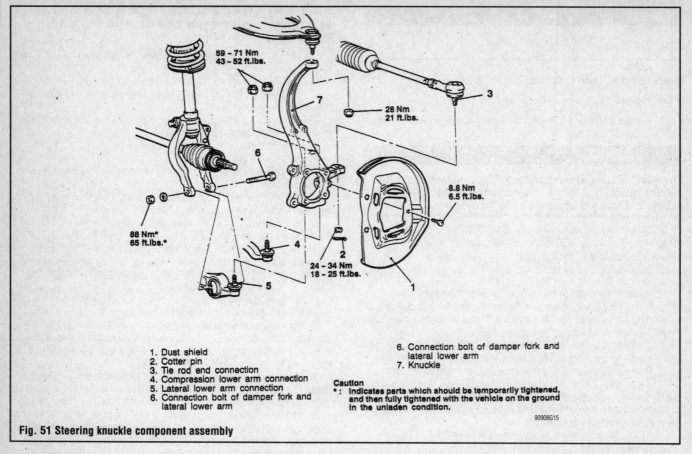

1. Dust shield
2. Cotter pin
3. Tie rod end connection
4. Compression lower arm connection
5. Lateral lower arm connection
6. Connection bolt of damper fork and lateral lower arm

6. Connection bolt of damper fork and lateral lower arm
7. Knuckle

Caution
* : Indicates parts which should be temporarily tightened, and then fully tightened with the vehicle on the ground in the unladen condition.

90908G15

Fig. 51 Steering knuckle component assembly

10. Separate the tie rod end from the steering knuckle with a tie rod end presser.

11. If equipped with an Anti-lock Brake System (ABS), remove the speed sensor from the steering knuckle.

12. Remove the locknuts from the lateral and compression lower control arm ball joints.

13. Detach the 2 ball joint studs from the steering knuckle by utilizing a ball joint separator tool.

➡**Be sure not to separate the inner CV-joint during this operation. Do not let the halfshaft hang by the inner CV-joint; the halfshaft MUST be supported.**

14. Lift up on the steering knuckle to separate it from the lower ball joint studs.

15. Pull the steering knuckle out and away from the outer CV-joint.

16. Remove the locknut from the upper ball joint stud-to-steering knuckle attachment.

17. Using a ball joint separator tool, remove the upper control arm ball joint stud from the steering knuckle.

18. Remove the steering knuckle from the vehicle.

To install:

19. If necessary, install a new hub and bearing assembly onto the steering knuckle.

20. Slide the halfshaft into the hub/bearing assembly, then install the steering knuckle onto the lateral and compression lower control arm ball joint studs.

21. Install the lower ball joint stud locknuts.

22. Install the upper control arm ball joint stud into the steering knuckle. Install the locknut and tighten to 21 ft. lbs. (28 Nm). Then, using a crow's foot attachment and torque wrench, tighten the 2 lower ball joint locknuts to 43–52 ft. lbs. (59–71 Nm).

23. If equipped with ABS, install the speed sensor onto the steering knuckle.

24. Install the tie rod end into the steering knuckle. Install and tighten the attaching nut to 18–25 ft. lbs. (24–34 Nm).

25. Install the brake rotor.

26. Install the brake caliper assembly.

27. Clean all dirt and/or foreign matter from the threads of the outer CV-joint stub axle. Install the washer and hub nut onto the threads of the stub axle and hand-tighten.

28. With the brakes applied (to keep the rotor from turning), tighten the hub nut to 188 ft. lbs. (255 Nm).

29. Install the front wheel and tire assembly. Tighten the lug nuts in a star pattern to 95 ft. lbs. (129 Nm).

30. Carefully lower the vehicle.

31. Install the spring washer, locknut and a new cotter pin. Wrap the cotter pin prongs tightly around the locknut.

32. Take the vehicle to a reputable front end alignment shop to have the toe checked, and adjusted if necessary.

Front Hub and Bearing

The front hub and wheel bearing is designed for the life of the vehicle and requires no type of adjustment or periodic maintenance. The bearing is a sealed unit with the wheel hub and can only be removed and/or replaced as one unit.

REMOVAL & INSTALLATION

▶ **See Figure 52**

1. Raise and safely support the vehicle.
2. Remove the front tire and wheel.
3. Remove the steering knuckle assembly, as described previously.
4. Remove the bolts attaching the hub/bearing assembly to the steering knuckle.

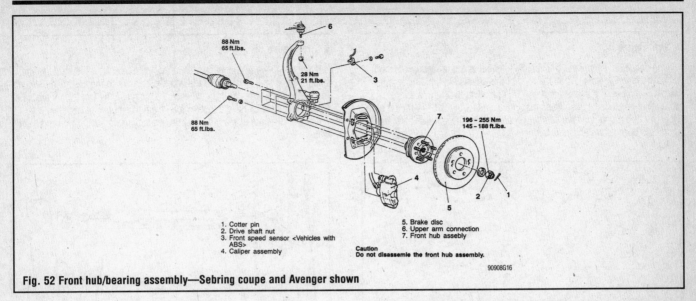

1. Cotter pin
2. Drive shaft nut
3. Front speed sensor <Vehicles with ABS>
4. Caliper assembly
5. Brake disc
6. Upper arm connection
7. Front hub assebly

Caution
Do not disassemle the front hub assembly.

90908G16

Fig. 52 Front hub/bearing assembly—Sebring coupe and Avenger shown

5. Remove the hub/bearing assembly from the front of the steering knuckle. The bolt-in front wheel bearing used on the vehicle is transferable to a replacement steering knuckle, if the bearing is in serviceable condition. If the bearing will not come out of the steering knuckle, it can be tapped out using a soft-faced hammer.

➡**The hub and wheel bearing assembly is not serviceable and should not be disassembled.**

To install:

6. Thoroughly clean all parts, including the hub/bearing assembly mounting surfaces on the steering knuckle.

7. Install the replacement hub/bearing assembly onto the steering knuckle, aligning the bolt holes of the bearing flange to the knuckle.

8. Install the attaching bolts and tighten evenly to make sure the bearing is square to the face of the steering knuckle. Tighten the attaching bolts to 80 ft. lbs. (110 Nm) on Cirrus, Stratus, Sebring convertible and Breeze, or 65 ft. lbs. (88 Nm) on Sebring coupe and Avenger.

9. Install the steering knuckle assembly, as previously described.
10. Install the tire and wheel.
11. Lower the vehicle and check for proper operation.

❋❋ CAUTION

Pump the brake pedal until it is hard, before attempting to move the vehicle.

Wheel Alignment

If the tires are worn unevenly, if the vehicle is not stable on the highway, or if the handling seems uneven in spirited driving, the wheel alignment should be checked. If an alignment problem is suspected, first check for improper tire inflation and other possible causes. These can be worn suspension or steering components, accident damage or even unmatched tires. If any worn or damaged components are found, they must be replaced before the wheels can be properly aligned. Wheel alignment requires very expensive equipment and involves minute adjustments which must be accurate; it should only be performed by a trained technician. Take your vehicle to a properly equipped shop.

Following is a description of the alignment angles which are adjustable on most vehicles and how they affect vehicle handling. Although these angles can apply to both the front and rear wheels, usually only the front suspension is adjustable.

CASTER

▶ **See Figure 53**

Looking at a vehicle from the side, caster angle describes the steering axis rather than a wheel angle. The steering knuckle is attached to a control arm or strut at the top and a control arm at the bottom. The wheel pivots around the line between these points to steer the vehicle. When the upper point is tilted back, this is described as positive caster. Having a positive caster tends to make the wheels self-centering, increasing directional stability. Excessive positive caster makes the wheels hard to steer, while an uneven caster will cause a pull to one side. Overloading the vehicle or sagging rear springs will affect caster, as will raising the rear of the vehicle. If the rear of the vehicle is lower than normal, the caster becomes more positive.

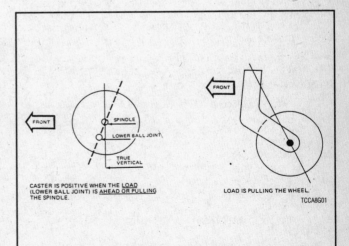

CASTER IS POSITIVE WHEN THE LOAD (LOWER BALL JOINT) IS AHEAD OR PULLING THE SPINDLE.

LOAD IS PULLING THE WHEEL.

TCCA8G01

Fig. 53 Caster affects straight-line stability. Caster wheels used on shopping carts, for example, employ positive caster

CAMBER

▶ **See Figure 54**

Looking from the front of the vehicle, camber is the inward or outward tilt of the top of wheels. When the tops of the wheels are tilted in, this is negative camber; if they are tilted out, it is positive. In a turn, a slight amount of negative camber helps maximize contact of the tire with the road. However, too much negative camber compromises straight-line stability, increases bump steer and torque steer.

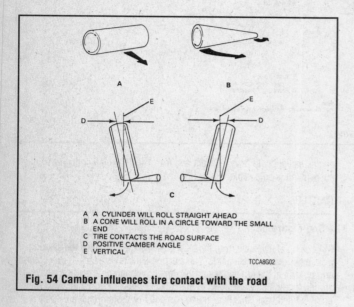

A A CYLINDER WILL ROLL STRAIGHT AHEAD
B A CONE WILL ROLL IN A CIRCLE TOWARD THE SMALL
   END
C TIRE CONTACTS THE ROAD SURFACE
D POSITIVE CAMBER ANGLE
E VERTICAL

TCCA8G02

Fig. 54 Camber influences tire contact with the road

TOE

▶ **See Figure 55**

Looking down at the wheels from above the vehicle, toe angle is the distance between the front of the wheels, relative to the distance between the back of the wheels. If the wheels are closer at the front, they are said to be toed-in or to have negative toe. A small amount of negative toe enhances directional stability and provides a smoother ride on the highway.

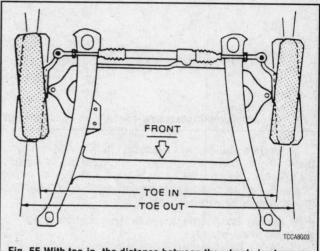

FRONT

TOE IN
TOE OUT

TCCA8G03

Fig. 55 With toe-in, the distance between the wheels is closer at the front than at the rear

REAR SUSPENSION

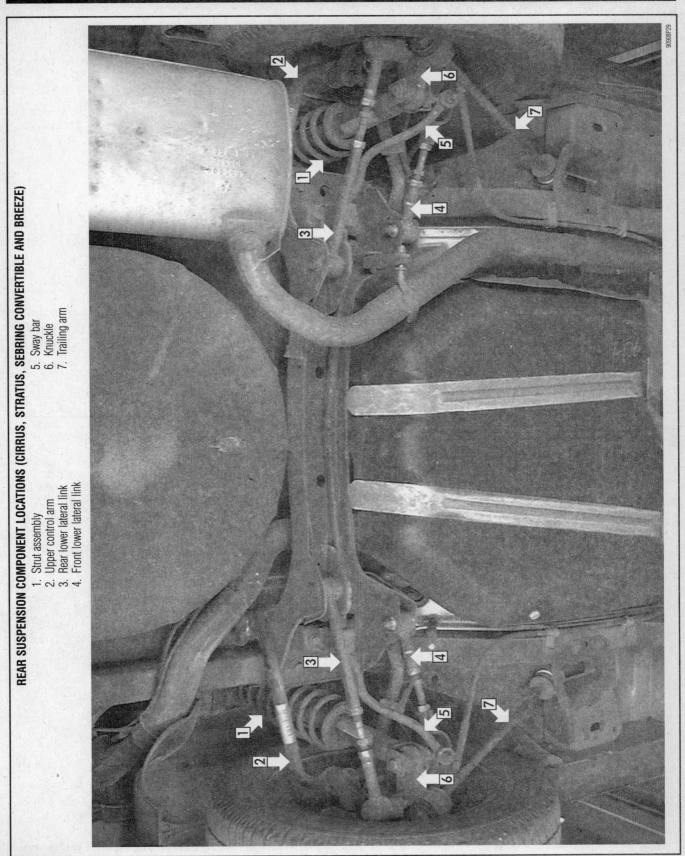

REAR SUSPENSION COMPONENT LOCATIONS (CIRRUS, STRATUS, SEBRING CONVERTIBLE AND BREEZE)

1. Strut assembly
2. Upper control arm
3. Rear lower lateral link
4. Front lower lateral link
5. Sway bar
6. Knuckle
7. Trailing arm

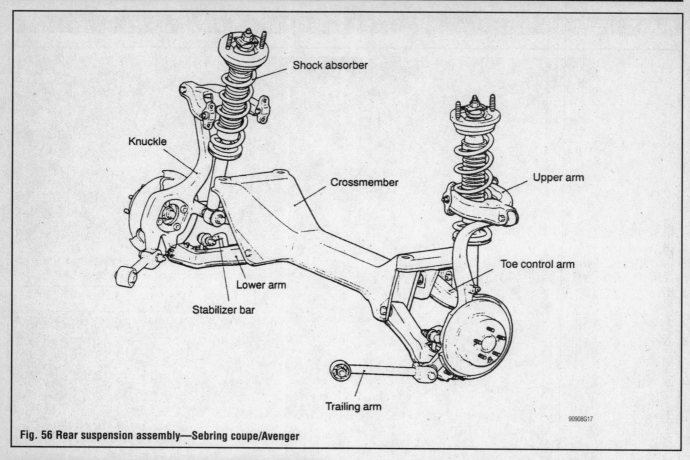

Fig. 56 Rear suspension assembly—Sebring coupe/Avenger

Labels:
- Shock absorber
- Knuckle
- Crossmember
- Upper arm
- Lower arm
- Stabilizer bar
- Toe control arm
- Trailing arm

90908G17

Struts

REMOVAL & INSTALLATION

Cirrus, Stratus, Sebring Convertible and Breeze

♦ See Figures 57 thru 64

1. Pull back the carpeting from the rear strut tower.
2. Remove the plastic cover from the top of the strut tower.

3. Remove the 2 nuts attaching the strut assembly to the body.
4. Raise and safely support the vehicle.
5. Remove the wheel and tire assembly.
6. Remove the bolt attaching the strut to the rear knuckle.
7. Push downward on the rear suspension and tilt the top of the strut outward.
8. Remove the strut from the vehicle.
To install:
9. Install the strut into the vehicle at the rear knuckle.
10. Push downward on the rear suspension and insert the top of the strut into the vehicle.

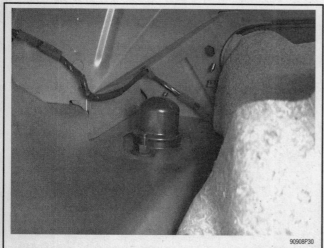

90908P30

Fig. 57 Pull back the trunk carpeting to locate the upper mounting portion of the rear strut assembly

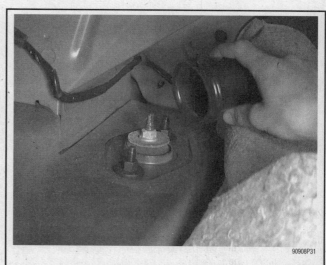

90908P31

Fig. 58 Remove the plastic cup from the top of the strut tower

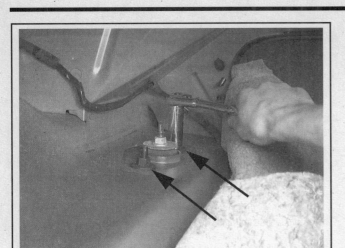

Fig. 59 Loosen, then remove, the 2 nuts attaching the strut assembly to the body

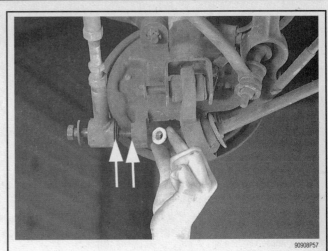

Fig. 62 . . . then remove the nut, and pull the bolt out just enough to allow clearance for removal of the clevis bolt

Fig. 60 Loosen the lower strut clevis-to-knuckle bolt

Fig. 63 Using a prybar between the strut clevis and knuckle, remove the strut clevis bolt

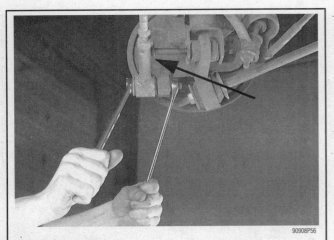

Fig. 61 If the strut's clevis bolt cannot be removed due to obstruction by the lower lateral link, loosen the link-to-knuckle nut and bolt . . .

Fig. 64 Carefully remove the rear strut assembly from the vehicle

11. Install the strut-to-rear knuckle attaching bolt. Tighten the bolt to 70 ft. lbs. (95 Nm).

12. Lower the vehicle enough to gain access to the trunk.

13. Install the strut upper mounting nuts and tighten to 40 ft. lbs. (54 Nm).

14. Install the strut top cover.

15. Install the rear wheel and tire assembly. Tighten the lug nuts to 95 ft. lbs. (125 Nm).

16. Lower the vehicle.

Sebring Coupe and Avenger

▶ **See Figure 65**

➡ **The strut assembly is a load bearing component; therefore, the vehicle's chassis and axle weight must be supported separately, requiring the use of two separate lifting devices.**

1. The rear package shelf front cover(s) must be removed to access the top mounting nuts. Most of the fasteners are plastic clips. Use care when removing these components to avoid unnecessary damage.

   a. Remove the rear shelf speaker covers.

   b. Remove the rear shelf top assembly.

   c. Remove the front cover(s) to access the strut top mounting nuts.

2. Raise and safely support the vehicle chassis.

3. Raise and support the lower control arm assembly slightly using a floor jack.

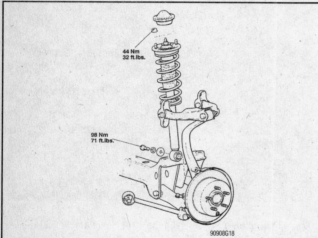

Fig. 65 Rear strut component assembly—Sebring coupe and Avenger

4. Remove the strut's upper mounting nuts.

5. Remove the strut's lower mounting bolt and remove the assembly from the vehicle.

To install:

6. Position the strut assembly so that the lower mounting bolt can be installed and lightly tightened.

7. Use a jack to raise or lower the lower control arm, so that the top strut plate studs align through the body. Raise the jack to hold the strut assembly in position.

8. Install the top plate mounting nuts on the studs and tighten them to 32 ft. lbs. (44 Nm).

9. Tighten the lower mounting bolt to 71 ft. lbs. (98 Nm).

10. Install the interior trim pieces to complete strut installation.

OVERHAUL

▶ **See Figures 26 thru 31**

1. Position the strut assembly firmly in a vise. With the strut mounted in a straight-up position, install a spring compressor tool. The tool must capture the first full top and bottom coil of the spring for it to work effectively. Tighten the compressor tool and compress the spring slowly. Make certain the compressor is properly engaged before tightening.

2. After tension has been removed from the strut assembly and strut plate, remove the piston rod nut and washer from the top of the strut assembly.

3. If the spring is to be replaced, slowly release the tension on the spring compressor. Allow the spring to expand fully. If only the strut cartridge is being replaced, the spring may remain in the compressor assembly.

4. By hand, remove any bushings, washers, shields or other components below the mounting bracket. Take notice of each component's location for proper reassembly. Examine the condition of these components, and replace any if necessary.

To install:

5. Install the lower insulator, strut bumper and uncompressed spring. Install the upper spring insulator, strut shield, mount and washer.

6. Install or align the spring compressor. Make certain the spring is correctly positioned relative to the upper and lower insulator rings. Smoothly compress the spring.

7. Install the washer and piston rod nut. Tighten the nut to 16 ft. lbs. (22 Nm) on Sebring coupe/Avenger and 40 ft. lbs. (55 Nm) on Cirrus/Stratus/Sebring convertible/Breeze.

8. Check to make sure that all the components of the strut assembly are accounted for and are installed correctly in their proper order.

9. Carefully release the spring compressor, watching the spring position as it seats. When the spring is properly seated, release/remove the compressor tools.

10. Reinstall the strut assembly.

Lower Control Arms

REMOVAL & INSTALLATION

Cirrus, Stratus, Sebring Convertible and Breeze

▶ **See Figures 66 and 67**

The Cirrus, Stratus, Sebring convertible and Breeze models use 2 lateral links, instead of a control arm, for the rear lower suspension.

1. Raise and safely support the vehicle.

2. Remove the wheel and tire assembly.

3. Disconnect the sway bar link and bushings from the lateral link.

➡ **The sway bar bushings are located on the front lateral link only. The rear lateral link does not have any connection to the sway bar.**

Fig. 66 Disconnect the sway bar link and bushings from the lateral link

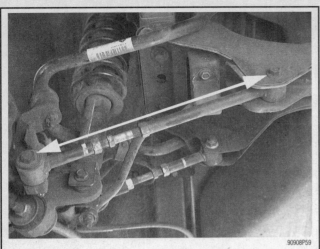

Fig. 67 Remove the 2 bolts attaching the lateral link to the rear knuckle and the crossmember

4. Remove the 2 bolts attaching the lateral link to the rear knuckle and the crossmember.

5. Remove the lateral link from the vehicle.

To install:

6. Install the lateral link into the vehicle.

7. Install the 2 attaching bolts and tighten to 70 ft. lbs. (95 Nm).

8. Install the sway bar bushings (front lateral link only).

9. Install the wheel and tire assembly.

10. Lower the vehicle.

11. Check the rear wheel alignment. If adjustment is necessary, have it perfomed by a reputable alignment shop.

Sebring Coupe and Avenger

LOWER ARM

▶ **See Figure 68**

1. Raise and safely support the vehicle.

2. Remove the appropriate wheel and tire assembly.

3. If equipped with an Anti-lock Brake System (ABS), disconnect the speed sensor harness brackets from the lower control arm.

4. Disconnect the stabilizer bar link from the lower arm.

5. Remove the through-bolt connecting the knuckle assembly to the lower arm.

6. Remove the mounting bolt connecting the lower arm to the suspension crossmember.

7. Remove the lower arm from the vehicle.

To install:

➡ **The control arm mounting bolts must not be fully tightened until the suspension is bearing the full weight of the vehicle.**

8. Install the lower arm to the suspension crossmember and temporarily tighten the mounting bolt.

9. Connect the knuckle to the lower arm and lightly tighten the through-bolt.

10. Connect the stabilizer bar link to the lower arm and tighten the nut to 28 ft. lbs. (39 Nm).

11. Install the wheel and tire assembly, then lower the vehicle to the floor.

12. Once the full weight of the vehicle is on the suspension, tighten the lower arm assembly mounting bolts to 71 ft. lbs. (98 Nm).

13. Check the rear wheel alignment. If adjustment is necessary, have it perfomed by a reputable alignment shop.

TOE CONTROL ARM

▶ **See Figure 68**

The lower ball joint is integral with the toe control arm. They are removed and replaced as an assembly.

1. Raise and safely support the vehicle.

2. Remove the appropriate wheel and tire assembly.

3. Matchmark the control arm adjusting bolt to aid in reassembly.

4. Using ball joint separator MB991113 or equivalent, disconnect the ball joint stud from the steering knuckle.

5. Remove the mounting bolts connecting the lower control arm to the suspension crossmember.

To install:

6. Connect the control arm to the suspension crossmember. Align the matchmarks on the adjustment bolt and lightly tighten the bolt.

7. Connect the ball joint stud to the knuckle and tighten the nut to 20 ft. lbs. (28 Nm).

8. Install the wheels and lower the vehicle to the floor.

9. With the full weight of the vehicle on the ground, tighten the control arm through-bolt to 50–56 ft. lbs. (69–78 Nm).

10. Check the rear wheel alignment. If adjustment is necessary, have it perfomed by a reputable alignment shop.

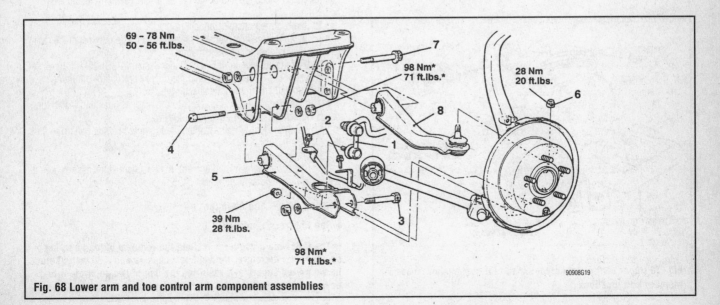

Fig. 68 Lower arm and toe control arm component assemblies

Upper Control Arms

REMOVAL & INSTALLATION

Cirrus, Stratus, Sebring Convertible and Breeze

▶ See Figures 69, 70 and 71

1. Raise and support the rear of the vehicle safely.
2. Remove the rear wheels.
3. Remove the strut-to-rear knuckle bolt on both sides of the vehicle.
4. Remove the muffler support bracket from the rear frame rail and the exhaust pipe hanger from the rear suspension crossmember. Allow the exhaust system to hang down.
5. Only on the side of the vehicle that requires upper control arm replacement, perform the following:
   a. Remove the cotter pin and castle nut from the upper control arm ball joint.
   b. Using puller tool CT-1106 or equivalent, separate the control arm ball joint stud from the knuckle.
6. Place a transmission jack and a block of wood underneath the center of the rear suspension crossmember for support.

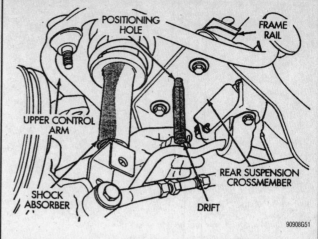

Fig. 71 Place a drift in each positioning hole to properly align the rear suspension crossmember

7. If equipped with an Anti-lock Brake System (ABS), remove the wheel speed sensor cable routing clips from the brackets on both upper control arms.
8. Remove the 4 rear suspension crossmember-to-frame rail mounting bolts.
9. Carefully lower the rear suspension crossmember just far enough to access the upper control arm pivot bar attaching bolts. Be careful not to put a strain on the flexible rear brake hoses.
10. Remove the 2 bolts that mount the upper control arm to the suspension crossmember. Remove the control arm.
11. Transfer any required components to the replacement control arm.

To install:

12. Align the upper control arm pivot bar with the mounting holes in the rear suspension crossmember. Install and tighten the 2 crossmember attaching bolts to 79 ft. lbs. (107 Nm).
13. Using the transmission jack, raise the rear suspension crossmember up to the frame rails and loosely install the 4 mounting bolts.
14. Place an appropriate size drift through the positioning hole on each side of the crossmember and into the locating hole in each frame rail. This is required to properly position the crossmember in the body of the vehicle. Then tighten the 4 crossmember mounting bolts to 70 ft. lbs. (95 Nm).
15. Remove the drifts from the crossmember.
16. Install the upper control arm ball joint stud in the knuckle. Install the ball joint stud castle nut and tighten to 50 ft. lbs. (67 Nm). Install a new cotter pin.
17. Remove the transmission jack.
18. Install the muffler support bracket to the frame rail. Install the rear exhaust pipe hanger to the crossmember.
19. If equipped with an Anti-lock Brake System (ABS), install the wheel speed sensor cable routing clip onto the upper control arm mounting brackets. Install and tighten the attaching bolts.
20. Install the strut clevis brackets to the rear knuckles and install the bolts. Tighten the bolts to 70 ft. lbs. (95 Nm).
21. Install the rear wheels. Tighten the lug nuts in a star pattern to 95 ft. lbs. (129 Nm).
22. Lower the vehicle.
23. Check the rear wheel alignment. If adjustment is necessary, have it perfomed by a reputable alignment shop.

Sebring Coupe and Avenger

▶ See Figures 72 and 73

➡The following procedures include the removal of load bearing components; therefore, the vehicle's chassis and axle weight must be supported separately, requiring the use of two separate lifting devices.

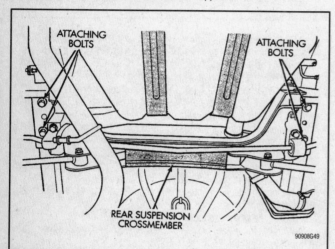

Fig. 69 Rear suspension crossmember-to-frame rail fastener locations

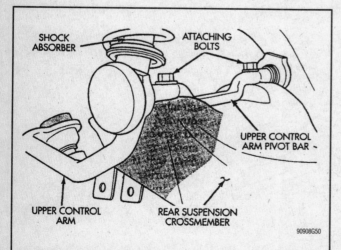

Fig. 70 Upper control arm pivot bar-to-rear suspension crossmember bolt locations

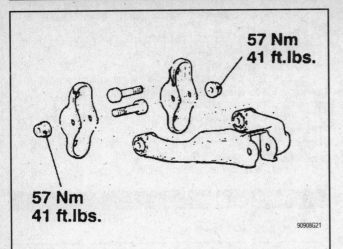

Fig. 72 Rear upper control arm components and torque specifications

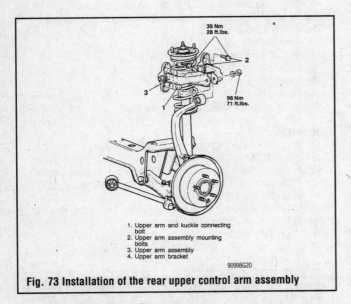

1. Upper arm and kuckle connecting bolt
2. Upper arm assembly mounting bolts
3. Upper arm assembly
4. Upper arm bracket

Fig. 73 Installation of the rear upper control arm assembly

1. Raise and safely support the vehicle.
2. Remove the appropriate wheel and tire assembly.
3. Support the lower arm assembly, and remove the mounting bolt connecting the upper control arm to the knuckle.
4. Remove the four bolts connecting the upper arm brackets to the subframe, then remove the upper control arm assembly.
5. Remove the mounting brackets from the control arm.

To install:
6. Install the mounting brackets to the control arm and tighten the mounting bolts to 41 ft. lbs. (57 Nm).
7. Install the upper control arm to the subframe and tighten the bolts to 28 ft. lbs. (39 Nm).
8. Connect the control arm to the knuckle and tighten the through-bolt to 71 ft. lbs. (98 Nm).
9. Install the wheel/tire assembly and lower the vehicle.
10. Check the rear wheel alignment. If adjustment is necessary, have it perfomed by a reputable alignment shop.

Sway (Stabilizer) Bar

REMOVAL & INSTALLATION

Cirrus, Stratus, Sebring Convertible and Breeze

▶ **See Figure 74**

1. Raise and safely support the vehicle.
2. Remove both rear wheel and tire assemblies.
3. Remove the nuts attaching the sway bar isolator bushings to the sway bar.
4. Remove the isolator bushings from the sway bar link.
5. Remove the 4 bolts attaching the sway bar clamps to the crossmember.
6. Remove the sway bar between the crossmember and the exhaust pipe.

To install:
7. Install the sway bar into the vehicle.

➡ **The bend in the end of the sway bar must be positioned upward (when viewed from the side) for proper installation.**

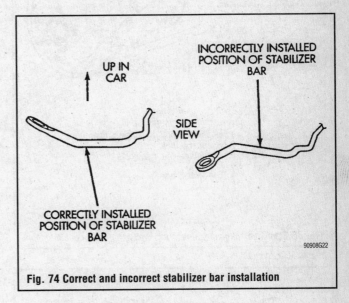

Fig. 74 Correct and incorrect stabilizer bar installation

8. Install the sway bar to the sway bar links.
9. Install the isolator bushings.
10. Tighten the sway bar link nuts to 40 ft. lbs. (55 Nm).
11. Install the sway bar hold-down clamps to the crossmember and center the sway bar in the vehicle.
12. Tighten the hold-down clamp bolts to 250 inch lbs. (28 Nm).
13. Install the wheel and tire assemblies. Tighten the lug nuts in a star pattern to 95 ft. lbs. (129 Nm).
14. Lower the vehicle and check for proper operation.

Sebring Coupe and Avenger

▶ **See Figures 75 and 76**

1. Raise and safely support the vehicle.
2. Disconnect the stabilizer links by removing the self-locking nuts.
3. Remove the stabilizer bar mounting brackets and bushings.
4. Remove the stabilizer bar from the vehicle.

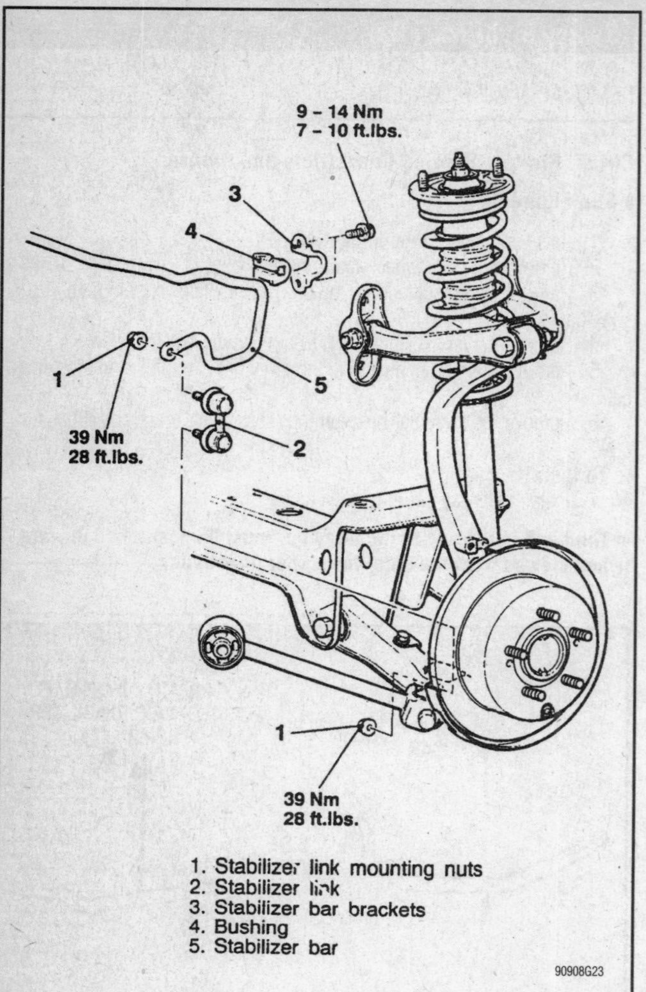

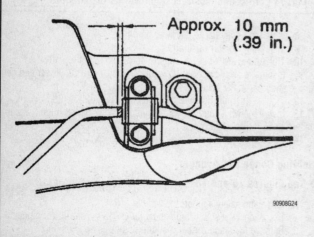

9 – 14 Nm
7 – 10 ft.lbs.

3
4

1

5

39 Nm
28 ft.lbs.

2

1

39 Nm
28 ft.lbs.

1. Stabilizer link mounting nuts
2. Stabilizer link
3. Stabilizer bar brackets
4. Bushing
5. Stabilizer bar

90908G23

Fig. 75 Stabilizer bar component assembly

5. Inspect all components for wear or damage, and replace parts as needed.

To install:

6. Install the stabilizer bar into the vehicle.

7. Loosely install the stabilizer bar brackets on the vehicle.

8. Align the side locating markings on the stabilizer bar, so that the marking on the bar extends approximately 0.39 inches (10mm) from the outer edge of the mounting bracket, on both sides.

9. With the stabilizer bar properly aligned, tighten the mounting bracket bolts to 28 ft. lbs. (39 Nm).

10. Connect the stabilizer links to the damper fork and the stabilizer bar. Tighten the locking nuts to 28 ft. lbs. (38 Nm).

11. Lower the vehicle and road test to check for noise.

Rear Wheel Bearings

REMOVAL & INSTALLATION

Cirrus, Stratus, Sebring Convertible and Breeze

▶ **See Figures 77 thru 82**

All vehicles are equipped with permanently lubricated and sealed-for-life rear wheel bearings. There is no periodic lubrication or maintenance recommended for these units.

1. Raise and safely support the vehicle.

2. Remove the wheel and tire assembly.

3. Remove the brake drum or rotor.

4. Remove the rear hub dust cap.

5. Remove the rear hub retaining nut.

6. Remove the rear hub and bearing assembly by pulling it straight off the spindle.

To install:

7. Install the replacement bearing on the rear spindle.

8. Install the hub with a new retaining nut.

9. Tighten the retaining nut to 185 ft. lbs. (250 Nm). Install the dust cap by tapping on it with a suitably sized socket and hammer.

10. Install the brake drum or rotor.

11. Install the wheel and tire assembly. Tighten the lug nuts in a star pattern to 95 ft. lbs. (129 Nm).

12. Lower the vehicle.

Approx. 10 mm
(.39 in.)

90908G24

Fig. 76 Correct installation of the stabilizer bar in the mounting bracket

90908P42

Fig. 77 Remove the dust cap using a hammer and chisel

Fig. 78 After loosening the cap, remove it from the center of the hub

Fig. 79 Using a breaker bar and socket, loosen the wheel hub/bearing center nut . . .

Fig. 80 . . . then remove the center nut from the vehicle

Fig. 81 Pull the wheel hub and bearing assembly straight off of the spindle

Fig. 82 Install the dust cap by tapping on it with a socket and a hammer

Sebring Coupe and Avenger

▶ See Figure 83

1. Raise and safely support the vehicle.
2. Remove the appropriate wheel and tire assembly.
3. If equipped with an Anti-lock Brake System (ABS), remove the vehicle speed sensor.
4. Remove the brake drum or rotor from the hub assembly.
5. From the back of the knuckle, remove the four bolts securing the hub to the knuckle.
6. Remove the hub and bearing assembly from the knuckle.

➡The hub assembly is not serviceable and should not be disassembled.

7. If replacing the hub, use special socket MB991248 and a press, to remove the wheel sensor rotor from the hub.

To install:

8. Press the wheel sensor rotor onto the hub.
9. Install the hub to the knuckle and tighten the mounting bolts to 54–65 ft. lbs. (74–88 Nm).

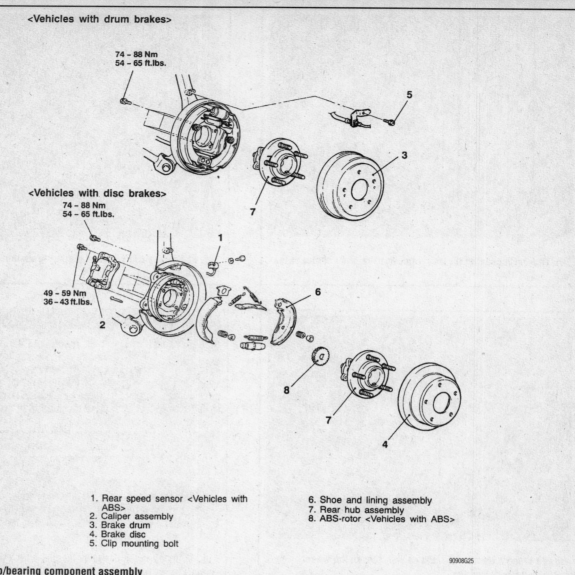

<Vehicles with drum brakes>

74 – 88 Nm
54 – 65 ft.lbs.

<Vehicles with disc brakes>

74 – 88 Nm
54 – 65 ft.lbs.

49 – 59 Nm
36 – 43 ft.lbs.

1. Rear speed sensor <Vehicles with ABS>
2. Caliper assembly
3. Brake drum
4. Brake disc
5. Clip mounting bolt
6. Shoe and lining assembly
7. Rear hub assembly
8. ABS-rotor <Vehicles with ABS>

90908G25

Fig. 83 Wheel hub/bearing component assembly

10. Install the brake drum or rotor on the hub.
11. If equipped with ABS, install the vehicle speed sensor.

12. Install the wheel and tire assembly. Tighten the lug nuts in a star pattern to 95 ft. lbs. (129 Nm).
13. Lower the vehicle.

STEERING

Steering Wheel

REMOVAL & INSTALLATION

Cirrus, Stratus, Sebring Convertible and Breeze

▶ **See Figures 84 thru 92**

❋❋ CAUTION

The Supplemental Inflatable Restraint (SIR) system must be disarmed before removing the steering wheel. Failure to do so may cause accidental deployment of the air bags, resulting in unnecessary SIR system repairs and/or personal injury.

1. Place the wheels in the straight ahead position.
2. Disarm the air bag system, as described in Section 6.

➡**The ground cable is equipped with an insulator grommet, which should be placed on the stud to prevent the negative battery cable from accidentally grounding.**

3. Remove the driver's air bag attaching bolts from the back of the steering wheel.
4. Lift the air bag module. While holding the module, raise the secondary latch and unfasten the wiring connector.

➡**Never use a metal tool to pry on the air bag wiring connector.**

5. Remove the air bag module and store it in a clean, dry place with the pad cover facing up. Do not place anything on top of the air bag module.

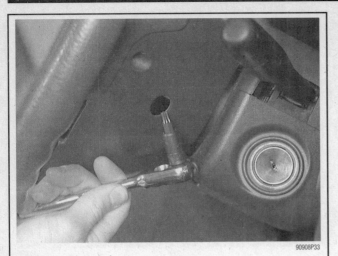

Fig. 84 Remove the driver's air bag attaching bolts from the back of the steering wheel

Fig. 85 While holding the air bag module, lift off the secondary latch from the connector . . .

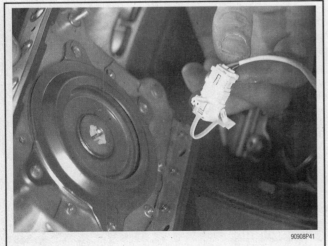

Fig. 86 . . . and remove the connector from behind the air bag module

Fig. 87 Carefully remove the air bag module from the steering wheel

> ※※ **CAUTION**
>
> When carrying a live air bag, make sure the bag and trim cover are pointed away from the body. In the unlikely event of an accidental deployment, the bag will then deploy with minimal chance of injury. When placing a live air bag on a bench or other surface, always face the bag and trim cover up, away from the surface. This will reduce the motion of the module if it is accidentally deployed.

6. Remove the speed control screws from the back of the steering wheel, lift out the pods and disconnect the wiring.

7. Disconnect the horn wire from the air bag bracket. Remove the speed control wires from under the bracket.

8. Remove the steering wheel retaining nut.

9. Attach a suitable steering wheel puller tool. Using a wrench, tighten the puller's center bolt until the steering wheel is removed.

To install:

10. Install the steering wheel onto the column.

11. Install the steering wheel retaining nut and tighten to 45 ft. lbs. (61 Nm).

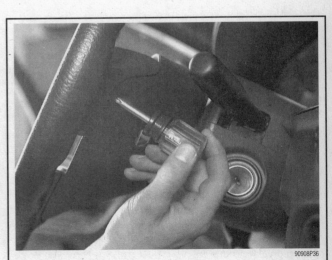

Fig. 88 Remove the speed control screws from behind the steering wheel

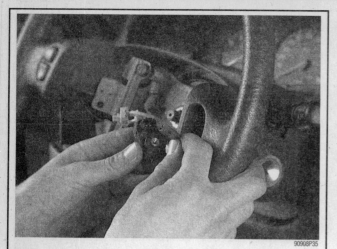

Fig. 89 Lift out the speed control pod and disengage the wiring connector

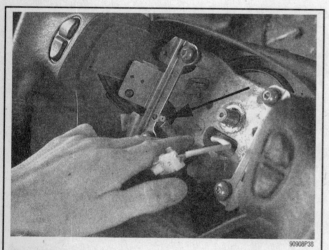

Fig. 90 Disengage the horn wiring connector from the air bag bracket

Fig. 91 Loosen, then remove, the steering wheel retaining nut

Fig. 92 Using a steering wheel puller, slowly draw the steering wheel off of its shaft

12. Connect the horn wire and the speed control wires.
13. Install the speed control pods and reattach the speed control unit to the steering wheel. Tighten the screws to 15 inch lbs. (2 Nm).
14. Connect the air bag lead and push the secondary latch into place.
15. Install the air bag module and tighten the screws to 85 inch lbs. (10 Nm).
16. Arm the air bag system, as described in Section 6.

Sebring Coupe and Avenger

▶ See Figures 93 and 94

✳✳ CAUTION

The Supplemental Inflatable Restraint (SIR) system must be disarmed before removing the steering wheel. Failure to do so may cause accidental deployment of the air bags, resulting in unnecessary system repairs and/or personal injury.

1. Disarm the air bag system, as described in Section 6.
2. Remove the air bag module mounting bolts from behind the steering wheel.
3. To unfasten the clock spring's connector from the air bag module, press the air bag's lock toward the module to spread the lock open. While holding the lock in this position, use a small tipped prying tool to gently pry the connector from the module.

✳✳ CAUTION

When carrying a live air bag, make sure the bag and trim cover are pointed away from the body. In the unlikely event of an accidental deployment, the bag will then deploy with minimal chance of injury. When placing a live air bag on a bench or other surface, always face the bag and trim cover up, away from the surface. This will reduce the motion of the module if it is accidentally deployed.

4. Remove the air bag module and store it in a clean, dry place with the pad cover facing up. Do not place anything on top of the air bag module.
5. Remove the steering wheel retaining nut and use a steering wheel puller to remove the wheel.

✳✳ WARNING

Do not use a hammer, or the collapsible mechanism in the column could be damaged.

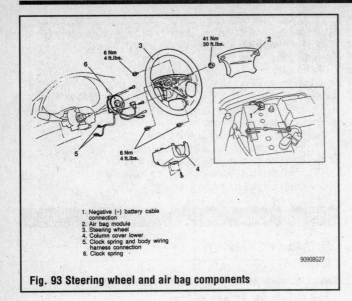

1. Negative (−) battery cable connection
2. Air bag module
3. Steering wheel
4. Column cover lower
5. Clock spring and body wiring harness connection
6. Clock spring

90908G27

Fig. 93 Steering wheel and air bag components

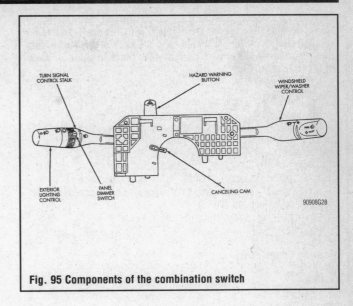

90908G28

Fig. 95 Components of the combination switch

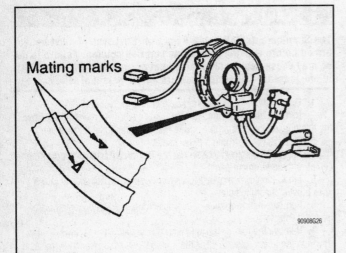

90908G26

Fig. 94 Center the clock spring by aligning the mating marks

To install:

6. Confirm that the front wheels are in a straight-ahead position. Center the clock spring by aligning the mating mark (small arrow) on the clock spring with the mating mark on the casing.

7. Install the steering wheel and tighten the retaining nut to 30 ft. lbs. (41 Nm).

8. Attach the air bag module wiring connector to clock spring connection. Install the air bag module and tighten the mounting bolts to 43 inch lbs. (5 Nm), then install the side covers.

9. Arm the air bag system, as described in Section 6.

Combination Switch

REMOVAL & INSTALLATION

Cirrus, Stratus, Sebring Convertible and Breeze
▶ **See Figures 95 and 96**

Should any function of the switch fail, the entire switch assembly must be replaced.

1. Set the steering wheel and the front wheels to the straight ahead position.

✱✱ CAUTION

The Supplemental Inflatable Restraint (SIR) system must be disarmed before working around the steering column. Failure to do so may cause accidental deployment of the air bags, resulting in unnecessary SIR system repairs and/or personal injury.

2. Disarm the air bag system, as described in Section 6.
3. Remove the steering column lower cover retaining screws.
4. Loosen the lower section of the instrument cluster hood for clearance, as necessary.
5. Remove the steering column upper cover.
6. Remove the combination switch mounting screws.
7. Unfasten the switch's wiring connectors.
8. Lift the switch upward to remove.

➡The turn signal flasher and hazard warning flasher are combined into one unit called a combination flasher (combo-flasher). An

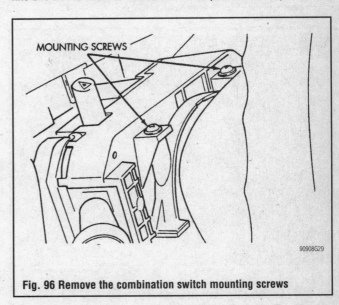

90908G29

Fig. 96 Remove the combination switch mounting screws

inoperative or incomplete turn signal circuit will result in an increase in flasher speed. The flasher, which is serviced separately from the switch, is mounted to the back of the multi-function (combination) switch. The flasher is black in color for ease of identification.

To install:

9. Install the combination switch.
10. Attach the wiring connectors.
11. Install the combination switch mounting screws and tighten to 20 inch lbs. (2.3 Nm).
12. Install the steering column covers as follows:
    a. Install the upper cover onto the steering column.
    b. Tighten the lower part of the instrument cluster hood.
    c. Install the lower steering column cover retaining screws and tighten to 17 inch lbs. (2 Nm).
13. Arm the air bag system, as described in Section 6.
14. Test the switch functions.

Sebring Coupe and Avenger

▶ See Figure 97

1. Set the steering wheel and the front wheels to the straight ahead position.

✳✳ CAUTION

The Supplemental Inflatable Restraint (SIR) system must be disarmed before removing the steering wheel. Failure to do so may cause accidental deployment of the air bags, resulting in unnecessary system repairs and/or personal injury.

2. Disarm the air bag system, as described in Section 6.
3. Remove the steering wheel.

✳✳ CAUTION

When carrying a live air bag, make sure the bag and trim cover are pointed away from the body. In the unlikely event of an accidental deployment, the bag will then deploy with minimal chance of injury. When placing a live air bag on a bench or other surface, always face the bag and trim cover up, away from the surface. This will reduce the motion of the module if it is accidentally deployed.

4. Remove the lower steering column cover and the column pad.
5. Remove the upper steering column cover.

6. Unfasten the clock spring/combination switch assembly retaining screws and electrical connectors, then remove the complete assembly.
7. Remove the 4 retaining screws and separate the clock spring from the combination switch.

To install:

8. Attach the clock spring to the combination switch with the 4 retaining screws.
9. Attach the electrical connectors and install the clock spring/combination switch assembly and secure it with the 2 retaining screws
10. Install the upper steering column cover.
11. Install the column pad and the lower steering column cover.
12. Install the steering wheel and air bag module.
13. Arm the air bag system, as described in Section 6.
14. Check the switch for proper operation.

Ignition Switch

REMOVAL & INSTALLATION

Cirrus, Stratus, Sebring Convertible and Breeze

▶ See Figures 98, 99, 100 and 101

✳✳ CAUTION

The Supplemental Inflatable Restraint (SIR) system must be disarmed before working around the steering column. Failure to do so may cause accidental deployment of the air bags, resulting in unnecessary SIR system repairs and/or personal injury.

1. Disarm the air bag system, as described in Section 6.
2. Remove the left end instrument panel cover/fuse panel and remove the retaining screw holding the end of the instrument panel top cover.
3. Remove the instrument panel center bezel.
4. Remove the screws that secure the instrument panel top cover to the center of the instrument panel.
5. Lift the instrument panel top cover enough to gain access to the knee bolster attaching screws.
6. Remove the lower knee bolster attaching screws and knee bolster from the vehicle.
7. Remove the lower steering column cover attaching screws. Pull down on the lower cover to clear the ignition key cylinder and key release (if equipped).
8. Remove the lower steering column cover, sliding the cover forward while holding down the steering wheel tilt lever.

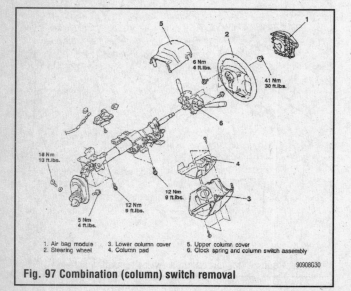

| 1. Air bag module | 3. Lower column cover | 5. Upper column cover |
| 2. Steering wheel | 4. Column pad | 6. Clock spring and column switch assembly |

Fig. 97 Combination (column) switch removal

90908G30

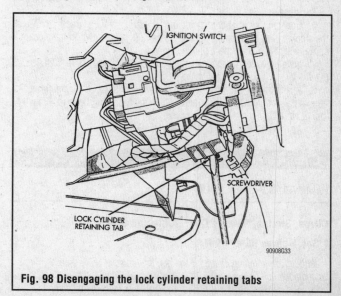

Fig. 98 Disengaging the lock cylinder retaining tabs

90908G33

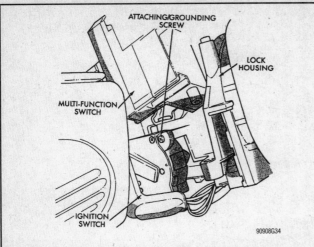

Fig. 99 Remove the ignition switch mounting screw using a No. 10 Torx® bit

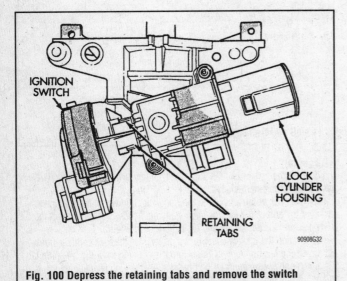

Fig. 100 Depress the retaining tabs and remove the switch

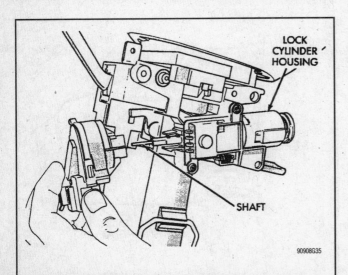

Fig. 101 Installing the ignition switch onto the lock cylinder

9. Tilt the steering wheel down to the fully lowered position and remove the upper steering column cover.

10. Remove the screws that hold the combination switch to the ignition lock housing.

11. Place the ignition lock cylinder in the **RUN** position.

12. Insert a small prying tool into the hole in the lower cover and depress the cylinder release tab.

13. Remove the ignition lock cylinder from the steering column.

14. Unfasten the electrical connectors from the switch.

15. Using a No. 10 Torx® bit, remove the ignition switch mounting screw.

16. Depress the retaining tabs and remove the switch.

To install:

17. Place the ignition switch in the **RUN** position. Be sure the actuator shaft in the lock housing is also in the **RUN** position.

18. Install the switch, making sure the switch snaps over the retaining tabs.

19. Install the retaining screw.

20. Connect the wiring to the ignition switch.

21. Install the ignition lock cylinder.

22. Install the 2 combination switch mounting screws.

23. Install the lower and upper shrouds.

24. Install the knee bolster to the lower dashboard panel and tighten the lower knee bolster attaching screws.

25. Install the screws that secure the instrument panel top cover to the center of the instrument panel.

26. Install the instrument panel center bezel.

27. Install and tighten the screw holding the end of the instrument panel top cover. Install the left side instrument panel/fuse panel cover.

28. Arm the air bag system, as described in Section 6. Check for proper ignition switch and key-in warning switch operation.

Sebring Coupe and Avenger

▶ See Figure 102

✳✳ CAUTION

The Supplemental Inflatable Restraint (SIR) system must be disarmed before working around the steering column. Failure to do so may cause accidental deployment of the air bags, resulting in unnecessary system repairs and/or personal injury.

1. Disarm the air bag system, as described in Section 6.
2. Remove the steering wheel.

✳✳ CAUTION

When carrying a live air bag, make sure the bag and trim cover are pointed away from the body. In the unlikely event of accidental deployment, the bag will then deploy with minimal chance of injury. When placing a live air bag on a bench or other surface, always face the bag and trim cover up, away from the surface. This will reduce the motion of the module if it is accidentally deployed.

3. Remove the hood lock release handle.
4. Remove the knee protector.
5. Remove the steering column upper and lower covers. Use care removing covers to prevent breakage of the alignment tabs.
6. Detach the combination switch and ignition switch harness connectors.
7. Unfasten the retaining screws and remove the entire column switch/clock spring assembly from the left side of the steering column.
8. Remove the mounting screws from the ignition switch and pull the switch from the lock cylinder.
9. To remove the lock cylinder, insert the key and place it in the **ACC** position. With a small pointed tool, push the lock pin of the steering lock cylinder inward, and pull the lock cylinder out.

To install:

10. Install the lock cylinder into the lock housing. Be sure the lock pin snaps into place.

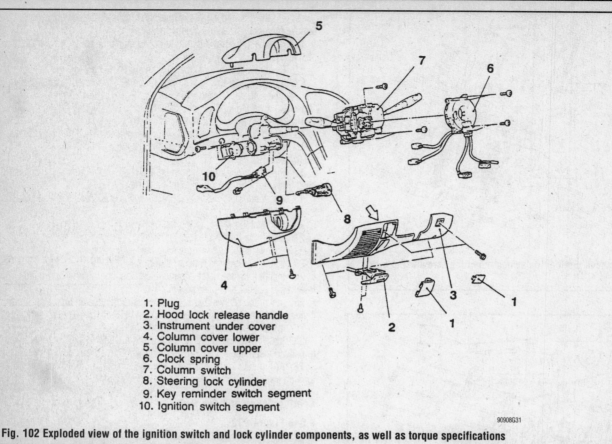

1. Plug
2. Hood lock release handle
3. Instrument under cover
4. Column cover lower
5. Column cover upper
6. Clock spring
7. Column switch
8. Steering lock cylinder
9. Key reminder switch segment
10. Ignition switch segment

90908G31

Fig. 102 Exploded view of the ignition switch and lock cylinder components, as well as torque specifications

11. Install the ignition switch into the lock housing. Align the ignition switch's keyway with the lock cylinder and secure with mounting screws.

12. Install the column switch/clock spring assembly to the steering column and fasten the harness connections.

13. Install the knee protector and the hood release handle.

14. Install the clock spring, steering wheel and air bag module.

15. Arm the air bag system, as described in Section 6. Check all functions of column-mounted switches and the ignition switch for proper operation.

Ignition Lock Cylinder

REMOVAL & INSTALLATION

Cirrus, Stratus, Sebring Convertible and Breeze

▶ See Figures 103 and 104

※ CAUTION

The Supplemental Inflatable Restraint (SIR) system must be disarmed before working around the steering column. Failure to do so may cause accidental deployment of the air bags, resulting in unnecessary SIR system repairs and/or personal injury.

1. Disarm the air bag system, as described in Scetion 6.
2. Remove the upper steering column shroud.
3. Pull down the lower steering column shroud enough to access the lock cylinder retaining tab.
4. Turn the ignition key to the **RUN** position.
5. Insert a small prying tool into the tab access hole and depress the tab.
6. Pull the ignition lock cylinder from the steering column.

To install:

7. With the ignition key in the lock cylinder, turn the key to the **RUN** position. Depress the lock cylinder retaining tab.

8. The shaft at the end of the ignition lock cylinder lines up to the socket at the end of the lock cylinder housing. The socket must be in the **RUN** position for the socket and lock cylinder to line up.

9. Line up the lock cylinder to the grooves in the lock cylinder housing. Insert the ignition lock cylinder into the housing until the retaining tab sticks through the opening in the housing.

10. Lightly pull on the ignition lock to make sure it has engaged the retaining tab.

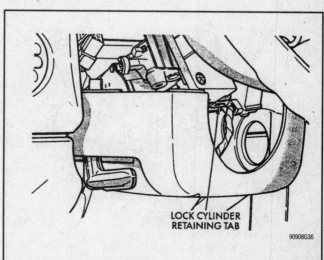

LOCK CYLINDER
RETAINING TAB

90908G36

Fig. 103 Depress the retaining tab and remove the lock cylinder

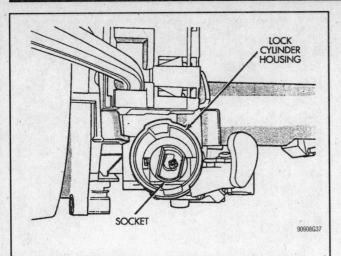

Fig. 104 The shaft at the end of the ignition lock cylinder lines up to the socket at the end of the lock cylinder housing

11. Turn the key to the **OFF** position. Remove the ignition key.
12. Install the steering column covers.
13. Arm the air bag system, as described in Section 6.

Sebring Coupe and Avenger

➡For information on removing/installing the Ignition Lock Cylinder, refer to the Ignition Switch removal and installation procedure, earlier in this section.

Steering Linkage

REMOVAL & INSTALLATION

Tie Rod Ends

▶ See Figures 105 thru 111

1. Raise and safely support the vehicle.
2. Remove the wheel and tire assembly.
3. Wire brush the threads on the steering shaft (tie rod) and lubricate them with penetrating oil. Loosen the tie rod jam nut. Mark the location of the tie rod end to the threads on the shaft.
4. Remove the cotter pin (if equipped) and nut, then press the tie rod end from the steering knuckle with a suitable tie rod end removal tool. If equipped, remove the tie rod end's seal boot heat shield.
5. Hold the steering shaft (tie rod) with locking pliers and unscrew the tie rod end. Counting the number of turns should make installation of the replacement tie rod end close to the previous alignment.

To install:

6. Install the tie rod end into the steering knuckle. Rotate the tie rod end the same amount of turns required to remove it. Do not tighten the jam nut at this time. Make sure the steering rack-to-tie rod boots are not twisted. Correct as necessary.
7. If equipped, install the tie rod end seal boot heat shield onto the tie rod end.
8. Install the tie rod end stud into the steering knuckle. Start the tie rod end-to-steering knuckle attaching nut onto the stud of the tie rod end. While holding the stud of the tie rod end stationary, tighten the tie rod end-to-steering knuckle nut. On Cirrus, Stratus, Sebring convertible and Breeze models, tighten the nut to 45 ft. lbs. (61 Nm). On Sebring coupe and Avenger models, tighten the nut to 18–25 ft. lbs. (24–34 Nm). Install a new cotter pin.
9. Check the front end alignment's toe setting.

➡If adjustment is necessary, have it performed by a qualified front end alignment shop.

Fig. 105 Loosen the jam nut on the steering shaft with an open end wrench

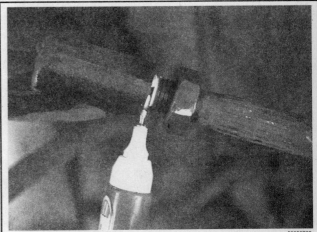

Fig. 106 Mark the location of the tie rod end on the steering shaft to ease installation

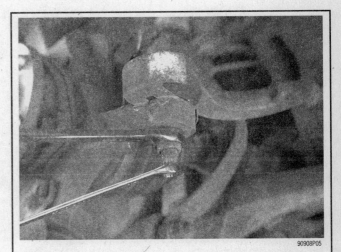

Fig. 107 Use a second wrench to secure the end of the ball joint stud while loosening the retaining nut

90908P06

Fig. 108 Use a ball joint separator tool to separate the tie rod end stud from the steering knuckle

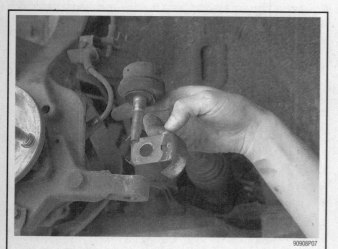

90908P07

Fig. 109 If equipped, remove the tie rod end's seal boot heat shield

90908P02

Fig. 110 Unscrew the tie rod end from the steering shaft while holding the shaft steady with a pair of locking pliers

90908P01

Fig. 111 Once it is free of the threads, remove the tie rod end from the steering shaft

10. On Cirrus, Stratus, Sebring convertible and Breeze, tighten the jam nut to 55 ft. lbs. (75 Nm). On Sebring coupe and Avenger, tighten the jam nut to 36–40 ft. lbs. (50–55 Nm).

11. Reinstall the wheel and lug nuts, then lower the vehicle. Tighten the lug nuts in a star pattern to 95 ft. lbs. (129 Nm).

Power Rack and Pinion

REMOVAL & INSTALLATION

Cirrus, Stratus, Sebring Convertible and Breeze

▶ **See Figures 112, 113, 114, 115 and 116**

✳✳ CAUTION

The Supplemental Inflatable Restraint (SIR) system must be disarmed before working around the steering column. Failure to do so may cause accidental deployment of the air bags, resulting in unnecessary SIR system repairs and/or personal injury.

1. Disarm the air bag system, as described in Section 6.

2. Siphon as much power steering fluid as possible from the remote power steering fluid reservoir.

3. From inside the vehicle, remove the retaining pin from the intermediate shaft coupler pinch bolt and remove the pinch bolt. Separate the intermediate shaft coupler from the steering gear shaft.

4. Raise and safely support the vehicle.

5. Remove the front wheels.

6. Disconnect the tie rod ends by holding the tie rod end stud with a $^{11}\!/_{32}$ in. socket while loosening the retaining nut with a wrench.

7. Detach the tie rod ends from the steering knuckles using a suitable ball joint separator tool.

➡**Before removing the front suspension crossmember from the vehicle, you must first scribe matchmarks on the front suspension crossmember and undercarriage. This must be done to retain the proper alignment. The caster and camber are not adjustable.**

8. Scribe a matchmark on the undercarriage and crossmember on all 4 sides of the crossmember.

9. Remove the stabilizer bar bushing clamp-to-body attaching bolts only. The stabilizer bar bushing clamp-to-front suspension crossmember bolts do not need to be removed.

10. If equipped with anti-lock brakes, remove the 3 bolts attaching the brake controller to the crossmember and tie the anti-lock brake controller to the vehicle body.

11. Disconnect the front strut clevis at each side of the vehicle from the lower control arms.

12. Remove the 2 bolts attaching the engine support bracket to the crossmember.

13. Remove the bolt attaching the engine support bracket to the transaxle mounting bracket.

14. Place a suitable lifting device under the front suspension crossmember.

15. Remove the 8 bolts attaching the crossmember to the body of the vehicle.

16. If necessary, lower the vehicle enough to gain access to the steering rack.

17. Disconnect the power steering lines and drain the fluid.

18. Disconnect the power steering pressure switch wiring.

19. If equipped with speed proportional steering, disconnect the solenoid control module wiring.

20. Remove the 2 steering rack isolator attaching bolts.

21. Remove the 2 steering rack saddle bracket attaching bolts.

22. Remove the rack and pinion assembly (steering rack) from the vehicle.

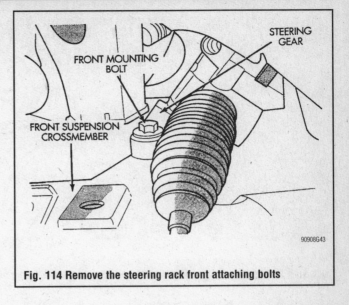

Fig. 114 Remove the steering rack front attaching bolts

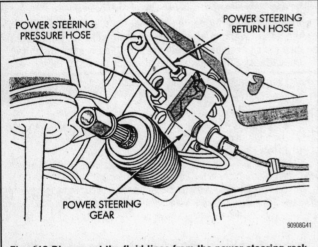

Fig. 112 Disconnect the fluid lines from the power steering rack assembly

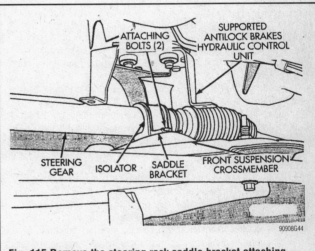

Fig. 115 Remove the steering rack saddle bracket attaching bolts (2 bolts per side)

To install:

23. Install the steering rack into the crossmember.

24. Install the isolator and saddle bracket bolts. Tighten the bolts to 50 ft. lbs. (68 Nm).

25. Install the power steering pressure and return lines. Tighten the fittings to 275 inch lbs. (31 Nm).

26. Raise the crossmember against the frame rails and install the 2 rear bolts.

27. Install the 2 front bolts.

28. Tighten all 4 bolts until the crossmember contacts the body.

29. Tighten the bolts to 20 inch lbs. (2 Nm).

30. Using a soft faced hammer, tap the crossmember into position.

➡ Be sure to align the scribed marks on the crossmember.

31. Starting with the rear bolts, tighten the crossmember bolts to 120 ft. lbs. (163 Nm).

32. Install the engine support bracket.

33. Install the 2 engine support bracket-to-crossmember bolts and tighten to 55 ft. lbs. (75 Nm).

34. Install the engine support bracket-to-transaxle mounting bracket bolt and tighten to 55 ft. lbs. (75 Nm).

35. Connect the power steering pressure switch.

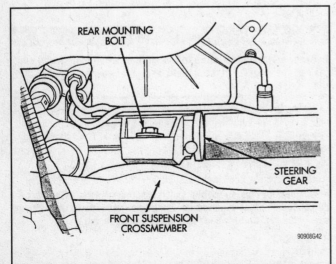

Fig. 113 Remove the steering rack rear isolator attaching bolts

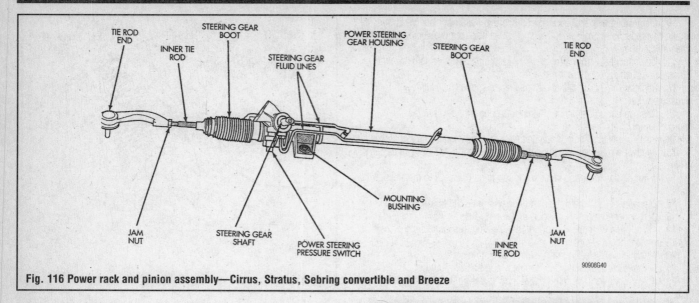

Fig. 116 Power rack and pinion assembly—Cirrus, Stratus, Sebring convertible and Breeze

36. Install the anti-lock brake control unit and tighten the mounting bolts to 21 ft. lbs. (28 Nm).

37. Attach each strut clevis to its lower control arm. Loosely install the nuts and bolts.

38. If applicable, install the heat shield on the tie rod ends.

39. Install the tie rod ends to the steering knuckles and tighten to 45 ft. lbs. (61 Nm).

40. Install and tighten the 2 stabilizer bar bushing clamp-to-body attaching bolts.

41. Lower the vehicle to the ground with a jackstand positioned under each front suspension lower control arm. Continue to lower the vehicle so that its total weight is supported by the jackstands and lower control arms.

42. Tighten each strut's clevis-to-lower control arm bushing through-bolt to 68 ft. lbs. (92 Nm).

43. Install the wheels and tighten the lug nuts in a star pattern to 95 ft. lbs. (129 Nm). Remove the jackstands.

44. Make sure the front wheels are pointing in the straight ahead position, and that the steering wheel is centered.

45. From inside the vehicle, reconnect the steering column intermediate shaft coupler on the steering gear shaft. Install the coupler's retaining pinch bolt and tighten to 20 ft. lbs. (27 Nm). Install the retaining pin.

46. Arm the air bag system, as described in Section 6.

47. Refill the reservoir with power steering fluid and properly bleed the power steering system.

48. Have the alignment professionally checked and adjusted at a properly equipped facility.

Sebring Coupe and Avenger

▶ See Figure 117

1. Drain the power steering fluid using the following procedure:
   a. Disconnect the power steering return (low side) hose.
   b. Connect a suitable container to the hose.
   c. Properly disable the ignition system.
   d. While cranking the engine, turn the wheels, several times, from side to side, until the fluid is removed.

✳✳ WARNING

Prior to removal of the steering rack and pinion unit, center the front wheels and remove the ignition key. Failure to do so may damage the Supplemental Inflatable Restraint (SIR) system's clock spring under the steering wheel and render the SIR system inoperative, risking serious driver injury.

✳✳ CAUTION

The Supplemental Inflatable Restraint (SIR) system must be disarmed before working around the steering column. Failure to do so may cause accidental deployment of the air bags, resulting in unnecessary SIR system repairs and/or personal injury.

2. Disarm the air bag system, as described in Section 6.

3. Raise and safely support the vehicle.

4. Remove both front wheels.

5. Remove the bolt holding the lower steering column joint to the rack and pinion input shaft.

6. Remove the stabilizer bar.

7. Remove the cotter pins and, using joint separator MB991113 or equivalent, disconnect the tie rod ends from the steering knuckles.

8. On vehicles equipped with Electronic Control Power Steering (EPS), disconnect the wiring harness from the solenoid connector.

9. Locate the two triangular braces near the crossmember and remove both.

10. Support the center crossmember. Remove the through-bolt from the front round roll stopper and remove the three bolts securing the center crossmember.

11. Remove the center crossmember.

12. Properly support the engine and remove the rear roll stopper through-bolt. Lower the engine slightly.

✳✳ WARNING

In order to prevent damage to the engine, when supporting and jacking the engine, place a block of wood between the jack and the oil pan.

13. Disconnect the power steering fluid pressure pipe and return hose from the rack fittings. Plug the fittings to prevent excessive fluid leakage.

14. Remove the clamp bolts and the two bolts securing the rack assembly to the chassis.

15. Remove the rack and pinion steering assembly and its rubber mounts.

➡When removing the rack and pinion assembly, tilt the assembly to the inner side of the compression lower arm, and remove from the left side of the vehicle. Use caution to avoid damaging the boots.

To install:

16. Align the rack assembly so the splines are inserted into the steering column shaft.

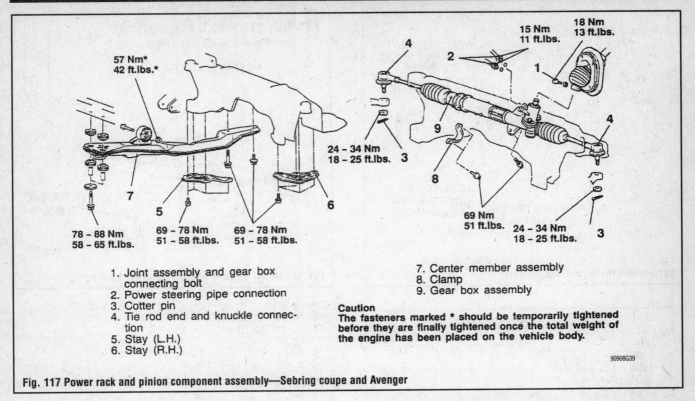

57 Nm*
42 ft.lbs.*

15 Nm
11 ft.lbs.

18 Nm
13 ft.lbs.

24 – 34 Nm
18 – 25 ft.lbs.

78 – 88 Nm
58 – 65 ft.lbs.

69 – 78 Nm
51 – 58 ft.lbs.

69 – 78 Nm
51 – 58 ft.lbs.

69 Nm
51 ft.lbs.

24 – 34 Nm
18 – 25 ft.lbs.

1. Joint assembly and gear box connecting bolt
2. Power steering pipe connection
3. Cotter pin
4. Tie rod end and knuckle connection
5. Stay (L.H.)
6. Stay (R.H.)
7. Center member assembly
8. Clamp
9. Gear box assembly

Caution
The fasteners marked * should be temporarily tightened before they are finally tightened once the total weight of the engine has been placed on the vehicle body.

90908G39

Fig. 117 Power rack and pinion component assembly—Sebring coupe and Avenger

17. Install the rack and pinion assembly with the mounting bolts. Tighten the mounting bolts to 51 ft. lbs. (69 Nm).

18. Install the pinch bolt and tighten the bolt to 13 ft. lbs. (18 Nm).

19. Connect the power steering fluid lines to the rack and tighten the high side fitting to 11 ft. lbs. (15 Nm). Secure the low side hose with the clamp.

20. Raise the engine into position. Install the rear roll stopper through-bolt and tighten to 32 ft. lbs. (43 Nm).

21. Raise the crossmember into position. Install the center member mounting bolts and tighten the front bolts to 58–65 ft. lbs. (78–88 Nm), and the rear bolt to 51–58 ft. lbs. (69–78 Nm).

22. Install the front roll stopper bolt and tighten the nut to 42 ft. lbs. (57 Nm).

23. Install the two triangular braces and tighten the mounting bolts to 51–58 ft. lbs. (69–78 Nm).

24. Install the stabilizer bar.

25. Attach the tie rod ends to the steering knuckles and tighten the nuts to 18–25 ft. lbs. (24–34 Nm).

26. On vehicles equipped with EPS, connect the wiring harness to the solenoid connector.

27. Install the wheels and lower the vehicle.

28. Arm the air bag system, as described in Section 6.

29. Refill the reservoir with power steering fluid and properly bleed the power steering system.

30. Have the alignment professionally checked and adjusted at a properly equipped facility.

Power Steering Pump

REMOVAL & INSTALLATION

Cirrus, Stratus, Sebring Convertible and Breeze

▶ **See Figures 118, 119, 120 and 121**

1. Disconnect the negative battery cable from the left strut tower. The ground cable is equipped with an insulator grommet, which should be placed on the stud to prevent the negative battery cable from accidentally grounding.

2. Siphon as much power steering fluid out of the reservoir as possible.

3. Raise and safely support the vehicle.

4. Remove the right front tire and wheel assembly.

5. Remove the splash shield from the right front wheel well.

6. Disconnect the power steering pressure hose from the pump.

7. Remove the hose connection on the power steering pump.

8. Remove the power steering adjusting bolt.

9. Remove the power steering pump rear attaching bolt.

10. If so equipped, remove the Anti-lock Brake System (ABS) hydraulic control unit heat shield.

11. Remove the wheel speed sensor retainer bracket from the right inner fender.

12. Remove the wheel speed sensor sealing grommet from the right inner fender.

13. Disconnect the speed sensor wiring.

14. Push the wiring through the hole in the inner fender.

➡ **If not equipped with anti-lock brakes, the hole will just have a sealing plug.**

15. Remove the bolt attaching the power steering front bracket to the mounting bracket. Access to the bolt is gained through the hole for the speed sensor wiring.

16. Remove the power steering pump drive belt.

17. Remove the power steering pump and the front bracket as an assembly.

To install:

18. Install the power steering pump and bracket.

19. Reinstall the bolt at the adjusting slot, but do not tighten.

20. Reinstall the bolt mounting the power steering pump to the rear mounting bracket, but do not tighten.

21. Reinstall the power steering pump top bolt, but do not tighten.

22. Reconnect the power steering hoses.

➡ **Use a new O-ring when reinstalling the power steering pressure hose.**

23. Reinstall the drive belt.

24. Adjust the drive belt and tighten the power steering pump bolts to 40 ft. lbs. (54 Nm).

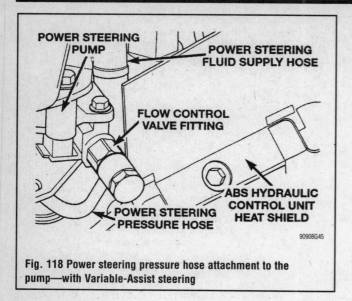

Fig. 118 Power steering pressure hose attachment to the pump—with Variable-Assist steering

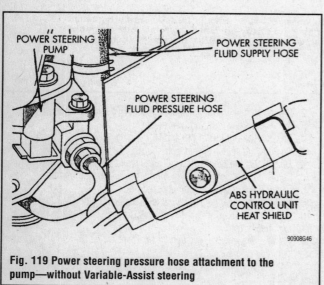

Fig. 119 Power steering pressure hose attachment to the pump—without Variable-Assist steering

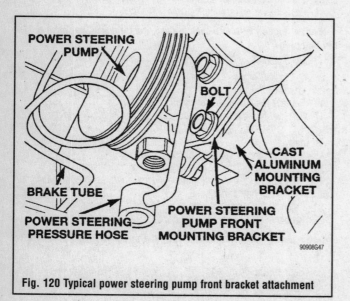

Fig. 120 Typical power steering pump front bracket attachment

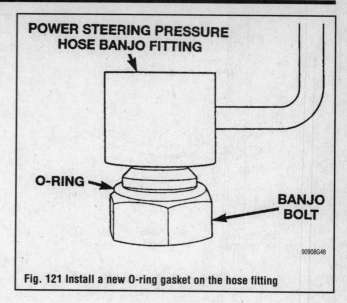

Fig. 121 Install a new O-ring gasket on the hose fitting

25. Reinstall the splash shield.
26. Reinstall the tire and wheel assembly.
27. Lower the vehicle.
28. Reconnect the negative battery cable.
29. Refill the reservoir and bleed the power steering system. For additonal information on fluid types and capacities, refer to Section 1.

Sebring Coupe and Avenger

▶ See Figures 122 and 123

1. Disconnect the negative battery cable.
2. Remove (drain, suction pump, etc.) as much power steering fluid as possible.
3. Disconnect the return fluid line. Remove the reservoir cap and allow the return line to drain the fluid from the reservoir. If the fluid is contaminated, disconnect the ignition high tension cable and crank the engine several times to drain the fluid from the gearbox.

➡**Cover any components located underneath the power steering pump with a shop towel to protect them from damage due to power steering fluid spillage. For example, the A/C compressor or alternator, depending on vehicle and engine, is below the power steering pump, so cover the A/C compressor or alternator with a shop towel before removing any hoses.**

4. Loosen (but do not remove) the power steering pump mounting bolts and remove the drive belt.
5. Remove the pressure switch connector from the side of the pump.
6. Disconnect the pressure line.
7. Unbolt and remove the pump from the mounting bracket.
To install:
8. Clean all parts well. Inspect the pump pulley for cracks. Check the hoses carefully for cracks or signs of weakness.
9. Install the pump, wrap the belt around the pulley and lightly tighten the mounting bolts.
10. Replace the O-rings and connect the pressure line. Connect the pressure line so the notch in the fitting aligns and contacts the pump's guide bracket. Tighten the fitting to 13 ft. lbs. (18 Nm).
11. Connect the return line and secure with the clamp.
12. Fasten the pressure switch connector.
13. Adjust the power steering belt for proper tension and tighten the adjusting bolts.

➡**Use only MOPAR ATF PLUS automatic transmission fluid type 7176, DEXRON II automatic transmission fluid, or equivalent, in the power steering system of Sebring coupe and Avenger models.**

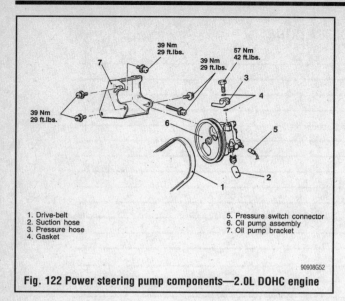

1. Drive-belt
2. Suction hose
3. Pressure hose
4. Gasket
5. Pressure switch connector
6. Oil pump assembly
7. Oil pump bracket

90908G52

Fig. 122 Power steering pump components—2.0L DOHC engine

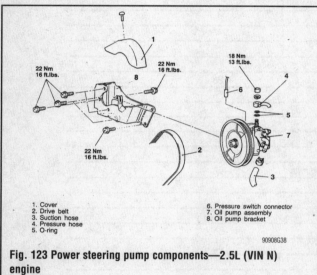

1. Cover
2. Drive belt
3. Suction hose
4. Pressure hose
5. O-ring
6. Pressure switch connector
7. Oil pump assembly
8. Oil pump bracket

90908G38

Fig. 123 Power steering pump components—2.5L (VIN N) engine

14. Refill the reservoir and bleed the power steering system. For additional information on fluid types and capacities, refer to Section 1.

BLEEDING

Cirrus, Stratus, Sebring Convertible and Breeze

❊❊ CAUTION

The power steering fluid level should be checked with the engine OFF to prevent injury from moving components. Power steering fluid, engine components and the exhaust system may be extremely hot if the engine has been running. Do not start the engine with any loose or disconnected hoses, or allow hoses to touch a hot exhaust manifold or catalyst.

➡ **In all power steering pumps, use only MOPAR® Power Steering Fluid or equivalent. DO NOT use any type of automatic transmission fluid in the power steering system.**

Wipe the filler cap clean, then check the fluid level. The dipstick should indicate FULL COLD when the fluid is at a normal room temperature of approximately 70–80°F (21–27°C).

1. Fill the power steering pump fluid reservoir to the proper level. Allow the fluid to settle for at least 2 minutes.
2. Start the engine and let it run for a few seconds. Turn the engine **OFF**.
3. Add fluid if necessary. Repeat this procedure until the fluid level remains constant after running the engine.
4. Raise the front wheels of the vehicle off the ground.
5. Start the engine. Slowly turn the steering wheel right and left, lightly contacting the wheel stops; then, turn the engine **OFF**.
6. Add more fluid if necessary.
7. Lower the vehicle and turn the steering wheel slowly from lock-to-lock.
8. Check the fluid level and refill as required.
9. If the fluid is extremely foamy, allow the vehicle to stand a few minutes and repeat the above procedure.

Sebring Coupe and Avenger

▶ **See Figure 123**

1. Check the power steering fluid level, and add if necessary.

➡ **Use only MOPAR ATF PLUS automatic transmission fluid type 7176, DEXRON II automatic transmission fluid, or equivalent, in the power steering system.**

2. Raise and safely support the vehicle to lift the front wheels off the ground.
3. Manually turn the pump pulley a few times.
4. Turn the steering wheel all the way to the left and to the right 5 or 6 times.

➡ **If bleeding is attempted with the engine running, air will be absorbed in the fluid. Bleed only while cranking the engine.**

5. Disconnect the ignition high tension cable and, while operating the starter motor intermittently, turn the steering wheel all the way to the left and right 5–6 times for 15–20 seconds. During the bleeding procedure, make sure the fluid in the reservoir never falls below the lower position of the filter.
6. Connect the ignition high tension cable, then start the engine and allow it to idle.
7. Turn the steering wheel left and right until there are no air bubbles in the reservoir. Confirm that the fluid is not milky and that the level is up to the specified position on the dipstick. Also confirm that there is very little change in the fluid level when the steering wheel is turned. If the fluid level changes more than 0.2 inches (about a ¼ inch), the air has not been completely bled. Repeat the process.

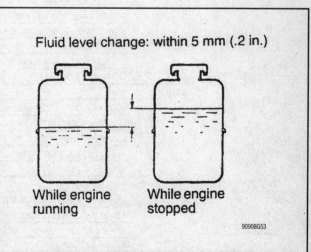

Fluid level change: within 5 mm (.2 in.)

While engine running

While engine stopped

90908G53

Fig. 123 Check whether or not the fluid level changes between when the engine is running and when it is stopped

TORQUE SPECIFICATIONS

System	Component	Ft. Lbs.	Nm
WHEELS			
	Lug Nuts	95	129
FRONT SUSPENSION			
	Struts		
	Cirrus/Stratus/Sebring conv./Breeze		
	Upper strut mounting bolts.	68	90
	Clevis-to-strut pin bolt	70	95
	Upper control arm ball joint castle nut	45	62
	Clevis-to-lower control arm mounting bolt	68	90
	Strut piston rod nut	40	55
	Sebring coupe/Avenger		
	Upper strut mounting nuts	32	44
	Upper damper fork pinch bolt	76	103
	Sway bar-to-damper fork link nut	29	39
	Strut piston rod nut	18	25
	Sway Bar		
	Cirrus/Stratus/Sebring conv./Breeze		
	Sway bar attaching link nuts	77	105
	Sway bar retainer bushing bolts	45	61
	Sebring coupe/Avenger		
	Sway bar mounting bracket bolts	28	39
	Damper fork-to-sway bar locking nuts	28	39
	Upper Control Arms		
	Cirrus/Stratus/Sebring conv./Breeze		
	Control arm-to-mounting bracket bolts	67	90
	Sebring coupe/Avenger		
	Control arm shaft-to-strut tower mounting nuts	62	86
	Ball joint-to-knuckle locking nut	20	28
	Lower Control Arms		
	Cirrus/Stratus/Sebring conv./Breeze		
	Control arm attaching bolts	85	115
	Control arm-to-steering knuckle nut	55	74
	Clevis-to-control arm bolt	65	88
	Front lower control arm nut and bolt	135	182
	Sebring coupe/Avenger		
	Damper fork-to-lateral lower control arm bolt	64	88
	Lateral lower arm ball joint nut	43-51	59-71
	Stay bracket-to-crossmember bolts	51-58	69-78
	Inner lateral lower arm mounting nut	71-85	98-118
	Compression lower arm-to-crossmember bolts	60	83
	Lower ball joint nut	43-51	59-71
	Steering Knuckle		
	Cirrus/Stratus/Sebring conv./Breeze		
	Upper control arm ball joint castle nut	45	62
	Lower ball joint castle nut	55	75
	Tie rod end-to-steering knuckle nut	45	62
	Wheel hub nut	180	244
	Sebring coupe/Avenger		
	Upper control arm ball joint nut	21	28
	Lower ball joint lock nuts	43-52	59-72
	Tie rod end-to-steering knuckle nut	18-25	24-34
	Wheel hub nut	188	255

90908C01

TORQUE SPECIFICATIONS

System	Component	Ft. Lbs.	Nm
FRONT SUSPENSION			
	Front Wheel Hub and Bearings		
	Cirrus/Stratus/Sebring conv./Breeze		
	Wheel hub nut	180	244
	Hub-to-steering knuckle bolts	80	110
	Sebring coupe/Avenger		
	Wheel hub nut	188	255
	Hub-to-steering knuckle bolts	65	88
REAR SUSPENSION			
	Struts		
	Cirrus/Stratus/Sebring conv./Breeze		
	Strut-to-rear knuckle bolt	70	95
	Upper strut mounting nuts	40	54
	Strut piston rod nut	40	55
	Sebring coupe/Avenger		
	Top plate mounting nuts	32	44
	Lower strut mounting bolt	71	98
	Strut piston rod nut	16	22
	Lower Control Arms		
	Cirrus/Stratus/Sebring conv./Breeze		
	Lateral link attaching bolts	70	95
	Sebring coupe/Avenger		
	Stabilizer bar link-to-lower control arm nut	28	39
	Lower control arm mounting nuts	71	98
	Lower ball joint-to-knuckle nut	20	28
	Toe control lower arm bolt	50-56	69-78
	Upper Control Arms		
	Cirrus/Stratus/Sebring conv./Breeze		
	Upper control arm-to-crossmember bolts	79	107
	Rear crossmember mounting bolts	70	95
	Upper control arm ball joint castle nut	50	67
	Strut clevis bracket-to-knuckle bolts	70	95
	Sebring coupe/Avenger		
	Control arm mounting bolts	41	57
	Upper control arm-to-subframe bolts	28	39
	Control arm-to-knuckle bolt	71	98
	Sway Bar		
	Cirrus/Stratus/Sebring conv./Breeze		
	Sway bar link nuts	40	55
	Hold-down clamp bolts	250 inch lbs.	28
	Sebring coupe/Avenger		
	Mounting bracket bolts	28	39
	Sway bar link locking nuts	28	39
	Rear Wheel Bearings		
	Cirrus/Stratus/Sebring conv./Breeze		
	Wheel hub retaining nut	185	250
	Sebring coupe/Avenger		
	Wheel hub-to-knuckle mounting bolts	54-65	74-88
STEERING			
	Steering Wheel		
	Cirrus/Stratus/Sebring conv./Breeze		
	Steering wheel retaining nut	45	61
	Speed control pod screws	15 inch lbs.	1.7
	Air bag module screws	85 inch lbs.	9.6

90908C02

TORQUE SPECIFICATIONS

System	Component	Ft. Lbs.	Nm
STEERING			
	Sebring coupe/Avenger		
	Steering wheel retaining nut	30	41
	Air bag module mounting bolts	43 inch lbs.	5
Combination Switch			
	Cirrus/Stratus/Sebring conv./Breeze		
	Combination switch mounting screws	20 inch lbs.	2.3
	Lower steering column cover retaining screws	17 inch lbs.	2
Tie Rod Ends			
	Cirrus/Stratus/Sebring conv./Breeze		
	Tie rod-to-steering knuckle nut	45	61
	Jam nut	55	75
	Sebring coupe/Avenger		
	Tie rod-to-steering knuckle nut	18-25	24-34
	Jam nut	36-40	50-55
Power Steering Gear (Rack and Pinion)			
	Cirrus/Stratus/Sebring conv./Breeze		
	Isolator and saddle bracket bolts	50	68
	Pressure and return line fittings	275 inch lbs.	31
	Crossmember bolts	120	163
	Engine support bracket-to-transaxle bracket bolts	55	75
	ABS control unit bolts	21	28
	Strut clevis-to-lower control arm bolt	68	92
	Tie rod end-to-steering knuckle nut	45	61
	Intermediate shaft pinch bolt	240 inch lbs.	27
	Sebring coupe/Avenger		
	Steering rack mounting bolts	51	69
	Pinch bolt	13	18
	Power steering fluid line high side fitting	11	15
	Engine rear roll stopper bolt	32	43
	Front center member mounting bolts	58-65	78-88
	Rear center member mounting bolts	51-58	69-78
	Engine front roll stopper bolt	42	57
	Triangular brace mounting bolts	51-58	69-78
	Tie rod end-to-steering knuckle nut	18-25	24-34
Power Steering Pump			
	Cirrus/Stratus/Sebring conv./Breeze		
	Power steering pump bolts	40	54
	Sebring coupe/Avenger		
	Pressure line fitting	13	18

90908C03

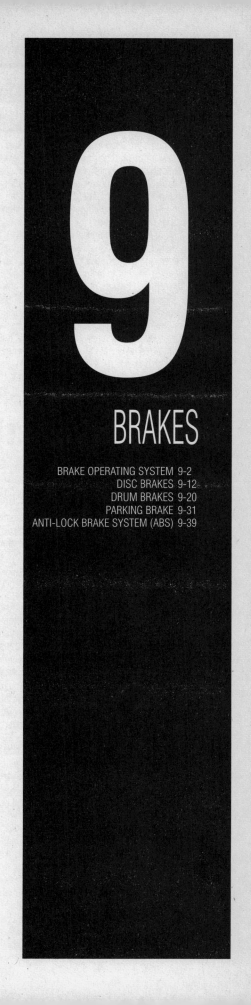

9

BRAKES

BRAKE OPERATING SYSTEM

Basic Operating Principles

Hydraulic systems are used to actuate the brakes of all modern automobiles. The system transports the power required to force the frictional surfaces of the braking system together from the pedal to the individual brake units at each wheel. A hydraulic system is used for two reasons.

First, fluid under pressure can be carried to all parts of an automobile by small pipes and flexible hoses without taking up a significant amount of room or posing routing problems.

Second, a great mechanical advantage can be given to the brake pedal end of the system, and the foot pressure required to actuate the brakes can be reduced by making the surface area of the master cylinder pistons smaller than that of any of the pistons in the wheel cylinders or calipers.

The master cylinder consists of a fluid reservoir along with a double cylinder and piston assembly. Double type master cylinders are designed to separate the front and rear braking systems hydraulically in case of a leak. The master cylinder coverts mechanical motion from the pedal into hydraulic pressure within the lines. This pressure is translated back into mechanical motion at the wheels by either the wheel cylinder (drum brakes) or the caliper (disc brakes).

Steel lines carry the brake fluid to a point on the vehicle's frame near each of the vehicle's wheels. The fluid is then carried to the calipers and wheel cylinders by flexible tubes in order to allow for suspension and steering movements.

In drum brake systems, each wheel cylinder contains two pistons, one at either end, which push outward in opposite directions and force the brake shoe into contact with the drum.

In disc brake systems, the cylinders are part of the calipers. At least one cylinder in each caliper is used to force the brake pads against the disc.

All pistons employ some type of seal, usually made of rubber, to minimize fluid leakage. A rubber dust boot seals the outer end of the cylinder against dust and dirt. The boot fits around the outer end of the piston on disc brake calipers, and around the brake actuating rod on wheel cylinders.

The hydraulic system operates as follows: When at rest, the entire system, from the piston(s) in the master cylinder to those in the wheel cylinders or calipers, is full of brake fluid. Upon application of the brake pedal, fluid trapped in front of the master cylinder piston(s) is forced through the lines to the wheel cylinders. Here, it forces the pistons outward, in the case of drum brakes, and inward toward the disc, in the case of disc brakes. The motion of the pistons is opposed by return springs mounted outside the cylinders in drum brakes, and by spring seals, in disc brakes.

Upon release of the brake pedal, a spring located inside the master cylinder immediately returns the master cylinder pistons to the normal position. The pistons contain check valves and the master cylinder has compensating ports drilled in it. These are uncovered as the pistons reach their normal position. The piston check valves allow fluid to flow toward the wheel cylinders or calipers as the pistons withdraw. Then, as the return springs force the brake pads or shoes into the released position, the excess fluid reservoir through the compensating ports. It is during the time the pedal is in the released position that any fluid that has leaked out of the system will be replaced through the compensating ports.

Dual circuit master cylinders employ two pistons, located one behind the other, in the same cylinder. The primary piston is actuated directly by mechanical linkage from the brake pedal through the power booster. The secondary piston is actuated by fluid trapped between the two pistons. If a leak develops in front of the secondary piston, it moves forward until it bottoms against the front of the master cylinder, and the fluid trapped between the pistons will operate the rear brakes. If the rear brakes develop a leak, the primary piston will move forward until direct contact with the secondary piston takes place, and it will force the secondary piston to actuate the front brakes. In either case, the brake pedal moves farther when the brakes are applied, and less braking power is available.

All dual circuit systems use a switch to warn the driver when only half of the brake system is operational. This switch is usually located in a valve body which is mounted on the firewall or the frame below the master cylin-

der. A hydraulic piston receives pressure from both circuits, each circuit's pressure being applied to one end of the piston. When the pressures are in balance, the piston remains stationary. When one circuit has a leak, however, the greater pressure in that circuit during application of the brakes will push the piston to one side, closing the switch and activating the brake warning light.

In disc brake systems, this valve body also contains a metering valve and, in some cases, a proportioning valve. The metering valve keeps pressure from traveling to the disc brakes on the front wheels until the brake shoes on the rear wheels have contacted the drums, ensuring that the front brakes will never be used alone. The proportioning valve controls the pressure to the rear brakes to lessen the chance of rear wheel lock-up during very hard braking.

Warning lights may be tested by depressing the brake pedal and holding it while opening one of the wheel cylinder bleeder screws. If this does not cause the light to go on, substitute a new lamp, make continuity checks, and, finally, replace the switch as necessary.

The hydraulic system may be checked for leaks by applying pressure to the pedal gradually and steadily. If the pedal sinks very slowly to the floor, the system has a leak. This is not to be confused with a springy or spongy feel due to the compression of air within the lines. If the system leaks, there will be a gradual change in the position of the pedal with a constant pressure.

Check for leaks along all lines and at wheel cylinders. If no external leaks are apparent, the problem is inside the master cylinder.

DISC BRAKES

Instead of the traditional expanding brakes that press outward against a circular drum, disc brake systems utilize a disc (rotor) with brake pads positioned on either side of it. An easily-seen analogy is the hand brake arrangement on a bicycle. The pads squeeze onto the rim of the bike wheel, slowing its motion. Automobile disc brakes use the identical principle but apply the braking effort to a separate disc instead of the wheel.

The disc (rotor) is a casting, usually equipped with cooling fins between the two braking surfaces. This enables air to circulate between the braking surfaces making them less sensitive to heat buildup and more resistant to fade. Dirt and water do not drastically affect braking action since contaminants are thrown off by the centrifugal action of the rotor or scraped off the by the pads. Also, the equal clamping action of the two brake pads tends to ensure uniform, straight line stops. Disc brakes are inherently self-adjusting. There are three general types of disc brake:

1. A fixed caliper.
2. A floating caliper.
3. A sliding caliper.

The fixed caliper design uses two pistons mounted on either side of the rotor (in each side of the caliper). The caliper is mounted rigidly and does not move.

The sliding and floating designs are quite similar. In fact, these two types are often lumped together. In both designs, the pad on the inside of the rotor is moved into contact with the rotor by hydraulic force. The caliper, which is not held in a fixed position, moves slightly, bringing the outside pad into contact with the rotor. There are various methods of attaching floating calipers. Some pivot at the bottom or top, and some slide on mounting bolts. In any event, the end result is the same.

DRUM BRAKES

Drum brakes employ two brake shoes mounted on a stationary backing plate. These shoes are positioned inside a circular drum which rotates with the wheel assembly. The shoes are held in place by springs. This allows them to slide toward the drums (when they are applied) while keeping the linings and drums in alignment. The shoes are actuated by a wheel cylinder which is mounted at the top of the backing plate. When the brakes are applied, hydraulic pressure forces the wheel cylinder's actuating links outward. Since these links bear directly against the top of the brake shoes, the tops of the shoes are then forced against the inner side of the drum. This action forces the bottoms of the two shoes to contact the brake drum by rotating the entire assembly slightly (known as servo action). When pressure within the wheel cylinder is relaxed, return springs pull the shoes back away from the drum.

Most modern drum brakes are designed to self-adjust themselves during application when the vehicle is moving in reverse. This motion causes both shoes to rotate very slightly with the drum, rocking an adjusting lever, thereby causing rotation of the adjusting screw. Some drum brake systems are designed to self-adjust during application whenever the brakes are applied. This on-board adjustment system reduces the need for maintenance adjustments and keeps both the brake function and pedal feel satisfactory.

POWER BOOSTERS

Virtually all modern vehicles use a vacuum assisted power brake system to multiply the braking force and reduce pedal effort. Since vacuum is always available when the engine is operating, the system is simple and efficient. A vacuum diaphragm is located on the front of the master cylinder and assists the driver in applying the brakes, reducing both the effort and travel he must put into moving the brake pedal.

The vacuum diaphragm housing is normally connected to the intake manifold by a vacuum hose. A check valve is placed at the point where the hose enters the diaphragm housing, so that during periods of low manifold vacuum brakes assist will not be lost.

Depressing the brake pedal closes off the vacuum source and allows atmospheric pressure to enter on one side of the diaphragm. This causes the master cylinder pistons to move and apply the brakes. When the brake pedal is released, vacuum is applied to both sides of the diaphragm and springs return the diaphragm and master cylinder pistons to the released position.

If the vacuum supply fails, the brake pedal rod will contact the end of the master cylinder actuator rod and the system will apply the brakes without any power assistance. The driver will notice that much higher pedal effort is needed to stop the car and that the pedal feels harder than usual.

Vacuum Leak Test

1. Operate the engine at idle without touching the brake pedal for at least one minute.
2. Turn off the engine and wait one minute.
3. Test for the presence of assist vacuum by depressing the brake pedal and releasing it several times. If vacuum is present in the system, light application will produce less and less pedal travel. If there is no vacuum, air is leaking into the system.

System Operation Test

1. With the engine **OFF**, pump the brake pedal until the supply vacuum is entirely gone.
2. Put light, steady pressure on the brake pedal.
3. Start the engine and let it idle. If the system is operating correctly, the brake pedal should fall toward the floor if the constant pressure is maintained.

Power brake systems may be tested for hydraulic leaks just as ordinary systems are tested.

❋❋ WARNING

Clean, high quality brake fluid is essential to the safe and proper operation of the brake system. You should always buy the highest quality brake fluid that is available. If the brake fluid becomes contaminated, drain and flush the system, then refill the master cylinder with new fluid. Never reuse any brake fluid. Any brake fluid that is removed from the system should be discarded.

Brake Light Switch

REMOVAL & INSTALLATION

Cirrus, Stratus, Sebring Convertible and Breeze

▶ **See Figures 1 and 2**

1. Disconnect the negative battery cable.
2. Depress and hold the brake pedal while rotating the brake light switch in a counterclockwise direction, about 30 degrees.
3. Pull the switch rearward, then remove it from its mounting bracket.
4. Detach the electrical connector from the brake light switch, then remove the switch from the vehicle.

To install:

➡ **Before installing the switch, you must move the plunger into its fully extended position, as described in the following step.**

5. Hold the brake light switch firmly in one hand. Use your other hand to pull outward on the plunger of the switch until it has ratcheted out to its fully extended position.

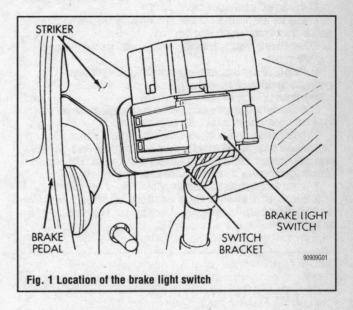

Fig. 1 Location of the brake light switch

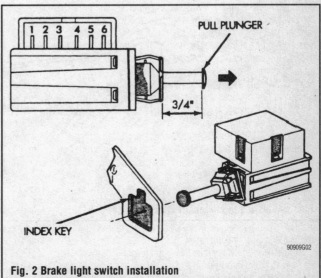

Fig. 2 Brake light switch installation

6. Attach the electrical connector to the brake light switch.
7. Mount the brake light switch into the bracket as follows:

   a. Depress the brake pedal as far down as possible, then install the switch in the bracket by aligning the index key on the switch with the slot at the top of the square hole in the mounting bracket.

   b. When the switch is fully installed in the bracket, rotate the switch clockwise about 30 degrees in order to lock the switch into the bracket.

❋❋ WARNING

Don't use extreme force when you pull on the brake pedal to adjust the switch. If too much force is used, you can damage the brake light switch or striker.

8. Gently pull back on the brake pedal until the pedal stops moving. This causes the switch plunger to ratchet backward to the proper position.
9. Connect the negative battery cable.

Sebring Coupe and Avenger

▶ **See Figures 3 and 4**

1. Disconnect the negative battery cable.
2. Depress and hold the brake pedal down while unscrewing the brake light switch in a counterclockwise direction.
3. Remove the brake light switch from the pedal support member assembly.
4. Detach the electrical connector from the brake light switch, then remove the switch from the vehicle.

To install:

5. Install the brake light switch into the pedal support member assembly by threading it in and rotating it clockwise.
6. Install the switch, but do not allow it to contact the brake pedal.
7. Adjust the height of the brake pedal by rotating the pedal pushrod with a pair of pliers. With the carpet turned back, the pedal height should measure approximately 7 inches from the foot panel of the floor.
8. Place the carpet back to its original position.
9. Screw in the brake light switch until it contacts the brake pedal stopper. Back off the brake light switch ½–1 turn and secure by tightening the switch locknut.

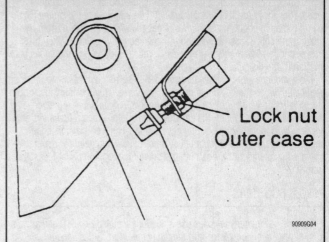

Fig. 4 Screw in the brake light switch until it contacts the brake pedal stopper

10. Attach the electrical connector to the brake light switch.
11. Connect the negative battery cable. Check the brake light for proper operation.

Master Cylinder

REMOVAL & INSTALLATION

Cirrus, Stratus, Sebring Convertible and Breeze

▶ **See Figures 5 thru 11**

1. With the ignition switch in the **OFF** position, pump the brake pedal until a firm pedal is achieved.
2. Before removing the master cylinder, remove the brake fluid in the reservoir using a hand held vacuum pump, equivalent tool.
3. Disengage the brake fluid level sensor electrical connector.

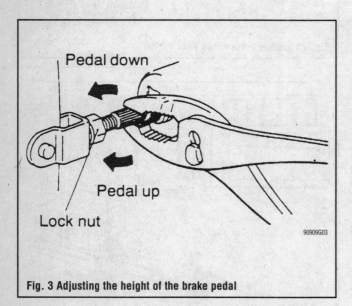

Fig. 3 Adjusting the height of the brake pedal

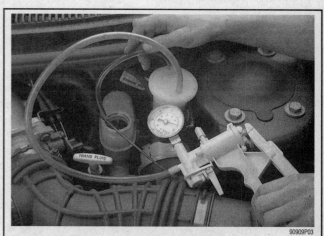

Fig. 5 Using a hand held vacuum pump, or equivalent, remove as much brake fluid as possible from the master cylinder reservoir

Fig. 6 Loosen the mounting nuts, then remove the speed control servo unit from the strut tower . . .

Fig. 7 . . . and swing the servo unit up. Disconnect the wiring harness and move it out of the way

Fig. 8 Unplug the brake fluid level sensor wiring connector

Fig. 9 Using a flare nut wrench, loosen, then disconnect the brake fluid lines from the master cylinder

Fig. 10 Remove the brake master cylinder mounting nuts . . .

Fig. 11 . . . then remove the brake master cylinder from the vehicle

4. Disconnect the hydraulic brake fluid lines from the master cylinder and plug off the openings to prevent dirt from contaminating the hydraulic system.

5. Clean the area around the mounting of the master cylinder with Brake Parts Cleaner, or equivalent.

6. Remove the master cylinder mounting nuts.

7. If equipped with ABS, remove the routing clip and chassis brake lines, as an assembly, from the inboard mounting stud for the master cylinder. Be careful not to bend or kink the chassis brake lines.

8. Remove the master cylinder.

To install:

9. Bench bleed the master cylinder before installing it into the vehicle.

10. Install the master cylinder onto the brake booster.

11. If equipped, install the routing clip and chassis brake lines on the inboard mounting stud for the master cylinder.

12. Tighten the master cylinder mounting nuts to 250 inch lbs. (28 Nm).

13. Connect the hydraulic lines to the master cylinder.

14. Tighten the hydraulic lines to 145 inch lbs. (17 Nm).

15. Connect the brake fluid level sensor electrical harness.

➡ **It is not necessary to the bleed the entire brake system after replacing the master cylinder. However, the master cylinder must have been properly bled and filled upon installation.**

16. Verify a firm brake pedal before attempting to move the vehicle. Carefully road test and check for proper operation.

Sebring Coupe and Avenger

▶ See Figure 12

✳✳ WARNING

Use care when working with brake fluid. Brake fluid is extremely harmful to painted surfaces.

1. Disconnect the negative battery cable first, then the positive battery cable.

2. Remove the battery from the vehicle.

3. If equipped with manual transaxle, remove the clutch fluid reservoir mounting bracket.

4. Remove the relay assembly mounting bolts and position off to the side.

5. Remove the windshield washer fluid tank.

6. Before removing the master cylinder, remove the brake fluid in the reservoir using a hand held vacuum pump, equivalent tool.

7. Disengage the fluid level sensor connector, if equipped.

8. Disconnect the hoses from the master cylinder to the fluid reservoir. Plug the hoses to prevent drainage.

9. Disconnect the brake lines from the master cylinder.

10. Remove the two nuts securing the master cylinder to the brake booster and remove the master cylinder.

To install:

11. Install the master cylinder to the booster mounting studs. Install the mounting nuts and tighten to 7 ft. lbs. (10 Nm).

12. Connect the reservoir hoses to the master cylinder and secure with clamps.

13. Connect the brake lines to the master cylinder and tighten to 11 ft. lbs. (15 Nm).

14. Connect the brake fluid level sensor wiring harness.

15. Install the windshield washer fluid tank.

16. Place the relay assembly back into correct position and tighten the mounting bolts.

17. If equipped, install the clutch fluid reservoir mounting bracket.

18. Install the battery. Connect the positive battery cable first, then the negative battery cable.

19. Fill the reservoir to the proper level with clean DOT 3 or DOT 4 brake fluid. Bleed the master cylinder.

20. Apply the brake pedal and check for firmness. If the pedal is spongy, air is present in the system and bleeding of the entire system is required.

21. Check the brakes for proper operation and leaks.

Power Brake Booster

REMOVAL & INSTALLATION

Cirrus, Stratus, Sebring Convertible and Breeze

2.0L AND 2.4L ENGINES

▶ See Figures 13, 14, 15 and 16

1. Disconnect the negative battery cable.

2. If equipped, disconnect the wiring harness from the speed control servo located on the left strut tower.

3. Remove the speed control servo mounting nuts. Move the speed control servo and cable assembly up and out of the way.

4. Remove the EVAP canister purge solenoid.

5. Disconnect the vacuum hoses from the power brake booster check valve.

6. Remove the electric EGR transducer solenoid.

7. Disconnect the brake fluid level sensor wiring harness from the side of the master cylinder.

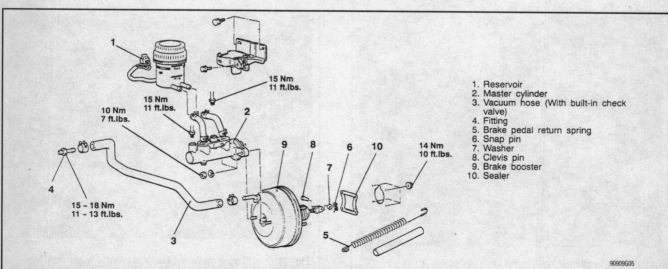

1. Reservoir
2. Master cylinder
3. Vacuum hose (With built-in check valve)
4. Fitting
5. Brake pedal return spring
6. Snap pin
7. Washer
8. Clevis pin
9. Brake booster
10. Sealer

15 Nm 11 ft.lbs.

15 Nm 11 ft.lbs.

10 Nm 7 ft.lbs.

15 – 18 Nm 11 – 13 ft.lbs.

14 Nm 10 ft.lbs.

90909G05

Fig. 12 Brake master cylinder and power booster component assembly—Sebring coupe and Avenger

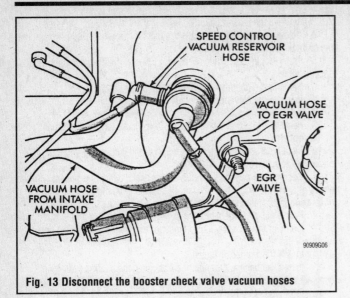

Fig. 13 Disconnect the booster check valve vacuum hoses

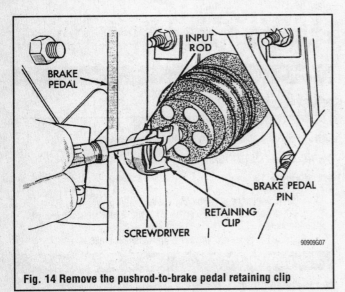

Fig. 14 Remove the pushrod-to-brake pedal retaining clip

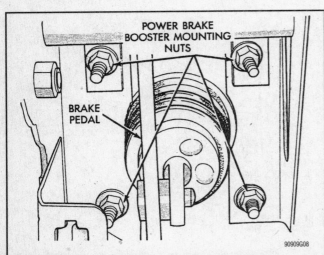

Fig. 15 From inside the vehicle, remove the power brake booster mounting nuts

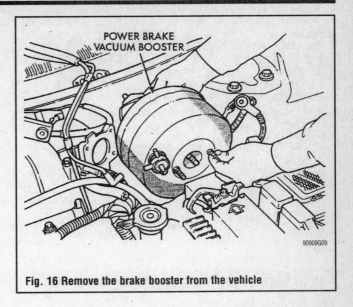

Fig. 16 Remove the brake booster from the vehicle

8. Remove the master cylinder mounting nuts and, without disconnecting any brake lines, separate the master cylinder from the vacuum booster unit. Carefully position the master cylinder and brake lines on top of the transaxle.

9. From inside the vehicle at the brake pedal, disengage the pushrod-to-brake pedal retaining clip. Discard the retaining clip and replace with a new one.

10. Remove the 4 brake booster mounting nuts, which are accessible from inside the vehicle against the firewall.

11. Remove the power brake booster from the vehicle through the engine compartment.

To install:

12. Place the power brake booster in proper position against the firewall and tighten the mounting nuts to 250 inch lbs. (29 Nm).

13. Using Lubriplate®, or equivalent multi-purpose lubricant, coat the surface of the brake pedal-to-booster pushrod retaining pin.

14. Connect the booster pushrod to the brake pedal pin and install a new retaining clip.

15. Place the master cylinder onto the brake booster and secure with the mounting nuts. Tighten the mounting nuts to 250 inch lbs. (28 Nm).

16. Connect the brake fluid level sensor wiring harness.

17. Install the EVAP canister purge solenoid.

18. Install the electric EGR transducer solenoid.

19. Connect the vacuum hoses to the power brake booster check valve.

20. Place the speed control servo unit in correct position on the mounting studs of the left strut tower and install the 2 retaining nuts. Tighten the nuts to 55 inch lbs. (6 Nm).

21. Connect the negative battery cable.

22. Check the brake system for proper operation.

2.5L ENGINE

▶ See Figures 13, 14, 15, 16 and 17

1. Disconnect the negative battery cable.

2. Remove the air cleaner/inlet duct assembly.

3. Remove the throttle body.

4. Remove the throttle and speed control cable bracket from the intake manifold.

5. Remove the EGR tube.

6. If equipped, disconnect the wiring harness from the speed control servo located on the left strut tower.

7. Remove the speed control servo mounting nuts. Move the speed control servo and cable assembly up and out of the way.

8. Remove the master cylinder.

9. Remove the EVAP canister purge solenoid and mounting bracket, as an assembly, from the vehicle.

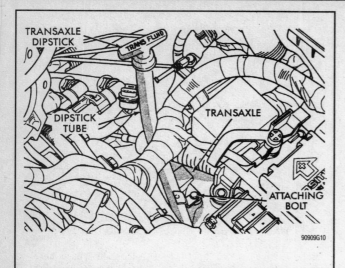

Fig. 17 Remove the transaxle fluid level dipstick and tube

10. Remove the mounting bolt, then pull out the transaxle fluid dipstick and tube from the vehicle.

11. Disconnect the vacuum hoses from the power brake booster check valve.

12. From inside the vehicle at the brake pedal, disengage the pushrod-to-brake pedal retaining clip. Discard the retaining clip and replace with a new one.

13. Remove the 4 brake booster mounting nuts, which are accessible from inside the vehicle against the firewall.

14. Remove the power brake booster from the vehicle through the engine compartment.

To install:

15. Place the power brake booster in proper position against the firewall and tighten the mounting nuts to 250 inch lbs. (29 Nm).

16. Using lubriplate, or equivalent, coat the surface of the brake pedal-to-booster pushrod retaining pin.

17. Connect the booster pushrod to the brake pedal pin and install a new retaining clip.

18. Connect the vacuum hoses to the power brake booster check valve.

19. Install the master cylinder.

20. Install the transaxle fluid dipstick and tube. Install and tighten the mounting bolt.

21. Install the EVAP canister purge solenoid and mounting bracket.

22. Place the speed control servo unit in correct position on the mounting studs of the left strut tower and install the 2 retaining nuts. Tighten the nuts to 55 inch lbs. (6 Nm).

23. Install the EGR tube.

24. Install the throttle and speed control cable bracket onto the intake manifold.

25. Install the throttle body.

26. Install the air cleaner/inlet duct assembly.

27. Connect the negative battery cable.

28. Check the brake system for proper operation.

Sebring Coupe and Avenger

▶ See Figure 12

❋❋ WARNING

Use care when working with brake fluid. Brake fluid is extremely harmful to painted surfaces.

1. Disconnect the negative battery cable first, then the positive battery cable.

2. Remove the battery from the vehicle.

3. Remove the master cylinder.

4. Disengage the clamp and disconnect the rubber vacuum hose at the power brake booster.

5. From inside the vehicle at the brake pedal, disengage the return spring.

6. Remove the pushrod clevis-to-brake pedal snap pin.

7. Remove the clevis pin and washer.

8. Remove the 4 booster mounting nuts from inside the vehicle.

9. Remove the power brake booster from the engine compartment.

To install:

10. Install the power brake booster into the vehicle and tighten the 4 mounting nuts to 10 ft. lbs. (14 Nm).

11. Position the pushrod clevis over the brake pedal and secure with the clevis pin, washer and snap pin. Lightly lubricate the clevis pin with a multi-purpose grease before installation.

12. Install the brake pedal return spring.

13. Connect the rubber vacuum hose to the power booster and secure with the hose clamp.

14. Install the master cylinder.

15. Install the battery. Connect the positive battery cable first, then the negative battery cable.

16. Fill the reservoir to the proper level with clean DOT 3 or DOT 4 brake fluid.

17. Apply the brake pedal and check for firmness. If the pedal is spongy, air is present in the system and bleeding of the entire system is required.

18. Check the brakes for proper operation and leaks.

Proportioning Valves

REMOVAL & INSTALLATION

Cirrus, Stratus, Sebring Convertible and Breeze

VEHICLES WITHOUT ABS

▶ See Figure 18

1. Disconnect the negative battery cable.

2. Using a back-up wrench, unfasten the brake tube from the faulty proportioning valve.

3. Remove the proportioning valve from the rear brake line.

❋❋ WARNING

Never attempt to disassemble a proportioning valve.

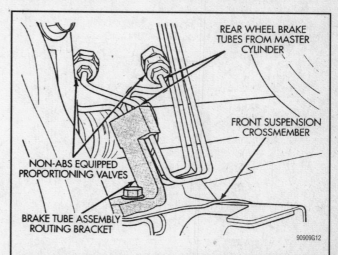

Fig. 18 Location of the proportioning valves on Cirrus, Stratus, Sebring convertible and Breeze

To install:

4. Install the proportioning valve in the rear brake line and hand-tighten both tube nuts until fully seated in the proportioning valve. Tighten the brake line tube nuts at the proportioning valve to 145 inch lbs. (17 Nm).

5. Connect the negative battery cable.

6. Bleed the brake system, as outlined later in this section.

VEHICLES WITH ABS

For proportioning valve removal on vehicles with ABS, please refer to the ABS portion of this section.

Sebring Coupe and Avenger

VEHICLES WITHOUT ABS

▶ **See Figure 19**

1. Disconnect the negative battery cable.

➡ **The official Chrysler Sebring Coupe/Avenger Factory Manual states that removing the entire engine assembly is required to remove the proportioning valve.**

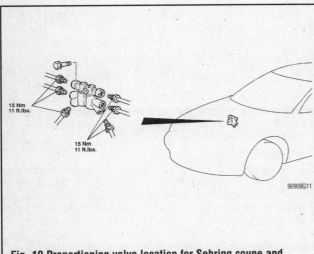

Fig. 19 Proportioning valve location for Sebring coupe and Avenger

2. If necessary, remove the engine assembly.

3. First label, then, using a flare nut wrench, unfasten the brake lines from the proportioning valve.

4. Loosen the mounting bolt and remove the proportioning valve from the vehicle.

To install:

5. Install the proportioning valve into the vehicle and tighten the mounting bolt.

6. Thread each brake line into its correct opening on the proportioning valve. Tighten each brake line fitting to 11 ft. lbs. (15 Nm).

7. If removed, install the engine assembly.

8. Connect the negative battery cable.

9. Bleed the brake system, as outlined later in this section.

VEHICLES WITH ABS

For proportioning valve removal on vehicles with ABS, please refer to the ABS portion of this section.

Brake Hoses and Lines

Metal lines and rubber brake hoses should be checked frequently for leaks and external damage. Metal lines are particularly prone to crushing

and kinking under the vehicle. Any such deformation can restrict the proper flow of fluid and therefore impair braking at the wheels. Rubber hoses should be checked for cracking or scraping; such damage can create a weak spot in the hose and it could fail under pressure.

Any time the lines are removed or disconnected, extreme cleanliness must be observed. Clean all joints and connections before disassembly (use a stiff bristle brush and clean brake fluid); be sure to plug the lines and ports as soon as they are opened. New lines and hoses should be flushed clean with brake fluid before installation to remove any contamination.

REMOVAL & INSTALLATION

▶ **See Figures 20 thru 25**

1. Disconnect the negative battery cable.

2. Raise and safely support the vehicle on jackstands.

3. Remove any wheel and tire assemblies necessary for access to the particular line you are removing.

4. Thoroughly clean the surrounding area at the joints to be disconnected.

5. Place a suitable catch pan under the joint to be disconnected.

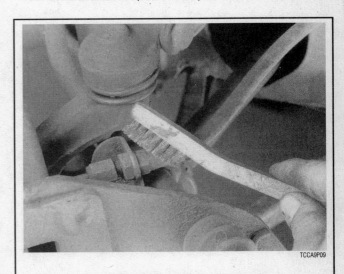

Fig. 20 Use a brush to clean the fittings of any debris

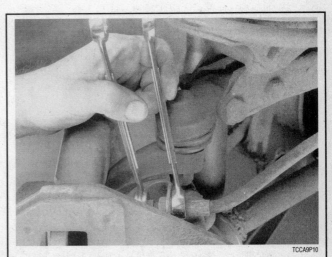

Fig. 21 Use two wrenches to loosen the fitting. If available, use flare nut type wrenches

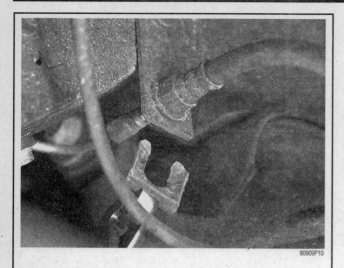

Fig. 22 Remove any retaining clip securing the line in position

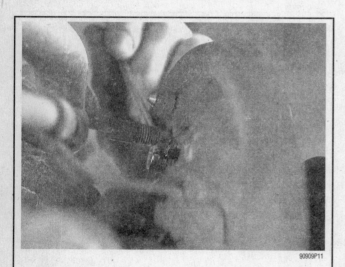

Fig. 23 Example of a rear wheel cylinder brake line fitting

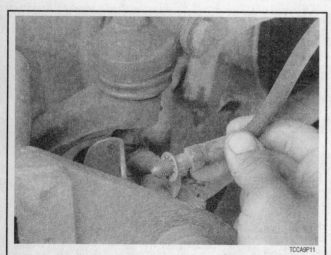

Fig. 24 Any gaskets/crush washers should be replaced with new ones during installation

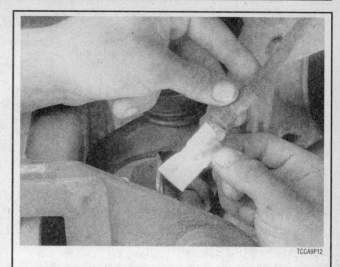

Fig. 25 Tape or plug the line to prevent contamination

6. Using two wrenches (one to hold the joint and one to turn the fitting), disconnect the hose or line to be replaced.

7. Disconnect the other end of the line or hose, moving the drain pan if necessary. Always use a backup wrench to avoid damaging the fitting.

8. Disconnect any retaining clips or brackets holding the line and remove the line from the vehicle.

➡**If the brake system is to remain open for more time than it takes to swap lines, tape or plug each remaining clip and port to keep contaminants out and fluid in.**

To install:

9. Install the new line or hose, starting with the end farthest from the master cylinder. Connect the other end, then confirm that both fittings are correctly threaded and turn smoothly using finger pressure. Make sure the new line will not rub against any other part. Brake lines must be at least ½ in. (13mm) from the steering column and other moving parts. Any protective shielding or insulators must be reinstalled in the original location.

✳✳ WARNING

Make sure the hose is NOT kinked or touching any part of the frame or suspension after installation. These conditions may cause the hose to fail prematurely.

10. Using two wrenches as before, tighten each fitting.
11. Install any retaining clips or brackets on the lines.
12. If removed, install the wheel and tire assemblies, then carefully lower the vehicle to the ground.
13. Refill the brake master cylinder reservoir with clean, fresh brake fluid, meeting DOT 3 specifications. Properly bleed the brake system.
14. Connect the negative battery cable.

Bleeding the Brake System

➡**For vehicles equipped with an Anti-lock Brake System (ABS), please refer to the ABS bleeding procedure at the end of this section.**

The purpose of bleeding the brakes is to expel air trapped in the hydraulic system. The system must be bled whenever the pedal feels spongy, indicating that compressible air has entered the system. It must also be bled whenever the system has been opened or repaired. If you are not using a pressure bleeder, you will need a helper for this job.

WARNING

Never reuse brake fluid which has been bled from the brake system.

MASTER CYLINDER

▶ **See Figure 26**

If the master cylinder is off the vehicle, it can be bench bled.

1. Secure the master cylinder in a bench vise.
2. Connect 2 short pieces of brake line to the outlet fittings, bend them until the free end is below the fluid level in the master cylinder reservoirs.
3. Fill the reservoir with fresh DOT 3 type brake fluid.
4. Using a wooden dowel, or equivalent, pump the piston slowly several times until no more air bubbles appear in the reservoirs.

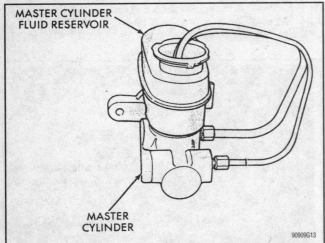

MASTER CYLINDER
FLUID RESERVOIR

MASTER
CYLINDER

90909G13

Fig. 26 Attach bleeding tubes to the master cylinder and position them as shown

5. Disconnect the 2 short lines, refill the master cylinder and securely install the cylinder cap.
6. If the master cylinder is on the vehicle, it can still be bled, using a flare nut wrench.
7. Open the brake lines slightly with the flare nut wrench, while pressure is applied to the brake pedal by a helper inside the vehicle.
8. Be sure to tighten the line before the brake pedal is released.
9. Repeat the process with both lines until no air bubbles come out.
10. Bleed the complete brake system, if necessary.

➡ **If the master cylinder has been thoroughly bled and filled to the proper level upon installation into the vehicle, it is not necessary to bleed the entire hydraulic system.**

PRESSURE BLEEDING

When bleeding the brakes, air may be trapped in the brake lines or valves far upstream, as much as 10 feet from the bleeder screw. Therefore, it is very important to have a fast flow of a large volume of brake fluid when bleeding the brakes, to make sure all of the air is expelled from the system.

On Cirrus, Stratus, Sebring convertible and Breeze models, the following wheel sequence should be used to ensure that all the air is removed from the system:
- Left rear wheel
- Right front wheel
- Right rear wheel
- Left front wheel

On Sebring coupe and Avenger models, the following wheel sequence should be used to ensure that all the air is removed from the system:
- Right rear wheel
- Left front wheel
- Left rear wheel
- Right front wheel

1. You should use bleeder tank tool C-3496-B or equivalent, with the required adapter for the master cylinder reservoir to pressurize the hydraulic system for bleeding. Make sure to follow the manufacturer's directions for using a pressure bleeder.
2. Attach a clear plastic hose to the bleeder screw located at the right rear wheel, then place the hose into a clean jar that has enough fresh brake fluid to submerge the end of the hose.
3. Open the bleeder screw at least one full turn or more to get a steady stream of fluid.
4. After about 4–8 oz. of fluid has been bled through the brake system and an air-free flow is maintained in the hose and jar, close the bleeder screw.
5. Repeat the procedure at all the other remaining bleeder screws. Then, check the pedal for travel. If pedal travel is excessive or has not improved, enough fluid has not passed through the system to expel all of the trapped air. Be sure to monitor the fluid level in the pressure bleeder. It must stay at the proper level so air will not be allowed to re-enter the brake system through the master cylinder reservoir.
6. Once the bleeding procedure is complete, remove the pressure bleeding equipment from the master cylinder.

MANUAL BLEEDING

▶ **See Figure 27**

➡ **Proper manual bleeding of the hydraulic brake system will require the use of an assistant.**

On Cirrus, Stratus, Sebring convertible and Breeze models, the following wheel sequence should be used to ensure that all the air is removed from the system:
- Left rear wheel
- Right front wheel
- Right rear wheel
- Left front wheel

On Sebring coupe and Avenger models, the following wheel sequence should be used to ensure that all the air is removed from the system:
- Right rear wheel

90909P24

Fig. 27 With a clear plastic hose in a container of clean brake fluid, open the bleeder screw at least one full turn

- Left front wheel
- Left rear wheel
- Right front wheel

1. Attach a clear plastic hose to the bleeder screw located at the right rear wheel, then place the hose into a clean jar that has enough fresh brake fluid to submerge the end of the hose.

2. Have an assistant pump the brake pedal 3–4 times, and hold it down before the bleeder screw is opened.

3. Open the bleeder screw at least one full turn. When the bleeder screw opens, the brake pedal will drop.

DISC BRAKES

✳✳ CAUTION

Older brake pads or shoes may contain asbestos, which has been determined to be cancer causing agent. Never clean the brake surface with compressed air! Avoid inhaling any dust from any brake surface! When cleaning brake surfaces, use a commercially available brake cleaning fluid.

Brake Pads

REMOVAL & INSTALLATION

Cirrus, Stratus, Sebring Convertible and Breeze

▶ **See Figures 28 thru 36**

1. Raise and safely support the vehicle.
2. Remove the appropriate wheel and tire assemblies.

➡**Regardless of their wear pattern, when brake pads are replaced on one side of the vehicle, they must also be replaced on the other side. It is advisable, however, to complete one side before beginning the other.**

3. Remove the 2 caliper-to-steering knuckle guide pin bolts.

4. Lift the caliper away from the steering knuckle by first rotating the free end of the caliper away from the steering knuckle. Then slide the opposite end of the caliper out from under the machined end of the steering knuckle.

5. Remove the brake pads from the caliper. Pull the inboard brake pad away from the piston until the retaining clip is free from the cavity in the piston. Remove the outboard brake pad by prying the pad retaining clip over the raised area on the caliper. Then slide the pad down and off the caliper.

4. Close the bleeder screw. Release the brake pedal only AFTER the bleeder screw is closed.

5. Repeat the procedure 4 or 5 times at each bleeder screw, then check the pedal for travel. If the pedal travel is not excessive, or has not been improved, enough fluid has not passed through the system to expel all of the trapped air. Make sure to watch the fluid level in the master cylinder reservoir. It must stay at the proper level so air will not re-enter the brake system.

6. Test drive the vehicle to be sure the brakes are operating correctly and that the pedal is solid.

6. Support the caliper from the upper control arm or coil spring to prevent the weight of the caliper from being supported by the brake flex hose, which will damage the hose.

To install:

7. Thoroughly clean all parts. Inspect the caliper for piston seal leaks (brake fluid in and around the boot area and inboard lining) and for any ruptures of the piston dust boot. If the boot is damaged or fluid leakage is visible, disassemble the caliper and install a new seal and boot (and piston, if scored).

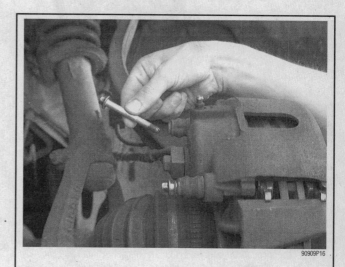

Fig. 29 . . . then pull them out of the caliper assembly

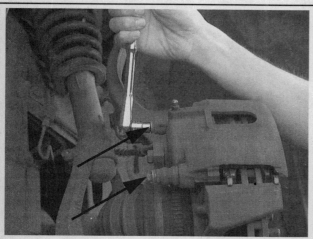

Fig. 28 Loosen the 2 caliper-to-steering knuckle guide pin bolts . . .

Fig. 30 Lift the brake caliper assembly away from the steering knuckle

Fig. 31 Remove the inboard pad by pulling it away from the caliper piston

Fig. 32 Remove the outboard brake pad by disengaging the retaining clip from the caliper assembly

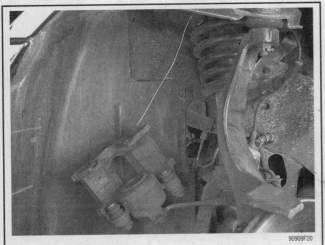

Fig. 33 Support the caliper assembly from the coil spring or upper control arm, using a strong piece of wire

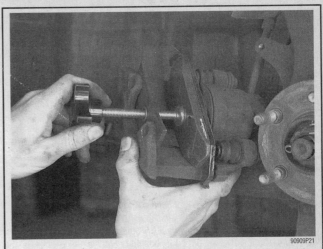

Fig. 34 Completely depress the brake piston into the caliper bore

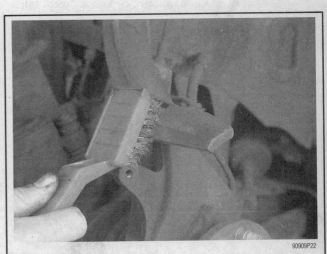

Fig. 35 Using a metal bristle brush, clean the area on the steering knuckle where the caliper slides . . .

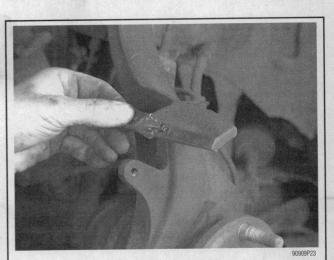

Fig. 36 . . . then lubricate the area with high temperature grease

8. Inspect the caliper pin bushings. Replace if damaged, dry or brittle.

9. Completely depress the piston into the caliper using a large C-clamp or other suitable tool.

10. Lubricate the area on the steering knuckle where the caliper slides with high temperature grease.

11. Install the new inboard brake pad into the caliper piston by firmly pressing into the piston bore. Install the brake pads into the caliper. Note that the inboard and outboard pads are different. Make sure the inboard brake pad assembly is positioned squarely against the face of the caliper piston.

➡**Be sure to remove the noise suppression gasket paper cover if the pads come so equipped.**

12. Install the new outboard brake pad onto the caliper assembly.

13. Carefully position the caliper and brake pad assemblies over the rotor by hooking the upper end of the caliper over the steering knuckle. Then, rotate the caliper into position at the bottom of the steering knuckle. Make sure the caliper guide pin bolts, bushings and sleeves are clear of the steering knuckle bosses.

14. Install the caliper guide pin bolts and tighten to 16 ft. lbs. (22 Nm).

15. Repeat Steps 2–14 for the corresponding position (front or rear) on the other side of the vehicle.

16. Install the wheel and tire assemblies. Tighten the lug nuts in 2 steps, in a star pattern to 95 ft. lbs. (129 Nm).

17. Lower the vehicle.

18. Pump the brake pedal until the brake pads are seated and a firm pedal is achieved before attempting to move the vehicle.

19. Road test the vehicle to check for proper operation.

Sebring Coupe and Avenger

➡ **See Figures 37 and 38**

1. Remove some of the brake fluid from the master cylinder reservoir. The reservoir should be no more than ½ full. When the pistons are depressed into the calipers, excess fluid will flow up into the reservoir.

2. Raise and safely support the vehicle.

3. Remove the appropriate tire and wheel assemblies.

4. Remove the caliper guide and lock pins and lift the caliper assembly from the caliper support. Tie the caliper out of the way using wire. Do not allow the caliper to hang by the brake line.

➡**On some models, the caliper can be flipped up by leaving the upper pin in place and using it as a pivot point.**

5. Remove the brake pads, spring clip and shims. Take note of the positioning to aid installation.

6. Install the wheel lug nuts onto the studs and lightly tighten. This is done to hold the disc on the hub.

To install:

7. Use a large C-clamp to compress the piston(s) back into the caliper bore.

8. Lubricate the slide points and install the brake pads, shims and spring clip onto the caliper support. Install the caliper over the brake pads.

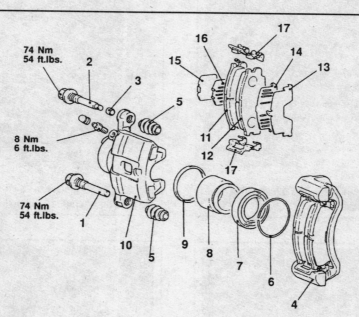

1. Guide pin
2. Lock pin
3. Bushing
4. Caliper support (pad, clip, shim)
5. Boot
6. Boot ring
7. Piston boot
8. Piston
9. Piston seal
10. Caliper body
11. Pad and wear indicator assembly
12. Pad assembly
13. Outer shim (stainless)
14. Outer shim (coated with rubber)
15. Inner shim (stainless)
16. Inner shim (coated with rubber)
17. Clip

Fig. 37 Front brake caliper and pad assembly—Sebring coupe and Avenger

90909G16

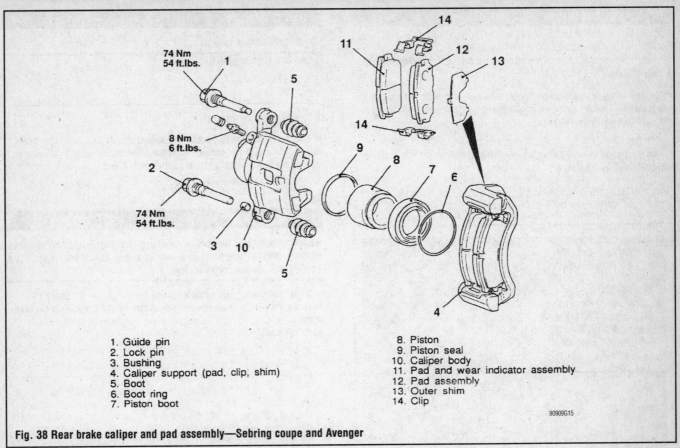

1. Guide pin
2. Lock pin
3. Bushing
4. Caliper support (pad, clip, shim)
5. Boot
6. Boot ring
7. Piston boot

8. Piston
9. Piston seal
10. Caliper body
11. Pad and wear indicator assembly
12. Pad assembly
13. Outer shim
14. Clip

90909G15

Fig. 38 Rear brake caliper and pad assembly—Sebring coupe and Avenger

➡ **Be careful that the piston boot does not become caught when lowering the caliper onto the support. Do not twist the brake hose during caliper installation.**

9. Lubricate and install the caliper guide and lock pins in their original positions. Tighten the guide and locking pins to 54 ft. lbs. (74 Nm).
10. Install the tire and wheel assemblies. Lower the vehicle.

✳✳ CAUTION

Pump the brake pedal several times, until firm, before attempting to move the vehicle.

11. Road test the vehicle and check brakes for proper operation.

INSPECTION

▶ **See Figure 39**

1. If you can't accurately determine the condition of the brake pads by visual inspection, you must remove the caliper, then remove the brake pads.
2. Measure the thickness of the brake pad's lining material at the thinnest portion of the assembly. Do not include the pad's metal backing plate in the measurement.
3. On Cirrus, Stratus, Sebring convertible and Breeze models, when a set of brake pads are worn to a total thickness of ⅜ in. (9.0mm) for front brakes, or ⅛ in. (3.0mm) for rear brakes, they should be replaced.
4. On Sebring coupe and Avenger models, when a set of brake pads are worn to a total thickness of ³⁄₃₂ in. (2.0mm), they should be replaced.

5. Replace both brake shoe assemblies (inboard and outboard). It is necessary that both front wheel sets be replaced whenever the brake shoe assemblies on either side are replaced.
6. If the brake shoes do not require replacement, reinstall the assemblies making sure each brake shoe is returned to the original position.

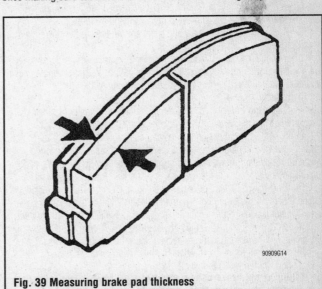

90909G14

Fig. 39 Measuring brake pad thickness

Brake Caliper

REMOVAL & INSTALLATION

▶ See Figure 40

➥Do not allow the master cylinder reservoir to empty. An empty reservoir will allow air to enter the brake system and complete system bleeding will be required.

1. Remove about half of the brake fluid from the master cylinder.
2. Raise and safely support the vehicle, then remove the tire and wheel assembly.
3. Position a C-clamp, or other suitable tool, over the caliper. Smoothly apply pressure, forcing the caliper piston into the caliper bore until it bottoms. Remove the C-clamp or other tool.

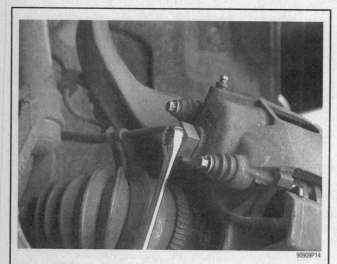

90909P14

Fig. 40 Loosen the brake hose-to-caliper attaching bolt

4. If the caliper is to be completely removed from the vehicle, remove the brake hose attaching bolt, then disconnect the brake hose from the caliper and plug the hose to prevent fluid contamination or loss.
5. Remove the caliper mounting bolts and lift the caliper off of the support bracket.
6. Remove the caliper from the vehicle. If the caliper is only removed for access to other components, support the caliper, with the brake hose attached, so that there is no strain on the brake hose.

To install:

7. Clean and lubricate both steering knuckle abutments or support brackets with a coating of multi-purpose grease.
8. Position the caliper and brake pad assembly over the brake rotor. Be sure to properly install the caliper assembly into the abutments of the steering knuckle or support bracket. Be sure the caliper guide pin bolts, rubber bushings and sleeves are clear of the steering knuckle bosses.
9. On Cirrus, Stratus, Sebring convertible and Breeze models, install the caliper guide pin bolts and tighten to 16 ft. lbs. (22 Nm). On Sebring coupe and Avenger models, tighten the caliper guide pin bolts to 54 ft. lbs. (74 Nm).
10. On Cirrus, Stratus, Sebring convertible and Breeze models, connect the brake line hose to the caliper and tighten to 35 ft. lbs. (48 Nm). On Sebring coupe and Avenger models, connect the brake line hose to the caliper and tighten to 22 ft. lbs. (29 Nm).
11. Fill the master cylinder with fresh brake fluid and, if the brake hose was removed, bleed the brake system.
12. Install the wheel and tire. Tighten the lug nuts in a star pattern to 95 ft. lbs. (129 Nm).
13. Lower the vehicle.
14. Depress the brake pedal 3–4 times to seat the brake linings and to restore pressure in the system.

✷✷ CAUTION

Do not move the vehicle until a firm pedal is obtained.

15. Road test the vehicle and check for proper operation.

OVERHAUL

▶ See Figures 41 thru 48

➥Some vehicles may be equipped dual piston calipers. The procedure to overhaul the caliper is essentially the same with the exception of multiple pistons, O-rings and dust boots.

1. Remove the caliper from the vehicle and place on a clean workbench.

✷✷ CAUTION

NEVER place your fingers in front of the pistons in an attempt to catch or protect the pistons when applying compressed air. This could result in personal injury!

➥Depending upon the vehicle, there are two different ways to remove the piston from the caliper. Refer to the brake pad replacement procedure to make sure you have the correct procedure for your vehicle.

2. The first method is as follows:
   a. Stuff a shop towel or a block of wood into the caliper to catch the piston.
   b. Remove the caliper piston using compressed air applied into the caliper inlet hole. Inspect the piston for scoring, nicks, corrosion and/or worn or damaged chrome plating. The piston must be replaced if any of these conditions are found.
3. For the second method, you must rotate the piston to retract it from the caliper.
4. If equipped, remove the anti-rattle clip.
5. Use a prytool to remove the caliper boot, being careful not to scratch the housing bore.
6. Remove the piston seals from the groove in the caliper bore.
7. Carefully loosen the brake bleeder valve cap and valve from the caliper housing.
8. Inspect the caliper bores, pistons and mounting threads for scoring or excessive wear.
9. Use crocus cloth to polish out light corrosion from the piston and bore.

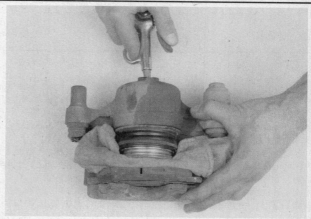

TCCA9P01

Fig. 41 For some types of calipers, use compressed air to drive the piston out of the caliper, but make sure to keep your fingers clear

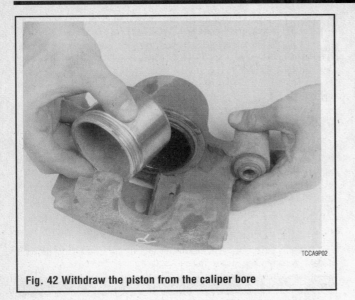

Fig. 42 Withdraw the piston from the caliper bore

Fig. 45 . . . then remove the boot from the caliper housing, taking care not to score or damage the bore

Fig. 43 On some vehicles, you must remove the anti-rattle clip

Fig. 46 Use extreme caution when removing the piston seal; DO NOT scratch the caliper bore

Fig. 44 Use a prytool to carefully pry around the edge of the boot . . .

Fig. 47 Use the proper size driving tool and a mallet to properly seal the boots in the caliper housing

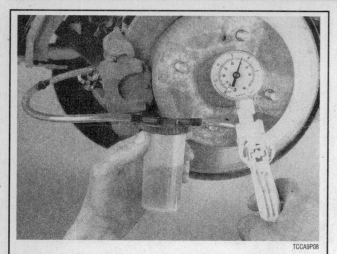

Fig. 48 There are tools, such as this Mighty-Vac, available to assist in proper brake system bleeding

10. Clean all parts with denatured alcohol and dry with compressed air.
To assemble:
11. Lubricate and install the bleeder valve and cap.
12. Install the new seals into the caliper bore grooves, making sure they are not twisted.
13. Lubricate the piston bore.
14. Install the pistons and boots into the bores of the calipers and push to the bottom of the bores.
15. Use a suitable driving tool to seat the boots in the housing.
16. Install the caliper in the vehicle.
17. Install the wheel and tire assembly, then carefully lower the vehicle.
18. Properly bleed the brake system.

Brake Disc (Rotor)

REMOVAL & INSTALLATION

▶ **See Figure 49**

1. Remove about half of the brake fluid from the master cylinder.
2. Raise and safely support the vehicle and remove the tire/wheel assembly.

Fig. 49 Remove the brake rotor by pulling it straight off the wheel mounting studs

3. Remove the 2 caliper guide pin or mounting bolts.
4. Lift the caliper assembly away from the brake rotor.
5. Support the caliper assembly from the upper control arm to prevent the weight of the caliper from being supported by the brake flex hose which will damage the hose.
6. Remove the brake rotor by pulling it straight off the wheel mounting studs.

To install:

7. Completely retract the piston into the caliper using a large C-clamp or other suitable tool.
8. Install the brake rotor onto the wheel hub.
9. Install the caliper assembly over the brake rotor and install the guide pin or mounting bolts.
10. On Cirrus, Stratus, Sebring convertible and Breeze models, tighten the caliper guide pin bolts to 16 ft. lbs. (22 Nm). On Sebring coupe and Avenger models, tighten the support bracket bolts to 65 ft. lbs. (88 Nm).
11. Fill the master cylinder to the proper level with fresh brake fluid.
12. Install the tire/wheel assembly and lower the vehicle.
13. Pump the brake pedal until the brake pads are seated and a firm pedal is achieved before attempting to move the vehicle.

✳✳ CAUTION

Do not move the vehicle until a firm pedal is obtained.

14. Road test the vehicle to check for proper operation.

INSPECTION

Cirrus, Stratus, Sebring Convertible and Breeze

▶ **See Figures 50, 51 and 52**

Whenever the brake calipers or pads are removed, inspect the rotors for defects. The brake rotor is an extremely important component of the brake system. Cracks, large scratches or warpage can adversely affect the braking system, at times to the point of becoming very dangerous.

Light scoring is acceptable. Heavy scoring or warping will necessitate refinishing or replacement of the disc. The brake disc must be replaced if cracks or burned marks are evident.

Check the thickness of the disc using a micrometer. Measure the thickness at 12 equally spaced points 1 in. (25mm) from the edge of the disc. If thickness varies more than 0.0005 in. (0.013mm), the disc should be refinished, provided equal amounts are cut from each side and the thickness does not fall below 0.843 in. (21.4mm). Be sure to remove as little as necessary from each rotor side.

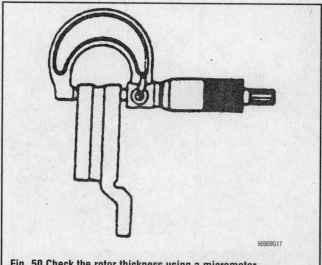

Fig. 50 Check the rotor thickness using a micrometer

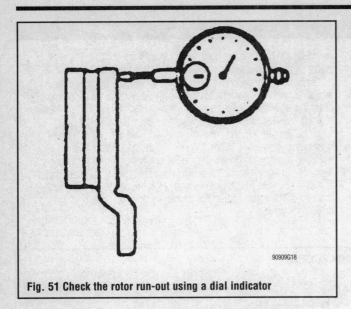

Fig. 51 Check the rotor run-out using a dial indicator

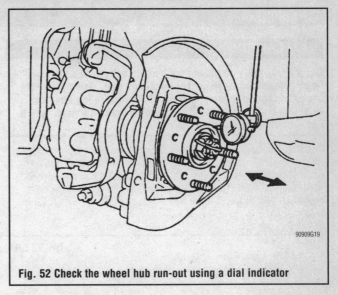

Fig. 52 Check the wheel hub run-out using a dial indicator

Check the run-out (warpage) of the disc using a dial indicator. Total run-out of the disc installed on the car should not exceed 0.005 in. (0.013mm). The disc can be resurfaced to correct minor variations, as long as equal amounts are cut from each side and the thickness is at least 0.882 inch (22.4mm) after resurfacing.

Check the run-out of the hub (disc removed). It should not be more than 0.002–0.003 inch (0.050–0.076mm). If so, the hub should be replaced.

All rotors have markings for MINIMUM allowable thickness cast on an unmachined surface or an alternate surface. Always use this specification as the **minimum** allowable thickness or refinishing limit. Refer to a local auto parts store or machine shop, if necessary, where rotors are resurfaced.

If the rotor needs to be replaced with a new part, the protective coating on the braking surface of the rotor must be removed with an appropriate solvent before installing the rotor to the vehicle.

Sebring Coupe and Avenger

▶ **See Figures 50, 51 and 52**

Whenever the brake calipers or pads are removed, inspect the rotors for defects. The brake rotor is an extremely important component of the brake system. Cracks, large scratches or warpage can adversely affect the braking system, at times to the point of becoming very dangerous.

Light scoring is acceptable. Heavy scoring or warping will necessitate refinishing or replacement of the disc. The brake disc must be replaced if cracks or burned marks are evident.

Check the thickness of the disc using a micrometer. Measure the thickness at 8 equally spaced points approximately 45° apart and 0.39 inch (10mm) in from the outer edge of the disc. If thickness varies more than 0.0006 inch (0.015mm), the disc should be refinished, provided equal amounts are cut from each side. The rotor's thickness must not fall below 0.880 inch (22.4mm) for the front, 0.330 inch (8.40mm) for rear solid rotors, or 0.720 inch (18.4mm) for rear ventilated discs. Be sure to remove as little as necessary from each rotor side.

Check the run-out (warpage) of the disc using a dial indicator placed 0.2 inch (5mm) from the outer edge of the rotor. Total run-out of the disc installed on the car should not exceed 0.0031 inch (0.08mm). The disc can be resurfaced to correct minor variations, as long as equal amounts are cut from each side and the thickness does not exceed the minimum thickness after resurfacing.

Check the run-out of the hub (disc removed). It should not be more than 0.002 inch (0.050mm). If so, the hub should be replaced.

All brake discs or rotors have markings for MINIMUM allowable thickness cast on an unmachined surface or an alternate surface. Always use this specification as the **minimum** allowable thickness or refinishing limit. Refer to a local auto parts store or machine shop, if necessary, where rotors are resurfaced.

If the rotor needs to be replaced with a new part, the protective coating on the braking surface of the rotor must be removed with an appropriate solvent before installing the rotor to the vehicle.

DRUM BRAKES

✳✳ CAUTION

Older brake pads or shoes may contain asbestos, which has been determined to be cancer causing agent. Never clean the brake surface with compressed air! Avoid inhaling any dust from any brake surface! When cleaning brake surfaces, use a commercially available brake cleaning fluid.

Cirrus, Stratus and Breeze models are equipped with a 2 shoe (leading/trailing), internal expanding type of rear drum brakes with automatic self-adjuster mechanisms. The automatic self-adjuster mechanisms used on these vehicles are new designs and function differently than the screw type adjusters used in the past. These new self-adjusters are still actuated each time the vehicle's service brakes are applied. The new adjusters are located directly below the wheel cylinders.

The Sebring coupe, convertible and Avenger models are equipped with a rear wheel, 2 shoe (leading/trailing) internally expanding type of drum brakes with an automatic self-adjuster mechanism. The automatic self-adjuster mechanism used on these vehicles is the screw type adjuster. The self-adjuster mechanism is actuated each time the vehicle's service brakes are applied. Generally, drum brakes with a self-adjusting mechanism do not require manual brake shoe adjustment. Although, in the event that the brake shoes are replaced, it is advisable to make the initial adjustment manually to speed up the initial adjustment time. The initial adjustment procedure must be done prior to driving the vehicle.

DRUM BRAKE COMPONENTS

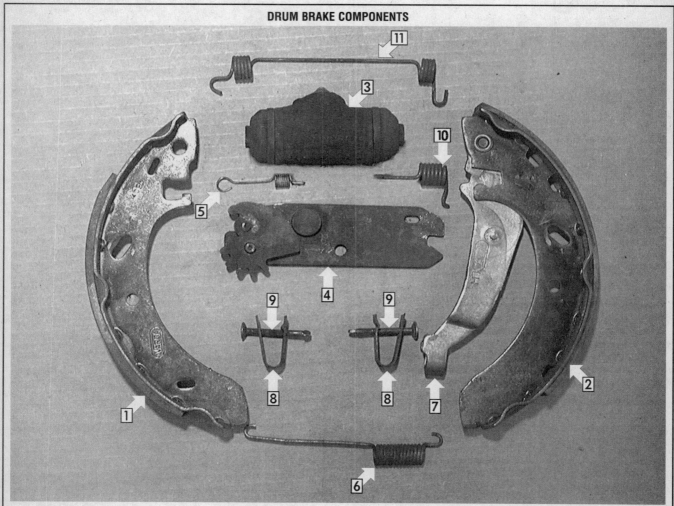

90909P12

1. Leading brake shoe
2. Trailing brake shoe
3. Wheel cylinder
4. Automatic self-adjuster mechanism
5. Self-adjuster mechanism spring
6. Lower return spring
7. Parking brake lever
8. Hold-down clips
9. Hold-down clip retaining pins
10. Actuating spring
11. Upper return spring

Brake Drums

REMOVAL & INSTALLATION

▶ **See Figures 53 and 54**

1. Raise and safely support the vehicle.
2. Remove the rear tire and wheel assembly.

➡**If the vehicle has high mileage, the brake drums may have a ridge worn in them by the brake shoes. This ridge causes the brake drum to interfere with the brake shoes, thereby preventing drum removal. Clearance can be obtained by backing off the brake's automatic self-adjuster mechanism, using the following procedures.**

3. For Cirrus, Stratus and Breeze models, use the following procedure:
   a. Locate and remove the rubber plug from the brake support plate (backing plate).
   b. Insert a brake adjuster tool or similarly-shaped prytool through the automatic adjuster access hole and engage the teeth on the adjuster wheel. Rotate the adjuster wheel so it is moved toward the front of the vehicle. Continue moving the adjuster until it stops; this will back off the adjustment of the rear brake shoes.

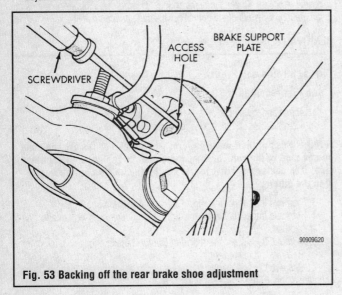

Fig. 53 Backing off the rear brake shoe adjustment

Fig. 54 After removing the rear wheel, pull off the brake drum

4. For Sebring coupe, convertible and Avenger models, use the following procedure for releasing the self-adjusting mechanism:
   a. Locate and remove the rubber plug from the brake support plate (backing plate).
   b. Insert a brake adjuster tool or similarly shaped prytool through the automatic adjuster access hole and carefully push the adjuster actuating lever out of engagement with the adjuster star wheel. While holding the lever away from the star wheel, insert a second prytool through the access hole and engage the teeth on the adjuster wheel. Rotate the adjuster wheel upward away from the ground; this will back off the adjustment of the rear brake shoes.
5. Remove the brake drum from the hub assembly.

To install:

6. Inspect the brake drum for cracks or signs of overheating. Measure the drum run-out and diameter. If not to specification, resurface the drum. Run-out should not exceed 0.006 in. (0.15mm). The diameter variation (oval shape) of the drum braking surface must not exceed either 0.0025 in. (0.064mm) in 30 degrees of rotation, or 0.0035 in. (0.089mm) in 360 degrees of rotation. All brake drums are marked with the maximum allowable brake drum diameter on the face of the drum.
7. Install the brake drum onto the hub assembly.
8. Install the tire and wheel assembly. Tighten the lug nuts in a star pattern to 95 ft. lbs. (129 Nm).
9. If necessary, repeat Steps 2–8 for the other brake drum.
10. Properly adjust the rear brakes.
11. Lower the vehicle.
12. Road test the vehicle to check for proper brake operation.

INSPECTION

▶ **See Figures 55 and 56**

1. Inspect the brake drums for cracks, signs of overheating or excessive wear.
2. On Cirrus, Stratus, Sebring convertible and Breeze models, perform the following inspection checks:
   a. Measure the drum run-out and diameter. If not to specification, resurface the drum. Run-out should not exceed 0.006 inch (0.15mm). The diameter variation (oval shape) of the drum braking surface must not exceed either 0.0025 inch (0.064mm) in 30° rotation, or 0.0035 inch (0.089mm) in 360° rotation.
3. On the Sebring coupe and Avenger models, measure the brake drum's inside diameter. Wear limit on the brake drum inside diameter is 230.6mm (9.0 inches).

➡**All brake drums are marked with the maximum allowable brake drum diameter on the face of the drum.**

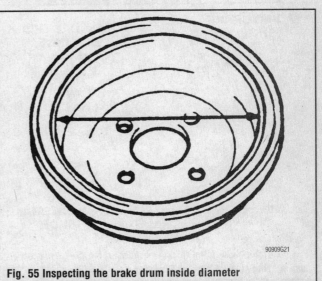

Fig. 55 Inspecting the brake drum inside diameter

Fig. 56 The maximum machining diameter is cast into the outer rim of the brake drum

Brake Shoes

INSPECTION

▶ See Figures 57 and 58

1. On Cirrus, Stratus, Sebring convertible and Breeze models, measure the combined thickness of the brake shoe rim and lining. The minimum leading brake shoe rim and lining thickness specification is ⅛ inch (3.0mm). The minimum trailing brake shoe rim and lining thickness specification is ⁷⁄₆₄ inch (2.8mm).

2. On Sebring coupe and Avenger models, measure the thickness of the brake shoe lining material only. The minimum brake shoe lining thickness specification is ³⁄₆₄ inch (1.0mm).

3. If any of the measurements fall below the minimum specifications, replace the brake shoes.

4. Thoroughly clean all parts. The brake lining should show contact across the entire width and from heel to toe; otherwise, replace. Clean and inspect the brake support plate and the automatic adjuster mechanism. Be sure that the adjuster mechanism has full movement throughout it adjustment range and that its teeth should be in good condition. If the adjuster is worn or damaged, replace it. If the adjuster is serviceable, lubricate the moving parts with high-

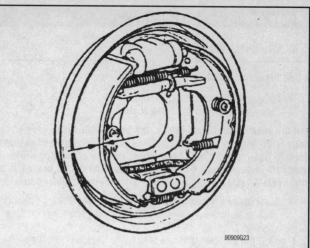

Fig. 58 Brake shoe lining thickness measurement—Sebring coupe and Avenger

temperature grease. Check the brake springs. Overheating indications are paint discoloration or distorted end coils. Replace parts as required.

REMOVAL & INSTALLATION

Cirrus, Stratus and Breeze

▶ See Figures 59 thru 70

1. Raise and safely support the vehicle.
2. Remove the rear tire and wheel assemblies.

➡Regardless of their wear pattern, when brake shoes are replaced on one side of the vehicle, they must also be replaced on the other side. It is advisable, however, to complete one side before beginning the other.

3. Remove the brake drum from the hub assembly.
4. Remove the actuating spring from the adjuster mechanism and trailing brake shoe.
5. Remove the upper return spring from the brake shoes.
6. Remove the lower return spring from the brake shoes.
7. Remove the brake shoe retainer and pin attaching the leading brake shoe assembly to the brake support plate.

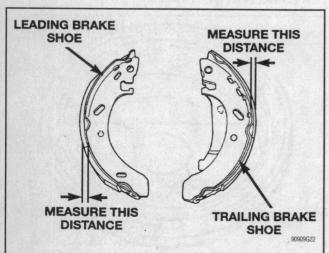

Fig. 57 Brake shoe lining thickness measurement—Cirrus, Stratus, Sebring convertible and Breeze

Fig. 59 Remove the actuating spring from the adjuster mechanism and trailing brake shoe

Fig. 60 Remove the upper spring using needlenose pliers

Fig. 63 Unfasten the trailing brake shoe retainer support plate

Fig. 61 Notice that the hooks on each end of the spring are different, so it can only be installed one way

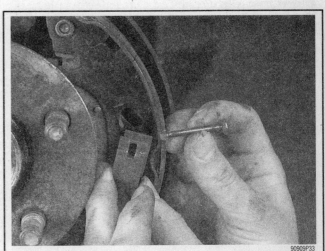

Fig. 64 Remove the retainer and pin attaching the trailing brake shoe assembly to the brake support plate

Fig. 62 Remove the lower return spring from the brake shoes

Fig. 65 Remove the leading brake shoe and adjuster mechanism as an assembly

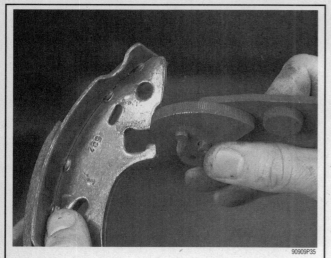

Fig. 66 Remove the adjuster mechanism from the brake shoe

Fig. 67 Use pliers to separate the parking brake cable from the actuating lever

Fig. 68 Unlike most actuating levers, this actuator is permanently attached to the shoe by a rivet

Fig. 69 Clean the brake shoe contact points of the backing plate . . .

Fig. 70 . . . then lubricate the contact points

8. Remove the leading brake shoe and adjuster mechanism as an assembly from the rear brake support plate. The adjuster mechanism cannot be separated from the leading brake shoe until the brake shoe and adjuster mechanism is removed from the support plate.

9. Remove the trailing brake shoe retainer and pin attaching the trailing brake shoe assembly to the brake support plate. Remove the trailing brake shoe assembly.

➡**On this vehicle, the parking brake actuating lever is permanently attached to the trailing brake shoe assembly. Do not attempt to remove it from the original brake shoe assembly or reuse the original actuating lever on a replacement brake shoe assembly. All replacement brake shoe assemblies for this vehicle must have the actuating lever as part of the trailing brake shoe assembly.**

10. Remove the parking brake cable from the parking brake lever. Do not remove the lever from the brake shoe.

11. Remove the automatic adjuster mechanism from the brake shoe by fully extending the adjuster, then rotating the adjuster to release from the brake shoe.

To install:

12. Lubricate the 8 brake shoe contact points with high-temperature grease.

➡The trailing brake shoe assemblies used on the rear brakes of this vehicle are unique (handed) for the left and right side of the vehicle. Care must be taken to ensure that the brake shoes are properly installed on their correct side of the vehicle. When the trailing shoes are properly installed on their correct side of the vehicle, the parking brake actuating lever will be positioned under the brake shoe web.

13. Install the parking brake cable onto the parking brake lever, then install the trailing brake shoe and attaching pin.

14. Install the automatic self-adjuster on the leading brake shoe by rotating it inward to attach. Install the leading shoe and adjuster assembly to the brake support plate.

15. Make sure the leading brake shoe is squarely seated on the brake support plate shoe contact areas and install the brake retainer on the retainer pin.

16. Install the lower return spring.

➡The upper brake shoe return spring and adjuster mechanism actuating spring are unique for each side of the vehicle. The springs are colored for identification. The left side springs are green and the right side springs are blue.

17. Install the upper return spring (blue on right side; green on left side) on the leading brake shoe first, then on the trailing brake shoe.

18. Install the self-adjuster spring on the trailing brake shoe first, then attach it to the adjuster.

19. Install the brake drum.

20. Repeat Steps 3–19 for the other rear wheel's brake assembly.

21. Install the tire and wheel assemblies. Tighten the lug nuts in a star pattern to 95 ft. lbs. (129 Nm).

22. Lower the vehicle.

23. Adjust the rear brakes shoes.

24. Road test the vehicle to check for proper brake operation.

Sebring Convertible

▶ See Figures 71 thru 79

➡When removing the rear brake shoes, replace the brake shoes from only one side of the vehicle at a time. This is due to the automatic adjustment feature of the parking brake system. If the brake shoes are removed from both sides of the vehicle at the same time, the automatic adjuster will remove all slack from the parking brake cables, which will make brake shoe installation extremely difficult.

1. Raise and safely support the vehicle.

2. Remove the rear wheel assembly.

3. Remove the brake drum from the hub assembly.

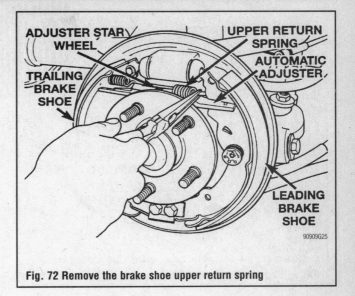

Fig. 72 Remove the brake shoe upper return spring

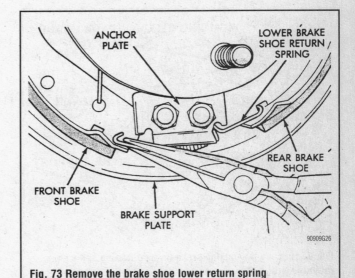

Fig. 73 Remove the brake shoe lower return spring

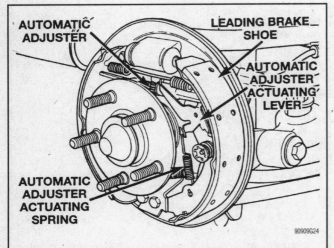

Fig. 71 Note the location of the automatic adjuster's actuating spring and lever

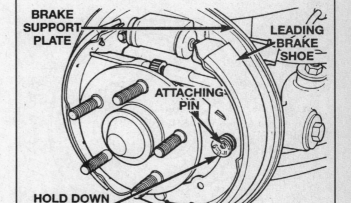

Fig. 74 Remove the leading brake shoe hold-down spring and pin

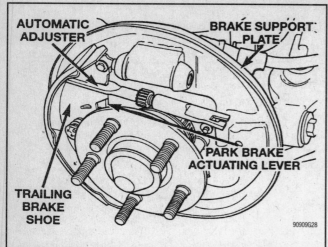

Fig. 75 Remove the automatic adjuster from the trailing brake shoe

4. Remove the adjusting lever actuating spring from the leading brake shoe. Remove the automatic adjuster actuating lever from the leading brake shoe.

5. Thread the adjuster star wheel all the way into the adjuster, which will remove all tension from the adjuster.

6. Remove the upper and lower return springs from the brake shoes.

7. Remove the brake shoe hold-down spring and pin attaching the leading brake shoe assembly to the brake support plate.

8. Remove the leading brake shoe from the support plate.

9. Remove the automatic adjuster from the parking brake actuating lever and trailing brake shoe.

10. Remove the retaining clip securing the parking brake actuating lever to the trailing brake shoe.

11. Remove the trailing brake shoe hold-down spring and pin attaching the trailing brake shoe assembly to the brake support plate.

12. Remove the trailing brake shoe from the brake support plate and separate the shoe from the parking brake actuating lever.

To install:

13. Lubricate the 6 brake shoe contact points and the brake shoe anchor points with high-temperature grease.

14. Install the wave washer on the pivot pin of the parking brake actuating lever.

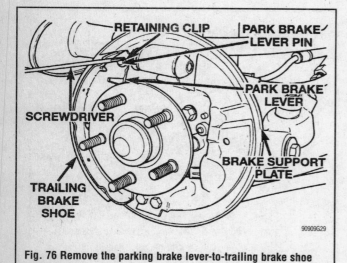

Fig. 76 Remove the parking brake lever-to-trailing brake shoe retaining clip

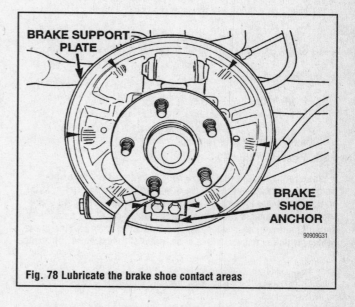

Fig. 78 Lubricate the brake shoe contact areas

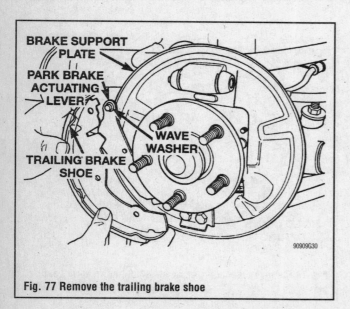

Fig. 77 Remove the trailing brake shoe

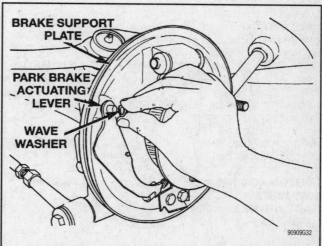

Fig. 79 Install the wave washer onto the pin of the parking brake actuating lever

15. Install the trailing brake shoe onto the attaching pin of the parking brake actuating lever.

16. Position the trailing brake shoe onto the brake support plate and be sure the trailing brake shoe is squarely seated on the support plate shoe contact areas and install the brake shoe hold-down spring on the hold-down pin.

17. Install the parking brake actuating lever-to-trailing brake shoe retaining clip.

18. Install the automatic adjuster on the trailing brake shoe and the parking brake actuating lever.

19. Place the leading brake shoe onto the brake support plate in proper position and install the attaching pin and hold-down spring.

20. Install the lower and upper return springs.

21. Install the automatic adjuster actuating lever and spring onto the leading brake shoe.

22. Manually adjust the brake shoes to the furthest adjusted position but not so far as to interfere with the installation of the brake drum.

23. Install the brake drums. Check and adjust the brake shoes as necessary.

24. Install the wheel and tire. Tighten the lug nuts in a star pattern to 95 ft. lbs. (129 Nm).

25. Lower the vehicle.

26. Road test the vehicle to check for proper brake operation.

Sebring Coupe and Avenger

1. Raise and safely support the vehicle and remove the wheel assembly.

2. Remove the brake drum.

➡Note the location of all springs and clips for proper reassembly.

3. Remove the shoe-to-lever spring and remove the adjuster lever.

4. Remove the auto adjuster assembly.

5. Remove the retainer spring.

6. Remove the hold-down springs, washers and pins.

7. Remove the shoe-to-shoe spring.

8. Remove the brake shoes from the backing plate.

9. Using a flat-tipped tool, open up the parking brake lever retaining clip. Remove the clip and washer from the pin on the shoe assembly and remove the shoe from the lever assembly.

To install:

10. Thoroughly clean and dry the backing plate. Lubricate the backing plate at the brake shoe contact points.

11. Lubricate backing plate bosses, anchor pin, and parking brake actuating mechanism with a lithium-based grease.

12. Install the parking brake lever assembly on the lever pin. Install the wave washer and a new retaining clip. Use pliers or the like to install the retainer on the pin. If removed, connect the parking brake lever to the parking brake cable and verify that the cable is properly routed.

13. Clean and lubricate the adjuster assembly. Make sure the nut-adjuster is drawn all the way to the stop, but the nut must NOT lock firmly at the end of the assembly.

14. Install the brake shoes on the backing plate with the hold-down springs, washers and pins.

15. Install the shoe-to-shoe spring.

16. Install the retainer spring.

17. Install the auto adjuster assembly and install the adjuster lever and the shoe-to-lever spring.

18. Pre-adjust the shoes so the drum slides on with a light drag and install the brake drum.

19. Adjust the rear brake shoes and install the rear wheels.

20. Adjust the parking brake cable.

21. Lower the vehicle and check for proper brake operation.

ADJUSTMENTS

Sebring and Avenger

▶ **See Figures 53 and 80**

➡**Usually, self-adjusting drum brakes do not necessitate manual adjustment. However, in the event of a brake reline, you should make the initial adjustment to speed up the adjustment period.**

1. Make sure the parking brake is fully released.

2. Raise and safely support the vehicle so that all wheels are free to turn.

3. Remove the rear brake adjusting hole rubber plug from the rear of the brake shoe support plate.

4. Insert a suitable brake adjusting tool through the adjusting hole in the support plate and against the star wheel of the adjusting screw. Move the handle of the tool downward until a slight drag is felt when the tire is rotated.

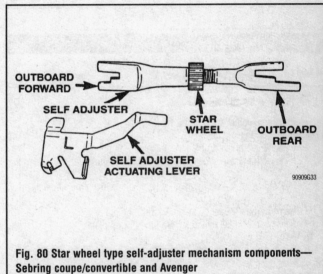

Fig. 80 Star wheel type self-adjuster mechanism components—Sebring coupe/convertible and Avenger

5. Insert a thin screwdriver or equivalent into the adjusting hole. Push the adjusting lever out of engagement with the star wheel. Be very careful not to bend the adjusting lever or contort the lever spring. While holding the adjusting lever out of engagement with the star wheel, back off the star wheel to guarantee a free wheel with no drag.

6. Repeat the adjustment procedure at the other rear wheel. After the procedure is complete, install the adjusting hole rubber plugs in the rear brake support plates.

7. After adjustment, apply and release the parking brake lever one time.

8. Carefully lower the vehicle.

Cirrus, Stratus and Breeze

▶ **See Figures 53 and 81**

1. Adjust the rear brakes by depressing the brake pedal. Brake shoe adjustment will occur the first time the brake pedal is depressed, pushing the rear brake shoes against the braking surface of the brake drums. The brake shoes should now be correctly adjusted and will not require any type of manual adjustment.

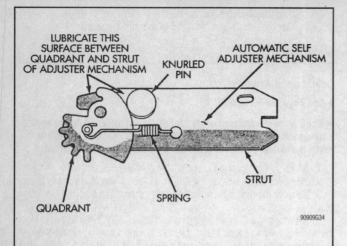

Fig. 81 Automatic self-adjuster mechanism—Cirrus, Stratus and Breeze

Wheel Cylinders

REMOVAL & INSTALLATION

▶ See Figures 82, 83 and 84

1. Raise and safely support the vehicle.
2. Remove the rear wheels.
3. Remove the brake drums.
4. Remove the brake shoes. Replace if soaked with grease or brake fluid.
5. Disconnect and plug the rear brake flex hose from the wheel cylinder.
6. Remove the 2 wheel cylinder attaching bolts.
7. Remove the wheel cylinder from the backing plate.

To install:

8. Apply a small bead of silicone sealer around the mating surface of the backing plate and the wheel cylinder.
9. Position the wheel cylinder on the backing plate and install the 2 wheel cylinder attaching bolts. Tighten the wheel cylinder attaching bolts as follows:

Fig. 82 Using a flare nut wrench, loosen the brake line fitting to the wheel cylinder . . .

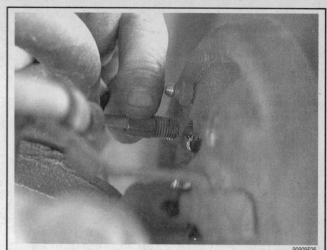

Fig. 83 . . . then unscrew the fitting from behind the wheel cylinder

Fig. 84 After removing the mounting bolts, remove the wheel cylinder from the brake backing plate

- Cirrus, Stratus and Breeze—97 inch lbs. (11 Nm)
- Sebring convertible—115 inch lbs. (13 Nm)
- Sebring coupe and Avenger—7 ft. lbs. (10 Nm)

10. Hand-start the brake line to the wheel cylinder. Tighten the brake line fitting as follows:

- Cirrus, Stratus, Sebring convertible and Breeze—145 inch lbs. (17 Nm)
- Sebring coupe and Avenger—11 ft. lbs. (15 Nm)

11. Install the rear brake shoes. Install the brake drum onto the wheel hub.
12. Install the tire and wheel assembly. Tighten in a star pattern to 95 ft. lbs. (129 Nm).
13. Adjust the rear brakes.
14. Bleed the entire brake hydraulic system.
15. Road test the vehicle to check for proper brake operation.

OVERHAUL

▶ See Figures 85 thru 94

Wheel cylinder overhaul kits may be available, but often at little or no savings over a reconditioned wheel cylinder. It often makes sense with these components to substitute a new or reconditioned part instead of attempting an overhaul.

If no replacement is available, or you would prefer to overhaul your wheel cylinders, the following procedure may be used. When rebuilding and installing wheel cylinders, avoid getting any contaminants into the system. Always use clean, new, high quality brake fluid. If dirty or improper fluid has been used, it will be necessary to drain the entire system, flush the system with proper brake fluid, replace all rubber components, then refill and bleed the system.

1. Remove the wheel cylinder from the vehicle and place on a clean workbench.

2. First remove and discard the old rubber boots, then withdraw the pistons. Piston cylinders are equipped with seals and a spring assembly, all located behind the pistons in the cylinder bore.

3. Remove the remaining inner components, seals and spring assembly. Compressed air may be useful in removing these components. If no compressed air is available, be VERY careful not to score the wheel cylinder bore when removing parts from it. Discard all components for which replacements were supplied in the rebuild kit.

4. Wash the cylinder and metal parts in denatured alcohol or clean brake fluid.

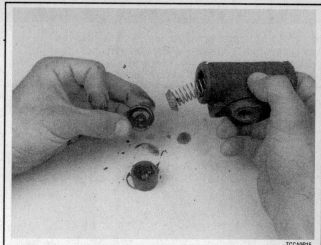

Fig. 87 Remove the pistons, cup seals and spring from the cylinder

Fig. 85 Remove the outer boots from the wheel cylinder

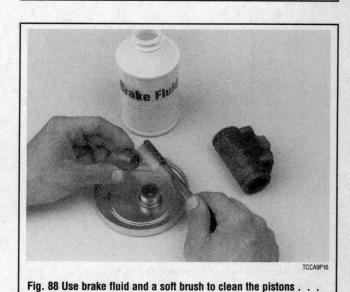

Fig. 88 Use brake fluid and a soft brush to clean the pistons . . .

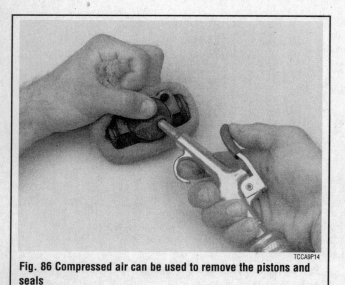

Fig. 86 Compressed air can be used to remove the pistons and seals

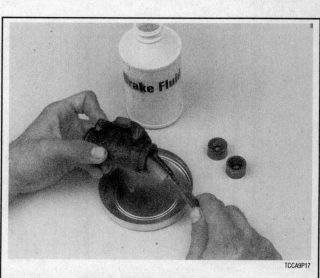

Fig. 89 . . . and the bore of the wheel cylinder

⁂ WARNING

Never use a mineral-based solvent such as gasoline, kerosene or paint thinner for cleaning purposes. These solvents will swell rubber components and quickly deteriorate them.

5. Allow the parts to air dry or use compressed air. Do not use rags for cleaning, since lint will remain in the cylinder bore.

6. Inspect the piston and replace it if it shows scratches.

7. Lubricate the cylinder bore and seals using clean brake fluid.

8. Position the spring assembly.

9. Install the inner seals, then the pistons.

10. Insert the new boots into the counterbores by hand. Do not lubricate the boots.

11. Install the wheel cylinder.

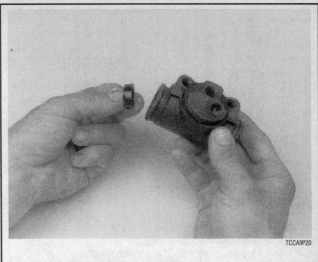

Fig. 92 Install the spring, then the cup seals in the bore

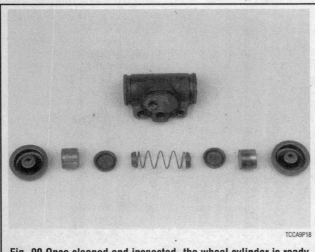

Fig. 90 Once cleaned and inspected, the wheel cylinder is ready for assembly

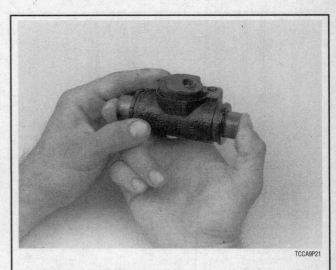

Fig. 93 Lightly lubricate the pistons, then install them

Fig. 91 Lubricate the cup seals with brake fluid

Fig. 94 The boots can now be installed over the wheel cylinder ends

PARKING BRAKE

REMOVAL & INSTALLATION

Cirrus, Stratus and Breeze

▶ **See Figures 95, 96 and 97**

1. Disconnect the negative battery cable.
2. Remove the floor console assembly from the vehicle.
3. Lower the parking brake lever.
4. Loosen the output cable adjuster nut. This will relieve tension from the parking brake cables allowing for easy removal.
5. Remove the floor console rear mounting bracket. Disconnect the parking brake cable requiring replacement from the cable tension equalizer.
6. Remove the rear seat cushion.
7. Carefully remove the right and left side rear scuff plates by prying scuff plate retaining clips out of the door sills.
8. Fold the rear section of carpet forward to expose the rear parking brake cables.
9. Remove the rear parking brake cables-to-floor pan routing clip.

10. Compress the parking brake cable retainer tabs at the console bracket using a ½ inch box wrench. Pull the parking brake cable straight out of the console bracket.
11. Raise and safely support the vehicle. Remove the rear wheel(s) requiring parking brake cable replacement.
12. Remove the brake drum.
13. Remove the rear wheel hub and bearing assembly.
14. Disconnect the parking brake cable from the parking brake actuating lever on the trailing brake shoe.
15. Remove the parking brake cable from the rear brake support plate by compressing the locking tabs on the cable retainer using a ½ inch box wrench or equivalent tool.
16. Remove the 2 parking brake cable routing brackets located on the vehicle frame rail.
17. Remove the parking brake cable and cable sealing grommet from the vehicle's floor pan.

To install:

18. Install the cable into the vehicle's floor pan. Be sure the sealing grommet is installed into the floor pan as far as possible to guarantee a proper seal.
19. Install the parking brake cable into the rear brake support plate. Be sure the cable retainer locking tabs are expanded to ensure that the cable is securely locked in the brake support plate.
20. Install the 2 parking brake cable routing brackets onto the vehicle frame rail. Install and securely tighten the bracket mounting bolts.
21. Connect the parking brake cable end to the parking brake actuating lever of the trailing brake shoe.
22. Install the wheel hub and bearing assembly.
23. Install the brake drum.
24. Install the rear wheel(s) and lug nuts. Tighten the lug nuts in a star pattern to 95 ft. lbs. (129 Nm).
25. Lower the vehicle.
26. Grasp the parking brake cable-to-floor pan sealing grommet from inside the vehicle. Pull the sealing grommet into the floor pan to ensure that it is fully seated into the floor pan.
27. Route the parking brake cable under the carpet and up to the hole in the console bracket on the floor pan. Insert the cable into the console bracket hole and engage the cable retainer locking tabs. Be sure the locking tabs are expanded to ensure that the locking tab will lock into place.
28. Install the parking brake cable routing/retaining clip to the floor pan of the vehicle and tighten the mounting nut.

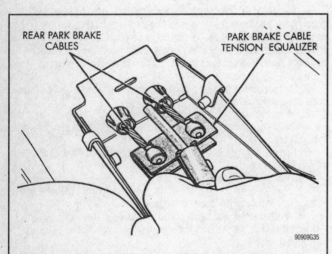

Fig. 95 Disconnect the parking brake cable from the tension equalizer

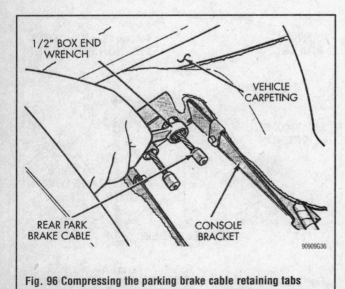

Fig. 96 Compressing the parking brake cable retaining tabs

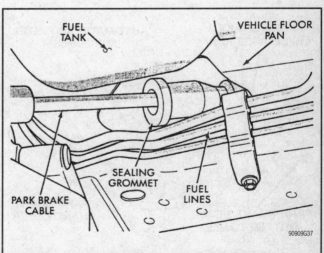

Fig. 97 Remove the parking brake cable and cable sealing grommet from the vehicle's floor pan

29. Using a suitable prytool, unseat the parking brake output cable retainer. Remove cable retainer and parking brake cable tension equalizer from the parking brake lever output cable and discard components.

30. Install a NEW parking brake cable tension equalizer on the parking brake lever output cable and rear parking brake cables.

31. Install a NEW parking brake lever output cable to tension equalizer retaining clip on tension equalizer. The cable retainer must be closed and securely latched.

32. Adjust the parking brake cable tension.

33. Slightly raise and support the vehicle. Check the rear wheels with the parking brake lever fully released, to make sure they rotate freely without dragging.

34. Lower the vehicle to the ground.

35. Check the parking brake lever for free-play. The parking brake lever should feel firm at all clicks. Maximum lever travel should only be 15 clicks.

36. Install the floor console into the vehicle.

37. Place the rear carpet back into its proper position in the rear of the vehicle interior.

38. Install both right and left rear door sill plate scuff moldings by snapping them into place on the rear door sills.

39. Install the rear lower seat cushion.

40. Check and adjust the rear brakes, if necessary.

41. Connect the negative battery cable.

42. Check that the parking brake holds the vehicle on an incline.

Sebring Convertible

▶ **See Figures 98, 99 and 100**

➡️ **To avoid extreme difficulty during the installation procedure, remove only one rear parking brake cable from the vehicle at a time.**

1. Disconnect the negative battery cable.

2. Remove the floor console from the vehicle. Fully release the parking brake lever.

3. Disconnect the wiring harness from the ground switch on the parking brake lever and unclip the harness from the parking brake lever.

✳✳ CAUTION

The parking brake lever contains an auto adjusting feature which consists of a clock spring loaded to approximately 20 lbs. (89 N). The auto adjuster must be reloaded before releasing the parking brake cables from the equalizer. Serious injury could result if the adjuster mechanism is not reloaded before removal of the parking brake cables from the equalizer.

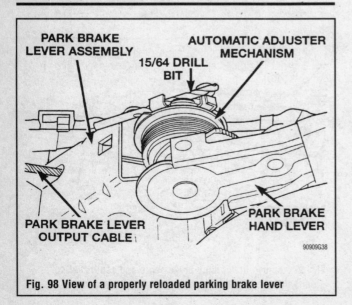

Fig. 98 View of a properly reloaded parking brake lever

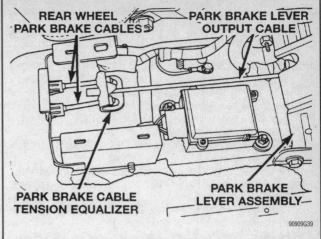

Fig. 99 The rear parking brake cables converge at the tension equalizer

4. Reload the adjuster mechanism on the parking brake lever by grasping the parking brake lever output cable and pulling upward by hand. Pull upward until a $^{15}/_{16}$ in. drill bit can be inserted into the adjuster mechanism. This will relieve any tension from the output cable making it easier to disconnect the rear parking brake cables from the equalizer.

5. Disconnect the parking brake cable requiring replacement from the cable tension equalizer.

6. Remove the rear seat cushion from the vehicle.

7. Carefully remove the right and left side door sill scuff plates by prying scuff plate retaining clips out of the door sills.

8. Remove the right and left side interior quarter trim panels from the vehicle as follows:

a. Lower the convertible top.

b. Pull the lower section of the rear seat back forward until the seat back brackets clear the studs on the floor pan.

c. Push the rear seat back upward to disengage the hooks that secure the seat back to the rear seat back support. Remove the rear seat back from the vehicle.

d. Remove the door sill trim panel and push-in fastener securing the quarter trim panel to the door sill panel.

e. Remove the speaker grille.

f. Remove the all of the quarter trim panel mounting screws.

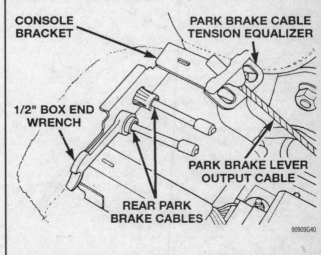

Fig. 100 Compressing the parking brake cable retaining tabs

g. Remove the push-in fasteners securing the quarter trim panel to the inner quarter panel at the front of the trim panel.

h. Remove the quarter trim panel from the inner quarter panel. Disconnect the speaker wiring connector. Remove the quarter trim panel from the vehicle.

9. Remove the 2 wiring harness routing clips from the cross-car beam and the 2 clips that hold down the carpet to the cross-car beam.

10. Fold the rear section of carpet forward to expose the rear parking brake cables.

11. Remove the rear parking brake cables-to-floor pan routing clip.

12. Compress the parking brake cable retainer tabs at the console bracket using a ½ in. box wrench. Pull the parking brake cable straight out of the console bracket.

13. Raise and safely support the vehicle. Remove the rear wheel(s) requiring parking brake cable replacement.

14. Remove the brake drum.

15. Remove the rear wheel hub and bearing assembly.

16. Disconnect the parking brake cable from the parking brake actuating lever on the trailing brake shoe.

17. Remove the parking brake cable from from the rear brake support plate by compressing the locking tabs on the cable retainer using a ½ in. box wrench.

18. Remove the 2 parking brake cable routing brackets located on the vehicle frame rail.

19. Remove the parking brake cable and cable sealing grommet from the vehicle floor pan.

To install:

20. Install the cable into the vehicle floor pan. Be sure the sealing grommet is installed into the floor pan as far as possible to guarantee a proper seal.

21. Install the 2 parking brake cable routing brackets onto the vehicle frame rail. Install and securely tighten the bracket mounting bolts.

22. Install the parking brake cable into the rear brake support plate but **DO NOT** engage the cable retainer locking tabs into the brake support plate at this time.

23. Reconnect the parking brake cable end to the parking brake actuating lever of the trailing brake shoe. Be sure the end of the spring is under the lip on the parking brake actuating lever.

24. Fully push the parking brake cable into the rear brake support plate. Be sure the cable retainer locking tabs are securely locked into the rear brake support plate.

25. Install the wheel hub and bearing assembly.

26. Install the brake drum.

27. Install the rear wheel(s) and lug nuts. Tighten the lug nuts in a star pattern to 95 ft. lbs. (129 Nm).

28. Lower the vehicle.

29. Grasp the parking brake cable-to-floor pan sealing grommet from inside the vehicle. Pull the sealing grommet into the floor pan to ensure that it is fully seated into the floor pan.

30. Route the parking brake cable under the carpet and up to the hole in the console bracket on the floor pan. Insert the cable into the console bracket hole and engage the cable retainer locking tabs. Be sure the locking tabs are expanded to ensure that the locking tab will lock into place.

31. Install the parking brake cable routing/retaining clip to the floor pan of the vehicle and tighten the mounting nut.

✳✳ CAUTION

This parking brake lever contains an auto adjusting feature which consists of a clock spring loaded to approximately 20 lbs. (89 N). DO NOT unload the auto adjuster mechanism using any procedure other than the one outlined in this procedure. Serious injury could result if the adjuster mechanism is unloaded using an alternative procedure.

32. Unload the adjuster mechanism by grasping the parking brake lever output cable by hand and pulling upward on it until all tension is relieved from the drill bit. Remove the drill bit from the clock spring of the adjuster mechanism. Then slowly release the cable until all the slack is removed from the cable.

33. Clip the wiring harness onto the parking brake lever bracket.

34. Connect the wiring harness connector to the ground switch of the parking brake lever.

35. Cycle the parking brake lever to its fully applied position and then lower it to its fully released position. This will position the parking brake cables and fully adjust them to the proper tension.

36. Slightly raise and support the vehicle. Check the rear wheels with the parking brake lever fully released, to make sure they rotate freely without dragging.

37. Lower the vehicle to the ground.

38. Raise the parking brake lever to approximately a 45 degree angle to provide proper clearance for console installation.

39. Install the floor console into the vehicle.

40. Place the rear carpet back into its proper position in the rear of the vehicle interior.

41. Install the 2 clips retaining the carpet to the cross-car beam.

42. Install the 2 wiring harness routing clips onto the cross-car beam.

43. Install the rear interior quarter trim panels.

44. Install both right and left door sill plate scuff moldings by snapping them into place on the rear door sills.

45. Install the rear lower seat cushion into the vehicle.

46. Check and adjust the rear brakes, if necessary.

47. Connect the negative battery cable.

48. Check that the parking brake holds the vehicle on an incline.

Sebring Coupe and Avenger

▶ See Figures 101 and 102

✳✳ CAUTION

The Supplemental Restraint System (SRS) must be disarmed before working around the interior of the vehicle. Failure to do so may cause accidental deployment of the air bags, resulting in unnecessary system repairs and/or personal injury.

1. Disarm the air bag system, as described in Section 6.

✳✳ CAUTION

The air bag control unit is mounted beneath the center console. Use care when working with the center console assembly not to impact or shock the control unit.

2. Remove the center floor console assembly.

3. Loosen the cable adjuster nut and then remove the parking brake cable, by pulling it from the passenger compartment.

4. Raise and safely support the vehicle.

5. If equipped with rear drum brakes, remove the brake drum and shoes. If equipped with rear disc brakes, remove the brake caliper, rotor and parking brake shoes.

6. Disconnect the cable end from the parking brake strut lever. Compress the retaining strips to remove the cable from the backing plate.

7. Unfasten any other frame retainers and remove the cables.

To install

8. Install the cable to the rear actuator. Secure in place with the parking brake cable clip and retainer spring.

9. If equipped with rear drum brakes, install the brake shoes and drum. If equipped with rear disc brakes, install the parking brake shoes, rotor and caliper assemblies.

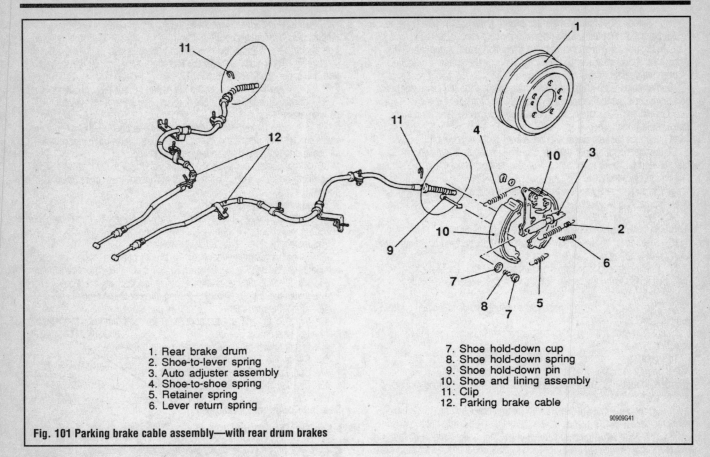

1. Rear brake drum
2. Shoe-to-lever spring
3. Auto adjuster assembly
4. Shoe-to-shoe spring
5. Retainer spring
6. Lever return spring
7. Shoe hold-down cup
8. Shoe hold-down spring
9. Shoe hold-down pin
10. Shoe and lining assembly
11. Clip
12. Parking brake cable

90909G41

Fig. 101 Parking brake cable assembly—with rear drum brakes

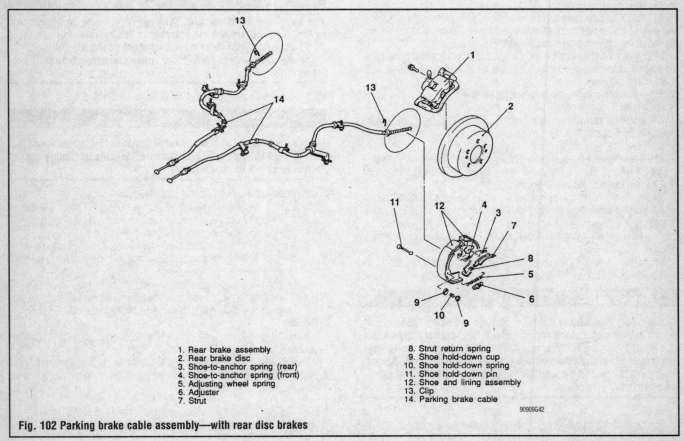

1. Rear brake assembly
2. Rear brake disc
3. Shoe-to-anchor spring (rear)
4. Shoe-to-anchor spring (front)
5. Adjusting wheel spring
6. Adjuster
7. Strut
8. Strut return spring
9. Shoe hold-down cup
10. Shoe hold-down spring
11. Shoe hold-down pin
12. Shoe and lining assembly
13. Clip
14. Parking brake cable

90909G42

Fig. 102 Parking brake cable assembly—with rear disc brakes

10. Position the cable in under the vehicle and install retainers loose.

11. Attach the parking brake cables to the actuator inside the vehicle. Tighten the adjusting nut until the proper tension is placed on the cable. Adjust the parking brake stroke.

12. Secure all cable retainers. Apply and release the parking brake a number of times once all adjustments have been made.

13. Assemble the interior components which were removed.

14. Adjust the rear brake shoes and parking brake cables. Check the rear wheels to confirm that the rear brakes are not dragging.

15. Arm the air bag system, as described in Section 6.

16. Check that the parking brake holds the vehicle on an incline.

ADJUSTMENT

Cirrus, Stratus and Breeze

▶ **See Figures 103, 104, 105 and 106**

This vehicle uses a "bent nail" type parking brake tension cable equalizer. The tension equalizer can only be used one time to set the parking brake cable tension. If the parking brake cables require adjustment during the life of the vehicle, a NEW tension equalizer MUST be installed before the adjustment is made.

1. Remove the floor console from the vehicle.

2. Lower the parking brake handle.

3. Loosen the brake cable adjusting nut on the parking brake cable output cable. This will take tension off the output cable, allowing it to be easily removed from the tension equalizer.

✳✳ CAUTION

Discard the output cable retaining clip after removing it from the parking brake cable tension equalizer. The retainer is not to be reused. A new retainer is to be installed when attaching output cable to the tensioner equalizer.

4. Using a flat bladed prytool, unlatch the parking brake output cable retainer. Then remove the cable retainer from the parking brake cable tension equalizer. Remove the equalizer from the cables.

5. Install a NEW tension equalizer and NEW retaining clip. The cable retainer must be closed and securely latched.

6. Adjust the cable tension using the following steps:

a. Position the parking brake lever so it is in the fully released position.

b. Tighten the adjusting nut on the parking brake lever output cable until 12mm of thread is out past the top edge of the adjustment nut.

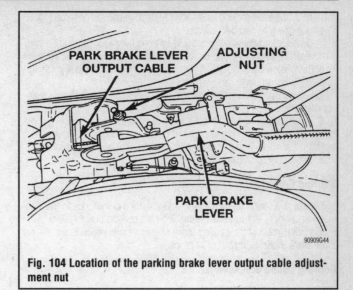

Fig. 104 Location of the parking brake lever output cable adjustment nut

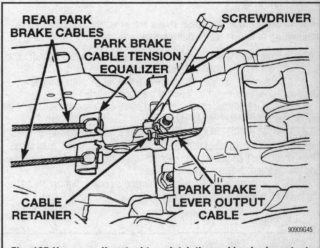

Fig. 105 Use a small prytool to unlatch the parking brake output cable retainer

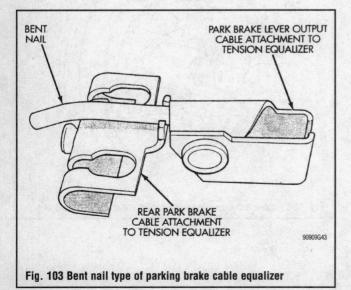

Fig. 103 Bent nail type of parking brake cable equalizer

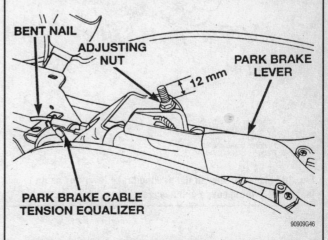

Fig. 106 Tighten the adjusting nut until 12mm of thread is out past the top edge of the adjusting nut

c. Actuate the parking brake lever to its fully applied position (15 clicks) one time and then release.

d. Actuating the parking brake lever to its fully applied position one time after tightening the adjustment nut will stretch the bent nail portion of the tension equalizer about ¼ in. (6mm). This process will correctly set the parking brake cable tension.

7. Check the rear wheels of the vehicle. They should rotate freely without dragging.

8. After the parking brake cable tension has been properly adjusted, check for free-play in the parking brake lever. The parking brake hand lever should feel firm at all clicks with a maximum of 15 clicks of lever travel possible.

9. Install the floor console.

Sebring Convertible

Manual adjustment of the parking brake is not required, due to the automatic adjustment feature used on this vehicle's parking brake system. Proper adjustment of the parking brake on this vehicle depends on the rear drum brake shoes being adjusted properly.

Sebring Coupe and Avenger

WITH REAR DRUM BRAKES

▶ **See Figure 107**

➡ **Make certain that the brake shoes are properly adjusted before attempting to adjust the parking brake.**

1. Pull the parking brake lever up with a force of about 45 pounds. The total number of clicks heard should be 5 to 7.

2. If the number of clicks was not within that range, release the lever. Uncover the inner compartment mat of the floor console.

3. Loosen the adjusting nut to the end of the cable rod at the base of the lever, freeing the parking brake cable.

4. With the engine idling, forcefully depress the brake pedal five or six times and confirm that the pedal stroke stops changing. If the pedal stroke stops changing, the automatic adjustment mechanism is working correctly and the clearance between the shoe and drum is correct.

5. After verifying that the brake adjustment is correct, tighten the adjusting nut until there is no more slack in the cable.

6. Operate the lever and brake pedal several times, and verify no more clicks are heard from the automatic adjuster.

7. Turn the adjusting nut to give the proper number of clicks when the lever is raised full travel.

8. Raise and safely support the rear of the vehicle.

9. Release the brake lever and make sure that the rear wheels turn freely. If they do not, then back off the adjusting nut until they do.

WITH REAR DISC BRAKES

▶ **See Figure 107**

1. Pull the parking brake lever up with a force of about 45 pounds. The total number of clicks heard should be 3 to 5 clicks. If the number of clicks was not within that range, the system requires adjustment.

➡ **The parking brake shoes must be adjusted before attempting to adjust the cable mechanism**

2. Adjust the parking brake shoes.

3. After adjusting the parking brake shoes have been properly adjusted, adjust the cable mechanism, by performing the following steps:

a. Turn the adjusting nut to give the proper number of clicks when the lever is raised full travel.

b. Raise and safely support the rear of the vehicle.

c. Release the brake lever and make sure that the rear wheels turn freely. If they do not, then back off on the adjusting nut until they do.

Brake Shoes

REMOVAL & INSTALLATION

Sebring Convertible

▶ **See Figures 108, 109, 110 and 111**

➡ **This procedure only applies to vehicles with rear disc brakes.**

1. Raise and safely support the vehicle. Remove the wheel and tire assembly.

2. Remove the rear disc brake caliper and rotor assembly.

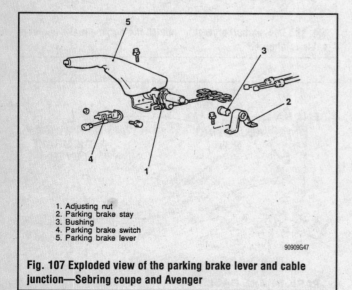

1. Adjusting nut
2. Parking brake stay
3. Bushing
4. Parking brake switch
5. Parking brake lever

90909G47

Fig. 107 Exploded view of the parking brake lever and cable junction—Sebring coupe and Avenger

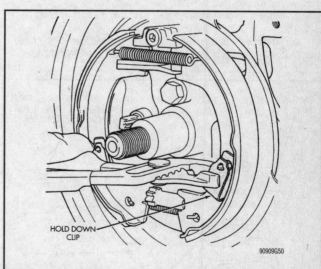

HOLD DOWN CLIP

90909G50

Fig. 108 Remove the rear parking brake shoe's hold-down clip

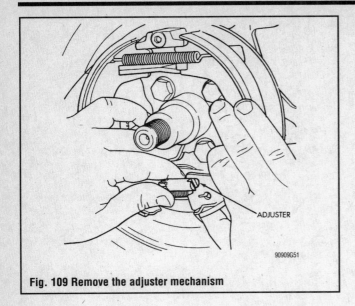

Fig. 109 Remove the adjuster mechanism

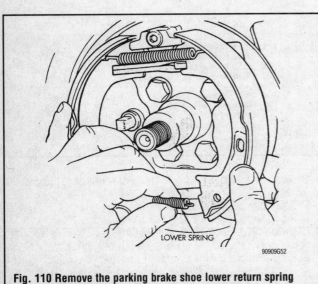

Fig. 110 Remove the parking brake shoe lower return spring

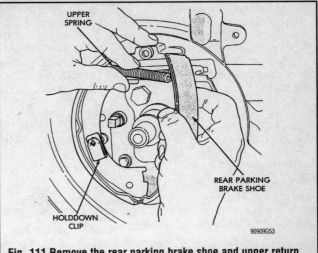

Fig. 111 Remove the rear parking brake shoe and upper return spring

13. Install the lower shoe-to-shoe return spring.
14. Install the brake shoe adjuster with the star wheel rearward.
15. Instal the rear brake shoe hold-down clip.
16. Adjust the brake shoes to an outside diameter of 6.75 inch (171mm).
17. Install the rear hub and bearing assembly.
18. Install the rotor and brake caliper assemblies.
19. Install the wheel and tire assembly, then carefully lower the vehicle.

Sebring Coupe and Avenger

▶ See Figure 112

➡ This procedure only applies to vehicles with rear disc brakes.

1. Raise and safely support the vehicle. Remove the wheel and tire assembly.
2. Remove the rear disc brake caliper and rotor assembly.
3. Remove the hub and bearing assembly.
4. Remove the upper shoe to anchor springs.
5. Remove the adjusting wheel spring.
6. Remove the adjuster from the parking brake shoe assemblies.
7. Remove the strut and strut return spring
8. Remove the brake shoe hold-down cups, springs and pins.
9. Disconnect the parking brake cable from the actuating lever.
10. Remove the parking brake shoes.

To install:

11. Place the front parking brake shoe into position and secure with the hold-down pin spring and cup.
12. Place the rear parking brake shoe into position and secure with the hold-down pin spring and cup.
13. Install the strut and strut return spring
14. Install the adjuster mechanism.
15. Install the adjusting wheel spring.
16. Install the front upper shoe to anchor spring, then the rear upper shoe to anchor spring.
17. Adjust the parking brake shoes.
18. Install the rear hub and bearing assembly.
19. Install the rotor and brake caliper assemblies.
20. Install the wheel and tire assembly, then carefully lower the vehicle.

3. Remove the hub and bearing assembly.
4. Remove the rear brake shoe hold-down clip.
5. Turn the brake shoe adjuster wheel until the adjuster is at its shortest length.
6. Remove the adjuster from the parking brake shoe assemblies.
7. Remove the lower shoe-to-shoe spring.
8. Pull the rear brake shoe assembly away from the anchor. Then, remove the rear brake shoe and upper spring.
9. Remove the front brake shoe hold-down clip, then remove the front brake shoe assembly.

To install:

10. Install the front brake shoe and hold-down clip.
11. Install the rear brake shoe and the upper brake shoe-to-shoe return spring.
12. Pull the rear brake shoe over the anchor block until it is properly located on the adapter.

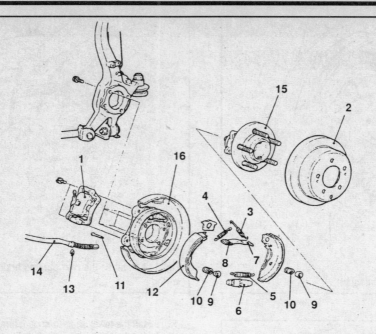

1. Rear brake assembly
2. Rear brake disc
3. Shoe-to-anchor spring (rear)
4. Shoe-to-anchor spring (front)
5. Adjusting wheel spring
6. Adjuster
7. Strut
8. Strut return spring
9. Shoe hold-down cup
10. Shoe hold-down spring
11. Shoe hold-down pin
12. Shoe and lining assembly
13. Clip
14. Parking brake cable
15. Rear hub assembly
16. Backing plate

90909G48

Fig. 112 Parking brake shoe assembly—Sebring coupe and Avenger

ADJUSTMENT

Sebring Convertible

1. Raise and safely support the rear of the vehicle. Remove the wheel and tire assemblies.

➡ **Unlike other rear disc brake models, the parking brake shoe adjustment cannot be performed through a hole in the rotor and hub assembly.**

2. Remove the rear brake caliper and rotor.
3. Remove the hub and bearing assembly.
4. Check the brake shoe outside diameter using a brake drum reset gauge, or equivalent. The outside diameter should measure 6.75 inches (171mm).
5. If out of specification, adjust the shoe diameter by rotating the star wheel adjuster mechanism using a small prying tool.
6. Install the hub and bearing assembly.
7. Install the rotor and brake caliper.
8. Install the wheel and tire assembly.
9. Repeat Steps 2–7 for the other rear wheel, then lower the vehicle.

Sebring Coupe and Avenger

▶ **See Figure 113**

1. Raise and safely support the rear of the vehicle. Remove the wheel and tire assemblies.
2. Remove the rubber adjustment hole plug on the hub of the brake rotor.
3. Use a flat bladed screwdriver to rotate the star wheel downward, until the brake rotor cannot rotate.

4. Return the adjuster 5 notches in the upward direction to complete the adjustment.
5. Install the rubber adjustment hole plug.
6. Repeat Steps 2–5 for the other rear wheel.
7. If necessary, adjust the parking brake cable, as outlined earlier in this section.
8. Install the wheel and tire assemblies, then lower the vehicle.

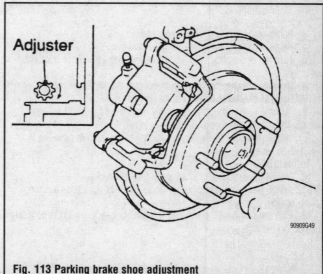

Adjuster

90909G49

Fig. 113 Parking brake shoe adjustment

ANTI-LOCK BRAKE SYSTEM (ABS)

General Information

The Bendix ABX-4 type 4 Anti-lock Brake System (ABS) was an option on the 1995–97 Cirrus, Stratus, Sebring convertible and Breeze models. Beginning in 1998, these same models are equipped with the Teves Mark 20 ABS system. Both of these ABS systems operate in basically the same manner, however, they may use some different components.

When conventional brakes are applied in an emergency stop or on ice, one or more wheels may lock. This may result in loss of steering control and vehicle stability. The purpose of the Anti-lock Brake System (ABS) is to prevent lock up under heavy braking conditions. This system offers the driver increased safety and control during braking. Anti-lock braking operates only at speeds above 3 mph (5 km/h).

Under normal braking conditions, the ABS functions the same as a standard brake system with a diagonally split master cylinder and conventional vacuum assist.

If wheel locking tendency is detected during application, the system will enter anti-lock mode. During anti-lock mode, hydraulic pressure in the four wheel circuits is modulated to prevent any wheel from locking. Each wheel circuit is designed with a set of electrical valves and hydraulic line to provide modulation, although for vehicle stability, both rear wheel valves receive the same electrical signal. The system can build or reduce pressure at each wheel, depending on signals generated by the Wheel Speed Sensors (WSS) at each wheel and received at the Controller Anti-lock Brake (CAB).

PRECAUTIONS

Failure to observe the following precautions may result in system damage:
- Before performing electric arc welding on the vehicle, disconnect the control module and the hydraulic unit connectors.
- When performing painting work on the vehicle, do not expose the control module to temperatures in excess of 185°F (85°C) for longer than 2 hours. The system may be exposed to temperatures up to 200°F (95°C) for less than 15 minutes.
- Never disconnect or connect the control module or hydraulic modulator connectors with the ignition switch ON.
- Never disassemble any component of the Anti-Lock Brake System (ABS) which is designated unserviceable; the component must be replaced as an assembly.
- When filling the master cylinder, always use brake fluid which meets DOT-3 specifications; petroleum-based fluid will destroy the rubber parts.
- Working on ABS system requires extreme amount of mechanical ability, training and special tools. If you are not familiar have your vehicle repaired by a certified mechanic or refer to a more advanced publication on this subject.

Diagnosis and Testing

For the proper diagnostic procedure for either the entire ABS system or a single component of the system, a scan tool (DRB or equivalent) is necessary. Because of the complexity of the ABS system and the importance of correct system functioning, it is a good idea to have a qualified automotive mechanic test the system if any problems have been detected.

The self-diagnostic ABS start up cycle begins when the ignition switch is turned to the **ON** position. An electrical check is completed on the ABS components, such as the wheel speed sensor continuity and other relay continuity. During this check the amber anti-lock light is turned on for approximately 1–2 seconds.

Further functional testing is accomplished once the vehicle is set in motion.
- The solenoid valves and the pump/motor are activated briefly to verify function

- The voltage output from the wheel speed sensors is verified to be within the correct operating range

If the vehicle is not set in motion within 3 minutes from the time the ignition switch is set in the **ON** position, the solenoid test is bypassed, but the pump/motor is activated briefly to verify that it is operating correctly.

For the ABX-4 system, fault codes are kept in a non-volatile memory until either erased by the DRB or erased automatically after 50 ignition cycles (key **ON-OFF** cycles). The only fault that will not be erased after the 50 ignition cycles is the CAB fault. On the Teves Mark 20 system, DTCs are kept in the controller's memory until erased with the DRB scan tool, or they are erased automatically after 3,500 miles or 255 key cycles which ever occurs first. A CAB fault can only be erased by the DRB scan tool. More than one fault can be stored at a time. The number of key cycles since the most recent fault was stored is also displayed. Most functions of the CAB and ABS system can be accessed by the DRB scan tool for testing and diagnostic purposes.

To read the Diagnostic Trouble Codes (DTC's) perform the following:
1. Inspect the ABS components and connectors for damage and/or proper connections. Keep in mind that the brake light circuit also provides an input to to the ABS system. If the brake lights do not work, they must be fixed before proceeding.
2. Connect a DRB or equivalent scan tool to the Data Link Connector (located under the driver's side instrument panel). A scan tool must be used to access these codes.
3. Turn the ignition to the **ON** position. Wtih the scan tool, select "ABS".
4. Use the scan tool to select "Inputs/Outputs", and read the brake switch status. While pressing on the brake pedal, check the scan tool display. Select "Read DTC" and record any trouble codes which may appear. Sometimes, the cause of one trouble code may trigger additional codes to be set. If more than one code appear, a certain sequence of tests may be necessary. The beginning of each test will indicate if another test should be performed first.
5. Once the problem is corrected, use the scan tool to erase the trouble code(s).

Trouble Codes

▶ See Figure 114

The following is a list of the ABS system trouble codes for 1995–98 Sebring coupe and Avenger models:
- Code 11: Front right-hand wheel speed sensor open circuit
- Code 12: Front left-hand wheel speed sensor open circuit
- Code 13: Right rear anti-lock sensor wheel speed sensor open circuit
- Code 14: Left rear anti-lock sensor wheel speed sensor open circuit
- Code 15: Wheel speed sensor system abnormal output signal
- Code 16: Power supply system
- Code 21: Front right wheel speed sensor short circuit
- Code 22: Front left wheel speed sensor short circuit
- Code 23: Rear right wheel speed sensor short circuit
- Code 24: Rear left wheel speed sensor short circuit
- Code 38: Stop light switch system
- Code 41: Front right inlet solenoid valve
- Code 42: Front left inlet solenoid valve
- Code 43: Rear right inlet solenoid valve
- Code 44: Rear left inlet solenoid valve
- Code 45: Front right outlet solenoid valve
- Code 46: Front left outlet solenoid valve
- Code 47: Rear right outlet solenoid valve
- Code 48: Rear left outlet solenoid valve
- Code 51: Valve power supply
- Code 53: Pump motor
- Code 63: ABS—ECU

DIAGNOSTIC TROUBLE CODE (DTC) DISPLAYED

ABS WARNING LAMP CIRCUIT
ABS WARNING LAMP DIODE CIRCUIT
BLANK DRB SCREEN
CAB MALFUNCTION
CAB MEMORY ERROR
CAB SENSOR CIRCUIT
CHECKING STOP LAMP SWITCH INPUT TO CAB
CONTROLLER ANTILOCK BRAKE (CAB)
CONTROLLER ENABLE
DRB "NO RESPONSE" MESSAGE
EXCESS DECAY
INTERMITTENT CAB WSS SIGNAL
INTERMITTENT LF WSS SIGNAL
INTERMITTENT LR WSS SIGNAL
INTERMITTENT RF WSS SIGNAL
INTERMITTENT RR WSS SIGNAL
LEFT FRONT WHEEL SPEED SENSOR
LEFT REAR WHEEL SPEED SENSOR
LF SOLENOID CIRCUIT OPEN
LF SOLENOID CIRCUIT SHORTED
LF WHEEL SPEED SENSOR CONTINUITY
LF WSS DYNAMIC CONTINUITY
LF WSS ERRATIC SIGNAL
LF WSS MISSING SIGNAL
LF WSS STATIC CONTINUITY
LR SOLENOID CIRCUIT OPEN
LR SOLENOID CIRCUIT SHORTED
LR WHEEL SPEED SENSOR CONTINUITY
LR WSS DYNAMIC CONTINUITY
LR WSS ERRATIC SIGNAL
LR WSS MISSING SIGNAL

LR WSS STATIC CONTINUITY
MODULATOR CIRCUIT
PUMP/MOTOR CIRCUIT
PUMP/MOTOR MONITOR CIRCUIT
PUMP/MOTOR RELAY CONTROL CIRCUIT
PUMP/MOTOR RELAY OUTPUT CKT
PUMP/MOTOR STALLED
RED BRAKE WARNING LAMP PROBLEM
RF SOLENOID CIRCUIT OPEN
RF SOLENOID CIRCUIT SHORTED
RF WHEEL SPEED SENSOR CONTINUITY
RF WSS DYNAMIC CONTINUITY
RF WSS ERRATIC SIGNAL
RF WSS MISSING SIGNAL
RF WSS STATIC CONTINUITY
RIGHT FRONT WHEEL SPEED SENSOR
RIGHT REAR WHEEL SPEED SENSOR
RR SOLENOID CIRCUIT OPEN
RR SOLENOID CIRCUIT SHORTED
RR WHEEL SPEED SENSOR CONTINUITY
RR WSS DYNAMIC CONTINUITY
RR WSS ERRATIC SIGNAL
RR WSS MISSING SIGNAL
RR WSS STATIC CONTINUITY
SOLENOID UNDERVOLTAGE
SYSTEM RELAY CIRCUIT
SYSTEM RELAY GND CIRCUIT OPEN
SYSTEM RELAY OUTPUT CIRCUIT
VERIFICATION PROCEDURE (IN STALL)
VERIFICATION PROCEDURE (ROAD TEST)
WSS SPEED COMPARISON

90909G90

Fig. 114 ABS system trouble codes for 1995–98 Cirrus, Stratus, Sebring convertible and Breeze

Controller Anti-lock Brakes

→The Controller Anti-lock Brakes (CAB) is the electronic control module for the anti-lock brake system on Cirrus, Stratus, Sebring convertible and Breeze models.

REMOVAL & INSTALLATION

Bendix ABX-4 System

▶ See Figures 115, 116 and 117

→The CAB is mounted in the right front corner of the engine compartment of the vehicle. It is mounted in the vehicle using an integral mounting bracket. It uses a 60-way system connector.

1. Turn the ignition switch **OFF**.
2. Disconnect the negative battery cable.
3. Unplug the 60-pin wiring harness connector from the CAB.
4. Remove the 2 bolts attaching the CAB mounting bracket to the inner fender and front upper crossmember, then remove the CAB from the vehicle.

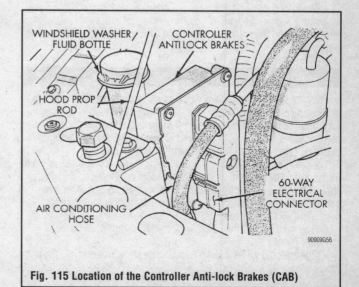

Fig. 115 Location of the Controller Anti-lock Brakes (CAB)

To install:

5. Install the CAB module and bracket into the vehicle. Secure the CAB in place with the 2 mounting bolts. Tighten the mounting bolts to 75 inch lbs. (8 Nm).

6. Attach the 60-way connector to the CAB by hand as far as possible, then use the CAB connector retaining bolt to fully seat the wiring harness connector into the CAB.

7. Tighten the 60-way connector retaining bolt and tighten to 38 inch lbs. (4 Nm).

➡If you are installing a new CAB, it must be initialized before driving the vehicle. You can initialize the CAB using the DRB or equivalent scan tool and the initializing procedure. All new controllers come programmed to flash the ABS warning lamp until initialization.

8. Connect the negative battery cable.

Teves Mark 20 System

▸ See Figures 118 and 119

➡To replace the Controller Anti-lock Brakes (CAB) on these vehicles, the Integrated/Hydraulic Control Unit (ICU/HCU) and CAB need to be removed from the vehicle as a unit. The CAB can then be separated from the control unit. Do not try to replace the CAB with the control unit in the vehicle.

1. Disconnect the negative battery cable.

2. Remove the ICU/HCU from the vehicle, as outlined in this section.

3. Unplug the pump motor wiring harness from the CAB.

4. Unfasten the 4 bolts attaching the CAB to the HCU, then remove the CAB from the unit.

To install:

5. Install the CAB on the HCU. Install the 4 mounting bolts and tighten to 17 inch lbs. (2 Nm).

6. Attach the pump/motor wiring harness to the CAB.

7. Install the ICU/HCU assembly, as outlined in this section.

8. Properly bleed the base brakes and the ABS brakes hydraulic system, as outlined in this section.

9. Connect the negative battery cable.

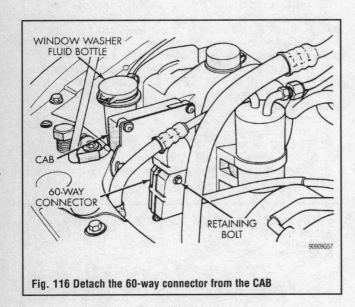

Fig. 116 Detach the 60-way connector from the CAB

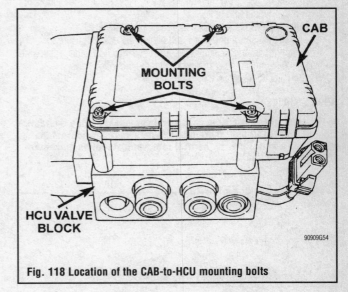

Fig. 118 Location of the CAB-to-HCU mounting bolts

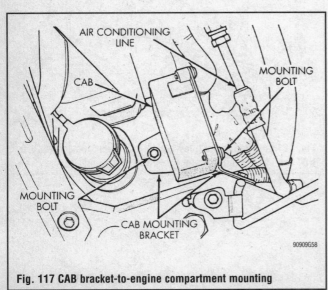

Fig. 117 CAB bracket-to-engine compartment mounting

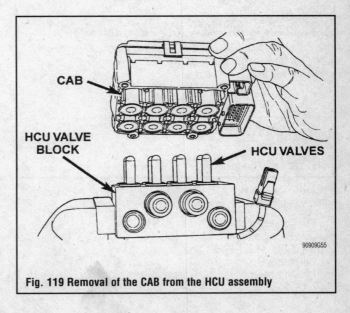

Fig. 119 Removal of the CAB from the HCU assembly

ABS-ECU

➡The ABS-ECU is the electronic control module for the anti-lock brake system on Sebring coupe and Avenger models.

REMOVAL & INSTALLATION

1995–97 Vehicles

▶ See Figure 120

➡The ABS-ECU is mounted underneath the instrument panel, against the firewall on the passenger side.

1. Turn the ignition switch OFF.
2. Disconnect the negative battery cable.
3. Loosen the mounting screws, then remove the cowl side trim panel and front door scuff plate by disengaging the metal clips.
4. Loosen the mounting screws and remove the control unit cover.
5. Unplug the wiring harness connector from the ABS-ECU.
6. Loosen the mounting screws and remove the ABS-ECU from the vehicle.

To install:

7. Install the ABS-ECU module into the vehicle. Secure the module in place with the 2 mounting bolts.
8. Attach the wiring harness connector to the ABS-ECU.
9. Install the control unit cover and tighten the mounting screws.
10. Install the front door scuff plate and cowl side trim panel. Push in to engage the metal retaining clips and tighten the mounting screws.
11. Connect the negative battery cable.

1998 Vehicles

➡For 1998, the ABS-ECU is an integral component of the Hydraulic Control Unit (HCU) and, therefore, can only be removed from the vehicle as a unit. Refer to the HCU removal/installation procedure later in this section.

Relay Box

REMOVAL & INSTALLATION

Cirrus, Stratus, Sebring Convertible and Breeze

▶ See Figures 121, 122 and 123

1. Disconnect the negative battery cable, then wrap it with insulated tape in order to isolate it.
2. Remove the Hydraulic Control Unit (HCU) from the vehicle, as outlined in this section.
3. Unfasten the 2 screws attaching the relay box to the HCU. Remove ONLY the 2 screws mounting the relay box to the HCU; do NOT remove the pump motor mounting screws.
4. Grasp the relay box. Without rocking or twisting, pull the relay box away from the pump motor housing until the connector on the relay box unplugs from the pump motor terminal. This is a tight connection and will require some effort to separate from the pump motor.
5. Remove the relay box from the HCU.

To install:

6. Make sure the electrical connector seal is installed in the pump motor housing before installation of the relay body. If the seal is in any way damaged, it must be replaced before the relay box is installed.
7. Position the relay box on the HCU, and carefully align the terminals on the relay box with the terminals on the pump motor.
8. Hold the relay box with both hands. Then, without rocking or twisting, push the relay box onto the pump motor electrical connector as far as you can.
9. Install and securely tighten the 2 screws attaching the relay box assembly to the HCU.
10. Install the HCU into the vehicle.
11. Connect the negative battery cable.
12. Bleed the base brake system in the usual fashion, then bleed the ABS system following the correct sequences and procedure.
13. Road test the vehicle to be sure the brake system is working properly.

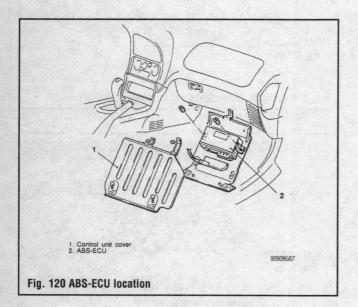

1. Control unit cover
2. ABS-ECU

90909G67

Fig. 120 ABS-ECU location

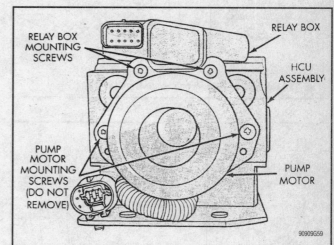

RELAY BOX MOUNTING SCREWS

RELAY BOX

HCU ASSEMBLY

PUMP MOTOR MOUNTING SCREWS (DO NOT REMOVE)

PUMP MOTOR

90909G59

Fig. 121 Location of the relay box-to-HCU mounting screws. DO NOT remove the pump motor mounting screws

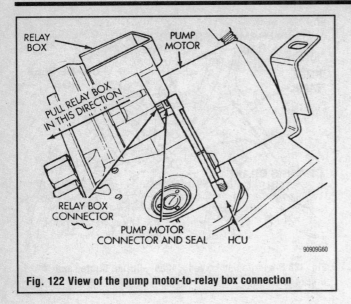

Fig. 122 View of the pump motor-to-relay box connection

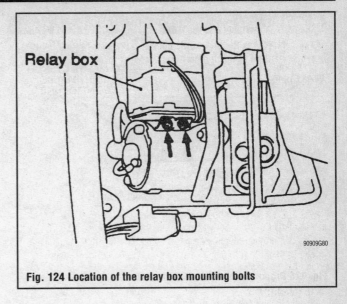

Fig. 124 Location of the relay box mounting bolts

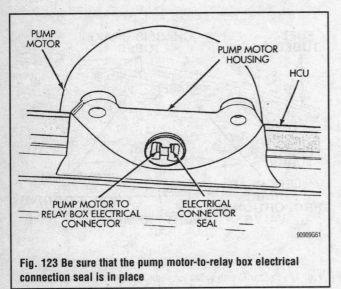

Fig. 123 Be sure that the pump motor-to-relay box electrical connection seal is in place

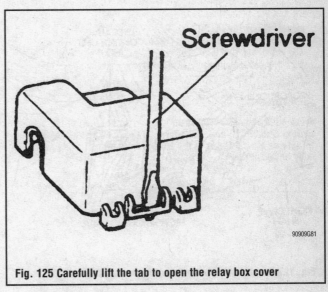

Fig. 125 Carefully lift the tab to open the relay box cover

Sebring Coupe and Avenger

▶ See Figures 124 and 125

1. Disconnect the negative battery cable.
2. Raise and support the vehicle safely.
3. Remove the left wheel.
4. Remove the left inner fender splash shield.
5. Remove the relay box mounting bolts.
6. Insert the tip of a small flat blade pry tool into the space between the HCU and the relay box cover, opening the tab at one place and removing the cover.
7. Remove the relays from the relay box.

To install:

8. Install the relays into the relay box.
9. Install the relay box cover.
10. Install and tighten the relay box mounting bolts.
11. Install the left inner fender splash shield.
12. Install the left wheel. Tighten the lug nuts in a star pattern to 95 ft. lbs. (129 Nm).
13. Lower the vehicle.
14. Connect the negative battery cable.

Proportioning Valves

REMOVAL & INSTALLATION

Cirrus, Stratus, Sebring Convertible and Breeze

BENDIX ABX-4 SYSTEM

▶ See Figures 126 and 127

You do not have to remove the HCU when replacing the proportioning valves.

1. Disconnect the negative battery cable.
2. Disconnect the brake line fitting from the faulty proportioning valve in the HCU.
3. Unscrew and remove the proportioning valve requiring replaced from the HCU.

To install:

4. Lubricate the O-ring seal on the new proportioning valve with clean brake fluid, from a fresh sealed container.

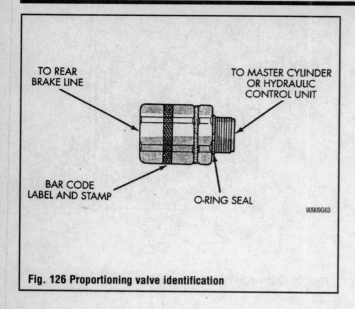

Fig. 126 Proportioning valve identification

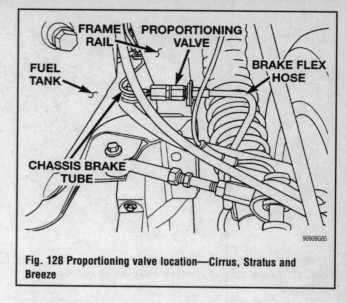

Fig. 128 Proportioning valve location—Cirrus, Stratus and Breeze

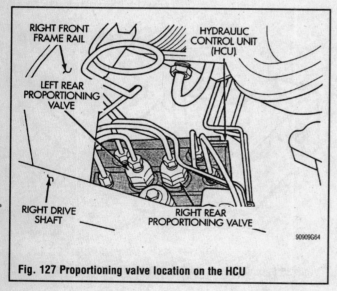

Fig. 127 Proportioning valve location on the HCU

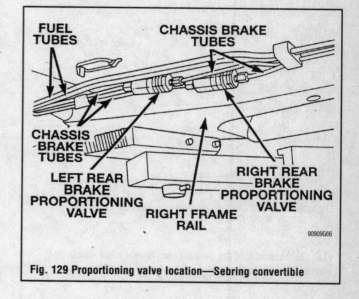

Fig. 129 Proportioning valve location—Sebring convertible

5. Install the proportioning valve in the HCU and hand-tighten it until it is fully installed and the O-ring seal is seated in the HCU. Then, tighten the valve to 30 ft. lbs. (40 Nm).

6. Connect the brake line to the proportioning valve and tighten the line nut to 12.5 ft. lbs. (17 Nm).

7. Bleed the base brake system in the usual fashion.

TEVES MARK 20 SYSTEM

▶ See Figures 128 and 129

➡Never attempt to disassemble a proportioning valve.

1. Raise and safely support the vehicle.
2. Remove the chassis brake tube nuts from the proportioning valve controlling the rear wheel of the vehicle which has premature wheel skid.
3. Remove the proportioning valve from the brake flex hose.

To install:

4. Install the proportioning valve on the brake flex hose.
5. Tighten the 2 chassis brake tube nuts to 12.5 ft. lbs. (17 Nm).
6. Bleed the affected brake line, as outlined in this section.

Sebring Coupe and Avenger

▶ See Figure 130

1. Disconnect the negative battery cable.
2. Remove the engine intake manifold assembly.
3. First label, then, using a flare nut wrench, unfasten the brake lines from the proportioning valve.
4. Loosen the mounting bolt and remove the proportioning valve from the vehicle.

To install:

5. Install the proportioning valve into the vehicle and tighten the mounting bolt.
6. Thread each brake line into its correct opening on the proportioning valve. Tighten each brake line fitting to 11 ft. lbs. (15 Nm).
7. Install the engine intake manifold assembly.
8. Connect the negative battery cable.
9. Bleed the brake system, as outlined later in this section.

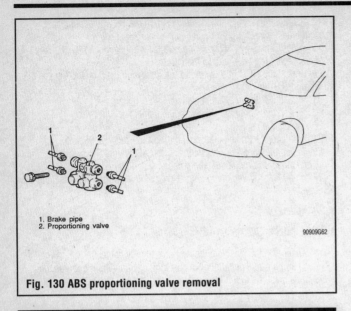

Fig. 130 ABS proportioning valve removal

1. Brake pipe
2. Proportioning valve

Hydraulic Control Unit

REMOVAL & INSTALLATION

Cirrus, Stratus, Sebring Convertible and Breeze

1995–1997 MODELS

▶ See Figures 131 thru 136

1. Disconnect and isolate the negative battery cable.
2. Using a brake pedal positioning tool, or equivalent, depress the brake pedal past the first 1 inch of travel and hold in this position. This will isolate the master cylinder reservoir from the brake hydraulic system, which will prevent the brake fluid from draining out of the reservoir.
3. Raise and support the vehicle safely.
4. Using Brake Parts Cleaner, thoroughly clean all surfaces, brake line fittings and connections to the HCU.
5. Remove the entire exhaust system.
6. Remove the right inner fender splash shield.
7. Remove the HCU heat shield from the mounting bracket.
8. Disengage the 6-way HCU wiring harness connector and the 10-way connector from the relay box on the HCU.

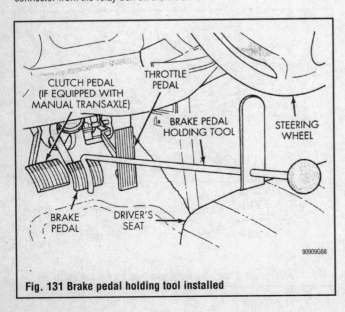

Fig. 131 Brake pedal holding tool installed

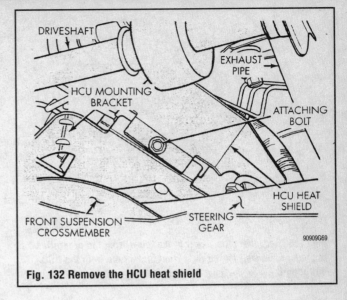

Fig. 132 Remove the HCU heat shield

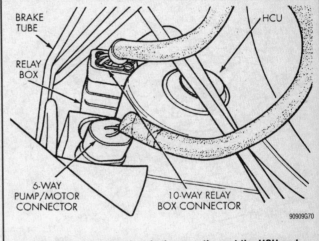

Fig. 133 Disengage the electrical connections at the HCU and relay box

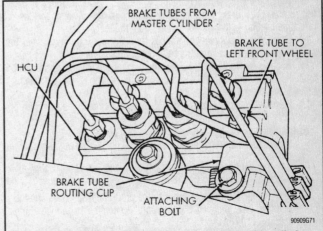

Fig. 134 Disconnect the 2 brake tubes from the master cylinder, as well as the brake tube leading to the left front wheel at the HCU ports

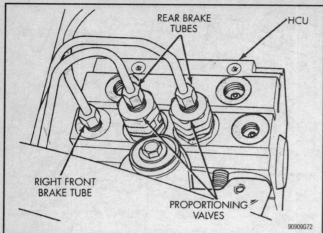

Fig. 135 Disconnect the 2 rear brake tubes from the proportioning valves, as well as the right front brake tube from the HCU outlet port

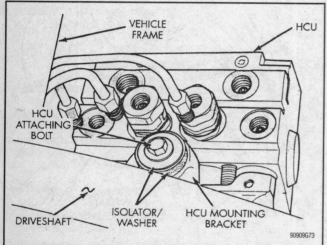

Fig. 136 Remove the front HCU-to-mounting bracket bolt, isolator and washer

9. Remove the brake tube routing clip from the HCU mounting bracket. Then remove the 2 brake tubes coming from the master cylinder and the brake tube leading to the left front wheel from the HCU ports.

10. Disconnect the 2 rear brake tubes from the proportioning valves and the right front brake tube from the HCU outlet port.

11. Remove the front HCU-to-mounting bracket bolt, isolator and washer.

12. Remove the 2 rear HCU-to-mounting bracket bolts, isolators and washers.

13. Remove the HCU out through the exhaust tunnel in the floor pan of the vehicle.

To install:

14. Install the HCU into the vehicle correctly positioned on its mounting bracket.

15. Install the HCU-to-mounting bracket bolts, isolators and washers. Tighten the 3 mounting bolts to 248 inch lbs. (28 Nm).

16. Connect the 2 rear brake tubes to the proportioning valves and the right front brake tube to the HCU outlet port. Tighten the brake tube fittings to 159 inch lbs. (18 Nm).

17. Connect the 2 brake tubes coming from the master cylinder and the tube leading to the left front wheel to the HCU ports. Tighten the fittings to 159 inch lbs. (18 Nm).

18. Connect the brake tube routing clip to the HCU mounting bracket and tighten the attaching bolt.

19. Install the 6-way HCU wiring harness connector and the 10-way connector from the relay box to the HCU.

20. Install the HCU heat shield to the mounting bracket and tighten the attaching bolt.

21. Install the entire exhaust system.

22. Install the right inner fender splash shield.

23. Lower the vehicle.

24. Remove the brake pedal positioning tool from the vehicle.

25. Bleed the base brake system and the ABS hydraulic system.

26. Connect the negative battery cable.

27. Road test the vehicle to ensure proper operation of the base and ABS systems.

1998 MODELS

♦ See Figures 137 thru 142

1. Disconnect and isolate the negative battery cable.

2. Using a brake pedal positioning tool, or equivalent, depress the brake pedal past the first 1 inch of travel and hold in this position. This will

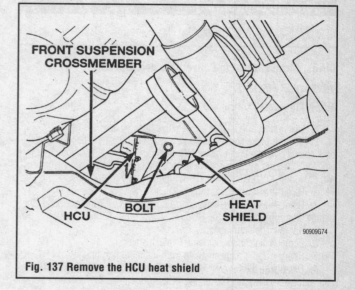

Fig. 137 Remove the HCU heat shield

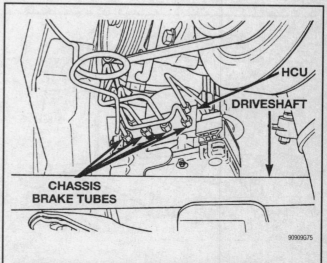

Fig. 138 Disconnect the chassis brake tubes from the HCU

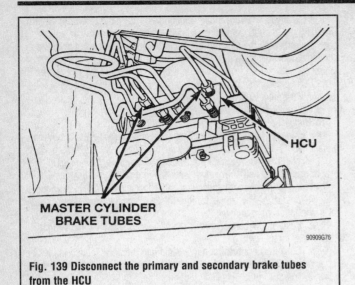

Fig. 139 Disconnect the primary and secondary brake tubes from the HCU

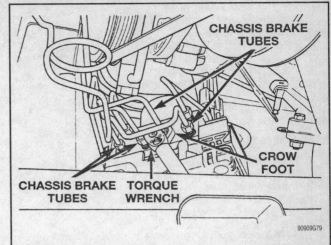

Fig. 142 Use a torque wrench and crow's foot to properly tighten the brake tube fittings to the HCU

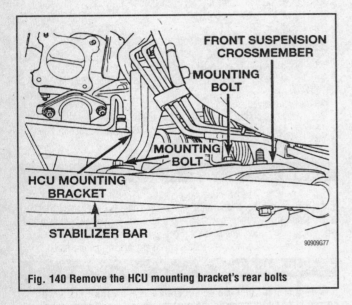

Fig. 140 Remove the HCU mounting bracket's rear bolts

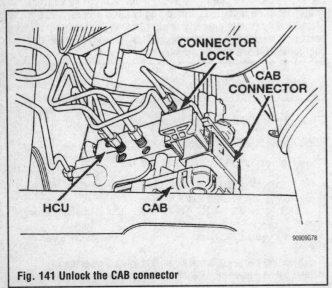

Fig. 141 Unlock the CAB connector

isolate the master cylinder reservoir from the brake hydraulic system, which will prevent the brake fluid from draining out of the reservoir.

3. Raise and support the vehicle safely.

4. Remove the entire exhaust system.

5. Remove the right inner fender splash shield.

6. Remove the HCU heat shield from the mounting bracket.

7. Using Brake Parts Cleaner, thoroughly clean all surfaces, brake line fittings and connections to the HCU.

8. Label and disconnect the 4 chassis brake tubes from the outlet ports of the HCU.

9. Disconnect the primary and secondary brake tubes coming from the master cylinder from the HCU inlet ports.

10. Remove the bolt attaching the front leg of the HCU mounting bracket to the front suspension crossmember.

11. Remove the 2 bolts attaching the back legs of the HCU mounting bracket to the front suspension crossmember.

12. Remove the side HCU-to-mounting bracket bolt.

13. Remove the 2 bolts attaching the top of the HCU to the mounting bracket.

14. Disengage the 25-way wiring harness connector from the CAB by grasping the lock on the connector and pulling it out from the connector as far as it will go. This will remove the connector out from the CAB socket.

15. Remove the HCU from the vehicle by pulling it out through the area between the right halfshaft and frame rail.

To install:

16. Install the HCU into the vehicle correctly positioned on its mounting bracket.

17. Install the HCU-to-mounting bracket bolts, isolators and washers. Tighten the 3 mounting bolts to 97 inch lbs. (11 Nm).

18. Install the 25-way connector into the CAB socket. Install the connector in the following manner:

a. Position the connector into the CAB socket and carefully push it down as far as it will go.

b. Once the connector is fully seated into the socket, push in the connector lock as far as it will go. This pulls the connector into the socket which locks it in the installed position.

19. Install the 3 mounting bracket-to-suspension crossmember bolts and tighten to 250 inch lbs. (28 Nm).

20. Install the brake tubes to the HCU. Make sure that the correct brake tubes are installed in the correct openings. Using a crow foot and torque wrench, tighten the brake tube fittings to 145 inch lbs. (17 Nm).

21. Install the HCU heat shield to the mounting bracket and tighten the attaching bolt.

22. Install the entire exhaust system.
23. Install the right inner fender splash shield.
24. Lower the vehicle the vehicle.
25. Remove the brake pedal positioning tool from the vehicle.
26. Bleed the base brake system and the ABS hydraulic system.
27. Connect the negative battery cable.
28. Road test the vehicle to ensure proper operation of the base and ABS systems.

Sebring Coupe and Avenger

▶ See Figures 143 and 144

1. Disconnect the negative battery cable.
2. Raise and support the vehicle safely.
3. Remove the left wheel.
4. Remove the left inner fender splash shield.
5. Remove the left headlight assembly.
6. Remove the air cleaner/inlet duct assembly.
7. Remove the Powertrain Control Module (PCM).
8. Remove the relay box bracket.
9. Using a flare nut wrench, disconnect and label the brake pipe connections.

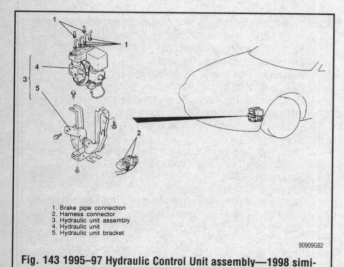

1. Brake pipe connection
2. Harness connector
3. Hydraulic unit assembly
4. Hydraulic unit
5. Hydraulic unit bracket

90909G82

Fig. 143 1995–97 Hydraulic Control Unit assembly—1998 similar

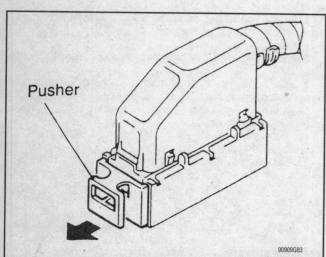

Pusher

90909G83

Fig. 144 On the 1998 HCU wiring harness, pull the pusher out to remove the connector

10. Disengage the wiring harness connector from the Hydraulic Control Unit (HCU). On 1998 models, disengage the 25-way wiring harness connector by grasping the lock on the connector and pulling it out from the connector as far as it will go. This will remove the connector out from the socket.
11. Loosen the mounting bolts and remove the HCU/mounting bracket assembly from the vehicle.
12. Separate the HCU from the mounting bracket assembly.
To install:
13. Install the HCU to the mounting bracket and tighten the mounting bolts.
14. Install the HCU/mounting bracket assembly into the vehicle in proper position. Install and tighten the mounting bolts.
15. Plug in the wiring harness connector to the HCU. On 1998 models only, install the 25-way connector into the HCU socket. Install the connector in the following manner:
   a. Position the connector into the HCU socket and carefully push it down as far as it will go.
   b. Once the connector is fully seated into the socket, push in the connector lock as far as it will go. This pulls the connector into the socket which locks it in the installed position.
16. Install the brake pipe connections to the correct openings in the HCU. Tighten the brake pipe fittings to 11 ft. lbs. (15 Nm).
17. Install the relay box bracket.
18. Install the PCM.
19. Install the air cleaner/inlet duct assembly.
20. Install the left headlight assembly.
21. Install the left inner fender splash shield.
22. Install the left wheel. Tighten the lug nuts in a star pattern to 95 ft. lbs. (129 Nm).
23. Lower the vehicle.
24. Check the brake fluid level and add the proper amount.
25. Bleed the base brake system and the ABS hydraulic system.
26. Connect the negative battery cable.

Wheel Speed Sensor

Each wheel has its own wheel speed sensor and sends a small AC signal to the control module. Correct ABS operation depends on accurate wheel speed signals. The vehicle's wheels and tires must all be the same size and type in order to generate accurate signals. If there is a variation between wheel and tire sizes, inaccurate wheel speed signals will be produced.

✳✳ WARNING

It is very critical that the wheel speed sensor(s) be installed correctly to ensure continued system operation. The sensor cables must be installed, routed and clipped properly. Failure to install the sensor(s) properly could result in contact with moving parts or overextension of sensor cables. This will cause ABS component failure and an open circuit.

REMOVAL & INSTALLATION

Cirrus, Stratus, Sebring Convertible and Breeze

FRONT WHEEL SPEED SENSOR

▶ See Figures 145, 146, 147, 148 and 149

1. Disconnect the negative battery cable at strut tower.
2. Raise and safely support the vehicle.
3. Remove the front wheel(s) of the wheel speed sensor(s) requiring removal.
4. Remove the speed sensor cable routing bracket from the steering knuckle.
5. Remove the speed sensor wiring harness sealing grommet retainer/routing bracket from the inner fender.

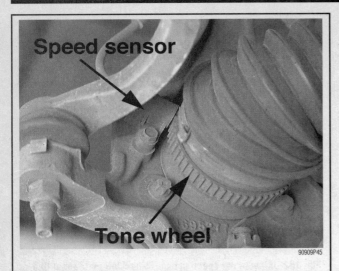

Fig. 145 Location of the front wheel speed sensor and tone ring

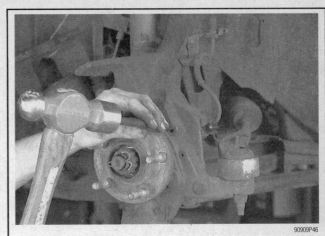

Fig. 148 If the speed sensor head cannot be removed from the steering knuckle due to corrosion, insert a pin punch through the hole in the front part of the knuckle and drive out the sensor

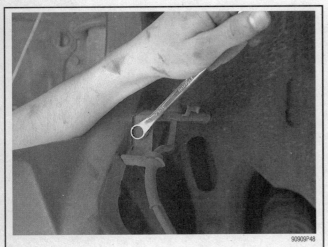

Fig. 146 Remove the speed sensor cable routing bracket from the steering knuckle

Fig. 149 Inspect the condition of the sensor head and tone wheel for broken or missing teeth, which can cause erratic signals

Fig. 147 Remove the speed sensor wiring harness sealing grommet retainer/routing bracket from the inner fender

6. Remove the sealing grommet from the inner fender and disconnect the speed sensor cable from the vehicle wiring harness.

7. Remove the speed sensor head-to-steering knuckle retaining bolt. Remove the speed sensor head from the steering knuckle.

8. If the speed sensor head cannot be removed from the steering knuckle due to corrosion, remove the brake caliper from the brake rotor and support from the knuckle using a strong piece of wire. Then remove the brake rotor from the vehicle and insert a pin punch through the hole on the front part of the steering knuckle for the sensor head locating pin. Tap the locating pin for the wheel speed sensor out of the steering knuckle.

9. Carefully inspect the condition of the sensor head and tone wheel for broken or missing teeth which can cause erratic sensor signals.

To install:

10. Connect the wheel speed sensor wiring connector to the vehicle wiring harness.

11. Install the sensor cable sealing grommet into the front inner fender. Install the sensor cable sealing grommet retainer/routing bracket on the front inner fender. Install and tighten routing bracket mounting bolt.

12. Install the speed sensor cable routing bracket onto the steering knuckle. Install the bracket mounting bolt and tighten the bolt to 105 inch lbs. (12 Nm). Be sure the sensor cable is looped toward the strut. If the

sensor cable is not routed in this direction, it will contact the wheel or tire, causing serious damage to the speed sensor cable.

13. Apply a light coating of MOPAR® Multi-Purpose Grease, or equivalent, to the locating pin of the speed sensor. Install the speed sensor head onto the steering knuckle. Install the sensor head mounting screw and tighten to 55 inch lbs. (6 Nm).

14. Install front wheel(s) and lug nuts. Tighten the lug nuts in a star pattern to 95 ft. lbs. (129 Nm).

15. Lower the vehicle. Connect the negative battery cable. Test drive the vehicle to check for proper operation of the base and ABS systems.

REAR WHEEL SPEED SENSOR

♦ See Figures 150, 151, 152, 153 and 154

1. Disconnect the negative battery cable at strut tower.
2. Disconnect the speed sensor cable electrical connector from the vehicle wiring harness. The wiring connection is located in the trunk of the vehicle.
3. Raise and safely support the vehicle.
4. Remove the rear wheel(s) of the wheel speed sensor(s) requiring removal.
5. Remove the speed sensor cable sealing grommet retainer from the vehicle rear frame rail.

Fig. 152 Unfasten the speed sensor-to-backing plate mounting bolts

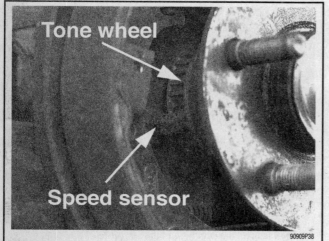

Fig. 150 Location of the rear wheel speed sensor and tone wheel

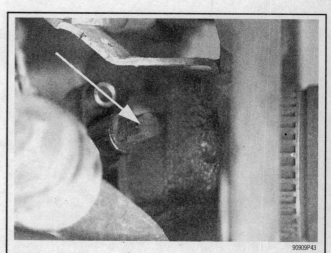

Fig. 153 Remove the wheel speed sensor (arrow) from the brake backing plate

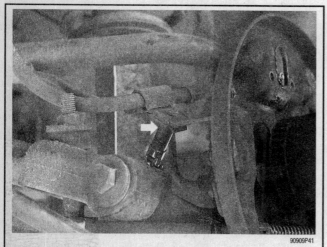

Fig. 151 Unfasten the speed sensor routing clip from the brake flex hose routing bracket

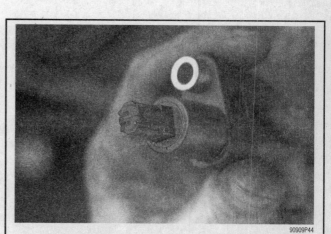

Fig. 154 Remove the speed sensor head from the rear brake support plate. Inspect the condition of the sensor head and tone wheel for broken or missing teeth, which can cause erratic signals

6. Remove the sealing grommet and sensor cable from the hole in the body of the vehicle.

7. Remove the speed sensor routing clips from the rear upper control arm and brake line flex hose routing bracket.

8. Remove the speed sensor head from the rear brake support plate.

9. Carefully inspect the condition of the sensor head and the tone wheel for broken or missing teeth which can cause erratic sensor signals.

To install:

10. Install the wheel speed sensor head into the brake support plate. Install the speed sensor retaining bolt and torque to 75 inch lbs. (8 Nm).

11. Install the speed sensor cable routing clips on the brake line flex hose bracket and upper control arm. Install and tighten the mounting bolts for the routing clip.

12. Install the wheel speed sensor wiring connector through the hole in the inner fender and into the vehicle trunk.

13. Install the speed sensor sealing grommet into the hole in the inner fender. Install the sensor sealing grommet retainer and attaching bolt on the rear frame rail.

14. Install the front wheel(s) and lug nuts. Tighten the lug nuts in a star pattern to 95 ft. lbs. (129 Nm).

15. Lower the vehicle.

16. Attach the sensor cable connector to the vehicle wiring harness, and slide the foam insulation sleeve over the wiring connection to prevent it from rattling against the body of the vehicle.

17. Connect the negative battery cable. Test drive the vehicle to check for proper operation of the base and ABS systems.

Sebring Coupe and Avenger

FRONT ABS WHEEL SPEED SENSOR

▶ See Figure 155

1. Disconnect the negative battery cable.
2. Remove the inner fender splash shield.
3. Remove the clips securing the speed sensor lead.
4. Remove the retaining screw and remove the speed sensor.

To install:

5. Attach the wheel speed sensor with the retaining screw.
6. Secure the speed sensor lead with the clips.

✳✳ WARNING

Make sure the lead wire is properly routed in its original position. If the lead wire is improperly installed it could be damaged by moving parts.

7. Install the inner fender splash shield.
8. Connect the negative battery cable and check the ABS system for proper operation.

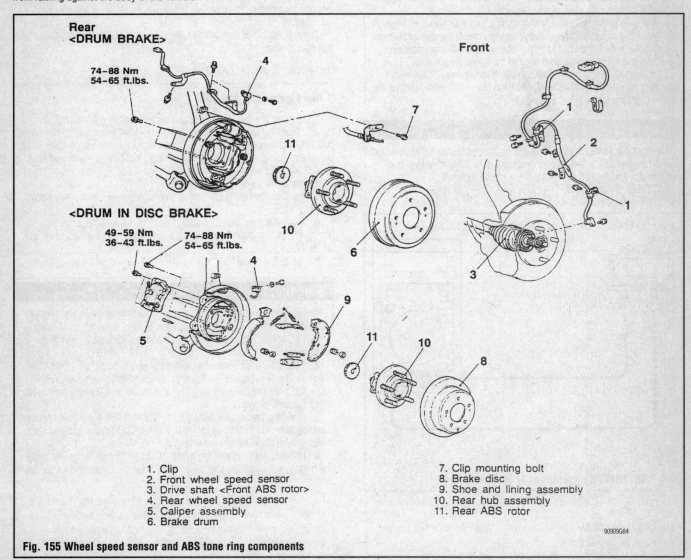

1. Clip
2. Front wheel speed sensor
3. Drive shaft <Front ABS rotor>
4. Rear wheel speed sensor
5. Caliper assembly
6. Brake drum
7. Clip mounting bolt
8. Brake disc
9. Shoe and lining assembly
10. Rear hub assembly
11. Rear ABS rotor

Fig. 155 Wheel speed sensor and ABS tone ring components

90909G84

REAR ABS WHEEL SPEED SENSOR

▶ **See Figure 155**

1. Disconnect the negative battery cable.
2. Remove the clips securing the speed sensor lead.
3. Remove the retaining screw and remove the speed sensor.
To install:
4. Attach the wheel speed sensor with the retaining screw.
5. Secure the speed sensor lead with the clips.

✳✳ WARNING

Make sure the lead wire is properly routed in its original position. If the lead wire is improperly installed it could be damaged by moving parts.

6. Connect the negative battery cable and check the ABS system for proper operation.

TESTING

▶ **See Figures 156 and 157**

1. Using an ohmmeter, measure the resistance between the wheel speed sensor connector terminals.
2. The resistance should measure 1.0–1.5k ohms. If the resistance measures outside this value, replace the wheel speed sensor.
3. Remove the wheel speed sensor from the vehicle, and then measure the speed sensor insulation resistance between one of the connector terminals and the body of the speed sensor. Then measure the resistance between the other connector terminal and the speed sensor body.
4. The resistance should measure 100k ohms or more. If the wheel speed sensor insulation resistance measures below this value, replace the wheel speed sensor.

Tone Ring

The front ABS tone ring is an integral component of the halfshaft assemblies and therefore, cannot be serviced separately. If the front tone ring requires service, the halfshaft assembly must be replaced.

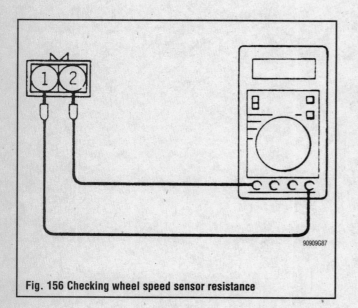

Fig. 156 Checking wheel speed sensor resistance

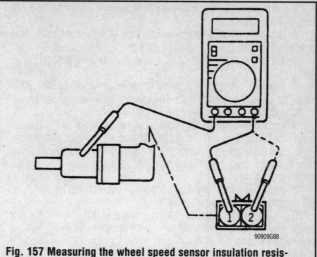

Fig. 157 Measuring the wheel speed sensor insulation resistance

On Cirrus, Stratus, Sebring convertible and Breeze models, the rear ABS tone ring is an integral component of the wheel hub/bearing assembly. If the rear tone ring requires service, the wheel hub/bearing assembly must be replaced.

The rear ABS tone ring can be serviced separately on Sebring coupe and Avenger models.

REMOVAL & INSTALLATION

▶ **See Figures 158 and 159**

1. Remove the rear wheel hub/bearing assembly from the vehicle.
2. Mount the assembly upside down in special inner shaft removal tool MB991248, or equivalent. With the assembly placed on top of 2 blocks of wood and, using a socket, tap the tone ring off of the back of the wheel hub/bearing assembly.
To install:
3. Position the hub/bearing assembly upside down on top of a small block of wood.
4. Place the tone ring in position over the back of the assembly. Using a socket and a hammer, tap the tone ring onto the hub/bearing assembly.
5. Install the wheel hub/bearing assembly onto the vehicle.

Bleeding the ABS System

The bleeding procedure is a 2-step process, one of which will require use of the DRB scan tool or its equivalent. Bleed the system as follows:
1. Locate the diagnostic connector under the dash panel next to the left kick panel.
2. Connect the DRB scan tool to the connector. Install the correct cartridge for the Anti-Lock Brake systems. Check to make sure the CAB or ABS-ECU does not have any fault codes stored in it. If it does, remove them using the DRB scan tool.
3. Bleed the base brake system using the non-ABS manual or pressure bleeding method as outlined earlier in this section. Be sure to bleed the brake system in the correct sequence.
4. Utilizing the scan tool, go to the "Bleed ABS" routine. Firmly apply the brake pedal to initiate the "Bleed ABS" cycle one time. Release the brake pedal.

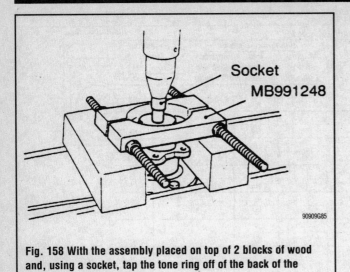

Fig. 158 With the assembly placed on top of 2 blocks of wood and, using a socket, tap the tone ring off of the back of the wheel hub/bearing assembly

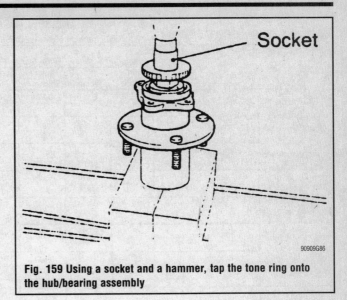

Fig. 159 Using a socket and a hammer, tap the tone ring onto the hub/bearing assembly

5. Using the scan tool, go on to bleed the Anti-Lock Brake System according to the scan tool literature.

6. Once bleeding with the scan tool is complete, repeat the conventional bleed procedure for the base brake system.

7. Perform this procedure until the brake fluid flows clear and free of air bubbles. Check brake fluid level periodically to prevent the reservoir from running low on fluid. Top off the master cylinder reservoir to the proper level with DOT 3 type brake fluid only.

8. Road test the vehicle to check for proper brake system operation.

BRAKE SPECIFICATIONS
All measurements in inches unless noted

Year	Model		Master Cylinder Bore	Brake Disc Original Thickness	Brake Disc Minimum Thickness	Maximum Runout	Brake Drum Diameter Original Inside Diameter	Max. Wear Limit	Maximum Machine Diameter	Minimum Lining Thickness Pad	Minimum Lining Thickness Shoe
1995	Cirrus	F	0.874	0.900	0.843	0.005	-	-	-	0.375	-
		R	-	-	-	-	7.874	NA	7.921	-	④
	Stratus	F	0.874	0.900	0.843	0.005	-	-	-	0.375	-
		R	-	-	-	-	7.874	NA	7.921	-	④
	Sebring Coupe	F	①	0.940	0.880	0.003	-	-	-	0.093	-
		R	-	0.400	0.330	0.003	NA	NA	9.000	0.093	0.039
	Avenger	F	①	0.940	0.880	0.003	-	-	-	0.093	-
		R	-	0.400	0.330	0.003	NA	NA	9.000	0.093	0.039
1996	Cirrus	F	0.874	0.900	0.843	0.005	-	-	-	0.375	-
		R	-	-	-	-	7.874	NA	7.921	-	④
	Stratus	F	0.874	0.900	0.843	0.005	-	-	-	0.375	-
		R	-	-	-	-	7.874	NA	7.921	-	④
	Breeze	F	0.874	0.900	0.843	0.005	-	-	-	0.375	-
		R	-	-	-	-	7.874	NA	7.921	-	④
	Sebring Conv.	F	0.874	0.900	0.843	0.005	-	-	-	0.375	-
		R	-	-	-	-	8.660	NA	8.690	-	④
	Sebring Coupe	F	①	0.940	0.880	0.003	-	-	-	0.093	-
		R	-	②	③	0.003	NA	NA	9.000	0.093	0.039
	Avenger	F	①	0.940	0.880	0.003	-	-	-	0.093	-
		R	-	②	③	0.003	NA	NA	9.000	0.093	0.039
1997	Cirrus	F	0.874	0.900	0.843	0.005	-	-	-	0.375	-
		R	-	-	-	-	7.874	NA	7.921	-	④
	Stratus	F	0.874	0.900	0.843	0.005	-	-	-	0.375	-
		R	-	-	-	-	7.874	NA	7.921	-	④
	Breeze	F	0.874	0.900	0.843	0.005	-	-	-	0.375	-
		R	-	-	-	-	7.874	NA	7.921	-	④
	Sebring Conv.	F	0.874	0.900	0.843	0.005	-	-	-	0.375	-
		R	-	-	-	-	8.660	NA	8.690	-	④
	Sebring Coupe	F	①	0.940	0.880	0.003	-	-	-	0.093	-
		R	-	②	③	0.003	NA	NA	9.000	0.093	0.039
	Avenger	F	①	0.940	0.880	0.003	-	-	-	0.093	-
		R	-	②	③	0.003	NA	NA	9.000	0.093	0.039
1998	Cirrus	F	0.874	0.900	0.843	0.005	-	-	-	0.375	-
		R	-	-	-	-	7.874	NA	7.921	-	④
	Stratus	F	0.874	0.900	0.843	0.005	-	-	-	0.375	-
		R	-	-	-	-	7.874	NA	7.921	-	④
	Breeze	F	0.874	0.900	0.843	0.005	-	-	-	0.375	-
		R	-	-	-	-	7.874	NA	7.921	-	④
	Sebring Conv.	F	0.874	0.900	0.843	0.005	-	-	-	0.375	-
		R	-	0.350	0.285	0.005	8.660	NA	8.690	0.125	④
	Sebring Coupe	F	①	0.940	0.880	0.003	-	-	-	0.093	-
		R	-	②	③	0.003	NA	NA	9.000	0.093	0.039
	Avenger	F	①	0.940	0.880	0.003	-	-	-	0.093	-
		R	-	②	③	0.003	NA	NA	9.000	0.093	0.039

NA: Not Available

① Non-ABS: 0.938 inch
   ABS: 1.0 inch
② Solid disc: 0.400 inch
   Vented disc: NA
③ Solid disc: 0.330 inch
   Vented disc: 0.720 inch
④ Leading brake shoe: 0.125 inch
   Trailing brake shoe: 0.110 inch

90909C01

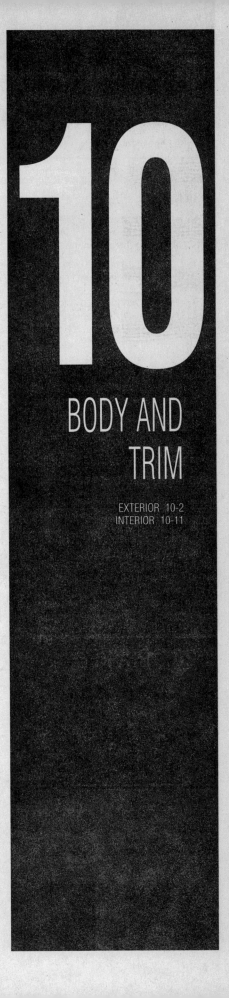

10

BODY AND
TRIM

EXTERIOR

Doors

REMOVAL & INSTALLATION

Cirrus, Stratus, Sebring Convertible and Breeze

▶ **See Figure 1**

➡ **The retaining clips used on the door hinge pins are not reusable after they have been removed. Make sure to have new clips on hand before beginning the procedure.**

1. Disconnect the negative battery cable.
2. Open the door, then support it either with the help of an assistant or a padded jack.
3. Detach the electrical connector at the hinge pillar.
4. Unfasten the bolts securing the door check strap to the hinge pillar.
5. Remove and discard the clip securing the hinge pin in the lower door hinge.

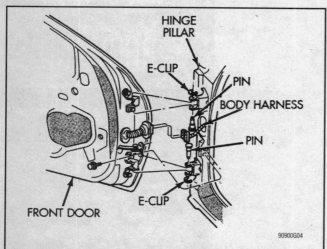

Fig. 1 Door and hinge components—Cirrus, Stratus, Sebring convertible and Breeze

6. Remove the pin from the lower hinge.
7. Remove and discard the clip holding the hinge pin in the upper door hinge, then remove the pin from the upper hinge.
8. Carefully remove the door from the vehicle.

To install:

9. Apply a suitable multi-purpose grease to the inside of the door hinge bushings.
10. Position the door on the vehicle and install the pin in the upper hinge. Align the knurling on the pin with the grooves in the door hinge before driving in the pin.
11. Install the pin in the lower hinge.

➡ **Make sure the head of each hinge pin is fully seated into the door hinge.**

12. Install a new clip securing the pin in the upper hinge and a new clip to hold the pin in the lower hinge.
13. Install the bolts holding the door check strap to the hinge pillar.
14. Attach the electrical connector at the hinge pillar.
15. Connect the negative battery cable. Perform the door adjustment procedure.

Sebring Coupe and Avenger

▶ **See Figure 2**

1. Disconnect the negative battery cable.
2. Open the door, then suitable support it either with the help of an assistant or a padded jack.
3. Detach the electrical connector at the hinge pillar.
4. Remove the spring pin securing the door check strap to the hinge pillar.
5. Remove the door-to-hinge mounting bolts.
6. Carefully remove the door from the vehicle.

To install:

7. Apply a suitable multi-purpose grease to the door hinges and door strap spring pin.
8. Position the door on the vehicle and install the door-to-hinge mounting bolts.
9. Tighten the door-to-hinge mounting bolts to 16 ft. lbs. (22 Nm).
10. Install the spring pin securing door check strap to the hinge pillar.
11. Attach the electrical connector at the hinge pillar.
12. Connect the negative battery cable. Perform the door adjustment procedure.

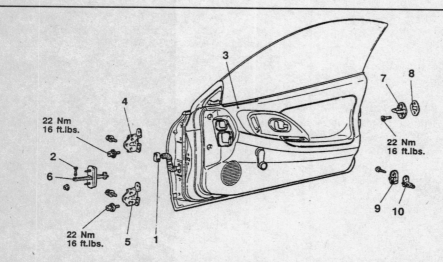

1. Harness connector
2. Spring pin
3. Door assembly
4. Door upper hinge
5. Door lower hinge
6. Door check
7. Striker
8. Striker shim
9. Door switch cap
10. Door switch

Fig. 2 Door and hinge components—Sebring Coupe and Avenger

ADJUSTMENT

Cirrus, Stratus, Sebring Convertible and Breeze

▶ See Figure 3

➡The only adjustment for the doors is a latch adjustment.

1. Insert a hex wrench through the elongated hole in the door end frame, near the latch striker opening.

2. Loosen the socket head screw on the side of the latch linkage ½–1 full turn.

3. Lift upward on the outside door handle, then release it. Do this two times.

4. Tighten the adjusting screw to 30 inch lbs. (3 Nm).

5. Check for proper latch operation.

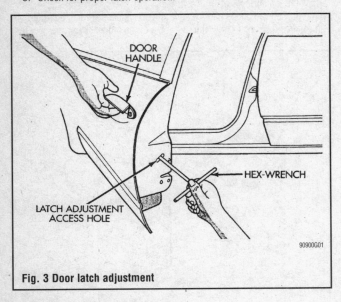

Fig. 3 Door latch adjustment

Sebring Coupe and Avenger

▶ See Figures 4 and 5

➡Mount protection tape to the fender edges where the hinge is installed.

1. Use special door adjusting wrench MB990834 or equivalent to loosen the hinge mounting bolts on the body side.

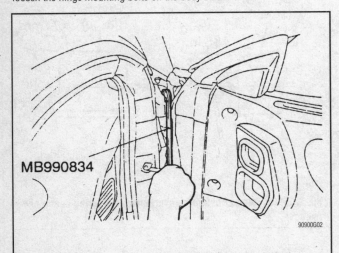

Fig. 4 Use a special door adjusting wrench to loosen the hinge mounting bolts

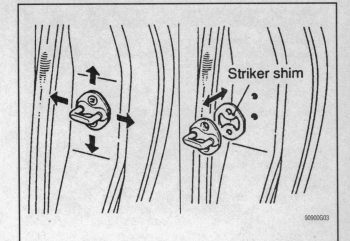

Fig. 5 The door striker mounting can be adjusted up-and-down, left-and-right, and in-and-out

2. When there is a stepped section in the door and body, use the special door adjusting wrench to loosen the door hinge mounting bolt on the door side and adjust the door to fit.

3. If the door is difficult to open or close, use the shim or move the striker plate up-and-down or left-and-right to adjust the linking of the striker and door latch.

Hood

REMOVAL & INSTALLATION

▶ See Figures 6, 7 and 8

➡You will need an assistant to perform this procedure.

1. Raise the hood to the full up position.

2. Disconnect the negative battery cable.

3. If equipped, detach the underhood lamp connector from the engine compartment wire harness.

4. Use a grease pencil or paint marker to outline the installed position of all of the bolts and hinges, for alignment during installation.

5. Disconnect the windshield washer fluid hose from the hood.

6. With an assistant supporting the hood, remove the top bolts holding

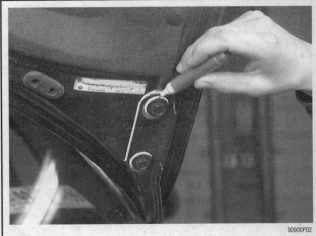

Fig. 6 For installation purposes, be sure to matchmark the correct hood mounting bolt-to-hinge position on each side of the hood

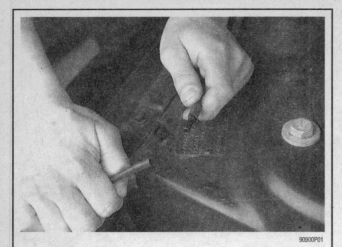

Fig. 7 Disconnect the windshield washer fluid hose at the plastic fitting

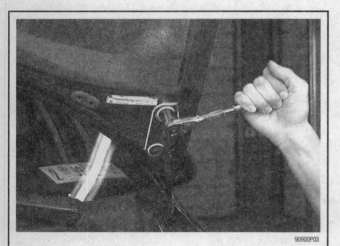

Fig. 8 With an assistant's help, unfasten the 4 mounting bolts, then remove the hood

the hood to the hinge, then loosen the bottom bolts until they can be removed by hand.

7. With the hood still supported, remove the bottom bolts securing the hood to the hinge.

8. Carefully remove the hood from the vehicle. If space does not permit flat storage of the hood, be sure to store it leaning straight up against a wall, with the front edge of the hood to the ground on a blanket to prevent scratches.

To install:

9. With the help of an assistant, place the hood in position on the vehicle. Have the assistant hold the hood at the opposite side of the vehicle from which you are working, then install the bottom bolts finger-tight to hold the hood to the hinges.

10. Install the top hood-to-hinge bolts finger-tight.

11. Position the bolts at the marks made during removal, then tighten the bolts securely.

12. Connect the windshield washer hose.

13. Attach the connector to the underhood lamp, if equipped.

14. Connect the negative battery cable.

15. Check for proper hood operation and alignment.

ALIGNMENT

▶ See Figures 9 and 10

1. The correct height is achieved by rotating the hood adjuster bumpers up or down. These bumpers are located on the radiator support member, in the front of the engine compartment.

2. The correct side gap between the hood and fenders can be achieved by loosening the hood-to-hinge bolts. With the bolts loosened, the hood can be moved front-to-back or side-to-side.

3. On Cirrus, Stratus, Sebring convertible and Breeze models, the hood should be aligned to a 0.160 inch (4mm) gap to the front fenders and flush across the top surfaces along the fenders.

4. On Sebring coupe and Avenger models, rotate the small bumper until it measures 0.55 inch (14mm) fom the top of the radiator crossmember to

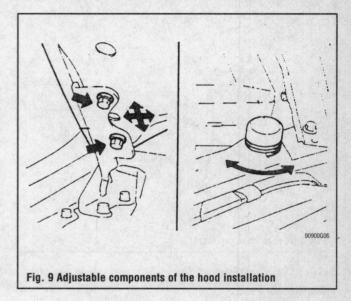

Fig. 9 Adjustable components of the hood installation

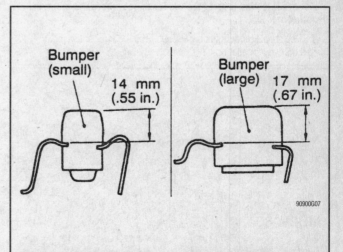

Fig. 10 Hood bumper height measurements—Sebring coupe and Avenger

the top of the bumper. Then, rotate the large bumper until it measures 0.67 inch (17mm) fom the top of the radiator crossmember to the top of the bumper.

Trunk Lid

REMOVAL & INSTALLATION

▶ **See Figures 11 and 12**

1. Disconnect the negative battery cable.
2. Open the trunk lid.
3. Matchmark the bolt locations on the inside of the trunk lid for alignment during installation.
4. Disengage the clips holding the wire harness and trunk lid release cable to the trunk lid.
5. Detach the wire connector and release cable from the trunk latch. Separate the wiring harness rubber boot from the trunk lid.
6. Unfasten the 4 bolts holding the top of the hinge to the trunk lid.
7. With an assistant supporting the trunk lid, remove the bolts holding the bottom of the hinge to the trunk lid.

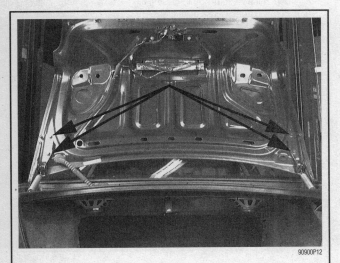

Fig. 11 Location of the trunk lid-to-hinge mounting bolts

Fig. 12 Before removing the trunk lid, separate the rubber boot

To install:

8. Place the trunk lid in position on the vehicle.
9. With an assistant holding the trunk lid in position, install the bolts to hold the bottom of the hinge to the lid.
10. Install the bolts securing the top of the hinge to the trunk lid.
11. Align the trunk lid to obtain a flush fit with equal spacing on all sides.
12. Check for proper trunk lid operation and sealing.
13. Attach the wire connector and release cable to the latch.
14. Install the clips which hold the wire harness and cable to the trunk lid.
15. Connect the negative battery cable.

Grille

REMOVAL & INSTALLATION

Cirrus

▶ **See Figures 13 and 14**

1. Open and support the hood.
2. Remove the plastic push-in fasteners and remove the front wheel housing splash shields.
3. Remove the push-in fasteners securing the bottom of the fascia to the radiator closure panel.
4. If equipped, disengage the fog lamp wiring connectors.
5. Remove the push-in fasteners securing the fascia to the front fenders.
6. Disengage the fascia from the hooks on the bottom of the front fenders and remove it from the vehicle.
7. Using a drill, remove the grille-to-fascia rivets.
8. Remove the grille.

To install:

9. Place the grille in position on the fascia and secure with new rivets, or small nuts and bolts.
10. Place the fascia/grille assembly into position on the front of the vehicle.
11. Engage the fascia onto the hooks at the bottom of the front fenders.
12. Install the push-in fasteners to secure the fascia to the front fenders.
13. If equipped, engage the fog lamp wiring connectors.
14. Install the push-in fasteners securing the bottom of the fascia to the radiator closure panel.

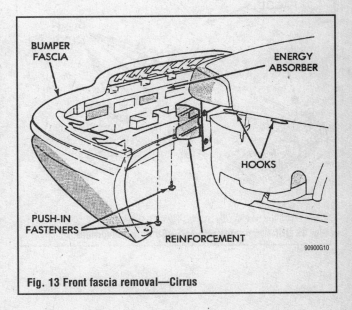

Fig. 13 Front fascia removal—Cirrus

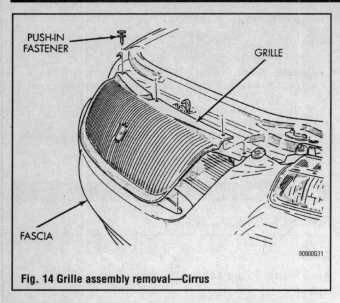

PUSH-IN FASTENER

GRILLE

FASCIA

90900G11

Fig. 14 Grille assembly removal—Cirrus

15. Install the front wheel housing splash shields and secure with the plastic push-in fasteners.

Sebring Convertible

▶ See Figure 15

1. Release the hood latch, then open and support the hood on the prop rod.
2. Remove the screws holding the grille to the headlamp adapter assembly.
3. Pull forward on the grille slightly and remove the clips securing grille to fascia.
4. Remove the grille from the vehicle.

To install:

5. Place the grille into position on the vehicle.
6. Install the clips securing the grille to the fascia.
7. Install the screws holding the grille to the headlamp adapter assembly.
8. Close the hood.

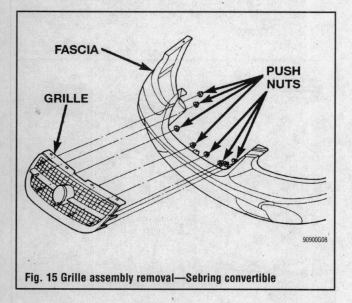

FASCIA

GRILLE

PUSH NUTS

90900G08

Fig. 15 Grille assembly removal—Sebring convertible

1997–98 Sebring Coupe

▶ See Figure 16

1. Disconnect the negative battery cable.
2. Remove the mounting screws and push-pin fasteners, then remove the inner fender wheelhouse splash shields.
3. Remove the front license plate bracket.
4. Remove the front turn signal housings from the fascia assembly.
5. Remove the front bumper center plate at the top of the fascia.
6. Remove the plastic retainer clips behind the top of the fascia.
7. Remove the front fascia assembly from the vehicle.
8. Remove the grille-to-fascia mounting fasteners from behind the assembly.
9. Separate the grille from the fascia assembly.

To install:

10. Place the grille into position on the fascia and secure with the mounting fasteners.
11. Place the front fascia assembly into position on the vehicle. Install and tighten the fascia assembly mounting fasteners.
12. Install the plastic retainer clips behind the top of the fascia.
13. Install the front bumper center plate at the top of the fascia.
14. Install the front turn signal housings to the fascia assembly.
15. Install the front license plate bracket.
16. Install the inner fender wheelhouse splash shields and secure with mounting screws and push-pin fasteners.
17. Connect the negative battery cable.

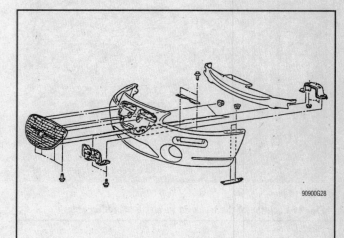

90900G28

Fig. 16 Front fascia and grille assembly—1997–98 Sebring coupe

Outside Mirrors

REMOVAL & INSTALLATION

▶ See Figures 17 thru 22

1. Disconnect the negative battery cable.
2. Remove the door trim panel, as outlined later in this section.
3. If equipped with a manually operated mirror, remove the control knob.
4. If equipped with power mirrors, perform the following:
   a. Remove the watershield.
   b. Detach the electrical connector from the power mirror motor.

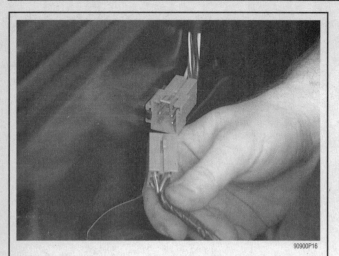

Fig. 17 Detach the electrical connector from the power side view mirror

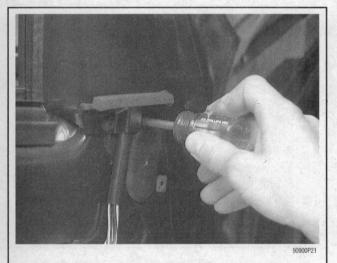

Fig. 18 Remove the 2 mirror trim panel mounting screws

Fig. 19 Remove the side view mirror interior trim panel from the door

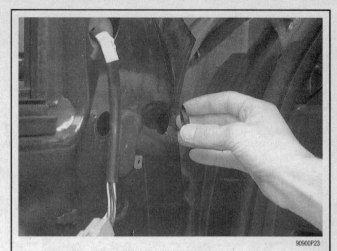

Fig. 20 If equipped, remove the fastener covers from the door panel

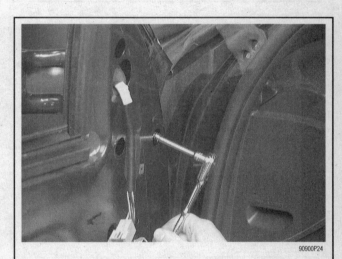

Fig. 21 Remove the 3 side view mirror-to-door mounting fasteners

Fig. 22 Pull the side view mirror assembly out from the door

5. Remove the mirror trim panel mounting screws. Remove the side view mirror interior trim panel from the door.

6. If equipped, remove the fastener covers from the door panel.

7. Unfasten the bolts holding the mirror to the door panel, then remove the mirror from the vehicle.

To install:

8. Position the side view mirror on the vehicle, then install the nuts attaching the mirror to the door panel.

9. If equipped with power mirrors, perform the following:

    a. Attach the electrical connector to the power window motor.

    b. Install the watershield.

10. If equipped, install the fastener covers to the door panel.

11. Install the side view mirror cover.

12. If equipped with a manually operated mirror, install the control knob.

13. Install the door trim panel, as outlined later in this section.

14. Connect the negative battery cable.

Antenna

REPLACEMENT

▶ **See Figure 23**

1. Disconnect the negative battery cable.

2. Open the trunk lid and move the right side trunk liner aside on Sebring coupe and Avenger models; move the left side trunk liner aside on Cirrus, Stratus, Sebring convertible and Breeze models.

3. Unplug the antenna lead from the base of the antenna body.

4. Remove the antenna mast by unscrewing it from the antenna body.

5. Remove the mounting bracket fastener.

6. Remove the antenna from the vehicle.

To install:

7. Install the antenna into the vehicle.

8. Align the mounting bracket and install the fastener.

9. Install the antenna mast.

10. Connect the antenna cable to the cable lead.

11. Place the inner trunk liner back into the correct position.

12. Connect the negative battery cable.

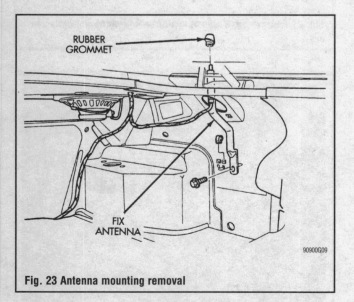

Fig. 23 Antenna mounting removal

Fenders

REMOVAL & INSTALLATION

Cirrus, Stratus, Sebring Convertible and Breeze

▶ **See Figures 24 and 25**

1. Disconnect the negative battery cable.

2. Remove all components mounted to the inside of the fender which must be removed.

3. Remove the front headlamp/side marker lamp assembly. For more details, refer to Section 6.

4. Remove the front bumper, as necessary, to gain clearance to remove the front fender.

5. Remove the front wheel well splash shield.

6. Remove the bolts holding the bottom front fender at the rear of the wheel opening.

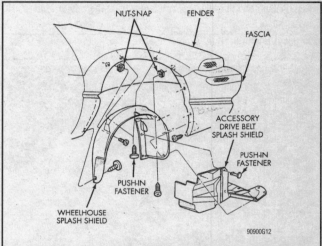

Fig. 24 Right front wheelhouse splash shield assembly—Cirrus, Stratus, Sebring convertible and Breeze

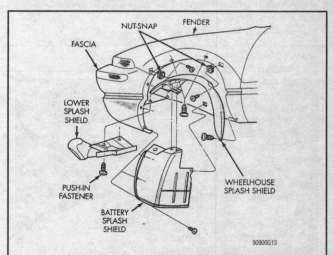

Fig. 25 Left front wheelhouse splash shield assembly—Cirrus, Stratus, Sebring convertible and Breeze

7. Remove the bolt holding the front fender at the top of the front door opening.

8. Remove the bolts holding the front fender to the front of the radiator closure panel.

9. Raise the hood and support the hood with a suitable holding device. Mark the hinge on the fender for installation indexing. Remove the lower hood hinge attaching bolts and separate the hinge from the front fender.

10. Remove the bolts holding the front fender to the inner wheel well along the hood.

11. Separate the front fender from the vehicle.

To install:

12. Position the fender onto the vehicle.

13. Loosely install the bolts to mount the front fender on the inner wheel well along the hood opening.

14. Loosely install the bolts to mount the front fender on the front of the radiator closure panel.

15. Loosely install the bolts to mount the front fender at the top of the front door opening.

16. Loosely install the bolts to mount the front fender at the rear of the wheel opening.

➡**When all mounting bolts are installed, adjust the fender to achieve a gap of 0.16 in. (4mm) between the fender and the hood, and a gap of 0.24 in. (6mm) to the front door edge. All surfaces across the gaps should be flush.**

17. Adjust the front fender to achieve the designated gap between the fender and the front door.

18. Tighten the attaching and mounting bolts.

19. Install the hood hinge-to-fender attaching bolts and the front wheel well splash shield, then tighten the bolts.

20. Install the front fascia and push-in fasteners.

21. Install the headlamp/side marker lamp assembly. Refer to Section 6 for more details.

22. Install all components removed from the inside of the fender. Refer to the necessary procedures depending on the various components.

23. Connect the negative battery cable.

Sebring Coupe and Avenger

▶ **See Figures 26, 27 and 28**

1. Disconnect the negative battery cable.

2. Remove the mounting screws and push-pin fasteners, then remove the inner fender wheelhouse splash shields.

3. On Sebring coupe models, remove the mounting fasteners, then separate the front side ground effect panel from the front fender, between the wheel well and the door.

4. Remove the front turn signal housings from the fascia assembly.

5. Remove the front bumper center plate at the top of the fascia.

6. On Sebring coupe models, remove the plastic retainer clips behind the top of the fascia.

7. Remove the front fascia assembly from the vehicle.

8. Remove the bolts holding the bottom front fender at the rear of the wheel opening.

9. Remove the bolt holding the front fender at the top of the front door opening.

10. Remove the bolts holding the front fender to the front of the radiator closure panel.

11. Remove the bolts holding the top edge of the front fender to the engine compartment outer side panel.

12. Remove the fender from the vehicle.

To install:

➡**Before installing the fender, apply silicone rubber sealer to the inner top edge.**

13. Place the fender in proper position on the vehicle.

14. Install and tighten the bolts holding the top edge of the front fender to the engine compartment outer side panel.

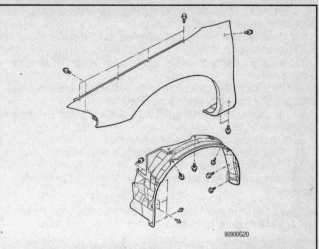

Fig. 26 Fender and inner wheelhouse splash shield—Sebring coupe and Avenger

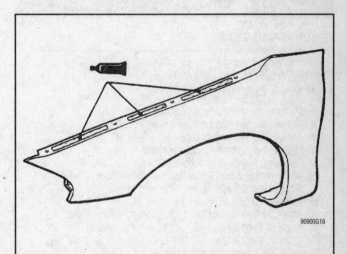

Fig. 27 Apply silicone rubber sealer to the inner top edge of the fender

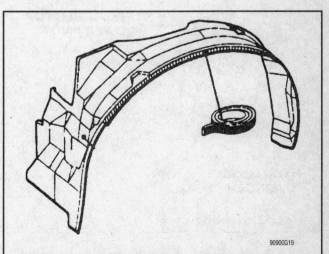

Fig. 28 Apply silicone rubber sealer to the outer top edge of the splash shield

15. Install and tighten the bolts holding the front fender to the front of the radiator closure panel.

16. Install and tighten the bolts holding the front fender at the top of the front door opening.

17. Install and tighten the bolts holding the bottom front fender at the rear of the wheel opening.

18. Place the front fascia assembly into position on the vehicle. Install and tighten the fascia assembly mounting fasteners.

19. On Sebring coupe models, install the plastic retainer clips behind the top of the fascia.

20. Install the front bumper center plate at the top of the fascia.

21. Install the front turn signal housings to the fascia assembly.

22. On Sebring coupe models, install the front side ground effect panel to the front fender, between the wheel well and door. Install the mounting fasteners.

➡**Apply silicone rubber sealer around the top outer edge of the fender wheelhouse splash shield.**

23. Install the inner fender wheelhouse splash shields, and secure with mounting screws and push-pin fasteners.

24. Connect the negative battery cable.

Convertible Top

MOTOR REPLACEMENT

Hydraulic Cylinder

▶ **See Figure 29**

1. Disconnect the negative battery cable.
2. Remove the rear seat cushion and seat back.
3. Remove the quarter trim panel.
4. Remove the cylinder mounting bracket and nut.
5. Remove the cylinder shaft-to-top linkage pivot bolt.
6. Disconnect and plug the hydraulic lines from the cylinder.
7. Remove the hydraulic cylinder from the vehicle.

To install:

8. Install the hydraulic cylinder into position in the vehicle.
9. Install and tighten the hydraulic lines to the cylinder.
10. Install and tighten the cylinder shaft-to-top linkage pivot bolt.
11. Install the cylinder mounting bracket and nut.
12. Install the quarter trim panel.

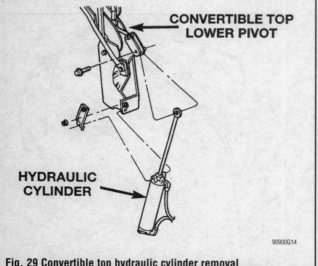

Fig. 29 Convertible top hydraulic cylinder removal

13. Install the rear seat cushion and back.
14. Connect the negative battery cable.
15. Fill the hydraulic system and check for proper operation.

Hydraulic Motor Pump Assembly

▶ **See Figure 30**

1. Disconnect the negative battery cable.
2. Remove the rear seat cushion and seat back.
3. Disengage the pump wire connector and ground connection.
4. Disconnect and plug the hydraulic lines from the motor pump assembly.
5. Remove the motor pump assembly from the vehicle. The rubber mounts are pressed and locked into the bracket, so pull up on the motor assembly to remove.

To install:

6. Position the motor pump assembly into the vehicle.
7. Press the motor pump into the rubber mounts.
8. Connect the hydraulic lines to the pump.
9. Connect the wiring harness and ground wire.
10. Install the rear seat cushion and back.
11. Connect the negative battery cable.
12. Fill the hydraulic system and check for proper operation.

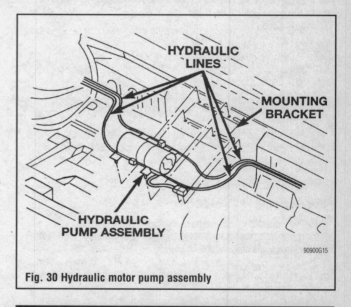

Fig. 30 Hydraulic motor pump assembly

Power Sunroof

REMOVAL & INSTALLATION

Motor

✳✳ WARNING

Do NOT cycle the new motor before installation. Replacement motors are shipped in the closed position. The sunroof vent position is programmed into the motor and is dependent on the closed position of the motor. If the drive motor and sunroof mechanism are not both in the closed position, the sunroof vent height will not be correct.

1. Disconnect the negative battery cable.
2. Move the sunroof panel to the fully closed position.
3. Remove the A-pillar trim, sun visors and map lamps.
4. Detach the control switch wiring harness.

5. Remove the headliner until the sunroof motor is accessible.

6. If the motor is to be reused, cycle the sunroof to the full forward position.

7. Detach the wiring harness connector from the motor.

8. Remove the screws attaching the motor-to-sunroof module bracket.

9. Separate the motor from the bracket.

To install:

10. With the help of an assistant, hold the sunroof glass panel in the closed position and engage the motor into the sunroof drive cables.

11. Install the screws holding the motor to the bracket.

12. Connect the wiring harness to the motor.

13. Install the headliner.

14. Connect the negative battery cable. Check for proper sunroof operation.

Glass Panel

1. Disconnect the negative battery cable.

2. Place the sunroof sunshade in the fully open position.

3. Remove the 6 glass mounting screws.

4. Push the glass panel upward from the underside, until the glass panel clears the roof panel.

5. Lift the glass panel from the vehicle.

To install:

6. Position the glass panel in the opening in the roof.

7. Install, but do not tighten, the glass attaching screws.

8. With the help of an assistant, hold the glass panel in place, then tighten the 6 mounting screws.

9. Check the sunroof to make sure it is the proper height, as outlined in the following procedure.

INTERIOR

Instrument Panel and Pad

REMOVAL & INSTALLATION

Cirrus, Stratus, Sebring Convertible and Breeze

▶ **See Figures 31 and 32**

✳✳ CAUTION

These models are equipped with a Supplemental Restraint System (SRS), which uses air bags. Whenever working near any of the SRS components, such as the impact sensors, air bag modules, steering column and instrument panel, disable the SRS.

1. Disarm the air bag system, as described in Section 6.

2. Open both front doors of the vehicle.

3. Remove the left end cover by pulling outward. Remove the right end cover by pulling rearward.

4. Remove the floor console.

5. Disconnect the air bag control module harness.

6. Remove the instrument cluster.

7. Remove the 5 knee bolster mounting screws.

8. Open the glove box door and press the side walls inboard to lower the door from the panel for access to the forward floor console.

9. Remove the 9 forward floor console mounting screws and one push-pin at the forward driver's side.

10. Pull the driver side underpanel silencer away from the distribution duct.

11. Remove the passenger side instrument panel top cover attaching screw.

12. Lift the right rear edge of the top cover to release the retaining clips along the rear edge, moving from right to left. Do not use a nylon trim stick to avoid scuffing the cover or panel.

13. Lift the rear edge and slide the top cover rearward to release the clips and remove the cover.

GLASS HEIGHT ADJUSTMENT

Flushness

1. Place the sun shade in the fully open position.

2. To adjust the front of the glass, perform the following:

   a. Loosen the front and middle glass attachment screws.

   b. Adjust the front of the sunroof glass panel so that the corners are flush to 1.0mm below the top surface of the roof panel.

   c. Tighten all of the glass attachment screws.

3. To adjust the rear of the glass, perform the following:

   a. Loosen the rear and middle glass attachment screws.

   b. Adjust the rear of the sunroof glass panel so that the corners are flush to within 1.0mm of the top surface of the roof panel.

   c. Tighten all of the glass attachment screws.

Vent Height

1. Cycle the sunroof module to the vent position using the drive motor.

2. Check the glass tilt-in height using an appropriate measuring tool.

3. If the vent height is greater than 35mm, use the switch to slowly set to the proper height.

4. After setting the correct height, remove the drive motor.

5. With the motor removed, use the switch to set the tilt by operating the gear to the fully closed position.

6. Using the tilt switch only, operate the motor until it comes to a full stop at the tilt position.

7. Install the drive motor and verify correct operation.

14. Remove the HVAC control mounting screws and center distribution duct screws from behind the radio and duct.

15. Remove the radio.

16. Remove the HVAC mounting screws from the duct, panel and cross-car beam.

17. Close the glove box door and remove the 5 screws mounting the panel retainer to the plenum.

18. Remove the steering column intermediate shaft mounting bolt.

19. Unplug the engine and body wiring harness from the junction block.

20. Remove the following mounting fasteners:

- Four at the left end and three at the right end of the cross-car beam
- Two at the steering column plenum

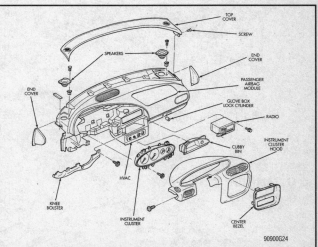

90900G24

Fig. 31 Exploded view of the instrument panel assembly—Cirrus, Stratus, Sebring convertible and Breeze

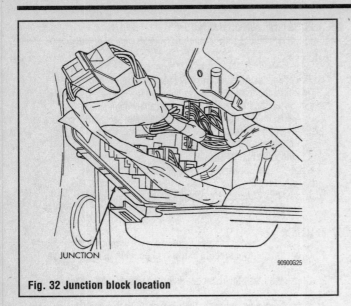

Fig. 32 Junction block location

- One at glove box hinge to cowl
- Two at the center support to the floor pan bracket.

21. Remove the mounting screw at the rear of the HVAC to the center support bracket.

22. Lift up the instrument panel and remove from the vehicle.

To install:

23. Place the instrument panel into the vehicle in correct position.

24. Install the mounting screw at the rear of the HVAC to the center support bracket.

25. Install the following mounting fasteners:
- Four at the left end and three at the right end of the cross-car beam
- Two at the steering column plenum

- One at glove box hinge to cowl
- Two at the center support to the floor pan bracket.

26. Plug in the engine and body wiring harness to the junction block.

27. Install and tighten the steering column intermediate shaft mounting bolt.

28. Open the glove box door and install the 5 screws mounting the panel retainer to the plenum.

29. Install the HVAC mounting screws to the duct, panel and cross-car beam.

30. Install the radio.

31. Install the HVAC control mounting screws and center distribution duct screws behind the radio and duct.

32. Slide the top cover forward into position and engage the retaining clips.

33. Install the passenger side instrument panel top cover attaching screw.

34. Install the driver's side under panel silencer onto the distribution duct.

35. Install the 9 forward floor console mounting screws and and 1 push-pin at the forward driver's side.

36. Close the glove box door.

37. Install the 5 knee bolster mounting screws.

38. Install the instrument cluster.

39. Connect the air bag control module harness.

40. Install the floor console.

41. Install the left and right instrument panel end covers.

42. Arm the air bag system, as described in Section 6.

Sebring Coupe and Avenger

▶ **See Figures 33 and 34**

❊❊ CAUTION

These models are equipped with a Supplemental Restraint System (SRS), which uses air bags. Whenever working near any of the SRS components, such as the impact sensors, air bag modules, steering column and instrument panel, disable the SRS.

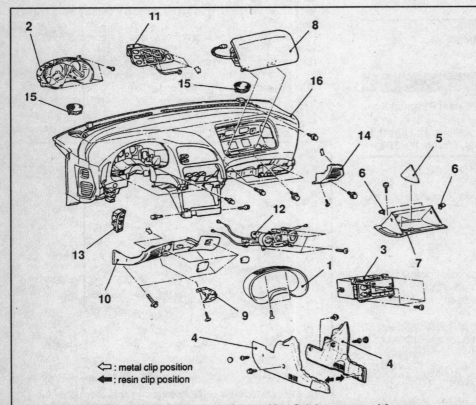

1. Meter bezel
2. Combination meter
3. Radio and tape player
4. Console side cover
5. Sunglasses holder
6. Stopper
7. Glove box
8. Passenger's side air bag module assembly
9. Hood lock release handle
10. Instrument under cover L.H.
11. Center air outlet assembly
12. Heater control assembly
13. Instrument panel switch
14. Instrument under cover R.H.
15. Front speaker
16. Instrument panel assembly

⇦ : metal clip position
⬅ : resin clip position

Fig. 33 Exploded view of the instrument panel assembly—Sebring coupe and Avenger

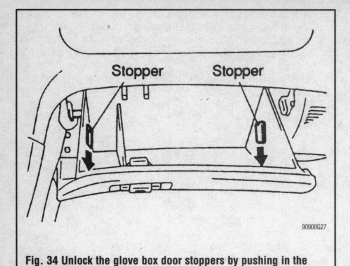

Fig. 34 Unlock the glove box door stoppers by pushing in the direction shown

1. Disarm the air bag system, as described in Section 6.
2. Remove the floor console.
3. Remove the steering wheel.
4. Remove the steering column cover.
5. Remove the instrument cluster (meter).
6. Remove the radio.
7. Remove the mounting screw and plastic retaining clip. Remove the console side cover.
8. Open the glove box door and unlock the door stoppers by pushing them down.
9. Detach the wiring harness connector to the passenger side air bag module.
10. Remove the passenger side air bag module mounting fasteners, through the glove box opening, and remove the module from the vehicle.

✳✳ CAUTION

When carrying a live module, the trim cover should be pointed away from the body to minimize injury in the event of accidental deployment. In addition, if the module is placed on a bench or other surface, the plastic trim cover should be face up to minimize movement in case of accidental deployment.

11. Remove the hood lock relaease handle.
12. Remove the driver side lower instrument panel.
13. Remove the center air outlet assembly.
14. Remove the heater control assembly.
15. Remove the instrument panel switch.
16. Remove the passenger side lower instrument panel.
17. Remove the front speakers.
18. Remove the instrument panel assembly from the vehicle.

To install:

19. Place the instrument panel assembly into the vehicle.
20. Install the passenger side lower instrument panel.
21. Install the instrument panel switch.
22. Install the heater control assembly.
23. Install the center air outlet assembly.
24. Install the driver side lower instrument panel.
25. Install the hood lock release handle.

✳✳ CAUTION

When carrying a live module, the trim cover should be pointed away from the body to minimize injury in the event of accidental deployment.

26. Install the passenger side air bag module into the instrument panel. Install the mounting fasteners through the glove box opening and connect the wiring harness.
27. Close the glove box door.
28. Install the console side cover and secure with the mounting screw and plastic retaining clip.
29. Install the radio.
30. Install the instrument cluster (meter).
31. Install the steering column cover.
32. Install the steering wheel.
33. Install the floor console.
34. Arm the air bag system, as described in Section 6.

Console

REMOVAL & INSTALLATION

Cirrus, Stratus and Breeze

▶ See Figure 35

1. Disconnect the negative battery cable.
2. Remove the mounting screws securing the rear of the floor console assembly to the floor bracket.
3. If equipped with an automatic transaxle, disengage the clips securing the PRNDL plate from the console and remove the plate.
4. If equipped with a manual transaxle, remove the shifter boot and knob as follows:
    a. Pull down the shift boot enough to expose the shifter roll pin.
    b. Using a flat blade tool, pry open the legs of the shift knob away from the roll pin and remove the knob from the shift lever.
    c. Squeeze the shift boot at its base and pull up to remove.
5. Remove the 2 front floor console mounting screws. Raise the parking brake lever as high as it will go to allow for removal clearance.
6. Remove the floor console from the vehicle.

To install:

7. With the parking brake lever in the fully applied position, install the floor console into the vehicle. Install the front and rear floor console mounting screws.
8. If equipped with an automatic transaxle, install the PRNDL plate onto the console and secure it into place by engaging the mounting clips.

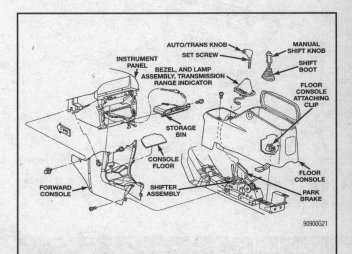

Fig. 35 Floor console and forward console component assembly—Cirrus, Stratus and Breeze

9. If equipped with a manual transaxle, install the shift boot and knob as follows:

a. Slide the rubber boot down over the shift lever and squeeze at the base of the boot to engage it into position on the console.

b. Install the shift knob onto the shift lever and bend the legs of the shift knob tightly on the shift lever over the roll pin.

10. Connect the negative battery cable.

Sebring Convertible

▶ **See Figure 36**

1. Disconnect the negative battery cable.

2. Using a 2mm Allen wrench, remove the setscrew securing the shifter knob to the shift lever. Remove the shifter knob by pulling it up off the shift lever.

3. Remove the 3 mounting screws securing the rear of the console to the console bracket.

4. Remove the screw hole garnish cap and the PRNDL bezel from the console.

5. Remove the 2 mounting screws attaching the console to the shifter. Raise the parking brake lever to a 45 degree angle to allow for removal clearance of the console.

6. Raise the rear of the console high enough to access the console wiring harness connector. Disconnect the 8-way wiring harness connector.

7. Remove the console from the vehicle.

To install:

8. Raise the parking brake lever to approximately a 45 degree angle to provide proper clearance for console installation.

9. Install the floor console into the vehicle. Engage the center console wiring harness connector to the vehicle wiring harness. Install the front and rear floor console mounting screws.

10. Install the PRNDL bezel onto the console and screw hole garnish cap.

11. Install the shifter knob down onto the shift lever. Install and securely tighten the shifter knob setscrew.

12. Connect the negative battery cable.

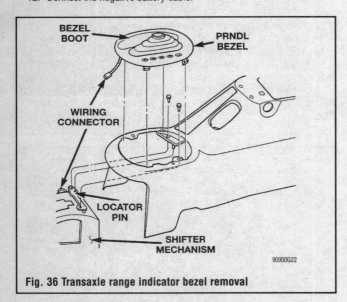

Fig. 36 Transaxle range indicator bezel removal

Sebring Coupe and Avenger

▶ **See Figure 37**

1. Disconnect the negative battery cable.

✳✳ CAUTION

The air bag control unit is mounted beneath the center console. Use care when working with the center console assembly not to impact or shock the control unit.

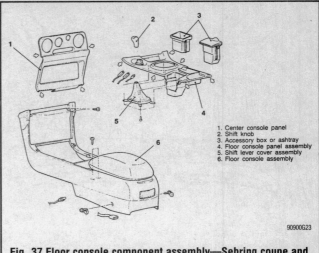

1. Center console panel
2. Shift knob
3. Accessory box or ashtray
4. Floor console panel assembly
5. Shift lever cover assembly
6. Floor console assembly

90900G23

Fig. 37 Floor console component assembly—Sebring coupe and Avenger

2. Remove the center floor console assembly as follows:

3. Remove the shifter knob on models equipped with a manual transaxle.

4. Remove the shifter trim panel.

5. Remove the center instrument panel.

6. Remove the panel box from the console assembly.

7. Remove the two screws from the center of the console.

8. Remove the four side panel screws and remove the console from the vehicle.

To install:

9. Place the center console into position in the vehicle.

10. Install the two screws to the center of the console.

11. Install the panel box to the console assembly.

12. Install the center instrument panel.

13. Install the shifter trim panel.

14. Install the shifter knob on models equipped with a manual transaxle.

15. Connect the negative battery cable.

Door Panels

REMOVAL & INSTALLATION

▶ **See Figures 38 thru 50**

1. Disconnect the negative battery cable.

2. Open the door, then lower the window.

3. If equipped with manual windows, slide a window crank removal tool behind the crank to unfasten the retaining clip, then remove the crank.

4. On all vehicles except Sebring coupe and Avenger, perform the following steps:

a. Disengage the clips that secure the speaker grille to the trim panel.

b. Remove the screws securing the trim panel to the door from around the speaker opening.

5. On Sebring convertible models, use a small flat tipped pry tool to remove the trim cap at the rear end of the door arm rest and remove the trim panel mounting screw.

6. On Sebring coupe and Avenger vehicles, perform the following:

a. Remove the 2 trim panel mounting screws from the rear end of the door.

b. Remove the 2 trim panel mounting screws from the front end of the door.

7. Using a small pry tool, remove the screw cap from the bottom of the arm rest pull cup.

8. Unfasten the screw attaching the pull cup to the door panel.

Fig. 38 Place a small piece of cloth or paper towel behind the tool to prevent scuffing the door panel when removing the speaker grille

Fig. 39 After releasing the locating tabs, remove the door speaker grille. Be careful not to bend the grille while removing

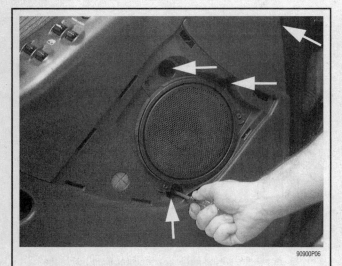

Fig. 40 Remove the door panel mounting screws

Fig. 41 Using a small prying tool, remove the screw hole cover in the bottom of the armrest pull cup

Fig. 42 Remove the retaining screw in the armrest pull cup

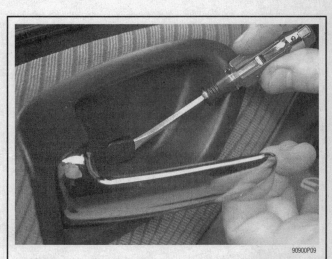

Fig. 43 Using a small prying tool while holding the inside door latch handle outward, remove the screw hole cover

9. Pull the inside door latch release handle, in order to remove the screw cap from behind the latch handle.

10. While holding out the inside door latch release handle, remove the screw.

➡**Use a fork-type trim panel fastener removal tool to disengage the push-in fasteners. Pulling on the trim panel to disengage the fasteners will damage the panel.**

11. Disengage all hidden push-in fasteners attaching the trim panel to the door. Make sure that all of the fasteners are detached using the removal tool.

12. Tilt the trim panel out to clear the locator pins on the back side of the trim panel.

13. Lift the trim panel to disengage it from the retainer channel on the inner belt weatherstrip at the top of the door and to clear the lock button.

14. Disengage the clip holding the door latch linkage to the back of the inside door handle, then separate the latch rod from the handle.

➡**Do not allow the door trim panel to hang by the wire connector or wiring.**

15. Detach the wire connector(s) from the power door lock switch, mirror switch and/or power window switch, as applicable.

16. Remove the trim panel from the vehicle.

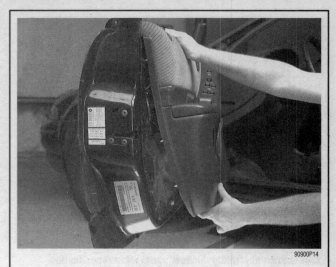

Fig. 46 Pull off the trim panel at the bottom

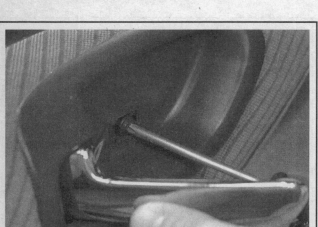

Fig. 44 Remove the retaining screw behind the inside door latch handle

Fig. 47 Using a flat tipped prying tool, unsnap the plastic clip from the inner door latch rod mechanism

Fig. 45 Use a fork-type trim panel fastener removal tool to disengage the door trim panel push-in fasteners

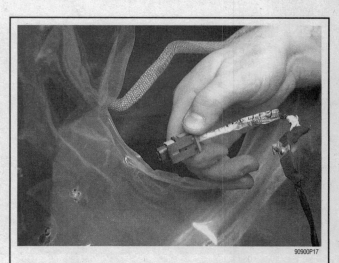

Fig. 48 Detach the wiring harness connector from inside the door to enable trim panel removal

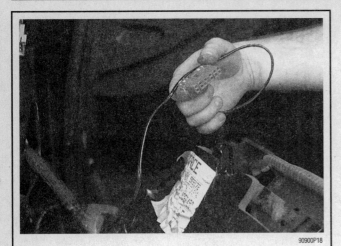

Fig. 49 Detach any electrical switch connectors from the door trim panel

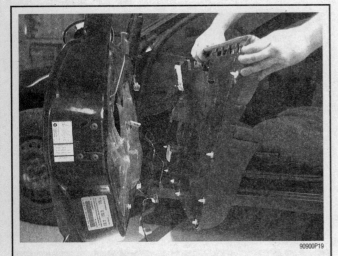

Fig. 50 Lift the trim panel upward and pull it away from the door

To install:

17. Replace any missing or damaged push-in retainers with new ones of the same type and quality.

18. Position the trim panel near the door.

19. Attach the connectors to the power components (window, mirror, locks), as applicable.

20. Insert the latch rod into the inside latch release.

21. Engage the clip holding the door latch linkage to the back of the inside door handle.

22. Place the trim panel into the retainer channel at the top of the door and push it down to seat.

23. Locate the door trim panel to the inner door panel by aligning the locating pins on the backside of the trim panel to the mating holes in the inner door panel. Gently shift the panel forward or rearward, as necessary.

24. Engage the hidden push-in fasteners holding the trim panel to the door from around the perimeter of the trim panel.

25. With the window still all the way down, position the window regulator crank handle (if equipped with manual windows). On the right door, install the handle at the 10 o'clock position; on the left door, install the handle at the 2 o'clock position.

26. Install the screw securing the trim panel to the door from behind the inside door latch release handle. Install the screw cap.

27. Install and tighten the screw inside the pull cup holding the door trim panel to the bracket. Install the screw cap.

28. On all vehicles except Sebring coupe and Avenger, perform the following steps:

   a. Install and tighten the screws securing the trim panel to the door around the speaker opening.

   b. Engage the clips that secure the speaker grille to the trim panel.

29. On Sebring convertible models, install and tighten the trim panel mounting screw at the rear end of the door armrest. Install the screw cover trim cap.

30. On Sebring coupe and Avenger models, perform the following:

   a. Install and tighten the 2 trim panel mounting screws to the front end of the door.

   b. Install and tighten the 2 trim panel mounting screws to the rear end of the door.

31. Connect the negative battery cable.

Door Locks

REMOVAL & INSTALLATION

▶ **See Figures 51 and 52**

1. Disconnect the negative battery cable.

2. Remove the door trim panel, as described previously in this section.

3. Close the door glass.

4. Carefully peel the watershield away from the adhesive around the edge of the inner door panel.

5. Disconnect the latch linkage from the door handle latch.

6. Remove the door handle-to-outer door panel mounting nuts.

7. Separate the door latch handle from the vehicle.

8. If equipped with an electric central door locking system, disengage the wiring harness connector.

9. Disconnect the clip holding the lock linkage to the back of the lock cylinder.

10. Separate the linkage from the lock cylinder.

11. Remove the lock cylinder-to-outer door panel retaining clip.

12. Remove the lock cylinder from the vehicle.

To install:

13. Install the lock cylinder into the outer door panel and secure with a retaining clip.

14. Connect the linkage to the lock cylinder and install the clip.

15. If equipped with an electric central door locking system, engage the wiring harness connector.

Fig. 51 Door latch handle removal

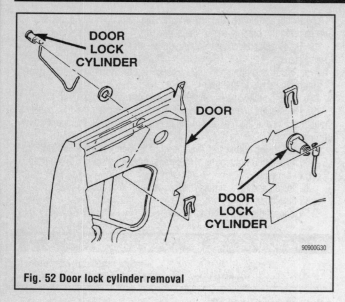

Fig. 52 Door lock cylinder removal

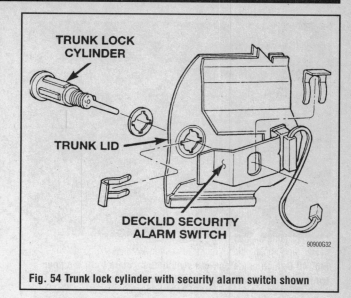

Fig. 54 Trunk lock cylinder with security alarm switch shown

16. Install the door latch handle into the door and connect the latch linkage. Tighten the door latch handle mounting nuts.

17. Place the watershield into position and secure with duct tape, if the shield does not stick to the original adhesive.

18. Install the interior door trim panel.

19. Connect the negative battery cable.

Trunk Lock

REMOVAL & INSTALLATION

▶ **See Figures 53 and 54**

1. Disconnect the negative battery cable.
2. Open the trunk lid.
3. Remove the trunk latch, as follows:
   a. Mark the position of the trunk latch on the lid to aid in installation.
   b. If equipped, disengage the wiring harness connectors from the latch.

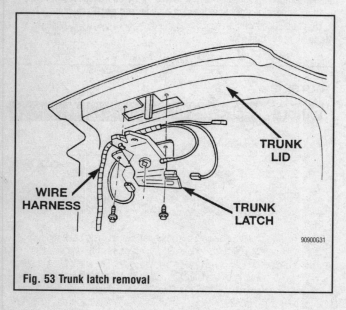

Fig. 53 Trunk latch removal

c. Unfasten the bolts securing the trunk latch to the trunk lid.

d. If equipped, disconnect the remote trunk latch release cable from the trunk latch.

e. Separate the latch from the vehicle.

4. If equipped, remove the clip holding the security alarm switch to the lock cylinder and remove the switch.

5. Remove the clip securing the lock cylinder to the trunk lid, then pull the lock cylinder from the trunk lid.

To install:

6. Place the lock cylinder in the trunk lid, then install the retaining clip.

7. If equipped, install the security alarm switch to the lock cylinder and retain with the clip.

8. Install the trunk latch, as follows:
   a. Position the latch in the trunk and, if equipped, engage the wiring harnesses to the latch.
   b. Connect the remote trunk latch release cable to the trunk latch.
   c. Install the bolts holding the trunk latch to the trunk lid. Close the trunk lid.

9. Connect the negative battery cable.

Window Regulator

REMOVAL & INSTALLATION

➡**Power and manual window regulators are removed and installed using the same procedure.**

2-Door Vehicles

1. Disconnect the negative battery cable.

2. Remove the door trim panel and watershield, as described earlier in this section.

3. If equipped with power windows, detach the wire connector from the power window motor.

4. Unfasten the nuts securing the regulator lift channel to the door glass.

5. Secure the window in the upright position.

6. Matchmark the position of the rear bolt of the roller channel to the inner door panel for installation purposes.

7. Remove the bolt securing the rear of the roller channel to the door panel.

8. Loosen the bolt holding the front of the roller channel to the door panel.

9. Separate the roller channel from the door panel.

10. Loosen the bolts holding the window regulator to the inner door panel.

11. Separate the bolt heads from the keyhole slots in the inner door panel.

12. Remove the window regulator through the large hole in the inner door panel.

13. If equipped, remove the power window motor from the regulator.

To install:

14. If equipped, install the power window motor on the regulator.

15. Move the regulator into position in the door, then engage the bolt heads into the keyhole slots in the inner door panel and tighten the bolts.

16. Install the roller channel to the door panel.

17. Install the bolt at the rear of the roller channel, making sure to align it to the mark on the inner door panel made during removal.

18. Tighten the front and rear roller channel bolts.

19. Install the nuts holding the regulator lift channel to the door glass.

20. If equipped, attach the electrical connector to the power window motor.

21. If equipped, install the door speaker.

22. Install the watershield and door trim panel.

23. Connect the negative battery cable.

4-Door Vehicles

1. Disconnect the negative battery cable.

2. Remove the door trim panel and watershield.

3. Remove the window glass.

4. If equipped with power windows, detach the wire connector from the power window motor.

5. Remove the nuts securing the top of the regulator to the inner door panel.

6. Remove the nuts holding the bottom of the regulator to the door panel.

7. Loosen the bolts holding the regulator crank/motor to the door panel.

8. Disengage the bolts from the keyhole slots in the door panel.

9. Remove the window regulator from the access hole in the door panel.

10. Remove the power window motor from the regulator, if equipped.

To install:

11. If equipped, install the power window motor onto the regulator.

12. Move the window regulator into position in the door, then engage the bolt heads in the keyhole slots in the inner door panel.

13. Tighten the bolts attaching the regulator crank/motor to the door panel.

14. Install the nuts holding the top and bottom of the window regulator to the door panel.

15. If equipped, attach the electrical connector to the power window motor.

16. Connect the negative battery cable.

17. Install the door glass. Check and adjust the glass alignment, as necessary.

Electric Window Motor

REMOVAL & INSTALLATION

♦ See Figure 55

✳✳ CAUTION

Do NOT place your hands or fingers in the sector gear area where they can be pinched by the small movements of the regulator linkage.

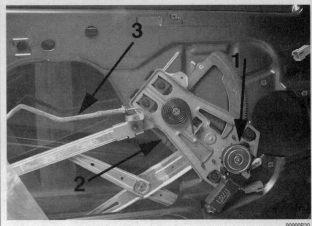

Fig. 55 Electric window motor (1), window regulator mechanism (2) and interior door handle latch rod (3)

90900P20

1. If possible, move the window to the fully closed position.

2. Remove the door trim panel and window regulator assembly, as described earlier in this section.

✳✳ CAUTION

Failure to clamp the sector gear to the mounting plate when removing the motor can result in injury.

3. Secure the sector gear and mounting plate with a C-clamp. This will prevent a sudden and forceful movement of the regulator when the motor is removed.

4. Remove the 3 mounting screws that secure the motor gear box to the regulator.

5. Remove the motor from the regulator.

To install:

6. Install the replacement motor on the regulator by positioning the motor's gear box so that it engages the regulator's sector teeth.

➡**A slight rotational or rocking motion may be necessary to bring the 3 motor gear box screw holes into proper position.**

7. Install the 3 gear box screws and one tie-down bracket screw, if applicable.

8. Tighten the mounting bolts to 50–74 inch lbs. (5.6–8.5 Nm).

9. Install the regulator assembly and door trim panel.

10. Connect the negative battery cable.

Windshield and Fixed Glass

REMOVAL & INSTALLATION

If your windshield, or other fixed window, is cracked or chipped, you may decide to replace it with a new one yourself. However, there are two main reasons why replacement windshields and other window glass should be installed only by a professional automotive glass technician: safety and cost.

The most important reason a professional should install automotive glass is for safety. The glass in the vehicle, especially the windshield, is designed with safety in mind in case of a collision. The windshield is specially manufactured from two panes of specially-tempered glass with a thin layer of transparent plastic between them. This construction allows the glass to "give" in the event that a part of your body hits the windshield during the collision, and prevents the glass from shattering, which could cause lacerations, blinding and other harm to passengers of the vehicle. The other fixed windows are designed to be tempered so that if they break during a collision, they shatter in such a way that there are no large pointed glass pieces. The professional automotive glass technician knows how to install the glass in a vehicle so that it will function optimally during a collision. Without the proper experience, knowledge and tools, installing a piece of automotive glass yourself could lead to additional harm if an accident should ever occur.

Cost is also a factor when deciding to install automotive glass yourself. Performing this could cost you much more than a professional may charge for the same job. Since the windshield is designed to break under stress, an often life saving characteristic, windshields tend to break VERY easily when an inexperienced person attempts to install one. Do-it-yourselfers buying two, three or even four windshields from a salvage yard because they have broken them during installation are common stories. Also, since the automotive glass is designed to prevent the outside elements from entering your vehicle, improper installation can lead to water and air leaks. Annoying whining noises at highway speeds from air leaks or inside body panel rusting from water leaks can add to your stress level and subtract from your wallet. After buying two or three windshields, installing them and ending up with a leak that produces a noise while driving and water damage during rainstorms, the cost of having a professional do it correctly the first time may be much more alluring. We here at Chilton, therefore, advise that you have a professional automotive glass technician service any broken glass on your vehicle.

WINDSHIELD CHIP REPAIR

▶ **See Figures 56 thru 70**

➥Check with your state and local authorities on the laws for state safety inspection. Some states or municipalities may not allow chip repair as a viable option for correcting stone damage to your windshield.

Although severely cracked or damaged windshields must be replaced, there is something that you can do to prolong or even prevent the need for replacement of a chipped windshield. There are many companies which offer windshield chip repair products, such as Loctite's® Bullseye™ windshield repair kit. These kits usually consist of a syringe, pedestal and a sealing adhesive. The syringe is mounted on the pedestal and is used to create a vacuum which pulls the plastic layer against the glass. This helps make the chip transparent. The adhesive is then injected which seals the chip and helps to prevent further stress cracks from developing. Refer to the sequence of photos to get a general idea of what windshield chip repair involves.

➥**Always follow the specific manufacturer's instructions.**

TCCA0P01

Fig. 57 To repair a chip, clean the windshield with glass cleaner and dry it completely

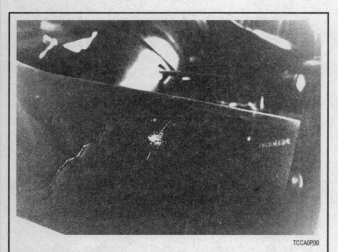

TCCA0P00

Fig. 56 Small chips on your windshield can be fixed with an aftermarket repair kit, such as the one from Loctite®

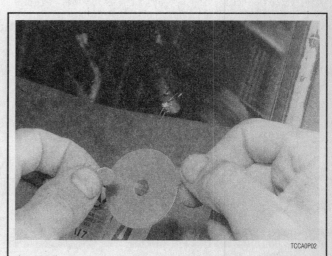

TCCA0P02

Fig. 58 Remove the center from the adhesive disc and peel off the backing from one side of the disc . . .

Fig. 59 . . . then press it on the windshield so that the chip is centered in the hole

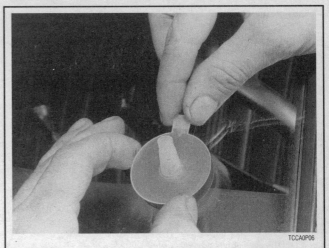

Fig. 62 . . . then position the plastic pedestal on the adhesive disc, ensuring that the tabs are aligned

Fig. 60 Be sure that the tab points upward on the windshield

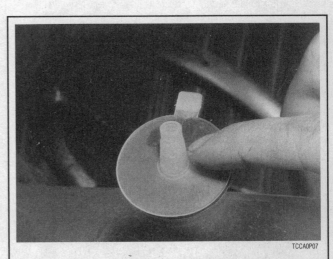

Fig. 63 Press the pedestal firmly on the adhesive disc to create an adequate seal . . .

Fig. 61 Peel the backing off the exposed side of the adhesive disc . . .

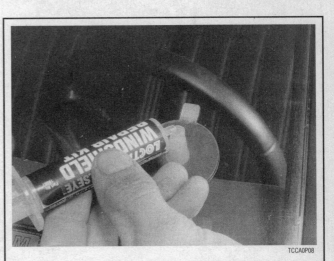

Fig. 64 . . . then install the applicator syringe nipple in the pedestal's hole

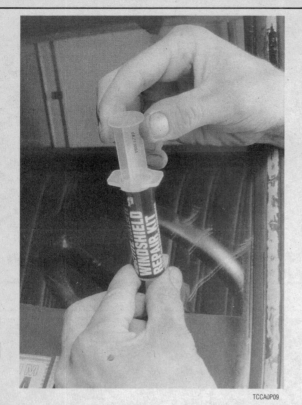

TCCA0P09

Fig. 65 Hold the syringe with one hand while pulling the plunger back with the other hand

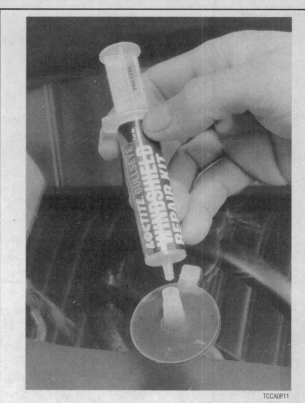

TCCA0P11

Fig. 67 After the solution has set, remove the syringe from the pedestal . . .

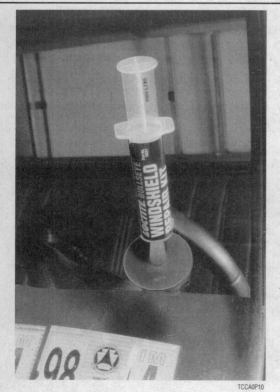

TCCA0P10

Fig. 66 After applying the solution, allow the entire assembly to sit until it has set completely

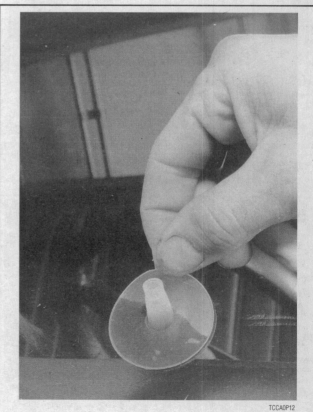

TCCA0P12

Fig. 68 . . . then peel the pedestal off of the adhesive disc . . .

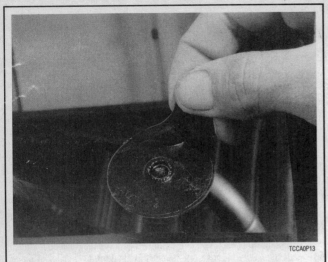

Fig. 69 . . . and peel the adhesive disc off of the windshield

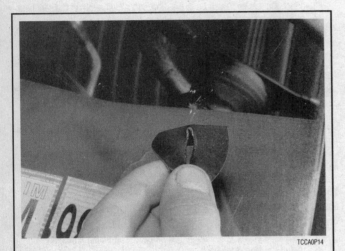

Fig. 70 The chip will still be slightly visible, but it should be filled with the hardened solution

Inside Rear View Mirror

REPLACEMENT

Cirrus, Stratus and Breeze

1. Disconnect the negative battery cable.
2. If equipped, detach the reading lamp wiring connector.
3. Loosen the mirror setscrew.
4. Lift the mirror from the mounting bottom.
5. Installation is the reverse of the removal procedure.

Sebring Convertible

▶ See Figure 71

1. Disconnect the negative battery cable.
2. Remove the inside rear view mirror mounting screws.

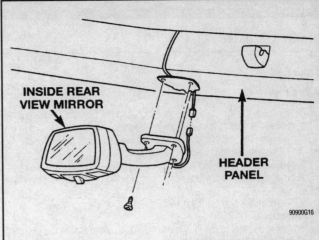

Fig. 71 Inside rear view mirror removal/installation—Sebring convertible

3. If equipped, detach the wiring harness connector from the mirror.
4. Separate the mirror from the vehicle.
5. Installation is the reverse of the removal procedure.

Sebring Coupe and Avenger

▶ See Figure 72

1. Insert a narrow, flat tipped prytool into the slit on the inside rear view mirror mounting bracket.
2. Push in the spring while moving the mirror in an upward direction.
3. Remove the inside rear view mirror from the vehicle.

➡ **While the spring is pushed in, the connection between the spring and pawl of the button is released.**

4. Installation is the reverse of the removal procedure.

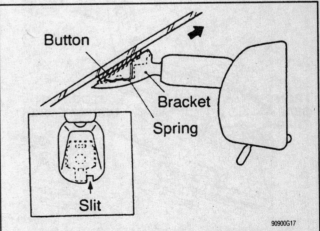

Fig. 72 Insert a narrow, flat tipped prytool into the slit on the inside rear view mirror mounting bracket—Sebring coupe and Avenger

Seats

REMOVAL & INSTALLATION

Front Seats

▶ **See Figure 73**

1. Remove any trim components concealing the seat track mechanism.
2. Move the seat to the fully forward position.
3. Remove the bolts holding the rear of the seat track to the floor.
4. Move the seat to the rearward position.
5. Remove the bolts securing the front of the seat to the floor.
6. If equipped with power seats, disengage the power seat wiring harness.
7. Remove the seat from the vehicle.

To install:

8. Move the seat to the fully rearward position and make sure both seat tracks are locked into position.
9. Place the seat in position in the vehicle. Do not use the head restraint, side shield, recliner handle, or adjuster lift bar to move the seat.
10. If equipped with power seats, connect the wiring harness.
11. Make sure that the mounting bolt holes are aligned with the bolt holes in the vehicle floor pan.
12. Install the front inboard bolt holding the seat track to the floor crossmember. Install the front outboard bolt holding the seat track to the floor crossmember.
13. Move the seat to the forward position. Check to make sure the inboard and outboard tracks are latched in the full forward position.
14. Install the bolts holding the rear of the seat track to the floor.
15. Tighten the indicated mounting bolts to the following specifications:
   - Cirrus, Stratus, Sebring convertible and Breeze (all bolts): 45 ft. lbs. (61 Nm)
   - Sebring coupe and Avenger—front mounting bolts: 22 ft. lbs. (29 Nm); rear mounting bolts: 33 ft. lbs. (44 Nm)
16. Install any trim components concealing the seat track mechanism.
17. Check the front seat adjuster mechanism for proper operation.

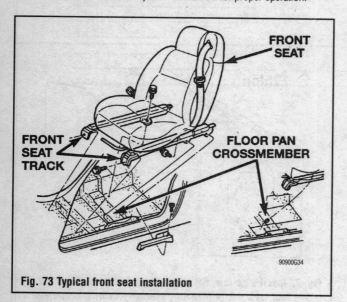

FRONT SEAT

FRONT SEAT TRACK

FLOOR PAN CROSSMEMBER

90900G34

Fig. 73 Typical front seat installation

Rear Seats

REAR SEAT BACK

1. Remove the rear seat cushion.
2. Unfasten the bolts securing the rear seat back to the floor.
3. On fold-down rear seats, remove the seat back side bolsters.
4. On non-fold-down rear seats, push the rear seat back upward to disengage the hooks at the top of the seat back, then remove the seat back from the vehicle.

To install:

5. Place the rear seat back into position in the vehicle.
6. On non-fold-down rear seats, push the seat back downward to engage the hooks at the top of the seat back.
7. Install the bolts holding the rear seat back and side bolsters (if equipped) to the floor. Tighten the retainers to 16 ft. lbs. (22 Nm).
8. Install the rear seat cushion.

REAR SEAT CUSHION

1. Pull upward at each end of the front edge of the rear seat cushion to disengage the retainer loops from the cups in the floor.
2. Remove the rear seat cushion from the vehicle.

To install:

3. Place the rear seat cushion in position under the bottom of the seat back.
4. Position the inboard seat belts on top of the seat cushion.
5. Guide the seat cushion loops into the retainer cups in the floor pan.
6. Push downward on the front corners of the seat cushion to engage the retainers.

Power Seat Motor

REMOVAL & INSTALLATION

Sebring Convertible

1. Disconnect the negative battery cable.
2. Remove the front seat from the vehicle.
3. Remove the front seat back.
4. Separate the power seat switch and wiring harness from the seat adjuster.

To install:

5. Install the power seat switch and harness to the seat adjuster.
6. Install the front seat back.
7. Install the front seat into the vehicle.
8. Connect the negative battery cable.

Sebring Coupe and Avenger

▶ **See Figure 74**

1. Disconnect the negative battery cable.
2. Remove the front seat.
3. Remove the bolts which mount the gear box to the left and right ends of the rails.
4. Remove the gear shaft from the left side.
5. Pull the gear box at the right side toward you to disengage the gear shaft from the side rail.
6. Remove the power seat motor.
7. Installation is the reverse of the removal steps.

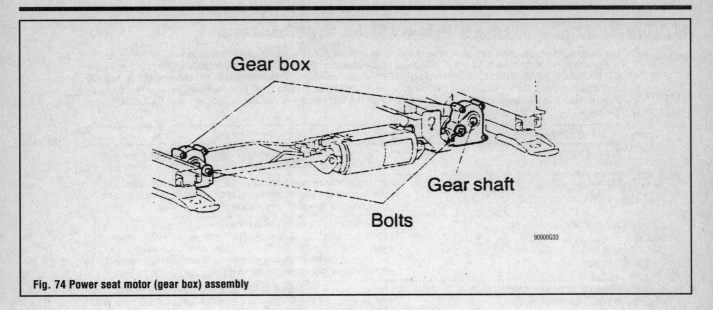

Fig. 74 Power seat motor (gear box) assembly

TORQUE SPECIFICATIONS

System	Component	Ft. Lbs.	Nm
EXTERIOR			
	Doors		
	Sebring Coupe and Avenger		
	Door-to-hinge mounting bolts	16	22
	Cirrus, Stratus, Sebring Convertible and Breeze		
	Adjustment screw	30 inch lbs.	3
INTERIOR			
	Electric window motor	50-74 inch lbs.	5.6-8.5
	Seats		
	Cirrus, Stratus, Sebring Convertible and Breeze		
	Front seats	45	61
	Sebring Coupe and Avenger		
	Front seat front mounting bolts	22	29
	Front seat rear mounting bolts	33	44
	Rear seats		
	Seat back lower retainers	16	22

90900C01

How to Remove Stains from Fabric Interior

For rest results, spots and stains should be removed as soon as possible. Never use gasoline, lacquer thinner, acetone, nail polish remover or bleach. Use a 3' x 3" piece of cheesecloth. Squeeze most of the liquid from the fabric and wipe the stained fabric from the outside of the stain toward the center with a lifting motion. Turn the cheesecloth as soon as one side becomes soiled. When using water to remove a stain, be sure to wash the entire section after the spot has been removed to avoid water stains. Encrusted spots can be broken up with a dull knife and vacuumed before removing the stain.

Type of Stain	How to Remove It
Surface spots	Brush the spots out with a small hand brush or use a commercial preparation such as K2R to lift the stain.
Mildew	Clean around the mildew with warm suds. Rinse in cold water and soak the mildew area in a solution of 1 part table salt and 2 parts water. Wash with upholstery cleaner.
Water stains	Water stains in fabric materials can be removed with a solution made from 1 cup of table salt dissolved in 1 quart of water. Vigorously scrub the solution into the stain and rinse with clear water. Water stains in nylon or other synthetic fabrics should be removed with a commercial type spot remover.
Chewing gum, tar, crayons, shoe polish (greasy stains)	Do not use a cleaner that will soften gum or tar. Harden the deposit with an ice cube and scrape away as much as possible with a dull knife. Moisten the remainder with cleaning fluid and scrub clean.
Ice cream, candy	Most candy has a sugar base and can be removed with a cloth wrung out in warm water. Oily candy, after cleaning with warm water, should be cleaned with upholstery cleaner. Rinse with warm water and clean the remainder with cleaning fluid.
Wine, alcohol, egg, milk, soft drink (non-greasy stains)	Do not use soap. Scrub the stain with a cloth wrung out in warm water. Remove the remainder with cleaning fluid.
Grease, oil, lipstick, butter and related stains	Use a spot remover to avoid leaving a ring. Work from the outisde of the stain to the center and dry with a clean cloth when the spot is gone.
Headliners (cloth)	Mix a solution of warm water and foam upholstery cleaner to give thick suds. Use only foam—liquid may streak or spot. Clean the entire headliner in one operation using a circular motion with a natural sponge.
Headliner (vinyl)	Use a vinyl cleaner with a sponge and wipe clean with a dry cloth.
Seats and door panels	Mix 1 pint upholstery cleaner in 1 gallon of water. Do not soak the fabric around the buttons.
Leather or vinyl fabric	Use a multi-purpose cleaner full strength and a stiff brush. Let stand 2 minutes and scrub thoroughly. Wipe with a clean, soft rag.
Nylon or synthetic fabrics	For normal stains, use the same procedures you would for washing cloth upholstery. If the fabric is extremely dirty, use a multi-purpose cleaner full strength with a stiff scrub brush. Scrub thoroughly in all directions and wipe with a cotton towel or soft rag.

TCCA0C01

GLOSSARY

AIR/FUEL RATIO: The ratio of air-to-gasoline by weight in the fuel mixture drawn into the engine.

AIR INJECTION: One method of reducing harmful exhaust emissions by injecting air into each of the exhaust ports of an engine. The fresh air entering the hot exhaust manifold causes any remaining fuel to be burned before it can exit the tailpipe.

ALTERNATOR: A device used for converting mechanical energy into electrical energy.

AMMETER: An instrument, calibrated in amperes, used to measure the flow of an electrical current in a circuit. Ammeters are always connected in series with the circuit being tested.

AMPERE: The rate of flow of electrical current present when one volt of electrical pressure is applied against one ohm of electrical resistance.

ANALOG COMPUTER: Any microprocessor that uses similar (analogous) electrical signals to make its calculations.

ARMATURE: A laminated, soft iron core wrapped by a wire that converts electrical energy to mechanical energy as in a motor or relay. When rotated in a magnetic field, it changes mechanical energy into electrical energy as in a generator.

ATMOSPHERIC PRESSURE: The pressure on the Earth's surface caused by the weight of the air in the atmosphere. At sea level, this pressure is 14.7 psi at 32°F (101 kPa at 0°C).

ATOMIZATION: The breaking down of a liquid into a fine mist that can be suspended in air.

AXIAL PLAY: Movement parallel to a shaft or bearing bore.

BACKFIRE: The sudden combustion of gases in the intake or exhaust system that results in a loud explosion.

BACKLASH: The clearance or play between two parts, such as meshed gears.

BACKPRESSURE: Restrictions in the exhaust system that slow the exit of exhaust gases from the combustion chamber.

BAKELITE: A heat resistant, plastic insulator material commonly used in printed circuit boards and transistorized components.

BALL BEARING: A bearing made up of hardened inner and outer races between which hardened steel balls roll.

BALLAST RESISTOR: A resistor in the primary ignition circuit that lowers voltage after the engine is started to reduce wear on ignition components.

BEARING: A friction reducing, supportive device usually located between a stationary part and a moving part.

BIMETAL TEMPERATURE SENSOR: Any sensor or switch made of two dissimilar types of metal that bend when heated or cooled due to the different expansion rates of the alloys. These types of sensors usually function as an on/off switch.

BLOWBY: Combustion gases, composed of water vapor and unburned fuel, that leak past the piston rings into the crankcase during normal engine operation. These gases are removed by the PCV system to prevent the buildup of harmful acids in the crankcase.

BRAKE PAD: A brake shoe and lining assembly used with disc brakes.

BRAKE SHOE: The backing for the brake lining. The term is, however, usually applied to the assembly of the brake backing and lining.

BUSHING: A liner, usually removable, for a bearing; an anti-friction liner used in place of a bearing.

CALIPER: A hydraulically activated device in a disc brake system, which is mounted straddling the brake rotor (disc). The caliper contains at least one piston and two brake pads. Hydraulic pressure on the piston(s) forces the pads against the rotor.

CAMSHAFT: A shaft in the engine on which are the lobes (cams) which operate the valves. The camshaft is driven by the crankshaft, via a belt, chain or gears, at one half the crankshaft speed.

CAPACITOR: A device which stores an electrical charge.

CARBON MONOXIDE (CO): A colorless, odorless gas given off as a normal byproduct of combustion. It is poisonous and extremely dangerous in confined areas, building up slowly to toxic levels without warning if adequate ventilation is not available.

CARBURETOR: A device, usually mounted on the intake manifold of an engine, which mixes the air and fuel in the proper proportion to allow even combustion.

CATALYTIC CONVERTER: A device installed in the exhaust system, like a muffler, that converts harmful byproducts of combustion into carbon dioxide and water vapor by means of a heat-producing chemical reaction.

CENTRIFUGAL ADVANCE: A mechanical method of advancing the spark timing by using flyweights in the distributor that react to centrifugal force generated by the distributor shaft rotation.

CHECK VALVE: Any one-way valve installed to permit the flow of air, fuel or vacuum in one direction only.

CHOKE: A device, usually a moveable valve, placed in the intake path of a carburetor to restrict the flow of air.

CIRCUIT: Any unbroken path through which an electrical current can flow. Also used to describe fuel flow in some instances.

CIRCUIT BREAKER: A switch which protects an electrical circuit from overload by opening the circuit when the current flow exceeds a predetermined level. Some circuit breakers must be reset manually, while most reset automatically.

COIL (IGNITION): A transformer in the ignition circuit which steps up the voltage provided to the spark plugs.

COMBINATION MANIFOLD: An assembly which includes both the intake and exhaust manifolds in one casting.

COMBINATION VALVE: A device used in some fuel systems that routes fuel vapors to a charcoal storage canister instead of venting them into the atmosphere. The valve relieves fuel tank pressure and allows fresh air into the tank as the fuel level drops to prevent a vapor lock situation.

COMPRESSION RATIO: The comparison of the total volume of the cylinder and combustion chamber with the piston at BDC and the piston at TDC.

CONDENSER: 1. An electrical device which acts to store an electrical charge, preventing voltage surges. 2. A radiator-like device in the air conditioning system in which refrigerant gas condenses into a liquid, giving off heat.

CONDUCTOR: Any material through which an electrical current can be transmitted easily.

CONTINUITY: Continuous or complete circuit. Can be checked with an ohmmeter.

COUNTERSHAFT: An intermediate shaft which is rotated by a mainshaft and transmits, in turn, that rotation to a working part.

CRANKCASE: The lower part of an engine in which the crankshaft and related parts operate.

CRANKSHAFT: The main driving shaft of an engine which receives reciprocating motion from the pistons and converts it to rotary motion.

CYLINDER: In an engine, the round hole in the engine block in which the piston(s) ride.

CYLINDER BLOCK: The main structural member of an engine in which is found the cylinders, crankshaft and other principal parts.

CYLINDER HEAD: The detachable portion of the engine, usually fastened to the top of the cylinder block and containing all or most of the combustion chambers. On overhead valve engines, it contains the valves and their operating parts. On overhead cam engines, it contains the camshaft as well.

DEAD CENTER: The extreme top or bottom of the piston stroke.

DETONATION: An unwanted explosion of the air/fuel mixture in the combustion chamber caused by excess heat and compression, advanced timing, or an overly lean mixture. Also referred to as "ping".

DIAPHRAGM: A thin, flexible wall separating two cavities, such as in a vacuum advance unit.

DIESELING: A condition in which hot spots in the combustion chamber cause the engine to run on after the key is turned off.

DIFFERENTIAL: A geared assembly which allows the transmission of motion between drive axles, giving one axle the ability to turn faster than the other.

DIODE: An electrical device that will allow current to flow in one direction only.

DISC BRAKE: A hydraulic braking assembly consisting of a brake disc, or rotor, mounted on an axle, and a caliper assembly containing, usually two brake pads which are activated by hydraulic pressure. The pads are forced against the sides of the disc, creating friction which slows the vehicle.

DISTRIBUTOR: A mechanically driven device on an engine which is responsible for electrically firing the spark plug at a predetermined point of the piston stroke.

DOWEL PIN: A pin, inserted in mating holes in two different parts allowing those parts to maintain a fixed relationship.

DRUM BRAKE: A braking system which consists of two brake shoes and one or two wheel cylinders, mounted on a fixed backing plate, and a brake drum, mounted on an axle, which revolves around the assembly.

DWELL: The rate, measured in degrees of shaft rotation, at which an electrical circuit cycles on and off.

ELECTRONIC CONTROL UNIT (ECU): Ignition module, module, amplifier or igniter. See Module for definition.

ELECTRONIC IGNITION: A system in which the timing and firing of the spark plugs is controlled by an electronic control unit, usually called a module. These systems have no points or condenser.

END-PLAY: The measured amount of axial movement in a shaft.

ENGINE: A device that converts heat into mechanical energy.

EXHAUST MANIFOLD: A set of cast passages or pipes which conduct exhaust gases from the engine.

FEELER GAUGE: A blade, usually metal, or precisely predetermined thickness, used to measure the clearance between two parts.

FIRING ORDER: The order in which combustion occurs in the cylinders of an engine. Also the order in which spark is distributed to the plugs by the distributor.

FLOODING: The presence of too much fuel in the intake manifold and combustion chamber which prevents the air/fuel mixture from firing, thereby causing a no-start situation.

FLYWHEEL: A disc shaped part bolted to the rear end of the crankshaft. Around the outer perimeter is affixed the ring gear. The starter drive engages the ring gear, turning the flywheel, which rotates the crankshaft, imparting the initial starting motion to the engine.

FOOT POUND (ft. lbs. or sometimes, ft.lb.): The amount of energy or work needed to raise an item weighing one pound, a distance of one foot.

FUSE: A protective device in a circuit which prevents circuit overload by breaking the circuit when a specific amperage is present. The device is constructed around a strip or wire of a lower amperage rating than the circuit it is designed to protect. When an amperage higher than that stamped on the fuse is present in the circuit, the strip or wire melts, opening the circuit.

GEAR RATIO: The ratio between the number of teeth on meshing gears.

GENERATOR: A device which converts mechanical energy into electrical energy.

HEAT RANGE: The measure of a spark plug's ability to dissipate heat from its firing end. The higher the heat range, the hotter the plug fires.

HUB: The center part of a wheel or gear.

HYDROCARBON (HC): Any chemical compound made up of hydrogen and carbon. A major pollutant formed by the engine as a byproduct of combustion.

HYDROMETER: An instrument used to measure the specific gravity of a solution.

INCH POUND (inch lbs.; sometimes in.lb. or in. lbs.): One twelfth of a foot pound.

INDUCTION: A means of transferring electrical energy in the form of a magnetic field. Principle used in the ignition coil to increase voltage.

INJECTOR: A device which receives metered fuel under relatively low pressure and is activated to inject the fuel into the engine under relatively high pressure at a predetermined time.

INPUT SHAFT: The shaft to which torque is applied, usually carrying the driving gear or gears.

INTAKE MANIFOLD: A casting of passages or pipes used to conduct air or a fuel/air mixture to the cylinders.

JOURNAL: The bearing surface within which a shaft operates.

KEY: A small block usually fitted in a notch between a shaft and a hub to prevent slippage of the two parts.

MANIFOLD: A casting of passages or set of pipes which connect the cylinders to an inlet or outlet source.

MANIFOLD VACUUM: Low pressure in an engine intake manifold formed just below the throttle plates. Manifold vacuum is highest at idle and drops under acceleration.

MASTER CYLINDER: The primary fluid pressurizing device in a hydraulic system. In automotive use, it is found in brake and hydraulic clutch systems and is pedal activated, either directly or, in a power brake system, through the power booster.

MODULE: Electronic control unit, amplifier or igniter of solid state or integrated design which controls the current flow in the ignition primary circuit based on input from the pick-up coil. When the module opens the primary circuit, high secondary voltage is induced in the coil.

NEEDLE BEARING: A bearing which consists of a number (usually a large number) of long, thin rollers.

OHM: (Ω) The unit used to measure the resistance of conductor-to-electrical flow. One ohm is the amount of resistance that limits current flow to one ampere in a circuit with one volt of pressure.

OHMMETER: An instrument used for measuring the resistance, in ohms, in an electrical circuit.

OUTPUT SHAFT: The shaft which transmits torque from a device, such as a transmission.

OVERDRIVE: A gear assembly which produces more shaft revolutions than that transmitted to it.

OVERHEAD CAMSHAFT (OHC): An engine configuration in which the camshaft is mounted on top of the cylinder head and operates the valve either directly or by means of rocker arms.

OVERHEAD VALVE (OHV): An engine configuration in which all of the valves are located in the cylinder head and the camshaft is located in the cylinder block. The camshaft operates the valves via lifters and pushrods.

OXIDES OF NITROGEN (NOx): Chemical compounds of nitrogen produced as a byproduct of combustion. They combine with hydrocarbons to produce smog.

OXYGEN SENSOR: Use with the feedback system to sense the presence of oxygen in the exhaust gas and signal the computer which can reference the voltage signal to an air/fuel ratio.

PINION: The smaller of two meshing gears.

PISTON RING: An open-ended ring with fits into a groove on the outer diameter of the piston. Its chief function is to form a seal between the piston and cylinder wall. Most automotive pistons have three rings: two for compression sealing; one for oil sealing.

PRELOAD: A predetermined load placed on a bearing during assembly or by adjustment.

PRIMARY CIRCUIT: the low voltage side of the ignition system which consists of the ignition switch, ballast resistor or resistance wire, bypass, coil, electronic control unit and pick-up coil as well as the connecting wires and harnesses.

PRESS FIT: The mating of two parts under pressure, due to the inner diameter of one being smaller than the outer diameter of the other, or vice versa; an interference fit.

RACE: The surface on the inner or outer ring of a bearing on which the balls, needles or rollers move.

REGULATOR: A device which maintains the amperage and/or voltage levels of a circuit at predetermined values.

RELAY: A switch which automatically opens and/or closes a circuit.

RESISTANCE: The opposition to the flow of current through a circuit or electrical device, and is measured in ohms. Resistance is equal to the voltage divided by the amperage.

RESISTOR: A device, usually made of wire, which offers a preset amount of resistance in an electrical circuit.

RING GEAR: The name given to a ring-shaped gear attached to a differential case, or affixed to a flywheel or as part of a planetary gear set.

ROLLER BEARING: A bearing made up of hardened inner and outer races between which hardened steel rollers move.

ROTOR: 1. The disc-shaped part of a disc brake assembly, upon which the brake pads bear; also called, brake disc. 2. The device mounted atop the distributor shaft, which passes current to the distributor cap tower contacts.

SECONDARY CIRCUIT: The high voltage side of the ignition system, usually above 20,000 volts. The secondary includes the ignition coil, coil wire, distributor cap and rotor, spark plug wires and spark plugs.

SENDING UNIT: A mechanical, electrical, hydraulic or electro-magnetic device which transmits information to a gauge.

SENSOR: Any device designed to measure engine operating conditions or ambient pressures and temperatures. Usually electronic in nature and designed to send a voltage signal to an on-board computer, some sensors may operate as a simple on/off switch or they may provide a variable voltage signal (like a potentiometer) as conditions or measured parameters change.

SHIM: Spacers of precise, predetermined thickness used between parts to establish a proper working relationship.

SLAVE CYLINDER: In automotive use, a device in the hydraulic clutch system which is activated by hydraulic force, disengaging the clutch.

SOLENOID: A coil used to produce a magnetic field, the effect of which is to produce work.

SPARK PLUG: A device screwed into the combustion chamber of a spark ignition engine. The basic construction is a conductive core inside of a ceramic insulator, mounted in an outer conductive base. An electrical charge from the spark plug wire travels along the conductive core and jumps a preset air gap to a grounding point or points at the end of the conductive base. The resultant spark ignites the fuel/air mixture in the combustion chamber.

SPLINES: Ridges machined or cast onto the outer diameter of a shaft or inner diameter of a bore to enable parts to mate without rotation.

TACHOMETER: A device used to measure the rotary speed of an engine, shaft, gear, etc., usually in rotations per minute.

THERMOSTAT: A valve, located in the cooling system of an engine, which is closed when cold and opens gradually in response to engine heating, controlling the temperature of the coolant and rate of coolant flow.

TOP DEAD CENTER (TDC): The point at which the piston reaches the top of its travel on the compression stroke.

TORQUE: The twisting force applied to an object.

TORQUE CONVERTER: A turbine used to transmit power from a driving member to a driven member via hydraulic action, providing changes in drive ratio and torque. In automotive use, it links the driveplate at the rear of the engine to the automatic transmission.

TRANSDUCER: A device used to change a force into an electrical signal.

TRANSISTOR: A semi-conductor component which can be actuated by a small voltage to perform an electrical switching function.

TUNE-UP: A regular maintenance function, usually associated with the replacement and adjustment of parts and components in the electrical and fuel systems of a vehicle for the purpose of attaining optimum performance.

TURBOCHARGER: An exhaust driven pump which compresses intake air and forces it into the combustion chambers at higher than atmospheric pressures. The increased air pressure allows more fuel to be burned and results in increased horsepower being produced.

VACUUM ADVANCE: A device which advances the ignition timing in response to increased engine vacuum.

VACUUM GAUGE: An instrument used to measure the presence of vacuum in a chamber.

VALVE: A device which control the pressure, direction of flow or rate of flow of a liquid or gas.

VALVE CLEARANCE: The measured gap between the end of the valve stem and the rocker arm, cam lobe or follower that activates the valve.

VISCOSITY: The rating of a liquid's internal resistance to flow.

VOLTMETER: An instrument used for measuring electrical force in units called volts. Voltmeters are always connected parallel with the circuit being tested.

WHEEL CYLINDER: Found in the automotive drum brake assembly, it is a device, actuated by hydraulic pressure, which, through internal pistons, pushes the brake shoes outward against the drums.

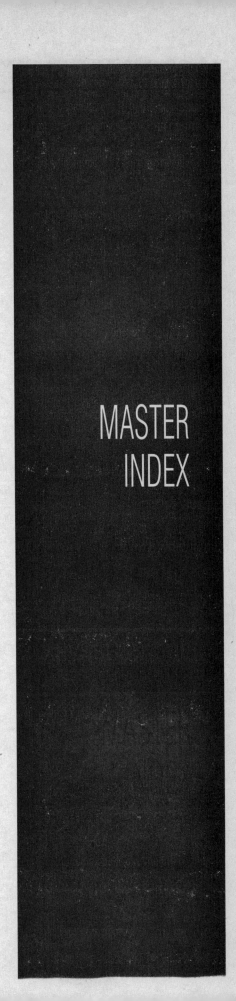

MASTER
INDEX